URBAN LIFE

Third Edition

D0024301

URBAN LIFE

Readings in Urban Anthropology
Third Edition

George Gmelch   **Walter P. Zenner**

WAVELAND
PRESS, INC.
Prospect Heights, Illinois

For information about this book, write or call:
Waveland Press, Inc.
P.O. Box 400
Prospect Heights, Illinois 60070
(847) 634-0081

Cover photograph: Self-service laundry in Rennes, France, by Shelton Schmidt.

Contents

Preface   ix

Part One: Urbanism   1

Introduction, *Walter P. Zenner and George Gmelch*   2

Urbanism As a Way of Life, *Louis Wirth*   14

The Urban Experience: A Psychological Analysis,   35
   Stanley Milgram

Urban Danger: Life in a Neighborhood of Strangers,   47
   Sally Engle Merry

The Metropolis and Everyday Life, *Robert Rotenberg*   60

The Preindustrial City, *Gideon Sjoberg*   82

The Preindustrial City: Reflections Four Decades Later,   94
   Gideon Sjoberg and Andrée F. Sjoberg

Cities and Human Health, *Lawrence M. Schell*   104

Part Two: Urban Fieldwork:
Anthropologists in Cities   129

Introduction, *George Gmelch*   130

Anthropological Fieldwork in Cities,   135
   George M. Foster and Robert V. Kemper

v

Doing It: Urban Research in Popayán, Colombia,   **151**
  Michael Whiteford

An Urban Field Experience: Irish Travellers in Dublin,   **169**
  Sharon Bohn Gmelch

Part Three: Migration and the Adaptation   187
of Migrants to City Life

Introduction, George Gmelch   **188**

Migration and Adaptation: Tzintzuntzeños in Mexico City   **196**
  and Beyond, Robert V. Kemper

Bogdan's Story: The Adaptation of a Rural Family   **210**
  to Yugoslavian Urban Life, Andrei Simić

A West Indian Life in Britain, George Gmelch   **228**

Women are Migrants Too: A Portuguese Perspective,   **245**
  Caroline B. Brettell

Surviving in the City: Coping Strategies of Female   **259**
  Migrants in Nairobi, Kenya, Nici Nelson

European Cyclical Migration and Economic Development: **279**
  The Case of Southern Spain, Robert Rhoades

Reflections of an Urban Anthropologist, Walter P. Zenner   **293**

Part Four: Urban Family, Kinship, and   297
Interpersonal Relations

Introduction, Walter P. Zenner   **298**

The Myth of the Declining Family: Extended Family   **308**
  Ties Among Urban Mexican-Americans and
  Anglo-Americans, Susan Emley Keefe

The Kindred of Viola Jackson: Residence and Family   **323**
  Organization of an Urban Black American Family,
  Carol B. Stack

Urban Chinese: Family Life in a Communist Society,   **335**
  William Jankowiak

Wives and Servants: Women in Middle-Class Households, **353**
Guatemala City, *Laurel Bossen*

Part Five: Urban Class and Ethnicity   367

Introduction, Walter P. Zenner   **368**

Coping with Poverty: A Cross-Cultural View of the   **378**
Behavior of the Poor, *Edwin Eames and Judith Goode*

The Culture of Poverty, *Oscar Lewis*   **393**

An Anthropological Critique of the Culture of Poverty,   **405**
Judith Goode and Edwin Eames

Office Work and the Crack Alternative Among Puerto Rican   **418**
Drug Dealers in East Harlem, *Philippe Bourgois*

A South Indian Caste in a Bombay Slum, *Owen M. Lynch*   **432**

Urban Women as Political Activists, Mérida, Yucatán,   **445**
Mexico, *Kathleen Logan*

The Transnational Web of Syrian-Jewish Relations,   **459**
Walter P. Zenner

Part Six: Urban Places and Spaces   473

Introduction, Walter P. Zenner   **474**

Within the Wall and Beyond: Ethnicity in Harar, Ethiopia,   **479**
Sidney R. Waldron

Territoriality and Social Organization in Islamic Cities,   **491**
Janet Lippman Abu-Lughod

The Genesis and Function of Squatter Settlements in   **510**
Brasília, *David Epstein*

Forging Tradition: Social Life and Identity in a Tokyo   **524**
Neighborhood, *Theodore C. Bestor*

Ordinary People/Everyday Life: Folk Culture in   **548**
New York City, *Barbara Kirshenblatt-Gimblett*

References   **563**

About the Authors   **597**

Preface

Our primary aim in putting together this book has been to communicate the research findings of anthropologists and others on urban life and culture to students. In our selection of readings, we have sought broad coverage of the topics and types of analysis central to urban anthropology. We have also chosen work that provides a wide geographic range. And finally, we have sought a balance between classic studies of enduring interest and important recent work. *Urban Life* includes twenty-four articles published here for the first time.

Fourteen years ago, when we were preparing the first edition of *Urban Life*, we looked for essays that were clearly written, that would capture and hold the interest of our students. Eight years later (1985) we re-edited the book, and replaced one-third of the essays with new articles, written expressly for *Urban Life*. Now, ten years later, we have repeated this process, continuing our search for articles written with insight and clarity and soliciting original essays from scholars doing important new research in the field. The third edition of *Urban Life* includes eight new selections, such as Janet Abu-Lughod on Islamic cities, William Jankowiak on family life in urban China, Caroline Brettell on women migrants in Portugal, Nici Nelson on women migrants in Kenya, and Gideon and Andrée Sjoberg's reflections on the preindustrial city forty years after their original conception. Seven authors of original essays who had been back to the field since the second edition have reworked their essays or written epilogues on changes that have occurred in their field settings. Altogether, over half of the material in this edition is new or updated. We have also reworked most of our introductory essays, noting new directions in urban anthropology.

And, for the first time, we have illustrated the essays in order to better communicate a sense of place to the reader. Most photographs were taken by anthropologists in the field.

These changes reflect the many conversations we have had with students and urban anthropologists we know who have used *Urban Life*. Waveland Press also distributed a questionnaire to instructors to learn what was beneficial in the previous edition and what needed to be changed. We believe that this new edition will capture students' interest. But we encourage you to continue to send us your comments and ideas for improving *Urban Life*.

Urban Life, Third Edition, is organized into six parts, each corresponding to a major focus in the field and each introduced by an editorial essay. These essays offer an overview of the general topic addressed by the readings and provide background and context for the selections. Each article is prefaced by a brief note highlighting its particular significance.

The selections in Part One discuss the effects of urbanism on the social life, personality, and health of city dwellers. Part Two looks at the manner in which anthropologists have changed their outlook and their methods in response to the study of urban life. In Part Three the cityward migration of rural peoples and their adaptation to city life are examined. Part Four focuses on family and kin, personal relations, and gender roles in urban society. Part Five treats ethnicity and class in the city. Finally, Part Six deals with community formation and urban neighborhoods.

The parts of this collection are interwoven by several underlying themes made explicit in the introductory essays. One theme is that of cross-cultural comparison, the testing of generalizations based on one culture with the experiences of other groups and contexts. A second theme is the importance of small intimate groups for most city people; such groups serve as a focus of urban life and help members maintain a meaningful pattern of expressive emotional relations. Most important is the familiar anthropological theme of *adaptation*, the strategies that people, both as individuals and as members of groups, use to cope with the demands of life in the city. Our chief concern here is with the unique demands posed by urban social environments and the ways in which human cultures have dealt with them. Implicit in this orientation is a comparison of the urban with the rural; in particular, how customs and institutions that evolved in small-scale societies have been transformed in urban settings. While the focus is often on the urban adaptation of individuals and groups, the city is also seen as part of the broader national and international system.

Our publishers, Neil Rowe and Tom Curtin at Waveland Press and

Bob Woodbury at St. Martin's Press for the first edition, gave us wise counsel and were generous in the extreme in offering assistance. Sharon Gmelch, Meredith Melzer, Robert V. Kemper, Polly Wheeler, Jennifer Unterberg, and the professors who returned the questionnaire created by Laurie Prossnitz at Waveland Press made valuable suggestions which guided our selection of articles. Gillian Scott gave advice on editorial matters. Megan Donovan, Kerry Cassidy, and Rita Michalec typed the essays. Above all, we are indebted to our colleagues who have written original essays for this volume.

George Gmelch
Walter P. Zenner

Part One

Urbanism

The Origins of Urbanism

If one were to draw a line across a classroom chalkboard to represent all the time of human evolution, it would only be a fraction of an inch from the end of the line that the first cities emerged. The agglomerations of humans in large settlements is a phenomenon that only began about seven thousand years ago.

The first cities appeared in Mesopotamia, in the river valleys of the Tigris and Euphrates in what is now Iraq. Like all early cities, their populations were tiny by today's standards, rarely exceeding thirty thousand. However, their inhabitants were concentrated in a small area, as most early cities were bounded by walls; in fact, population densities (up to ten thousand per square mile) were comparable to those of many small American cities today. Crowding and urban congestion has been a characteristic since the first cities (Jordan and Rowntree 1990).

These early cities had other characteristics that we would instantly recognize as urban: monumental religious and government buildings, armed forces, taxation, fashion, class distinctions, and artisans, merchants, officials, and priests who were not directly involved in food-producing activities.

By 3000 B.C. cities began to appear outside the "fertile crescent" of the Tigris-Euphrates region, with the earliest of these other cities arising in the Nile valley of Egypt. The similarity of early Egyptian cities and the earlier Mesopotamian cities raises the question of whether the city was invented once or twice and then diffused elsewhere, or whether cities developed independently of one another (Basham 1978). Clearly, the close proximity of the two regions meant that early Egyptians had some knowledge of the cities of Mesopotamia. But the mere knowledge of city life could not in itself have been "sufficient to induce the generation of urban forms." However, it is plausible that the diffusion of certain technology and ideas from Mesopotamia to the Nile region would have hastened urban development. This hypothesis, that urbanism spread from Mesopotamia to Egypt, is supported by the five-hundred-year time lag between the appearance of the first Mesopotamian cities and the later Egyptian ones, by the similarity in architectural styles, and by the sudden appearance of an advanced writing system in Egypt.

A millennium after the emergence of these cities, other urban forms appeared in Pakistan's Indus River Valley, the Yellow River

Valley of China and, later, in Mesoamerica. These cities had many of the same architectural and spatial characteristics: they had a citadel (temple or pyramid) monopolizing the central place; their streets were winding and narrow, unlike the grid plan we are accustomed to in modern cities; and along their crooked streets were clustered low houses of one or two stories. The elites and more affluent citizens lived near the center, with the poorest citizenry being on the outskirts, nearest the encircling wall. Yet there were also some significant differences, especially between those of the early Old World (Mesopotamia, Egypt, Indus Valley, and China) cities and the earliest New World urban forms in Mesoamerica where cities were less dense and were spread over larger areas. Mesoamerica is the one region where archaeologists can say with some certainty that its early cities developed independently, uninfluenced by other civilizations. In fact, Mesoamerican cities developed without the benefit of many of the technological advances found in the Old World civilizations, notably the wheel, the plow, metallurgy, and draft animals.

If we had the space to continue looking at the development of urbanism over time, we would next turn to the cities of ancient Greece, which are the immediate roots of Western civilization and the Western city. There were more than five hundred towns and cities on the Greek mainland and surrounding islands by 600 B.C. Proceeding along we would shift our lens to Rome. As the Romans expanded their empire across western Europe, towns and cities sprang up in their path, often beginning as garrisons for Roman troops and promoted by trade. But by A.D. 400 the Roman empire had fallen and with it urban life also declined. Outposts of the Roman empire like Paris and London shrank to little more than small towns, which they remained throughout the dark ages. Six hundred years would pass before cities would again expand in western Europe, and more than a thousand years before the industrial modern cities that we know today would begin to take shape. We would also want to examine early cities in Africa, such as Benin, and the Chinese cities which, in many respects, were more advanced than European cities until the Industrial Revolution in the West.

Defining the City

When we use the term "city" and "urban," what exactly do we mean? What kinds and sizes of settlements count? Where do we draw the line between town and city, between rural, suburban, and urban? Scholars of urbanism would like to define "city" and "urban" in a manner that encompasses the same kinds of community throughout the world and throughout all periods of human history. But is it possible to adopt a single definition that will pertain equally to the early, preindustrial cities of Mesopotamia as well as to contemporary New York, Hong Kong, and Beijing? The different ways the *American Heritage Dictionary* defines "city" gives us a clue to the difficulty. Its entry reads: "(1) a town of significant size. (2) In the U.S. an incorporated municipality with definite boundaries and legal powers set forth in a charter granted by the state. (3) In Canada a municipality of high rank, usually determined by population varying by province. (4) In Great Britain, a large incorporated town, usually the seat of the Bishop with its title conferred by the Crown. (5) The inhabitants of a city as a group. (6) An ancient Greek city-state. (7) Formerly a walled area in the center of a community." So, the dictionary suggests that there are many ways to define "city," often specific to particular countries. Our dictionary doesn't even begin to take into account cities in the non-Western world.

Islamic cities, for example, can be quite different from Western ones. Unlike American cities, Islamic cities in the Middle East were subdivided into small residential quarters that persisted for long periods of time, even centuries, and in some older cities, these quarters still exist. The neighborhood or quarter in the Islamic city was seen as defensible turf, even when it did not involve ethnic or sectarian segregation. This is unlike the fluid boundaries of neighborhoods in American cities like New York or Chicago. The fluidity of neighborhood designations, however, does not prevent "street gangs" in these areas from marking out "turfs" that they defend violently. Gender segregation has been an important feature of Middle Eastern Islamic cities. Islamic law led to what amounted to building codes that prevented strange men from seeing the women of the house. The layout of houses, courtyards, and neighborhoods, as well as screening of windows, made it possible for women to see the men, but not vice versa. The causes of the differences between the Islamic and Western cities are not simply an entity such as "Islamic culture." While the regulations regarding gender segregation are found in Islamic law, the importance of neighborhood defensibility is the outgrowth of a wide variety of social, economic, and political forces over long periods of time (Abu-Lughod, "Territoriality and Social Organization").

Even within a single culture there may be little consensus about what the terms "city" and "urban" apply to. In an urban anthropology class, we found that our students variously referred to

Schenectady, New York (the city in which they were living and which has a population of sixty-six thousand) as a "town," "city," and "suburb." The students from the rural areas and small towns of upstate New York saw Schenectady as a proper city, while those from Manhattan and Boston defined it as a "town" or "suburb" of Albany. It is no wonder that it is difficult to arrive at a definition that will stand up cross-culturally.

Urban scholars often focus on different characteristics in defining the city. Some definitions emphasize demographic attributes, particularly the size and density of the population. Others reserve the term "city" for communities with certain specific institutions, such as an autonomous political elite, or a commercial market (Wheatley 1971) . Some scholars define the city in cultural and behavioral terms. Ulf Hannerz, a Swedish anthropologist, takes relative density and size for granted and concentrates on the quality of heterogeneity in his attempt at defining the city. He points to the fact that in a city one has access to a wider variety of services and goods than is generally accessible in smaller communities (Hannerz 1980: 109–118).

Richard Fox (1977) connects cities to their societal contexts. For instance one of the types that he delineates is the "regal-royal city," such as that of Charlemagne, the medieval emperor of the Franks and founder of the Holy Roman Empire. The government founded by Charlemagne centered around the ruler's entourage, which included his kin and personal retainers; it was based around a fortress which housed the royal court and the warriors who protected it and was supported by an agrarian economy and serf labor. This contrasts sharply with the administrative capital of a highly bureaucratic state, full of "civil servants," or a mercantile city-state in which traders control most resources, built around a market and an international port.

After our review of the many attempts at defining the city, we are not surprised that governments have favored a simple definition based on population size. But even that kind of definition varies from one country to another. In Denmark and Sweden, a city could have two hundred people, while in Greece and Senegal there needs to be ten thousand (Brunn and Williams 1983).

The Consequences of Urbanism

Problems of definitions aside, urban anthropologists and sociologists have been most concerned with understanding the way of life peculiar to cities. There is a parable that speaks to what it means to live in a city. It goes something like this. Once upon a time there was a mouse who lived in the country. He played out in the fields and lived off the simple products of the land in a poor hole. One day the mouse was visited by its cousin from the city. The city mouse complained about the hard work that the country mouse put in to get its simple food and poor accommodations. When he left, he suggested that his country cousin come with him to the city. And he did. The city mouse lived in an apartment. There was much excitement and variety in the city and many kinds of free food. When the shadow of the cat appeared, however, the mice shivered with fear in a small corner. The country mouse then fled from the city and was happy to return to the country.

The mouse's fear expresses the common-sense view of the differences between country life and city ways. Country life is tranquil but dull, while city life has variety and excitement but also fear. Country people are plain and moral. They know and care about each other. Indeed, they know so much about each other's doings that there is little or no privacy. While material concerns, loneliness, and privacy are the hallmarks of city life, in the country "life is with people," to quote the title of a book presenting such a folk society (Zborowski and Herzog 1952).

This stereotype of the differences between the village (country) and the city was the starting point for social scientific research on rural-urban differences. It found its way into Louis Wirth's model of "Urbanism As a Way of Life," in what was until recently the most widely read article in all of sociology. The interest of sociologists in the city, which led to Wirth's formulation, had its roots in the rapid growth of industrial cities in Europe and North America. Chicago, where Wirth lived, was an excellent example of this explosion; Chicago started as a village in the early 1800s and within a century had become a metropolis of more than three million inhabitants. While clearly emphasizing modern industrial urbanism, Wirth wrote as if he was describing a universal model. The model stressed size, population density, and heterogeneity as characteristics of the city. Wirth related these features of the city to the breakdown of primary groups, such as the family and the community, and the resultant individualism and anomie (normlessness, alienation, anarchy). Bureaucracy—an impersonal type of social structure—arises, and people have a sense of individual impotence.

Wirth's theory has prompted a great deal of research by anthropologists and sociologists. For example, Robert Redfield (1947), a colleague of Wirth's at the University of Chicago, compared four communities in the Yucatán area of Mexico that ranged from a city (Mérida) to a small Indian village, and developed the concept of "folk society" as an opposite of Wirth's urbanism. Where urban society was impersonal, heterogeneous, and secular, folk society was posited to be personal, homogeneous, and sacred. Village life was seen to be satisfying, peaceful, well integrated, and comparatively free of strife. This idealization of the rural strengthened the perception of the urban as being negative, as having harmful effects on its inhabitants.

Oscar Lewis, an anthropologist who followed villagers from Tepoztlan to Mexico City, found that the Tepoztecos maintained close kinship ties and kept many of their religious practices in the city (Lewis 1952). In general, anthropologists challenged the idea that a single model or paradigm could apply to all cities in time and space. The difficulty in applying Wirth's paradigm cross-culturally has encouraged some scholars to explore the variation in cities.

Horace Miner (1953) applied the Wirthian urban paradigm to the small African city of Timbuctoo (pop. 6,000), with mixed success. He found that while it worked for the macro-level characteristics of the city it did not hold true at the neighborhood and family level which were more integrated and personal than Wirth would have predicted. Similarly, Bascom (1955) studied the Yoruba of western Nigeria, who lived in dense concentrations comparable to cities elsewhere. Yet they did not exhibit traits hypothesized by Wirth as characteristic of urban places and of people in such circumstances (Bascom 1955; Wheatley 1970).

In some parts of the world, like the Mediterranean, anthropologists note a pervasive urbanity which makes even villages seem like cities and where peasants show a sophisticated knowledge of urban ways. Sally Engle Merry ("Urban Danger") in a study of a multiethnic neighborhood in an American city, also finds that Wirth's vision of the effects of urbanism are not wrong, but partial. She agrees that the anonymity, disorder, and exploitation that Wirth described are characteristic of the city, but they are found mainly at the boundaries between different groups of people (e.g., the Chinese, blacks, Hispanics, and whites in the neighborhoods Merry studied). Residents live in the social world of their own localized ethnic groups. They do not interact or get to know their neighbors who belong to the other groups.

Wirth's view of the city stresses negative features, yet various scholars have shown the positive sides of urban life (cf. Gulick 1989). Hannerz (1980) has shown that in cities, especially concentrated city centers, a wide range of services are easily available. This accessibility applies to preindustrial, as well as industrial, cities. Robert Rotenberg ("The Metropolis and Everyday

Life'') likewise points to the continuing attractions of metropolises and how ordinary people adapt to the large monumental structures often imposed upon them by the political and economic elites. What he writes about the metropolis can also be applied to our consideration of the suburban ''edge cities'' which have emerged in the past half-century. Thus Rotenberg, Hannerz, and others have shown the positive sides of city life which were downplayed by Wirth.

Other social scientists have criticized Wirth's model of urbanism for not being applicable to cities outside of Europe and North America. Conrad Arensberg believed that a closer examination of the ''green cities'' of India, pre-Columbian America, and West Africa would lead to a very different conceptualization of what is urban. A sociologist, Gideon Sjoberg (''The Preindustrial City''), who spent ten years trying to distill the essential characteristics of the preindustrial cities of Europe and parts of the Third World today, concluded that Wirth's model only applied to industrial cities. The preindustrial city, according to Sjoberg, is based on a technology which relies on the power of humans and animals, rather than on machines. While the majority of people in the whole society are cultivators, the society is ruled by an elite living in cities. Strong kin and other particularistic ties unite the ruling elite. Who you are, not what you are, is the guiding principle. Such a city is obviously quite different from the one seen in Wirth's model.

Many anthropologists, however, have been as critical of Sjoberg's theory of preindustrial urbanism as of Wirth's. Some of these reject the effort to find a universal definition of cities as a futile exercise in what is called ''essentialism.'' ''Essentialism'' is a philosophic term, which means that the object which is defined has a real essence that can be perceived. For instance, to essentialists, all chairs share the property of ''chairness.'' The opposite view, ''nominalism,'' asserts that abstractions, general terms, and universals exist only as names and have no objective reference. To nominalists, there is no such thing as ''chairness.'' Humans simply name certain objects ''chairs,'' but each of these objects is different from others which are so named. In this view, the word ''city'' is simply a label and the search for a universal urbanism is futile. Thus it is not surprising that Yoruba and Dahomeans had cities, for instance, without having social heterogeneity or a system of writing (Bascom 1955; Arensberg 1968). Nominalistic critics also oppose efforts to see cities of particular regions as qualitatively different from Western cities. They strive to resist stereotyping other cultures in either a romantic or pejorative way.

Industrial Urbanism

There have been several adaptations of the Wirth model as an explanation of modern urbanism. Nels Anderson (1962), for instance, has interpreted Wirth's formulation as one which shows how modern society as a whole—not just urban settlements—differs from its predecessors. Modern industrial society in Anderson's view has the following characteristics:

1. a high degree of specialization in labor and mass production of goods and services;
2. almost total commitment to mechanical power, both in work and nonwork situations;
3. increasing detachment of the individual from traditional controls, greater transiency in contracts and loyalties, and increasing dependence on secondary institutions (such as corporate and government bureaucracies);
4. high mobility—in daily movements, changes of jobs and residences, as well as changes in social status;
5. continuous change in the man-made elements of the urban environment, including structural renewal and technological innovation;
6. the almost complete subordination of the individual and the group to mechanical time and increasing control by clock time over appointments and coordination of movement;
7. considerable anonymity, which is related to transiency (nos. 3 and 4);
8. expectancy and devotion to continuous change;
9. increasing commitment to records and conformity to their use in verification of actions, contacts, pledges, and presences.

Rather than stressing such features as heterogeneity and density, Anderson emphasized the impact of the new technology, such as the use of mechanical power, the clock, and the computer, on modern society. While the full impact of such devices is felt most fully in urban areas, their effects can be seen in the countryside as well. Corn and pig farmers in Iowa, for example, rely on fertilizers and on tractors, which often are air-conditioned and have tape decks. Farmers use machines produced far away and are acutely aware of the international markets for their grain and meat, which affect their yearly fortunes.

Anderson's definition of modern industrial urbanism is a fine complement to Sjoberg's delineation of preindustrial society.

Sjoberg and others emphasized the importance of a complex society based on animal and human power. Anderson's formulation sees the importance in technological elements like transportation, clock time, and record keeping in accounting for the relative impersonality of modern society, including the transiency of relations, easy mobility, and the expectancy of change. But like Wirth, he does not devote much thought to how such devices may lead to countervailing tendencies as well. For instance, the letter, the telegram, and the telephone call make it possible for individuals to maintain meaningful intimate relationships over long distances without face-to-face contact. To quote a Bell system ad, "It's the next best thing to being there" (Aronson 1971).

The Urban Environment

The themes of heterogeneity and density have been elaborated by other scholars. Milgram's article ("The Urban Experience") is a good example of this genre. Laboratory psychologists use mice and rats to experiment on the behavioral effects of crowding on rats in cages. They have suggested that the behavior of rats in these situations is analogous to humans in small rooms and apartments. The psychologists have also conducted research that places human subjects in actual situations of crowding. These studies, particularly those of American and British college students, tend to confirm that crowding produces detrimental effects. These effects include aggressive acts and lack of concern for others (Mercer 1975).

Laboratories used by psychologists are not natural settings. The short-term encounters characteristic of such experiments do not permit the rearrangement of living patterns that humans may adopt in crowded conditions. Moreover, different cultures maintain different expectations of physical contact among individuals, including the normal space between individuals while having a conversation, touching each other, and feeling the breath or smelling the odors of others. Many sociologists and anthropologists remain unconvinced that crowding, noise, and the increase of stimulation present in the urban environment produce the detrimental effects attributed to them (Fischer 1976:154–164). On the other hand, some research on the relationship of overcrowding to health tends to confirm the theory that crowding does affect humans adversely, at least in Western settings (Gove, Hughes, and Galle 1979).

Obviously more research on this problem needs to be done. While anthropologists in the past have made few contributions to crowding theory, the observational and cross-cultural approaches of cultural anthropology can add a valuable dimension to this research. Actual observation of how individuals react to crowding in natural settings can be enhanced through the use of videotapes and other new devices. Lawrence Schell ("Cities and Human Health") deals with crowding as well as other consequences of urbanism. He finds that there is no one-to-one relationship between unhealthfulness and urbanism per se. Various factors such as noise and chemical pollution can, however, change either cities or rural settings into unhealthy places to live. Anthropologists also can be expected to carry out such research in cities outside North America.

Small Groups in the Large City

The major contribution that urban anthropologists, in conjunction with community sociologists, have made to the theory of modern urbanism has been in the criticism of one aspect of Wirth's theory— the thesis that the modern metropolitan environment leads to a breakdown of primary social relationships, to powerlessness, and to lawlessness. Initially, Wirth and his followers stressed the loss of community in the modern urban setting. The first wave of critics, however, discovered the existence of intense intimate relations and community solidarity in urban slums, in middle-class suburbs, and among some elites of modern society. The heterogeneity and population density of the city was seen as less important than it did to Wirth, while the economic position of individuals, their cultural characteristics, and their familial status seemed more important in determining their membership in primary groups. The work of anthropologists like Oscar Lewis ("The Culture of Poverty"), Elliott Liebow (1967), and Carol Stack ("The Kindred of Viola Jackson") and sociologists utilizing ethnographic approaches like Whyte, Gans, and Young and Willmott, were among those showing the persistence of "communities" in the city.

Herbert Gans (1962), for instance, described an Italian-American neighborhood in Boston as an "urban village." Indeed, the title of his highly acclaimed book was *The Urban Villagers*. Social life, according to this view, takes place at the level of small groups, such as the family, the church, and the block; on most occasions one is not merely "lost in the crowd." Proponents of this view, like Herbert Gans and Oscar Lewis, stressed the need urbanites have for social solidarity, sociability, and mutual assistance both in work and leisure situations. They were not concerned with and they downplayed the effects of population density on urban groups.

Of late, a synthesis between the Wirthian view and its critics has begun to emerge. While acknowledging the crucial roles that the family, the neighborhood, and the ethnic and occupational communities continue to play in contemporary urban society, these social scientists (e.g., Claude Fischer) also point to the following as primary influences on urban life: the concentration of large numbers of different kinds of people in cities, the new forms of communication, and the high degree of mobility of people today. A large number of people sharing a common ethnic identity or a particular interest (e.g., opera, chess, soccer) makes it possible for them to form a group that develops the traits of a "subculture," which offers its participants a sense of solidarity and shared interest. Wirthians believed that such solidarity was found mainly in folk/rural societies, but this is not the case (Fischer 1976). The new forms of communication and greater mobility make it possible for individuals to maintain a sense of community with people who are far away while these same individuals can be indifferent to their next-door neighbors.

In traditional villages, there was often an overlap between neighbors, kin, and friends. Urbanites today may have many different kinds of alliances, cliques, and other kinds of links to their fellows. While spatial propinquity is still important, many significant relationships are with those who are not in the next house or on the next block, but many miles away. Many urbanites do have people on whom they can rely for assistance in an emergency, but they may lack a sense of community because of this multiplicity of relationships. The fact that an individual in Boston has relatives in Chicago, neighbors who are friends across the street, and another set of friends from work in the suburbs—most of whom rarely meet—does not provide one with the feeling of a closely knit society.

While anthropologists once went out to study communities—which were localized in space—urban social scientists today are more inclined to look at social networks. A network is a set of links between individuals. Each individual in a particular place has a different series of links with others, many of whom live in other places and cities. For example, in a typical college student's network are some fellow students on campus, old friends back home, friends who have moved away or attend other colleges, families, and scattered relatives. With some persons they have strong ties, while with other people the links are casual and weak. The network perspective provides a new view of modern society, as Carol Stack makes clear in "The Kindred of Viola Jackson."

In this volume, we have chosen to concentrate on the way in which groups have persisted and been transformed in modern urban settings. The study of this phenomenon has been the forte of urban anthropologists. As indicated in this section, anthropologists together with their colleagues in other social sciences have made important contributions to the general theory of urbanism. They have provided a cross-cultural perspective to such a general consideration. Anthropologists such as Gulick (1967; 1989), Price (1972), Waldron ("Within the Wall and Beyond"), and Fox (1972) have tried to study cities as a whole. In recent years, Marxist anthropologists have adopted the perspective of Marxian economics in relating the groups, networks, and cities that they study to the larger socioeconomic system in which these are embedded. The example of how rural-urban migration in a Third World country is affected by decisions made in the commodities markets of Europe and America is an example of this interdependency. It requires looking at cities as part of a world system (see Rhoades, "European Cyclical Migration"; Bossen, "Wives and Servants"; and Zenner, "The Transnational Web of Syrian-Jewish Relations").

All these contributions by anthropologists to urban studies are welcome and often exciting. Still, the main task of urban anthropology is to describe and analyze the lives of the people who live in cities and their satellites. The macroscopic perspectives of holists and Marxists are needed to sharpen our analyses, but it has been our singular function to provide the "worm's-eye view."

Walter P. Zenner and George Gmelch

Urbanism As a Way of Life

LOUIS WIRTH

In this famous essay Louis Wirth speculates on how cities influence the social organization, attitudes, and personality of their inhabitants. Wirth begins his analysis by defining the city sociologically as a type of community which is large, dense, and comprised of socially heterogeneous individuals. He then deduces the essential properties of urban existence—anonymity, transitory and impersonal relationships, secularization of thought, and so on. In short, Wirth is less concerned with the ecological and demographic aspects of urbanism than with its social and individual properties. Elsewhere in this section, Milgram ("The Urban Experience") and Merry ("Urban Danger") test and expand upon Wirth's model.

The City and Contemporary Civilization

Just as the beginning of Western civilization is marked by the permanent settlement of formerly nomadic peoples in the Mediterranean basin, so the beginning of what is distinctively modern in our civilization is best signalized by the growth of great cities. Nowhere has mankind been farther removed from organic nature than under the conditions of life characteristic of great cities. The contemporary world no longer presents a picture of small isolated groups of human beings scattered over a vast territory, as Sumner described primitive society.[1] The distinctive feature of the

Source: *American Journal of Sociology*, XLIV (1938): 1–24, © 1938 by University of Chicago. Reprinted by permission of the University of Chicago Press.

mode of living of man in the modern age is his concentration into gigantic aggregations around which cluster lesser centers and from which radiate the ideas and practices that we call civilization.

The degree to which the contemporary world may be said to be "urban" is not fully or accurately measured by the proportion of the total population living in cities. The influences which cities exert upon the social life of man are greater than the ratio of the urban population would indicate, for the city is not only in ever larger degrees the dwelling-place and the workshop of modern man, but it is the initiating and controlling center of economic, political, and cultural life that has drawn the most remote parts of the world into its orbit and woven diverse areas, peoples, and activities into a cosmos.

The growth of cities and the urbanization of the world is one of the most impressive facts of modern times. Although it is impossible to state precisely what proportion of the estimated total world-population of approximately 1.8 billion is urban, 69.2 percent of the total population of those countries that do distinguish between urban and rural areas is urban.[2] Considering the fact, moreover, that the world's population is very unevenly distributed and that the growth of cities is not very far advanced in some of the countries that have only recently been touched by industrialism, this average understates the extent to which urban concentration has proceeded in those countries where the impact of the industrial revolution has been more forceful and of less recent date. This shift from a rural to a predominantly urban society, which has taken place within the span of a single generation in such industrialized areas as the United States and Japan, has been accompanied by profound changes in virtually every phase of social life. It is these changes and their ramifications that invite the attention of the sociologist to the study of the differences between the rural and the urban mode of living. The pursuit of this interest is an indispensable prerequisite for the comprehension and possible mastery of some of the most crucial contemporary problems of social life since it is likely to furnish one of the most revealing perspectives for the understanding of the ongoing changes in human nature and the social order.[3]

Since the city is the product of growth rather than of instantaneous creation, it is to be expected that the influences which it exerts upon the modes of life should not be able to wipe out completely the previously dominant modes of human association. To a greater or lesser degree, therefore, our social life bears the imprint of an earlier folk society, the characteristic modes of settlement of which were the farm, the manor, and the village. This historic influence is reinforced by the circumstance that the population of the city itself is in large measure recruited from the countryside, where a mode of life reminiscent of this earlier form of existence persists. Hence we should not expect to find abrupt and discontinuous variation between urban and rural types of personality. The city and the country may be regarded as two poles in reference to one or the other of which all human settlements tend to arrange themselves. In viewing urban-industrial and rural-folk society as ideal types of communities, we may obtain a perspective for the analysis of the basic models of human association as they appear in contemporary civilization.

A Sociological Definition of the City

Despite the preponderant significance of the city in our civilization, however, our knowledge of the nature of urbanism and the process of urbanization is meager. Many attempts have indeed been made to isolate the distinguishing characteristics of urban life. Geographers, historians, economists, and political scientists have incorporated the points of view of their respective disciplines into diverse definitions of the city. While in no sense intended to supersede these, the formulation of a sociological approach to the city may incidentally serve to call attention to the interrelations between them by emphasizing the peculiar characteristics of the city as a particular form of human association. A sociologically significant definition of the city seeks to select those elements of urbanism which mark it as a distinctive mode of human group life.

The characterization of a community as urban on the basis of size alone is obviously arbitrary. It is difficult to defend the present census definition which designates a community of twenty-five hundred and above as urban and all others as rural. The situation would be the same if the criterion were four thousand, eight thousand, ten thousand, twenty-five thousand, or one hundred thousand population, for although in the latter case we might feel that we were more nearly dealing with an urban aggregate than would be the case in communities of lesser size, no definition of urbanism can hope to be completely satisfying as long as numbers are regarded as the sole criterion. Moreover, it is not difficult to demonstrate that communities of less than the arbitrarily set number of inhabitants lying within the range of influence of metropolitan centers have greater claim to recognition as urban communities than do larger ones leading a more isolated existence in a predominantly rural area. Finally, it should be recognized that census definitions are unduly influenced by the fact that the city, statistically speaking, is always an administrative concept in that the corporate limits play a decisive role in delineating the urban area. Nowhere is this more clearly apparent than in the concentrations of population on the peripheries of great metropolitan centers which cross arbitrary administrative boundaries of city, county, state, and nation.

As long as we identify urbanism with the physical entity of the city, viewing it merely as rigidly delimited in space, and proceed as if urban attributes abruptly ceased to be manifested beyond an arbitrary boundary line, we are not likely to arrive at any adequate conception of urbanism as a mode of life. The technological developments in transportation and communication which virtually mark a new epoch in human history have accentuated the role of cities as dominant elements in our civilization and have enormously extended the urban mode of living beyond the confines of the city itself. The dominance of the city, especially of the great city, may be regarded as a consequence of the concentration in cities of industrial and commercial, financial and administrative facilities and activities, transportation and communication lines, and cultural and recreational equipment such as the press, radio stations, theaters, libraries, museums, concert halls, operas, hospitals, higher educational institutions, research and publishing centers, professional organizations, and religious and welfare institutions. Were it not for the attraction and suggestions that the city exerts through these instrumentalities upon the rural population, the differences between the rural and the urban modes of life would be even greater than they are. Urbanization no longer denotes merely the process by which persons are attracted to a place called the city and incorporated into its system of life. It refers also to that cumulative accentuation of the characteristics distinctive of the mode of life which is associated with the growth of cities, and finally to the changes in the direction of modes of life recognized as urban which are apparent among people, wherever they may be, who have come under the spell of the influences which the city exerts by virtue of the power of its institutions and personalities operating through the means of communication and transportation.

The shortcomings which attach to number of inhabitants as a criterion of urbanism apply for the most part to density of population as well. Whether we accept the density of ten thousand persons per square mile as Mark Jefferson[4] proposed, or one thousand, which Wilcox[5] preferred to regard as the criterion of urban settlements, it is clear that unless density is correlated with significant social characteristics it can furnish only an arbitrary basis for differentiating urban from rural communities. Since our census enumerates the night rather than the day population of an area, the locale of the most intensive urban life—the city center— generally has low population density, and the industrial and commercial areas of the city, which contain the most characteristic economic activities underlying urban society, would scarcely anywhere be truly urban if density were literally interpreted as a mark of urbanism. Nevertheless, the fact that the urban community is distinguished by a large aggregation and relatively dense con- centration of population can scarcely be left out of account in a definition of the city. But these criteria must be seen as relative to the general cultural context in which cities arise and exist and are sociologically relevant only in so far as they operate as conditioning factors in social life.

The same criticisms apply to such criteria as the occupation of the inhabitants, the existence of certain physical facilities, institu- tions, and forms of political organization. The question is not whether cities in our civilization or in others do exhibit these distinctive traits, but how potent they are in molding the character of social life into its specifically urban form. Nor in formulating a fertile definition can we afford to overlook the great variations between cities. By means of a typology of cities based upon size, location, age, and function, such as we have undertaken to establish in our report to the National Resources Committee,[6] we have found it feasible to array and classify urban communities ranging from struggling small towns to thriving world-metropolitan centers; from isolated trading-centers in the midst of agricultural regions to thriving world-ports and commercial and industrial conurbations. Such differences as these appear crucial because the social characteristics and influences of these different "cities" vary widely.

A serviceable definition of urbanism should not only denote the essential characteristics which all cities—at least those in our culture—have in common, but should lend itself to the discovery of their variations. An industrial city will differ significantly in social respects from a commercial, mining, fishing, resort, university, and capital city. A one-industry city will present different sets of social characteristics from a multi-industry city, as will an industrially balanced from an imbalanced city, a suburb from a satellite, a residential suburb from an industrial suburb, a city within a metropolitan region from one lying outside, an old city from a new one, a southern city from a New England, a middle-western from a Pacific Coast city, a growing from a stable and from a dying city.

A sociological definition must obviously be inclusive enough to comprise whatever essential characteristics these different types of cities have in common as social entities, but it obviously cannot be so detailed as to take account of all the variations implicit in the manifold classes sketched above. Presumably some of the characteristics of cities are more significant in conditioning the nature of urban life than others, and we may expect the outstanding features of the urban-social scene to vary in accordance with size, density, and differences in the functional type of cities. Moreover, we may infer that rural life will bear the imprint of urbanism in the measure that through contact and communication it comes under the influence of cities. It may contribute to the clarity of the statements that follow to repeat that while the locus of urbanism as a mode of life is, of course, to be found characteristically in places that fulfill the requirements we shall set up as a definition of the city, urbanism is not confined to such localities but is manifest in varying degrees wherever the influences of the city reach.

While urbanism, or that complex of traits that makes up the characteristic mode of life in cities, and urbanization, which denotes the development and extensions of these factors, are thus not exclusively found in settlements that are cities in the physical and demographic sense, they do, nevertheless, find their most pronounced expression in such areas, especially in metropolitan cities. In formulating a definition of the city it is necessary to exercise caution in order to avoid identifying urbanism as a way of life with any specific locally or historically conditioned cultural influences that, while they may significantly affect the specific character of the community, are not the essential determinants of its character as a city.

It is particularly important to call attention to the danger of confusing urbanism with industrialism and modern capitalism. The rise of cities in the modern world is undoubtedly not independent of the emergence of modern power-driven machine technology, mass production, and capitalistic enterprise. But different as the cities of earlier epochs may have been by virtue of their development in a preindustrial and precapitalistic order from the great cities of today, they were, nevertheless, cities.

For sociological purposes a city may be defined as a relatively large, dense, and permanent settlement of socially heterogeneous individuals. On the basis of the postulates which this minimal definition suggests, a theory of urbanism may be formulated in the light of existing knowledge concerning social groups.

A Theory of Urbanism

In the rich literature on the city we look in vain for a theory of urbanism presenting in a systematic fashion the available knowledge concerning the city as a social entity. We do indeed have excellent formulations of theories on such special problems as the growth of the city viewed as a historical trend and as a recurrent process,[7] and we have a wealth of literature presenting insights of sociological relevance and empirical studies offering detailed information on a variety of particular aspects of urban life. But despite the multiplication of research and textbooks on the city, we do not as yet have a comprehensive body of compendent hypotheses that may be derived from a set of postulates implicitly contained in a sociological definition of the city and from our general sociological knowledge which may be substantiated through empirical research. The closest approximations to a systematic theory of urbanism that we have are to be found in a penetrating essay, "Die Stadt," by Max Weber,[8] and a memorable paper by Robert E. Park on "The City: Suggestions for the Investigation of Human Behavior in the Urban Environment."[9] But even these excellent contributions are far from constituting an ordered and coherent framework of theory upon which research might profitably proceed.

In the pages that follow we shall seek to set forth a limited number of identifying characteristics of the city. Given these characteristics we shall then indicate what consequences or further characteristics follow from them in the light of general sociological theory and empirical research. We hope in this manner to arrive at the essential propositions comprising a theory of urbanism. Some of these propositions can be supported by a considerable body of already available research materials; others may be accepted as hypotheses for which a certain amount of presumptive evidence exists but for which more ample and exact verification would be required. At least such a procedure will, it is hoped, show what in the way of systematic knowledge of the city we now have and what are the crucial and fruitful hypotheses for future research.

The central problem of the sociologist of the city is to discover the forms of social action and organization that typically emerge in relatively permanent, compact settlements of large numbers of heterogeneous individuals. We must also infer that urbanism will assume its most characteristic and extreme form in the measure in which the conditions with which it is congruent are present. Thus the larger, the more densely populated, and the more heterogeneous a community, the more accentuated the characteristics associated with urbanism will be. It should be recognized, however, that in the social world institutions and practices may be accepted and continued for reasons other than those that originally brought them into existence, and that accordingly the urban mode of life may be perpetuated under conditions quite foreign to those necessary for its origin.

Some justification may be in order for the choice of the principal terms comprising our definition of the city. The attempt has been made to make it as inclusive and at the same time as denotative as possible without loading it with unnecessary assumptions. To say that large numbers are necessary to constitute a city means, of course, large numbers in relation to a restricted area or high density of settlement. There are, nevertheless, good reasons for treating large numbers and density as separate factors, since each may be connected with significantly different social consequences. Similarly the need for adding heterogeneity to numbers of population as a necessary and distinct criterion of urbanism might be questioned, since we should expect the range of differences to increase with numbers. In defense, it may be said that the city shows a kind and degree of heterogeneity of population which cannot be wholly accounted for by the law of large numbers or adequately represented by means of a normal distribution curve. Since the population of the city does not reproduce itself, it must recruit its migrants from other cities, the countryside, and—in this country until recently—from other countries. The city has thus historically been the melting pot of races, peoples, and cultures, and a most favorable breeding ground of new biological and cultural hybrids. It has not only tolerated but rewarded individual differences. It has brought together people from the ends of the earth *because* they are different and thus useful to one another, rather than because they are homogeneous and like-minded.[10]

There are a number of sociological propositions concerning the relationship between (*a*) numbers of population, (*b*) density of settlement, (*c*) heterogeneity of inhabitants and group life, which can be formulated on the basis of observation and research.

Size of the Population Aggregate

Ever since Aristotle's *Politics*,[11] it has been recognized that increasing the number of inhabitants in a settlement beyond a certain limit will affect the relationships between them and the character of the city. Large numbers involve, as has been pointed out, a greater range of individual variation. Furthermore, the greater the number of individuals participating in a process of interaction, the greater is the *potential* differentiation between them. The personal traits, the occupations, the cultural life, and the ideas of the members of an urban community may, therefore, be expected to range between more widely separated poles than those of rural inhabitants.

That such variations should give rise to the spatial segregation of individuals according to color, ethnic heritage, economic and social status, tastes and preferences, may readily be inferred. The bonds of kinship, of neighborliness, and the sentiments arising out of living together for generations under a common folk tradition are likely to be absent or, at best, relatively weak in an aggregate the members of which have such diverse origins and backgrounds. Under such circumstances competition and formal control mechanisms furnish the substitutes for the bonds of solidarity that are relied upon to hold a folk society together.

Increase in the number of inhabitants of a community beyond a few hundred is bound to limit the possibility of each member of the community knowing all the others personally. Max Weber, in recognizing the social significance of this fact, pointed out that from a sociological point of view large numbers of inhabitants and density of settlement mean that the personal mutual acquaintanceship between the inhabitants which ordinarily inheres in a neighborhood is lacking.[12] The increase in numbers thus involves a changed character of the social relationships. As Simmel points out:

> [If] the unceasing external contact of numbers of persons in the city should be met by the same number of inner reactions as in the small town, in which one knows almost every person he meets and to each of whom he has a positive relationship, one would be completely atomized internally and would fall into an unthinkable mental condition.[13]

The multiplication of persons in a state of interaction under conditions which make their contact as full personalities impossible produces that segmentalization of human relationships which has sometimes been seized upon by students of the mental life of the cities as an explanation for the "schizoid" character of urban personality. This is not to say that the urban inhabitants have fewer acquaintances than rural inhabitants, for the reverse may actually be true; it means rather that in relation to the number of people whom they see and with whom they rub elbows in the course of daily life, they know a smaller proportion, and of these they have less intensive knowledge.

Characteristically, urbanites meet one another in highly segmental roles. They are, to be sure, dependent upon more people for the satisfactions of their life-needs than are rural people and thus are associated with a greater number of organized groups, but they are less dependent upon particular persons, and their dependence upon others is confined to a highly fractionalized aspect of the other's round of activity. This is essentially what is meant by saying that the city is characterized by secondary rather than primary contacts. The contacts of the city may indeed be face to face, but they are nevertheless impersonal, superficial, transitory, and segmental. The reserve, the indifference, and the blase outlook which urbanites manifest in their relationships may thus be regarded as devices for immunizing themselves against the personal claims and expectations of others.

The superficiality, the anonymity, and the transitory character of urban-social relations make intelligible, also, the sophistication and the rationality generally ascribed to city-dwellers. Our acquaintances tend to stand in a relationship of utility to us in the sense that the role which each one plays in our life is overwhelmingly regarded as a means for the achievement of our own ends. Whereas, therefore, the individual gains, on the one hand, a certain degree of emancipation or freedom from the personal and emotional controls of intimate groups, he loses, on the other hand, the spontaneous self-expression, the morale, and the sense of participation that comes with living in an integrated society. This constitutes essentially the state of *anomie* or the social void to which Durkheim alludes in attempting to account for the various forms of social disorganization in technological society.

The segmental character and utilitarian accent of interpersonal relations in the city find their institutional expression in the proliferation of specialized tasks that we see in their most developed form in the professions. The operations of the pecuniary nexus lead to predatory relationships, which tend to obstruct the efficient functioning of the social order unless checked by professional codes and occupational etiquette. The premium put upon utility and efficiency suggests the adaptability of the corporate device for the organization of enterprises in which individuals can engage only in groups. The advantage that the corporation has over the individual entrepreneur and the partnership in the urban-industrial world derives not only from the possibility it affords of centralizing the resources of thousands of individuals or from the legal privilege of limited liability and perpetual succession, but from the fact that the corporation has no soul.

The specialization of individuals, particularly in their occupations, can proceed only, as Adam Smith pointed out, upon the basis of an enlarged market, which in turn accentuates the division of labor. This enlarged market is only in part supplied by the city's hinterland; in large measure it is found among the large numbers that the city itself contains. The dominance of the city over the surrounding hinterland becomes explicable in terms of the division of labor which urban life occasions and promotes. The extreme degree of interdependence and the unstable equilibrium of urban life are closely associated with the division of labor and the specialization of occupations. This interdependence and instability is increased by the tendency of each city to specialize in those functions in which it has the greatest advantage.

In a community composed of a larger number of individuals than can know one another intimately and can be assembled in one spot, it becomes necessary to communicate through indirect mediums and to articulate individual interests by a process of delegation. Typically in the city, interests are made effective through representation. The individual counts for little, but the voice of the representative is heard with a deference roughly proportional to the numbers for whom he speaks.

While this characterization of urbanism, in so far as it derives from large numbers, does not by any means exhaust the sociological inferences that might be drawn from our knowledge of the relationship of the size of a group to the characteristic behavior of the members, for the sake of brevity the assertions made may serve to exemplify the sort of propositions that might be developed.

Density

As in the case of numbers, so in the case of concentration in limited space, certain consequences of relevance in sociological analysis of the city emerge. Of these only a few can be indicated.

As Darwin pointed out for flora and fauna and as Durkheim[14] noted in the case of human societies, an increase in numbers when area is held constant (i.e., an increase in density) tends to produce differentiation and specialization since only in this way can the area support increased numbers. Density thus reinforces the effect of numbers in diversifying men and their activities and in increasing the complexity of the social structure.

On the subjective side, as Simmel has suggested, the close physical contact of numerous individuals necessarily produces a shift in the mediums through which we orient ourselves to the urban milieu, especially to our fellow men. Typically, our physical contacts are close but our social contacts are distant. The urban world puts a premium on visual recognition. We see the uniform which denotes the role of the functionaries and are oblivious to the personal eccentricities that are hidden behind the uniform. We tend to acquire and develop a sensitivity to a world of artifacts and become progressively farther removed from the world of nature.

We are exposed to glaring contrasts between splendor and squalor, between riches and poverty, intelligence and ignorance, order and chaos. The competition for space is great, so that each area generally tends to be put to the use which yields the greatest economic return. Place of work tends to become dissociated from place of residence, for the proximity of industrial and commercial establishments makes an area both economically and socially undesirable for residential purposes.

Density, land values, rentals, accessibility, healthfulness, prestige, aesthetic consideration, absence of nuisances such as noise, smoke, and dirt determine the desirability of various areas of the city as places of settlement for different sections of the population. Place and nature of work, income, racial and ethnic characteristics, social status, custom, habit, taste, preference, and prejudice are among the significant factors in accordance with which the urban population is selected and distributed into more or less distinct settlements. Diverse population elements inhabiting a compact settlement thus tend to become segregated from one another in the degree in which their requirements and modes of life are incompatible with one another and in the measure in which they are antagonistic to one another. Similarly, persons of homogeneous status and needs unwittingly drift into, consciously select, or are forced by circumstances into, the same area. The different parts of the city thus acquire specialized functions. The city consequently tends to resemble a mosaic of social worlds in which the transition from one to the other is abrupt. The juxtaposition of divergent personalities and modes of life tends to produce a relativistic perspective and a sense of toleration of differences that may be regarded as prerequisites for rationality and that lead toward the secularization of life.[15]

The close living together and working together of individuals who have no sentimental and emotional ties foster a spirit of competition, aggrandizement, and mutual exploitation. To counteract irresponsibility and potential disorder, formal controls tend to be resorted to. Without rigid adherence to predictable routines a large compact society would scarcely be able to maintain itself. The clock and the traffic signal are symbolic of the basis of our social order in the urban world. Frequent close physical contact, coupled with great social distance, accentuates the reserve of unattached individuals toward one another and, unless compensated for by other opportunities for response, gives rise to loneliness. The necessary frequent movement of great numbers of individuals in a congested habitat gives occasion to friction and irritation. Nervous tensions which derive from such personal frustrations are accentuated by the rapid tempo and the complicated technology under which life in dense areas must be lived.

Heterogeneity

The social interaction among such a variety of personality types in the urban milieu tends to break down the rigidity of caste lines and to complicate the class structure, and thus induces a more ramified and differentiated framework of social stratification than is found in more integrated societies. The heightened mobility of the individual, which brings him within the range of stimulation by a great number of diverse individuals and subjects him to fluctuating status in the differentiated social groups that compose the social structure of the city, tends toward the acceptance of instability and insecurity in the world at large as a norm. This fact helps to account, too, for the sophistication and cosmopolitanism of the urbanite. No single group has the undivided allegiance of the individual. The groups with which he is affiliated do not lend themselves readily to a simple hierarchical arrangement. By virtue of his different interests arising out of different aspects of social life, the individual acquires membership in widely divergent groups, each of which functions only with reference to a single segment of his personality. Nor do these groups easily permit a concentric arrangement so that the narrower ones fall within the circumference of the more inclusive ones, as is more likely to be the case in the rural community or in primitive societies. Rather the groups with which the person typically is affiliated are tangential to each other or intersect in a highly variable fashion.

Partly as a result of the physical footlooseness of the population and partly as a result of their social mobility, the turnover in group membership generally is rapid. Place of residence, place and character of employment, income, and interests fluctuate, and the task of holding organizations together and maintaining and promoting intimate and lasting acquaintanceship between the members is difficult. This applies strikingly to the local areas within the city into which persons become segregated more by virtue of differences in race, language, income, and social status, than through choice or positive attraction to people like themselves. Overwhelmingly the city-dweller is not a home-owner, and since a transitory habitat does not generate binding traditions and sentiments, only rarely is he truly a neighbor. There is little opportunity for the individual to obtain a conception of the city as a whole or to survey his place in the total scheme. Consequently he finds it difficult to determine what is to his own "best interests" and to decide between the issues and leaders presented to him by the agencies of mass suggestion. Individuals who are thus detached from the organized bodies which integrate society comprise the fluid masses that make collective behavior in the urban community so unpredictable and hence so problematical.

Although the city, through the recruitment of variant types to perform its diverse tasks and the accentuation of their uniqueness through competition and the premium upon eccentricity, novelty, efficient performance, and inventiveness, produces a highly differentiated population, it also exercises a leveling influence. Wherever large numbers of differently constituted individuals congregate, the process of depersonalization also enters. This leveling tendency inheres in part in the economic basis of the city. The development of large cities, at least in the modern age, was largely dependent upon the concentrative force of steam. The rise of the factory made possible mass production for an impersonal market. The fullest exploitation of the possibilities of the division of labor and mass production, however, is possible only with standardization of processes and products. A money economy goes hand in hand with such a system of production. Progressively as cities have developed upon a background of this system of production, the pecuniary nexus which implies the purchasability of services and things has displaced personal relations as the basis of association. Individuality under these circumstances must be replaced by categories. When large numbers have to make common use of facilities and institutions, an arrangement must be made to adjust the facilities and institutions to the needs of the average person rather than to those of particular individuals. The services of the public utilities, of the recreational, educational, and cultural institutions must be adjusted to mass requirements. Similarly, the cultural institutions, such as the schools, the movies, the radio, and the newspapers, by virtue of their mass clientele, must necessarily operate as leveling influences. The political process as it appears in urban life could not be understood without taking account of the mass appeals made through modern propaganda techniques. If the individual would participate at all in the social, political, and economic life of the city, he must subordinate some of his individuality to the demands of the larger community and in that measure immerse himself in mass movements.

The Relation Between a Theory of Urbanism and Sociological Research

By means of a body of theory such as that illustratively sketched above, the complicated and many-sided phenomena of urbanism may be analyzed in terms of a limited number of basic categories. The sociological approach to the city thus acquires an essential unity and coherence enabling the empirical investigator not merely to focus more distinctly upon the problems and processes that properly fall in his province but also to treat his subject matter in a more integrated and systematic fashion. A few typical findings of empirical research in the field of urbanism, with special reference to the United States, may be indicated to substantiate the theoretical propositions set forth in the preceding pages, and some of the crucial problems for further study may be outlined.

On the basis of the three variables—number, density of settlement, and degree of heterogeneity—of the urban population, it appears possible to explain the characteristics of urban life and to account for the differences between cities of various sizes and types.

Urbanism as a characteristic mode of life may be approached empirically from three interrelated perspectives: (1) as a physical structure comprising a population base, a technology, and an ecological order; (2) as a system of social organization involving a characteristic social structure, a series of social institutions, and a typical pattern of social relationships; and (3) as a set of attitudes and ideas, and a constellation of personalities engaging in typical forms of collective behavior and subject to characteristic mechanisms of social control.

Urbanism in Ecological Perspective

Since in the case of physical structure and ecological processes we are able to operate with fairly objective indices, it becomes possible to arrive at quite precise and generally quantitative results. The dominance of the city over its hinterland becomes explicable through the functional characteristics of the city which derive in large measure from the effect of numbers and density. Many of the technical facilities and the skills and organizations to which urban life gives rise can grow and prosper only in cities where the demand is sufficiently great. The nature and scope of the services rendered by these organizations and institutions and the advantage which they enjoy over the less developed facilities of smaller towns enhance the dominance of the city and the dependence of ever wider regions upon the central metropolis.

The urban-population composition shows the operation of selective and differentiating factors. Cities contain a larger proportion of persons in the prime of life than rural areas, which contain more old and very young people. In this, as in so many other respects, the larger the city the more this specific characteristic of urbanism is apparent. With the exception of the largest cities, which have attracted the bulk of the foreign-born males, and a few other special types of cities, women predominate numerically over men. The heterogeneity of the urban population is further indicated along racial and ethnic lines. The foreign born and their children constitute nearly two-thirds of all the inhabitants of cities of one million and over. Their proportion in the urban population declines as the size of the city decreases, until in the rural areas they comprise only about one-sixth of the total population. The larger cities similarly have attracted more Negroes and other racial groups than have the smaller communities. Considering that age, sex, race, and ethnic origin are associated with other factors such as occupation and interest, it becomes clear that one major characteristic of the urban-dweller is his dissimilarity from his fellows. Never before have such large masses of people of diverse traits as we find in our cities been thrown together into such close physical contact as in the great cities of America. Cities generally, and American cities in particular, comprise a motley of peoples and cultures, of highly differentiated modes of life between which there often is only the faintest communication, the greatest indifference and the broadest tolerance, occasionally bitter strife, but always the sharpest contrast.

The failure of the urban population to reproduce itself appears to be a biological consequence of a combination of factors in the complex of urban life, and the decline in the birth rate generally may be regarded as one of the most significant signs of the urbanization of the Western world. While the proportion of deaths in cities is slightly greater than in the country, the outstanding difference between the failure of present-day cities to maintain their population and that of cities of the past is that in former times it was due to the exceedingly high death rates in cities, whereas today, since cities have become more livable from a health standpoint, it is due to low birth rates. These biological characteristics of the urban population are significant sociologically, not merely because they reflect the urban mode of existence but also because they condition the growth and future dominance of cities and their basic social organization. Since cities are the consumers rather than the producers of men, the value of human life and the social estimation of the personality will not be unaffected by the balance between births and deaths. The pattern of land use, of land values, rentals, and ownership, the nature and functioning of the physical structures, of housing, of transportation and communication facilities, of public utilities—these and many other phases of the physical mechanism of the city are not isolated phenomena unrelated to the city as a social entity, but are affected by and affect the urban mode of life.

Urbanism as a Form of Social Organization

The distinctive features of the urban mode of life have often been described sociologically as consisting of the substitution of secondary for primary contacts, the weakening of bonds of kinship, and the declining social significance of the family, the disappearance of the neighborhood, and the undermining of the traditional basis of social solidarity. All these phenomena can be substantially verified through objective indices. Thus, for instance, the low and declining urban-reproduction rates suggest that the city is not conducive to the traditional type of family life, including the rearing of children and the maintenance of the home as the locus of a whole round of vital activities. The transfer of industrial, educational, and recreational activities to specialized institutions outside the home has deprived the family of some of its most characteristic historical functions. In cities, mothers are more likely to be employed, lodgers are more frequently part of the household, marriage tends to be postponed, and the proportion of single and unattached people is greater. Families are smaller and more frequently without children than in the country. The family as a unit of social life is emancipated from the larger kinship group characteristic of the country, and the individual members pursue their own diverging interests in their vocational, educational, religious, recreational, and political life.

Such functions as the maintenance of health, the methods of alleviating the hardships associated with personal and social insecurity, the provisions for education, recreation, and cultural advancement have given rise to highly specialized institutions on a community-wide, statewide, or even national basis. The same factors which have brought about greater personal insecurity also underlie the wider contrasts between individuals to be found in the urban world. While the city has broken down the rigid caste lines of preindustrial society, it has sharpened and differentiated income and status groups. Generally, a larger proportion of the adult-urban population is gainfully employed than is the case with the adult-rural population. The white-collar class, comprising those employed in trade, in clerical, and in professional work, are proportionately more numerous in large cities and in metropolitan centers and in smaller towns than in the country.

On the whole, the city discourages an economic life in which the individual in time of crisis has a basis of subsistence to fall back upon, and it discourages self-employment. While incomes of city people are on the average higher than those of country people, the cost of living seems to be higher in the larger cities. Home ownership involves greater burdens and is rarer. Rents are higher and absorb a larger proportion of the income. Although the urban-dweller has the benefit of many communal services, he spends a large proportion of his income for such items as recreation and advancement and a smaller proportion for food. What the communal services do not furnish the urbanite must purchase, and there is virtually no human need that has remained unexploited by commercialism. Catering to thrills and furnishing means of escape from drudgery, monotony, and routine thus becomes one of the major functions of urban recreation, which at its best furnishes means for creative self-expression and spontaneous group association, but which more typically in the urban world results in passive spectatorism on the one hand, or sensational record-smashing feats on the other.

Being reduced to a state of virtual impotence as an individual, the urbanite is bound to exert himself by joining with others of similar interest into organized groups to obtain his ends. This results in the enormous multiplication of voluntary organizations directed toward as great a variety of objectives as there are human needs and interests. While on the one hand the traditional ties of human association are weakened, urban existence involves a much greater degree of interdependence between man and man and a more complicated, fragile, and volatile form of mutual interrelations over many phases of which the individual as such can exert scarcely any control. Frequently there is only the most tenuous relationship between the economic position or other basic factors that determine the individual's existence in the urban world and the voluntary groups with which he is affiliated. While in a primitive and in a rural society it is generally possible to predict on the basis of a few known factors who will belong to what and who will associate with whom in almost every relationship of life, in the city we can only project the general pattern of group formation and affiliation, and this pattern will display many incongruities and contradictions.

Urban Personality and Collective Behavior

It is largely through the activities of the voluntary groups, be their objectives economic, political, educational, religious, recreational, or cultural, that the urbanite expresses and develops his personality, acquires status, and is able to carry on the round of activities that constitute his life-career. It may easily be inferred, however, that the organizational framework that these highly differentiated functions call into being does not of itself insure the consistency and integrity of the personalities whose interests it enlists. Personal disorganization, mental breakdown, suicide, delinquency, crime, corruption, and disorder might be expected under these circumstances to be more prevalent in the urban than in the rural community. This has been confirmed in so far as comparable indices are available; but the mechanisms underlying these phenomena require further analysis.

Since for most group purposes it is impossible in the city to appeal individually to the large number of discrete and differentiated individuals, and since it is only through the organizations to which men belong that their interests and resources can be enlisted for a collective cause, it may be inferred that social control in the city should typically proceed through formally organized groups. It follows, too, that the masses of men in the city are subject to manipulation by symbols and stereotypes managed by individuals working from afar or operating invisibly behind the scenes through their control of the instruments of communication. Self-government either in the economic, the political, or the cultural realm is under these circumstances reduced to a mere figure of speech or, at best, is subject to the unstable equilibrium of pressure groups. In view of the ineffectiveness of actual kinship ties we create fictional kinship groups. In the face of the disappearance of the territorial unit as a basis of social solidarity we create interest units. Meanwhile the city as a community resolves itself into a series of tenuous segmental relationships superimposed upon a territorial base with a definite center but without a definite periphery and upon a division of labor which far transcends the immediate locality and is worldwide in scope. The larger the number of persons in a state of interaction with one another the lower is the level of communication and the greater is the tendency for communication to proceed on an elementary level, i.e., on the basis of those things which are assumed to be common or to be of interest to all.

It is obviously, therefore, to the emerging trends in the communication system and to the production and distribution technology that has come into existence with modern civilization that we must look for the symptoms which will indicate the probable future development of urbanism as a mode of social life. The direction of the ongoing changes in urbanism will for good or ill transform not only the city but the world. Some of the more basic of these factors and processes and the possibilities of their direction and control invite further detailed study.

It is only in so far as the sociologist has a clear conception of the city as a social entity and a workable theory of urbanism that he can hope to develop a unified body of reliable knowledge, which what passes as "urban sociology" is certainly not at the present time. By taking his point of departure from a theory of urbanism such as that sketched in the foregoing pages to be elaborated, tested, and revised in the light of further analysis and empirical research, it is to be hoped that the criteria of relevance and validity of factual data can be determined. The miscellaneous assortment of disconnected information which has hitherto found its way into sociological treatises on the city may thus be sifted and incorporated into a coherent body of knowledge. Incidentally, only by means of some such theory will the sociologist escape the futile practice of voicing in the name of sociological science a variety of often insupportable judgments concerning such problems as poverty, housing, city planning, sanitation, municipal administration, policing, marketing, transportation, and other technical issues. While the sociologist cannot solve any of these practical problems—at least not by himself—he may, if he discovers his proper function, have an important contribution to make to their comprehension and solution. The prospects for doing this are brightest through a general, theoretical, rather than through an ad hoc approach.

Notes

[1] William Graham Sumner, *Folkways* (Boston, 1906), p. 12.
[2] S. V. Pearson, *The Growth and Distribution of Population* (New York, 1935), p. 211.
[3] Whereas rural life in the United States has for a long time been a subject of considerable interest on the part of governmental bureaus, the most notable case of a comprehensive report being that submitted by the Country Life Commission to President Theodore Roosevelt in 1909, it is worthy of note that no equally comprehensive official inquiry into urban life was undertaken until the establishment of a Research Committee on Urbanism of the National Resources Committee. (Cf. *Our Cities: Their Role in the National Economy* [Washington: Government Printing Office, 1937].)
[4] "The Anthropogeography of Some Great Cities," *Bulletin of the American Geographical Society*, XLI (1909), 537–66.

34   Urbanism As a Way of Life

[5] Walter F. Wilcox, "A Definition of 'City' in Terms of Density," in E. W. Burgess, *The Urban Community* (Chicago, 1926), p. 119.

[6] *Op. cit.*, p. 8.

[7] See Robert E. Park, Ernest W. Burgess, et al., *The City* (Chicago, 1925), esp. chaps. ii and iii; Werner Sombart, "Städtische Siedlung, Stadt," *Handwörterbuch der Soziologie*, ed. Alfred Vierkandt (Stuttgart, 1931); see also bibliography.

[8] Max Weber, *Wirtschaft und Gesellschaft* (Tübingen, 1925), Part II, chap. viii, pp. 514–601.

[9] Park, Burgess, *et al.*, *op. cit.*, chap. i.

[10] The justification for including the term *permanent* in the definition may appear necessary. Our failure to give an extensive justification for this qualifying mark of the urban rests on the obvious fact that unless human settlements take a fairly permanent root in a locality the characteristics of urban life cannot arise, and conversely the living together of large numbers of heterogeneous individuals under dense conditions is not possible without the development of a more or less technological structure.

[11] See esp. vii. 4. 4–14. Translated by B. Jowett.

[12] *Op. cit.*, p. 514.

[13] Georg Simmel, "Die Grossstädte und das Geistesleben," *Die Grossstadt*, ed. Theodor Petermann (Dresden, 1903), pp. 187–206.

[14] E. Durkheim, *De la division du travail social* (Paris, 1932), p. 248.

[15] The extent to which the segregation of the population into distinct ecological and cultural areas and the resulting social attitude of tolerance, rationality, and secular mentality are functions of density as distinguished from heterogeneity is difficult to determine. Most likely we are dealing here with phenomena which are consequences of the simultaneous operation of both factors.

The Urban Experience
A Psychological Analysis

STANLEY MILGRAM

*Some social scientists have tested Wirth's theory of ways in
which large concentrations of people can affect the individual.
These scientists have refined the concepts of density and
heterogeneity so that specific operations could be performed in
these experiments which would prove or disprove Wirth's
theory. In this article Milgram reviews the results of such
experiments. Milgram presents the concept of "psychic
overload" to explain why crowding has certain effects on
people, such as their politeness to strangers. Milgram's stress is
on crowding in public places. See Oscar Lewis's "The Culture of
Poverty" for a consideration of the effects of crowding in the home.*

When I first came to New York it seemed like a nightmare. As
soon as I got off the train at Grand Central I was caught up in
pushing, shoving crowds on 42nd Street. Sometimes people
bumped into me without apology; what really frightened me was
to see two people literally engaged in combat for possession of
a cab. Why were they so rushed? Even drunks on the street were
bypassed without a glance. People didn't seem to care about
each other at all.

This statement represents a common reaction to a great city, but
it does not tell the whole story. Obviously cities have great appeal
because of their variety, eventfulness, possibility of choice, and the
stimulation of an intense atmosphere that many individuals find

Source: "The Experience of Living in Cities: A Psychological Analysis," Stanley
Milgram, *Science*, Vol. 167 (March 13, 1970), pp. 1461–68. Copyright 1970 by the
American Association for the Advancement of Science. Reprinted by permission of
Science.

35

a desirable background to their lives. Where face-to-face contacts are important, the city offers unparalleled possibilities. It has been calculated by the Regional Plan Association[1] that in Nassau County, a suburb of New York City, an individual can meet 11,000 others within a 10-minute radius of his office by foot or car. In Newark, a moderate-sized city, he can meet more than 20,000 persons within this radius. But in midtown Manhattan he can meet fully 220,000. So there is an order-of-magnitude increment in the communication possibilities offered by a great city. That is one of the bases of its appeal and, indeed, of its functional necessity. The city provides options that no other social arrangement permits. But there is a negative side also, as we shall see.

Granted that cities are indispensable in complex society, we may still ask what contribution psychology can make to understand the experience of living in them. What theories are relevant? How can we extend our knowledge of the psychological aspects of life in cities through empirical inquiry? If empirical inquiry is possible, along what lines should it proceed? In short, where do we start in constructing urban theory and in laying out lines of research?

Observation is the indispensable starting point. Any observer in the streets of midtown Manhattan will see (1) large numbers of people, (2) a high population density, and (3) heterogeneity of population. These three factors need to be at the root of any sociopsychological theory of city life, for they condition all aspects of our experience in the metropolis. Louis Wirth,[2] if not the first to point to these factors, is nonetheless the sociologist who relied most heavily on them in his analysis of the city. Yet, for a psychologist, there is something unsatisfactory about Wirth's theoretical variables. Numbers, density, and heterogeneity are demographic facts but they are not yet psychological facts. They are external to the individual. Psychology needs an idea that links the individual's *experience* to the demographic circumstances of urban life.

One link is provided by the concept of overload. This term, drawn from systems analysis, refers to a system's inability to process inputs from the environment because there are too many inputs for the system to cope with, or because successive inputs come so fast that input A cannot be processed when input B is presented. When overload is present, adaptations occur. The system must set priorities and make choices. A may be processed while B is kept in abeyance, or one input may be sacrificed altogether. City life, as we experience it, constitutes a continuous set of encounters with overload, and of resultant adaptations. Overload characteristically deforms daily life on several levels, impinging on role performance, the evolution of social norms, cognitive functioning, and the use of facilities.

The concept has been implicit in several theories of urban experience. In 1903 George Simmel[3] pointed out that, since urban dwellers come into contact with vast numbers of people each day, they conserve psychic energy by becoming acquainted with a far smaller proportion of people than their rural counterparts do, and by maintaining more superficial relationships even with these acquaintances. Wirth[4] points specifically to "the superficiality, the anonymity, and the transitory character of urban social relations."

One adaptive response to overload, therefore, is the allocation of less time to each input. A second adaptive mechanism is disregard of low-priority inputs. Principles of selectivity are formulated such that investment of time and energy are reserved for carefully defined inputs (the urbanite disregards the drunk sick on the street as he purposefully navigates through the crowd). Third, boundaries are redrawn in certain social transactions so that the overloaded system can shift the burden to the other party in the exchange; thus, harried New York bus drivers once made change for customers, but now this responsibility has been shifted to the client, who must have the exact fare ready. Fourth, reception is blocked off prior to entrance into a system; city dwellers increasingly use unlisted telephone numbers to prevent individuals from calling them, and a small but growing number resort to keeping the telephone off the hook to prevent incoming calls. More subtly, a city dweller blocks inputs by assuming an unfriendly countenance, which discourages others from initiating contact. Additionally, social screening devices are interposed between the individual and environmental inputs (in a town of five thousand anyone can drop in to chat with the mayor, but in the metropolis, organizational screening devices deflect inputs to other destinations). Fifth, the intensity of inputs is diminished by filtering devices, so that only weak and relatively superficial forms of involvement with others are allowed. Sixth, specialized institutions are created to absorb inputs that would otherwise swamp the individual (welfare departments handle the financial needs of a million individuals in New York City, who would otherwise create an army of mendicants continuously importuning the pedestrian). The interposition of institutions between the individual and the social world, a characteristic of all modern society, and most notably of the large metropolis, has its negative side. It deprives the individual of a sense of direct contact and spontaneous integration in the life around him. It simultaneously protects and estranges the individual from his social environment.

Many of these adaptive mechanisms apply not only to individuals but to institutional systems as well, as Meier[5] has so brilliantly shown in connection with the library and the stock exchange.

In sum, the observed behavior of the urbanite in a wide range of situations appears to be determined largely by a variety of adaptations to overload. I now deal with several specific consequences of responses to overload, which make for differences in the tone of city and town.

Social Responsibility

The principal point of interest for a social psychology of the city is that moral and social involvement with individuals is necessarily restricted. This is a direct and necessary function of excess of input over capacity to process. Such restriction of involvement runs a broad spectrum from refusal to become involved in the needs of another person, even when the person desperately needs assistance, through refusal to do favors, to the simple withdrawal of courtesies (such as offering a lady a seat, or saying "sorry" when a pedestrian collision occurs). In any transaction more and more details need to be dropped as the total number of units to be processed increases and assaults an instrument of limited processing capacity.

The ultimate adaptation to an overloaded social environment is to totally disregard the needs, interests, and demands of those whom one does not define as relevant to the satisfaction of personal needs, and to develop highly efficient perceptual means of determining whether an individual falls into the category of friend or stranger. The disparity in the treatment of friends and strangers ought to be greater in cities than in towns; the time allotment and willingness to become involved with those who have no personal claim on one's time is likely to be less in cities than in towns.

Bystander Intervention in Crises

The most striking deficiencies in social responsibility in cities [occur] in crisis situations, such as the Genovese murder in Queens. In 1964, Catherine Genovese, coming home from a night job in the early hours of an April morning, was stabbed repeatedly, over an extended period of time. Thirty-eight residents of a respectable New York City neighborhood admit to having witnessed at least a part of the attack, but none went to her aid or called the police until after she was dead. Milgram and Hollander, writing in *The Nation*,[6] analyzed the event in these terms:

Urban friendships and associations are not primarily formed on the basis of physical proximity. A person with numerous close friends in different parts of the city may not know the occupant of an adjacent apartment. This does not mean that a city dweller has fewer friends than does a villager, or knows fewer persons who will come to his aid; however, it does mean that his allies are not constantly at hand. Miss Genovese required immediate aid from those physically present. There is no evidence that the city had deprived Miss Genovese of human associations, but the friends who might have rushed to her side were miles from the scene of her tragedy.

Further, it is known that her cries for help were not directed to a specific person; they were general. But only individuals can act, and as the cries were not specifically directed, no particular person felt a special responsibility. The crime and the failure of community response seem absurd to us. At the time, it may well have seemed equally absurd to the Kew Gardens residents that not one of the neighbors would have called the police. A collective paralysis may have developed from the belief of each of the witnesses that someone else must surely have taken that obvious step.

Gaertner and Bickman[7] of The City University of New York have extended the bystander studies to an examination of help across ethnic lines. Blacks and whites, with clearly identifiable accents, called strangers (through what the caller represented as an error in telephone dialing), gave them a plausible story of being stranded on an outlying highway without more dimes, and asked the stranger to call a garage. The experimenters found that the white callers had a significantly better chance of obtaining assistance than the black callers. This suggests that ethnic allegiance may well be another means of coping with overload: the city dweller can reduce excessive demands and screen out urban heterogeneity by reasoning along ethnic lines; overload is made more manageable by limiting the "span of sympathy."

In any quantitative characterization of the social texture of city life, a necessary first step is the application of such experimental methods as these to field situations in large cities and small towns. Theorists argue that the indifference shown in the Genovese case would not be found in a small town, but in the absence of solid experimental evidence the question remains an open one.

More than just callousness prevents bystanders from participating in altercations between people. A rule of urban life is respect for other people's emotional and social privacy, perhaps because physical privacy is so hard to achieve. And in situations for which the standards are heterogeneous, it is much harder to know whether taking an active role is unwarranted meddling or an appropriate response to a critical situation. If a husband and wife are quarreling in public, at what point should a bystander step in? On the one hand, the heterogeneity of the city produces substantially greater tolerance about behavior, dress, and codes of ethics than is generally found in the small town, but this diversity also encourages people to withhold aid for fear of antagonizing the participants or crossing an inappropriate and difficult-to-define line.

Moreover, the frequency of demands present in the city gives rise to norms of noninvolvement. There are practical limitations to the Samaritan impulse in a major city. If a citizen attended to every needy person, if he were sensitive to and acted on every altruistic impulse that was evoked in the city, he could scarcely keep his own affairs in order.

Willingness to Trust and Assist Strangers

We now move away from crisis situations to less urgent examples of social responsibility. For it is not only in situations of dramatic need but in the ordinary, everyday willingness to lend a hand that the city dweller is said to be deficient relative to his small-town cousin. The comparative method must be used in any empirical examination of this question. A commonplace social situation is staged in an urban setting and in a small town—a situation to which a subject can respond by either extending help or withholding it. The responses in town and city are compared.

One factor in the purported unwillingness of urbanites to be helpful to strangers may well be their heightened sense of physical (and emotional) vulnerability—a feeling that is supported by urban crime statistics. A key test for distinguishing between city and town behavior, therefore, is determining how city dwellers compare with town dwellers in offering aid that increases their personal vulnerability and requires some trust of strangers. Altman, Levine, Nadien, and Villena[8] of The City University of New York devised a study to compare the behaviors of city and town dwellers in this respect. The criterion used in this study was the willingness of householders to allow strangers to enter their home to use the telephone. The student investigators individually rang doorbells, explained that they had misplaced the address of a friend nearby, and asked to use the phone. The investigators (two males and two females) made one hundred requests for entry into homes in the city and sixty requests in the small towns. The results for middle-income housing developments in Manhattan were compared with data for several small towns (Stony Point, Spring Valley, Ramapo, Nyack, New City, and West Clarkstown) in Rockland County, outside of New York City. As table 1 shows, in all cases there was a sharp increase in the proportion of entries achieved by an experimenter when he moved from the city to a small town. In the most extreme case the experimenter was five times as likely to gain admission to homes in a small town as to homes in Manhattan. Although the female experimenters had notably greater success both in cities and in towns than the male experimenters had, each of the four students did at least twice as well in towns as in cities. This suggests that the city-town distinction overrides even the predictably greater fear of male strangers than of female ones.

Table 1 Percentage of Entries Achieved by Investigators for City and Town Dwellings

	ENTRIES ACHIEVED (%)	
Experimenter	*City**	*Small town†*
Male		
No. 1	16	40
No. 2	12	60
Female		
No. 3	40	87
No. 4	40	100

*Number of requests for entry, 100.
†Number of requests for entry, 60.

   The lower level of helpfulness by city dwellers seems due in part to recognition of the dangers of living in Manhattan, rather than to mere indifference or coldness. It is significant that 75 percent of all the city respondents received and answered messages by shouting through closed doors and by peering out through peepholes; in the towns, by contrast, about 75 percent of the respondents opened the door.
   Supporting the experimenters' quantitative results was their general observation that the town dwellers were noticeably more friendly and less suspicious than the city dwellers. In seeking to explain the reasons for the greater sense of psychological vulnerability city dwellers feel, above and beyond the differences in crime statistics, Villena points out that, if a crime is committed in a village, a resident of a neighboring village may not perceive

the crime as personally relevant though the geographic distance may be small, whereas a criminal act committed anywhere in the city, though miles from the city-dweller's home, is still verbally located within the city; thus, Villena says, "the inhabitant of the city possesses a larger vulnerable space."

Civilities

Even at the most superficial level of involvement—the exercise of everyday civilities—urbanites are reputedly deficient. People bump into each other and often do not apologize. They knock over another person's packages and, as often as not, proceed on their way with a grumpy exclamation instead of an offer of assistance. Such behavior, which many visitors to great cities find distasteful, is less common, we are told, in smaller communities, where traditional courtesies are more likely to be observed.

In some instances it is not simply that, in the city, traditional courtesies are violated; rather, the cities develop new norms of noninvolvement. These are so well defined and so deeply a part of city life that *they* constitute the norms people are reluctant to violate. Men are actually embarrassed to give up a seat on the subway to an elderly woman; they mumble "I was getting off anyway," instead of making the gesture in a straightforward and gracious way. These norms develop because everyone realizes that, in situations of high population density, people cannot implicate themselves in each other's affairs, for to do so would create conditions of continual distraction which would frustrate purposeful action.

In discussing the effects of overload I do not imply that at every instant the city dweller is bombarded with an unmanageable number of inputs, and that his responses are determined by the excess of input at any given instant. Rather, adaptation occurs in the form of gradual evolution of norms of behavior. Norms are evolved in response to frequent discrete experiences of overload; they persist and become generalized modes of responding.

Overload on Cognitive Capacities: Anonymity

That we respond differently toward those whom we know and those who are strangers to us is a truism. An eager patron aggressively cuts in front of someone in a long movie line to save time only to confront a friend; he then behaves sheepishly. A man is involved in an automobile accident caused by another driver, emerges from his car shouting in rage, then moderates his behavior on discovering a friend driving the other car. The city dweller, when walking through the midtown streets, is in a state of continual anonymity vis-à-vis the other pedestrians.

Anonymity is part of a continuous spectrum ranging from total anonymity to full acquaintance, and it may well be that measurement of the precise degrees of anonymity in cities and towns would help to explain important distinctions between the quality of life in each. Conditions of full acquaintance, for example, offer security and familiarity, but they may also be stifling, because the individual is caught in a web of established relationships. Conditions of complete anonymity, by contrast, provide freedom from routinized social ties, but they may also create feelings of alienation and detachment.

Empirically one could investigate the proportion of activities in which the city dweller or the town dweller is known by others at given times in his daily life, and the proportion of activities in the course of which he interacts with individuals who know him. At his job, for instance, the city dweller may be known to as many people as his rural counterpart. However, when he is not fulfilling his occupational role—say, when merely traveling about the city— the urbanite is doubtless more anonymous than his rural counterpart.

Another direction for empirical study is investigation of the beneficial effects of anonymity. The impersonality of city life breeds its own tolerance for the private lives of the inhabitants. Individuality and even eccentricity, we may assume, can flourish more readily in the metropolis than in the small town. Stigmatized persons may find it easier to lead comfortable lives in the city, free of the constant scrutiny of neighbors. To what degree can this assumed difference between city and town be shown empirically? Judith Waters,[9] at The City University of New York, hypothesized that avowed homosexuals would be more likely to be accepted as tenants in a large city than in small towns, and she dispatched letters from homosexual and heterosexual individuals to real estate agents in cities and towns across the country. The results of her study were inconclusive. But the general idea of examining the protective benefits of city life to the stigmatized ought to be pursued.

Role Behavior in Cities and Towns

Another product of urban overload is the adjustment in roles made by urbanites in daily interactions. As Wirth has said: "Urbanites meet one another in highly segmental roles. . . . They are less dependent upon particular persons, and their dependence upon others is confined to a highly fractionalized aspect of the other's round of activity."[10] This tendency is particularly noticeable in the transactions between customers and individuals offering professional or sales services. The owner of a country store has time to become well acquainted with his dozen-or-so daily customers, but the girl at the checkout counter of a busy supermarket, serving hundreds of customers a day, barely has time to toss the purchases into one customer's shopping bag before the next customer confronts her with his pile of groceries.

Meier, in his stimulating analysis of the city,[11] discusses several adaptations a system may make when confronted by inputs that exceed its capacity to process them. Meier argues that, according to the principle of competition for scarce resources, the scope and time of the transaction shrink as customer volume and daily turnover rise. This, in fact, is what is meant by the "brusque" quality of city life. New standards have developed in cities concerning what levels of services are appropriate in business transactions. . . .

McKenna and Morgenthau,[12] in a seminar at The City University of New York, devised a study (1) to compare the willingness of city dwellers and small-town dwellers to do favors for strangers that entailed expenditure of a small amount of time and slight inconvenience but no personal vulnerability, and (2) to determine whether the more compartmentalized, transitory relationships of the city would make urban salesgirls less likely than small-town salesgirls to carry out, for strangers, tasks not related to their customary roles.

To test for differences between city dwellers and small-town dwellers, a simple experiment was devised in which persons from both settings were asked (by telephone) to perform increasingly onerous favors for anonymous strangers.

Within the cities (Chicago, New York, and Philadelphia), half the calls were to housewives and the other half to salesgirls in women's apparel shops; the division was the same for the thirty-seven small towns of the study, which were in the same states as the cities. Each experimenter represented herself as a long-distance caller who had, through error, been connected with the respondent by the operator. The experimenter began by asking for simple information about the weather for purposes of travel. Next the experimenter excused herself on some pretext (asking the respondent to "please hold on"), put the phone down for almost a full minute, and then picked it up again and asked the respondent to provide the phone number of a hotel or motel in her vicinity at which the experimenter might stay during a forthcoming visit. Scores were assigned the subjects on the basis of how helpful they had been. McKenna summarizes her results in this manner:

> People in the city, whether they are engaged in a specific job or not, are less helpful and informative than people in small towns; . . . People at home, regardless of where they live, are less helpful and informative than people working in shops.

However, the absolute level of cooperativeness for urban subjects was found to be quite high and does not accord with the stereotype of the urbanite as aloof, self-centered, and unwilling to help strangers. The quantitative differences obtained by McKenna and Morgenthau are less great than one might have expected. This again points up the need for extensive empirical research in rural-urban differences, research that goes far beyond that provided in the few illustrative pilot studies presented here. At this point we have very limited objective evidence on differences in the quality of social encounters in city and small town.

But the research needs to be guided by unifying theoretical concepts. As I have tried to demonstrate, the concept of overload helps to explain a wide variety of contrasts between city behavior and town behavior: (1) the differences in role enactment (the tendency of urban dwellers to deal with one another in highly segmented, functional terms, and of urban sales personnel to devote limited time and attention to their customers); (2) the evolution of urban norms quite different from traditional town values (such as the acceptance of noninvolvement, impersonality, and aloofness in urban life); (3) the adaptation of the urban dweller's cognitive processes (his inability to identify most of the people he sees daily, his screening of sensory stimuli, his development of blasé attitudes toward deviant or bizarre behavior, and his selectivity in responding to human demands); and (4) the competition for scarce facilities in the city (the subway rush; the fight for taxis; traffic jams; standing in line to await services). I suggest that contrasts between city and rural behavior probably reflect the responses of similar people to very different situations, rather than intrinsic differences in the personalities of rural and city dwellers. The city is a situation to which individuals respond adaptively.

Notes

1 *New York Times* (June 15, 1969).
2 L. Wirth, *American Journal of Sociology*, Vol. 44, No. 1 (1938). Wirth's ideas have come under heavy criticism by contemporary city planners, who point out that

the city is broken down into neighborhoods, which fulfill many of the functions of small towns. See, for example, H. J. Gans, *People and Plans: Essays on Urban Problems and Solutions* (New York: Basic Books, 1968); J. Jacobs, *The Death and Life of Great American Cities* (New York: Random House, 1961); G. D. Suttles, *The Social Order of the Slum* (Chicago, The University of Chicago Press, 1968).

[3] G. Simmel, *The Sociology of Georg Simmel*, ed. K. H. Wolff (New York: Macmillan, 1950). [English translation of G. Simmel, "Die Grossstädte und das Geistesleben," *Die Grossstadt* (Dresden: Jansch, 1903).]

[4] L. Wirth, *American Journal of Sociology.*

[5] R. L. Meier, *A Communications Theory of Urban Growth* (Cambridge: M.I.T. Press, 1962).

[6] S. Milgram and P. Hollander, *Nation*, Vol. 25, No. 602 (1964).

[7] S. Gaertner and L. Bickman (Graduate Center, The City University of New York), unpublished research.

[8] D. Altman et al. (Graduate Center, The City University of New York), unpublished research.

[9] J. Waters (Graduate Center, The City University of New York), unpublished research.

[10] L. Wirth, *American Journal of Sociology.*

[11] R. L. Meier, *A Communications Theory of Urban Growth.*

[12] (Graduate Center, The City University of New York), unpublished research.

Urban Danger
Life in a Neighborhood of Strangers

SALLY ENGLE MERRY

*In a landmark study, Wirth argued that the urban way of life is
characterized by relations between strangers. Despite
considerable research that shows that urbanites' social lives
include intimate and enduring social ties, relations between
strangers continue to define an essential and problematic
quality of urban social life. Sally Engle Merry's ethnographic
study of a multiethnic housing project in a high-crime
neighborhood shows how the boundaries between social groups
contribute to the sense that the city is dangerous. The existence
of social boundaries makes the project a fertile place for crime,
while the residents' awareness of danger comes from their
belief that they live in a world of dangerous and unpredictable
strangers. These strangers are people in other social networks,
known across the social boundaries which divide the intimate
worlds of the project.*

In "Urbanism As a Way of Life," Wirth describes cities as places
of anonymity and disorder, as settlements in which people treat
each other with indifference, competition, and exploitation. A city
is a place of strangers. The web of gossip, social pressure and
concern about the opinions of others is unable to hold in check the
criminal, the prostitute, and the social deviant or to prevent the
personal breakdown of the increasingly isolated individual. Wirth's
famous article, written in 1938, distills the ideas of two decades of

Source: Article written expressly for *Urban Life*.

urban research done by sociologists and anthropologists at the University of Chicago during the early twentieth century. He argues that the ecological conditions of size, density, permanency, and heterogeneity create a social world of impersonal, superficial, transitory relationships in which individuals are detached from close ties to social groups, such as communities and families, and are freed from the constraints of social control. Intimate ties of family and neighborhood become less important, while more impersonal and instrumental relationships come to predominate. Cities are characterized by anomie: by a sense of normlessness, both in the sense of the individual's lack of attachment to a moral code and of a collective loss of moral consensus.

In the fifty years since Wirth's article was published, numerous studies of the social life of cities have challenged his theory. Many researchers have described neighborhoods, workplaces, religious communities, and other urban settings in which people know one another and treat each other in terms of intimacy and interdependence (e.g., Whyte 1955; Young and Willmott 1957; Gans 1962; Hannerz 1969; Lewis 1952; Stack 1974; Hannerz 1980). In these places, the close community life which Wirth saw as characteristic of villages flourished. Other critics argued that Wirth was really describing the impact of industrialization, not urbanism. Preindustrial cities lacked the anonymity and disorder of large industrial cities (Sjoberg 1960; Krapf-Askari 1969; Fox 1977). Still others claimed that, despite the apparent disorder of the city, particularly its lack of cohesive neighborhood communities, new forms of community have emerged in modern industrial cities based on social networks, voluntary associations, and other more ephemeral, yet important, *quasi-groups* which stretch across neighborhoods and regions (Mitchell 1969; Boissevain 1974).

Despite these serious and legitimate criticisms of Wirth's vision of the city, however, sociologists and anthropologists still return to his article because they have a lingering sense that he has special insight into the issues; that there are some features of the city life he describes which do resonate with the experience of living in the modern industrial city. Such cities do have many strangers, and strangers are particularly taxing and troubling for urbanites. They lie behind the problems of urban crime, the fear of crime and even the fear of immigrants and newcomers, of people who are culturally strange and different.

Although Wirth's theory of urbanism does not describe the totality of urban social life, it does apply to particular aspects of city life. It describes the boundaries between separate social worlds. Neither Wirth nor Park, an early and influential sociologist at the

University of Chicago, thought that the city lacked close-knit urban villages, but saw the city as a collection of these small communities. Park described the city as "a mosaic of little worlds which touch but do not interpenetrate" (1952:47). It is at these boundaries that the characteristic features of urban social life, as Wirth described them, appear. Such social boundaries within a single housing project—Dover Square—and how they generate both crime and a sense of danger will be explored in this article.

Life in a High-Crime Neighborhood

Inspired by Wirth's vision of urban social life, I decided to conduct a cultural study of urban danger. I wanted to learn how people who live in high-crime urban areas think about danger, how they deal with it on a daily basis, and how anonymity fosters crime. After perusing crime statistics and neighborhood descriptions, I selected a subsidized housing project located deep in a neighborhood with one of the highest crime rates in a major northeastern city. Since the intent was also to investigate the impact of several ethnic groups living side-by-side, a neighborhood which had a broad mixture of residents was chosen. After locating an ideal small development housing 300 white, black, Chinese, and Hispanic families, I moved into an apartment three blocks from the project and spent a year and a half carrying out anthropological field research. The residents were questioned regarding how they thought about danger and about how they handled the high rate of crime surrounding them. Project residents who committed crimes against their neighbors were also interviewed concerning their views of crime and danger.

In the mid-1970s, when the study was conducted, the neighborhood was slowly changing from a depressed area populated by homeless alcoholics and characterized by deteriorating housing projects to a trendy neighborhood attractive to wealthy professionals. More daring members of this group bought the old buildings, some of which had a tarnished elegance about them, and renovated them into attractive townhouses. In the ten years since the completion of the study, this process of gentrification in the surrounding neighborhood has continued, but the project has remained much the same. The ethnographic present will be employed to describe the project.

The residents of the Dover Square project are 55 percent Chinese, 14 percent black, 9 percent white, and 9 percent Hispanic, by population, although the number of families is more evenly distributed. The Chinese residents, most of whom are recent immigrants from Hong Kong, speak little or no English, although their children are typically fluent in English. They plan to stay in the United States. Many of the blacks arrived in the city in the 1950s during the massive black migration from the South and have lived in less attractive parts of the city for ten years or more. A substantial number of the whites are connected to an established Syrian-Lebanese community nearby dating from the early 1900s. Some of this community was razed to build the project. The Hispanics are recent arrivals from Puerto Rico and many do not speak fluent English. Many plan to return to their homeland and consider their stay in the city temporary.

The project is federally subsidized, designed to house both low- and moderate-income families. It opened in the mid-1960s and, ten years later, had a remarkably stable population for a housing project: well over half the families had lived in the development since it opened, and the rate of turnover was under 5 percent per year. Yet, despite this stability, the neighborhood has not become a community. It is not a cohesive, integrated social system, but rather a series of distinct, unconnected social networks occupying the same geographical space. Each ethnic group is scattered throughout the development, yet residents maintain virtually all of their close social relationships with neighbors of the same ethnicity. Consequently, neighbors who belong to different ethnic groups often remain strangers, despite years of sharing the same stairwells, porches and walkways.

A social network is a way of conceptualizing those parts of social life which do not form bounded, enduring social groups (see Barnes 1954; Bott 1957; Epstein 1961; Mitchell 1969; Boissevain 1974). Each person is the center of a group of friends and kinsmen, the central point from which radiates a series of links to other people. This constellation forms an egocentric social network. Members of this network also know others, some of whom the first person does not. These are second-order links, friends of friends. By extension, each second-order link also has social contacts, so that one can imagine a network of social relationships extending outward from any individual to first, second, and further orders of contact. Since these networks of relationship are also potential communication channels, mapping their structure and boundaries provides important clues to the flow of gossip and information through a social system (Merry 1984). Boundaries in social networks tend to be gaps in the flow of information.

In Dover Square, intimate networks—links to close friends and relatives—are almost always restricted to a single ethnic group. An extended network of acquaintances crosscuts ethnic lines at a few points, but also tends to remain within a single ethnic group. A few individuals have social networks consisting almost entirely of a different ethnic group, such as the white youths who regularly hang out with a gang of young black men and women. Since each ethnic group is scattered throughout the area, the social organization of the project consists of a series of discrete, overarching social networks. One can imagine this social composition as several layers of fishnet strung over the same space with a few threads running between the layers.

The social boundaries between ethnic groups persist because each group is encapsulated within a network of social relationships and a set of institutions which stretches to nearby black, white, Chinese, and Hispanic communities. The majority of families in the project regularly visit kinsmen, friends, religious groups, and social organizations in their nearby ethnic communities. Chinatown lies on one side of the project, an established Syrian-Lebanese community on another, the black community is close by on another side, and a substantial Hispanic settlement is in the middle of the slowly gentrifying neighborhood nearby. Jobs, friends, marriage partners, churches, social services, and recreational opportunities are all primarily available within these communities. Consequently, relations with members of the same ethnic group carry an expectation of continuity that is not characteristic of relations with neighbors in Dover Square. Neighbors are only temporary associates, here today but gone whenever they move away, while people in the same ethnic group are connected by enduring ties. The denser mesh of personal ties and group affiliations within ethnic groups means that Dover Square residents are far more accountable to their fellow ethnics than they are to their neighbors of different ethnicity.

Because of the boundaries between ethnic groups, neighbors are often anonymous. This anonymity provides opportunities for crime, since criminals can rob their neighbors with little fear of apprehension. Many project residents observed that, in general, criminals prefer not to work close to home where they can too easily be identified by their neighbors, but here, where neighbors are often strangers, a resident can rob or burglarize people close to home without fear of identification. This means that a project resident can commit crimes on his home territory, which is relatively safe, predictable, and familiar, while appearing to victims as a stranger from a distant area. The same people can be robbed whose daily habits and material possessions are easily visible.

At the same time, the widespread fear and distrust of neighbors undermines community efforts at controlling crime. As one of the leaders of the youth group active in committing crimes in the area put it:

> The people who are being affected by crime don't understand that they are the cause of crime. I think a lot of people around here don't want other people's houses to be safe. People are beginning to be cold-hearted, not caring enough, because, if people cared enough about other people, they would care about theirs. In order to protect your house, you have to protect your neighbor's.

Social control is undermined by this structure of social networks since the implementation of sanctions, of punishments for rule-breaking, is unlikely across the social boundaries. For sanctions to be effective in discouraging rule-breaking, they must be both powerful and certain of implementation. A sanction which is severe will have little deterrent effect if the offender feels that there is little chance that she will feel its weight. When the offender is anonymous to his victim, it is obviously difficult to catch him or to impose any penalty on him. If the person who observes a crime knows who the perpetrator is or even where he lives or who his friends are, she might be able to impose some kind of pressure on him. When the perpetrator is a stranger, however, even observing the crime act leaves the observer powerless. The strategies Dover Square residents develop to cope with living in a hazardous environment reveal the critical role played by this knowledge of who the dangerous people are, both in protecting the individual from victimization and in reducing the sense of danger.

Conceptions of Danger

As I became further acquainted with the residents who lived in the project, I discovered that they differed greatly in their perceptions of and approaches to the dangers in their environment. One young Chinese woman, for example, never returned home alone on foot after dark. When she arrived by car, she honked the horn to alert her parents and then dashed the twenty feet to her door. A white man cautiously packed his suitcases into his car under cover of darkness before leaving for a trip to escape being noticed by potential burglars. A middle-aged black woman sneaked surreptitiously from her home at 6:00 A.M. to do her laundry before the neighborhood youths gathered in the laundromat to visit and smoke. She was anxious not to leave her home vacant, even for a few minutes, lest the burglars she constantly feared notice that her house was unguarded.

Yet, in the same neighborhood, a young black woman moved freely, visiting neighbors late at night with no thought of danger. Young men would rendezvous in dark secluded hallways even though they were aware that they risked being mugged. A Chinese man, reputed to possess marvelous skill in the martial arts, was studiously avoided by youths seeking safe and profitable robbery victims. He walked through the project without fear. Lastly, an adult black man declared that his neighborhood was very safe because he knows everyone, and everyone knows him.

All of these people face the same hazards, yet their attitudes, fears, and modes of coping vary enormously. Why do they respond so differently to the same risks? Urbanites, in general, continually make decisions about which situations and persons they consider dangerous, but these judgments are rarely based on detailed statistics about where and when crimes occur. Nor are such peoples' attitudes proportional to the statistical risks of victimization, either in this project or nationwide. A survey of the victimization experiences of two-thirds of the three hundred households suggested that the rates of victimization of black and Chinese households are roughly the same: about half of each had experienced a robbery, burglary, or assault since moving into the development ten years earlier. Yet, when asked how dangerous they found their environment, the Chinese residents reported much higher levels of fear: 30 percent of those interviewed said the project was dangerous in contrast to only 13 percent of the black respondents, and 18 percent said it was not at all dangerous, while 65 percent of the blacks interviewed felt this way. National statistics show a similar discrepancy between fear and the chance of victimization: although fear focuses on the random, unpredictable attack of the stranger, the risk of assault and murder by friends is far greater.

Clearly, danger cannot be equated with the statistical probability of being the victim of a crime. Instead, it is the individual's interpretation of the surrounding environment. The process of forming attitudes about which kinds of people, places, and times of day and night are safe or dangerous, and the cues which identify them, is one facet of the elaborate process by which an individual comes to know her world. Information from the mass media, from friends and neighbors, and from the urbanite's own experience is constructed into a mental map of the city which guides behavior and creates a sense of safety in the midst of danger. What the individual considers harmful is itself a cultural product. For some, danger is the risk of losing property; for others, it is name calling and personal humiliation; and for others, the degradation of abusive police and social service workers.

The term *risk* is used to refer to the likelihood of experiencing a crime or some other harm. It is thus a concept which refers to the external world and to the hazards it contains. Danger is a cultural construct which describes the way an individual conceptualizes the hazards and risks in his or her world and assesses what they mean to him or her. Fear refers to the inner emotional state an individual experiences as he or she contemplates the danger he or she believes to exist. Thus, both danger and fear are subjective in a way in which risk is not. On the other hand, they are not inevitably connected. Some may see a situation as dangerous but not regard it with fear, while others may see the same situation as dangerous and feel fearsome about it. Ideas about danger are a component of culture: they are learned, shared within groups, and influence the way the world is interpreted and understood. Fear is more individualized, depending on each person's experience with harm, sense of competence and control, sense of vulnerability in general, and other psychological characteristics.

Other cultures similarly define danger in terms of more general belief systems about their world. For example, a group of Indians living in remote forest settlements in Canada, the Salteaux, do not fear wolves or bears but consider snakes, toads, and frogs dangerous (Hallowell 1938). Although these are among the most harmless of the inhabitants of the forest, they are believed to be emanations of powerful supernatural forces, capable of acting as emissaries for sorcerers, of exuding malevolent magic, and of serving as omens of ill fortune. Monster toads and frogs roam the forest. On the other hand, the Azande farmers of East Africa consider dangerous the man who is quarrelsome, spiteful, and dirty, as well as the person who defecates in others' gardens and eats house rats, since he is believed to possess witchcraft, the power to inflict misfortune, wasting disease, and death on others (Evans-Pritchard 1937).

Notions of danger in American cities, as in other cultural settings, draw on more general social understandings of who and what is dangerous, the kinds of persons who are believed to be violent and immoral and the characteristics of people who are believed likely to commit crimes. In both simple and complex societies, those who suffer misfortune do not always know exactly where the final responsibility lies. In small-scale societies, the witch or supernatural forces are blamed; whereas in American cities, the faceless criminal receives the blame. Yet, in both, it is the outsider, the stranger, who is held responsible. Such persons are not full members of the observer's social and cultural world, but are people whose behavior appears strange and irrational.

The attitudes of the project residents I talked to vividly illustrate these images of danger. Danger has a variety of meanings for project residents. It means encounters with muggers on deserted streets, invasion by culturally alien neighbors, or the nuisance of disheveled drunks asleep on the sidewalk. Essentially, danger is fear of the stranger, the person who is potentially harmful and whose behavior seems unpredictable and beyond control. Those residents who are the most convinced that their environment is dangerous tend not to be those most victimized, but rather those who lack any social connection to street youths. Such people see themselves awash in a sea of dangerous strangers.

To Chinese residents, the blacks, all of whom seem to look alike and are thought to be robbers whose favorite victims are Chinese, appear most dangerous. Whites seem dangerous because they are members of a dominant group which has long excluded the Chinese from full membership in its social institutions and has treated them with disdain and indifference. Yet, to blacks, who recognize that only a small proportion of the project youths are actually involved in crime (only 10 percent of the black families have children who commit crimes), the project appears as a safe place in which they know almost everyone and can anticipate which few youths might be inclined to rob them. As one young black woman said to a young Chinese woman, also a resident of the project:

> To you, all the blacks are dangerous because you can't tell them apart, but to me they are George, Johnny, and Jamesy, and I know who to look out for and who will not bother me.

Black adults who endeavor to guide their children into a life of steady jobs and stable family ties find the project youths who pursue a glamorous life of hustling, easy money, and the *fast lane* dangerous in that they threaten to tempt their children away from their values. Some whites find the blacks dangerous, but those who know the black families and have watched their children grow up know which youths are active in crime and hustling and which are not and take comfort in the belief that, because they know them, they will not bother them.

Places which seem dangerous are not those where crimes occur most often, but those which are unfamiliar or are favorite hangouts of tough-looking youths. Nor are places thought to be safe free from crime. A playground in the center of the project, a favorite hangout for a group of youths blamed for local crime, was generally seen as very dangerous, although few crimes actually took place there.

On the other hand, the area seen most often as safe was the street in front of each person's house. Yet this was also one of the most common places for robberies. Most people said that their side of the project was safe, but they feared to venture to the other, more dangerous side. Those who lived in the center of the project avoided the edges and those who lived on the periphery regarded the center of the project as a dangerous place to be carefully avoided. The victimization survey revealed no differences in the rate of robberies on any one side of the project. Thus, notions of safe and dangerous places do not simply reflect crime rates, but take into account ideas about territory, ethnic hostilities and conflicts, the presence of hostile strangers, familiarity, the availability of allies, and the design of spaces.

Not all crimes are dangerous, nor are all dangerous events crimes. Some crimes which are technically serious are not so perceived by their victims, while others which are not considered serious by the police loom large as dangerous experiences. For example, crimes of violence or threatened violence committed by strangers seem dangerous even if little or no property is taken, such as unsuccessful robbery attempts or attempted burglaries. These incidents are reported when residents are asked if they have been the victims of crimes but rarely elicit a phone call to the police. On the other hand, assaults by people who know each other are not perceived as crimes, even though they are technically defined as crimes by the police. Those who were assaulted in vicious, interpersonal battles never mentioned these incidents when queried about their experiences with victimization. Assaults by strangers on the other hand, are regarded as crimes and engender fear, not knife fights between rivals for a woman's affection or punches between neighbors over barking dogs or damaging gossip.

Residents of this high-crime environment respond to the dangers which surround them by constructing mental maps of the kinds of people and locations which are dangerous and safe. These maps are subjective representations imposed on the physical realities of space and time, constructions of reality that reflect the individual's past experience and knowledge. They guide movements through the project and channel behavior toward strangers. Yet not all mental maps are equally accurate or helpful. The process of constructing these maps involves drawing distinctions and making generalizations. Maps of areas that are well known are more finely differentiated, while maps of unfamiliar areas are blank or vague. Those with greater knowledge of the potentially hazardous people around them and of the particular uses of the surrounding spaces develop more accurate and differentiated mental maps. Such people also find their environment far less dangerous.

Chinese residents, for example, were generally unable to tell the black residents apart, lumping them all into a criminal and predatory population, despite the fact that 90 percent of the families had no connection to crime. They also failed to make fine distinctions between the relative danger of different parts of the development. On the other hand, the blacks were far more sophisticated in drawing distinctions between black residents and were equipped with highly differentiated locational maps of the project. Yet, they lumped all Chinese together into the category of rich restaurant owners, despite the fact that the vast majority were poor cooks and waiters in Chinese restaurants. The use of these unsophisticated mental maps thus exacerbates residents' feelings that they are surrounded by a faceless mass of dangerous strangers.

How do these people cope with their dangerous environment? Some residents adopt a defensive strategy, turning their homes into fortresses barricaded with expensive locks and elaborate window bars, stockpiling guns, learning to live with large guard dogs in small apartments and calling the police to report every incident. They are always cautious, staying at home at night and avoiding social contact with anyone but close friends and relatives. These are the people whose lives are most constricted by the fear of crime: the elderly, residents who speak only Chinese, and social isolates. Their mode of defense is escape and retreat, but, if the fragile shell of safety around their homes is violated by a crowbar mark on the door or an attempted purse snatch on the porch, the loss of a sense of security is devastating.

Others adopt offensive strategies, developing reputations as dangerous, tough people who are willing to fight back if abused, either by violence, by calling the police, or by going to court. These people are still vulnerable to victimization by outsiders who do not know their reputations or by insiders who are angry at them, but they do not feel the same sense of helplessness in the face of anonymous dangers. Unlike the defensive residents, who are vulnerable every time they leave their homes, those who adopt offensive strategies carry their protective armor around with them. Thus, the residents of this project range from those who cower in fear in a barred haven of safety to those who traverse the city at any time of day or night with a sense of confidence and ease springing from their mastery of the urban environment and their extensive knowledge of its locations, its residents, and its cultural patterns.

A Theory of Danger

This analysis suggests a more general theory: that the sense of danger is rooted in feelings of uncertainty, helplessness, and vulnerability triggered by encounters with strangers who belong to unfamiliar, hostile, and potentially harmful groups. A stranger is not perceived as a unique individual having a personal history, reputation, and location in social space. Instead, visible cues such as age, sex, dress, demeanor, ethnicity, location, and mode of speaking are used to place a stranger in a social category associated with certain expected behaviors. Mitchell terms this a categorical relationship, one which arises in situations in which interactions are superficial and perfunctory (1966:52). Such categories codify and order social interaction in otherwise uncertain, unstructured urban situations. These categories are constructed through experience and shared cultural conceptions, but the process of construction is rarely conscious or deliberate; rather, it proceeds through the creation of implicit categories which feel like instinctive descriptions of the world.

Categorical identities inevitably ignore individual variation and are likely to lump very different individuals together. Because finely honed categories develop through familiarity and contact, socially distant and unfamiliar strangers will be assigned to grosser and less refined categories than those who inhabit more familiar social worlds. The less contact an individual has with members of other groups, the less accurately will she categorize these groups. Entire ethnic or age groups can be lumped into the dangerous, immoral or threatening camp. The dangerous group generally differs in ethnic background, but suspicions may also arise due to differences in class and lifestyle.

Predictions of behavior based on categorical identities are far less certain than predictions based on knowledge of the particular habits and propensities of a specific person. The stranger's behavior is likely to appear unexpected and unprovoked, leaving the observer with the feeling that there is little she can do to avoid attack. Psychological research suggests that fear comes from the experience of helplessness in the face of harm, the sense that there is no place or time of safety nor any course of action which will guarantee safety (Seligman 1975).

In Dover Square, the coexistence of separate social worlds divided by sharp social boundaries creates conditions under which residents are likely to experience their environment as dangerous. Those who make contacts across the boundaries, who come to know those in other social networks, see the project as much less dangerous than those who do not, who consequently function with far less differentiated and accurate categorical identities and who lack the sense of certainty and control provided by knowing who the potentially harmful people are. Knowing their identities does not protect one from harm, but it does diminish the sense of living in a world of unpredictable and uncontrollable strangers.

Wirth argued that individuals who are detached from organizations and groups pose the greatest threat to social order because they are not controlled by any social group or moral code (1938:76). However, it is not those who are detached, but those who appear detached, who are responsible for crime, disorder, and fear. These individuals are least susceptible to social control. Although they are firmly anchored in existing social groups, their social moorings are unknown to the observer, who sees them as *detached* persons. Criminals in Dover Square actively fostered their appearance of anonymity, of detachment, in order to escape punishment from their victims. Thus, it is the separation between social worlds, as much as the detachment of individuals, that produces anomie and social disorder.

Urban Social Theory and Social Boundaries

This description of life in a multiethnic neighborhood suggests that Wirth's vision of urbanism as a way of life was not wrong, but only a partial view. Primary and intimate relationships exist within urban villages and social networks, but the problematic interactions are those that lurk in the gaps between these worlds. Wirth and the Chicago sociologists hinted at the problem of the relationship between the pieces of the urban social mosaic, but it was generally ignored. These pieces may be geographically based communities or nonlocalized social networks (Jacobson 1971). Several nonlocalized networks can occupy the same space, as they do in Dover Square. Whatever their configuration, the question of how these networks articulate with one another is a critical problem for urban anthropology. It is here that the breakdown of social control is the greatest and the freedom to be different the greatest challenge. Anthropologists tend to focus on enduring ties yet it is these fleeting relationships and social boundaries between enduring groups which are most problematic for urban social life.

The Metropolis and Everyday Life

ROBERT ROTENBERG

In urban studies, many scholars focus on negative aspects of city life, especially when dealing with central cities. It is refreshing to read studies which point out the attractions the metropolis holds for many people. Here, Robert Rotenberg, who has devoted much of his research to the analysis of life in Vienna, Austria, reminds us of this fact. He also points out that each city has its own individual features, which must be learned anew, every time we go from one city to another. He documents this through examining the Viennese identity, an analysis of how life is scheduled, and the meaning and use of places in Vienna.

In reading Rotenberg's article, students may wish to contrast his description of the Austrian capital with the accounts of other cities in this book, such as Kirshenblatt-Gimblett's New York City, Bestor's Tokyo, Epstein's Brasilia, and Abu-Lughod's Cairo.

With each crossing of the street, with the tempo and multiplicity of economic, occupational and social life, the city sets up a deep contrast with small town and rural life with reference to the sensory foundations of psychic life.

Georg Simmel, *The Metropolis and Mental Life*

We must always infer that urbanism will assume its most characteristic and extreme form in the measure in which the conditions with which it is congruent are present. Thus, the

Source: Article written expressly for *Urban Life*.

larger, the more densely populated, and the more heterogeneous
a community, the more accentuated the characteristics associated
with urbanism will be.

Louis Wirth, *Urbanism As a Way of Life*

A metropolis is not merely a populous city. It is a city with a strong
identity that it projects internationally. The identity of the city
relates to its importance as the home of significant people or
institutions, the source of unique ideas. The identity of the
metropolis is not dependent on the economic fortunes of a region
or a state, although these factors do influence the comfort of the
people living there. Instead the metropolis participates in international flows of people, capital, and information that tie its fate
to other metropolises. Within its region and state, the metropolis
is the most important city, socially, economically, politically, and
artistically. Even when it is not the political capital of the state, it
is still the most powerful city. Only very large states will have more
than one metropolis. Metropolises are attractive places to live. Their
residents are likely to enjoy a disproportionate share of career
opportunities. The ever-growing administrative institutions in the
metropolis are voracious employers. New industries are likely to
locate there. The largest market for artistic and craft production
is located there, as are markets catering to rare and expensive
tastes. The metropolis will have museums, theaters and concert
halls, universities and research institutes, charitable organizations
and religious centers, and similar institutions judged to be of great
value to the society as a whole. If you look up the word "metropolis"
in a good dictionary, you will find that the word is often used to
describe a city of enduring political, economic, and cultural power.
Other cities may specialize in politics, possess culturally valued
institutions or hoard economic wealth. In the metropolis, all three
resources of power are fully developed, sustained over time, and
dominant within the surrounding region.

The large, concentrated population of the metropolis guarantees
that two conditions will be present. First, compared to other cities
in the region, there will be many more local communities, neighborhoods, and enclaves. These will persist through time and will be
highly varied. There are plenty of local places for people to come
from, and remain in, if they so choose. Second, the problems of
maintaining the stability and security of the large and dense
population in the metropolis are overwhelming. This guarantees
that the various civic institutions will be powerful shapers of public
life, competitive with each other and heavily invested in a particular

view of urban life. It is difficult for metropolitans to resist the influence of these institutions in their lives.

This tension between the institutional momentum of the large city and the private struggles of individuals and households leads to an interesting wrinkle on what is otherwise a well-known social experience. Metropolitans develop a widely dispersed, shared knowledge of their world even though frequent face-to-face communication among millions of people is impossible. In some areas of metropolitan experience, this knowledge includes shared values. In other areas, it does not. This shared knowledge is a direct result of the power of the metropolitan and state institutions to impose rules that constrain all metropolitan residents without regard to the social distinctions between them. Of course, the more powerful residents can occasionally find ways around some of the constraints. The sharing of this knowledge is obvious. Some of it forms the silent backdrop of everyday life, such as the arrangements of schedules, the meanings of places, and the identities of people that permit metropolitans to find each other. This shared knowledge constitutes the culture of the metropolis. It represents the contribution by residents of large cities to the pan-human effort to make sense of the world. I call this *metropolitan knowledge*.

Metropolitan knowledge, like all of culture, is composed of the symbols through which people impose meaning on the features of their everyday lives. This means that people do not live in a city of streets, buildings, and parks. That set of symbols belongs to the abstract worlds of geographers, elementary school teachers, and urban planners. Ordinary metropolitans live in a city of paths between destinations, building addresses that refer to different levels of social status, and places of safety or harm in a dangerous environment. This knowledge is crucial for negotiating everyday life in large cities. While people living everywhere participate in this everyday knowledge, each metropolis generates its own particulars. These can be so city-specific that it is impossible to predict where the paths, addresses, and safe places are before actually living in a city and learning its ways. For newcomers to the city, the need to learn so many things for the first time can be so exhausting that it leads to a form of culture shock. Among those who move from one large city to another, the experience of learning the previous city's peculiarities prepares them to know that more learning must take place. This awareness provides metropolitans with a different knowledge of the world than that possessed by residents of small towns. Metropolitans share this awareness with residents of other large cities.

Metropolitan knowledge is different from shared understandings created by what urban anthropologists call "complex social organization," the institutions of power that link localities of different sizes together in a single regional system. Metropolitan knowledge is a specific description of the rarities that occur at the pinnacle of this organization. It can be argued that even people in the smallest villages of an urbanized region experience their world and gain knowledge that is exactly like what I am describing for metropolitans. The difference lies in how critical that knowledge becomes for the people involved. The best way to fathom the difference is to consider the traffic jam. These arise whenever more vehicles try to use a road than the road can accommodate. Theoretically, traffic jams can occur in small villages in an urbanized region, as, say, when trucks carrying agricultural produce compete with donkey-carts for the same stretch of road leading to the local market. At the local market, the influx of vehicles from many directions can produce a heavier jam. As we move up the hierarchy of urban places in the region, the jams become still longer and involve more people. Eventually they become a significant problem for every resident, whether they drive or not! This condition increases with urban scale. For the metropolitan, the traffic jam is a condition of existence. Metropolitan life is, among other conditions that intensify with increased scale, a series of jams of people, commodities, and information that no resident can escape. The metropolis defines the most pervasive interference of these jams in everyday life. Thus, even though the villager might experience a jam, the metropolitan never ceases to experience the jam. The jam is critical to understanding the metropolitan experience. It is not critical to understanding the village experience.

If the everyday knowledge of metropolitans was nothing more than knowing how to find one's way around the streets, or knowing the best pizza shop in town, it would not hold our interest for very long. This knowledge has a more significant side. A portion of the meaning that metropolitans impose on their everyday world is representational. That means that streets are not merely paths between destinations. Among a set of routes of approximately equal length, people choose to use one because of considerations that are unrelated to the destination. People might choose a path that takes them past a place full of childhood memories, or along a street with high status, high design housing. Among safe parks, they might choose one where there is tacit permission for adults to lie on the grass or climb in the trees, activities that are unrelated to the desire to be in a park. These facets of metropolitan knowledge tell us about the people who live there, about their priorities and their goals. They inform about people's understanding of their relationship to each other, their institutions, their world. A willingness to explore metropolitan knowledge permits us to use the city as a mirror of these unique and powerful social experiences.

Much of metropolitan knowledge is so obvious that we pay no attention to it. Our efforts to talk about culture require us to create categories that focus on some aspects of the invented world while ignoring others. In my research, I have found three such categories particularly useful. They are not the only categories available. They may not even be the best categories. They are only the categories that I find interesting. These are identities, schedules, and places. I want to give you an example of metropolitan knowledge for each of these categories. I hope to show that in Vienna, Austria, the scale of metropolitan life determines people's understandings of their identities, their schedules, and their places. For each category, I will begin by showing the particular issues that life in the metropolis brings to the category. Then I describe how these issues are dealt with by individuals and institutions in Vienna.

Knowledge of Identity

The metropolis generates a particular knowledge of one's identity and the identities of others, all of which is bound up in the issue of who can consider themselves to be metropolitans. Like most of us, the Viennese live in a world in which their city is part of a large state that contains other provinces, cities, towns, and villages. How, then, among all these other kinds of Austrians do the Viennese know who is a Viennese and who is not? Does it matter that one is or is not a Viennese? When you are far from home, and people ask you where you are from, what do you answer? People from nonmetropolitan regions will answer defensively, "You've never heard of the place, but it's called Elmwood." If you live in a metropolitan region, the image of your street or neighborhood might briefly come to mind, but you will quickly seek another image. The center of the large city is the part of your metropolitan region that strangers are most likely to know. This is appropriate because for foreigners the center of the metropolis symbolically represents the seat of power in every realm of social experience: the political, the economic, the social, the artistic, the technological. The center of the metropolis is where it all happens.

Another example of the metropolitan construction of identity can be seen in the attraction of fans to a successful sports team. How

far away from the home stadium do you have to live before you are
no longer automatically considered to be a fan of the successful
metropolitan team? I specify the successful team because the
experience of the collective joy associated with a winning team is
so rare, that the greatest numbers of people are likely to be caught
up in it. I know that sports are important to nonmetropolitan people.
Metropolitans use the sport-fan experience in original, metropolitan-
specific ways that nonmetropolitan sport fans then imitate. Successful sport teams generate a class of highly significant,
community-defining events. Metropolitans derive elation from these
events that they can sustain for years afterward. Metropolitans
derive optimism and self-confidence from such successes. Participating in them through the fan experience is another way in which
people allege their metropolitan identities, even if they live in the
farthest reaches of the metropolitan region.

   Associating yourself with life in the center of the metropolis is
a more powerful, more important statement of who you are, or of
who you want to be. Since the metropolis is more like an onion,
with many layers of boundaries, than it is like an avocado, with a
clear boundary between the core and the outlying region, everyone
who lives within bragging distance of the metropolitan center can
claim it as their home. All of these metropolitan-identified people
form an imaginary community that distinguishes them through an
elevated, more sophisticated and more powerful social experience.
Metropolitans claim the center as their home, even if they do not
live there, because their sense of who they are as persons is bound
up with the powerful images of that central place.

   These statements may seem impolite to a North American
audience accustomed to minimizing the social differences within
the majority group. We all enjoy equal protection under the law.
We can travel and live wherever we can find a job. The metropolitan
I just described seems to be putting on airs, inappropriately raising
himself or herself above the rest of us.[1] In Europe, this tension
between the metropolitan and the person from the provinces reflects
a long-standing conflict between two views of what is the most
meaningful in defining one's place in the world. Is it more
meaningful for the individual to give priority to local ties, particular
duties, and personal obligations? This is referred to in Europe as
provincialism. Or, is it more appropriate to give priority to ties with
strangers, universal duties, and international opportunities? This
is referred to as *cosmopolitanism*. The metropolitan identity is a
dramatic assertion of cosmopolitanism. The Viennese engage in this
European debate. The question of who is a Viennese is important
because to be a Viennese is to associate oneself not only with the

seat of enormous cultural power, but with universal law, with cosmopolitan political attitudes, and against narrow provincialism.

We can now return to the question that introduced this section: How do the Viennese know who is a Viennese and who is not? When I ask the people who live there how they identify other Viennese the most common answer is through the way people talk. Most Austrians speak the southern dialect of German, along with Bavarians. This dialect differs from other dialects of German, including the one you may be learning in German class. It includes the substitution of certain vocabulary terms and a shortening of final consonant sounds. These sound shifts contribute a softer, drawling sound quality to the dialect. The Viennese start with this dialect, but they have a peculiar way of pronouncing certain vowels, even when they are speaking the educated standard language.[2] On television, one can always tell the Viennese on the panel of a television game show or interview program because it is very difficult to overcome the habit of pronouncing words this way. How we pronounce our words is fixed at puberty and it is very difficult to overcome these habits. This means that people who speak with a Viennese accent must have lived in Vienna as children. This is certainly a sign that they are true Viennese.

Beyond the pronunciation of words, the Viennese dialect also includes thousands of words that do not exist in the Austrian dialect. These words are borrowings from the Italian, Jewish, Slavic, and Hungarian communities that existed at various times in the history of the city. The words came into wide usage in Vienna through the languages that were spoken by those minority groups. Most of the people who use these words think of them as Viennese words and are not aware of their histories. To use these words in ordinary speech and pronounce them in the appropriate way signals a complete Viennese upbringing. These words rarely diffused into the Austrian dialect.

It is very difficult to distinguish between Viennese dialect and the dialect of the people who live in the towns immediately surrounding the city. Language does not recognize political boundaries. Crossing the boundary between Vienna and Lower Austria, the province that surrounds Vienna, produces only the beginning of a very gradual shift away from Viennese-specific pronunciations toward the standard southern dialect. Thus, language alone is a necessary sign of being a Viennese, but by itself it is not sufficient.

Another common answer among my Viennese acquaintances is the question of family composition. They say that a true Viennese is someone whose family includes at least one grandparent from Hungary, Bohemia, Moravia, or Slovakia. These were the provinces in the old Austro-Hungarian Empire from which many industrial workers emigrated to Vienna in the nineteenth century. So many people migrated that by 1900, only 40 percent of the Viennese population of two million had been born in the city! It is quite rare to meet someone who could claim that all of their grandparents came from families that lived in Vienna before 1848. Vienna was a melting pot. To be Viennese in this sense means to come from a multicultural family. It also means that one's family is directly related to the pluralistic society of the old Austro-Hungarian empire. This is different from families in the provinces. While selected regions experienced some in-migration in the nineteenth century, most Austrian towns contain the same family names they did two hundred years ago. There is a deeper sense of rootedness in a local tradition in these towns. Even in large cities, like Graz and Innsbruck, people are proud to point out grandparents who were natives of the town, rather than those who were immigrants. This way of constructing identity through family history separates the cosmopolitan Viennese from other provincial Austrians. It is a boundary the Viennese and the provincials like to maintain.

Both of these ways of understanding the Viennese identity are private features of people's lives. People do not have to speak in public, giving away their accent. People certainly do not have to relate their family history in public. The Viennese recognize each other by observing these subtle signs of identity: a certain pronunciation of a standard word, a certain last name, or the use of a word known only to the Viennese. Even I can signal my membership in this exclusive Viennese identity by dropping the few dialect phrases I have learned to pronounce properly at the appropriate moments in the conversation. This usually delights my conversation partners. Up to this point, there is nothing specifically urban or metropolitan about using family history or language to construct identity. The real metropolitan character of this problem comes into focus only when there is an institutional interest in who is a Viennese. Without that institutional interest, the secret signs of Viennese identity are merely a game that people throughout the world can play.

The institutional interest in identity comes from a Central European legal tradition known as the *Heimatsrecht*, the hometown law. According to this tradition, individuals and the communities in which they live are parties to a special kind of contract. The community will recognize a person as a member of the community if they can support themselves and contribute to that community. Then, if the person should fall on hard times, the community will give that person whatever supports they need to stay alive.

Residence in a place involved duties to that community and the right to make claims against the community under certain circumstances. Historically, the rights included medical care, protection from military threat, special import and export tax considerations, and, under certain circumstances, the right to vote for municipal leaders.[3] Today, those rights include catastrophic medical care, legal assistance, welfare and housing payments of various kinds, and the unrestricted right to vote for local council government.

There is a lot of money involved in providing these services to the current population of 1.2 million people. The issue of who is a Viennese and who is not a Viennese is very important to the officials who must manage these large sums of money. There is an institutional interest in providing the necessary assistance to everyone who is entitled to it, but not to anyone else. To simplify their identification of needy Viennese, the rule the bureaucrats have come up with is that everyone must register their address with the authorities. Everyone who is registered as residing at a Viennese address at the time that their needs arise is entitled to Viennese assistance, regardless of how they pronounce words or where their grandparents were born. On the other hand, anyone registered at a non-Viennese address when they become ill is not eligible for Viennese assistance, regardless of how they pronounce words or where their grandparents were born.

The problems of an elderly aunt of an acquaintance of mine will illustrate the difficulties this regulation creates. The woman is over ninety and infirm. Five years ago, when she was relatively fit, she moved from Vienna, where she had lived all her life, to Salzburg, another city, to help care for a sick friend. There she registered her address with the Salzburg authorities. The old woman began to get sick herself before her friend died. Soon she found herself incapacitated in a Salzburg nursing home away from her own family. Her national pension paid her medical bills and Salzburg paid for her stay in the nursing home, as they were required to do for all their registered residents. She was too far away for her family to visit her frequently. As she became too infirm to take care of her own affairs, my acquaintance had to travel more often to Salzburg to pay bills and look after her apartment. She and her family wanted her to move back to Vienna, not only because it would be easier to organize her affairs, but also because the people who knew her could continue to visit her. The Viennese authorities had nothing against her moving back. Since she became sick while living in Salzburg, they refused to support this life-long Viennese in a nursing home, citing the residence registration law as the reason for their refusal. The woman's family was forced to finance her nursing home care through their private means in order to bring her back to Vienna.

There is a tension between the interest of metropolitan institutions charged with administering to the needs of the large urban population and people's everyday knowledge of who is a Viennese. This produces two different understandings of Viennese identity: a communal sense of self, shared among the broad urban population and based on the echoes of language and family history; and the public identification of self, as understood by the city's administrative institutions and based on registered address. People act on their communal knowledge of self. The woman wanted to come back to the place where she felt herself to be at home. They do so in an institutional climate that constrains their actions. She could come home, but she was not entitled to exercise the rights of a Viennese resident for a pre-existing health condition. In the end, it is clear where the power lies. As people act on their understandings of who they are in the metropolis, they must eventually encounter administrative institutions that define their identities in a different way, thwarting or redirecting their actions. Through this interaction, they become enculturated to the possibilities for resisting, circumventing, or transforming the institutional rules to suit their sense of themselves, a highly particularized form of metropolitan knowledge.

Knowledge of Schedules

Schedules are a fundamental dimension of all social life. In the metropolis, time is a contested resource. Institutions compete with each other to claim the attention of the residents. Often the claims made on the lives of metropolitans can add up to more than the number of hours available in a waking day. To manage the conflicting claims of institutions, cities evolve public schedules. These include the operating hours of workplaces, shops, schools, offices, and agencies. These schedules permit potential conflicts to become known, so that steps can be taken to avoid them. The process of putting a public schedule in place is itself highly contested. Consider the political conflicts that might revolve around the proposal of adding Saturday as a sixth public school day in your hometown. As the schedule develops through history, different constellations of local forces shape its fate. This results in each metropolis developing its own unique public schedule (Rotenberg 1992b).

It is possible to describe activities as having a certain duration, as occurring in a certain sequence, as recurring at a certain rate, or as taking place at the same time as alternative activities. These constitute the four dimensions of social time. One of the ways in which institutions can exert influence over people is to emphasize some of these dimensions to the exclusion of the others. The public schedule concerns itself with fixing the duration of certain public activities, especially work, school, and shopping hours, and the rate of their recurrence. The effect is to make these activities highly predictable. The emphasis on these dimensions creates a system of activity limits. Within these limits people can choose to do less work, shopping, or school, but they cannot choose to do more. In this way these activities can be better coordinated with each other and conflict less often with nonpublic activities.

While the public schedule emphasizes the duration and the rate of recurrence of activities, household schedules emphasize the other two dimensions, sequence and timing. Fixed sequences of activities permit family members to know where each other is at different times of the day. When you lived at home, you probably knew where each of your family members was when he or she was not at home. Knowledge of these sequences permits family members to better meet the needs of the household by occasionally choosing among demands that occur at the same time. On Saturday, some could shop while others clean the house. The roles could be reversed the next week. This cannot happen in the public schedule. The household and the metropolitan schedules treat activities so differently that they are antagonistic to each other. By fixing duration the public schedule makes it impossible for household members to choose among co-occurring demands. This is well known to those stem families where both adults work and a child must stay home from school with an illness. There is no flexibility in the work segment of the public schedule to permit a parent to postpone work to care for a sick child. The inflexible rhythms of recurring activities in the public schedule make it difficult for household members to alter their sequences of activities. The routine that this imposes on household life can be stifling to creativity and change. Routine can be stressful. When families try to break out of their routines, they come into direct conflict with the public schedule. Often the employed members must change their place of work, their school program, or where and how they will shop. Time conflicts occur between households and metropolitan institutions far more often than they do between competing institutions.

A concrete example of the differences will point out not only the antagonisms in organizing metropolitan time but also the special knowledge of schedules that metropolitan residents require. Retail shops in Vienna have very restrictive shopping hours. They must follow a store closing ordinance that puts limits on the number of hours they can be open. This ordinance applies to all of Austria, but the mayor of Vienna has the power to grant variances that adapt the national law to the specific needs of the Viennese market.

The current system of limits began in 1959. Though based on social justice principals that were progressive in the post-war period, many argue these laws are irrelevant today. In that era, store clerks were mostly women who worked in small shops with few employees. If the government did not regulate store hours, their employers could demand that these women work during the hours when their households were not working. This was felt to undermine the healthy development of family life and add to the economic exploitation of the clerks. The law was created out of a social consensus that it was unfair for some employees to be forced to work shifts that conflict with the family life. For that reason, shops must close at 6:00 or 6:30 P.M. on weekdays and 12:00 P.M. on Saturday. All shops are closed on Sunday.

This ordinance is a good example of how the public schedule evolves. A group representing an institutional interest within the metropolis comes to power in government. From that position, they are able to pass regulations that channel the behavior of residents in ways that favor the agenda of their clients. In this case, the labor parties that ruled Austria after the war were able to pass laws that institutionalized their principles of social justice. Over the last forty-odd years, there have been amendments and variances granted, but the basic principle remains persuasive for many policy makers.

Since the mid-1970s there have been efforts to liberalize this store closing ordinance. Not being able to shop whenever they wanted frustrated many families whose household schedules did not follow the norm imagined by the policy makers. More and more people found themselves caught up in this conflict over the years. Initially, the store closing ordinance insured that people would have at least ninety minutes to shop before the stores closed on weekdays. Throughout the 1960s and 1970s, legislation reduced the standard workweek. Soon the work schedule and the shopping schedule were no longer coordinated with each other. People were working fewer days, but more hours per day. By 1975, many wage-earners had won a thirty-eight-hour, five-day workweek, but could no longer shop after work on Monday through Friday. The ninety minutes reserved for shopping at the end of the workday had evaporated. Shopping activities migrated to Saturday morning. Since the 1960s, there has been a 70 percent decline in the number of family-run shops employing less than five employees. Large chain stores employing hundreds of people replaced the small shops. There are a number of reasons for this. One is that small shops could not handle the volume of shoppers or goods when people shop on a once-a-week basis, instead of every day. The chain stores do this much better.

The shift in the market structure of the neighborhoods was not without cost. The small shopkeepers had been neighbors. They had multiple ties to their clients and knew each other's names and backgrounds. The shops were places to socialize. Store owners extended credit to long-standing clients. The quality of the goods was very high. Customers were treated with respect. On the other hand, the chain stores were impersonal and foreign. Their prices were initially cheaper, but it required more time and effort to shop in them. Carrying a week's worth of groceries from the neighborhood shop to the apartment even a few doors away was an extra burden. People began to use their automobiles to travel to large supermarkets where they could cart shopping bags directly to the car. This increased car traffic on Saturday morning, making the shopping trip longer. Once the groceries were home, there was not enough room to store all the goods. Refrigerators are small and pantry space is at a premium in Viennese apartments. People either invested in rebuilding their kitchens, buying larger refrigerators, or figured out some way to return to shopping on a daily basis. The protests against the shopping ordinance in the mid-1970s came from this effort to return to daily shopping.

After much political soul-searching, a variance went into effect in 1988. It permitted stores to stay open either one Saturday afternoon, or one Thursday evening per month. For the first six months of the experiment, the neighborhood shops reported that very few customers were taking advantage of the liberal shopping hours. The large drive-in supermarkets were reporting only moderate sales on Saturday afternoon. The variance had come too late. The households had rearranged their lives to cope with the restrictions and these rearrangements had become rigid parts of the household schedule. It will take a decade of new households establishing themselves in the new conditions for the neighborhood shops to fill up during these new hours.

As households change and grow, they collide with the limits imposed by the public schedule. In this case, it was the changes occurring in the standard working hours that set the collision in motion. Since so many institutional interests are involved in setting these public schedules, they are not easily changed. In Vienna, it took twelve years from the initial protest until some liberalization of the ordinance was possible.

Changing durations in the public schedule are not immediately taken advantage of because household schedules can become rigid too. Changing the known sequences of household activities also changes the choices available among various activities for household members. Finding time to shop is not merely a matter of not having other conflicting activities. It is also a matter of who in the household is free from other activities to do the shopping. Large shopping trips may require help with carrying the bags. Small children may require supervision. Since the household schedule evolves to deal with many different problems, people could not radically alter it without upsetting the balance. This prevented many households from taking advantage of the new shopping hours that became available in the late 1980s.

How does this relate to metropolitan knowledge? First, this shopping schedule conflict is exclusively a metropolitan problem. The concentration of people in a confined commercial strip makes the rush to shop all that much more uncomfortable. This forces people to find ways of solving their shopping problem in a more relaxed fashion. The problem does not exist in the smaller suburbs that surround Vienna. There, a similar ordinance applies, but the shops are open far fewer hours than they could be.[4]

Second, the metropolitan ethic that underlies the public schedule is a universal one. Everyone is affected equally by the constraints of the law. One cannot call up the manager of the supermarket on a Sunday morning to buy a liter of milk. It is not even clear who among the nameless employees would have the key. This is not the case in smaller communities. It was not the case in Viennese neighborhoods before the demise of the small shops in the 1960s and 1970s.

Third, there is no other previous social experience that prepares one for negotiating the placement of shopping activities within the household in Vienna. It is a fact of life that applies to this particular metropolis. There may be other cities that restrict shopping hours in different ways or not at all. These evolved under different circumstances and reflect the noncomparable particularities of metropolitan knowledge systems. It doesn't take long to figure out the system when encountering the schedule of a metropolis for the first time, but one cannot figure it out ahead of time.

The solutions to the shopping problem depend upon a knowledge of the entire Viennese public schedule, including school hours, working hours, and transportation times. In some households, shopping must involve cooperation between different household members to shop for different items independently of each other. This is the only way the household can find the time to get their shopping done. There are specifically Viennese alternatives to what people eat at different mealtimes. Eating a warm meal in a restaurant during the lunch break from work and cold cuts at home in the evening reduce pressure on the daily shopping and meal preparation responsibilities. There is the judicious use of the automobile to visit large supermarkets. There people can buy particularly heavy items in large quantities every few weeks, such as bottled water or beer, reducing the weight of the daily shopping bags. I could list still more tactics. The point here is that the institution of the public schedule not only engenders conflict, but also inspires solutions. In the end, it is clear where the power to shape the flow of public activities really lies. As people act to fulfill their household's needs in the metropolis, they must eventually encounter institutional entanglement in scheduling that constrains or redirects their actions. Through this experience, metropolitans become knowledgeable of the public schedule.

Knowledge of Places

As occurred with identity and time, conflicts arise between individuals and institutions over the meaning and use of places in the metropolis. Knowledge of this conflict is particular to a specific city, pertains only to the city and not to the surrounding region, and must be learned within the contexts of that city. This is because places are not only containers for activity. They also include the permission to engage in some activities, but not others. Metropolitan institutions have an interest in restricting as much activity in public as possible. All use of public space increases maintenance costs. From the point of view of the people who must manage the city, everything would work much better if there were no people. People, on the other hand, need public spaces of various kinds, from roads to parks, to recreate the social ties that make their lives meaningful. This is a problem that all cities have in common. Large cities experience this conflict in even greater measure because of the increased scale in the size and use of public space. The following example shows how the different needs of institutions and people in a metropolitan park produce knowledge that is specific to that metropolis.

Like Paris and London, Vienna modernized its downtown area in the middle of the nineteenth century. The name of this massive redevelopment project was the *Ringstrasse Project*. The Ringstrasse is a circular boulevard the surrounds the oldest part of the city. The walls of the old city were torn down to create the Ringstrasse, as well as many new streets and new apartment buildings. In the process, a large open area in front of the city walls was destroyed. People had used this esplanade, known as the *Glacis*, as a public park for centuries. In the late 1700s, the emperor Joseph II planted trees along its myriad paths. In the early 1800s, gas lights were installed to help people find their way at night. It was an urban place that contained hundreds of different activities, from begging and selling of handicrafts to music concerts and the consummation of love affairs. It was what McDonogh has called an ''empty'' urban space: ''empty'' of having its function pre-defined, and therefore, a place that was full of possibilities (1993). It was loved by the people because it was a place that permitted them the freedom to do whatever they wanted to do. Thieves and other criminals also used the park, but frequent police patrol on horseback guaranteed the safety of ordinary citizens. All of this was destroyed when the Ringstrasse was built.

The Ringstrasse was not something ordinary people had demanded. It was an effort at increasing the cultural and economic importance of the city in Europe and was the project of the city's business elite. Ordinary Viennese were very angry at the destruction of the Glacis. To make amends, the planners pushed the completion of a much smaller park on the edge of the Glacis as the first completed piece of the redevelopment project. The smaller park is called the City Park. It is a lovely landscape that includes many of the park ideas that Olmstead was putting into use in the large downtown parks in U.S. cities. People immediately adopted it as the successor to the Glacis. This was precisely what the city council feared. In the discussions surrounding the planning of the park, many councilmen expressed the fear that the many trees in the park would permit hiding places for thieves, prostitutes, and people wanting to use the park as a toilet. They preferred an open landscape of low flower beds and statues, like the old aristocratic gardens that were all over the imperial city. They believed the new style in landscaping parks permitted too many activities to occur beyond the ability of the police to observe them. Others on the city council argued that giving the people a park that was beautiful would instill a sense of pride. This would make them responsible citizens who would self-consciously restrict their activities to those which in the socially conservative climate of the 1860s were publicly acceptable. Their view prevailed, and the park was opened with only a few posted restrictions: no tobacco smoking, no dogs, no cooking fires, and no walking on the grass.

The park opened in September and was an immediate success. After the first hard freeze of the winter, a new crisis developed.

People were ice skating on the small, shallow duck pond in the center of the park. The city council was scandalized. They had never discussed using the pond for this purpose and saw the activities of the ice skaters as anarchy. Police were posted to prevent people from ice skating. There then followed a long exchange of letters in the newspapers that focused on how absurd it was for the city council to respond so forcefully to what was a perfectly reasonable park activity. The police were withdrawn and the ice skating resumed. The second year, the council attempted to prevent the ice skaters again, citing safety concerns. Another exchange of letters pointed out the absurdity of this position since the pond was barely four feet deep at its deepest place. The ice skating resumed. The third year, the city council appropriated funds to build a small shack with benches where people could sit to put on their skates and get warm. They also licensed a vendor to sell coffee and roasted chestnuts to the skaters. The people had won a victory for recreating the kind of space the Glacis had been where anything that is not harmful was permitted.

To this day, the City Park is the most socially permissive of all public spaces in Vienna. This does not mean that there are prostitutes and drug addicts everywhere. The prediction that a beautiful park would attract many middle-class people to help care for it proved true. The park is full of people every day who want to do nothing more than enjoy its landscape. They bring their dogs on leashes and they sunbathe on the grass in summer. Once while I was showing the park to some visiting American students, we observed a young couple about fifty feet behind a row of crowded benches. The couple was obviously engaged in the preliminaries to making love. Their movements attracted the attention of the mostly older people sitting on the benches who turned to watch them. When the young people became aware that they were being watched, they reluctantly got up and moved a few hundred feet farther up the meadow toward a stand of trees. There it was harder to see them, and they resumed their activity.

No one on the benches commented at the inappropriateness of the couple's behavior. A few were heard to joke that the City Park was truly a lively place. The couple's activities would not have been so easily tolerated in other parks in the city. The Viennese are not prudish, but like most Europeans they do not consider sex an appropriate public activity. The young couple were not trying to be exhibitionists. They were enjoying their affection for each other in a space that they believed permitted that. When they were observed, they did not leave in shame. They merely moved to a more private, though still visible, part of the meadow. Clearly, what is appropriate in the City Park because of its historical connection with the free-wheeling atmosphere of the Glacis is not appropriate everywhere else.

This was not an isolated incident of people using the City Park in creative ways. I have observed unofficial art exhibitions, women sunbathing topless, people openly gambling with cards or backgammon, teenagers dancing to tape-recorded rock music right next to the outdoor cafe where tourists listened to a live band play waltz music, and similar affronts to official park behavior. The City Park has developed a unique set of rules that are interesting to us for their permissiveness. Every public space has such rules. They are never posted. Because I have spent years studying them, I know of other parks that are unique in other ways. One permits drug addicts to loiter there under the watchful eyes of a pair of police officers. Another is primarily used as a dog toilet. Some public swimming pools permit topless sunbathing. Others do not. There is an entire class of parks that are as restrictive as these are permissive. These are parks where you really cannot walk on the grass or even talk in loud voice. They have the behavioral atmosphere of an art museum. Once again, none of these permissions or restrictions are posted or advertised. They are the stuff of people's everyday experience with these places as these have evolved over time. They were learned on school outings and on trips with parents. The levels of what is permitted were tested during adolescence and early adulthood. As part of this testing process, some places came to tolerate new behaviors. The stranger can learn them, as I have had the opportunity to do. Still, nothing in our previous experience with cities predisposes us to know what specific public behavior possibilities have evolved for each place in a particular city.

The examples of identity and schedules emphasize the obscure ways in which institutional arrangements necessitated by large-scale social organization in cities thwart or redirect people's actions. This example of park behavior focuses on how people play around the edges of these constraints to find the permissive underbelly of the institutional framework. In the end, it is clear where the power to circumscribe public behavior really lies. With the stroke of a pen, the responsible bureaucrat can wipe out specific behaviors from public places, as was the case during the skateboarding craze of the 1980s. As these young people learned to their frustration, the permission to engage in new public behaviors exists only as long as the public administrators are willing to tolerate it.

Defining the Metropolitan Experience

For each of these examples from Vienna, I keep referring to the size and scale of the metropolis determining people's experience of the forces that shape their everyday lives. I want to emphasize that what makes these understandings different from those of people in a small town is not simply a matter of either degree or kind. The increased size and scale of the metropolis introduce unique issues and singular solutions in people's everyday lives. People in smaller cities or towns may experience special circumstances owing to geography or history, but this could be true of any human settlement. All metropolises must contend with the effects of their size and scale.

We can imagine a metropolitan experience where the total size of the city was a mere ten thousand people, barely the size of a small town in many parts of the world. Place this metropole in a region in which all the other settlements are villages of no more than one hundred people and you have recreated the difference in scale between our actual metropolises and the towns surrounding them. Would such a tiny city generate the kind of metropolitan knowledge as I have described it here? I have argued elsewhere that, at least in the case of schedules, this mini-metropole would not produce a metropolitan experience unless one other crucial factor is taken into account: the political organization of the region (Rotenberg 1992a). In each of the examples of Viennese metropolitan experience, I described a conflict between people's needs and the goals of the institutions charged with regulating social life. Regulatory institutions are part of the larger political organization that creates and legitimates authority in society. These political organizations vary considerably in place and time.[5]

Having invented our tiny metropolis, we can now look for cases of real urban experiences in small cities in which the likelihood of conflict between people's needs and institutional goals was small. In the archeological and historical development of cities it is possible to identify some where the system of authority is closely related to family organization. The royal cities of the old West African trade states of Mali and Songhai could serve as examples of these kin-based cities. As these are described in epic stories of those civilizations, such as the "Sundiata" (Niane 1965), each was closely identified as the residence of a clan leader and the overwhelming majority of residents were members of the leader's clan. Islamic mosques existed, but Islam was primarily a religion of the clan elite and the various traders from other ethnic groups who lived in the city. Only they were influenced by the Muslim prayer schedule and ritual calendar. Everyone else followed a schedule of everyday life that was shaped by family obligations and clan-oriented rituals. We lack detailed accounts of everyday life for ordinary people in these cities. Still, it is possible to make educated guesses about it from the observations of anthropologists in various parts of the world where family obligations form the primary pattern of people's daily activities.[6] What we find is a pattern of activity that has no set sequence or pattern of repetition, in which the durations of individual activities vary from day to day. In other words, there is no schedule in community life in which family organizations dominate the authoritative institutions. The urban experience in this kin-oriented political organization would not produce a special understanding of the schedule of everyday activities. Therefore, we cannot assume that a relatively large population size alone will generate all of the experiential features of an advanced post-industrial metropolis, like Vienna.[7]

Does this mean that there is an absolute threshold in population below which one cannot describe an urban experience as metropolitan? I believe the answer to this question is yes, but not in the sense of an absolute number of people. Instead, the metropolitan threshold lies in the size and importance of groups in the city with different goals from those of the authoritative institutions. This multigroup social environment was one of the features I cited at the beginning of this essay as distinguishing the metropolis from other cities. These groups may be defined through race and ethnicity, class, place of birth, language, or political characteristics. Regardless of the criteria used, the effect is the same. Some groups will see themselves as closely aligned with the institutional agenda of the city. Others will feel themselves at odds with it and seek to mitigate its influence on their lives. Almost every human settlement distinguishes between people to some extent. What makes social stratification in the metropolis different is that the size and significance of the minority groups empower them to resist the influence of the dominating institutions.[8]

Sometimes this resistance is successful and the institutional goals become more inclusive. Think of the group of ordinary citizens who insisted on skating on the ice pond in the park in spite of the city council's efforts to make them stop. More often the resistance is unsuccessful. The minority groups find themselves in an increasingly precarious balance between competing demands on their understanding of who they are, where they are supposed to be, and what they are supposed to be doing when they get there. Remember the decades that employed households waited to get some relief from the restrictive store closing laws.

People experience the city as a metropolis only when history, economy, and politics converge to create a settlement of enduring regional and international influence. Because of this role, the metropolitan life becomes an attractive one for different people. The by-product of this lasting importance is the growth over time of increasingly significant minority groups. This is what produces the contest over needs and goals between the urban institutions and the city's constitutive groups. This is why the contest is peculiarly apparent in the metropolis. A similar process may occur in smaller cities among certain groups and over certain issues but it must occur in the metropolis. The evidence of this process is the knowledge it produces. Look for a group of urbanites with the experience of contesting issues of identity, schedule, and place, and you will have found a metropolitan group.

Conclusion

By focusing on the knowledge that people create to adapt to and give meaning to their lives in large cities, the anthropologist can write about urban culture as a dynamic, changing force in people's lives. In metropolitan knowledge, we discover that part of the human experience that only large cities can produce. Ultimately, the question of what we mean when we describe a human experience as urban, or city-based, may depend on demonstrating the nature of the linkage between the needs of households and goals of institutions. This focus on the meaning that people give to schedules, places, and identities is one way of describing the linkage between power centers, and groups or classes in the city. These linkages need as broad a base as possible in order to encompass the large and variable urban population. When we demonstrate that an experience is indeed metropolitan, we are then compelled to explore the processes that permitted it to become so widespread within the population. In this way, metropolitan knowledge becomes the basis for an anthropology of the city.

Notes

[1] What is true of American culture in general is also true of urban anthropology. A quick glance at the companion papers in this volume will reveal a definite resistance to treating the power of large cities in a positive light. The city is mostly the problem in anthropological studies, the grave backdrop against which local people fight valiantly to survive. To turn the telescope around, as I am trying to do, and see the city as the valuable object of study, submerging the local

experience, will offend the philosophical and political sensibilities of many colleagues. In spite of this, the metropolitan perspective must be addressed.

2 For those of you who understand a bit about phonology, the crucial sounds include the interconsonantal diphthong /ie/, as in the word *Zeit*, meaning 'time.' In the standard dialect, this word is pronounced /tsiet/. In Viennese dialect, the diphthong is medialized to become /tsait/. Initial /u/ as in the word *und*, the conjunction 'and,' is also medialized to /ont/. Overall there is a tendency to bring vocalic sounds toward the center of the mouth, and this is the quality that stands out when Viennese are trying to speak standard German. When they speak their home dialect, there are a number of consonantal shifts that take place, especially with /l/ and /r/, that are too technical to go into here.

3 These laws are not ancient. They began as unwritten customs commonly found throughout Europe that pertained only to people born within a community. In the 1820s, state power began to exert itself over these communities. It did so by insisting that communities take responsibility for any proper citizen of the state residing there. This shift from community member to state citizen is an important one in the development of modern states in Europe. In Austria, because of the use of the term *Heimatsrecht* in the Nazi period to dispossess minority groups of their property, the current law is called the residence registration law.

4 For a full discussion of the setting of shopping hours and the difference between metropolitan and suburban market hours, see Rotenberg 1992b.

5 By emphasizing only the political organization of the region, I realize that I am skirting a more complicated understanding of the organization of power that includes both authoritative institutions and economically productive institutions. Wolf has used the term *mode of production* for this combined organization of politics and the economy, which he defines as the strategic social relationships through which a society organizes its productive and reproductive capabilities (Wolf 1982). What makes this complicated is that every society produces its own variation on one of three possible types of the strategic relationships. Rather than shifting the focus of this section away from defining the experience of metropolitan life, I have decided to focus only on the political aspects of the process. For a more detailed discussion of how cities with different modes of production differ from each, consult the article cited in the paragraph.

6 One of the most detailed of these comes from a group of Southern African farmers studied by Audrey Richards in the 1930s (1939). She recorded the activities of every adult in a village of sixty people for three weeks in the wet season and two weeks in the dry season. The lack of any recurring pattern to an individual's activities is immediately evident from her summary chart in the end paper of the book. Another might be Tedlock's study of the role of Mayan timekeepers in the social life of a small town in highland Guatemala (1982). Here the needs of individuals and their families, rather than the demands of institutions, dominate people's experience of time.

7 In a study on landscape and power (1995), I show that the special experience of place we observe in the contemporary metropolis is also a product of some kinds of political organizations but not all of them. While I suspect that the same may be true of metropolitan identity, I can recommend only two published studies that take on the subject, Borneman (1992) and Bestor (1989).

8 I am using the term minority here in the sense of lacking certain qualifications for power, as in being a minor in age, not in its numerical sense of belonging to the smaller group. As we have seen in Vienna, groups can be the numerical majority and still have their needs ignored by metropolitan institutions.

The Preindustrial City

GIDEON SJOBERG

In this pioneering study of the preindustrial city, Sjoberg seeks to understand the characteristics of cities before they are transformed through industrialization. Preindustrial cities throughout the world, he claims, show certain similarities. For one, their technology is based on the use of human and animal power, rather than on machines; and their relationship to the countryside differs from that of industrial cities. The prein-dustrial city also differs from the industrial city in its lifeways. For these people, city living does not mean participation in a society marked by impersonalization. At the same time there is a sharp division between the ruling elite and the rest of the population. For a portrait of a contemporary preindustrial city, read Waldron's article "Within the Wall and Beyond."

In the past few decades social scientists have been conducting field studies in a number of relatively non-Westernized cities. Their recently acquired knowledge of North Africa and various parts of Asia, combined with what was already learned, clearly indicates that these cities are not like typical cities of the United States and other highly industrialized areas but are much more like those of medieval Europe. Such communities are termed herein "preindustrial," for they have arisen without stimulus from that form of production which we associate with the European industrial revolution.

Recently Foster, in a most informative article, took cognizance of the preindustrial city.[1] His primary emphasis was upon the peasantry (which he calls "folk"); but he recognized this to be part of a broader social structure which includes the preindustrial city. He noted certain similarities between the peasantry and the city's

Source: *American Journal of Sociology*, LX (1955): 438–445. © 1955 by University of Chicago. Reprinted by permission of the University of Chicago Press.

lower class. Likewise the present author sought to analyze the total society of which the peasantry and the preindustrial city are integral parts.[2] For want of a better term this was called "feudal." Like Redfield's folk (or "primitive") society, the feudal order is highly stable and sacred; in contrast, however, it has a complex social organization. It is characterized by highly developed state and educational and/or religious institutions and by a rigid class structure.

Thus far no one has analyzed the preindustrial city per se, especially as it differs from the industrial-urban community, although Weber, Tönnies, and a few others perceived differences between the two. Yet such a survey is needed for the understanding of urban development in so-called underdeveloped countries and, for that matter, in parts of Europe. Such is the goal of this paper. The typological analysis should also serve as a guide to future research.

Ecological Organization

Preindustrial cities depend for their existence upon food and raw materials obtained from without; for this reason they are marketing centers. And they serve as centers for handicraft manufacturing. In addition, they fulfill important political, religious, and educational functions. Some cities have become specialized; for example, Benares in India and Karbala in Iraq are best known as religious communities, and Peiping in China as a locus for political and educational activities.

The proportion of urbanites relative to the peasant population is small, in some societies about 10 percent, even though a few preindustrial cities have attained populations of one hundred thousand or more. Growth has been by slow accretion. These characteristics are due to the nonindustrial nature of the total social order. The amount of surplus food available to support an urban population has been limited by the unmechanized agriculture, transportation facilities utilizing primarily human or animal power, and inefficient methods of food preservation and storage.

The internal arrangement of the preindustrial city, in the nature of the case, is closely related to the city's economic and social structure.[3] Most streets are mere passageways for people and for animals used in transport. Buildings are low and crowded together. The congested conditions, combined with limited scientific knowledge, have fostered serious sanitation problems.

More significant is the rigid social segregation which typically has led to the formation of "quarters" or "wards." In some cities (e.g., Fez, Morocco, and Aleppo, Syria) these were sealed off from each other by walls, whose gates were locked at night. The quarters reflect the sharp local social divisions. Thus ethnic groups live in special sections. And the occupational groupings, some being at the same time ethnic in character, typically reside apart from one another. Often a special street or sector of the city is occupied almost exclusively by members of a particular trade; cities in such divergent cultures as medieval Europe and modern Afghanistan contain streets with names like "street of the goldsmiths." Lower-class and especially "outcaste" groups live on the city's periphery, at a distance from the primary centers of activity. Social segregation, the limited transportation facilities, the modicum of residential mobility, and the cramped living quarters have encouraged the development of well-defined neighborhoods which are almost primary groups.

Despite rigid segregation the evidence suggests no real specialization of land use such as is functionally necessary in industrial-urban communities. In medieval Europe and in other areas city dwellings often serve as workshops, and religious structures are used as schools or marketing centers.[4]

Finally, the "business district" does not hold the position of dominance that it enjoys in the industrial-urban community. Thus, in the Middle East the principal mosque, or in medieval Europe the cathedral, is usually the focal point of community life. The center of Peiping is the Forbidden City.

Economic Organization

The economy of the preindustrial city diverges sharply from that of the modern industrial center. The prime difference is the absence in the former of industrialism which may be defined as that system of production in which *inanimate* sources of power are used to multiply human effort. Preindustrial cities depend for the production of goods and services upon *animate* (human or animal) sources of energy—applied either directly or indirectly through such mechanical devices as hammers, pulleys, and wheels. The industrial-urban community, on the other hand, employs inanimate generators of power such as electricity and steam which greatly enhance the productive capacity of urbanites. This basically new form of energy production, one which requires for its development and survival a special kind of institutional complex, effects striking changes in the ecological, economic, and social organization of cities in which it has become dominant.

Other facets of the economy of the preindustrial city are associated with its particular system of production. There is little fragmentation or specialization of work. The handicraftsman participates in nearly every phase of the manufacture of an article, often carrying out the work in his own home or in a small shop nearby and, within the limits of certain guild and community regulations, maintaining direct control over conditions of work and methods of production.

In industrial cities, on the other hand, the complex division of labor requires a specialized managerial group, often extra-community in character, whose primary function is to direct and control others. And for the supervision and coordination of the activities of workers, a "factory system" has been developed, something typically lacking in preindustrial cities. (Occasionally, centralized production is found in preindustrial cities—e.g., where the state organized slaves for large-scale construction projects.) Most commercial activities, also, are conducted in preindustrial cities by individuals without a highly formalized organization; for example, the craftsman has frequently been responsible for the marketing of his own products. With a few exceptions, the preindustrial community cannot support a large group of middlemen.

The various occupations are organized into what have been termed "guilds."[5] These strive to encompass all, except the elite, who are gainfully employed in some economic activity. Guilds have existed for merchants and handicraft workers (e.g., goldsmiths and weavers) as well as for servants, entertainers, and even beggars and thieves. Typically the guilds operate only within the local community, and there are no large-scale economic organizations such as those in industrial cities which link their members to their fellows in other communities.

Guild membership and apprenticeship are prerequisites to the practice of almost any occupation, a circumstance obviously leading to monopolization. To a degree these organizations regulate the work of their members and the price of their products and services. And the guilds recruit workers into specific occupations, typically selecting them according to such particularistic criteria as kinship rather than universalistic standards.

The guilds are integrated with still other elements of the city's social structure. They perform certain religious functions; for example, in medieval European, Chinese, and Middle Eastern cities each guild had its "patron saint" and held periodic festivals in his honor. And, by assisting members in time of trouble, the guilds serve as social security agencies.

The economic structure of the preindustrial city functions with little rationality, judged by industrial-urban standards. This is shown in the general nonstandardization of manufacturing methods as well as in the products and is even more evident in marketing. In preindustrial cities throughout the world a fixed price is rare; buyer and seller settle their bargain by haggling. (Of course, there are limits above which customers will not buy and below which merchants will not sell.) Often business is conducted in a leisurely manner, money not being the only desired end.

Furthermore, the sorting of goods according to size, weight, and quality is not common. Typical is the adulteration and spoilage of produce. And weights and measures are not standardized: variations exist not only between one city and the next but also within communities, for often different guilds employ their own systems. Within a single city there may be different kinds of currency, which, with the poorly developed accounting and credit systems, signalize a modicum of rationality in the whole of economic action in preindustrial cities.[6]

Social Organization

The economic system of the preindustrial city, based as it has been upon animate sources of power, articulates with a characteristic class structure and family, religious, educational, and governmental systems.

Of the class structure, the most striking component is a literate elite controlling and depending for its existence upon the mass of the populace, even in the traditional cities of India with their caste system. The elite is composed of individuals holding positions in the governmental, religious, and/or educational institutions of the larger society, although at times groups such as large absentee landlords have belonged to it. At the opposite pole are the masses, comprising such groups as handicraft workers whose goods and services are produced primarily for the elite's benefit.[7] Between the elite and the lower class is a rather sharp schism, but in both groups there are gradations in rank. The members of the elite belong to the "correct" families and enjoy power, property, and certain highly valued personal attributes. Their position, moreover, is legitimized by sacred writings.

Social mobility in this city is minimal; the only real threat to the elite comes from the outside—not from the city's lower classes. And a middle class—so typical of industrial-urban communities, where it can be considered the "dominant" class—is not known in the preindustrial city. The system of production in the larger society provides goods, including food, and services in sufficient amounts to support only a small group of leisured individuals; under these conditions an urban middle class, a semileisured group, cannot arise. Nor are a middle class and extensive social mobility essential to the maintenance of the economic system.

Significant is the role of the marginal or "outcaste" groups (e.g., the Eta of Japan), which are not an integral part of the dominant social system. Typically they rank lower than the urban lower class, performing tasks considered especially degrading, such as burying the dead. Slaves, beggars, and the like are outcastes in most preindustrial cities. Even such groups as professional entertainers and itinerant merchants are often viewed as outcastes, for their rovings expose them to "foreign" ideas from which the dominant social group seeks to isolate itself. Actually many outcaste groups, including some of those mentioned above, are ethnic groups, a fact which further intensifies their isolation. (A few, like the Jews in the predominantly Muslim cities of North Africa have their own small literate religious elite which, however, enjoys no significant political power in the city as a whole.)

An assumption of many urban sociologists is that a small, unstable kinship group, notably the conjugal unit, is a necessary correlate of city life. But this premise does not hold for preindustrial cities.[8] At times sociologists and anthropologists, when generalizing about various traditional societies, have imputed to peasants typically urban kinship patterns. Actually, in these societies the ideal forms of kinship and family life are most closely approximated by members of the urban literate elite, who are best able to fulfill the exacting requirements of the sacred writings. Kinship and the ability to perpetuate one's lineage are accorded marked prestige in preindustrial cities. Children, especially sons, are highly valued, and polygamy or concubinage or adoption help to assure the attainment of large families. The pre-eminence of kinship is apparent even in those preindustrial cities where divorce is permitted. Thus, among the urban Muslims or urban Chinese divorce is not an index of disorganization; here, conjugal ties are loose and distinctly subordinate to the bonds of kinship, and each member of a dissolved conjugal unit typically is absorbed by his kin group. Marriage, a prerequisite to adult status in the preindustrial city, is entered upon at an early age and is arranged between families rather than romantically, by individuals.

The kinship and familial organization displays some rigid patterns of sex and age differentiation whose universality in preindustrial cities has generally been overlooked. A woman, especially of the upper class, ideally performs few significant functions outside the home. She is clearly subordinate to males, especially her father or husband. Recent evidence indicates that this is true even for such a city as Lhasa, Tibet, where women supposedly have had high status.[9] The isolation of women from public life has in some cases been extreme. In nineteenth-century Seoul, Korea, "respectable" women appeared on the streets only during certain hours of the night when men were supposed to stay at home.[10] Those women in preindustrial cities who evade some of the stricter requirements are members of certain marginal groups (e.g., entertainers) or of the lower class. The role of the urban lower-class woman typically resembles that of the peasant rather than the urban upper-class woman. Industrialization, by creating demands and opportunities for their employment outside the home, is causing significant changes in the status of women as well as in the whole of the kinship system in urban areas.

A formalized system of age grading is an effective mechanism of social control in preindustrial cities. Among siblings the eldest son is privileged. And children and youth are subordinate to parents and other adults. This, combined with early marriage, inhibits the development of a "youth culture." On the other hand, older persons hold considerable power and prestige, a fact contributing to the slow pace of change.

As noted above, kinship is functionally integrated with social class. It also reinforces and is reinforced by the economic organization: the occupations, through the guilds, select their members primarily on the basis of kinship, and much of the work is carried on in the home or immediate vicinity. Such conditions are not functional to the requirements of a highly industrialized society.

The kinship system in the preindustrial city also articulates with a special kind of religious system, whose formal organization reaches fullest development among members of the literate elite.[11] The city is the seat of the key religious functionaries whose actions set standards for the rest of society. The urban lower class, like the peasantry, does not possess the education or the means to maintain all the exacting norms prescribed by the sacred writings. Yet the religious system influences the city's entire social structure. (Typically, within the preindustrial city one religion is dominant; however, certain minority groups adhere to their own beliefs.) Unlike the situation in industrial cities, religious activity is not separate from other social action but permeates family, economic, governmental, and other activities. Daily life is pervaded with religious significance. Especially important are periodic public festivals and ceremonies like Ramadan in Muslim cities. Even distinctly ethnic outcaste groups can through their own religious festivals maintain solidarity.

Magic, too, is interwoven with economic, familial, and other social activities. Divination is commonly employed for determining the "correct" action on critical occasions; for example, in traditional Japanese and Chinese cities, the selection of marriage partners. And nonscientific procedures are widely employed to treat illness among all elements of the population of the preindustrial city.

Formal education typically is restricted to the male elite, its purpose being to train individuals for positions in the governmental, educational, or religious hierarchies. The economy of preindustrial cities does not require mass literacy, nor, in fact, does the system of production provide the leisure so necessary for the acquisition of formal education. Considerable time is needed merely to learn the written language, which often is quite different from that spoken. The teacher occupies a position of honor, primarily because of the prestige of all learning and especially of knowledge of the sacred literature, and learning is traditional and characteristically based upon sacred writings.[12] Students are expected to memorize rather than evaluate and initiate, even in institutions of higher learning.

Since preindustrial cities have no agencies of mass communication, they are relatively isolated from one another. Moreover, the masses within a city are isolated from the elite. The former must rely upon verbal communication, which is formalized in special groups such as storytellers or their counterparts. Through verse and song these transmit upper-class tradition to nonliterate individuals.

The formal government of the preindustrial city is the province of the elite and is closely integrated with the educational and religious systems. It performs two principal functions: exacting tribute from the city's masses to support the activities of the elite and maintaining law and order through a "police force" (at times a branch of the army) and a court system. The police force exists primarily for the control of "outsiders," and the courts support custom and the rule of the sacred literature, a code of enacted legislation typically being absent.

In actual practice little reliance is placed upon formal machinery for regulating social life.[13] Much more significant are the informal controls exerted by the kinship, guild, and religious systems, and here, of course, personal standing is decisive. Status distinctions are visibly correlated with personal attributes, chiefly speech, dress, and personal mannerisms which proclaim ethnic group, occupation, age, sex, and social class. In nineteenth-century Seoul, not only did the upper-class mode of dress differ considerably from that of the masses, but speech varied according to social class, the verb forms and pronouns depending upon whether the speaker ranked higher or lower or was the equal of the person being addressed.[14] Obviously, then, escape from one's role is difficult even in the street crowds. The individual is ever conscious of his specific rights and duties. All these things conserve the social order in the preindustrial city despite its heterogeneity.

Conclusions

Throughout this paper there is the assumption that certain structural elements are universal for all urban centers. This study's hypothesis is that their form in the preindustrial city is fundamentally distinct from that in the industrial-urban community. A considerable body of data not only from medieval Europe, which is somewhat atypical,[15] but from a variety of cultures supports this point of view. Emphasis has been upon the static features of preindustrial city life. But even those preindustrial cities which have undergone considerable change approach the ideal type. For one thing, social change is of such a nature that it is not usually perceived by the general populace.

Most cities of the preindustrial type have been located in Europe or Asia. Even though Athens and Rome and the large commercial centers of Europe prior to the industrial revolution displayed certain unique features, they fit the preindustrial type quite well.[16] And many traditional Latin-American cities are quite like it, although deviations exist, for, excluding pre-Columbian cities, these were affected to some degree by the industrial revolution soon after their establishment.

It is postulated that industrialization is a key variable accounting for the distinctions between preindustrial and industrial cities. The type of social structure required to develop and maintain a form of production utilizing inanimate sources of power is quite unlike that in the preindustrial city.[17] At the very least, extensive industrialization requires a rational, centralized, extra-community economic organization in which recruitment is based more upon universalism than on particularism, a class system which stresses achievement rather than ascription, a small and flexible kinship system, a system of mass education which emphasizes universalistic rather than particularistic criteria, and mass communication. Modification in any one of these elements affects the others and induces changes in other systems such as those of religion and social control as well. Industrialization, moreover, not only requires a special kind of social structure within the urban community but provides the means necessary for its establishment.

Anthropologists will in the future devote increased attention to the study of cities throughout the world. They must therefore recognize that the particular kind of social structure found in cities in the United States is not typical of all societies. Miner's recent study of Timbuctoo,[18] which contains much excellent data, points to the need for recognition of the preindustrial city. His emphasis upon the folk-urban continuum diverted him from an equally significant problem: How does Timbuctoo differ from modern industrial cities in its ecological, economic, and social structure? Society there seems even more sacred and organized than Miner admits.[19] For example, he used divorce as an index of disorganization, but in Muslim society divorce within certain rules is justified by the sacred literature. The studies of Hsu and Fried would have considerably more significance had the authors perceived the generality of their findings. And, once the general structure of the preindustrial city is understood, the specific cultural deviations become more meaningful.

Beals notes the importance of the city as a center of acculturation.[20] But an understanding of this process is impossible without some knowledge of the preindustrial city's social structure. Although industrialization is clearly advancing throughout most of the world, the social structure of preindustrial civilizations is conservative, often resisting the introduction of numerous industrial forms. Certainly many cities of Europe (e.g., in France or Spain) are not so fully industrialized as some presume; a number of preindustrial patterns remain. The persistence of preindustrial elements is also evident in cities of North Africa and many parts of Asia; for example, in India and Japan,[21] even though great social change is currently taking place. And the Latin-American city of Mérida, which Redfield studied, had many preindustrial traits.[22] A conscious awareness of the ecological, economic, and social structure of the preindustrial city should do much to further the development of comparative urban community studies.

Notes

[1] George M. Foster, "What Is Folk Culture?" *American Anthropologist*, LV (1953), 159–73.

[2] Gideon Sjoberg, "Folk and 'Feudal' Societies," *American Journal of Sociology*, LVIII (1952), 231–39.

[3] Sociologists have devoted almost no attention to the ecology of preindustrial centers. However, works of other social scientists do provide some valuable preliminary data. See, e.g., Marcel Clerget, *Le Caire: Étude de géographie urbaine et d'histoire économique* (2 vols.; Cairo: E. & R. Schindler, 1934); Robert E. Dickinson, *The West European City* (London: Routledge & Kegan Paul, 1951); Roger Le Tourneau, *Fès: Avant le protectorat* (Casablanca: Société Marocaine de Librairie et d'Édition, 1949); Edward W. Lane, *Cairo Fifty Years Ago* (London: John Murray, 1896); J. Sauvaget, *Alep* (Paris: Librairie Orientaliste Paul Geuthner, 1941); J. Weulersse, "Antioche: Essai de géographie urbaine," *Bulletin d'études orientales*, IV (1934), 27–79; Jean Kennedy, *Here Is India* (New York: Charles Scribner's Sons, 1945); and relevant articles in American geographical journals.

[4] Dickinson, *op. cit.*, p. 27; O. H. K. Spate, *India and Pakistan* (London: Methuen & Co., 1954), p. 183.

[5] For a discussion of guilds and other facets of the preindustrial city's economy see, e.g., J. S. Burgess, *The Guilds of Peking* (New York: Columbia University Press, 1928); Edward T. Williams, *China, Yesterday and Today* (5th ed.; New York: Thomas Y. Crowell Co., 1932); T'ai-ch'u Liao, "The Apprentices in Chengtu during and after the War," *Yenching Journal of Social Studies*, IV (1948), 90–106; H. A. R. Gibb and Harold Bowen, *Islamic Society and the West* (London: Oxford University Press, 1950), Vol. I, Part I, chap. vi; Le Tourneau, *op. cit.*; Clerget, *op. cit.*, James W. Thompson and Edgar N. Johnson, *An Introduction to Medieval Europe* (New York: W. W. Norton Co., 1937), chap. xx; Sylvia L. Thrupp, "Medieval Guilds Reconsidered," *Journal of Economic History*, II (1942), 164–73.

[6] For an extreme example of unstandardized currency cf. Robert Coltman, Jr., *The Chinese* (Philadelphia: F. A. Davis, 1891), p. 52. In some traditional societies (e.g., China) the state has sought to standardize economic action in the city by setting up standard systems of currency and/or weights and measures; these efforts, however, generally proved ineffective. Inconsistent policies in taxation, too, hinder the development of a "rational" economy.

[7] The status of the true merchant in the preindustrial city, ideally, has been low; in medieval Europe and China many merchants were considered "outcastes." However, in some preindustrial cities a few wealthy merchants have acquired considerable power even though their role has not been highly valued. Even then most of their prestige has come through participation in religious, governmental, or educational activities, which have been highly valued (see, e.g., Ping-ti Ho, "The Salt Merchants of Yang-Chou: A Study of Commercial Capitalism in Eighteenth-Century China," *Harvard Journal of Asiatic Studies*, XVII [1954], 130–68).

[8] For materials on the kinship system and age and sex differentiation see, e.g., Le Tourneau, *op. cit.*; Edward W. Lane, *The Manners and Customs of the Modern Egyptians*, 3d ed. (New York: E. P. Dutton Co., 1923); C. Snouck Hurgronje, *Mekka in the Latter Part of the Nineteenth Century*, trans. J. H. Monahan (London: Luzac, 1931); Horace Miner, *The Primitive City of Timbuctoo* (Princeton: Princeton University Press, 1953); Alice M. Bacon, *Japanese Girls and Women*, rev. ed. (Boston: Houghton Mifflin Co., 1902); J. S. Burgess, "Community Organization in China," *Far Eastern Survey*, XIV (1945), 371–73; Morton H. Fried, *Fabric of Chinese Society* (New York: Frederick A. Praeger, 1953); Francis L. K. Hsu, *Under*

the *Ancestors' Shadow* (New York: Columbia University Press, 1948); Cornelius Osgood, *The Koreans and Their Culture* (New York: Ronald Press, 1951), chap. viii; Jukichi Inouye, *Home Life in Tokyo*, 2d ed. (Tokyo: Tokyo Printing Co., 1911).

[9] Tsung-Lien Shen and Shen-Chi Liu, *Tibet and the Tibetans* (Stanford: Stanford University Press, 1953), pp. 143–44.

[10] Osgood, *op. cit.*, p. 146.

[11] For information on various aspects of religious behavior see, e.g., Le Tourneau, *op. cit.*; Miner, *op. cit.*, Lane, *Manners and Customs*; Hurgronje, *op. cit.*; André Chouraqui, *Les Juifs d'Afrique du Nord* (Paris: Presses Universitaires de France, 1952); Justus Doolittle, *Social Life of the Chinese* (London: Sampson Low, 1868); John K. Shryock, *The Temples of Anking and Their Cults* (Paris: Privately printed, 1931); Derk Bodde, ed., *Annual Customs and Festivals in Peking* (Peiping: Henri Vetch, 1936); Edwin Benson, *Life in a Medieval City* (New York: Macmillan Co., 1920); Hsu, *op. cit.*

[12] Le Tourneau, *op. cit.*, Part VI; Lane, *Manners and Customs*, chap. ii; Charles Bell, *The People of Tibet* (Oxford: Clarendon Press, 1928), chap. xix; O. Olufsen, *The Emir of Bokhara and His Country* (London: William Heinemann, 1911), chap. ix; Doolittle, *op. cit.*

[13] Carleton Coon, *Caravan: The Story of the Middle East* (New York: Henry Holt & Co., 1951), p. 259; George W. Gilmore, *Korea from Its Capital* (Philadelphia: Presbyterian Board of Publication, 1892), pp. 51–52.

[14] Osgood, *op. cit.*, chap. viii; Gilmore, *op. cit.*, chap. iv.

[15] Henri Pirenne, in *Medieval Cities* (Princeton: Princeton University Press, 1925), and others have noted that European cities grew up in opposition to and were separate from the greater society. But this thesis has been overstated for medieval Europe. Most preindustrial cities are integral parts of broader social structures.

[16] Some of these cities made extensive use of water power, which possibly fostered deviations from the type.

[17] For a discussion of the institutional prerequisites of industrialization see, e.g., Bert F. Hoselitz, "Social Structure and Economic Growth," *Economia internazionale*, VI (1953), 52–77, and Marion J. Levy, "Some Sources of the Vulnerability of the Structures of Relatively Non-industrialized Societies to Those of Highly Industrialized Societies," in Bert F. Hoselitz, ed., *The Progress of Underdeveloped Areas* (Chicago: University of Chicago Press, 1952), pp. 114 ff.

[18] *Op. cit.*

[19] This point seems to have been perceived also by Asael T. Hansen in his review of Horace Miner's *The Primitive City of Timbuctoo*, *American Journal of Sociology*, LIX (1954), 501–2.

[20] Ralph L. Beals, "Urbanism, Urbanization and Acculturation," *American Anthropologist*, LIII (1951), 1–10.

[21] See, e.g., D. R. Gadgil, *Poona: A Socio-economic Survey* (Poona: Gokhale Institute of Politics and Economics, 1952), Part II; N. V. Sovani, *Social Survey of Kolhapur City* (Poona: Gokhale Institute of Politics and Economics, 1951), Vol. II; Noel P. Gist, "Caste Differentials in South India," *American Sociological Review*, XIX (1954), 126–37; John Campbell Pelzel, "Social Stratification in Japanese Urban Economic Life" (unpublished Ph.D. dissertation, Harvard University, Department of Social Relations, 1950).

[22] Robert Redfield, *The Folk Culture of Yucatan* (Chicago: University of Chicago Press, 1941).

The Preindustrial City
Reflections Four Decades Later
GIDEON SJOBERG and ANDRÉE F. SJOBERG

In this short article, Gideon and Andrée Sjoberg answer criticisms made of their original model of the "preindustrial city." They begin by reviewing why the original article and subsequent book were written. They then answer particular critiques and show how recent research, such as that on Mayan cities, has, in fact, supported their original conclusions.

For a different approach to the problem of defining types and making generalizations across different cultures and periods of time, see Janet L. Abu-Lughod's article, "Territoriality and Social Organization in Islamic Cities." Whereas the Sjobergs distinguish sharply between preindustrial and industrial cities, she shows that there are also features that some preindustrial cities share with modern Western cities.

Reflecting upon one's earlier endeavors some decades later is not without pitfalls. There is the ever-present danger of indulging in mere self-justification. Nevertheless, looking back on a journal article (Sjoberg 1955) and a more fully developed book on the preindustrial city (Sjoberg 1960) affords us an opportunity to set this effort within a broader intellectual context.

This essay is a collaborative effort for several reasons. Andrée F. Sjoberg, who co-authored two chapters in the book, *The Preindustrial City*, has, because of the nature of her teaching and research, made special efforts to keep up with the burgeoning literature on preindustrial urban life. During the decades since we carried out research for the book we have returned at frequent

Source: Article written expressly for *Urban Life*.

intervals to intense discussion of this general topic, hardly a subject of ongoing conversation among couples.

After considering why the project was undertaken in the first instance, we shall respond to some of the criticisms that have been leveled against our formulation. We also point to new directions for research (ever mindful of the fact that the present essay provides only a general sketch of our reasoning).

The article and the book were to a considerable degree written in reaction to the existing analyses of urban centers by American sociologists and anthropologists. At the time the article was published in 1955, social scientists in the United States were relying heavily on Redfield's (1947) "The Folk Society" and Wirth's (1938) "Urbanism As a Way of Life" in their interpretation of cities worldwide and, implicitly, since the dawn of civilization. Contemporary urban life in the United States and elsewhere was often contrasted with Redfield's "folk society" (or small, nonliterate social order), or, following Wirth, American cities were taken as the standard for interpreting urban communities in diverse historical and cross-cultural settings. Although the perspectives of Redfield and Wirth have stimulated a considerable amount of useful research, they provide too narrow a foundation for an adequate understanding of urban life on a global basis prior to the scientific and industrial revolutions.[1] The impressive body of data collected during the past few decades in differing social and cultural settings has highlighted the contrasts between industrial cities and cities of the world before industrialization.[2]

Still, a number of objections have been raised to the basic conceptualization of the preindustrial city. One major criticism has been voiced by social scientists who stress the cultural distinctions among cities in diverse preindustrial civilized societies—for example, they argue that cities in China differed appreciably from those in India, and that these in turn deviated from urban communities in pre-Columbian America. One group of scholars would align themselves with the geographer Paul Wheatley (1971), whose magnificent work, *The Pivot of the Four Quarters*, describes how the cosmology of the ancient Chinese provided a framework for constructing their leading cities. We do not question the thesis that religious beliefs (and other cultural values) affected the spatial arrangements of preindustrial urban settlements, and we have always assumed that significant cultural variations existed. But our emphasis has been on the common structural patterns in preindustrial cities. Certainly, cultural values such as the cosmological led to distinctive spatial arrangements in different areas. Nevertheless, we can isolate shared features in the ecology of cities in traditional societies. To cite one such pattern, the central core of preindustrial cities was inhabited by the ruling elite, whereas the lower orders settled at a greater distance from the center and toward the city's periphery. Residence at or near the city's hub, with its major religious and governmental edifices, was a prime consideration, especially so in a society characterized by limited means of transportation and communication. Ongoing interpersonal interaction among members of the ruling class was vital to the maintenance and enhancement of their power and status in the urban communities and the broader society. It must be added that lower-status occupational groups who met the immediate needs of the dominant class—household servants, merchants, craftsmen, and others—also tended to cluster in or about the city center.

Commonalities existed in spheres other than the ecological (or spatial): family structure, political and economic organization, religion, education, and the accumulation of knowledge. For example, in preindustrial cities it was the upper class that was able to realize and sustain the extended kin arrangements considered the ideal in traditional civilizations. The urban lower class and the peasantry generally found it economically and socially impossible to maintain an extended kinship group within a common household—though most aspired to this goal.

It was only within the privileged class that extreme forms of gender segregation were attainable. Upper-status women were restricted to the home and thereby excluded from public activities—in the economic, political, and educational realms. Even in the home women and men occupied separate social space (e.g., Murray and Price 1990). In the urban lower class and among ruralites women's labor was too essential for survival to permit a high degree of gender segregation.

No one, to our knowledge, has examined gender relationships specifically within the upper class in traditional cities across a broad spectrum of societies. Even the renowned anthropologist Jack Goody (1990), in his major synthesis of data on kinship systems of Eurasia, fails to consider the privileged sector in preindustrial cities. Yet the patterns adhered to by the elite served as the ideal for many urbanites and the more privileged sectors of the peasantry. Over time many such patterns spread, though in somewhat muted form, to virtually all families in the society. Gender segregation, championed by preindustrial elite males, and acceded to by adult females, found striking cultural expression in footbinding in China and purdah (veiling and other forms of seclusion) in Muslim societies. In the course of the centuries these patterns came to affect even the poorer segments of society. The norms adhered to by the privileged class, established in the cities, set the tone for the society as a whole.

The technology of traditional civilizations and its associated knowledge systems, as well as the supporting political and economic organizations, were far more complex than anything developed in folk, or nonliterate, orders. All this made possible the construction of cities and the maintenance of a privileged ruling class and a substantial body of full-time specialists. Certainly, the literati (the educated elite) in these societies could not have produced and sustained the knowledge systems they did had they not been freed from the need to engage in the production of food and other essential goods.

However, the technology that characterized the preindustrial civilization, advanced though it was over that in preliterate orders, still was largely dependent on human and animal muscle power (to a modest extent the energy of water and wind was harnessed), and such severely limited the size of the privileged class who could be freed from basic forms of production. Not until the emergence of industrialism, in which machines came to perform the heavy labor required for human survival or otherwise deemed essential by the ruling class (e.g., pyramid building), was it possible to achieve the patterns we associate with modernity.

A second line of criticism of the preindustrial city framework is more complex and has many ramifications. We can only touch on these here. The criticism emanates from scholars who take "capitalism" as the master concept.[3] A number of social scientists contend that capitalism has shaped, or been shaped, by urban life in the West. A significant outgrowth of this emphasis on capitalism has been world-system analysis (Wallerstein 1974). Its proponents have perceived capitalism as spreading out of Europe (its core or center) to the rest of the world. Consequently, cities in the core have profited, through the accumulation of capital, at the expense of those in the periphery. However, the proponents of the world-system perspective neglect the political structures that sustain social and, especially, economic life in urban centers. Moreover, the rather narrow economism that characterizes studies of the relationship among cities in the core and the periphery blinds scholars to the social arrangements that are part and parcel of preindustrial city life (e.g., Kasaba 1991; King 1990). The central issues raised in the article and the book fall outside the purview of world-system analysis (see e.g., Chase-Dunn and Hall 1991).[4]

Somewhat in tandem with, as well as overlapping with, world-system analysis has been a heightened awareness of the considerable commerce and travel throughout Eurasia that occurred prior to the scientific and industrial revolutions (e.g., Curtin 1984). Many of the leading preindustrial cities did maintain extensive trade and other connections, often over vast distances.

While we acknowledge the major contributions of this new scholarship, we nevertheless stand convinced that the preindustrial city framework is essential for an understanding of the nature of urban life prior to the scientific and industrial revolutions.

If we were to rework our description of the preindustrial city type, we would take greater account of the substantial trading activity referred to above. We would also incorporate aspects of the world-system perspective into our analysis. In particular we would be attentive to the fact that some leading cities in Asia today (Bombay and Calcutta come to mind) were established by European colonialists and displayed certain features that deviated from preindustrial-urban patterns (e.g., Basu 1985). Still, the early colonial cities that were creations of the Spaniards in Latin America were essentially preindustrial in their form. Spain had not yet experienced the scientific and industrial revolution, which emerged in northwestern Europe a couple of centuries after the conquest of Mexico.

The idea of the preindustrial city type will not disappear. Although we do not subscribe to any crass form of linear evolutionary theory, we do recognize that the social patterns in small nonliterate (or folk) societies have differed markedly from those in preindustrial civilized orders—most notably in cities, the centers of social power. Researchers who lump together data from nonliterate and preindustrial civilized orders overlook certain critical aspects of preindustrial city life. Thus Martin Whyte (1978) in his study of women in preindustrial orders in general, in both literate and nonliterate societies, was unable to discern the striking gender patterns of the preindustrial urban elite. We learn nothing from him about the virtual monopoly of literacy by elite males and the exclusion of women from the public sphere.

It is not surprising that a number of major scholars today rely on the distinction between preliterate and preindustrial civilized societies, and industrial ones as well, when theorizing about the social and cultural development of human beings from the past to the present. Thus, preeminent theorists such as Anthony Giddens (1985), in Britain, and Jürgen Habermas (1975), in Germany, who have been shaping the manner in which social scientists (from various disciplines) view societal and cultural arrangements, rely on distinctions among types of society. Habermas in a general sense distinguishes among preliterate, preindustrial civilized, and industrial ("capitalist") orders, and Giddens explicitly acknow-ledges the contrasts between preindustrial cities and modern urban forms.[5]

Today, rethinking our original formulations, especially in light of recent findings, we would make a special effort to analyze the differences between earlier and later forms of the preindustrial city. In so doing, we could advance our analysis in a more compelling manner and more effectively demonstrate the relevance of the concept of the preindustrial city for social investigation. The inhabitants of the more developed cities were far more able to harness wind, water, and animal power than were their earlier counterparts. Coastal cities throughout Europe and Asia profited from improvements in shipbuilding and navigation. So too, large-scale construction projects such as the Colosseum, the aqueducts, and the roads leading to Rome were predicated on certain technological developments that ultimately helped to lay the basis for the scientific/industrial revolution (the latter did not invent itself).

To more fully grasp the nature of preindustrial city life, we can focus on particular cultural settings, keeping one question foremost in mind—How does the particular relate to the general? The Mayan cities are an informative case in point. At the time the article and the book were published, the idea of the Maya having created fully developed cities was largely unrecognized by, and contrary to, the conventional wisdom of social scientists. It was often assumed that even the more extensive archaeological remains that had been excavated were simply "ceremonial centers" to which people from the nearby countryside thronged periodically in order to engage in a variety of activities, mainly of a ceremonial nature. The assumption was that no permanent settlements had ever been established around the often imposing public edifices. In *The Preindustrial City* we briefly advanced the argument that the Mayan "ceremonial centers," even in the pre-Classic era, must each have been the core of true cities. We assumed, on theoretical grounds, that a privileged class (including a well-developed intellectual elite whose impressive advances in astronomy and mathematics surpassed the accomplishments of Europe at the time) could not have survived without a substantial supportive body of bureaucrats, craftsmen, merchants, and servants functioning as permanent residents of urban centers.

Now, after several decades of archaeological research, essentially all specialists on the Maya recognize that these people did develop true cities. Some urban communities, such as Tikal, were of impres-sive size.[6]

Although the *conquistadores* destroyed great numbers of Mayan manuscripts, the surviving *stelae*, or inscriptions on stone, are being deciphered, and their contents lend strong support to the notion of a powerful ruling class. Specialists on the Maya, however, have not yet recognized the fact that the cities rather closely fit our constructed preindustrial urban type, something that is best illustrated in the ecological patterns, with the privileged elite residing at the city's core, persons of humbler status spread farther out, and ruralites at the periphery and beyond. A systematic comparison of the Mayan cities with those in traditional societies in Eurasia would be a worthy endeavor.

A second profitable line of inquiry is to examine the great literatures of civilized orders specifically within a preindustrial city framework. This would cast additional light on the early cities and perhaps refine the preindustrial city typology. We made far too limited use of these materials in our previous work. Though primarily oriented toward religion, these literatures are, along with archaeological and linguistic data, a vital source for deciphering a variety of social arrangements in older cities. Yet it must be emphasized that they were composed by a minute segment of the urban populace: the educated male elite. These persons wrote about their own privileged world and virtually ignored the lives of ordinary people, particularly marginal groups such as non-upper class women, outcast groups, the urban poor, and ruralites in general. Little wonder that we have highly limited data on, for example, the slaves of ancient Greek cities (and elsewhere).

For data on social arrangements in traditional cities one could draw, for example, on the great literatures of earlier China, the Middle East, or Greece. But we elect to focus here briefly on the literary texts of ancient India associated with Hinduism, the dominant religious orientation of the Indian people.[7] Preindustrial urban arrangements in India, one of the world's great civilizations, have generally been overlooked. Moreover, many of the traditional patterns, particularly with respect to religion, continue to affect the lives of what is today the second most populous nation in the world.

Among the vast body of religious-philosophical texts from ancient India, the most useful for an understanding of preindustrial urban life are the two great epics, the *Mahabharata* and the *Ramayana*. These rank among the longest single poems in world literature. They have been seen as analogous in certain respects to the *Iliad* and the *Odyssey*. Like the Greek epics, they are in a sense encyclopedic compendia of mythology and of the deeds of heroic figures, always members of the ruling elite. At various points they provide useful hints about the life of the upper classes in the early cities. Although much has been written about the epic poetry of India, no one, to our knowledge, has analyzed the content of these works within a preindustrial urban framework. Yet these literary creations were clearly the work of a male literati who resided in urban centers. The social patterns that can be teased out of these texts reflect the life of the privileged strata in early traditional civilized societies.

Examination of the content of the Indian epics within a preindustrial city framework reveals a number of significant social patterns. Here again gender serves as a useful point of departure. As in traditional cities everywhere, elite women were considered mere appendages of men and were excluded from participation in the public sphere of activity wherein men ruled supreme. But gender relations were more complex than they might appear on the surface. In ancient India, as in many other preindustrial civilized orders, women were viewed in highly ambiguous, even contradictory, terms. They were to be both revered and honored and feared and denigrated. In addition, they were viewed as simultaneously powerful and powerless. Elite women, whose actions were highly constrained and who were subject to rigid social and spatial segregation, even within the confines of the home, had at the same time the greatest potential among all women to enhance or undermine the social status and power of the family and the males within it. Women were especially crucial to the continuance of the lineage through the production of male children. Even highly advantaged males in the society depended for their status and power to a considerable degree on the rockbed of the supporting family, and unacceptable behavior on the part of the women seriously threatened their power and prestige. (It may be significant also that Hinduism, which personalizes the many forms of the divine that it embraces, plays out this same theme in its hierarchy of the divinities. All of the male deities are dependent on their female consorts for their very power and energy to act in the realm of human beings.) Though many of the aforementioned arrangements were perhaps more starkly illustrated in India than elsewhere, these kinds of gender patterns are typical of preindustrial urban life.

The patterns associated with the preindustrial city are significant for more than just their historical interest. The persistence today of traditional social forms in many societies of Eurasia has escaped the attention of most American social scientists, who lack personal acquaintance with the "heavy hand of tradition" associated with a preindustrial civilized past. These traditional norms continue to affect family, religious, and stratification patterns even in the face of the great transformation that has resulted from industrialization, urbanization, and bureaucratization. The place of tradition in defining familial and gender roles has special import. In Japan, India, the Middle East, and many other areas, complex honorifics in the language, typical of preindustrial cities, continue to reinforce class, gender, and age distinctions.

Much work on preindustrial urban life remains to be done.[8] A fuller description of the details of traditional preindustrial urban arrangements would serve to clarify a host of thorny problems regarding urban centers, both past and present.

Notes

[1] That Redfield's "folk society" continues to be employed to organize research data is attested to by Edgerton (1992).

[2] The preindustrial city framework has been used in a variety of ways by researchers in a number of disciplines. For example, Simić (1983), discussing Serbian cities in the nineteenth century, observes how these closely approximated the preindustrial city type. Highly informative is the research by Dray-Novey (1993) on Imperial Beijing. On the basis of a study of the spatial order and the police in Beijing in about 1650–1850, the author criticizes the preindustrial city framework for its failure to examine the nature of formal social control. Any full-scale revision of the original work would need to take careful account of findings of this sort.

[3] To do justice to the connection between capitalism and cities requires advances in knowledge on a variety of fronts. First, we need to consider the relationship of capitalism to city life in Western Europe (e.g., Holton 1986). Unlike scholars who conceive of capitalism as the central force in history, we contend that capitalist cities in Europe prior to the scientific and industrial revolutions were far closer to the preindustrial city type than to the modern urban. Only after capitalism converged with the scientific and industrial revolutions did the modern urban form come into full bloom.

Second, we need to look closely at those cities in Western Europe, especially in Spain and Portugal, that built up vast commercial (or mercantilist) empires. If we were to pursue such a project we would chide our critics for their failure to give due attention not only to the social arrangements in preindustrial cities but also to the way in which capitalism in the urban centers of Europe was supported by powerful political structures. This was clearly the case in the expansion of the Portuguese and Spanish empires (e.g., Tracy 1990). The political stability that made possible rather extensive commercial activities is frequently brushed aside by classical economists and neo-Marxists. The champions of world-system analysis can be seriously faulted along these lines.

The case against some of the assumptions underlying world-system analysis finds support not just in European expansionism but also in the East Asian experience in the twentieth century. The case of the Japanese empire prior to World War

II documents how political control facilitated and solidified further economic expansion. In more recent decades capitalism in nations of the East Asian rim is likewise being driven by state power.

Interestingly, some East Asian scholars (both in East Asia and in Europe) have been drawing rather heavily on the work of a neglected German political economist, Friedrich List (1974), who wrote in the first half of the nineteenth century. Essentially, List challenged Adam Smith's emphasis on free trade in England after it had achieved political dominance, on the grounds that Smith's argument served the cause of the British empire. With free trade, the British could export manufactured goods and import raw materials and agricultural products. They thus gained at the expense of other nations.

The ideas associated with List, properly modified, can readily be directed against the proponents of world-system analysis, for its economism (or materialism) downgrades the role of political power. *The Preindustrial City* plays up the essentiality of political organizations in establishing economic and commercial activities. Major issues of this sort can be only briefly discussed in this essay.

[4] Although Ward (1993), among others, attacks world-system analysis for ignoring gender, the book on the preindustrial city did take gender patterns into account (though these need to be considerably elaborated).

[5] Giddens is one of the few major contemporary social theorists to pay special heed to the role of urban centers in shaping the nature and development of social orders.

[6] Sources that survey the relevant recent research include Hammond (1988) on the Maya and Weaver (1993) on the Maya and the Aztecs.

[7] Andrée F. Sjoberg (1990; 1994) has written on the broad sweep of Indian cultural history as she has sought to demonstrate the unrecognized impact of the leading minority people, the Dravidians, on the course of Indian civilization and Hinduism. In conducting her research, she has confronted firsthand the failure of leading Indologists to recognize the nature of the preindustrial city in their interpretation of the historical evidence.

[8] The relationship between Eurocentrism and the preindustrial city type is a methodological problem that demands careful attention. It is not a mere artifact of what Said (1979) terms "Orientalism." In the article and the book, we did not draw, as many authors do, a marked distinction between Western and "Oriental" cities. European cities, prior to the scientific and industrial revolutions, far more closely approximated the preindustrial urban type than the modern one. The earlier cities fitted the preindustrial type quite well. Yet, just how the "West" is set apart from the "East" haunts any researcher engaged, as we are, in generalizing about urban life.

We thank the editors, George Gmelch and Walter Zenner, for their constructive criticisms of an earlier version of this essay. We are also indebted to Boyd Littrell and Leonard Cain for their careful reading of the manuscript and their suggestions for improvements.

Cities and Human Health

LAWRENCE M. SCHELL

What is the relationship of urbanism to human health? How does living in cities affect our biological adaptation? In this essay, Lawrence Schell examines how urban environments influence human biology. He critically looks at the stereotype of the city as a dreadfully artificial and unhealthy place and disentangles the characteristics of the urban environment that are linked to health and disease.

In this exploration of the relationship of urbanism to health, the stereotype of the city as an artificial and unhealthy place will be undermined by identifying specific characteristics of urban environments that pertain to health and disease. In addition, the influence of urbanism on human biology and the significant challenge to human biological adaptation which it poses will be discussed. While it is customary to think of human biological adaptation and evolution as processes which were replaced by culture as the means of human adaptation, it is precisely the environment most conditioned by culture, the urban environment, that poses the greatest challenge *biologically* and to which *Homo sapiens* must now adapt.

The Problem of Urbanism

The characteristics of hominids evolved over five or more million years and became established in the hominid line at least fifty thousand years before today's cities. Virtually all human evolution,

Source: Article written expressly for *Urban Life*.

from the first hominids to the appearance of *Homo sapiens sapiens*, occurred in response to the demands of a physical and social environment which modern humans in urban environments never experience. Indeed, the genus Homo, for more than 99 percent of the time that it has existed on earth, has congregated in numerically small, technologically simple bands of migratory hunters and gatherers. The extreme difference between the environment of our early biological adaptation and the environment of today's populations has consequences for modern people in urban surroundings.

Human Settlements and Health in the Past

The Transition to Settled Village Life

One way to gauge the effect of urbanism on health is to examine human societies before the appearance of permanent settlement. In presettled societies, human beings lived in small, loosely organized bands or tribes. The populations of hunter-gatherers were small, usually not more than fifty individuals, and there was little contact with other bands. People had a migratory subsistence pattern based on hunting and gathering which involved much physical activity and a highly varied diet that was low in animal protein, animal fats, and sodium. Resources (food, shelter, tools) were distributed without sharp inequalities within the society. The only domesticated animal was the dog.

With the advent of village life, the earliest form of urbanization, most of this changed. Agriculture replaced hunting and gathering and made possible settled village life. Population size increased slightly, the variety of the diet decreased, and the domestication of animals (e.g., sheep, goats, cattle) resulted in increased contact between people and animals. All these changes had a profound impact on human health, slowly at first and then more powerfully as each trend became more pronounced.[1]

When agriculture replaces hunting and gathering as the primary source of nutrients, a narrower range of nutrients is consumed. This focus on a few domesticated foods makes possible nutritional diseases, especially vitamin or mineral deficiencies. In hunting and gathering societies, these are rare because of the wide variety of food sources utilized. In addition, agriculture involves risk. If only a few crops provide all the foods, there is a greater risk of famine and of dietary deficiency. Seasonal fluctuations in supply occur, and crops may be lost to drought, insects, or plant diseases at any time.

Malnutrition due to protein or calorie deficiency is more character-istic of poor agricultural societies than of today's isolated hunting and gathering ones. Early agriculturally based villages and small cities may have been characterized by occasional malnutrition or by vitamin and mineral deficiencies.

Increases in population size can also have a profound impact on health. Many diseases require a minimum population size year after year. These diseases, often called acute community infections, either kill those they infect or, if the host recovers, leave the host permanently immunized against the disease. Measles is an example of an acute community infection, but the flu is not. A natural bout of measles (not the vaccine) leaves permanent, lifelong immunity among the survivors, but people get influenza year after year, there being no permanent immunity to every influenza type. Diseases that leave surviving hosts with permanent immunity need new hosts or the disease-causing organism (pathogen) will perish and no new cases of the disease will occur. If all the adults in a community are the survivors from previous years of infection, the only new hosts are immigrants and newborns. In small populations, like bands, there are not enough of either to sustain an acute community infection. In larger societies with high birth rates, new hosts are produced faster than the rate of natural immunity building, and the disease persists. The population size necessary for maintaining measles is well over five hundred thousand. This urban size was not attained in any one city until rather recently (consider table 1). Infectious diseases may not have been prevalent in early agricultural villages because of their small population size. Skeletal remains from these villages do not show much infectious disease; however, our samples of skeletal remains are too scanty at present to rule out the possibility of an increase in infectious disease before the advent of large urban centers one thousand years ago, at which time acute community infections were prevalent in European cities.

A major change that occurred with sedentariness and agricul-turally based subsistence was increased contact with animals. Humans had increased contact with two kinds of animals: the domesticated animals such as cats, dogs, horses, and sheep, and, secondly, the pests such as rats, raccoons, mice, and insects that share human domiciles. Human settlements provided stable environments to which these pests adapted and which were thus instrumental in their evolution. Both types of animals increase the variety of pathogens with which humans come into contact, as well as increase the frequency of their appearance.

Table 1 The World's Largest Cities
(*from* Chandler and Fox 1974)

Era	Number of Cities with Population over:		Largest City	
	50,000	100,000	Name	Population
1360 BC	3	0 or 1	Thebes, Egypt	100,000
1200	4	0 or 1	Memphis, Egypt	?
430	25	12	Babylon, Mid. East	250,000
200	35	14	Patna, India	
100 AD	45	16	Rome, Europe	650,000
361	25	14	Constantinople, Rome	350,000
622	46	10	Constantinople, Bzy.	500,000
800	58	16	Changan, China	800,000
900	60	15	Bagdad, Persia	900,000
1000	61	19	Cordova, Spain	450,000
1200	69	25	Hangchow, China	255,000
1400	74	24	Nanking, China	473,000
1600	75+	37	Peking, China	706,000
1800	179	66	Peking, China	1,100,000

The problems posed by more frequent contact with disease-harboring animals are made worse by rudimentary sanitary engineering. While there are reports of drained latrines, piped drinking water, and water-cleansed lavatories from archeological excavations of ancient cities in India, Greece, and Egypt, these facilities were available only to the elite. For the masses, hygiene and sanitation were probably ineffective, and infectious material of animal or human origin sometimes contaminated food and drink. Because many parasites are transmitted from feces to the mouth via food or drink, settled villagers with rudimentary sanitary facilities can develop a heavy burden of parasitic disease. In contrast, the migratory hunters and gatherers had less contact with animals, moved too often for pests to adapt to people's domiciles, and left their own waste behind with each move to a new camp. Only parasites with exceptional powers of survival outside a host can survive the drying and heat or cold to remain infectious long enough for migratory hunters and gatherers to reinfect themselves.[2]

Health problems stemming from ineffective sanitation were probably new during early urbanization, and they may have become endemic (always present at a constant level) in the populations as urbanization increased. Lewis Mumford (1961) distinguishes two stages in the history of the city pertaining to health: an early stage of small houses, usually of one or two stories and separated by kitchen gardens with some domesticated animals, with farms nearby, and a second stage characterized by greater population, multistoried dwellings so close together that there is no room for kitchen gardens, and fields at a greater distance from the city. In the first stage, the production of waste was balanced by its use as fertilizer in adjacent kitchen gardens and nearby fields. In the second stage, however, the production of waste was much greater, and there were no uses for waste within the city—cesspits contaminated local wells, and, by each multistoried dwelling, there accumulated a dung pile waiting for removal to the countryside. Unsanitary cesspits and dung piles provided an opportunity for contamination of water and food that was far greater than in earlier, small cities or villages, and certainly greater than the hunting and gathering existence of human societies that had preceded the development of village settlements.

The Preindustrial City: Plagues and Pestilences

Given the characteristics of early city life just described, it is no surprise that, for many centuries, human populations experienced substantial mortality and morbidity due to infectious diseases. Actually, in many countries today, infectious diseases still are responsible for much morbidity and mortality, especially in children. The features of urban life so important to the spread of infectious disease are common in many cities: poor hygiene and sanitation, crowding, large population size, malnutrition or suboptimal nutrition, and contact with infected individuals (pests, domesticated animals, and humans).

Although Europe was not alone in its experience of infectious disease, the chronicles of its history provide a rich and detailed story of human experience with infectious disease. From the rise of large towns to the development of cities with a half million or more inhabitants, epidemic after epidemic of infectious disease is recorded in great detail as an essential part of the history of Europe.

Leprosy provides but one example. While some historians of medicine claim that leprosy was present during biblical times, this conclusion assumes that ancient investigators could distinguish the disease from other skin disorders. Indisputable evidence is lacking, but the disease is well known from the time just following the fall of Rome. It was widely disseminated in the eleventh and twelfth centuries, probably by the Crusades, and pandemics (the spread of disease over large land areas) are known from the thirteenth, fourteenth, and fifteenth centuries. The reason for its subsequent decrease is something of a mystery. Today, the disease still afflicts thousands, though not in Europe. A curious feature of leprosy is that its transmission requires prolonged contact, and its incubation takes years. It is plausible that hygienic conditions in medieval Europe were so poor that infected parents transmitted the disease to their children before the parents showed any symptoms.

In contrast to leprosy, the Plague is easily transmitted. The Bubonic Plague, as it is sometimes known, can take several forms, all of which are caused by a bacterium, *Pastuerella pestis*. The Plague is a city disease, because, in cities, the transmission of *P. pestis* is greatly facilitated. *P. pestis* infects the fleas that infest rats. It is believed that wild animals first harbored the disease, and they transmitted it, through their fleas, to the rats which shared habitations with humans. There, infected fleas could spread the disease to humans either directly or after living on domesticated animals. The flea can also survive on pigs, cats, calves, chickens, and geese. Unlike the rich, common people shared their living quarters with domesticated animals, slept on straw as a family, stored grain in the home, and generally provided few barriers to rats. Once the disease was started in humans, it could spread from person to person by an aerosol route. In a cough, droplets of saliva carrying *P. pestis* from the lungs would have been inhaled by anyone living in close quarters. In a crowded city, the disease would be able to spread quickly. Since the disease is often fatal and survival does not provide immunity for very long, if at all, the disease could kill millions. In Europe in the sixth, the fourteenth and, again, in the seventeenth centuries, it did. By some accounts, half of the European population perished in each of the first two epidemics. The epidemics, some of which lasted for decades, were accompanied by a variety of social changes including urban outmigrations, debauchery, religious piety, and the development of a number of now quaint remedies and preventive measures. One of these was a scented water that was meant to prevent infection and was named after its town of origin, Cologne (Eau de Cologne).

A variety of other infectious diseases related to sanitation, contact with animals, and crowding in cities became epidemic at one time or during several periods. When several epidemics raged at once, the world must have seemed hideous indeed. One can imagine a resident of sixteenth-century Europe gauging the disposition of infectious disease epidemics across the continent in somewhat the same way that an average citizen of the United States watches the television news of severe weather conditions across North America.

A district physician of Regensburg, Lammert comments in the year 1602 (from Zinsser 1935, p. 272):

> There was severe winter, a cold April, a hailstorm in the summer. The wine was scarce and of poor quality. In this year, there was plague in the Palantine, through Saxony and Prussia. In Danzig 12,000 people died in one week. There was a smallpox epidemic in Bohemia; another in Silisia. In southern Germany, there raged the terrible *Bauch krankheit* [probably dysentery or typhoid]. There was a famine in Russia accompanied by pestilences of plague and typhus, and in Moscow alone [probably a gross exaggeration] 127,000 people are said to have died of pestilence.

Transition to the Twentieth Century

Many of the factors that contributed to the high rates of morbidity and mortality in preindustrial cities are no longer characteristic of cities in developed countries. Historians of health point to the beginning of the twentieth century as a turning point in health for the United States, especially for cities. At this time, piped water, sanitary removal of wastes, eradication of vermin and pests, food industry regulation, and reduction of overcrowded dwellings became prevalent. These improvements are generally credited with the decline in deaths from infectious disease which occurred in the late nineteenth and early twentieth centuries (Omran 1977; Perry 1975). However, public health reforms cannot be held completely responsible. Tuberculosis deaths began their decline before most reforms were initiated, and the twentieth century has been characterized by several major infectious disease epidemics: poliomyelitis in the 1940s and 1950s, influenza in 1918, and Acquired Immune Deficiency Syndrome in the 1980s. Despite the threat of future epidemics, infectious diseases do not cause most deaths now. They have been replaced by deaths due to heart disease and cancer. The reason for the ascendance of these new common causes of death may be found in changes in the urban environment.

Cities in Developed Nations

There are still many cities that struggle with the problems of sanitation, hygiene, crowding, nutrition, and the control of infectious

◀ An inner courtyard bordered by prewar-vintage buildings and served by a single cold-water tap provides home for a dozen families only a few blocks from Belgrade's center.

disease; still other cities have solved these problems and now face others that affect human health, such as pollution and psychosocial stress. There are other problems which stem from population size and the economic hardships of the underclass, as well as their related effects on health, but these subjects are too large and complex to be considered here.

Cities in developed nations can be classified by their health problems. Those cities characterized by problems with psychosocial stress and from pollution caused by current industrial activities or from past industrialization (e.g., toxic waste dumps) can be called *postindustrial* cities. Health-related environmental factors distinguish these cities from industrializing ones in which problems with industrial pollution are just beginning to surface, and in which problems with sanitation, nutrition, and crowding likewise prevail.

In considering health and cities, there are two ways to proceed: by direct comparison of rural and urban rates of diseases, deaths, and other measures of well-being, such as child growth and longevity, or by identifying the factors or characteristics of cities that should affect human health. Both approaches offer insight into the complex relationship between urbanism and health.

Urban Environmental Features Related to Health

Stress

Stress can be a difficult concept to define. Although noise may be considered an urban pollutant, biologically it is usually classed as a stressor. Other common urban stressors are crowding, light, and psychological stress. Considering noise as a stressor rather than as a pollutant has to do with the definition of stress. Although, in nonscientific literature, *stress* refers to the stimulus that provokes the body, in biology, *stress* refers to the body's *response* rather than to the stimulus, and *stressor* is reserved for reference to the *stimulus* for that response (Selye 1956). Stimuli that do not provoke the body to react in certain, well-defined ways are not, strictly speaking, stressors (Selye 1956). By this definition, noise is a stressor because it provokes a particular constellation of features.

Figure 1 shows the major features that define the stress response. After experiencing a physical stressor, a perceived stressor, or an imagined one, reactions occur along two interconnected pathways: the neurological and the endocrine. The overall reaction used to be called the "fight or flight" response, but this label may be an over-interpretation—the response may have many functions. Nevertheless, the immediate reaction does enable a fast energetic

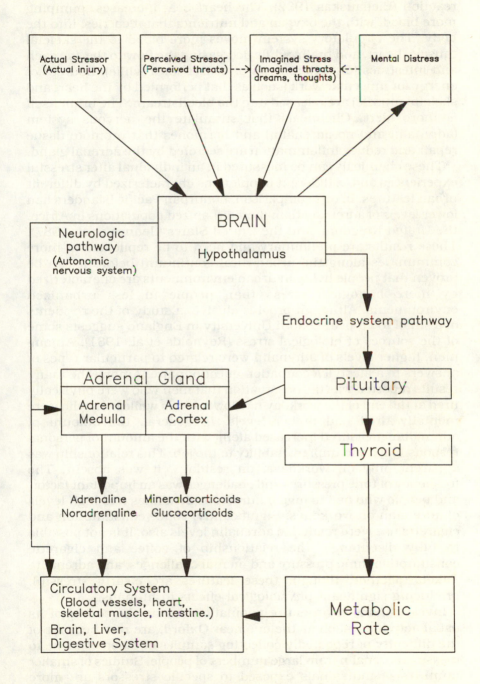

Figure 1 Pathways of the Stress Response

reaction (Bieliauskas 1982). The heart beat increases, pumping more blood, with the oxygen and nutrients that it carries, into the body. The circulatory system moves more blood to the skeletal muscle, heart, and brain, while decreasing the flow to the stomach and intestines (digestion slows or ceases for a while). Sources of energy for muscular work (such as that performed by the heart and skeletal muscle) are released into the bloodstream. The brain itself is more alert. Chemicals that stimulate the nervous system (adrenalin and noradrenalin) and hormones that promote tissue repair and reduce inflammation are secreted by the adrenal gland.

These chemicals can be measured in an individual after stressful experiences and in different populations characterized by different urban features. In one comparison, nonurban Pacific Islanders had lower levels of adrenalin than more urbanized populations in Africa, the United Kingdom, and the United States (Jenner et al. 1987). These results are preliminary and need to be replicated in more communities along the urban-rural continuum before it can be proven that people living in urban environments are characterized by more biological stress than people in less urbanized environments. Although proof is elusive, a study of the residents of a small town near Oxford University in England suggests some of the sources of biological stress (Reynolds et al. 1981). Among men, higher levels of adrenalin were related to particular types of answers to a lifestyle/occupation questionnaire. Among the many results reported was the observation that men who were physically tired at the end of the workday had lower levels while men who were mentally tired had higher levels. In general, the amount of adrenaline measured increased along with the amount of personal responsibility and unpredictability in the job. This relationship was apparent only on workdays; on restdays, it was absent. The frequency of time pressures and challenges was an important factor, and people who had to juggle numerous deadlines had high levels of adrenalin on workdays. Significantly, coffee consumption and cigarette use were related to adrenalin levels also. It is not possible to fully disentangle the relationship of coffee and cigarette consumption, time pressure and mental challenges, and adrenalin. Taken together, though, these features are clearly stressful, producing significant physiological effects in humans.

Investigations of an entire population during the course of its usual activities, such as the one near Oxford, are rare because of the difficulty of repeatedly collecting samples of blood or urine to measure adrenalin from large numbers of people. Studies of smaller numbers of individuals exposed to specific stressors are more common and still reveal pertinent information. One study examined race car drivers during and after a race (reviewed in Carruthers 1976). As you might expect, heart rate went up to nearly two hundred beats per minute (a common resting heartbeat is seventy beats per minute), adrenalin and noradrenalin levels rose steeply, and energy reserves were released into the bloodstream. A similar study was done of people driving in rush hour traffic. After a half-hour drive during rush hour, adrenalin and noradrenalin levels were significantly increased. Distinctively urban experiences such as driving during rush hour are difficult to pick apart scientifically. Is driving a stressor because of the activity itself or because of the competition, the rude road companions, or the noise? Each one of these may be a stressor.

Noise, itself, is a physiological stressor and is usually louder and more continuous in urban environments where transportation and manufacturing produce much noise. Noise is usually defined as unwanted sound; thus, one person's music, or celebration, or desired home repair is another's noise. As a component of the urban scene, noise can raise blood pressure, increase heart rate, alter breathing patterns, stimulate the endocrine system and stimulate the release of adrenalin (Welch and Welch 1970). These are all short-term responses, but there are other effects that are longer lasting.

Noise exposure has been associated with a number of chronic health problems. One of these is mental illness (Tarnopolsky and Clark 1984). Although the causes of mental illness are always difficult to specify, the contribution of emotional stress is rarely doubted. Noise is such a stress, and two studies have noted that, in the areas they studied, mental hospitals had more patients from the communities adjacent to nearby airports than from communities away from the airports, suggesting that the noise contributed to increasing the rate of mental illness (Abey-Wickrama et al. 1969; Kryter 1987; Meecham and Smith 1977). Other studies, however, have not been able to link noise exposure and mental hospital admissions (Gattoni and Tarnopolsky 1973; Frerichs, Beeman, and Coulson 1980). One study of the population adjacent to the international airport serving Amsterdam found an increased rate of consumption of remedies for conditions related to stress (counting pharmacy prescriptions written in an area is one way of learning which maladies are being treated there) and more self-reports of anxiety (Knipschild 1977a; Knipschild and Oudshoorn 1977). Also, rates of cardiovascular diseases were higher among the residents closest to the airport (Knipschild 1977b). Researchers also found that the birthweights were smaller among the children born to mothers who had lived nearest to the airport (Knipschild, Meijer, and Salle 1981). Reduced birthweights were also observed by scientists working independently who studied communities near airports in Japan (Ando and Hattori 1973, 1977) and in the United States (Schell 1981, 1984). One study of births around the Los Angeles airport reported that the number of congenital malformations was higher among the most noise exposed areas (Jones and Tauscher 1978). This last finding needs to be replicated (Frerichs, Beeman, and Coulson 1980) by other human biologists working independently at other locations before we can classify noise as a human teratogen (causer of malformations).

All of these effects are believed to occur because of the body's stress reaction to noise; however, in addition to these effects, noise also has a direct effect on hearing. Loud noise can make the ear temporarily less sensitive to sound. Too much noise exposure over a short period of time without break can lead to permanent loss of hearing. In both cases, the ear usually first becomes less sensitive to higher frequencies (Kryter 1970). Considering both the auditory and nonauditory effects, it is important to realize that the ear need not be damaged in order to have more profound physiological effects. Sounds may affect our physiology at a level too low to affect the ear itself. In summary, noise is both a physiological and auditory stressor that affects numerous aspects of human biology, from the auditory to the cardiovascular to the reproductive systems, and it may affect mental health as well.

Pollutants

A large variety of materials in urban environments act as pollutants. Lead, PCBs (polychlorinated biphenyls), mercury, carbon monoxide, and even naturally occurring substances such as methane, are pollutants. A pollutant may be defined as an unwanted substance, in much the same way that a weed, however beautiful or useful, is defined as an unwanted plant. Pollutants cannot be defined by their origin, composition, or distribution in the environment. In fact, many urban pollutants are common in rural areas. Some are a consequence of manufacturing or of farm use and, since rural areas have frequently been used as dumping grounds for industrial waste, many others are also present. For example, waste disposal sites in rural areas of eastern New York State may contain substantial amounts of PCBs. Likewise, biologically significant chemicals are likely to turn up in pesticides used on farms; thus, rural areas and the people living there may be carrying a higher chemical burden than urban dwellers. Dairy farmers in upstate Michigan were exposed to PBBs (polybromated biphenyls) that were accidentally added to cattlefeed and subsequently entered the food chain. While some of the worst cases of widespread mercury poisoning are in fishing communities, the source of the mercury which poisoned so many people in the Japanese cities of Minamata and Niigata was an industrial process. Cities are not free of responsibility, but rural areas are not as ecologically separate from urban ones as we might wish.

Despite the conceptual problems with dividing pollution into urban and rural types, some pollutants do appear to be more characteristic of urban environments, particularly air and lead pollution. A problem with any classification of urban pollution is that air pollution contains many elements, including lead, carbon monoxide, ozone, sulfur, and nitrogen. Furthermore, any element can come in a variety of forms, such as an air pollutant or as a water pollutant.

Let us first examine the major components of urban air pollution: carbon monoxide and nitrogen and sulfur compounds, all of which result from combustion. Sulfur is produced from the combustion of fossil fuels, such as oil and coal, which contain high levels of sulfur. When burned to generate heat or electricity, for example, oxides of sulfur are produced (SO_2, SO_3, and SO_4) with varying health effects (Waldbott 1978) and the ability to combine with other elements to form new toxic materials. Mild exposure to oxides of sulfur is corrosive to the upper respiratory tract and severe exposure to concentrated sulfur oxides can cause constriction of small passageways in the lungs, coughing, constriction of larger bronchial passages, and even pulmonary edema or the release of fluid into the lung (Waldbott 1978).

Nitrogen is also produced as a result of the combustion of a variety of materials, most commonly automobile emissions. Combustion produces nitric oxide which, when rapidly cooled, becomes nitrogen dioxide. Nitrogen dioxide is four times more toxic than nitric oxide (Waldbott 1978). When formed as nitrous acid or nitric acid, it is corrosive to lung tissue, but, unlike the oxides of sulfur, it is less soluble and is not absorbed into the lining of the upper respiratory tract. Instead, it damages the terminal branches of the lung, the alveoli. Small doses in humans lead to temporary airway resistance (closing down of the small passages). Larger doses over an extended period may cause emphysema, a pathological condition of the lung in which the alveoli coalesce, reducing the available surface area for oxygen exchange and, ultimately, reducing the amount of oxygen getting into the tissues. There are other direct effects and important secondary effects, such as strain on the pulmonary side of the heart, that impair living and shorten life. Carbon monoxide

(CO) is another important component of air pollution. Carbon monoxide binds to hemoglobin, the oxygen-bearing protein present in red blood cells. If too much hemoglobin binds with carbon monoxide instead of with oxygen, cells will malfunction and die. The brain is extremely sensitive to oxygen deprivation.

Air contains oxygen (about 21 percent), nitrogen (about 78 percent), argon (just under 1 percent) and CO_2 (about 0.03 percent). In good, clean air, oxides of sulfur amount to perhaps 0.0001 percent, while CO and oxides of nitrogen are even rarer. Air in urban environments contains measurable amounts of oxides of sulfur and nitrogen; levels can reach 0.5 parts per million parts of air. Nevertheless, gauging the effects in humans is difficult, and special situations of higher exposure are examined closely to study the effects of environmental pollutants.

Occupational exposures to polluted air provides important information. A classic example is the study of workers in automobile tunnels. In one study of employees of the Triborough Bridge and Tunnel Authority in New York City, the average CO level over thirty days was sixty-three parts per million (Ayres et al. 1973). Forty-seven of the nonsmoking workers had 3 percent of their red blood cells' hemoglobin bound with CO instead of oxygen (a significant percentage), and there was a high percentage of workers with symptoms suggesting bronchitis. Another study, which examined lung function in children in a number of United States cities, found a relationship between forced expiratory volume, a useful measure of lung function, and pollutant levels (Shy et al. 1973).

Air pollution may even affect reproduction. One study of birthweight, a common measure of newborn health, found that the average weight of babies born in parts of Los Angeles with heavy air pollution was less than that of the babies born in the areas with cleaner air. This was true even after taking into consideration some socioeconomic factors and mothers' cigarette smoking (Williams et al. 1977). The effect of air pollution may also be seen in mortality rates. Increased mortality rates in Los Angeles have been tied at specific times to increased carbon monoxide levels there (Hexter and Goldsmith 1971), and increased mortality in the New York metropolitan region has been related to increased levels of SO_2 (Buechley et al. 1973). Thus, it has been established that air pollution, a characteristic of cities where combustion of fossil fuels is common, is associated with significant effects on human physiology, reproduction, and survival.

Lead is also a component of air pollution. Although it constitutes less than the contribution made by carbon monoxide and sulfur or nitrogen oxides, it is important. Lead produces significant biological effects in people and is plentiful in dust around and in homes. Unlike the air pollutants discussed earlier, lead dust gets absorbed primarily through ingestion rather than through respiration (Barltrop 1982). In terms of exposure to children, dust gets onto toys and hands, both of which get into the mouth. Also, children generally pass less lead through the gastrointestinal system than adults, and they absorb more into the bloodstream where it then reaches the brain and the blood-forming portions of the bone (Annest et al. 1982). The source of lead in city dust is the emissions from vehicles that burn leaded gasoline (now much less common) and from the rubble and paint scrapings from houses that had been painted with lead-based paint. Other, lesser sources include materials such as solder, while major occupational sources that affect groups of workers include, for example, fabricators of lead storage batteries for automobiles. The latter sources, however, affect fewer people or are not unique to cities.

The effect of lead varies with the type of exposure, from a poisoning (a large dose over a short period of time) to a chronic low-level lead exposure. Chronic exposure is more prevalent in cities (poisoning has been more common in occupational exposures), and is associated with several biological effects, including the impairment of the process by which new red blood cells are built, and neuropsychologic deficits (Lin-Fu 1979; Needleman 1983). The most troublesome of the latter are subtle effects on cognition and attentiveness, which together may impair the ability of children to learn in school. The number of children with lead in their blood at levels that might produce some of these effects is high in urban areas in comparison to rural locations (Annest et al. 1982; Brody et al. 1994). While levels of blood lead have decreased over the last decade (Pirkle et al. 1994), we now know that even low levels of lead can cause detrimental effects, and the blood lead level officially termed "elevated" by the Centers for Disease Control is set lower now than it was ten years ago.

Place of residence within the city and race are substantial risk factors for elevated blood lead among urban children. According to a recent survey of the U.S. population by the U.S. Center for Health Statistics (Brody et al. 1994), nearly 20 percent of 1–5 year old children living in the central areas of large cities have elevated lead levels, and among 1–5 year old black children living in the same areas, one in three have elevated lead levels!

To make matters worse, children who are on diets poor in minerals, especially calcium and phosphorous, generally absorb more lead than children on mineral-rich diets. In animal studies, a high-fat, low-mineral diet was associated with blood lead levels fifty times higher than in animals on the better diet (Barltrop 1982). Between the diet and the higher levels of lead in the dust in urban areas, cities may be breeding children who are experiencing biological effects of lead exposure that may be hindering their education and job preparation. This, in turn, may make it harder for them to find well-paying jobs and may result in their residence in poor areas of cities where their children, in turn, will be exposed to lead. Hence, lead pollution may be influencing the social and cultural characteristics of our cities (Schell 1992).

Comparison of Disease Rates Between Urban and Rural Areas

Heart Disease

According to the American Heart Association and the National Center for Health Statistics, heart disease (diseases of heart and blood vessels) was responsible for 975,550 deaths in the United States in 1979, establishing it as the leading cause of death. In comparison, cancer killed less than half as many people in the United States. The number of deaths due to heart disease, specifically ischemic heart disease (obstruction of the blood supply), is usually higher in urban than in rural areas, but the size of the difference varies. The reason for this variation should help us to understand the disease itself.

In one study, Kleinman and associates (1981) found that deaths due to ischemic heart disease occurred more often in urban than in suburban counties in the United States, although the difference was slight among the age groups at highest risk (sixty-five to seventy-four years of age). Marmot (1980) reviewed urban-rural differences in heart disease around the world. In developed countries such as the United States and Britain, the difference is small, with the rate of death among males due to ischemic heart disease in the urban centers being 13 percent more than the rate in rural areas. In Yugoslavia, where urban-rural differences in the environment are more pronounced than in England and Wales, the urban rate is approximately 200 percent of the rural rate. In traditional, rural societies, such as the Samburu of east Africa, rates of death from heart disease are very low to nonexistent. In summation, the rate of deaths due to heart disease differs greatly between rural and urban areas when there are marked environmental or lifestyle differences between them, but, in developed countries where specific risk factors for heart disease (cigarette smoking, for example) are more evenly distributed between urban and rural areas, the differences in disease rates are very slight or nonexistent. Urban residence per se is not clearly the cause of heart disease in cities. On the contrary, lifestyle differences among people are likely to be more important causes.

Cancer

Cancer has long been associated with the urban environment. In 1775, the British surgeon, Percivall Pott, noted that chimney sweeps in London had a high rate of cancer of the scrotum. Sweeps climbed into chimneys to clean them, and the soot that lodged in the dermal crevices is now known to contain carcinogens (cancer-causing elements). Today, the urban environment is still associated with cancer. Studies of the distribution of cancer in developed countries show a higher rate of cancer in urban areas (urban areas are often defined differently in different studies, thus hindering a broad generalization). Table 2 shows the difference in cancer rates between thirteen urban and 957 rural counties in the United States (Goldsmith 1980). The differences are substantial and consistent: urban rates are always higher than rural ones. The reason for the difference is interesting and may aid scientists in understanding the disease itself. The cause may not be urban living per se, but rather, in the case of the chimney sweeps, there are occupations

Table 2 Urban-Rural County Ratios of Cancer Mortality Rates (adjusted for age), U.S. White Populations, 1950–1969[1] (*from* Goldsmith 1980)

Male		Female	
Site	Urban-Rural	Site	Urban-Rural
Esophagus	3.08	Esophagus	2.12
Larynx	2.96	Rectum	2.11
Mouth & Throat	2.88	Larynx	1.92
Rectum	2.71	Nasopharynx	1.66
Nasopharynx	2.17	Lung	1.64
Bladder	2.10	Breast	1.61
Colon	1.97	Bladder	1.58
Lung	1.89	Other Endocrine Glands	1.52
All Malignant Neoplasms	1.56	All Malignant Neoplasms	1.36

[1]957 counties are 100% rural and 13 counties are 100% urban.

in urban areas that employ carcinogens. Usually, employees who use such chemicals are at greater risk for cancer. Insofar as these jobs, and their chemicals, are more common in urban areas, these areas have higher incidence rates of cancer. In short, some of the excess cancer in cities may be due to the occupations of the residents.

The problem of determining the true causes of the differences between urban and rural cancer rates has been intensively examined by Goldsmith (1980). Because air pollution contains carcinogens and is more common in cities where lung cancer is also prevalent, we are tempted to attribute increased lung cancer to the air pollution characteristic of cities. However, Goldsmith points out that the greatest difference between urban and rural rates of lung cancer is between rural counties and the small urban counties with populations of ten thousand to fifty thousand. The rate in large

Suburban tract homes in Westlake, California. This is the suburb on which the 1960s popular song ''Little Boxes'' was based. [Photo by George Gmelch]

urban centers with populations greater than five hundred thousand lies between the two. This does not support the theory that the pollution of cities increases the rate of lung cancer, since larger, more polluted cities do not seem to have the highest rate of lung cancer. Also, life-long residents of cities do not necessarily have the highest rate of lung cancer when compared to other city residents. If exposure to pollution is related to lung cancer, then the life-long residents who have had the most exposure should have the highest rate, but, in fact, migrants to the city have the highest rate (Goldsmith 1980).

To discover the true causes of urban-rural differences in cancer, we should look beyond air pollution to the behaviors of urban and rural people. Cigarette smoking may be related to the urban-rural difference and to the higher rate among migrants, and stress might also play a role. In studies of the distribution of any disease, it is difficult to extract the role of one factor, in this case urban living, from the interconnected network of many other factors such as stress, smoking, and diet. Cigarette smoking is a very difficult factor

to control in urban-rural comparisons because it is believed to strongly influence the risk of lung cancer, yet, at the same time, it is difficult to measure an individual's exposure to it. Interestingly, in a study of nonsmoking doctors in Britain, no rural-urban difference was found in the rate of lung cancer (Doll 1978).

Mental Health

Considerable controversy exists over the relationship between urbanism and mental health. Results from different studies do not always agree. Again, some of the reasons for this discrepancy are similar to those impeding generalizations about urbanization and other diseases (e.g., heart disease and lung cancer): definitions of urban vary from study to study; definitions of the disease also vary. One generalization does emerge though, namely, that extremely isolated communities have higher rates of certain types of mental impairments or psychiatric disorders than do more settled and diversified communities (Webb 1984). Beyond the impact of isolation, few generalizations are not contradicted by one study or another. One review of many studies concluded that there is a consistently higher rate of psychiatric disorder in urban areas (Dohrenwend and Dohrenwend 1974). On the other hand, in individual studies, rural and suburban areas are sometimes found to have a higher rate than cities (Wagenfeld 1982; Engelsmann et al. 1972). Webb (1984) persuasively argues that whatever differences do exist among rural areas, small and large towns, and cities, they are not large differences. Results from his study of scores of psychiatric symptoms derived from interviews of persons in rural and urban areas show that the differences between rural and urban areas are small and not consistent (Webb 1978). It is important to remember that the variety of results from studies is due partly to the variety of approaches taken to study a difficult problem, and from the simple fact that the studies have been conducted at different times and in different places. Indeed, a variety of results among well-conducted studies can be beneficial, since it may suggest specific factors within the rural and urban environments that contribute to psychiatric disorders whether in urban or rural places.

Child Growth

Measuring child growth, unlike mental health, is more straight-forward and nonsubjective. If the children are measured accurately, the assessment of the pattern of physical growth of a community's children can provide important information about the health of the children and, indirectly, about the suitability or healthfulness of the habitat for children and adults (Schell 1986). Child growth depends on a large variety of physiological pathways, and untoward environmental factors can influence many of these and impede physical growth. Provided that the communities under comparison are similar genetically and that nutrition is adequate, comparison of child growth patterns becomes a comparison of the habitability of the respective environments.

Comparisons of the heights of urban and rural children in the United States show no differences (Hamill, Johnston, and Lemeshow 1972). In Canada, the difference in height is small, although, when present, it favors rural children (Thiebault et al. 1985). In other parts of the world, urban children are generally taller (Eveleth and Tanner 1976). There is variation in the amount of the urban advantage, depending on the age of the children being compared and whether the comparison is between girls or between boys. Even at the same age and within one sex, the urban-rural difference varies. Rural Finnish eight-year-old boys are about one inch shorter than their age- and sex-matched peers from the capital, Helsinki. In Greece, the difference is nearly two inches. The urban-rural difference is larger at adolescence, as adolescence is a time of very rapid growth. Since urban children in most countries reach adolescence earlier (Eveleth and Tanner 1990), the increase in size contributes to the urban-rural difference. Figure 2 shows that, for girls, there is an earlier age at menarche (first menses) among urban girls. After adolescence, when the slower growers have caught up, some small urban-rural differences remain among adults.

There may be a pattern to urban-rural differences in child growth. The differences are small in developed countries such as Canada, the United States, and Australia, and are larger in Finland, Poland, and Greece, (Eveleth 1986; Eveleth and Tanner 1976). In the 1960s, when studies of urban-rural growth differences in Finland, Poland, and Greece were conducted, they may have had more marked differences between rural and urban areas in economy and in health services for pregnant women and children than when studies of Canada, Australia, and the United States were conducted. There are probably factors other than economy and health services, but the urban environment itself does necessarily promote or retard growth. Studies of urban slum children show the depressing effect of poverty, regardless of the degree of urbanization.

Generally, as rural environments around the world become better, and urban-rural differences lessen, we expect to see the

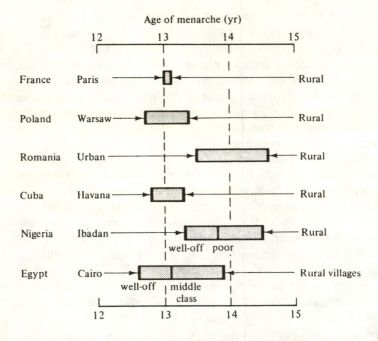

Figure 2 Median ages of menarche in rural and urban population samples. Shaded areas show difference between median ages in each geographical area.

(From *Worldwide Variation in Human Growth, Second Edition*, by Phyllis B. Eveleth and James M. Tanner. Copyright 1990. Reprinted with the permission of Cambridge University Press.)

difference in child growth lessen also. However, in well-off, industrialized countries, pollution, crowding, and stress may cause urban environments to deteriorate, and then the physical growth of children may become poorer in urban areas in comparison to rural ones. This possibility is presented by the few studies that have isolated specific factors that, for now, are more common in urban environments, such as noise (Ando and Hattori 1973, 1977; Schell 1981, 1984; Schell and Ando 1991; Knipschild, Meijer, and Salle 1981), lead (Davis and Svendsgaard 1987; Mushak et al. 1989; Shukla et al. 1989), air pollution (Williams et al. 1977), and toxic waste (Fein et al. 1984; Jacobson et al. 1990; Paigen et al. 1987). These studies suggest that future urban areas may be less healthy; currently, however, the difference between urban and rural children appears to depend on many social factors rather than on the physical features of the two environments.

Conclusion

Cities have a reputation for unhealthfulness that is based on their history and a failure to understand their present characteristics. Although past comparisons of rural and urban health indicators have often revealed differences favoring rural areas, we now know that the advantage depends on the characteristics of the specific urban and rural environments that are compared. Some features of the environment are more important than others to human health, and, when urban and rural environments are similar in these respects, health differences are minimal. Current research focuses on those specific features of urban and rural environments that pertain to health and avoid gross generalization.

Notes

[1] Other essays have focused on changes over time in the relationship between settlement pattern and health (Armelagos and Dewey 1970; Black 1975; Cockburn 1971; Polgar 1964). The reader is encouraged to consult these valuable sources.

[2] Resource centers that may be shared with infected people or wild animals, waterholes for example, could have provided a source of parasitic infection for migratory hunters and gatherers, though the opportunities for infection and reinfection are far smaller than those open to villagers with domesticated animals and ineffective sanitation.

Part Two

Urban Fieldwork
Anthropologists in Cities

Although rural communities are rarely as simple as they are often characterized, they are markedly more homogeneous than cities. The anthropologist studying a tribal group or peasant village can assume that there is a certain degree of uniformity in the lifestyles and values of the population, although status and wealth differences exist even here. Such an assumption cannot be made by the urban fieldworker. As we saw in Part One, one of the defining characteristics of cities is complexity and heterogeneity. The typical city contains a wide spectrum of subcultures based upon class, ethnicity, occupation, religion, and so forth. In response to the problems of understanding such a diverse population, most urban anthropologists have restricted the scope of their inquiries to small, clearly segmented groups within the complex urban mosaic. There have only been a few attempts to understand cities as wholes, in the fashion of the traditional community study method.

Units of Analysis

The range of social units in which urban anthropologists work has been outlined by Eames and Goode (1977). They are: (1) units based on common residence such as a neighborhood or a cluster of blocks in a city; (2) groups based on common culture of origin such as ethnic or minority groups; (3) groups based on a common belief system—religious or political—such as Hare Krishna or radical political communes; (4) groups based on common work, notably occupational groups such as longshoremen, construction workers, or bankers; and (5) units based upon primary relationships such as households, kinship units, and social networks. Most urban research has been on the first type—residential units that have definable boundaries and in which the population is somewhat homogeneous. Such spatially bounded units, in which most of the inhabitants are of the same ethnic and class background, where there is a high degree of face-to-face interaction and a sense of community, are similar enough to the traditional units of the tribal or peasant village to enable the anthropologist to use conventional methods of field research. But even within such small bounded groups there may be numerous crosscutting components that the urban fieldworker must take into account. In a study of prostitutes in Seattle, Washington, Jennifer James (1976) found her research complicated by the diverse backgrounds and attitudes of her subjects. Instead of a homogeneous occupation, she encountered major differences between the prostitutes who were full-time professionals and the drug addicts who worked only when the need arose. Moreover, the attitudes of the women toward prostitution were influenced by their different ethnic backgrounds.

The People Anthropologists Study

Despite a growing interest in middle- and upper-class groups, the bulk of urban anthropology continues to be done in slums, ghettos, and squatter settlements. This concentration on the poor is due to several factors. First, anthropology's traditional techniques of collecting data, most importantly participant-observation, were designed for working with fairly homogeneous groups localized in one area. The condensed neighborhoods of the urban poor offer a field situation more suitable to the anthropologist's data-gathering techniques than do the more spread out, dormitory suburbs of the middle class. Second, poor people are more accessible. Perhaps harboring fewer image pretensions, perhaps gratified that someone cares, and perhaps less aware of their legal rights, the poor are not as resistant to being studied as those in the strata above them. In most societies, the middle and upper classes are less willing to tolerate the intrusions of anthropologists and their endless questions. Third, anthropologists have always been concerned primarily with people and societies that are marginal in terms of national political power and wealth. Tribal and peasant peoples, long the staple of anthropological fieldwork, are clearly outside the mainstream. It has been anthropologists' adopted role to study (and be the spokespersons for) the marginal peoples of the world. Other social sciences have focused primarily on the mainstream, and particularly on Western societies and their elites. And fourth, to some degree anthropologists may be attracted to the poor because they are "exotic." A middle-class Irishman is not terribly different from myself, but the gypsy-like nomadic Irish Travellers whom I studied certainly are. Apart from the added interest of working among people who possess a culture different from one's own, the more divergent the cultural patterns of the group being studied, the more clearly they stand out to the observer.

The Nature of Urban Fieldwork

The hallmark of anthropological fieldwork has been the intensive participation of the anthropologist in the life of the community. This is usually accomplished by the anthropologist taking up residence in a village. Unlike sociologists or political scientists who often commute to the people they study, anthropologists try to live among their subjects, participating in and observing activities as fellow residents. Among urban groups, however, residence is often not possible. A severe shortage of housing or dispersed residential pattern of the group under study may necessitate living outside the community. Michael Whiteford ("Doing It") recounts how he was unable to find accommodation in the poor urban barrio in which he was conducting research and instead had to live in a nearby middle-class neighborhood. In a study of cityward migrants to Belgrade, Yugoslavia, Andrei Simić ("Bogdan's Story") found private housing so scarce that he spent the first two months of his fieldwork looking for a suitable place to live. Sharon Gmelch ("An Urban Field Experience") describes living in an apartment and commuting to the camps of the Irish Travellers she was studying for the first seven weeks, before finally buying a horse and a covered

In a pub, anthropologist George Gmelch hangs out with the Irish Travellers he lived among on the outskirts of Dublin (1972). [Photo by Pat Langan]

wagon and moving into a camp. Because he was white, Elliott Liebow found it impractical to reside in the black Washington, D.C., ghetto he studied. It should be no surprise that nonresident fieldworkers often have more difficulty gaining the confidence of the people they study than do fieldworkers who live in the neighborhood. Moreover, important activities often take place at times when commuting anthropologists are not present.

Whether anthropologists live in the community or commute, gaining access to informants is usually more difficult in the city than in the village. With less outdoor space available than in rural areas, urbanites tend to spend more time inside and therefore are less observable and not as easily approached. Also important are the nature of urban work and the constraints of time. Most urbanites are employees: they work for someone else and receive an hourly wage. Unlike rural anthropologists who may accompany their informants in their gardens or fields or on a hunt, or sit with them while they are making a craft or repairing equipment, urban anthropologists generally cannot interview their informants in their workplace without interfering. Hence, in urban societies potential informants are unavailable for much of each day.

Anthropologists studying a nonlocalized group spread across an entire city, such as the Tzintzuntzeños studied by Robert Kemper ("Migration and Adaptation"), may lose much time just traveling to and from informants' homes. And without telephone and advance notice of their visit, anthropologists may arrive after a long journey through traffic to find their informant not at home. In one year of fieldwork, Kemper logged nine thousand miles on his car driving to the homes of migrants living in more than forty different neighborhoods in Mexico City. In a rather extreme case, James Watson (1974) estimated in his study of Chinese restaurant workers in London he spent four hours of travel time for every one hour of interviewing. Clearly, the urban anthropologist, not unlike the peasant migrant adapting to city life, must develop new strategies for working in urban settings.

Counterbalancing some of the difficulties of urban field research are certain benefits absent in peasant and tribal societies. Often available to urban anthropologists is an enormous amount of statistical data collected in government censuses and surveys. Sharon Gmelch ("An Urban Field Experience") also points out the psychological boost such sources of information can give fieldworkers during emotional lows or slack periods in their research. In tribal and many peasant villages the fieldworker must collect the necessary information on demography and household structure of the community through the time-consuming administration of a household census. In most urban societies this data can be obtained by a trip to the government statistics office. Because urbanites tend to be better educated and are more likely to be literate than their rural counterparts, they are often able to help in the research process. For example, they sometimes fill in questionnaires and keep detailed records of their own activities or expenses.

One psychological benefit of urban fieldwork is the ease with which the anthropologist can escape the stresses and insecurities of the field situation. In traditional rural fieldwork, especially in remote tribal societies, anthropologists are often isolated, completely cut off from their own society. When feeling lonely or alienated they must fall back on their own resources. They may retreat into the imaginary world of novels, but there is no physical escape. Whereas in the city anthropologists can leave the small world of their informants by simply hopping a bus for "downtown." In the city center, whether it be Bogotá or Katmandu, anthropologists may, if they need to, speak their own language, read *Time* or the *Herald Tribune*, watch an American film, or buy a hamburger. As Foster and Kemper note in the next essay, anthropologists may also make contact with local scholars, who can offer sound advice and assurances that field problems—real or imagined—are not as serious or unresolvable as they often appear.

George Gmelch

Anthropological Fieldwork in Cities

GEORGE M. FOSTER and
ROBERT V. KEMPER

This article traces the development of the fieldwork tradition in anthropology, placing the relatively new field of urban anthropology in its historical context. The authors discuss how the fieldwork tradition begun in rural areas, first among tribesmen and then peasants, has shaped the interests of anthropologists working in urban areas. They conclude with a discussion of some of the problems and advantages encountered in urban research, including which aspects of anthropology's conventional field methods remain useful. The need for survey and questionnaire data, as well as a reevaluation of anthropologists' traditional role as neutral observers rather than advocates for the people they study, is noted.

Anthropologists are latecomers to urban research. By the 1920s sociologists were doing systematic research in American cities, especially through the efforts of the "Chicago" school, and since that time most sociological research has dealt with urban phenomena. In contrast, the earliest anthropological research on city life took place only after World War II, and widespread interest in urbanization developed only in the 1960s and 1970s. Whereas urban sociology is a mature discipline, urban anthropology is still in its professional adolescence.[1] Only in the past two decades have

Source: Revised from George M. Foster and Robert V. Kemper, eds., *Anthropologists in Cities* (Boston: Little, Brown, 1974), pp. 1–17, "Introduction: A Perspective on Anthropological Fieldwork in Cities." Copyright © 1979 by G. M. Foster and R. V. Kemper. Reprinted by permission of the authors.

we defined the parameters of the field, identified the topics to be studied, settled upon the most appropriate research strategies, and come to grips with new problems of ethics and relevance.

This recent interest in cities is the third—and probably the final—major revolution in anthropology's definition of its subject matter. When anthropology emerged as a formal science at the end of the nineteenth century it was concerned exclusively with "primitive" (i.e., nonliterate) peoples. Then, about 1940, interest began to shift to peasant societies, the rural dimension of traditional cultures. Now, as we turn to cities, we again face a major change. During these transformations the research goals, the definitions of problems, and the kinds of hypotheses that intrigued anthropologists have varied greatly. One principle, however, has remained constant: the anthropologists' dedication to fieldwork as a primary data-gathering strategy. Whether interested in tribal peoples, peasant villagers, or city dwellers, anthropologists believe that the richest, most complete information on how people live comes from direct, personal participation in gathering this information.

In the Beginning

Anthropologists have not always insisted that fieldwork is their basic data-gathering technique. With rare exceptions nineteenth-century anthropologists relied upon the descriptions of native life published by missionaries, colonial administrators, and travelers for the data on which they based their theories and hypotheses. Only when anthropology became a legitimate academic discipline at the turn of the century, with formal Ph.D. graduate programs, was field research accepted as essential to professional preparation and practice. In America, Franz Boas was the teacher most influential in standardizing this new approach to data gathering.

In some ways research methods have changed very little since those early days. Most anthropologists still draw the greater part of their data from firsthand contact with relatively small numbers of people. In other ways, though, the changes have been great. New research goals have been formulated, and field trips have grown longer. When Boas, Clark Wissler, A. L. Kroeber, Robert Lowie, and others of their generation began their research, anthropology was assumed to be an historical discipline rather than a social science. Faced with a bewildering array of languages, cultures, and physical types, anthropologists saw as their task the discovery of the origins and migrations of the world's people, especially "primitive" societies lacking written histories. In the United States, most indigenous cultures had already changed greatly as a consequence of white contact. Because even greater changes seemed inevitable, a related goal of field research here was to draw upon the memories of the oldest surviving Indians to reconstruct as completely as possible the "untouched" precontact situation.

Since most data gathering consisted of sitting with elderly Indians (who were usually paid for their help) and writing down what they remembered of earlier years, anthropologists needed little field equipment. As late as 1937, when Foster was preparing for his first research among the Yuki Indians of California, the only advice he received from his professor, A. L. Kroeber, was to "buy a pencil and a stenographer's notebook." In the United States prior to World War II, field trips were usually short, often limited to a summer's vacation. Even the largest departments of anthropology had only three or four staff members, and long leaves were difficult to arrange. Moreover, the research goals of ethnographers led them to see little advantage in spending twelve or more continuous months in the field; instead, they worked over several summers, beginning again each year where they had stopped the summer before. In the first quarter of this century, most American Indian tribes were disrupted and acculturated. This fact, plus the "memory culture" orientation of fieldworkers, combined to convince anthropologists that no single group needed or justified more than a few months' study. Because native peoples appeared to be dying out, anthropologists felt it their scientific responsibility to survey all groups, rather than to study intensively a few and neglect the rest.

Even in these relatively short, early field trips the distinctive methodological characteristic of anthropology was apparent. From the beginning anthropologists formed close personal ties with the people they studied, and almost all anthropologists of that period have written affectionately about their key informants, some of whom became lifelong friends. Anthropologists quickly realized that the best and most accurate data come from persons who like and trust them. Hence, "establishing rapport" came to be an anthropologist's first assignment upon arriving in the field: to search out the most knowledgeable individuals, present oneself to them in a plausible and empathetic role, and make friends. Without fully realizing it, these early anthropologists were inventing the "depth" interview—the ability to talk with, to probe, to "pump" informants, day after day, in order to extract maximum information about their history and culture. Today, in cities as in rural areas, most anthropologists retain this basic philosophy: good rapport with good friends, trust and confidence, and abundant conversation over long periods of time.

Fieldwork in the United States during the first third of the century was strongly conditioned by restrictions of time, distance, and money. Research in the West involved train trips of from three to six days in each direction, often followed by stage coach, riverboat, or horseback rides to the final destination. Sources of financial support were limited, and long and costly trips of the type now routinely undertaken would have been difficult indeed. When, in the late 1920s and 1930s, American anthropologists began to embark on research in more distant areas, it was not unusual to spend six weeks in merely reaching the field site. Now that the most distant parts of the earth are rarely more than twenty-four hours away, young anthropologists often forget how huge the world was only a little over a generation ago.

As long as the emphasis of American anthropology was on the disappearing tribe, field research methods, including "scientific" equipment, changed very little. The first bulky portable typewriters, the Kodak camera, and primitive cylinder recording machines were occasionally carted to the reservation, but the pencil (or fountain pen) and the stenographer's notebook continued to be the only indispensable items of equipment.

The British Revolution

In England, meanwhile, a revolution in the concept of field research was occurring: long-term analysis of a viable community, emphasizing form and function in their synchronic rather than their diachronic dimensions. Tribal origins, it was assumed, were lost in dim antiquity; they could never be known. What *could* be known was the structure of the contemporary group, its form and content, and the way this system functioned. Anthropology was thus converted into a social science. Although he was not the first anthropologist to live for a long period with a single people, the Polish-born, British-naturalized Bronislaw Malinowski justly receives credit for introducing this new approach to fieldwork. Beginning in the early 1920s at the London School of Economics, he taught his students what he had discovered a few years earlier on the Trobriand Islands: live with the people, learn their language, observe their activities, question, speculate, theorize.

Malinowski and his students were favored in their revolutionary endeavors by conditions in the British Empire. Most of the Commonwealth's "native" peoples belonged to viable societies which functioned with much of their precontact vigor; they certainly were not disappearing. There was little need to press for "salvage" ethnography, to record while there was still time. Consequently, young anthropologists with enough financial support could afford to spend as much time as needed with a single group, untroubled by the nagging thought that they should turn their attention to disappearing groups elsewhere. Wherever they worked, field researchers were not foreigners; they were simply in parts of the Commonwealth where the societies were more exotic than at home. The British colonial service encouraged anthropological research, and the Union Jack flying at the District Officer's headquarters symbolized the special privileges that anthropologists could expect from government and native peoples alike. Under Malinowski's tutelage, and favored by the colonial setting—especially in Africa—a new generation of British social anthropologists produced superb monographs on a wide variety of topics which even today are required reading in most doctoral programs.

In the United States, research sophistication lagged behind that of England for a number of years; we lacked a Malinowski, and we were still committed to recording the ways of disappearing societies. The first American anthropologist to adopt the new approach, ten years after Malinowski's pioneering efforts, was Margaret Mead, who in 1925 set out for nine months' research in American Samoa. She was soon followed by Robert Redfield, who spent eight months in Tepoztlán, Mexico, during 1926–1927, and by Hortense Powdermaker, who went to Lesu, in New Ireland, for ten months during 1929–1930. (Although American-born, Powdermaker was a student of Malinowski, so she is perhaps best thought of as carrying on a British tradition in the United States rather than beginning an American style of fieldwork.)

In spite of the demonstrable advantages of long-term fieldwork, quickly brought to the attention of American anthropologists in *Coming of Age in Samoa* (Mead 1928), *Tepoztlán* (Redfield 1930), and *Life in Lesu* (Powdermaker 1933), extended field trips did not become commonplace until after World War II. Although a growing number of American anthropologists made long trips to India and Africa shortly before the war, most doctoral candidates (and their professors as well) continued the old tradition of short trips.

After the war, however, American researchers rapidly adopted the British research pattern, for several reasons. First, we had just about run out of Indians. The fairly exhaustive product of fifty years of North American research, coupled with the accelerating rate of acculturation of native North Americans, meant that these tribes looked much less attractive as research subjects than they had a generation earlier. Second, transportation to distant parts of the world had vastly improved; even in 300-mph piston planes, most places were no more than forty-eight hours from the United States. Research support, too, was becoming more abundant than in earlier years, and for the first time anthropologists could seriously contemplate prolonged research in foreign countries.

The Discovery of Peasants

In growing numbers American anthropologists now traveled to Latin America, Europe, Africa, and Asia. Some—particularly in Africa—studied tribal peoples, but a majority chose to work in small rural communities in modern or developing nations, for it was soon discovered that these peasant villages made ideal research sites. During the 1950s and 1960s, half or more of American anthropological fieldwork was carried out in such communities.

With the study of peasants came greatly improved data-gathering techniques. Now fully aware of the importance of observing as much as possible, of being present when significant events occurred, anthropologists tried to be as close as we could to the people we studied. Under ideal circumstances we were able to live with village families, to sleep and work in a spare room, and to share meals with them. When this was not feasible, we rented a house near the center of the village, usually hiring local women to cook, clean, wash clothes, babysit—and simultaneously to serve as informants to explain the meaning of what we saw. Now we had opportunities to attend weddings, funerals, baptisms, and other family and community rites on a scale that had never before been possible. For the first time that familiar, but much abused, phrase "participant observation" really came alive. We did not simply ask informants how people behaved; we saw with our own eyes what happened, so that our notes took on a richness, a depth, a detail rarely if ever achieved by earlier researchers.

Because we were observing real people acting out real roles, we needed to know more about them as individuals than in the earlier days of salvage ethnography: where they lived, who their relatives were, their occupations, their incomes and socioeconomic statuses, and the like. To gather this data we adopted the census as a basic technique to provide a factual and statistical framework for our observations and interviews. We also buckled down and learned the local language. Prior to this time relatively few American anthropologists had mastered the language of the people they studied, preferring to use bilingual informants or interpreters. Now we realized that language competence was essential to good fieldwork, and intensive language training became a basic part of every well-planned field trip.

In the post-World War II era more elaborate recording and coding techniques to control and retrieve ever greater quantities of data came into common use. For many anthropologists, the five-by-eight-inch card or sheet, filed according to the Human Relations Area File code, replaced the stenographer's notebook (Murdock et al. 1961). Technological advances likewise vastly facilitated fieldwork: portable typewriters became truly lightweight, miniature cameras replaced the old Kodaks, and flash equipment was perfected. Transistors made possible small tape recorders, which greatly simplified recording linguistic texts, folklore, and other data such as dreams and projective tests (e.g., the Rorschach and Thematic Apperception Tests), where textual accuracy is essential. Antibiotics reduced the apprehension of serious illness in the field, and with radios and telephones, anthropologists were usually less isolated even in remote countries than their professional ancestors had been among Indian tribes in Canada and the western United States. For those who had known the conceptual limitations and technological handicaps of earlier field research, the fifties and sixties were a great time to be a practicing anthropologist.

Urban Anthropology

After about a generation of intensive fieldwork in peasant communities, anthropologists realized that significant changes were occurring in the research situation. For one thing, we felt that we had defined rather completely the parameters of peasant societies and had constructed models to explain much of their cross-cultural variation. So, as with the Indians a generation earlier, we appeared to be approaching a point of diminishing returns. At the same time, many of our peasant friends were ceasing to be peasants. Influenced by radio and television, work experiences in foreign countries, and the modernity that follows new roads, many of them gave up their folk costumes and their fiestas; they adopted tractors, fertilizers, and insecticides in farming; and they sent their children to secondary schools and universities. Others simply packed up and moved to cities, where they found work in factories or service fields and after a few years became townsmen themselves.

To a large extent the transformation of traditional peasant societies and the mass exodus to the city explain the new interest of anthropologists in urban research. Beyond this, many of us are genuinely concerned with the social, ethnic, and economic problems so clearly seen in cities; we believe that anthropology, along with the other social sciences, can help to ameliorate these problems. Together these events and convictions have created a new field, *urban anthropology*.

From the beginning the urban research of anthropologists has differed significantly from that of other social scientists and historians. While they have been concerned primarily with the technologically developed countries of Europe and North America, we have been especially interested in the growing cities of Latin America, Africa, and Asia. Our theoretical orientation, too, is different. Because the first people we knew well in these countries were peasants and tribesmen, who today are moving to the cities in increasing numbers, we have been curious about what happens to them in urban environments. As a result, anthropological urban studies have dealt largely with *urbanization*, the process by which rural emigrants settle in and adjust to urban life, rather than with the way of life in cities, which is commonly referred to as *urbanism* (cf. Wirth 1938). In addition, because we have been interested primarily in how people adjust to urban life, we have paid much less attention than have other social scientists to broader issues involving the operation of the urban *system* (i.e., the network of cities within a nation, the ways in which these cities are interrelated, and how the lives of urbanites and rural residents are influenced by large-scale demographic, political, economic, and sociological processes). And finally, although anthropologists have occasionally utilized the results of comparative statistical studies, which have become so important in political science, economics, and sociology, we have continued to offer theories about urbanization on the basis of firsthand field research.

The anthropological urban studies that have appeared since World War II, and especially since the 1960s, make it possible for us to trace common patterns in the urbanization process and to discern fruitful directions for future work. But with few exceptions (e.g., Whyte 1943; Liebow 1967; Leeds 1968) these reports tell us little or nothing about the urban fieldwork experience. For anthropologists, how does this research compare with that undertaken in peasant villages and tribal groups? What research techniques are equally valuable in both settings? What new methodologies must be developed (or borrowed from other disciplines) to investigate urbanites? Are anthropologists working in a city a new breed of scientist, "urban anthropologists," or do we differ from our rural-based colleagues only by our choice of field site? That is, are urban anthropologists simply mirror images of rural sociologists?

In the second part of this essay we discuss how the rural fieldwork tradition consciously and unconsciously shapes the anthropologist's definition of urban problems, what features of conventional methodology are useful in the city, what urban research topics arise that require new approaches, and how urban research may force a reevaluation of the profession's present dilemma regarding "relevance" and ethics.

Urbanites as Rural People

Accustomed as we are to working in small, "bounded" rural communities, anthropologists are often disconcerted by the amorphous and heterogeneous populations of large cities. How are the boundaries of the urban sample to be determined, and how should the fieldworker proceed with his study? As Anthony Leeds has pointed out (1968:31), we often try to solve this problem by concentrating on slums, squatter settlements, or ethnic minorities, on the assumption that they are analogous to the small rural villages we know, and that they can be investigated in similar fashion. This tendency to see urban peoples in the light of our rural experiences may have serious consequences, as Peter Gutkind has pointed out for Africa:

> The methodological traditions brought to this [urban] field of research are mostly those acquired by social anthropologists working in rural areas. It is this background which for long fostered the view that we were studying tribesmen in town and not townsmen in town. (1967:136)

As a consequence, he continues, "Far less attention has been paid to those Africans who have been resident in urban areas for a considerable length of time than to migrants and those less committed to urban life" (1967:143–144). We believe that Gutkind is correct in noting that anthropologists have been shortsighted in ignoring long-settled urbanites.

In urban research anthropologists face one insurmountable problem: defining a population in the holistic context taken for granted in rural fieldwork. We may investigate a group of migrants from a single village, migrants from many regions, or a group composed of migrants and urban natives. The group may be dispersed throughout the metropolitan zone, clustered in a few neighborhoods, or restricted to a single spatial unit as small as an apartment house (as in Oscar Lewis's well-known studies of *vecindades* in Mexico City). Alternatively, the population may be defined in social terms, as members of a religious sect, a voluntary association, a professional or occupational category. Selecting and delineating the urban population segment to be investigated is *the* critical first step in urban anthropological research.

Once this decision is made, another issue emerges: should anthropologists concentrate on the internal structure of the group or on the relations of its members to the rest of the urban population? Most anthropologists, following the community study approach, have chosen the former. But, as Leeds argues, this "has led to a thorough failure to justify the units of study used and the failure to show mutual effects between the asserted 'units' of study and the city in which they are immersed" (1968:31–32).

Getting Settled

Although fieldworkers face different problems in defining the group to be studied in rural and urban settings, the difficulties of settling in—of finding a place to live, experiencing culture shock, establishing a plausible role, and finding informants—remain much the same. As we have seen, in village fieldwork anthropologists usually live with a family or maintain quarters in the middle of town, in either case residing among the people studied and constantly observing their daily life. In cities, arrangements of this kind are more difficult; families studied by anthropologists almost always live in crowded quarters with barely enough room for themselves, much less for a researcher and family. Rented rooms, too, are usually less attractive in urban slums than in peasant villages. Moreover, unless anthropologists decide to study a compact population—a suburban neighborhood, an inner-city slum, or a peripheral squatter settlement—we almost literally cannot live "with" the informants. As a result, when anthropologists study a general social institution or a group of people spread throughout the city, we nearly always find an apartment or house in a convenient area, then commute to visit informants.

This arrangement has advantages and disadvantages. On the one hand, anthropologists gain privacy, a comfort often denied us in tribal or village areas where we are a constant object of curiosity. When tired and irritated, and on those days when we hope never to see another informant, we can retire to comfortable lodgings to rest and recuperate. On the other hand, many anthropologists who have lived like this feel both guilty and cheated. Conditioned by colleagues to expect a close emotional identification with the people studied, even the most conscientious researchers may come to question whether they are doing a good job and whether they are in fact true anthropologists, if fieldwork must be carried out in circumstances where the anthropologist is isolated much of the time from the target population.

Meeting Informants

When beginning research in a village, anthropologists sometimes have letters to a few people, who in turn can introduce us to others. More often, though, for the first few days we simply wander the streets, talk to as many people as possible, lean over fences to chat and make friends, give candy and balloons to children, cigarettes to men, and in other encounters try to explain why we are in the village and what we hope to accomplish. In this informal way, friendships develop. Often anthropologists "scout" several communities, then choose the most accepting one. All of the people met in these early contacts are potential informants.

In contrast, only a few of the people urban anthropologists meet in the course of a day are potential informants. Although casual encounters may offer insights into city life, researchers must work at building a network of informants. As intermediaries we may use members of the group itself (e.g., a migrant whom we already know), local officials, or other social scientists who are known to the people we have selected for study.

Robert V. Kemper interviewing a Tzintzuntzan migrant in Mexico City (1974). [Photo by Rafael Campuzano]

Just as rapport-building techniques vary from one fieldworker to another, finding a suitable role depends as much on circumstances as on planning. For doctoral candidates, the role of students preparing themselves for teaching careers and required by their professors to learn about another way of life is usually satisfactory. For older anthropologists, the reverse role of professor seems to work best, at least outside of the United States. Sometimes it is as difficult to avoid a negative role as to establish a positive one; most anthropologists have at one time or another been accused of being a CIA agent, a Protestant missionary (if working in a Catholic community), a social worker, a tax collector, or even a misguided tourist.

Official and Professional Ties

Whether anthropologists undertake research in a foreign country or in the United States, it is considered proper—and usually it is essential—to notify the appropriate governmental and anthropological authorities of the research plan and to obtain their permission *before* beginning work. These formalities sometimes seem a nuisance, but for urban anthropologists they often provide an introduction to potential associates in the fieldwork setting. Precisely because cities are centers for universities and government agencies, urban fieldworkers need not be isolated from professional and official assistance.

Relationships with government officials are extremely important to all anthropologists, for an unsympathetic person in a position of power can make research impossible, while a helpful official can open otherwise closed doors. Ties with local anthropologists can be especially rewarding. As experts in residence, they can point out possible problems in the research design, suggest alternate groups for investigation, and introduce the newcomer to potential informants. Of course, local social scientists may not always be helpful, but taking them into our confidence at the outset may prevent subsequent misunderstandings and usually makes for good relationships in the future. This is especially important if an anthropologist plans to return later to continue the research project or wishes to carry out related fieldwork in other cities in the same country.

Urban anthropologists are more fortunate than rural anthropologists in that professional and social obligations to local colleagues can easily be repaid by attending their professional meetings, joining their societies, teaching part-time in their institutions, and (if a separate residence is maintained during fieldwork) bringing them into his or her home. In addition, local scholars and students may be included in the research project, an important advantage in equalizing anthropological skills and training throughout the world. Urban fieldwork also offers young anthropologists an opportunity to meet the community of scholars they will know and cooperate with throughout their careers.

Rural Research Models in the City

We have already seen that anthropologists tend to view urban populations from a rural perspective, to look upon them as transplanted villagers. Not surprisingly, then, research design and problem definitions are often based on rural models, on the assumption that what works well in the country will also work well in the city. This "jack-of-all-trades" approach stands in sharp contrast to most other social science models for urban research, where team members are chosen to provide interdisciplinary and interethnic perspectives. Although rich data and valuable theoretical insights have emerged from these anthropological studies, the size and complexity of urban environments clearly place limits on what can be accomplished by a lone fieldworker, even when aided by a trained spouse. Paid assistants are a partial solution to this problem, especially in taking a census and conducting social surveys, but they are no substitute for a genuine team approach, whose advantages have been summarized by John Price:

> The team represents a wide variety of academic skills and personalities that together produce a wider variety of ethnography than an individual does over a long period of time. Through formal and informal discussions, the team is able to create a productive information exchange. It also accelerates the generation and testing of hypotheses much more rapidly than individuals working alone (1972:27).

Although the lone researcher will continue to make important contributions to urban studies, we believe that anthropologists working in cities will increasingly do so as members of social science teams.

In still another way, urban anthropologists reflect a decidedly rural bias: often many of their best data come from the personal relationships rural fieldworkers have long cherished. Although it may not provide a full picture of city life, the ethnographic interview, with contact over a long period of time between anthropologist and respondent, continues to be a major research technique in the city. When combined with the statistical survey approaches favored in the other social sciences, it may well prove to be the single most important contribution anthropologists can make to urban studies.

But despite the benefits of such deep and continuing relationships, there is clearly a need for census and questionnaire data beyond the limits common in rural research. Chance contacts alone are insufficient to provide the balance that marks first-class research. The conclusion we draw is that anthropologists contemplating urban fieldwork will need to devote much more attention than they have in the past to sociological research techniques such as survey research and the design and pretesting of interview schedules. Familiarity with computers, too, is essential if anthropologists are to make the best use of census and questionnaire materials.

Whether urban anthropologists carry out fieldwork alone or as team members, we must strike a balance between "total immersion" and dependence on the more formal techniques of the other social sciences. Andrew Whiteford has described the dilemma we face:

> Such approaches as sampling techniques, the use of census data, and statistical analysis of masses of data would appear to be absolutely necessary for understanding [urban phenomena], but their use also tends to impersonalize the research and deprive the worker of his most satisfying experience, the personal identification with the people being studied (1960:2).

Anthropologists become easily disenchanted when close friendships with informants are replaced by limited, impersonal contacts with "subjects" or "respondents." But, however we might wish it were not so, we must recognize that in cities we can neither observe our informants with the same ease as in villages, nor expect as many contact hours with factory workers as with craftsmen who labor at home. Thus, unless we are content to limit ourselves to the "street corner" variety of urban research (e.g. Whyte 1943; Liebow 1967), we must learn to combine the most valuable features of traditional research models with the quantitative methods common in the other social sciences.

Ethics and Relevance

Urban research introduces many new ethical problems to anthropology. We are not dealing with nameless faces in the crowd when describing and commenting on important people in cities. Their roles are distinctive enough to make them easily identifiable no matter how we try to disguise them in our reports. And when the attitudes and lifestyles of the urban elite strike anthropologists as unattractive, and when our analyses are constantly unflattering, what are we to do? Like tribesmen or peasants, these upper-class urbanites have great power over us, to the point of making our research impossible.

Even the least visible city dwellers we study often are literate. They are more interested than villagers in the end product of our research, and they are anxious to see what we say about them. Increasingly, anthropological publications are translated into the languages of the people studied, and they can read about themselves. As anthropologists, we must become more concerned about their privacy, and about the harm that careless revelations might cause them.

Although most anthropologists have carried into their urban research the traditional anthropological stance of objectivity—the desire to find out about what life was like in the community in question, without major concern for resolving social problems—it seems inevitable that future urban research will be more concerned with "relevance," that it will be more "applied" than earlier work. Already we see signs of this. During her two years of fieldwork in the Ciudad Guayana project in Venezuela, Lisa Peattie found herself becoming an advocate of the poor people she studied and lived among, defending them against the "system" represented by the project coordinators and their elite clientele. Her description of the role of "The Social Anthropologist in Planning" (1967) and her "Reflections on Advocacy Planning" (1968a) make thought-provoking reading for urban anthropologists concerned with the relevancy of their work. In the same way, the Valentines have argued convincingly that urban fieldworkers owe a debt to the people we study, the people who make our job possible. This debt can best be repaid, they believe, when anthropologists become attentive to community needs and attempt to help our informants to cope with the urban system (Valentine and Valentine 1970).

This combined emphasis on ethics and applied urban anthropology has led to a reevaluation of the anthropological "prime directive"—our commitment not to interfere with "native" life unless it is absolutely necessary. This in turn has raised an even more fundamental question: Is the best fieldwork performed by "outsiders" or "insiders"? For instance, can Anglo anthropologists understand the lifestyles of urban African-Americans, Hispanic-Americans, or Native Americans—or, for that matter, any group outside the white middle class—without falling prey to unconscious prejudices? Anthropologists have assumed that on many points insiders are less perceptive observers than outsiders, just as a fish is unaware of the water it lives in until the tank is drained. As the literate, predominantly urban, ethnic minorities in the United States strive to establish their identities, and similar forces are at work in developing nations, this fundamental bias of anthropological research is being put to the test. And more often than not, it is urban anthropologists rather than our rural colleagues who must withstand these pressures.

The net result of these transformations is still unclear, but it seems unlikely that future anthropologists will be allowed to carry out their research without some regard to contemporary social problems or to the needs and feelings of their informants. Just as peasant migrants to the metropolis face a new world, so anthropologists moving from the "bush" to the city must adapt their ideas regarding fieldwork to fit a new environment.

The future of anthropology we believe, lies largely in urban research. Yet the available evidence indicates that urban fieldwork is more difficult than rural, and that it is often emotionally less satisfying, because of the problems of maintaining close affective ties with informants. At the same time urban research presents anthropology with challenges and opportunities that cannot be ignored if the profession is to increase its contributions to social science theory and to the resolution of society's problems.

And if, as Morris Freilich suggests, we ourselves are "the critical tool in anthropological research" (1970:33), then the ingenuity anthropologists have shown in working in tribal and peasant communities will serve in equal measure to master the problems of urban fieldwork. Just as in rural areas, urban anthropologists will find adequate housing, establish good rapport, define a suitable social role, overcome culture shock, deal successfully with government officials and anthropological colleagues, and ultimately combine the best in traditional research methods with the new techniques required for sound urban research.

Note

[1] For more information about the professional development of urban anthropology, see Kemper 1991a, 1991b, 1993a, 1993b; Kemper and Kracht 1991; Kemper, Kracht, and Campos 1991; and Kemper and Rollwagen 1995.

Doing It
Urban Research in Popayán, Colombia

MICHAEL WHITEFORD

*In this article Michael Whiteford offers a personal glimpse of his
experiences in the Colombian city of Popayán. The unit of
analysis is a working-class neighborhood, Barrio Tulcán, on the
edge of the city. Due to limited housing within the barrio,
Whiteford is forced to live outside the community, commuting
each day to work. But by using one family's home as a base, he
manages to approximate participant observation. He also uses
a range of other research techniques. Whiteford concludes with
some remarks on the role and value of anthropology's
traditional, personalistic fieldwork methods in urban settings.*

After months of planning and ten days of traveling through Mexico
and Central America, my wife, Patty, and I deplaned in Bogotá in
May, 1970. At last we had arrived in Colombia, where I would conduct thirteen months' fieldwork.[1] Two days later we arose with great
excitement: on this day we would fly to Popayán, a town I had lived
in twice as a child but had not seen for eight years. The day began
ominously; we had no Colombian pesos, and discovered that no one
would cash our traveler's checks since it was a holiday. At last, the
hotel manager agreed to cash enough checks—at far less than the
official rate of exchange—to cover our bill and taxi fare to the airport.

Still smarting from this gouging, we climbed into a taxi and
implored the driver to rush us to the airport, since we were now
late for our plane. No problem, we thought, as Colombian cabbies
drive like Grand Prix racers. But this one pampered his machine,

Source: Article written expressly for *Urban Life*.

driving at a leisurely pace, and despite my complaints, insisted on giving us a scenic tour of Bogotá. Perhaps he knew something we did not, for on arriving at the airport we were informed that our flight and the following one to Cali had been canceled. The airline agent was confident, though, that everyone could be accommodated on the afternoon flight.

For the next four hours we sat amid our suitcases and boxes watching other passengers leave for Mexico City, Los Angeles, and Madrid. Finally word came that our flight was scheduled to leave. En masse we turned and raced down the corridor, all of us hoping for a seat. Patty and I were among the lucky ones.

We debarked in Cali and staggered into a wave of heat and humidity. Anxious to finish our trip, we spent only enough time there to find another taxi for the two-hour trip to Popayán. Like a thoroughbred racer our driver sped by the huge fields of sugar cane and pastures of regal Brahman cattle.

When at last the lights of Popayán appeared, Patty and I gave simultaneous sighs of relief. We had made it. The streets, wet after a recent rain, gave back reflections of Popayán's colonial architecture. People walked alone, returning home from movies and restaurants or just taking an evening stroll. It was good to be back.

A Familiar Field

I first came to Popayán at the age of six, when my father, also an anthropologist, brought his family on a fieldwork expedition. In many ways this was an excellent prelude to becoming a fieldworker myself; I learned Spanish at an early age and experienced a different culture without really being conscious of it. We returned to the field several times while I was growing up, and as an undergraduate I took part in ethnological field sessions in Latin America.

Initially I had thought about working in Mexico. I had done my most recent fieldwork there, and I knew other research was under way which paralleled what I would be doing. Nevertheless, I had very pleasant memories of Colombia, and the idea of returning to Popayán to study migration intrigued me. Furthermore, I was aware that much of the current literature on Latin American urbanization dealt with peasants who arrive in large, industrialized, often capital cities. Comparable data on provincial towns were less abundant. Although these towns have little or no industry and relatively small populations (from ten or twenty thousand to two hundred thousand), they still receive many migrants, who see the towns either as stages in longer journeys or as a final destination.

Although Popayán has not grown as fast as Bogotá, Cali, or Medellín, between 1951 and 1964 the population showed a 46 percent increase from 31,866 to 58,500 (DNP 1969:21), and in 1970 the city had an estimated population of 77,000 (DNP 1969:57). As a result of this population growth, new barrios were springing up on Popayán's outskirts. This expansion had been fairly orderly, and the edges of the city lacked the jumbled appearance of many other Latin American cities. Although some of these new neighborhoods were being built for Popayán's upper and middle classes, who were gradually moving out from the city's center, most were built to accommodate the influx of working-class migrants.

Getting Organized

Unlike most anthropologists entering the field site, Patty and I had a place to stay when we arrived in Popayán. Old family friends graciously housed and fed us for two weeks while we looked for a house of our own. My father was also in Popayán doing fieldwork and was able to offer me on-the-spot advice during my first weeks in the field. After weighing various research alternatives, I eventually decided to concentrate my efforts on a single migrant population, Barrio Tulcán,[2] a low-income neighborhood of 1,780 inhabitants, built without government assistance.

Tulcán

Barrio Tulcán is in the southwest corner of Popayán, half an hour's walk from the city's central plaza. Geographically it stands apart from the city; a distance of no less than one kilometer separates the houses of the barrio from those of its nearest neighbor, Barrio Alfonso López. The barrio is hidden by a tall, thick barrier of willows, bamboos, eucalyptus, and cypress. Its entrance is a well-traveled road which skirts the perimeter of the municipal stockyards. Tulcán is situated at the juncture of two small streams, above which rise grassy hills speckled with grazing cattle.

To the casual observer, Tulcán appears more rural than urban. Chickens, ducks, sleeping dogs, and an occasional pig or horse vie for space in its narrow dirt streets with bicyclists, men pushing two-wheeled carts, and women balancing heavy shopping baskets on their heads. From time to time, even cattle are driven through the barrio. Large plots of sweet manioc, corn, coffee, and bananas, as well as a variety of other garden vegetables, add to the countryside ambience, while the hodgepodge of architectural styles further sets the barrio apart from the colonial Popayán. Even the bright yellow and green façades of the houses distinguish the barrio from the more subdued hues in the town.

Living Arrangements

Even after I made the choice to work in Tulcán, we continued to live in town. Rental houses in the barrio were few, and we were only a short distance—ten or fifteen minutes by foot or about three minutes on my motorcycle—from Tulcán. At first I was distressed not to live among Tulcaneses twenty-four hours a day, but in the long run I came to feel that the advantages of living in town adequately compensated for the disadvantages. Living where we did gave me a valuable opportunity to meet middle-class Payaneses, and in talking with them I gained another perspective on what the Tulcaneses told me. In the end this important if unforeseen contribution to my fieldwork allowed me to see Barrio Tulcán more objectively in the context of the entire city. Life in Tulcán shut down at night. Because most of the houses lacked electricity, families usually went to bed shortly after sundown. Even if I had lived in the barrio, most of my involvement in its activities would have been during the daylight hours.

Every day I parked my motorcycle in back of a house owned by the Arias family, and began the morning by talking to various members of the family before I set off to work. Whenever necessary, I could return there to rest or jot down notes. I visited with the Arias family at least three times a day and had complete freedom of access to the house and yard. Several times they remarked that I must be one of them because their dogs would never let others come and go as freely. In this way I did experience some of the advantages of living with a family in Tulcán.

Fieldwork Begins

Once I had made the decision to work in Tulcán, I was faced with the problem of getting people to talk to me. Would they be cooperative? Would they like me? Many such questions passed through my mind and, having no answers, I tried without success to block them out. Although I knew I had to stop *planning* the fieldwork and actually begin *doing* it, I kept procrastinating. One more trip to some office for a report on a new barrio that might be

better than the one I had chosen, one more search for a map of
Tulcán—these were what I occupied myself with. Finally, one day
I decided I would begin work the next morning. And to my amaze-
ment, I did.

A government office in Popayán had given me a list of leaders
of the barrio's governing body. Armed with the names of three of
its officers, I made my entrée. The first few people I approached had
never heard of any of the names—my initial clue to mobility in the
barrio—but they seemed friendly. Nobody snarled; people discussed
at length who the leaders might be and then accompanied me until
we found someone who told me that my list was a year old, and
that the barrio now had a new group of leaders. This led to an
informal discussion of how the barrio was organized and managed,
and gave me a chance to explain briefly to a polite and curious
audience of three my plans for studying the barrio. They nodded
in seeming comprehension.

I learned later that my idea to study Barrio Tulcán was not
entirely novel. Before my arrival various groups—among them
researchers from the *Instituto de Crédito Territorial* ([ICT] the
Colombian government's agency for housing and urban development) and engineering and medical undergraduates from the local
university—had undertaken short investigations of this, the city's
poorest barrio. With the exception of some medical students, who
came weekly for one semester to visit specific families, the studies
had lasted only a few weeks, and I now believe that the people I
talked to on my first day in Tulcán thought my study would be just
as brief. After several weeks, residents were amazed that my
interest was still keen, and this hastened their confidence and trust
in me. They were pleased and flattered that I was interested in doing
an in-depth study of them and was truly concerned with *their* views
on life.

It was two and a half months before I knew enough people in
Tulcán to feel comfortable. This initial phase was the most difficult
and discouraging part of my fieldwork. I tried to meet new people
every day, but at times it was tempting to believe that I had done
enough for the day. Coming upon some unsuspecting person in a
store or outside a house, I would walk up to him or her and make
small talk, generally asking questions about the barrio which almost
inevitably led to conversation. In this way I initially contacted a
number of people, noting who they were, where they lived, and
whether I wanted to interview them later.

During those first few months I felt that my interviewing was
inadequate to my needs. I questioned my ability to collect meaningful data, and I was aware that time was not standing still, and that

my apprenticeship counted in the total time we had in Colombia. After working in Tulcán for about a month, I woke up one morning having dreamed I had gone back to Berkeley with only enough data to write a one-page dissertation. Gradually my fear of not getting enough data subsided, although it never went away entirely.

I always explained my role to barrio residents candidly, saying I was a graduate student gathering materials for my doctorate in anthropology. Although this did not mean much to them, the concept of a thesis was not entirely foreign since the local university students who had worked in the barrio were preparing to write senior theses for their graduation.

Research Techniques

While my field techniques ranged from simple observation to a detailed questionnaire on migration, most of my information came from interviews. I used two kinds of interviews, lasting from thirty minutes to two and a half hours: in open-ended interviews, I tried to pursue a single line of questioning on a specific topic, but with considerable flexibility in the discussion; whereas the more rigorous and tightly organized interviews followed a written and numbered schedule.

Both casual and participant observation were important in acquiring data. In the former I would gather data just by watching, a technique helpful in learning about how children play, how people greet each other and interact, and countless other things. I participated to some degree in activities I would later describe—fiestas, baptisms, political discussions, and *cantina* (bar) culture. Some of my best insights on life in Tulcán came as a result of observation.

To record data, I always carried a small notebook in my back pocket. Tulcaneses knew what my notebook was for, and sometimes I asked whether or not I could write down interesting facts or the words of a saying or limerick. In some cases I asked to take notes, perhaps to record something I might not otherwise remember exactly. Some interviews, such as those involving life histories, involved considerable detail of a nonsensitive nature, and these too lent themselves to on-the-spot note taking. But sometimes I did not want to interrupt the speaker, and other times I did not take notes on sensitive topics such as politics, interpersonal relations with neighbors, and witchcraft. In these instances I stored the information in my head and left as quickly as possible, hoping to remember most of what I had heard when I wrote it up at home.

I recorded my thoughts in a permanent and organized way at least twice a day. Of all the aspects of fieldwork, this is perhaps the most tedious and boring, yet I learned early that recording notes is not something that can be postponed; otherwise bits and pieces will be forgotten. I organized my data according to the format of Murdock's *Outline of Cultural Materials* and typed my notes in triplicate on five-by-eight-inch paper, noting at the top the informant's name, the date, and the place. The original copy was a key-sort punch card which I kept with me in the field for reference, and every six weeks I mailed the others back to the States for safekeeping.

Three and a half months after I began work in the barrio, I hired three residents to help me conduct a house-by-house census. My chief assistant, president of the barrio Junta, was well known, respected, and extremely hardworking. At his suggestion, I hired two teenaged girls, one the Junta's secretary and the other the queen of Tulcán's soccer team. Choosing the Junta president was fortunate; he was very conscientious about his work, and people freely gave him the information we asked for. The girls, though, were not effective census takers. Taking a census is meticulous work because interviewees must understand all of the questions, and the work can become boring. In addition, when household heads were not at home we had to make several trips in order to complete the census for the family. Unfortunately, my assistants lacked the necessary patience; either they skipped houses where no one was home, claiming later that the dwelling was vacant, or they tried to get the information from small children. Moreover, a friend pointed out what I suspected and feared: some residents were reluctant to reveal personal information to teenagers. After two days, I dismissed the girls and recensused the area myself.

My camera was useful both in getting to know people and in recording events. After residents discovered my willingness to take pictures, I received many requests, and I soon became the unofficial barrio photographer. Taking pictures helped me to meet many people I would have otherwise missed, and returning later with a print provided a basis for further contact.

My cassette tape recorder also served a dual purpose. Music was a primary source of entertainment among barrio residents and I sometimes recorded singing. Many people played guitars or *tiples* (an eight-string, guitar-shaped instrument), and frequently men practiced together in informal groups. Recording singing was always a marathon event; the participants practiced every song before it was taped, then heard it replayed once when they finished and again when we were through with the session. Toward the end of our stay, I also used the cassette to record responses to Thematic Apperception Tests. Tulcaneses were not reticent about talking into the machine. On the contrary, they thoroughly enjoyed it and usually insisted that I replay everything in front of family and friends.

Finally, I collected what little printed material existed concerning Tulcán. The director of the Instituto de Crédito Territorial gave me a copy of the demographic study his office had conducted in October, 1969, and I found reports on the barrio in local and national newspapers, usually regarding government grants for improving Popayán's poor barrios.

Time was an important methodological intangible. Only long-term residence permits the fieldworker's picture of a community to develop accurately. For example, for many months Hernán Granada told me that he had come to Popayán to get a job—a common reason for migrating. But late in my stay, he told me a long story about how, when he was young, he had gotten into a machete fight with a drinking companion whose family forced him to flee his village. Incidents like this one convinced me that fieldwork cannot be rushed.

Leisure Time

One of the advantages of urban research is that the anthropologist can retreat from the field situation more easily than if he were in a peasant village. Although Popayán is a small, provincial city, it offered us periodic concerts, bullfights, soccer matches, and movies. We also had non-Tulcanese friends we visited on a regular basis. We read a great deal, too, and I cannot overemphasize the importance of having good books in the field. Our short-wave radio was an excellent source of entertainment and information; we enjoyed getting international and North American news, and we felt reassured to hear Eric Sevareid put it all in perspective.

Friendships

Certainly one of the most rewarding aspects of fieldwork is making friends. A number of people in Tulcán I never regarded as informants, but more as friends. On the other hand, some very good informants were not particularly good friends. Several Tulcaneses were protective of our friendship and were quite concerned about which of their neighbors we visited or interviewed. One family was quite upset when its members learned that I was getting information from another family they thought undesirable and "without culture." After he had seen me talking with María Molina, Jaime Arias informed me that she was no good, behaved in a scandalous manner, and probably was not telling me the truth. After coming to visit us, Carmen Martínez asked us not to mention her visit to one of her neighbors, some of our good friends, "because they would get mad at me for visiting you."

There were several reasons for this protectiveness. Occasionally we made small loans, all of which were reciprocated in one way or another. Some of our acquaintances did not want to strain our friendship by tapping our resources too often, nor did they want their neighbors to make such demands. Furthermore, our friendship was a source of prestige, since they ascribed to us high social and economic status. But in the end, friends grudgingly recognized that I had to establish contact with a large number of people throughout the barrio.

Leaving the Barrio

When the time came to leave the field, saying goodbye to our friends in Tulcán was awkward. When we arrived late at one party given in our honor, we found our host and most of the celebrants semi-comatose, an unusual occurrence in a barrio where drunkenness was rare. In some houses, people would stand looking at the floor, shuffling their feet in uncomfortable silence before saying simple goodbyes. With others we would sit drinking coffee or beer and visit just as though we would be back in a week or two. Our last stop was at the house of the Junta president, where we not only said goodbye but also offered our gratitude. I tried to speak eloquently about how grateful I was for the barrio inhabitants' cooperation in my study. I realized that they had done a great deal for me and felt guilty that I had not done more for them. We wanted to do something for the entire barrio but did not know just how, so we left many of our household goods with the parish priests and asked that they be distributed to the residents of Tulcán.

No matter how thorough I tried to be, I frequently worried that I would get back to Berkeley only to find large holes in my data. I envied friends working in Mexico, for they could always return to their field sites, while distance and cost precluded my returning to Colombia. Although I was unsure how much data I needed on a given topic before I could turn my attention elsewhere, I decided to consider my information sufficient when responses from several informants became repetitive. This problem was partially alleviated when, with five months remaining in the field, I wrote a forty-page paper on my work. Having to sort through my field notes and marshal my data into meaningful sections allowed me to see more clearly the areas on which I would have to concentrate during my remaining months in the field.

The following day, as we were driving to Cali, I thought about our year in Colombia. Thirteen months earlier we had arrived in Popayán, with ambivalent feelings: I was eager to begin fieldwork but was worried that I might not succeed. Now as we raced across the flatlands of the Cauca Valley, I had mixed feelings once again. Psychologically we were ready to leave. During the previous few weeks everything was done with departure in mind—yet nearly two hours before we left I found I missed Popayán already. I wondered how many of our friends we would see again and when we might return. As I reviewed the year's events—good and bad—I was amazed at how quickly the time had passed. It had been an unforgettable experience, and now it was over.

Thoughts on Neighborhood Studies

Since so many of our discipline's efforts have been directed at life in the countryside, it is natural that anthropological fieldwork conducted in the cities raises comparisons with that done in rural areas. This is particularly the case for anthropologists working in urban neighborhoods where the issues are germane and at times bewildering. Perhaps this is because in both village and neighborhood settings the investigator usually has a socially, geographically, and perhaps even a politically bounded unit of analysis. Yet there are some interesting similarities, as well as important differences, between them.

Because in both cases the investigator is dealing with relatively small populations, the traditional data-gathering tools used in village studies are convenient and generally adequate for looking at urban neighborhoods. But in working in the city we must be ready to adapt and expand our techniques. As George Gmelch notes in the introduction to this section, neighborhoods as units of analysis might be, and often are, more heterogeneous than most peasant villages. For example, although the majority of the adult population of the two neighborhoods I studied in Popayán were migrants from southern Colombia and certainly shared a number of very similar traits, they also were very different from each other in a variety of important ways. In most cases to talk about the Tulcaneses required gathering more individual data than would have been needed on any particular peasant community with its assumed homogeneity. Out of necessity, the urban anthropologist becomes more quantitatively oriented than students of peasant society often are.

We must be careful not to think of either of these settings as truly isolated units. In the past students of both neighborhoods and villages have been correctly chastised for treating these settings as discrete entities and often for failing to integrate villages into their regional contexts and neighborhoods into their urban ones, and in this way not considering the whole picture. Perhaps the urban anthropologist is more cognizant than his/her rural-oriented colleagues of linkages with the larger whole, in this case the city. We should ask: What does the study of a neighborhood tell us about life in general in a particular city? Unfortunately, one small area often tells us very little.

Finally, something should be said about the nature of the data-gathering and theory-generating process. One of the things which attracts people to ethnology is the personal work which the anthropologist has with the target population. In both village and urban neighborhood studies we interact intensively with a relatively small group of individuals, on a daily basis, over a prolonged period of time. We get to know them, and they us; we participate in the rites of passage of their children, and celebrate other important occasions with them. The nature of this relationship is not one of working with faceless individuals represented by IBM numbers on a fortran sheet, but of dealing with people who live and breathe, and have faces which smile and grimace. They are "real" people. Lamentably, as the units of analysis become larger than what the anthropologist can handle on a one-to-one basis, there is a tendency to lose some of this identity. Thus, while no neighborhood study can tell the reader everything he or she wants to know about any particular city, the reader will be provided with a view of it through the eyes of a certain, but real, segment of its population. These perspectives do convey particularistic experiences and interpretations from a personal point of view, something which should not be lost by anthropologists.

Returning to Popayán

By the fall of 1973, I had finished my graduate training, taken a job, and was in my second year of teaching. When I completed my initial fieldwork in Tulcán, several important changes were scheduled to take place during the next few years: after abandoning their original idea of simply bulldozing the barrio and completely rebuilding it, the municipal government designed a series of improvements. I wanted to return to see if these plans had come to fruition and what effects they might have had on the barrio.

In June, 1974, Patty, our one-year-old son Scott, and I left for Colombia. At first glance, Popayán seemed little changed: more residences for the upper, as well as for the working, classes had arisen on the outskirts of town, as had a shopping mall, which occupied an entire city block. In spite of occasional letters, the flow of correspondence had not been very regular, and, although we repeatedly promised to return, most of our barrio friends were very surprised to see us. It was a happy reunion indeed.

Work Begins

Since the primary objective of our return was to study change in the barrio, I wasted no time in beginning the research process. Among other obvious changes, I found the barrio now had regular bus service and, as a result, the bridge leading into the area had been replaced, and a new one permitted traffic to exit in a different location. Many of the old and dilapidated bamboo electrical poles had been replaced with sturdy concrete poles. Some new houses had been built by private individuals, but the ICT's scheme for a block-by-block renovation to improve existing houses and to build eighty new dwellings never transpired. Although the master plan had been approved in Bogotá, engineers in Popayán stated that the problems of getting access to all of the land titles kept the project from ever getting off the ground. The barrio sewer was still in the planning stage, and, while blueprints existed, funds were never appropriated.

I began interviewing residents about their attitudes toward the barrio and their feelings regarding what had (and had not) taken place. This went quite quickly, and it was during this time that I began to conduct a comparative investigation of another low-income neighborhood. Unlike Tulcán, Barrio Alberto Lleras was built by ICT. It, too, was a migrant neighborhood with close to two-thirds of the household heads born outside of Popayán. Prospective residents were required by ICT to apply to live in Alberto Lleras. As part of the application process, one had to supply the previous year's income tax receipt, furnish statements on employment, get police clearance, present records of military service, and provide a health certificate. The process of qualifying for housing alone provided some interesting and important contrasts with Tulcán.

It was at this time that an old friend, who was teaching a statistics course for anthropology students at the state university, asked me if I would give a couple of guest lectures on urban anthropology. I agreed and was surprised and pleased when, several days later, he approached me and said that the class wanted to know if I needed any research assistants. I jumped at the chance, and a team was prepared.

Because of my familiarity with the research setting, I was able to devise a culturally appropriate, semi-open-ended, structured interview schedule which would allow us to collect quantitative data for comparative purposes from the two barrios. This was supplemented by participant observation and long, intensive interviews along the same lines as the schedule. We divided the two neighborhoods into segments of approximately equal spatial representation and then began interviewing household heads. I was able to use interviews from about 35 percent of Barrio Tulcán's household heads, and we collected information from slightly more than 20 percent of the heads of households in Alberto Lleras.

It was an excellent training experience for the students, and it provided me with some data that, because of time constraints, I never would have collected on my own. Like anthropologists working in cultures other than their own, some of these students had to overcome stereotypes, not only ones which they had about the people they were interviewing, but also ones which these working-class people possessed about them as university students (a group that many in Tulcán and in Alberto Lleras felt was pampered and spoiled). A couple of students clearly were uncomfortable working in low-income neighborhoods, and two quit before the end of the first day. After talking with them, it was apparent that, as upper- or middle-class university students, it was difficult for them to relate to the people they were interviewing. Further, some of the migrants were tired of being surveyed again by university students whose attitudes in the past had tended to be patronizing and condescending. Yet, importantly, most of the students managed very well, with most enjoying the work and showing genuine understanding, empathy, and compassion.

New Roles with Old Friends

Not only had Barrio Tulcán changed, but I, too, had gone through a metamorphosis. When we left Popayán in 1971, my friends in the barrio bid goodbye to someone who had been in their midst for a year, poking around, asking questions, at times being somewhat of a nuisance, but always curious and ever-present. I was a university student and some had been puzzled that I seemed to need so much schooling. For example, it was immediately apparent that some of my barrio friends, with only a year or two of formal education, were undeniably more adept at math than I.

Three years later, I returned as a university professor. My status in the barrio increased with my age and profession. When I told friends in Tulcán that I was writing a book about them, they seemed truly pleased. I had been with them long enough, they reasoned, to be able to present an accurate picture. They wondered if having a book about them would improve their situation, and I was somewhat saddened at having to confess that it probably would not, but that it might make a difference to some.

When we returned to Popayán in the summer of 1974, some of the acquaintances of my youth, who had not been there in 1970–71, had returned to Popayán, and, although they were now only in their late twenties and early thirties, they definitely held positions of power and influence in the community. It was through my inter-actions with these community leaders, or people who would soon assume such ranks, that I obtained a sense of how Popayán operated, what directions the community would soon be taking, and how its leadership envisioned the role of low-income neighborhoods like Tulcán and Alberto Lleras in the grand scheme.

The Earthquake of 1983

About five minutes before my class was to begin, I was looking over some notes when a student rushed into my office and blurted out, "Did you hear about the earthquake in Popayán?" I looked up in amazement. No, I responded, what had she heard? She explained that, while driving to campus, she had been listening to a report of an earthquake striking southern Colombia and that the commen-tator had mentioned Popayán. Any student who has even taken a course from me has heard about Popayán, so it was not surprising that the name rang a bell with her. That evening, we watched the news with uneasy anticipation. There was a thirty-second clip on the destruction of Popayán, which showed the cathedral and a graphic display of several other scenes depicting the impact of the calamity.

At approximately 8:15, Thursday morning, March 31, 1983, Popayán's residents were awakened by the shaking of buildings accompanied by a thunderous, roaring sound, like that of a jet airplane, coming from the ground beneath them. The oscillations and the initial loud noises were followed by sounds which were described as *diabolical* moans and groans. Although the whole process lasted only eighteen seconds, when it was through one of the most beautiful cities in the New World had been severely damaged, at least two hundred people had been killed, and more than thirty thousand inhabitants were left homeless. The earthquake struck as Popayán was celebrating Easter week, the most important time in the lives of many of Popayán's residents. Not only is it a period of celebration of a series of events in the life of the Church, but it is also an occasion for families to gather together. In recent years, tourists from various parts of Colombia, as well as from other countries, have crowded into the city to visit its churches and to watch the nightly activities. Although the evening processions generally are solemn affairs, the hotels are jammed, the shops are full, and a carnival atmosphere pervades the air. The city is never more beautiful than during this time of year. Traditionally, Easter is the time when the exteriors of houses get new coats of paint. Mid-afternoon rains wash Popayán's streets clean, and the blooming hibiscus, jacaranda, and bougainvillea give the city an additional sprinkling of pinks, reds, yellows, and purples. Easter week of 1983, unfortunately, ended on a tragic note.

When the tremor struck, Samuel Samboni, a baker in Barrio Tulcán, was still in bed. Usually at this time, Samuel would be at work delivering bread, but that day was a holiday, and he was enjoying some extra sleep. When the shocks of the quake subsided, Samuel turned on his radio and heard that the center of the city had been destroyed, including the cathedral, whose roof collapsed on worshippers during the 8:00 A.M. mass. Knowing his mother and daughter were there, Samboni raced into town. For several hours, he and other rescuers dug through the rubble. Samboni helped uncover eleven bodies, some smashed beyond recognition. Exhausted, he finally returned home only to encounter his mother waiting for him with news that his daughter had been injured and was in the hospital.

Ignacio Gonzalez and his family lived on the second floor of a relatively new, four-story complex built for members of the city's middle class. At the moment of the quake, Gonzalez was preparing breakfast for himself, the other members of his family having already left for activities elsewhere in the city. When the building started to vibrate, Ignacio hurried to the front door and found that the frame had twisted to the point where the door would not open. Having no time to lose, he kicked out the kitchen window and jumped. By the time he smashed the glass, Gonzalez realized his apartment was now on the ground floor, and he gingerly stepped over the ledge and onto the rubble beneath his feet. Many of

Gonzalez's neighbors, who were still sleeping in the ground-floor apartments, were crushed to death in those brief seconds.

Everyone suffered. Families lost loved ones, and thousands of houses were destroyed, as were places of business—large commercial establishments, small stores, cottage industries, and the like. Only one of the city's beautiful baroque churches was left undamaged. Even the dead were disrupted. The walled tombs, in which the city's deceased are encased, were split open by the tremor. Caskets tumbled out, exposing their contents.

Popayán looked as if it had been bombed. For months afterward, the streets were filled with debris, making pedestrian and vehicular traffic tedious and dangerous. The city's parks and the green belt around its periphery became tent cities, as those left homeless crowded into makeshift housing, which lacked adequate, potable water and waste disposal systems. These were the lucky ones. For every family jammed into a tent, at least three were forced to huddle in dwellings made from unmortared bricks, flattened-out oil drums, sheets of plastic, strips of bamboo, and cardboard. Farther from the city's center, new squatter settlements spontaneously appeared. Within weeks, the hillsides of Popayán began to have an uncanny and disconcerting resemblance to the slums of larger cities elsewhere in Latin America.

Small communities outside of Popayán similarly experienced the force of the earthquake. The peasant village of Puelenje was turned into a series of small brick mounds. Ruins of the church stood out because the pile of debris was higher than those of residences. Julumito, a small coffee-growing community just outside of Popayán, appeared as though some supernatural force had taken a giant eraser and simply reduced the village to a fine pile of reddish pieces of brick.

However, like flowers in the spring, within days after the earthquake, shops popped up amidst the rubble. In other instances, merchants tacked up notices in empty buildings informing customers where they could be found. More commonly, many store owners lost entire inventories and lacked capital to replenish stocks and open their doors. While there were jobs on both demolition and construction crews, the unemployment situation became serious.

Relief Fund

Because of the long relationship between the city of Popayán and my family, when news of the disaster reached us, we immediately moved into action. An emergency relief fund, centered in Ames, collected funds raised by my parents and siblings in their respective cities. Six weeks after the earthquake, I arrived in Popayán to stay with an old childhood friend. After talking with acquaintances about how the funds could most effectively be spent, we decided to dispense most of the monies through the regional office of the Servicio Nacional de Aprendizaje (SENA). SENA is a Colombian government institution designed to train people in occupational skills. The branch in Popayán offers courses in such skills as masonry, pottery making, plumbing, typing, and bookkeeping. Immediately after the earthquake, people at SENA moved into some of the most impoverished rural and urban areas and began organizing teams of neighbors to build earthquake-proof housing. Under the direction of a *teacher*, groups of four or five neighbors rebuilt each other's homes. They were taught how to secure the rafters so that the roofs would not collapse during minor quakes. Steel reinforcement rods were employed in the construction as well. SENA was able to acquire building materials at reduced prices and sold them at cost.

Barrio Tulcán

The physical damage to Barrio Tulcán itself was minimal—an island of eerie tranquility, left untouched on the edge of such obvious destruction. Like people throughout the city, barrio residents talked of lost loved ones, of the disappearance of jobs, as their places of work often were destroyed, and about the nightmares they had that other quakes would soon follow. In the days after the quake, many Tulcaneses worked throughout the city, assisting the relief efforts. After this initial response, they settled back and concentrated on putting their own lives in order. Six weeks after the incident, residents were concerned that the promises made by the government to ease the problems of housing and to assist in the reconstruction of the city would be too slow in coming. Many sarcastically wondered if the monies would ever leave the capital, and, even if they did, how would the residents benefit? It seemed to some that, once again, they might be bypassed as the assistance went elsewhere. Realistically, they observed, there were many others in more desperate circumstances. Nevertheless, they hoped something positive would come out of this catastrophe for them.

Although there was not time to conduct any type of study, there were other observations about the barrio that indicated it was changing. Aside from some of the new growth, compounded by the nearby squatter settlements, the barrio that I had first studied almost a decade and a half before had aged nicely. Homes made from split bamboo, ill-fitting wooden planks, and brick facing now had evolved into stuccoed and painted abodes. Many of the sons and daughters of families I had previously worked with were now studying in high school or trade school, and some were at the local university—educational levels unobtained by anyone from previous generations in those families. Nemecio Cruz's father told me that his son, then six years old, would go to the university one day. The family had singled out Nemecio as the one who would receive a university degree and decided to make whatever sacrifices necessary to bring this to fruition. Over the next decade, both parents worked to this end. Likewise, after older siblings completed primary school and joined the work force, some of their income was put aside for Nemecio's education. In 1983, he was in his third year at the university and, according to his delighted mother, would graduate in a couple of years.

While I would have preferred to have returned under more pleasant circumstances, it was good to see the people in the barrio again, and I am convinced those strong feelings were reciprocated. For instance, Faustina Arias announced with great emotion to her daughter and husband that, after the earthquake, she knew I would return. We talked of the past, of the current situation, and of what the future held for them. By and large, as they had always done, they looked at life with an air of unbridled optimism, tempered by a generous dollop of reality.

Notes

[1] The original fieldwork was supported by the National Institute of Health, and 1974 research was funded by the Wenner-Gren Foundation for Anthropological Research. The author also appreciates the continued support of Iowa State University.
[2] The names of the barrio and its inhabitants are pseudonyms.

An Urban Field Experience
Irish Travellers in Dublin

SHARON BOHN GMELCH

*In this account of an urban field experience, Sharon Gmelch
discusses the personal adaptation required of the
anthropologist when studying another culture. Research was
carried out among Irish Travellers—a nomadic, impoverished,
gypsy-like population—living in Dublin, Ireland. From her
account we learn that fieldwork in cities need not be less
intimate or personal than that conducted in rural areas. We
also learn some of the advantages and special requirements of
urban field research, and of the dilemma anthropologists face
in deciding whether to remain neutral observers or become
needed advocates for the people they live among.*

I first went to Ireland in the summer of 1970 as a graduate student
participating in a field training program in anthropology.[1] The
program began with an orientation period in Dublin during which
we attended lectures on Irish society and research techniques. We
then left the city for small communities in the Irish countryside.
This was not surprising given the traditional focus of anthropology
on tribesmen and peasants. I went to a fishing village in the west.
Only once did I venture by bus into the nearby provincial town; to
do so more often, I felt, would diminish the experience of living in
an "isolated" community. In adopting this attitude I naively ignored
the crucial role played by urban centers in the lives of people
everywhere. My village, although small (pop. 342), was hardly

Source: Article written expressly for *Urban Life*.

isolated. To a large extent it was a bedroom community for the provincial town of Tralee, just seven miles away. Many of its residents drove to work there each morning, returning each evening; others commuted longer distances returning only at week's end. A number of my village neighbors had sons or daughters living in cities—in Dublin or "across the water" in London, Birmingham, and New York. Almost every home had television, and everyone read newspapers and listened to radio, which brought national and international news as well as urban values into their homes.

Irish Travellers

It was on my way to and from my village at the beginning and end of the summer that I first became aware of "tinkers" or Travellers[2]—

A Traveller family negotiating Dublin traffic in their flat cart. [Photo by Pat Langan]

Ireland's indigenous nomads who at that time still lived on the roadside in horse-drawn wagons, tents, and trailers and earned their living largely by begging and scavenging for scrap metal. They were a well-known yet little understood group in Ireland, more the subject of folklore and fiction than serious sociological or anthropological study. I was intrigued. To my eyes, they were exotic. They also matched my interests in poverty and ethnicity. By coincidence my husband, also an anthropologist, was at the same time becoming involved with the Travellers. He had arrived in Dublin at the end of the summer and while waiting for my field school to end, collected demographic data for a physical anthropologist who was conducting a genetic study of Travellers.[3]

Before leaving Ireland that summer we acquired a copy of a government report detailing what had become known in Ireland as the "itinerant problem." It outlined the plight of hundreds of Traveller families living in poverty as well as the problems their nomadic lifestyle created for the settled community, especially in urban areas. Reading the report and the most recent census figures forced the realization that if I pursued my interest in Travellers, I would be doing "urban anthropology." For although many Travellers still lived in rural areas, they were moving into Irish cities at an ever-increasing rate. And for good reason.

The rural-based trades of the Travellers, such as tinsmithing, chimney sweeping, and horse dealing, had become obsolete due to modernization. Moreover, the city and the advantages it offered exerted considerable pull; its high population density, for example, made begging and scrap metal collecting, the Travellers' newest economic specializations, easier. It was also easier to collect the "dole" (unemployment assistance) and obtain other social welfare benefits in the city. A Dublin-based, volunteer movement—the Itinerant Settlement Movement—had also been organized to help Travellers. But there were other attractions, too. City life meant street lights to brighten the night, more pubs, cinemas, and activity of all kinds. In the span of less than twenty years (1952–1971), the number of Travellers living in the capital city of Dublin had jumped from 158 to 1,435. The trend was the same in other Irish cities and provincial towns. Thus even the most isolated and traditional segment of the Irish population had been touched by urbanism and modernization.

The following account emphasizes my field experience more than research techniques, although the latter as they relate to urban areas are treated as well. Anthropological fieldwork, even in cities, is always an intensely personal experience. Unlike other social scientists, anthropologists attempt to live among the people they study, conducting research at all times of day for an extended period of time. It is their desire to know a culture from the inside, through the eyes of its members, and to observe actual behavior rather than rely solely on informants' verbal responses that separates anthropologists from other social scientists. It is for this reason that I focus on the field experience itself in this essay.[4]

Preparation and Arrival

While completing my formal graduate training at the University of California, Santa Barbara, I read everything I could on poverty, ethnicity, and outcast groups in other countries in order to refine my interests and formulate a research design. I was interested in understanding how Travellers—who, like the settled Irish community, are white, English-speaking, Roman Catholic, and indigenous to Ireland—had for so long maintained a separate ethnic identity. I decided to focus my research on the interaction that takes place between Travellers and settled people as one way of understanding the maintenance of social boundaries between two groups and the persistence of Traveller identity. The density of the population in Dublin made it an ideal place to examine the dynamics of this interaction. My husband George Gmelch, who was also doing doctoral research among the Travellers, planned to investigate their urbanization and adaptation to urban life. With a resolve that these were the two most significant issues to examine, we set off to Ireland.

First Impressions

The marriage ceremony took place in Our Good Shepherd Catholic Church in Churchtown, a suburb on the south side of Dublin. I had expectations of a large, gregarious crowd. Instead only thirteen people counting the bride and groom, my husband, the social worker, and myself attended. An air of disinterest and perfunctoriness pervaded the gathering. The fifteen-year-old bride appeared shy and woebegone in her wrinkled and ill-fitting wedding dress. The groom wore a dark, rumpled suit and an expression of detached resignation. The bride's father and the handful of women relatives present shifted uncomfortably in the pews, murmuring among themselves. The priest and his assistant arrived and taking the bride and groom by their elbows, jockeyed them into the proper position in front of the altar. Perhaps unnecessarily, I felt acutely embarrassed for them, especially as the priest instructed them in what

A 15-year-old Traveller bride and her mother at a Dublin wedding. [Photo by Pat Langan]

seemed like a loud and impatient tone on what to say and when to say it. About a dozen neighborhood children who had filtered in during the ceremony stood at the back of the church, gaping innocently at the spectacle before them. The customary mass was omitted, and then it was over. Outside, a young *gardai* (policeman), after calling Johnny over to the curb, leaned out of his car window and advised him to "start out right" and be "well-behaved." Johnny was out on bail for the ceremony. Larceny, the social worker informed us, was a growing problem among Travellers in the city. We left soon after, my head spinning from these glimpses of what was to come.

My first impressions of Travellers were not exactly flattering, nor did they help make interaction easy. The men looked tough and forbidding with their weather-beaten and unshaven faces, tattered suits, and dark, tobacco-stained fingers. They seldom smiled. The women were less threatening, if only because most were somewhat matronly and many were pregnant. But even they looked tough and acted wary and evasive. Fieldwork among Travellers, I feared, was not going to be easy.

Beginning Fieldwork

One of the first problems faced by any anthropologist when working in a city is delineating the boundaries of the population he or she intends to study. In my rural research, I had simply studied the small, nucleated village that I lived in. Dublin, on the other hand, was large and heterogeneous. My interest in Travellers defined in ethnic terms the group I was interested in, yet there were close to fifteen hundred Travellers spread across Dublin in more than fifty camps. Some of these were small roadside camps of two or three families; others were large government-sponsored, serviced "sites" for up to forty families. As a single researcher rather than a member of a large research team, I could not regularly visit them all.

After making an initial visit to most of the larger encampments, George and I decided to concentrate on two camps which seemed most appropriate for our purposes. Both had large, relatively stable populations and were within easy commuting distance of the apartment we had rented. One, Labre Park, was the first site built for Travellers in Dublin and one of the first of its kind in the country. It accommodated thirty-nine families in one-room, prefabricated dwellings (known as "tigins"); extra family members spilled over into trailers and wagons parked nearby. The second site, Holylands, was a temporary and undeveloped campsite located on the edge of a suburban housing estate on the south side of the city. It was little more than a large field ringed by trees with two strips of blacktop on either side to provide hard standing for the Travellers' wagons and trailers. A single water tap and a rarely used outhouse constituted the amenities for a population of about twenty families.

During this initial phase of fieldwork, we alternated our visits between the camps. Upon arriving in one, we would both get out of our car and walk off in separate directions, approaching individuals or groups of Travellers and attempting to engage them in conversation. A few people had met George the previous summer during his work with the physical anthropologist and had received the photographs he had sent back to them, so he was not a complete stranger. But I was. At first most of my contacts were with curious children, teenagers, and the elderly. I explained my *role*—an American university student who would some day be a teacher—and what I hoped to do, to learn what it was like to be a Traveller. I explained about writing a dissertation, which they interpreted to mean a book. When they asked how long I was going to stay and I said "a year," they were skeptical. Most of their contacts with outsiders similar to myself, primarily Irish students during one-term projects or journalists carrying out interviews, had been short-lived. After repeated visits, however, the realization that I intended to keep coming became clear. As I became more familiar to people, they in turn became friendlier. Gradually I was developing *rapport*. No doubt the fact that I was not Irish lessened their suspicions that I might be something other than what I had said. Nevertheless, I learned later that for a period of several months a few people in our camp suspected that we were police agents because of a suspicious death that had taken place just before our arrival.

The early weeks were not easy. I can remember the sinking feeling I got when people were cold or walked away from me. When in camp I was always on guard, monitoring my behavior, trying to act appropriately, wanting to be friendly but not too friendly, interested but not too curious. I ate whatever food was offered me, sat casually on the ground and on several occasions on urine-soaked mattresses, trying my best to seem indifferent to the odor of unwashed bodies and the filth of the surroundings some people lived in. I was repeatedly asked the same questions, often during the course of a single conversation, partially because Travellers were genuinely curious about me and partially because we had so few common experiences on which to base a conversation. But I also came to view this questioning as a test of my truthfulness and consistency. "Are you married? How long have you been married? Is he your husband? Do you have any children? Don't you like your children? Are you from America? Do you know Elvis?" Some days I thought I couldn't face driving into camp again. The thought of seeking out people to talk to, of giving the same explanations over and over, and of risking rejection was almost too much to bear.

Although rapport developed with some Travellers, commuting to the camps soon proved unsatisfactory. To begin with, there were logistical problems. Travellers lack defined work and leisure hours; plans, even major trips away, were made on the spur of the moment. Some days I would arrive in camp to find virtually everyone gone. Setting up an appointment to talk to a specific individual at a specific time was nearly impossible. Travellers do not live by a clock. And understandably, my appointments were far more important to me than to them.

I also felt that I was missing out on much of the important activity of Traveller life. This fear was reinforced each time I arrived in camp to be told something like, "You should have been here last night; the guards came up and took Biddy's Jim." Most importantly,

I wanted to lose my outsider status and get "backstage," in Erving Goffman's terms, to blend into the background of camp life so that people would act naturally in front of me. Travellers are used to dealing with outsiders in a superficial and manipulative way: the nature of many of their contacts with settled people such as in begging, second-hand dealing, and door-to-door sales requires them to be skilled at impression management. I felt it was important for me to view their lives from the inside, in hopes of learning what they really felt and to get beyond the settled community's stereotypes of them. Moreover, Travellers had never been studied in depth before, and I felt an obligation to collect as wide a range of ethnographic data as possible.[5] Only living in a camp would enable us to do this.

Moving into Camp

After seven weeks of commuting between camps, we selected Holylands as our main research site for a number of reasons. First, the layout of the camp was better for observation. Families were camped along opposite ends of a small central field and consequently the actions of one were readily observable to all. At Labre Park, in contrast, the tigins were lined up in a single row, each doorway facing the back of the house in front. Secondly, Holylands provided a better cross section of the Traveller community. Some families living there had lived in the Dublin area as long as ten years, others were new to the city, and many families were still mobile. Because Holylands was then a temporary site, Travellers were for the most part free to move on and off with their own wagons, trailers, and tents. Thus besides the stable core of families who remained for the entire year, we were also exposed to new families who stayed for shorter periods of time. Thirdly, and perhaps most important, families at Holylands had been more approachable and hospitable during our visits than those at the other camp. It was at the suggestion and with the help of some of Holylands' Travellers that we finally bought a wagon and horse and prepared to move in.

The wagon, which was in need of paint and a few repairs, gave us a tangible excuse for coming to camp each day. Moreover, now that it was apparent that we really intended to live and travel like Travellers, the social distance that had naturally existed between us lessened. Our relationship with Travellers improved steadily over the next few days. As we worked on the wagon, people stopped by

A Traveller camp in Finglas, a Dublin suburb. In the foreground is ▶ scrap metal collected from homeowners. [Photo by George Gmelch]

to give advice, lend a hand, or simply chat and question us about America, particularly about the wild West ("What are cowboys like? Are there still Indians?"). The transition from regular visitor to camp member was completed the first night we slept in the wagon.

I had spent most of the evening sitting around a wood stove in one of the trailers quietly talking to a family. I had then gone to bed, about ten. An hour or so later I woke to the roar and screech of vans and lorries racing into the site and the sounds of people laughing and talking. This lasted for a half hour and then the camp settled down to sleep once more. A few minutes later, a loud argument broke out in the trailer next door. Accusations, curses, and obscenities were hurled back and forth. I could hear screams, groans, and the sound of glass breaking. As I peered out the front window of my wagon, I saw the woman next door stagger from her trailer. A wave of irrational paranoia swept over me, and I envisaged being dragged from my wagon and beaten. But gradually things quieted down and the camp fell into a fitful third sleep. The next morning I acted as if nothing happened. Everyone I saw, however, seemed subdued and sheepish. I was coyly asked by one woman how well I'd slept, but no direct reference to the fight was made. The eight-year-old son of the family involved came closest when he said, "You must have learned a lot last night." Indeed I had; many of the pretenses and polite public fictions maintained for the "outsider" had been broken.

I soon learned that Thursdays, the day Dublin Travellers received their unemployment payments, were invariably days of heavy drinking and often fighting once the pubs had closed. Most fights started as arguments between husbands and wives, which sometimes escalated into physical beatings. Sometimes this domestic violence involved other family members, but rarely people outside the family. As the year progressed, I became inured to the sounds of Thursday-night violence.

Once living in camp, I fell into a more comfortable fieldwork routine. Much of the Travellers' time was spent out-of-doors, except in bad weather. Hence people were more accessible than villagers in the west of Ireland or most urban dwellers. Each family lit a campfire in the morning and kept it burning until they went to bed at night. A blackened kettle of water was kept boiling, and pots of tea were brewed throughout the day. Informal interviews consisted largely of extended conversations around the campfire and at the pub in the evening.

Each morning I made a list of questions and topics I needed to explore and during the course of the day steered conversations on to them, learning in the process when (and when not) to ask direct questions as well as what questions to ask and in front of whom. I started with what I regarded as the least intimate and least sensitive topics—with aspects of Travelling life that Travellers were proud of. Early weeks were spent learning about the art of Travelling itself, the traditional skills of tinsmithing and rural peddling, about what settled people were like in different parts of the country, and family history. As time passed, the historical and general were left behind and more contemporary and sensitive issues were discussed—begging, scavenging, welfare, discrimination in the city, drinking behavior, family problems, and trouble with the law. Much of this was discussed spontaneously and at the Travellers' instigation. The anthropologist, as a neutral outsider and someone who has shown great interest in the people he or she is living among, often becomes friend and counselor. Many people came to our wagon during the course of the year, shut the door, and talked about their problems to either George or me.

I rarely took field notes in front of Travellers. I felt it would act as a barrier, reminding them of the differences between us. I also felt it would be insensitive and raise unnecessary suspicions, since they themselves could not read. I tried to be as unobtrusive as possible. Moreover, the proximity of my wagon made note taking immediately after an event or discussion relatively easy. If I had time, I would write down a conversation in detail; at the very least I would jot down important information and reminders to myself to be typed up later as complete field notes.[6] During the last few months of research, I made numerous tape recordings to obtain details of family histories and to record the Travellers' own descriptions and explanations of aspects of their culture. I did not use the tape recorder as often as I would have liked, however, since it always attracted a crowd of children and young adults who wanted to take turns singing into it.

As with other anthropologists, I relied heavily upon the friendship and assistance of several key "informants" or native teachers. To balance the view of Travellers I was developing by living in one Dublin camp, however, I continued to make periodic visits to other camps in the city and even to areas outside of Dublin.[7] Regular attendance at the weekly meetings of Dublin social workers involved with Travellers also provided an opportunity to cross-check certain impressions and ask questions about Travellers in other parts of the city. For six weeks I acted as a substitute social worker in a nearby town. This provided me with an opportunity to directly experience some of the problems and misunderstandings that arise between Travellers and settled Irish working in the welfare sphere.

Fieldwork is a process of adjustment. Just as the anthropologist must adjust to the people he or she is studying, so the people must adjust to the presence of an anthropologist. I had numerous "unusual" habits. At first small children gathered around me in the morning to watch me brush my teeth, talking and pointing, "Ah, would you look. Sharon's scrubbing her teeth." More importantly, Travellers had traditional and conservative notions about the role of women. They were curious about why I did not have children (I told them about birth-control pills), that I knew how to drive a car, and that I often wore slacks or jeans. My most difficult adjustment was to the lack of privacy. Trailer and wagon walls were thin, and each family's camp was located only a few yards away from the next. Moreover, Travellers are gregarious, the result of being raised in large families and crowded living conditions.[8] They freely entered each other's dwellings without warning, sitting down to listen for awhile, and then leaving, perhaps without uttering a word themselves. As we became an accepted part of camp life, our wagon became a customary stop on the visiting rounds. If someone wanted to talk, he or she simply opened the wagon door and came in. We could expect visitors at any hour of the day or night. It was difficult to suggest that people leave without risking offending them. I put a latch on the door which deterred some, but most merely opened the double windows above the door and leaned in to talk or else tugged at the flimsy door until we were forced to open it.

Research in the City

Data Collection

One of the advantages of urban research over that conducted in most rural areas is the anthropologist's access to a variety of other sources of information—government agencies and personnel, research institutes and their reports, university departments and staff, the census bureau, and libraries and private archives. Depending upon the particular research problem, information from such sources can be as important as that obtained from the people the anthropologist is working with. I spent many hours in the National Library ferreting out information on the origins and history of Travellers and in the library of *The Irish Times* reading newspaper clippings that documented the growth of the Itinerant Settlement Movement and clashes between Travellers and settled Irish over housing, campsites, and trespassing. The latter provided important clues to the stereotypes and attitudes settled people held toward Travellers and their change over the years. The archives of the Department of Folklore at University College, Dublin contained a variety of information on Travellers, including the results of a questionnaire sent to school teachers across Ireland in the early 1950s. This yielded important data on rural Traveller culture before their urban migration. Whenever I was depressed or anxious or felt my interaction with Travellers had reached a point of diminishing returns, I went to one of these places and drowned my sorrows in solitary work. This never failed to cheer me up, providing me with a wealth of new information as well as further topics and questions to pursue with Travellers.

When a complete respite from research was needed, the city provided shops, restaurants, plays, movies, museums, art galleries, and the zoo—a range of diversions unavailable to anthropologists working in the countryside. The wide range of contacts with settled Irish we made during the course of the year meant that we were occasionally asked out for dinner or tea. Good food in comfortable surroundings helped place fieldwork in perspective.

An important part of my research involved observing Travellers outside the camp setting as they moved among and interacted with the settled community. Even had I not been interested in interethnic relations, it would have been impossible to view Travellers as an isolate, especially in an urban area. There was regular contact between the two groups. On any major shopping street, for example, I could observe the transactions that took place between Traveller women begging for alms and settled passers-by. I could also accompany Travellers when they went scrap collecting and begging and go out with them to pubs, shops, cinemas, courts, hospitals, and the like.

To supplement the observations and impressions I gained when in the company of Travellers and from informal encounters with settled Irish, I undertook a series of formal interviews. First I outlined the main institutions and spheres of activity within which interaction between Travellers and settled Irish takes place: the legal system, health care and social welfare, organized religion, with the members of the Itinerant Settlement Movement, and during economic exchanges. Interviews were then arranged with authorities and personnel from each of these spheres—justices, social workers, local police, nuns, priests, settlement committee members, doctors, nurses, and scrap metal merchants. In order to more systematically measure the settled community's attitude towards Travellers, however, a methodology requiring more than participant observation and interviewing was needed. Eight months into the research, using the insights gained from participant observation, I designed a questionnaire which elicited information on the frequency and contexts within which settled Irish people meet Travellers. Three hundred Irish men and women in Dublin and three rural areas filled out the questionnaire, which also explored settled Irish attitudes toward Travellers.

Few cultural groups are truly isolated; virtually all are part of larger political and economic systems. This is especially apparent when one is conducting research in urban areas. Most people today are also personally involved in the transnational community. Travellers, for example, not only have economic ties to the settled community in Ireland, but also have economic ties and social networks which extend into Northern Ireland, England, Scotland, and Wales. Many families travel in Great Britain for part of each year. A smaller number of Travellers have used the anonymity of English cities to shed their Traveller identity by finding wage employment and "passing" as working-class Irish. Recognizing this, I went to England to see for myself where many Travellers migrated and the conditions they lived in. My primary destination was Birmingham where I visited relatives of families I knew in Holy-lands and interviewed social workers, probation officers, and other people who had regular contacts with Travellers.

Neutral Observer or Advocate?

Urban research raises new dilemmas for the anthropologist. The groups studied by anthropologists in urban areas such as ethnic minorities and migrants are often faced with major social problems. This was true of Travellers who not only lived in poverty and suffered discrimination at the hands of the settled community but also had to cope with a new, urban environment and pressures to give up nomadism. The Itinerant Settlement Movement and govern-ment actively sought to settle them on official sites and in houses. At the time of my research the movement stressed integration with the settled community as the ultimate solution to the "itinerant problem." It was difficult in the circumstances not to become a spokesperson or advocate for Travellers' rights.

Travellers were then, and still are, an emotive subject in Ireland. The people working to help them wanted answers and reassurance that they were doing the right thing. Since I often attended settle-ment committee meetings, I was frequently asked my opinion. I resisted giving advice to settlement workers, however, during the course of my research. For one, I saw my role as that of a dispas-sionate observer—the perspective in which I had been trained in

graduate school. I also wished to avoid making ill-informed statements while I was still learning. What help I gave Travellers was
generally on a smaller, more personal level such as reading
medicine labels, filling out medical cards and housing applications,
interpreting the legal notices which arrived in the mail, writing and
reading personal letters to the families who received them,
obtaining telephone numbers, and when necessary acting as a
chauffeur.

Yet the pressures to give advice continually fought with my desire
to remain neutral and simply carry out my fieldwork. By the end
of the research, I decided that I was sufficiently knowledgeable to
make a few common-sense suggestions to settlement workers. I also
felt I owed it to Travellers. To be truly dispassionate when working
with people, particularly a poor and stigmatized group like Irish
Travellers, is in some ways inhuman. Moreover, anthropologists are
in a far better position than most outsiders to speak for the people
they have lived among. At the urging of a prominent settlement
worker, George and I wrote an open letter to the settlement
committees, assessing their work from the Traveller point of view.
Later we wrote a critique of the Itinerant Settlement Movement for
an Irish journal.[9] Our recommendations were modest and included
urging the provision of serviced campsites for Travellers who
wished to continue travelling rather than focusing all efforts on
permanent settlement. We strongly recommended that Travellers
be involved actively in settlement work, particularly that they be
given a voice in planning. In our letter to settlement workers we
advised against being patronizing in their dealings with Travellers
and against making promises that could not be kept. These
suggestions were endorsed by some settlement workers, resented
and ignored by others. It is difficult to assess their impact.

Since the time of our research, Travellers have become more
involved in organizations and policy making that affect their future.
Initially, a few Travellers joined the national organization of the
settlement movement—the National Council for Itinerant Settlement—although they had no decision-making power. In time,
however, their voices were heard, and the official goal of the
movement did change. Settlement was no longer promoted as the
sole path to integration but as an "alternative" to life on the road.
The national organization, renamed the National Council for
Travelling People, began to focus more on constructing campsites
for Travellers who wished to remain nomadic. By the early 1990s,
Travellers had established their own organizations to represent their
interests (or at least the interests of those Travellers in their

membership) and to lobby the government. They worked in opposition to the National Council for Travelling People which eventually disbanded.

Conclusions

Urban fieldwork, like urban life itself, is varied and complex. Most anthropologists employ a wider range of research techniques in the city than are typically used in rural areas. In my own work, participant observation and interviewing were supplemented by a survey and extensive archival research. Far more sources of data are available in the city than in rural areas. Thus fieldwork in urban areas often requires considerable imagination in order to take advantage of the wealth of information collected by government agencies, journalists, social scientists, and other academics which is pertinent to the anthropologist's own interests.

When an anthropologist conducts research in the city it is necessary to place the group under study in its larger political and economic context. This is also true of rural research, of course, but is especially important in the city where groups are less autonomous. This often requires research outside the bounded unit the anthropologist has chosen to study. I lived in a camp, yet I also worked outside it observing interactions between Travellers and settled Irish, administrating a questionnaire, and interviewing government officials and other settled Irish who had dealings with Travellers. I also spent time outside the country tracing the Travellers' wider familial and economic networks. In rural research the anthropologist, while aware of the influences of the larger system, is less likely to be drawn outside his or her community for actual fieldwork.

Yet urban research need not be any less intimate or personal than rural fieldwork. The principal goal of anthropology, whether conducted in rural or urban areas, remains that of gaining an understanding of human society. It is based on the belief that only intense, day-to-day involvement with people over an extended period of time can provide real understanding. Thus while urban anthropologists may, indeed should, make use of historical, demographic, and survey techniques, they should not do so at the expense of the insights gained from traditional methods such as participant observation. Even in cities anthropological fieldwork should remain an intensely personal experience, for only through in-depth interaction in small groups and intimate familiarity with the field setting can we truly understand other cultures.

Notes

[1] The field school was organized by the Department of Anthropology, University of Pittsburgh, supervised by Dr. Eileen Kane, and funded by the National Science Foundation.

[2] "Traveller" and "Travelling People" are the terms most frequently used by the people themselves. "Tinkers" was the term traditionally used by members of the settled community. It was also a name once used by some Travellers (mainly tinsmiths) and is the name by which many foreigners know the group. Within Ireland, however, it is now pejorative. "Itinerant" was the government designation and the term used by the news media during the 1970s; today they use "Traveller" and "Travelling People."

[3] See Crawford, M. H., and George Gmelch (1974).

[4] Few of the results of my research with Travellers are presented here. The interested reader can consult other accounts if he or she wishes (See S. Gmelch 1976, 1977, 1986, 1989, and 1991 and Gmelch and Gmelch 1974a, 1974b, 1978, 1985a, 1985b, 1987, and 1988).

[5] The only study of Travellers then completed was a master's thesis in sociology. See McCarthy, Patricia Walsh (1971).

[6] Even after moving into Holylands, we retained a room where we kept our typewriter, books, field notes, and the like, which we did not have space for in the wagon. It was also a place to take much needed baths, since Holylands had no bathing or toilet facilities.

[7] Travellers living in campsites or houses in the towns of Athlone, Ballinasloe, Bray, Carlow, Clones, Dundalk, Ennis, Ennisorty, Kilkenny, Loughrea, Monaghan, Roscrea, and Tuam as well as Galway City were also visited during the course of the year.

[8] Travellers families were large; most households contained six or seven children. The fertility rate of 10.4 children per prolific woman over the age of forty is one of the highest recorded. This high fertility rate can be explained in part by the long reproduction careers of the women who marry young and continue reproducing until they are forty-five and fifty years of age. At Holylands, three women had each given birth more than twenty times, although not all infants survived childhood.

[9] See Gmelch, Sharon Bohn, and George Gmelch (1974b).

Part Three

Migration and the Adaptation of Migrants to City Life

By 1990 nearly three of every four people in the industrialized countries were living in cities of more than one hundred thousand, while in the rest of the world one out of every three were urbanites. By the year 2000, 50 percent of the world's population will be urbanized, compared to 4 percent in 1900. Since World War II the increase in urban migration has been phenomenal. Mexico City is one of the most striking examples. From 1960 to 1993, the population of the metropolitan area grew from less than five million to over twenty-five million, with cityward migrants making up almost half of the increase. The flow continues today at a rate of more than fifteen thousand new migrants each month—an average of five hundred new persons each day. All new arrivals need food and water, shelter, employment, and schooling for their children.

Anthropology has given much attention to migration, as have some of the other social sciences, notably sociology, demography, and economics. Indeed, more urban anthropologists have conducted research on rural-urban migration than on any other single topic. There are several specialized journals devoted solely to migration studies, such as *International Migration Review* and *International Migration*, though they cross the lines of several disciplines. There are also a half-dozen anthologies on the topic and a similar number of bibliographies which list more than three thousand individual titles dealing with migration. In fact there is so much literature that many social scientists believe that migration has achieved status as an independent field of study (Kemper 1979:10).

Most anthropological interest in migration has been of rural peasants or tribal members moving to industrialized cities, usually within their own society but also internationally. There the peasants obtain unskilled or semiskilled work and frequently live among their own kind—co-ethnics and often co-villagers. While peasant migrants of this type comprise the vast bulk of rural-to-urban movements, there are also other groups in the migration stream. These groups include merchants, students, small-town elites moving to larger cities, and even some upper-class landowners. These middle- and upper-strata migrants, whose migration behavior and adaptation in the city tend to be individual-oriented, have not been the concern of many anthropologists.

Early Studies

Early studies of migration focused on mass movements, particularly the transatlantic movement of people from Europe to the New World in the late nineteenth and early twentieth centuries. In analyzing the causes of migration, the larger economic and social forces were stressed. Comparatively little attention was given to the characteristics and motives of individual migrants or to selectivity—why in the same circumstances some individuals choose to leave while others remain at home.

Once the migrants were in the city, researchers focused on problems of adjustment rather than the successful ways in which most migrants adapted. In large part this focus was the result of prevailing views about the differences between rural and urban society. The pioneering writings of Louis Wirth and Robert Redfield, for example, described urban society as disorganized, secular, and individualistic. This led observers to expect that cityward migration by rural peoples would be disruptive and would cause social disorganization, culture conflict, and even anomie (the breakdown of norms) and alienation. Oscar Lewis's (1952) landmark study "Urbanization Without Breakdown" was the first study to question this view. Among his Tepoztecan migrants, urbanization did not result in weakened kinship bonds, social disorganization, change in religious beliefs, or alienation. Lewis's findings were later corroborated by others such as Janet Abu-Lughod's (1962) study of Egyptian migrants in Cairo. The Egyptian migrants had to make some adjustments to nonagricultural wage labor and to reduced space caused by the high population density of the city, but otherwise no major shift in behavior occurred. They readily adapted to the city with little disruption of their traditional ways.

A New Approach

Since the 1950s more attention has been given to the individual migrant—to decision-making processes and the strategies migrants develop to cope with city life. Today's migrants are less likely to be viewed as pawns automatically responding to large structural forces than as volitional individuals who understand their situation and the alternatives open to them and who rationally choose among them (Kasdan 1970). Take the example of a poor Italian (or Spanish, Yugoslav, Turkish, Greek, Portuguese) peasant whose lands are not large enough or fertile enough to make a satisfactory living. He or she does not blindly migrate to a new land but rather has a number of alternatives to consider: he or she (1) may choose to continue working the land as best as he or she can; (2) may be able to remain at home while commuting to a nearby town to work; (3) may move to a large city, leaving family at home but returning on weekends; (4) may move the entire family to the city and give up the village home; or (5) may leave the country altogether and go to a city in one of the northern, industrialized nations such as Germany or Switzerland to work, either going alone or taking along the family. Not all of these alternatives, of course, are open to every rural villager, but there are nearly always a number of possibilities to be considered. Hence, migration must be viewed as a process in which individuals consciously change their own situations in search of a more rewarding life.

The decision to migrate is usually based on a complex and careful consideration of many variables. It is reached when the anticipated advantages of life in the city outweigh the strength of social bonds at home and the individual's attachment to the predictable and familiar. The attractions of the city must overcome the fears and insecurities associated with moving to an unfamiliar and alien environment in which the migrant must start a new life. Only in extreme cases of hardship such as famine (e.g., Ireland during the potato blight of 1847–48, or more recently, Somalia), genocide, and war (e.g., Bosnia, Rwanda) is migration motivated by a single factor.

The Push-Pull Framework

In describing the underlying factors that enter into the decision to migrate, anthropologists often speak in terms of "push" and "pull." Push factors are the conditions or attributes of the rural homeland which induce individuals to leave. Common among them are soil erosion, low crop yields, land shortage, disputes, and political factionalism. Pull factors are the attractions of the city which draw or pull individuals to it. These include jobs, educational opportunities, conveniences, the excitement and lure of "city lights," and hopes of success. Since few migrants have prior experience living in cities, pull factors often tend to be stereotypes of city life and what it has to offer. Not surprisingly then, expectations are sometimes inaccurate or unrealistic. Although the push-pull framework has been criticized as being simplistic, it is nevertheless a useful framework for categorizing the range of factors encouraging migration.

Adaptive Strategies

Once in the city the migrant must find a place to live, get a job, and develop a network of friends to satisfy his or her emotional and social needs. Of great concern to urban anthropologists are the strategies migrants adopt to do these things. These strategies may be *individualistic*, in that migrants may depend primarily upon their own resources and initiative, or they may be *group-oriented* with migrants relying upon others—usually kinfolk or fellow villagers—for assistance (Graves and Graves 1974). A migrant seeking housing, for example, may find accommodation on his or her own or may rely upon kinfolk for assistance. Often migrants who do the latter reside with their kinfolk for several months until suitable accommodation can be obtained. Similarly, in establishing friendships the migrant may seek contacts with other members of the wider urban society or may choose relationships solely from among kinfolk, fellow villagers, or co-ethnics.

Perhaps the best example of group-oriented strategy is the voluntary association. Comprised of members of the same ethnic group or simply individuals from the same rural village, voluntary associations assume many of the functions that were performed by kinship groups in the migrants' home villages. As Kenneth Little demonstrated, in a study of voluntary associations in Africa, the associations are much like guilds in preindustrial cities in that they give the migrant a sense of belonging; and they also provide financial aid in times of need, and organize dances and other recreational activities. In short, such associations provide a strong support group which eases the migrant into the urban world.

Similarly, squatter settlements are a group response to the shortage of low-cost housing in cities in much of the developing world, particularly Latin America. Through careful organization, migrants as well as longer-term urbanites have successfully invaded government-owned lands and constructed their own rent-free settlements (Mangin 1967, Safa 1974). In time the squatters are often able to secure title to their homesites as well as cajole the government into providing electricity and piped water. In some cities squatter settlements are so numerous that their populations comprise a major segment of the total urban population. The genesis of squatter settlements in the Brazilian capital, Brazilia, is examined by David Epstein in Part Five.

Most migrants develop and utilize both individual and group-oriented strategies. However, individualistic strategies tend to be more typical among migrants in Western society and particularly among better educated, middle-class migrants who have a better understanding of how the urban system operates. We get a sense of this in Walter Zenner's reflections on his migration from Chicago to Albany, New York in the afterword to this part. The more individualistic approach is also characteristic of the adjustment of students who go away to college, and again when they move to a new location after graduation. When my students leave Union College in a small town in upstate New York and begin their working careers in New York City, Boston, San Francisco, etc., they do it largely on their own. Seldom do they already have friends or family there who can assist them in getting settled and in getting acclimated to the new place and people.

Strategies in which the migrant relies upon kinfolk and fellow ethnics for help in getting established in the city are most common among tribal and peasant migrants in the cities of developing countries. Examples, however, also can be found in the United States, such as migrants from the hollows of Appalachia who rely heavily upon their kin already residing in midwestern industrial cities to help them find jobs and get a foothold in the city.

Migration Intentions

Not all migrants who arrive in the city remain permanently. Some return home; others move on to other cities or emigrate to a new country. Many persons moving to the city go as *temporary* migrants who do not intend to stay. They migrate only with the intention of accomplishing a specific objective, usually saving a sum of money. In some societies the dominant migration pattern is a circular one in which individuals move back and forth periodically between their rural homes and urban centers. This pattern, known as "circular migration," is essentially a movement between two economic systems, with villagers leaving the rural area where resources are limited for the city where they can obtain wage-earning jobs. While migrants may spend much time in the city and develop a network of social ties there, their primary identification remains with their home villages. Once enough money has been earned to satisfy their consumption needs at home, they return to their villages and remain there either permanently or until economic need propels them once again to the city in search of work.

There are also migrants who intend or at least hope to make the city their permanent home but are forced to return, often because of family circumstances, such as the need to look after ill or elderly parents, or because of a failure to find work. Still others may return because they cannot adapt. This is more often the case in international migration where persons are moving not only from a rural to an urban setting but to an unknown setting in a new society with language, customs, and people that are strange to them. Unless they have kinfolk or belong to a voluntary association or some other support group, the psychic pain of being separated from close friends and the familiarity and security of the home environment may be too much to bear.

Surprisingly, it's only been in the last two decades that many social scientists have given much attention to the tens of thousands of migrants worldwide who have returned home. Yet, as early as 1885, E.G. Ravenstein wrote an article, "The Laws of Migration," in which he included the principle of return migration in his renowned list of migration laws: "Each main current of migration produces a compensating counter-current." The view of migration as a once-and-only phenomenon probably arose from the nineteenth-century transatlantic migrations from Europe and Asia to North America. It was this transatlantic movement of peoples that captured the interest of early migration scholars and that dominated migration studies until after World War II. But even in this massive movement there were many migrants who later returned to their homelands, including an estimated one quarter of the sixteen million Europeans who arrived in the United States during the early decades of this century. Yet they were barely noticed by social scientists. In an exhaustive migration bibliography published by J.J. Mangalam in 1968, only ten of the more than two thousand titles listed were studies of return migration.

Robert Rhoades has suggested several other reasons for the neglect of return migration. The massive urbanization occurring in most parts of the world led to a "rural-urban" analytical framework in which geographical movements were viewed as occurring in one direction only—rural to urban. The nature of traditional anthropological fieldwork which involved research for a limited period of time (customarily one year) in a limited space (a single village) may have also led to a view of migration as a static event. Finally, return is the most difficult aspect of the migration cycle to quantify. Most nations do not have reliable means of gathering information on returning citizens. When returnees pass through the immigration lines at most airports they are indistinguishable from fellow expatriot citizens who are coming home for a vacation only, not to resettle.

In the last three decades, anthropology and its sister disciplines have begun to treat migration as a system, examining both stream and counter-stream, and working at both ends—sending and receiving societies. In this section, the essays by Caroline Brettell on Portuguese women migrants in Paris, George Gmelch on West Indians in London, and Robert Rhoades on Spanish migrants who had returned from Germany to their home villages, deal with migration as a cycle, treating migrants at both ends—Portugal and France, Barbados and England, and Spain and Germany, respectively.

Studying Migration

Migration, unlike weddings, festivals, funerals, and many other cultural phenomena, is not a readily observable event (cf. Gmelch 1992). There are no artifacts or special material culture; there are few if any rituals and little public behavior related to migration. If one is investigating the adaptations of migrants after they have arrived in the host society, then of course a wide range of behavior is observable. But ordinarily most of the stuff of migration involves spontaneous discussions, debates, and decisions, which usually take place in the privacy of the home. And in most communities few families are actively planning to migrate at any one time. There are exceptions: famine, natural disasters, and war provoke large-scale migration. (But we call the subjects or victims "refugees," rather than migrants.) In the course of an anthropologist's normal term of fieldwork, migration is a rare event. In fact, only one family emigrated from the Barbadian village during the three field seasons, totaling nine months, that I lived there doing a study of return migration. Hence, anthropologists often must rely on the migrants' own detailed accounts of their decision making and behavior. Such accounts are usually elicited in a series of intensive, open-ended interviews in which migration is explored in the larger context of an individual's life. In this section we see examples of this in the essays by Simić, Gmelch, and to a lesser degree, Brettell and Nelson.

Because migration invariably involves two or more locations—the community migrants leave and the places they move to—it is usually not feasible, financially or logistically, for the investigator to do research in both locations. This is particularly so when the migration is international. Traditionally, there has been a division of labor: some anthropologists work in the villages and towns of the sending societies, often examining the reasons for the migrants' departure and the impact of their absence, while others work in the host societies, often studying the migrants' adaptation in the new, usually urban setting (e.g., Kemper's study of Tzintzuntzeños in Mexico City, and Nelson's Kenyan women in Nairobi).

One consequence of social scientists working at only one end of the migration chain has been a failure to appreciate the systemic nature of migration, that while migrants may be far from their homelands, they are still embedded in and affected by social networks and dyadic relations that reach back to the village. As noted earlier, the kind of fieldwork that anthropologists traditionally do—participant-observation in a single community for a set period of time—led to a view of migration as a one-way movement, as a static event. And the snapshot view of migration produced by this fieldwork often failed to note that many migrants eventually returned home, that for every migration flow there was a counterstream. The life history approach (used in whole or part in the essays by Simić, Gmelch, Nelson, and Brettell in this section) has been one strategy for getting around this problem. Life history is not constrained by time and space, and thus it is well suited to exploring migration's cyclical nature.

An Alternative Approach: Macro-Level Analysis

It is important, also, to call attention to the work of a few scholars who are attempting macro-level analyses of migration. Their approach, sometimes termed the "historical-structural" (as opposed to the micro-level "culturalist" approach adopted in this book), focuses on the contexts of population movements (Kemper 1979:10). Migration is seen as the dependent variable in a larger process involving an economic imbalance between the highly urban, industrialized societies and regions of the world and the rural, largely agrarian societies and regions. This perspective is found in varying forms, including the "dependency theory" and the "internal colonialism" and "center-periphery" models.

The problem for future migration scholars will be how best to integrate the micro-level analyses, such as those of the anthropologists represented in this reader, with the macro-level analyses of some anthropologists, political economists, and others. As Robert Kemper states, the issue is "how can we cross the 'frontier' between the culturalist and historical-structuralist territories without, on the one hand, sacrificing the fine-grained ethnographic fieldwork among individuals and small groups or, on the other, ignoring the important national/international forces which influence the migration process" (1979:10).

George Gmelch

Migration and Adaptation
Tzintzuntzeños in Mexico City and Beyond

ROBERT V. KEMPER

Through the writings of George M. Foster, the Mexican village of Tzintzuntzan has become well known to students of peasant societies. Robert V. Kemper, a former student of Foster's, has followed the migration of Tzintzuntzeños to Mexico City and to many other destinations beyond the capital. In this essay, Kemper examines the adaptive strategies of the Tzintzuntzeño migrants in the areas of residential behavior, group organization, employment, and in their psychological adjustment to urban life. The Tzintzuntzeños rely more on themselves and their immediate families in coping with city life than do the Egyptian migrants described by Abu-Lughod. Moreover, Tzintzuntzan has become the focus of a spatially dispersed "extended community" involving both villagers and migrants.

During the half century since Oscar Lewis (1952) carried out his pioneering fieldwork in Mexico City, in which he suggested that migrants from the village of Tepoztlán undergo "urbanization without breakdown," anthropologists have devoted considerable attention to cityward migration in Latin America. The causes and patterns of migration, its effects on communities of origin and destination, and the characteristics of the migrants have been investigated. However, the emphasis of anthropological research has been on the processes and strategies of adaptation among

Source: Article written expressly for *Urban Life*.

metropolitan migrants. A common approach to studying migration and adaptation involves examination of migrants from a *single* community of origin to one or more urban destinations. Ideally, a fieldworker will generate a detailed longitudinal data base that will permit analysis of continuity and change over an entire generation. This was Lewis's plan for his Tepoztlán-Mexico City research project, and it is my plan for the study of migrants from the community of Tzintzuntzan in Mexico City and beyond.[1]

The Tzintzuntzan Migration Project

From the initial period of fieldwork in 1969–1970, this investigation has been conceived as a logical outgrowth of George M. Foster's (1948, 1967) long-term study of the people of Tzintzuntzan, a *mestizo* peasant village located on the shores of Lake Pátzcuaro about four hundred kilometers west of Mexico City. When I arrived (with my wife) in Mexico City, I had a list of about twenty migrants' names and just two addresses; when I departed the field sixteen months later, I had gathered information on nearly five hundred persons involved with Tzintzuntzan migrant households in Mexico City. During this first phase of fieldwork, I used the standard array of anthropological data-gathering procedures: participant observation, censuses, household budget surveys, in-depth interviews, questionnaires, projective tests (Thematic Apperception Test), and life histories.

Subsequently, I conducted a mid-decade ethnographic survey of the Tzintzuntzan migrants in the capital and, using a key informant in each village neighborhood, collected individual and family-level data on migrants' destinations—to Mexico City and elsewhere. Results of this fieldwork and the companion village survey showed that the migrant population had increased 23 percent to reach a total of about 630 persons in just four years. By summer 1974, there were at least 105 identifiable household units located in more than fifty *colonias* (neighborhoods) within the greater metropolitan area of Mexico City. The recent arrivals tended to move directly to peripheral housing areas, thus continuing the center to periphery pattern of mobility found among the earlier migrants.

In 1979–80, I (and my wife) spent nearly fifteen months in Mexico City among the migrants as well as with the people of Tzintzuntzan in the home village. We gathered data on around 1,000 persons living in some 200 households dispersed around the Mexico City metropolitan area. In addition, with the help of some of the migrants themselves, I obtained information on Tzintzuntzeños in several other Mexican provincial cities. I also extended my own fieldwork to the states of California and Illinois in the United States. This additional fieldwork yielded data on about 700 people living in 150 households beyond what we had found in Mexico City.

In 1982, 1984, 1986, and 1988, I continued the biennial village-based survey of population changes in Tzintzuntzan that I had begun in 1974 and had continued in 1976 and 1978 before assisting Foster with the complete census of the village in 1980. Thus, when I began to prepare for the 1990 census of the village and migrants of Tzintzuntzan, I had come to conceive of this population as a spatial and temporal social field focused on Tzintzuntzan, but with extensions to Mexico City, other urban and rural places in Mexico, and even sites across the border in the United States. In sum, my problem had expanded beyond the original study of migrants in Mexico City to become a comprehensive long-term study of the people of Tzintzuntzan, migrants and villagers alike.

Since completion of the 1990 ethnographic census—including more than 3,000 persons in Tzintzuntzan itself and another 3,000 migrants spread among metropolitan Mexico City, provincial Mexican communities, and diverse towns and cities in California, Illinois, and, the most recent destination of choice, the state of Washington—I have continued with the biennial surveys in 1992 and 1994. As a result, we have a substantial body of ethnographic information about the people and processes involved in migration from the community of Tzintzuntzan.

Buscar La Vida: The Decision to Emigrate

In the period since World War II, the forces of technology and economic modernization have permanently transformed life in thousands of Mexican villages, and Tzintzuntzan is no exception. Through the effects of health and sanitation campaigns, the once stable population of Tzintzuntzan had by 1970 more than doubled to 2,200 persons and by 1990 had surpassed 3,000. Penetration of the community by highway, rail, radio, and television networks has greatly increased its participation in national affairs. The growing tourist market for the locally produced pottery and crafts and the active involvement of villagers in the *bracero* program of the 1950s and early 1960s (and continuing involvement in legal and illegal labor migration to the United States) have combined to raise the standard of living for nearly all Tzintzuntzan residents. The construction of a secondary school in the village (in conjunction with the remodeling of the old primary school) in the mid-1970s also stimulated interest in the world beyond the local community.

In this context, migration is becoming a routine matter for the people of Tzintzuntzan. Between 1930 and 1940, when nearly one of every nine Mexicans was moving across state boundaries, only a handful of Tzintzuntzeños ventured outside of the state of Michoacán. In contrast, about 15 percent of all village households had one or more members leave the state between 1960 and 1970, and the proportion had passed 20 percent by the 1990s. This proportion is in line with the current national average for interstate migration. Although a small number of Tzintzuntzan peasants are forced to leave the village to avoid retribution or prosecution for criminal acts, the majority are eager to leave. In their words, they emigrate to *buscar la vida*, to search for life.

Tzintzuntzan migrants in Mexico City offer many reasons for having left the village to pursue the "good life" in the capital. Emiliano Guzmán, a twenty-nine-year-old factory worker, laments the lack of progress in Tzintzuntzan while reciting his opportunities for steady, albeit low-paying, employment in Mexico City. José Zavala, a middle-aged teacher, recalls the tranquility and pleasant pace of village life in contrast to the overcrowded, smoggy, and hectic metropolis—but in the same breath admits that there is no job for him in the village. Raúl Silva dislikes being separated from friends and relatives in the city but at the same time admits that he has no wish to go back to Tzintzuntzan to become a potter like his father. Others make similar comments when asked why they migrated. Taken as a whole, they weigh the good and bad of village and city, and—like peasants the world over—opt for urban life.

As these examples show, the people of Tzintzuntzan have learned to treat migration as an option to remaining in the village. The decision to migrate is not always simple, nor related directly to visible economic conditions. Tzintzuntzeños select destinations based on their perceptions of available opportunities which they learn about through friends and relatives who already have experiences beyond the local scene. In this regard, we may speak of migration *strategies* by which villagers manipulate (although not always maximize) available contacts to improve their situations.

Rufino, and many other Tzintzuntzeños like him, can survive their initial encounters with urban life because when they arrive in the capital they can stay *arrimado* ("up close to," i.e., as a guest) with relatives or friends already established in the city. These ties to "senior" migrants have been important in the initial urban experiences of more than 90 percent of Tzintzuntzeños now living in Mexico City. The *arrimado* network—with the promises of assistance in finding housing and work—is certainly responsible for much of the growth in the migrant group in Mexico City. Complex social networks now bridge the gap between village and metropolis, transforming what once were individual migration itineraries into a continuing and expanding social process. The set of actors is constantly changing, with each new migrant profiting from the experiences—pleasant and unpleasant—of friends and relatives who preceded him to the capital.

Although the migrants' first residence in Mexico City is usually arranged through friends or relatives, the choice is also constrained by governmental and private sector forces beyond their control. For instance, the prohibition on new residential subdivisions within the Federal District, which was in effect from 1952 to 1970, severely restricted the housing options for new arrivals and for the urban middle class. Rent control policies in the central city zones have had similar effects. As a result, most Tzintzuntzeños now live near the metropolitan periphery, with perhaps half living outside of Mexico City proper.

These limitations on the urban housing stock have encouraged many migrants to reconsider traditional family and household arrangements. Although the conjugal family remains important, enclaves of extended families have appeared in several neighborhoods. Some migrants rent adjacent rooms in a *vecindad* (low-income apartment units) while others purchase lots with kinfolk and share the burden of house building. These urban residential strategies are not mere recreations of the village patterns of living, but have evolved in an effort to conserve limited financial and social resources in an overcrowded metropolitan environment.

In recent years, especially since the 1985 earthquake, Mexico City has lost much of its appeal to migrants from Tzintzuntzan. The economic "crisis" of the 1980s has shifted many migrants' eyes to the north. Tzintzuntzeños who learned to use their connections earlier in Mexico City now use the same strategies on the other side of the border. The creation of small enclaves in certain areas—such as South Chicago, Orange County in California, and in and around Tacoma, Washington—provides the social support system they need to "search for life" beyond Tzintzuntzan.

Organizational Strategies: The Agrupación and Beyond

One way in which many migrant groups maximize their limited resources in urban settings is to establish village-based or regional associations. Until recently, however, the Tzintzuntzan migrants had no such voluntary association and they had little sense of "community" in Mexico City. Absence of such an association meant that social integration among the migrants rested solely on kinship, friendship, or *compadrazgo* (ritual co-parenthood) ties, often established before migration. In addition, the limited social relations among migrants has encouraged an outward search for potentially useful contacts in the city.

Expansion of a migrant's reference group beyond fellow migrants and villagers is a critical phase in the process of urban social adaptation. Urbanization thrusts Tzintzuntzeños into a new social domain: the two great categories of peasant life—"villagers" vs. "outsiders"—are blurred and ultimately obliterated through daily participation in city life. Surviving in the city beyond the initial period of adjustment requires ties with persons beyond the migrant group; the most successful migrants have often drifted away from the other Tzintzuntzeños in the capital as they pursue better jobs, housing, and education for themselves and their families.

In this context, can the *Agrupación* (association) of Tzintzuntzan migrants succeed in creating a sense of community among a

The banner of the Agrupación at the home of a Tzintzuntzan migrant family in Mexico City (1975). [Photo by Robert V. Kemper]

growing and increasingly diverse population? Founded in 1975 by a socially minded school principal nearing retirement age, the Agrupación is intended to provide the migrants a common identity by making annual pilgrimages to Tzintzuntzan during the village's patron saint's festival. Beyond this ritual activity, the Agrupación is chartered to provide nominal social assistance to needy migrants and its members pledge to "struggle to maintain a closeness that will permit them to help one another in their physical, spiritual, social, and cultural problems."

Until the establishment of the Agrupación, the Tzintzuntzeños in the capital never united to press for political favors, economic benefits, or social services. Their geographic and socioeconomic diversity prevented them from organizing. The Agrupación has been helpful in supporting village efforts to construct a secondary school in Tzintzuntzan and it has also made donations for the work of the church in Tzintzuntzan. On the other hand, the efforts of the Agrupación's leader to involve the entire membership in a campaign to "bring to justice" a villager who killed the leader's brother during a recent Tzintzuntzan fiesta created considerable controversy among members. In effect, the Agrupación is splitting along traditional kinship and friendship lines rather than providing a mechanism for consolidating the migrants.

More importantly, the Agrupación is primarily a middle-class professional phenomenon. Very few working-class migrants have been recruited into the membership, even though they represent two-thirds of all migrants. Thus, the Agrupación appears to perpetuate—and reinforce—the class barriers among Tzintzuntzan migrants in Mexico City. The differential success of certain migrant families—often linked to their status in Tzintzuntzan prior to emigration—has virtually created two migrant groups within the capital rather than one. Those in the working class turn to fellow workers for help; professionals limit their social interaction to middle- and upper-class colleagues. Extended family ties within the migrant population closely follow class lines and extensions of a migrant's reference group to non-Tzintzuntzeño urbanites do little to create a sense of community among the migrants.

This emphasis on individualistic solutions to social organizational issues does not mean that Tzintzuntzeños are floundering in an impersonal urban world. On the contrary, many belong to unions, neighborhood organizations (e.g., to maintain streets), and parish groups, although few appear to be active in the political arena. When they gather for weddings, baptisms, funerals, and holiday fiestas, the migrants usually entertain a mix of fellow migrants and other urban residents.

When the founder of the Agrupación was killed in an automobile crash in the early 1980s, the fate of the Agrupación was sealed. No leader emerged to assume his role and the pilgrimages to the village ceased. On the other hand, the strong orientation to the home community has not been abandoned. Most Tzintzuntzan migrants in the capital and elsewhere return to the village to celebrate important fiestas, to baptize and confirm their children within the Catholic parish located in Tzintzuntzan, and to renew their ties with family and friends on occasions such as weddings and funerals.

Palancas:
The Struggle for Economic Success

Tzintzuntzeños hold many types of jobs in Mexico City. They are employed as factory workers, school teachers, civil servants, store clerks, musicians, and even as pharmacists, translators, and computer analysts. Many migrant households have more than a single wage earner (the average is 1.75 workers per household), but few individuals attempt to maintain two separate jobs. The unemployment rate among the migrants is quite low (about 7 percent), and rates of upward economic mobility appear to be at least as high as for the rest of the urban population.

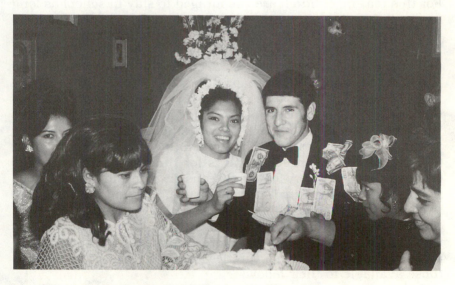

A wedding reception among middle-class Tzintzuntzan migrants in Mexico City (1970). Note the money attached to the groom's jacket. [Photo by Robert V. Kemper]

Most Tzintzuntzan migrants come to the capital without a job assured; instead, they hope to find work through the assistance of relatives and friends already working there. Thus, in addition to providing temporary lodging, the more experienced migrants often serve as *palancas* ("levers") in finding jobs for new arrivals. The length of time needed to find a "good" job depends on the migrant's personal attributes (especially, his previous work experience and educational background), on the sequence and quality of his experiences outside of Tzintzuntzan, and on his own definition of what constitutes adequate employment. Generally, the migrants find some work immediately upon arrival, but a satisfying job seldom comes quickly. After some initial job instability, most migrants settle into relatively permanent niches. This does not mean that they retain the same job year after year; on the contrary, they continually search for better opportunities, with the final decision to change careers or company affiliations determined by their perception of the best available combination of wages, tenure, and social security benefits.

Few migrants expect to get wealthy in Mexico City, but some hope to make the critical shift from manual to "professional" jobs, and most believe (or hope) that their children will enter the ranks of white-collar workers. The Tzintzuntzeños are well aware that it is difficult to get ahead without adequate educational and job training. For this reason, children are encouraged to stay in school as long as possible and to obtain the best "credentials" possible. Indeed, in recent years, one of the main reasons for the emigration of young people from Tzintzuntzan is to get an advanced education, which will then open doors to professional employment opportunities in Mexico City and in other urban centers.

A shift from traditional to modern concepts of "success" is an integral part of the process of economic adaptation to urban life. When the migrants compare their positions with those of their parents or siblings still in Tzintzuntzan, nearly all conclude that the city offers the better prospects for themselves and for their children. Moreover, very few would consider returning to the village as an alternative to seeking other urban employment if they were to lose their current positions. The most important shift, however, occurs when the migrants come to realize that a dependence on their fellow migrants poses severe limitations on their urban prospects, since their opportunities are unlikely to be superior to those available to their fellows.

Tzintzuntzeños in Mexico City eventually recognize that, while fellow migrants are keys to the initial job, long-term economic success is the result of individual initiative, hard work, and a good network of migrant and non-migrant palancas. As one migrant remarked, "What are my dreams? Well, with hard work a person begins to think about his future, in having his own home, in helping his children and in seeing them achieve a social and economic level that he himself doesn't enjoy."

The experiences of the migrants in Mexico City are also seen in the lives of those who have settled in provincial Mexican towns or have traveled great distances to work in the United States. They begin with their connections to other Tzintzuntzeños but soon look for others who can help them find stable, well-paying jobs. Even illegal migrants to the United States, most of whom spend only part of each year in the north, depend on their *palancas* for obtaining jobs and housing. The steady increase in the number of villagers who have experiences outside Tzintzuntzan has made an awareness of the importance of these social and economic ties a standard part of the "migrant culture" of Tzintzuntzeños.

Imagen Del Mundo: Psychological Adaptation to Migrant Life

Migrating from Tzintzuntzan not only involves people in new residential, organizational, and occupational strategies, it also may require modification of an individual's *imagen del mundo* ("worldview"). The psychological dimensions of urban adaptation must be understood not merely in terms of a rural-urban continuum but also in terms of the relative socioeconomic positions occupied by migrants before and after they leave the village. If a migrant holds values inappropriate for city life, these may not be *rural* values, but attitudes acquired in the process of interacting in situations where they have been defined as an inferior.

Tzintzuntzeños near the bottom of the socioeconomic scale in Mexico City face pressures and frustrations which parallel those of the poorest peasants in the village. For both groups, their concern is day-to-day survival, not upward mobility. Of course, since most migrants come from the better educated, more affluent, and more ambitious village families, their economic success in the capital is not surprising. Those migrants with steady urban jobs tend to have an optimistic worldview in which a pragmatic balance is struck between present needs and future hopes. The idea of most working-class Tzintzuntzeños in the capital is to provide a base upon which their children can build even better lives.

Downtown Mexico City, near the stock exchange. [Photo by Shelton Schmidt]

The small but growing number of professional-level migrants often face a frustration common to middle sectors of many urban societies. They may earn quite respectable wages, but they can rarely hope to belong to the elite groups whom they emulate. The psychological dangers of excessive "social climbing" haunt long-term as well as recent migrants. For example, the Zavala family was eager to send their daughter to a private academy—preferably, a French-speaking school—because they wanted her to receive a "proper" education (which to them meant an upper-class, foreign-oriented curriculum). Ultimately, however, the financial drain outweighed the benefits, and they enrolled her in the inexpensive public high school near their apartment. Subsequently, she has entered a professional school where she is being trained to work in the growing field of tourism. In this case, the Zavala's reference group was not compatible with their means. Their excessive drive brought with it a greater psychological malaise than if they had been content with their actual middle-class status.

This concern for education as the means to upward social and economic mobility is a key indicator that a "modern" worldview has become dominant among most migrants—as well as among the village families who are now sending their children to the secondary school in Tzintzuntzan or to boarding schools in other communities. The emphasis on education implies a strong achievement motivation and a healthy future orientation. These values are especially strong among young professionals. For example, Martin Calva works as a well-paid government employee in the computer analysis division of the Treasury Department. He has moved steadily up the job ladder so that he now has a nice home in which his wife, child, and younger siblings reside. Just as his relatives helped him through the university a decade ago, so he now assists a chain of his own brothers and sisters to get an education and move ahead in the urban system. Martín Calva and other migrants reason that if a primary school certificate was enough to lift an earlier generation of migrants out of the village and into a working-class job in Mexico City, then a secondary or university diploma should guarantee their children a professional position.

Unfortunately, the gap between working class and middle class is too wide for many people to bridge in a single generation. Furthermore, the competition for civil service jobs and professional (e.g., doctors, lawyers, engineers) positions throughout Mexican society has become increasingly arduous since the economic "crisis" of the 1980s. To fulfill their dreams of upward mobility, young migrants have had to reevaluate Mexico City as a destination. Often, they opt to go north to the United States, even if it means trading professional status for manual work. For instance, one man with an engineering degree left the capital in the late 1980s and took his family to live near Tacoma, where he continues to labor in the agricultural fields. He earns more money and feels better about the future for his children in the north than if he had remained in Mexico City.

Conclusion

Most early discussions of migrant adaptation in Latin American cities were framed in terms of the Great Dichotomy, usually labeled "folk-urban" or "rural-urban." A significant corollary of this dichotomous view suggested that cityward migrants from "rural" areas ought to experience major difficulties in adjusting to "urban" culture. Such difficulties were supposed to result in culture conflicts, disorganization of traditional lifestyles, personal anomie and alienation, and breakdown of primary group affiliations. This model of the urbanization process, which Lewis attacked so effectively in his study of Tepoztlán and Mexico City, suffers from a fatal flaw: it is static, and thus fails to account for the continuing changes in the rural communities of origin, in the urban communities of destination, and in the migrants themselves.

In contrast, numerous recent studies demonstrate that contemporary processes of economic and social development in countries such as Mexico are creating an increasingly unified system in which villages and cities each play important roles. Rather than focusing on the separation of city and countryside, social scientists now recognize the interdependencies that connect a metropolis like Mexico City with a village like Tzintzuntzan. The evidence gathered over the past twenty-five years shows clearly that, far from being passive pawns moved by impersonal economic and political forces, Tzintzuntzan migrants are active agents in shaping their own destinies and, in turn, the future of Mexico. Moreover, as Tzintzuntzan shifted from the "pioneer" migrations of the 1940s and 1950s to the "mass" migrations of the 1960s and 1970s, so a new phase dawned in the 1980s and continues in the 1990s.

Tzintzuntzeños have created an effective "extended community" as their migrations have spread beyond Mexico City to encompass other provincial towns and, increasingly, focused on temporary and permanent settlement in the United States. The people of Tzintzuntzan, like those of many other Mexican communities, have learned that they can sustain substantial levels of migration without losing their sense of local community and cultural distinctiveness. Migrants who live in Mexico City, in Guadalajara, in the border city of Tijuana, as well as those as far away as Tacoma, Washington, find their way back to Tzintzuntzan nearly every year to participate in the local fiestas and other special occasions—and thus to reconfirm their membership in this "extended community."

What will the situation be like in the year 2000 or in 2010 and beyond? By then, we will be working with the great-grandchildren of the adults known to Foster when he began his village fieldwork in 1945 and the grandchildren of those I first knew when I began my own work in 1969. If Tzintzuntzan continues to develop as a center for a spatially diverse population, spreading from Mexico City to the United States, it will represent a serious challenge to us as anthropologists to carry out long-term field research. In the process we also will discover if ideas about migration and adaptation developed in the 1960s and 1970s—when I began my field research in Mexico City—will still be useful in framing research questions about the international systems of social action and political-economy in which the lives of Tzintzuntzeño villagers and migrants are increasingly grounded.

Note

[1] For additional information about the Tzintzuntzan Migration Project, see Kemper 1977, 1981, 1994.

Bogdan's Story
The Adaptation of a Rural Family to Yugoslavian Urban Life

ANDREI SIMIĆ

*In the years following the Second World War, the rapid
expansion of the Yugoslav economy and the bureaucracy
brought about the migration of millions of peasants into urban
centers. Andrei Simić finds that, in contrast to some peoples in
other parts of the world, these migrants quickly became
assimilated into city life. They exhibited few of the signs of
social pathology or social breakdown described by Louis Wirth
in Part One. Simić concludes that this has been possible
because urbanization in Yugoslavia has taken place principally
during a period of economic growth and within the context of a
relatively stable system of traditional values shared by
urbanites and villagers alike. Simić looks at this phenomenon
through the life history of a single migrant, Bogdan, whose
success in Belgrade is largely typical of the experiences of
South Slav rural-urban migrants as a whole.*

*The use of life history in this essay, as well as in "A West
Indian Life" by G. Gmelch, provides an insider's account of
migration, revealing the subjective world of attitudes, feelings,
and emotions. This is a perspective not often found in most
studies of migration, which are typically based on etic methods,
where the emphasis is on the general rather than the
individual. In Bogdan's story, as in Roy Campbell's story in the
following essay, and in the experiences of the women migrants
in Nairobi described by Nici Nelson, we learn the context in*

Source: Article written expressly for *Urban Life*.

which decisions, choices, and social acts occur. These paint a picture of migration which is not only rich in detail and texture but shows migration to be more complex and varied than etically based generalizations often suggest.

Following the close of the Second World War, the Yugoslavs, like rural peoples all over the world, opted for urban life with an almost uncritical faith in the promises of industrialization and modernization. However, unlike many of their counterparts in other developing countries, their experience was largely a positive one. While this was especially true during the three decades of initial urbanization, even up to the recent dissolution of Yugoslavia one finds minimal evidence by world standards of the kinds of social and cultural marginality that typify what Lewis (1966) has labeled "the culture of poverty." This was despite the fact that the size of most Yugoslav towns and cities more than doubled and other, serious socioeconomic problems existed, such as runaway inflation (in 1987 exceeding 100 percent a year[1]), chronic unemployment, a cash-poor economy, low productivity and the relative lack of a work ethic, an acute housing shortage, inadequate and inefficient public services, and increasing ethnic and political unrest. The smooth integration of millions of former peasants into the fabric of urban life has largely contradicted the age-old stereotype that urbanism inevitably leads to every sort of social pathology and disorganization (cf. Wirth 1938). Rather, the South Slav experience confirms Lewis's (1952) contention that the process by which rural peoples move to cities and adapt to conditions there will differ from one historical and cultural setting to another.

Yugoslav Urbanization

Yugoslavia, like the rest of the Balkans, has a very ancient history of urban life. For instance, Belgrade, the national capital, was the site of a Roman citadel and town called Singidunum and, dating from at least A.D. 100, has been continuously occupied up to the present. However, through the mid-twentieth century, Yugoslav cities remained remote, provincial centers of traditional Middle Eastern, Mediterranean, or Central European types, thus reflecting the diverse influences of the three great civilizations which met on this southeastern frontier of Europe. For the most part, Balkan urban populations existed, until recently, as small islands in a vast sea of peasantry.

At the close of the Second World War, Yugoslavia ranked with Albania, Malta, and Portugal as one of the four least-urbanized countries in Europe, with under 20 percent of its people living in centers with populations over twenty thousand. Not a single paved road joined its two largest cities, Belgrade and Zagreb, and, even in 1961, only a little over 11 percent of the population gained its livelihood from industry, with almost 60 percent still dependent on peasant agriculture. However, under the influence of an ambitious plan of industrialization and modernization initiated by Tito's socialist government, there began a significant shift away from peasant agriculture, which, by 1964, accounted for only about 20 percent of the national income. Economic change and the rapid postwar expansion of the bureaucracy brought about mass migrations from the countryside into the towns and cities. Clearly, as elsewhere, the motivation to leave ancestral villages in favor of urban life can be explained as a reaction to perceived unfavorable rural conditions in contrast to positive expectations regarding the city, what social scientists have labeled the *push-pull syndrome.* In this respect, Hoyt, Hoffman, and Neal (1962:485) estimate that, in the period immediately following the war, the level of migration to Yugoslav urban centers was 380,000 migrants per year. The Belgrade experience is typical of this trend. Its population increased from approximately 365,000 in 1948 to 697,000 in 1965, and, by 1982, numbered almost 1.5 million (Savezni Zavod za Statistiku, 1982). This augmentation represents more than a fourfold increase in less than four decades, almost all of it attributable to the influx from the countryside.

Belgrade, which was, until recently, the capital of both Yugoslavia and the Republic of Serbia, reflects in microcosm the transformations wrought by the past 150 years of Balkan history. It was only a little over one hundred years ago that Ali Rizah Pasha, by order of the Ottoman Sultan, surrendered Belgrade's Kalemegdan Fortress, thus relinquishing the last symbol of almost five hundred years of Turkish domination. At that time, the Serbian capital was little more than a dusty Moslem market town and garrison. During the following decades, the city grew to become the modest intellectual and administrative center of Serbia with twenty-four thousand residents in 1867. The vacuum created by the retreating Turks was quickly filled by a new native artisan class, the bourgeoisie, and an elite, drawn to a large degree from the indigenous peasantry.

Another period of modest expansion followed the First World War, when Belgrade became the capital of the newly created Kingdom of the Serbs, Croats and Slovenes (later named Yugoslavia). However, the city remained an essentially quasi-Oriental backwater with a superficially Western European façade. During World War

II, many of the modest gains of the interwar period were lost when the city was severely damaged during the German invasion and occupation. With the defeat and expulsion of the Axis powers, due in large part to the efforts of the Yugoslavs themselves, Belgrade became the hub of a new Marxist state and, as Hammel (1969:25) points out, "the final Yugoslav station on the Serbian road to success in migration."[2]

Although Belgrade was the capital of the most multiethnic state in Europe, excluding the Soviet Union, it remained, at the same time, a predominantly Serbian city, Eastern Orthodox by religious tradition (if not practice) and non-Western in its historical and cultural orientation.[3] This ethnic specificity of Belgrade holds particular significance for the integration of peasants into urban life, since rural-urban mobility in Yugoslavia has largely followed internal cultural boundaries. Of equal importance is the fact that, while Yugoslav cities such as Belgrade have been profoundly influenced by rural culture, there has occurred a simultaneous modernization of the countryside (Halpern and Kerewsky-Halpern 1986). Thus, no sharp cleavage has developed between these two major segments of the society. Not only do most Yugoslav families trace direct origins from the peasantry, but, even today, they maintain close ties with village kin regardless of their socioeconomic and educational levels. In this respect, an ideology of kinship solidarity associated with an earlier period of Balkan history and typified by large, patrilocally extended households (the *zadruga*) continues to play a salient role, thus easing the stresses associated with rapid urbanization and economic development. This solidarity is expressed in the intense material and ritual reciprocity which links rural and urban kin and which demonstrates the ability of traditional South Slav culture to adapt to new conditions brought about by the transformation of Yugoslav society into a modern, industrial, urban state (Simić 1973; 1983).[4]

Rural-urban migration and urbanization are clearly the result of major economic and social trends rooted in large-scale historical antecedents; nevertheless, these phenomena are fundamentally the result of conscious choices made by individuals from among existing perceived alternatives. For instance, Max Weber (1892), in his classic study of German agrarian society at the close of the nineteenth century, found that, while migration of farm workers from eastern to western Germany could be explained in terms of fluctuations in the world market, in the final analysis, individual motivations played the decisive role. Thus, one way of understanding the dynamics of rural-urban migration and the accommodation to city life in Yugoslavia is to consider such

Peasants set up an informal marketplace in a Belgrade suburb. [Photo by Andrei Simić]

adaptation from the standpoint of the personal histories of those who have experienced this metamorphosis. In this respect, the story of Bogdan and his family is not atypical of the more than two hundred informants I have known over more than twenty years of periodic fieldwork in both rural and urban Yugoslavia. While the levels of success varied among the peasant migrants, in almost all of the case histories I have collected, the same motivations, values, and strategies appear. Thus, the character and fate of the nation can ultimately be seen to reside in the individual, and one is not intelligible without the understanding of the other.

Bogdan's Story*

The red-tiled roofs of Cerići's almost sixty households dot the green flanks of the valley, stretching for almost two kilometers, like so many Christmas ornaments, along the winding course of the Žabica

---

* The names of informants and their places of origin have been changed to protect their anonymity.

Creek. Today, a hard-surfaced, but narrow, road spans the twenty kilometers from the regional market town of Gornji Milanovac to the unpaved village plaza around which cluster the Byzantine-style Orthodox church, soccer field, four-year elementary school, and community meeting hall (*dom*). Parallel to the road, glistening wires stretched between crudely hewn trunks of young poplars unpredictably deliver power for the electric lights, sewing machines, television sets, stoves, and refrigerators which grace all but a few of the homes. Only a generation ago, Bogdan remembers, life was quite different here in the heart of Serbia, which is little more than an hour's drive south of Belgrade:

> In those days, there was no electricity, and we could barely afford the kerosene lamps which, in any case, we used sparingly. For the most part, we were up with the sun and to bed at dark. I often think of the late fall, when the village paths turned to mud, and how we sloshed through it in our leather moccasins [*opanci*] and scratchy, homespun wool socks. There were times, after the heavy snows, when we could not leave Cerići at all, and, in the best of weather, it took at least half a day to reach Gornji Milanovac by horse-drawn wagon. When we sold our produce at the town marketplace, we would leave in the middle of the night in order to be there by dawn. We were poor by any standard, yet our neighbors were no better off. We didn't feel inferior to anyone, and, after all, we are the descendants of generations of warriors who defended our Serbian traditions against the Turks! Nevertheless, I don't think I could return to the hardships of those times. But, the village is no longer like that, and I will never sever the ties to my birthplace or our kin who still live there.

As in many traditional agrarian societies, until recent times, much of rural Yugoslavia was characterized by widespread poverty. This was due in large part to the relative lack of land resources in respect to the size of the peasant population. In the case of Bogdan, this was a significant motivating factor for leaving the village:

> I lived in Cerići until I was 42—that was in 1950. I had only three hectares [about seven and a half acres] of unproductive land. Until just before my father's death in 1941, I lived in a *zadruga* [a patrilocally extended household] with my parents, my sister, and my five brothers and their families. There were twenty-two of us, including the children, and, even with fifteen hectares of land, we had a hard time. Just before my father died, he divided the holdings among us sons—my sister, of course, went to live on her husband's land after she got married. In order to support my wife and three children, I had to hire myself out doing any

jobs I could find. But the opportunities in the village were limited, and the pay almost nothing. After the war, I worked part time as a clerk in the Cerići agricultural cooperative, but this was barely enough to pay the taxes on our land. Between the five of us, we were somehow able to wrest a living from the soil—even our small children helped. Not that we lived well. We ate what we produced: fresh cheese, milk, beans, bread, onions, peppers, and cabbage for the most part. Meat was a rarity—we couldn't afford to slaughter our animals.

Among the most significant stimuli for migration was indirect contact with urban life through the experiences of relatives or neighbors who now lived in the city and who returned for frequent visits to the village. Through such relationships, it was possible not only to judge the chances of success in migration, but also to be assured of a helping hand during the difficult periods of settlement and accommodation to an unfamiliar environment and way of life:

After the war, we began hearing more and more about the opportunities in the city from neighbors and relatives who had gone to Gornji Milanovac or even Belgrade. I knew that there must be a better way of life than this. Actually, before the war, I had served a year in Zagreb while in the army, but in those days there were no jobs in town, and the urban poor lived worse than the peasants. In 1949, my wife's cousin, Panto, moved to Belgrade, where he found employment with a construction company, and, when my job with the village cooperative was abolished in 1950, I wrote him and asked him to help me obtain work there. Much to my surprise, he answered right away informing me that there was an opening with his concern as a clerk and that his boss would save the position for me, since he owed Panto a favor. I went immediately and stayed with Panto and his wife. My family remained in the village, and I visited them every weekend. Actually this worked out very well, since I could bring food from Cerići back to Belgrade and aid Panto by sharing it with him. I can't say I enjoyed living in Belgrade at first. I just worked and slept for the most part, saving as much money as I could. We ate what Panto and I would bring from the village, and I only spent my earnings for the bus tickets to Cerići. I wasn't like some others who, once they had a few dinars in their pockets, went wild, wasting their money in cafes on drink and Gypsy musicians!

After employment, the most basic problem facing a new migrant in Belgrade was housing. Without space for his family, he could not really be said to have put down roots in the city. The destruction due to the Second World War and the rapid increase in the urban population brought about a major housing crisis in all Yugoslav cities, and Belgrade was among the most acutely affected. In spite of the fact that one of the major tenets of the former Yugoslav socialist state when it came to power was that the government "owes each family an adequate dwelling unit with minimum standards," this remained largely empty rhetoric (Fisher 1966:144). Theoretically, housing could be obtained by impersonal means via the so-called socialist economic sector, that is, through government agencies or the enterprise where one is employed. In this respect, larger and more successful firms could frequently offer their workers modern housing, or an apartment could be obtained through the municipality, if one did not mind waiting for years. All of this could be expedited, of course, through friends or kin in important positions; however, most migrants had to fend for themselves. For an unskilled worker like Bogdan with a minimal education and few significant connections, the process of settling down was likely to be a long one. Thus, for the peasant migrant, there was usually a direct relationship between the length of time in the city and the quality of housing:

> I couldn't continue staying with Panto—he and Milena had only one room they rented from an old lady, and there was barely enough space for the two of them. After about two months, I managed to get a bed in a worker's barracks. There were about twenty of us in an old wooden building on the southern outskirts of the city. It was very cheap, but life was really worse than in the army or the village. There was only one cold-water tap outside, and the outhouse was always filthy. When it rained, the whole area flooded, and we had to wade through a mire of mud to get to the toilet. The entire place smelled of urine and feces. We workers tried to share our food and prepare meals together, but there was no kitchen, and we had only a small kerosene camp stove. In those days, I went home to Cerići as often as possible. About four months later, I found an old shack made of boards and galvanized iron sheets on an unpaved alley near the barracks. I was able to buy it, but not the land it stood on. It had one small room and a kitchen with a cold-water tap. There was no bathroom, just an outhouse, but, after all, that is what we were used to in the village. I bought a kerosene heater, but it did little to keep out the cold during the winter. In any case, I was able to call for my family and to provide a place for them to live. In the meantime, I found a better job through a distant relative as a clerk with the city government (*opština*). We stayed in the shack for almost three years, while we waited for the housing agency to give us an apartment. We were always short of money, and, if it weren't for the food from the village, we would have never made it. My wife finally found

Workers' "barracks" in the shadow of postwar Belgrade highrises. [Photo by Andrei Simić]

a job in a municipal office making Turkish coffee for the workers and cleaning up, a kind of caretaker, you might say. Finally, we received an apartment through the city in an old part of Belgrade. It was rather primitive, but very spacious with large porcelain stoves heated by coal. Also, for the first time in our lives, we had an indoor toilet, but no hot water. Nevertheless, we had never experienced better! My wife and I slept with the three children in one room just as we had in Cerići. We kept one room for a parlor, and another for guests from the village who were almost always with us. We discovered credit, and gradually began buying the furniture that we now have piece-by-piece. In the beginning, we simply borrowed a truck from a cousin who worked at a motor pool and brought what few things we needed from Cerići. I remember how we slept on homemade straw mattresses. I had no idea how uncomfortable we were! Well, finally they began the renewal of the neighborhood in which we lived, and our building was torn down. By law, when this occurs, a family must be given other housing of at least equal size. Since there was no such space then available, we received two apartments in this modern building where we live today. One was put in my name and the other in that of our son, Mile. We rent Mile's apartment out, even though this is not quite legal. When our daughter, Stana, gets married, it will be her dowry. Actually, we have had a good deal of luck, more than many others!

Bogdan's success in accommodating to Yugoslav urban life can be attributed, to a large degree, to the role of traditional culture and its associated values. In particular, kinship has provided this family with a ready-made set of resources, and, thus, precluded the kinds of alienation and social marginality that have typified rapid urbanization in many other parts of the world. Bogdan's case being not at all atypical, suggests that neither long residence nor even birth in the city necessarily weakens ties to the countryside. Indeed, many native Belgradians are as familiar with their parents', and even grandparents', villages as they are with the capital itself. Moreover, such rural-urban ties are not only of utility during the initial phase of settlement in the city, but may persist over an entire lifetime. For the urbanite, the village constitutes a source of foodstuffs, a place for summer vacations, and, perhaps most importantly, an insurance policy against failure in the city or economic crisis. For the peasant, city kin represent a source of cash for taxes and capital improvements, an initial base for the new migrant, and a place where children may stay while obtaining a higher education. In some cases, the urban household simply constitutes an extension of the village home, and many families continue to behave as if they were still a single unit with two or more residences. In other words, the urbanization of segments of rural-based kinship groups has simply opened up new avenues for continuing the same kinds of reciprocity that have always typified South Slav traditional culture. For example, twenty-four years after migrating to Belgrade, Bogdan was still interacting with both his and his wife's urban and rural kin as intensely as he had the day he left Cerići:

To tell you the truth, life in Cerići was not entirely bad, and, in some ways, it was much better than in the city. I particularly remember how we would look forward to village weddings, which usually lasted several days, and how we enjoyed going to Gornji Milanovac to the *vašar* [animal fair]. Actually, in reality, I still belong to the village. I never sold my land, but simply gave it to my brother, Branko, to work. Also, I have let

my nephew live in my house with his wife and three children.
That is the house where we were all born, and, even though it
is part of my share of the estate, it is really a family home, since
that is where our parents lived and died. You must understand
what I mean by family. In Cerići, there are seventeen households
of Mitrovići, and we are all related through our fathers. In fact,
the *mala* [neighborhood] where most of the family houses are
clustered is called Mitrovići. My wife is also close to her kin, and
we visit her village of Livadice as often as we do Cerići. Family
is family, and we remain close to our own no matter where they
may be or what they may have accomplished in life. We help
each other when we can. No one else will!

In 1974, when questioned about specific recent contacts with kin,
Bogdan gave the following account:

The fifteen-year-old daughter of my *sinovica* [brother's
daughter] spent ten days with us in August. Her mother,
Miroslava, spent two days here during the same month.
Miroslava's husband also visited us for a day in September.
Another sinovica, Jelena, came with her husband to stay for
several days in September. They are from the village of Beli
Potok near Belgrade. My brother Nikola came from the town of
Ivanjica for a day in October. My wife's unmarried sister from
Zemun [a town just across the Sava River from Belgrade] visits
us at least once a week. Another sister of my wife from Takovo
[a provincial town not far from Cerići] has already visited us four
times this year with her husband and five children. They always
bring us large amounts of food from their holdings in Livadice—
potatoes, garlic, onions, homemade sausages, and *rakija* [fruit
brandy]. The young daughter of my brother Milenko from Cerići
was with us for a month this summer, and Mira and Rada, the
two girls that are here right now, are cousins from the village.
Vaso, our *prijatelj* [in-law—the brother of Bogdan's wife's sister's
husband], who lives in Belgrade, drops by several times a week.
And, of course, my wife's cousin, Panto, and his wife live only
a few minutes walk from here, and we see each other quite often.
Frankly, we have so many visitors, it is hard to remember them
all. Our kin just come whenever they want. We don't expect
them to let us know ahead of time. And, we do the same! In June,
I went to Gornji Milanovac because I have been feeling badly
of late. There is a spa there and taking the water always makes
me feel better. I stayed with the daughter of my brother Branko
and her husband. He is an instructor in the secondary school
there. Of course, I didn't pay them anything, but I took a dress
for my niece and a sweater for her fifteen-year-old daughter. I
didn't go to Cerići while I was there, but at least a dozen of my
relatives came to see me in Gornji Milanovac. Some of my wife's

Bogdan celebrates his patriline Patron Saint's Day (the *slava*). [Photo by Andrei Simić]

kin also visited me: her *brat od tetke* [mother's sister's son], her *ujna* [mother's brother's wife], her *brat od strica* [father's brother's son], and my *šurak* [wife's brother] and his wife. Everyone I saw in Gornji Milanovac brought me food from the village to take back to Belgrade—so much I couldn't even carry it all. In late October, I will go to Cerići to visit the family graves on the Days of the Dead [Zadušnice]. This year, my three children spent almost the entire summer in Cerići and Livadice with their uncles. They still love village life, and it is a change from the dirt and confusion of Belgrade.

Bogdan is an example of a conservative peasant migrant whose social universe, even after settling in Belgrade, remained rooted almost entirely in kinship. In fact, his kinship network was so extensive and contained so many diverse social types, that he had no real need for friends apart from family members. Counted among his blood relatives and affines [relatives through marriage] were peasants, industrial and construction workers, skilled craftsmen, bureaucrats and other white-collar workers, a lawyer, an army colonel, an Orthodox priest, a secondary school instructor, an engineer, and a factory director. Among his close relatives were at least a dozen Communist Party members, and an equal number who were deeply religious and hostile to the Yugoslav regime. In this respect, Bogdan's family is not exceptional by Yugoslav standards, and the vast majority of the more than two hundred families I have studied over the past twenty years exhibit the same diversity. What is even more significant is that such differences in status, educational levels, and political orientation do not seem to inhibit kinship relationships to any appreciable degree.

As was the case with most peasant migrants at the time when Bogdan came to Belgrade, he left Cerići hoping to escape from what seemed to be the unrelenting and unchanging drudgery and poverty of peasant life. In exchange, he envisioned a more comfortable and economically secure existence in the city and dreamed of the social mobility that his children might enjoy. For Bogdan, as well as for the vast majority of peasants who settled in Belgrade during the three decades following the Second World War, this desire was largely fulfilled. His son Mile is a graduate of a secondary technical school, and now works as a skilled cabinetmaker for a furniture concern in Belgrade and lives with his widowed mother, wife, and two children in the modern apartment his father finally obtained after almost six years in Belgrade. Mile's wife, Zora, was born in a village only seven kilometers from Cerići and supplements the family income as a seamstress working in the private sector. Over the last ten years, they have gradually modernized the family home in Cerići, adding a contemporary kitchen and bathroom. They spend most of their holidays in the village and plan eventually to retire there in a comfort unknown to their parents' generation. Bogdan's daughter Stana finished secondary commercial school and, with the aid of the father of a student friend, found a job as a secretary in a small textile enterprise. She now lives with her husband, a secondary mathematics instructor and native Belgradian, in the apartment her father had promised her as a dowry. Zoran, Bogdan's oldest son, is an epileptic and consequently was unable to finish secondary school or to find permanent employment in the city. He has now returned to Cerići to work in agriculture with his uncles, cashing in the *village insurance policy* that his father had never allowed to lapse.

At the time of his death in 1981, Bogdan must have felt a deep sense of satisfaction from a lifetime of accomplishment. It was largely through his own initiative that he and his family had come to enjoy the best of two worlds. Together with masses of other rural migrants, Bogdan, as an agent of change, participated in a great historical process, the simultaneous peasantization of the cities and the modernization of the countryside (cf. Friedl 1959; Halpern 1965). However, it would be erroneous to suggest that all migrants experience the same level of success as had Bogdan. Many lack his extensive kinship ties, and others come from even poorer and more remote villages than Cerići, villages that are difficult to visit regularly or that can provide little material support. Still others, freed from the bonds of traditional social controls and norms, drift into various forms of maladaptive behavior: alcoholism, poor work habits, family violence, and even criminality. The latter, however, does not describe even a significant minority. For instance, there is nothing comparable in former Yugoslavia to the so-called American *underclass* or the slum dwellers of Latin America. Moreover, rural migrants in Belgrade do not form a class segment, nor are they, after a few years in the city, readily discernable from the general urban population. Although Belgrade folklore is full of stories about bewildered peasants washing potatoes in the bidet and stalling goats in the living room, the reality is that the cultural gap which separates the new urbanite from the city proletariat is minimal. My case studies and personal observations clearly show that the important cultural contrast does not exist between long-time urbanites and new migrants, but rather can be observed between intellectuals and professionals, on the one hand, and blue-collar workers and peasants on the other. Even this distinction is mitigated by the class-heterogeneous nature of most South Slav kinship groups.

Conclusion

One measure of successful urbanization is the degree to which rural migrants are able to integrate themselves into all levels of urban society. On the one hand, this depends on the migrant's ability to discard those markers and forms of behavior that readily identify him or her as of recent rural origins, and, on the other, the degree to which barriers exist on the part of the host population to the incorporation of the new settler. In this respect, the generally positive experience in Serbia can be explained in terms of the concurrence of a set of unique historical circumstances. The

Turkish conquest in the fourteenth century destroyed the existing indigenous aristocracy, and, in more than five hundred years of Moslem occupation, no native elite of any significance was to emerge until the nineteenth century. However, this small middle and upper class, which was derived largely from the peasantry, was to enjoy only a little more than a century of ascendancy before the socialist revolution following World War II destroyed the existing system of social stratification. Thus, unlike many of the countries of Western Europe and Latin America, in most of former Yugoslavia, a centuries-old continuity of asymmetrical class relationships has not prevailed. Until about thirty years ago, Yugoslav urban populations remained very small and were largely derived from peasant migrations of earlier periods. Similarly, contemporary urbanites have recent village roots and have brought with them a repertoire of folk customs which have been superimposed over earlier borrowings of rural culture. Thus, those cultural differences which do exist are not the product of the rural-urban dichotomy, but rather reflect various levels of occupational and educational achievement.

While migrants to Belgrade have encountered a congenial cultural atmosphere, that is, an existing population speaking the same language, sharing the same religious origins, and generally participating in the same kinship-oriented value system, economic factors have also contributed to the relatively trouble-free urbanization of South Slav society. The massive movement of rural peoples took place during the first three decades following the war, a time of accelerated economic expansion; therefore, not only was there a balance struck between the creation of new jobs and the rate of migration to cities, but also an expanding occupational pyramid made very rapid vertical mobility possible for many. Consequently, peasant migrants in such cities as Belgrade did not necessarily remain at the bottom of the urban prestige ladder; rather, they were able to enter every level of the productive and bureaucratic hierarchies. This initial phase of the modernization of Yugoslav society represents the simultaneous transformation of an entire people; yet, in many respects, this transformation has been more of an economic and demographic revolution than a cultural one.

It is doubtful that Bogdan's experience will ever be repeated again. He is the product of a particular period in his nation's history. With a deepening economic crisis, it is possible that his son Zoran, who returned to Cerići, represents the wave of the future. Recent reports indicate that land that has lain fallow for decades is again being cultivated. For at least the immediate future, rural-urban migration in Yugoslavia remains a two-way street.

Epilogue

When in 1987 I originally wrote that "it is doubtful that Bogdan's experience will ever be repeated again," I had in mind such factors as slowing economic growth, rising urban unemployment, a declining birth rate among the Serbs, and a constantly narrowing difference between urban and rural living standards, all of which seemed to make migration from the countryside less attractive. Although I had long been aware of underlying, but largely repressed, interethnic tensions, I little suspected that these would ultimately lead to the country's dissolution and a bitter civil war. Now looking back to the 1960s and 1970s, I wonder if, in spite of an authoritarian political system and a wide disparity between socialist ideology and practice, many Serbs, Croats, and Slav Moslems will not soon regard this period in their history as a kind of "golden age"? Surely, in most respects, it had been such for Bogdan and his family.

As previously mentioned, one of the elements contributing to Bogdan's success in adjusting to urban life was the fact that he found himself in a relatively homogeneous ethnic and cultural context. In this regard, it now seems clear that his decision to migrate specifically to Belgrade was neither entirely the result of proximity nor was it an isolated case. Among the many signs of the failure of the Titoist government to create a new pan-Yugoslav identity were patterns of internal migration, the majority of which were quite similar to Bogdan's. Contrary to expectations that the constituent Yugoslav republics would become increasingly heterogeneous, migration by individuals and families was largely within, or into, the republics dominated by their own ethnic groups (Spasojević 1984). The failure to create a single South Slav nation is further evidenced by the results of the 1971 census in which only 273,077 out of approximately 20 million respondents declared themselves as "Yugoslavs" (SFRJ 1974:3).

Bogdan, like many other Serbs, regarded his national identity as "sacred," immutable, and part of the "natural order." Nevertheless, it is my impression that he expressed this ideology largely in terms of personal and ancestral pride rather than as hostile or aggressive behavior toward members of other ethnic groups. Moreover, the period during which he had migrated and settled in Belgrade was one of relative ethnic latency, reflecting, on the one hand, rising expectations of social mobility and a more comfortable lifestyle, and, on the other, harsh repression of most overt expressions of nationalism.

The death of Tito in May of 1980 signaled a turning point in the history of Yugoslavia, and was soon followed by rapidly accelerating political, economic, and cultural decentralization. In this respect, two seemingly benign events dating from 1981 were in fact harbingers of the current chaos. In June of that year, six children in the remote and impoverished Hercegovinian town of Medjugorje claimed to have been visited by the Virgin Mary. Although the Catholic Church failed to recognize this as a "genuine miracle," Medjugorje quickly became an international pilgrimage center. Significantly, this phenomenon became associated with the Franciscan Order which had been closely tied to the pro-Nazi wartime Independent State of Croatia, underscoring its nationalist implications. At about the same time, in Belgrade, work had begun on the completion of a "memorial church" in honor of Serbia's patron, St. Sava, a project which had been prohibited by the communist government. This sanctuary, which now dominates Belgrade's skyline, is the largest Eastern Orthodox church in Europe. In effect, the lid was off public religious displays, and in former Yugoslavia, for the Croats, Serbs, and Slav Muslims, religion equals ethnicity.

The fragmentation of Yugoslavia continued unabated, culminating finally in the declarations of independence by first Slovenia, and then in 1991 by Croatia, and in 1992 by Bosnia-Hercegovinia. Unfortunately, the latter two nations received international recognition before a resolution could be found for the festering problem of approximately three million Serbs within their newly established borders, Serbs who refused to live in countries dominated by those whom they perceived as their former enemies. The resultant rebellion and civil war has brought about the largest dislocation of civilians in Europe since World War II. In respect to urban life, especially in Bosnia and Hercegovinia, there has been enormous physical destruction and loss of life, as well as both the voluntary and involuntary flight of hundreds of thousands of residents. Outside the combat zones, such cities as Zagreb and Belgrade have been forced to accommodate masses of refugees while segments of their own populations have been reduced to abject poverty by the collapse of the economy. For example, accounts in the American press reported that the rate of inflation in Serbia during May, 1993 was as high as 300 percent per month, and that industrial production had fallen between 40 percent and 50 percent since the beginning of hostilities. However, most pertinent to this discussion of urbanization are indications of changes in the very structure of Belgrade's population.

Commenting on the recent exodus of thousands of professionals and intellectuals abroad, Belgrade's mayor is quoted as saying, "The emigrants, who are urban and sophisticated, are being replaced by narrow-minded hillbillies from Bosnia and the countryside. They are imposing a new cultural model here. . . ." (Kinzer 1993:A7). Nevertheless, it should be kept in mind that this is not the first time that Belgrade has been populated from the hinterland, and it still remains, at least in part, a city of peasant urbanites. In fact, it is highly probable that some of these departing intellectuals are the children of migrants from Bogdan's village or others like his.

Notes

[1] A report by the Yugoslav News Agency Tanjug, cited in the *Los Angeles Times* (4 July, 1987), states that the rate of inflation increased from 93.3 percent in 1986 to 100.6 percent in June of 1987.

[2] For a more detailed discussion of Yugoslav urbanization and the history of Belgrade, see Simić (1973:28–71).

[3] Yugoslavia was composed of six republics and two autonomous regions roughly corresponding to the settlement of the major ethnic groups. Ethnicity is defined principally on the basis of language and religion. For example, the Serbs, who comprise the largest national category, are of the Eastern Orthodox faith and speak Serbo-Croatian.

[4] While traditional concepts governing kinship and other interpersonal relationships have made a positive contribution to the integration of rural migrants into urban life, this same ideology has significantly inhibited the building of efficient large-scale institutions within the economy and bureaucracy. For a detailed discussion of this phenomenon, see Simić (1983).

A West Indian Life in Britain

GEORGE GMELCH

In this essay, George Gmelch examines the migration and adaptation of West Indians to Britain. The oral history of a single migrant, Roy Campbell, is used to give the reader an insider's view of emigration. While the previous essays on Yugoslav and Mexican migration were concerned with rural-to-urban migration within a single culture, this West Indian case concerns international migration and the adaptation of migrants to a new culture. While the Yugoslav and Mexican examples dealt with linear migration in which migrants permanently left their rural homelands, most West Indian migrants only aim to be abroad long enough to satisfy certain economic or educational goals. This article is about return migration, as well as outmigration. Robert Rhoades's essay, also in Part Three, examines the impact of returning migrants.

About one of every ten current residents of Barbados has emigrated at one time or another; many others have left and have never returned. High rates of outmigration are common throughout the small, over-populated, and resource-poor islands of the Caribbean. It is so pervasive that, in most villages, nearly every household has a relative or close friend in Britain or North America. Beginning in the 1830s, when slavery was abolished in the British Caribbean, and slaves were free to move, migration has been of such fundamental importance to the islanders' economic adaptation that it has been referred to as "livelihood migration" (Richardson 1983). Success for most West Indians, economic as well as social, depends upon emigration.

Source: Article written expressly for *Urban Life.*

Most West Indian outmigration is not *permanent* or *linear*. Most migrants do not intend to settle abroad for good; rather, they see their migration as circular. At the time of their departure, they expect to be away only long enough to achieve a goal—to save enough money to build a respectable house at home, to complete a college education, or to learn a trade. Today, an estimated half million West Indian immigrants live in Britain; three times that number reside in the United States and Canada. Most have arrived since 1955, first going to Britain, and then, after she closed her doors to immigrants in the 1960s, to North America. Most have stayed away from their homeland much longer than they originally intended, yet they cling to the hope that someday, if only at retirement, they will be able to return home. Having an *ideology of return* is important, for it gives the migrants a psychological safety valve, an idea to fall back on when life abroad does not measure up to their expectations.

West Indian Migration

In the first fifty years after emancipation (1835 to 1885), the major movement of West Indians was away from the plantations on which they had been enslaved to small holdings and towns on their home islands (Marshall 1982). Some also migrated to other islands within the Caribbean, primarily to British colonies. Much of this inter-island migration was in response to the expansion of sugar cane cultivation in the newer colonies of British Guinea and Trinidad.

After the 1880s, the migrants went farther afield, traveling to Spanish and other non-British territories: to Cuba and the Dominican Republic to work on large sugar estates, to Central America to work on banana plantations, to Bermuda to construct a dry dock, to the United States to work in factories and in fields, and, most notably, to Panama to excavate and build the Canal.

In the following two decades, until World War II, little migration occurred. Likewise, at this time, many earlier migrants returned home. During the Depression, it was generally considered better to scratch out a living on a small parcel of land at home than to be unemployed abroad.

With the outbreak of World War II, a new wave of migration began as workers moved to Britain, the United States, and Canada to fill the jobs of citizens who were away in the armed forces. The war, however, was only a prelude to the mass migration to Britain that followed. The war, itself, provided the conditions which promoted such extensive migration, namely the enormous loss of life and the devastation of many British cities which created a high demand for labor. Hence, in the 1950s, West Indians migrated in large numbers to Britain, *the mother country*. In just a six-year period from 1955 to 1961, Barbados saw nearly nineteen thousand, or 8 percent, of its citizens leave.[1]

What prompted Barbadians and other West Indians to leave their homelands? In most of the Caribbean, population growth had outstripped development; on many islands, there were simply too many people for the available resources. On Jamaica, for example, population growth rates of 3 and 4 percent per year, which were double those of the nineteenth century, caused the rural population to become so concentrated on small holdings that further increases were not possible without a substantial drop in the standard of living or movement off the land (Lowenthal 1972). Many scholars, however, have argued that postwar migrants were reacting less to internal conditions in the West Indies than to an external stimulus, namely, the demand for labor in Britain (Peach 1968, Rose 1969, Foner 1978).[2]

Most West Indians migrated to England alone, not as couples or families. In most households, the male emigrated first, followed by his wife or girlfriend and by some, but seldom all, of their children. Why did men go first? Are they more ambitious, adventurous, or independent than West Indian women? Definitely not, according to Nancy Foner (1986) in a study of Jamaican migrants. Rather, in most households, there simply was not enough money for the entire family to emigrate together, and, as men were the principal breadwinners, it was natural that they would go first. If employment and housing conditions abroad were favorable and enough money could be saved for additional fares, women and children followed.

Most West Indian governments made no effort to prevent their citizens from leaving; in fact, emigration was often seen as a safety valve for excess population and high unemployment. Barbados assisted British companies and government agencies to recruit workers. London Transport and the Lyons Hotel and Restaurant Association, for example, set up offices in Bridgetown to interview Barbadians. A Barbadian from a tiny village in the north of the island could make his way to Bridgetown and apply for a job three thousand miles away as a bus conductor, a ticket taker on the platform at Euston Station, or a dishwasher in a Picadilly restaurant.

Who were the men and women who left the Caribbean to seek jobs in England? What was it like to be a black immigrant in a predominantly white society? How well did they adjust? Did they achieve their goals and were they able to return to the Caribbean? The following pages focus on the experiences of Roy Campbell, one of ten Barbadian migrants whose life histories I recorded in the late 1980s. I use Roy's account here because, in many respects, he comes closest to being *typical* of postwar Barbadian migrants in terms of education, jobs, housing, and social adjustment.

Roy Campbell: An Immigrant's Life

Roy grew up in a village in the parish of St. Lucy at the northern tip of Barbados. Like many Barbadian villages, this community is made up of small, brightly colored, wooden houses stretched single file along a narrow main road, with other houses connected by footpaths. Scattered among them is the occasional *wall* or cement-block house owned by a better-off family, often emigrants who have

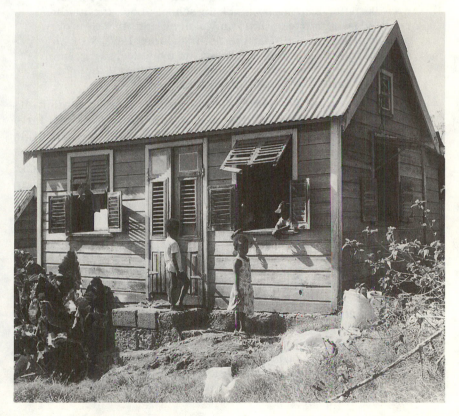

A typical village "chattel" or board house in rural Barbados, similar to the one Roy Campbell was raised in.

returned from abroad. Bordering the village are the pale green canefields, which cover much of Barbados, and bordering the fields are lines of cabbage palms and casurina trees imported from Australia by the early British planters.

Roy remained in school until age fifteen, earning his *leaving certificate* (equivalent to a high school diploma). He then obtained a job as an apprentice automobile mechanic in a garage in Bridgetown, the capital and Barbados' only city. Four years later, he was still earning apprentice wages of seven dollars per week when British Army recruiters came to Barbados.[3] Roy volunteered, took the physical exam and was accepted, but his father, fearing another war, refused to let his only son go. Instead, he gave Roy money to pay for his passage to England, a new suit of clothes and a suitcase.

> I wanted to go [to England], because I wasn't getting anywhere here in Barbados, and because I wanted to see what England was like after hearing so much in school about the mother country. I was nineteen, and many of my friends had gone over already. I left on the boat the 16th of June, 1962, with my suitcase full of warm underclothing and food: rice, sugar, rum, peppers, pepper sauce, flour, yams, and potatoes. I thought it would be hard to get West Indian food there.

In the early years of West Indian emigration to England, migrants traveled by sea. In 1955, thirteen ships made more than forty sailings, each carrying up to a thousand migrants (Patterson 1963). Over half the ships were Italian, and, in a curious reversal of migration streams, some of the ships carried Mediterranean emigrants to Venezuela on the outward voyage, then picked up West Indians bound for Britain on the return crossing. The fare was expensive and many emigrants sold their possessions and borrowed from relatives to raise the money. Most had never been on a ship before.

> I went on the *Serrienta*, an Italian ship. I was seasick for about three days, but, after I recovered, the days started going too quickly. I wanted to stay on a bit longer—the food was so good, and, at night, you could go down to the cinema. And they had a lounge where you could listen to the news, and they had comics so you could sit down and read if you wanted. And they had a bar where you could have a drink. The ship had an Italian band, but they played samba music so that both the Italians and the West Indians could dance to it. I'll tell you, I didn't want to come off the ship.
>
> After seven days at sea, we stopped at Tenerife in the Canary Islands, then Barcelona, then Naples and then we got off in

Genoa. I was seeing places I'd never seen, places I'd never heard of. In Tenerife, I saw policemen walking the streets with guns. I said to myself, "These people are not as free as our people back home." I'd never seen a policeman with a gun. At first, I was terrified. I was afraid if I said anything bad I'd be shot.

In Tenerife and Barcelona, I saw white people begging. I never knew of such things. Then I saw white people working as refuse collectors, and I thought to myself that I'd never do that job and here are whites doing it. Then I saw white taxi drivers. I said to myself, "Is it going to be like this in England?" My whole attitude began to change. I was going to England thinking of only picking the jobs that I wanted, but seeing white people doing those bad jobs made me think that I might have to do bad jobs too.

From Italy, we took the train across the continent to France and the English Channel, where we got the ferry over to the English side and then the train to Waterloo Station in London. There my sister met me.

More than half the arriving West Indians settled in London; the others gravitated to cities in the Midlands and the north of England, particularly Birmingham, Manchester, Bradford, and Nottingham. Where an immigrant settled was determined largely by where his relatives and friends had settled before him. They provided temporary accommodation, helped the new arrival find a job, and assisted in acclimating him to English life—how to ride the bus, where to shop, and so forth. As each new immigrant, in turn, assisted others, colonies of transplanted West Indians developed in particular neighborhoods of most major cities. Anthropologist Douglas Midgett (1977) found half of the 290 migrant households from the village he had studied on the island of St. Lucia in the same London neighborhood of Paddington. Roy remembers:

The first week, I stayed with my sister, her husband and their boy. Then she got me another room in the same house. I shared it with a Barbadian who worked for London Transport. He did his own cooking and sometimes he'd cook for me, but mostly I'd only sleep there, because I'd go up to my sister's to eat and watch television. When the landlord sold the house, we all had to move. My sister and her husband got a flat with three rooms, and she rented one of the rooms to me.

It was hard to find a place to stay in England. Rooms were available, but you'd see signs—"No Blacks," "No Coloured," "No Irish." Or you might see "English Only." And when you did get a room, the landlord would put restrictions on you, like telling you all visitors must be out of your place by ten o'clock.

West Indian immigrants waiting at Victoria Station in London after having disembarked from a ship at Southhampton, gone through customs, and traveled by train to London (1956). [Photo by Haywood Magee, the Hulton Deutsch Collection]

England was rough in the beginning; it wasn't what I expected. The first morning my sister and I walked down to the bus stop, and she didn't say good morning or hello to the people there, and I am thinking, "This is strange." Anywhere in Barbados, you say good morning and hello to people. The next morning, I go to fetch the milk off the stoop, and, when I get there, the lady next door was there to pick up her milk as well. I said, "Good morning." She just looked surprised and didn't answer. When I got upstairs, I told my sister, then she told me that was the custom in England. Nobody says good morning or hello, at least not to black people. I missed all the friendliness that you have in Barbados.

When I first saw all the houses joined together with all their chimneys up in the air and smoke coming out the top, I wondered where the people lived. I thought the houses were factories. I had never heard of people making fires in their houses, and they all looked the same, every building, every street, all the same way. I said to a man, "How do you know which is your house?" He said, "By the numbers." That alone put me off.

When I got to England my thinking was that I'd be away no more than five years. I wanted to save enough money to get a little home in Barbados. At that time, the pound was worth $4.80, and I thought that if I could save $10,000, I would be able to buy enough building materials to build a home. Building material was pretty cheap then; you'd get a [cement] block for thirty-six cents, a board for about forty cents, and labor was cheap. I wasn't thinking about getting married, settling down, or anything like that. I only wanted to make some quick money, see the country and come back home.

The first winter, I really wanted to go back home. It was so cold, the worst winter they had had in many years, but my father told me before I left Barbados that that was the last money he was going to spend on me and that I was on my own from now on. That stopped me from writing and asking him to send for me. After that winter, I wanted to get back to Barbados as fast as I could, but it took a long time to save any money. And by the time I saved enough for my passage, I was starting to get settled down.

My first job in England was working at a bakery as a porter. It was a Jewish bakery in East London. The pay was 8 pounds, 10 shillings per week. I had to load the van with the cakes, then I'd clean the bread trays, pack the frig with the cakes for the next day, and sometimes I'd sweep up. In Barbados, I wouldn't have done that kind of work, but, as I said, seeing white people doing those jobs, I knew I'd have to do them too. They didn't pay me enough for the work I was doing, but the bakery was walking distance from home, plus they let me have rolls and buns for lunch. I'd bring a piece of ham to work, and I'd eat their rolls. Plus they gave me free milk to put in my tea. So I saved an extra ten shillings a week that I'd have had to spend on lunch if I had worked somewhere else. I guess that's why I didn't leave the bakery, at least not for a long time.

In the bakery, there were a half dozen Barbadians, a couple of Jamaicans, and a half dozen Montserratians. The foreman, assistant foreman, oven man and storekeeper were all Jewish. Only the cakemaker was English. You had more West Indians there than anybody else. That was because we were cheap labor and did all the hard work. All the West Indians became very friendly. We used to go to each other's house to have a drink and party. There was a lot of mickey taking [poking fun] at each other, especially about the country you came from. Jamaicans would call us "small island" because Jamaica was so much bigger than our islands. Then we'd say that the cricket players from Montserrat can't bowl very fast because, if they take a long run, they'll land in the sea. Or we'd say, they can't even grow pumpkins in Montserrat because the vines have to run and land is so scarce they haven't got anywhere to go. We'd make fun of each other's speech, too. We used to laugh at the way Jamaicans talk, because they talk back to front. Bajans would say the "top of my head" is hurting me, where Jamaicans would say "my head top" is hurting me. I would say "bring me the bottle," but Jamaicans would say "go carry come the bottle." We laughed at them. But they'd just say all small islanders are "fou fou" [foolish].

About this time, in 1963, I met the woman that became my wife. I met her when I went to visit a friend of mine, and she was there. I got talking to her and her girlfriend (she was Barbadian too), and I spent the whole day there. I told Wendy about my work, and she told me about her work at the Lyons Restaurant at the corner of Oxford Street and Tottenham Court Road. She had come to England on a contract with Lyons Hotel and Restaurant; they were recruiting girls in Barbados, and she signed up.

The following day, my friend's girlfriend called me at work to tell me that Wendy wanted to see me again and that she was off from work that day. So I told my boss I had to go home. I caught the bus and went straight there. She made me a cup of tea and something to eat. After that, I'd meet her every night after work and take her home. After two or three months courting I said, "It is not profitable for you paying rent and me paying rent—why not live together?" So we moved in together, and she got pregnant. She lost the first baby, but got pregnant again and, in November, 1966, had the baby.

When she was pregnant, she said, "You know, this is not Barbados. Here, if you have children and you are not married, they look down on you." I said I would try to get a different job to make more money so that we could get married. At the time, there were a lot of colored immigrants working for London Transport, so I decided to give them a try. At the driving test [for bus driver] there were a half dozen of us, five white guys and me. We got in this old Routemaster double-decker bus. We all sat upstairs except for the guy who was being tested on driving. Each guy drove for fifteen to twenty minutes. Well, I drove pretty well, and the guy said, "You drive damn good." When all of us completed the driving, he took us back to the depot. The inspector said to us, "You all let me down; this black boy here drove better than any of you." So then I figured that everything was going to be okay, that I was going to get the job. But he called me to one side. "What I advise you to do," he says, "is take a conductor's job, and maybe later you'll get to drive the bus." Back in the room, I talked to the five white guys, and they told me that they all got through, that they were all going to be bus drivers. When I told them about me, they said, "Blimey, you drive better than us." That really put me off. I didn't bother with the conductor's job then, I just started for home.

On the train on the way back home, I got the *Midday Standard*, and I saw a position for a postman. So I sent in the form. Two days later, I got a reply asking me to come in for a test. Two dozen of us took the test, and after we finished, we all went out in the room and waited. They called out eight of us. I heard them tell the others that they would have to try another time, that they hadn't made it. I really felt good then. I had made it!

They sent me to postman's school to learn the towns and cities in England, Scotland, Ireland and Wales. And I had to learn the London districts, learn the whole of London from North 22, EC 1 to EC 4, WC to WC 2, E 1 to E 18, Northwest 1 to Northwest 11, West 1 to West 14, Southeast 1 to Southeast 27.

At the school we'd test each other:
"Where is Southeast 3?"
"Greenwich."
"Where is Tottenham?"
"North 15."
We had three days to learn all that and nine days to learn all the towns and cities. They gave us a pack of cards to take home at night so that we could study. I would give my girlfriend the cards, and she would test me, even when we were eating:
"Where is Wellingborough?"
"Northhampton."
"Yeah, you know that one. Okay, where is Limerick?"
"Ireland." and so on.

I learned them all with two days to spare. There were three of us colored fellows in a class of eighteen, and we all passed the exam early. Some of the white guys said they couldn't understand how these black people come here and learn these places faster than they who were born here and who lived here all the time. I'd think to myself, "Hey, I am doing great in this white man's country." We wanted to do well, so we really put our minds to it.

I started in the north London post office. There were about eight West Indians and a dozen Africans. At first, they gave us, the black fellows, the dirty jobs, like sorting parcels. Whatever they told us to do, we'd always try to do it to our best so that the governor [supervisor] couldn't come in and say that you, a black person, wasn't doing a good job. My boss used to call me Sam.

A West Indian immigrant on the streets of Birmingham, England in the late 1950s. [Photo by Thurston Hopkins, the Hulton Deutsch Collection]

I asked why he called me Sam and not my real name, Roy. He said that in his school days, they used to call all little black boys Sam, "You know, Sambo. So if I call you Sam," he says, "don't be annoyed."

Another English guy at the post office told me that when he was in school, he thought black boys had tails. He and his friend had followed a black man into a public lavatory to see if it was true. When the black man went into the toilet stall, they got up on the next toilet and looked over the top at him. The black guy pretended he didn't see them peeping on him, but then, when he was done, he rushed for them and banged their two heads together.

West Indians got on better with the whites than with the Africans. The white workers wouldn't show their prejudice. The Africans thought we were inferior to them. They would say that all West Indians are descended from slaves, and the slavemasters were white people who had sex with our great grandmothers and their mothers, and that is why we were much fairer in color than the Africans.

Roy's primary leisure activity in England was playing cricket. After several years in London, playing with other West Indians in the London Post Office League, Roy was invited to play for a white English club.

My friend Winston introduced me to the fellows from Trinity. They were all white except Winston, his brother and me. The first match, I did very badly. I made naught [didn't score any runs]. I felt bad for Winston because he had told them what a good bat I was. But the second match, I did a little better, and the third match I was still better. Eventually I was opening the batting [batting first in the order].[4] Playing on an English team was different from playing in the West Indies. If you did well, say you scored a century [100 runs in one match], you'd have to buy drinks. In the West Indies, they'd buy you the drinks. Playing with the English fellows, you always wanted to do well, but you also knew that if you did well it was going to cost you money.

After my girlfriend, Wendy, had the baby, I said to her that we had to be careful, because we want to go back to Barbados, and, if we have more children, we won't ever be able to afford to go back. So I said, "Let's quit for a while." Then we had a second kid in 1969, and I said "That's it, no more kids." I was eight years in England then, and it was time to start preparing to go home.

After we got married, her mom wrote from Barbados and told us that there was some land being sold, and if we would like a house spot, it would be a good place. We didn't have much money, but we withdrew what we had and sent it home to buy the spot. The price was $3,300.

I came back to Barbados on a visit for the first time in 1968, after being away for six years. You could see great improvement: there were many more cars, the roads were much better and

the people were doing better. In the stores, you'd see many of
the same things that you'd see in England. In 1973, Wendy and
I came back together and had a plan drawn up for a house, and
then we went back to England to save more money.

When Roy and Wendy returned to England in 1973 they left their
two children behind in Barbados with Wendy's parents. They did
so in order to save money and hasten their permanent return to
Barbados. Although their children were in good hands, the
separation was traumatic for Roy and Wendy. Roy had difficulty
even talking about it years afterward. In 1976, they returned to
Barbados again, but they still did not have enough money to build
the house they wanted. Nevertheless, they contracted a relative to
begin construction.

> We went to my wife's uncle and asked him if he could start the
> house and told him to build until our money was gone. He
> agreed, and he told me to open an account at Plantations
> Limited, the builders store in Bridgetown. When we left
> Barbados that time, I said to my wife that the next time we came
> back, it must be for good. There were the kids to think about,
> and I really wanted to be back in Barbados to enjoy my own
> country. Barbados looked so good to me, all the sunshine and
> the friendliness of the people. In England, you only get three
> or four months of what they call sunshine, in what they call
> summer. You always seem to be loaded down with lots of
> clothes—shoes, socks, t-shirt, shirt, vest, cardigan, coat and
> what not. The weight on you made you feel old. In Barbados,
> you can just put on a pair of shorts and walk outside barefoot.

In 1979, six years after leaving their children, Roy and Wendy
returned to Barbados for good, having saved enough to finish the
construction of their house. Roy, who had slipped and injured his
back while working at the post office, was given a medical disability
and a pension, which would help support them in Barbados.

> We arrived home on the 31st of November, 1979, which was
> Independence Day. We stayed at my mother-in-law's until our
> things arrived by boat, and then, just before Christmas, we
> moved into our own house. Coming home made me a bit
> nervous. I wondered if I could get a job and what kind of work
> I would do. My first job was as a security guard. The pay was
> small, but I didn't have much choice. I had to make some money
> because the kids were in school. My wife didn't have a job, and
> the house wasn't finished yet. My post office pension paid some
> of the bills, but it wasn't enough to support the whole family.
>
> Then I met a friend from England who had come back to
> Barbados and after a lot of trying he got me a job at the Transport

Roy Campbell in front of his Bridgetown, Barbados home, after his return from England. [Photo by George Gmelch]

Board. They made me an inspector. Being able to travel all around the island, riding on all the different bus routes, I was able to meet a lot of people. People on the buses or at the bus stops saying, "Good morning, Mr. Campbell," or "Hello, Roy," people knowing your name and wanting to speak to you and you just being back from England—well, that made me feel pretty good. It made me feel glad to be home.

Coming back to Barbados wasn't very hard on me, mostly because I'd come home a few times to visit. I knew what to expect. If I had stayed away for all those years and then come back and tried to settle down, it would have been hard. Plus, I got a job pretty quick, and we were able to move into our home so that we didn't have to pay rent.

Some things, however, do bother me. One thing is that people here are not good at timekeeping. If someone agrees to meet you at eight o'clock, they don't turn up until eight-thirty or maybe even nine, and they don't say they are sorry for being late. If the English say they will get here at eight o'clock, they will be here at eight o'clock. And people here aren't as mannerly. The

English always say "please" and "thank you," but you don't hear that said much here.

I wasn't able to adjust myself to the West Indian type of cricket either. I was thirty-five when I came home and the boys here were young and really fast [bowlers], and the pitches were hard. I decided that I had played enough, so I packed it in. I still watch a lot of cricket; when a touring team comes to Barbados, I go out to Kensington Oval to see the match. I meet a lot of the blokes who played for the post office teams in England there. I look around for them and during the intervals, or the lunch and tea breaks, we talk about what we used to do in England and how we used to play over there, and remember the old times.

About a fourth of the Barbadians who emigrated to Britain during the 1950s and 1960s have since returned home. More will return in the future, especially as they near retirement age and get pensions that will help support them in the Caribbean. Why do they return to their less developed homeland where good jobs are scarce, prices are high and services limited? How well do they readjust?

Some migrants are pushed home by unfavorable conditions abroad—unemployment, racial tension, and personal problems. The British economy has been recovering slowly from the last recession (1979–82), and what gains have been made have done little for West Indians. The unemployment rate among West Indians in British cities is double that among whites. West Indians have also been disturbed by new signs of racism in Britain, such as the rising popularity of extreme right-wing groups like the National Front. The rhetoric and policies of a conservative government have also contributed to the growing uneasiness. Some right-wing members of Parliament proposed that the government encourage West Indians to go home by offering them money, and the British Nationality Act of 1981, which declared that children born in Britain of West Indian parents would no longer qualify for British citizenship, was a slap in the face of West Indians who had given the best years of their lives to Britain.

Some return migration is precipitated by personal crisis: the breakup of a marriage, the death of a spouse, trouble with children, or ill health. One of Roy's neighbors who had been a hotel maid in an English resort town returned after being divorced. "After my husband left, it was just me and the kids in the house, and that's not good for anybody. I was lonely and bored. We needed more relatives around." In Britain, doctors often advise West Indians with serious health problems, especially mental disorders, to re-emigrate.

The change of scenery and climate may be good for the patient, but it also helps to reduce the burden on Britain's National Health Service.

While some emigrants go home because they are unhappy with their lives abroad, the vast majority, like Roy, return because of their attachments to Barbados and its people. Many want to be near aging parents and old friends again; others have patriotic reasons.

For most emigrants, however, return migration is best understood as merely the fulfillment of what they had always intended to do, the natural completion of the migration cycle. At the time of their initial emigration, most Barbadians only plan to be away long enough to save money to buy a house and perhaps a car or to acquire a college degree or a trade. Despite such intentions, however, most overseas Barbadians never manage to return for good. Some simply cannot afford the passage or plane ticket back to Barbados. Those who fare poorly overseas are also disinclined to return because they will lose face, since all emigrants are expected to come home with at least enough money to buy a home of their own. Unless they are receiving a pension, most migrants will not return home without good prospects of a job. Because Barbados has scarcely any benefits for the unemployed, they are better off staying abroad. Conversely, the very successful also seldom return. To do so would mean giving up well-salaried positions and a standard of living that cannot be equaled in Barbados. It can also mean costly obligations to share their wealth with less well-off kinfolk at home.

Not all returnees readjust to life in Barbados as easily as Roy Campbell. Many are disappointed with what they find. Barbados is not the same place they left more than a decade before. The number of cars on the roads has doubled, snarling traffic around Bridgetown; crime has increased; the development of tourist hotels has driven up land prices on the coast, putting the hope of buying a house near the sea out of reach; and young Barbadians seem less courteous than a generation ago. In short, the primary source of dissatisfaction among many returnees is the lack of fit between what they had expected to find at home and the modern reality. The most dissatisfied tend to be those who have been away the longest and those who made no or few visits home.

An estimated 15 percent of returnees are so unhappy that they re-emigrate to Britain or to North America. For others, the dreams and unrealistic fantasies of what the homeland was going to be like fade with the passage of time. They adjust to the comparative inefficiency and petty annoyances of life at home. Gradually, their expectations about what can be accomplished in a day's work are lowered, and the slow pace of island life, rather than being a source of frustration, is seen as a virtue. Many cope with the shortcomings of life at home by getting off the island occasionally. Whether it be a return trip to London or a cheap charter flight to Miami, in the metropole, they can satisfy their appetites for the things they cannot get in Barbados. When abroad, these Barbadians are also reminded of the drawbacks of life there—the impersonality, the unsafe feeling on the streets at night, racial prejudice, and the *rat race*—and, thus, tend to appreciate Barbados and island life all the more.

Notes

[1] During the 1950s, the doors to Britain were wide open to all immigrants from the Commonwealth, though the British government did try to ensure that passports were not given to people with serious criminal records, old people, or unaccompanied children (Fields and Haikin 1971). Although just about any Commonwealth citizen could enter, the emigrants were, generally speaking, better educated and more skilled than those who stayed behind (Richardson 1983). This changed in 1982 with the passage of the Commonwealth Immigrants Act, which restricted immigration. The Act was the outcome of a campaign that began in the mid-1950s, spearheaded by extreme right-wing political groups and some Conservative members of Parliament and widely publicized by the press, to control immigration—in particular, the immigration of colored people. Support for the Act came largely from those who believed, first, that immigrants were flooding the labor market and, thus, taking jobs away from native Britons, and, second, that too many colored immigrants were creating a *race problem* in Britain (Rose 1969).

[2] The sole exception to this pattern was the final year and a half before the imposition of the 1962 Commonwealth Immigration Act when, in the rush to beat the ban, the numbers of arrivals swelled out of proportion to labor demands.

[3] All figures are in Barbados dollars. One Barbados dollar equals fifty U.S. cents.

[4] Roy was a star batsman for the Trinity team; in 1972, he averaged more than eighty runs per game, and, by the time he left England, he had become the third highest run producer in the history of the Trinity team.

Women are Migrants Too
A Portuguese Perspective
CAROLINE B. BRETTELL

In this essay Caroline Brettell looks at the experiences of women as migrants—their decisions to migrate, their experiences in adapting to the societies they immigrate to, their incorporation into the urban labor force, and their desire to return to their homelands. Until the work of Caroline Brettell, Nancy Foner (1978), Rita Simon (Simon and Brettell 1986), and a few others in the 1970s and 1980s, women were largely neglected in migration studies. The pervasive assumption was, notes Brettell, that migrants, and particularly international migrants, were young males who left their homelands for economic reasons. Women who also left and wives who accompanied their husbands were largely absent from the scholarly accounts.

In this essay, Caroline Brettell not only informs us of gender differences in the experiences of migrants but also shows the complexity of migration phenomena. Virginia, the Portuguese woman that Brettell profiles, migrates to several places— Lisbon, France, Venezuela, and back to Portugal to retire in her natal village—and for a variety of reasons involving work, marriage, and family. Brettell also touches on the issue of political activity among immigrant women, a subject that Kathleen Logan treats at length ("Urban Women as Political Activists") in Part Five.

Virginia Fernandes dos Santos Caldas lives in the town of Viana do Castelo in northwestern Portugal. Fourteen kilometers to the east

Source: Article written expressly for *Urban Life*.

is the rural agricultural village where she was born in 1932. I first met Virginia in Paris in 1974.[1] At that time she was employed as a maid (*bonne à toute faire*) for a bourgeois French family who lived in the posh Parisian suburb of Neuilly. Her workday began before seven in the morning and ended well after nine in the evening. Normally she had a few hours off in the middle of the afternoon. For this work she was paid fourteen hundred francs per month (at the time about US $350 per month) plus room and board. Although not much by today's standards, it was significantly more than the 150 escudos per month (about $5 US in 1970) that she had earned as a maid in Lisbon, Portugal.

In France, Virginia did not work on Sundays. In the mornings she attended mass at a neighborhood church where a young Portuguese priest administered to the community of Portuguese immigrants who lived in the vicinity. Many of these immigrants were like Virginia—single women who had emigrated to France in the late 1960s and early 1970s. Virginia's dreams were their dreams—to make enough money to buy or build a house or apartment in Portugal where they could live in peace and security during their old age.

When I first met Virginia she was not married, but she had a son, born out-of-wedlock in 1954. Soon after his birth, the father left for South America. He wrote periodically but never returned to Portugal. When her son Joaquim was three years old, Virginia went to work for a well-to-do "aristocratic" family who owned a house in Lisbon as well as a *solar* (manor house and estate) in her natal village. Rather than take Joaquim with her to Lisbon, she left him in the village in the care of her mother and aunts. She saw him on holidays and during the summer when her employers returned to their solar. Virginia remained in the service of this family for eleven years.

Sometime in 1968 she was corresponding with Joaquim's father to ask him to send the papers that would allow her son to take his father's name in addition to her own. As a result of this process she discovered that her son's father, who was by this time living in Brazil, had married another woman. She was devastated. Two years later he wrote to say that his wife had left him and asked Virginia and her son to join him in Brazil. "I was so crazy about him," Virginia told me, "that I quit my job in Lisbon and returned to the village to make preparations for our departure. I even bought a new dress to wear when I arrived. I was very happy because my dream of marrying him was finally coming true." However, at the last moment the Portuguese government would not give her son a passport because he was sixteen and approaching the age for obligatory military service. Virginia would not leave without her son. "I was heartbroken, ashamed, and without work."

In the late 1960s Virginia's brother-in-law—the husband of her younger sister Rosa—had emigrated to France leaving his wife and four children behind in the village. Eventually Virginia's brother-in-law, who had developed a serious stomach ailment, asked his wife to join him in France. Rosa was frightened to go by herself and convinced Virginia to emigrate too—telling her that she had a lot of experience as a maid and would find work easily. Virginia and her sister arrived in France in October of 1971. Virginia was forty years old.

She found a job soon after her arrival and stayed in the same position until her departure in 1977. She had a very good relationship with her employers although she complained, at times, of having too much work. Everything had to be precise and just right for her *patroa* (mistress of the house). However, they were very generous with vacations and each summer she was able to return to Portugal for a month. Sometimes she also spent Christmas with her family.

In 1977 Virginia received a letter from her son Joaquim. His father, Manuel, had written from Venezuela and asked him to join him there. Unable to emigrate to France (after 1974 it became increasingly difficult), Joaquim decided to fly across the Atlantic Ocean to meet his father for the first time. His father gave him work and by the fall of 1977 he had suggested to his mother that she join them in Venezuela. In December of that year, Virginia quit her job in Paris and flew to South America to re-meet, and later marry, the father of her son—a man she had not seen since he abandoned her in 1954.

Virginia, her husband Manuel, and her son Joaquim (who married a young woman from a neighboring parish in Portugal) eventually returned to Portugal, but Virginia's marriage (a civil rather than a religious contract) had already failed. Manuel was constantly suspicious of Virginia's years of independence and particularly of her life in France. He started a relationship with his Venezuelan secretary, a woman much younger than he, whom he had brought with him to Portugal. Manuel asked Virginia for a divorce, offering her a small apartment in Viana do Castelo as a place to live. Although not without much emotional and spiritual pain, Virginia finally decided to give him the divorce. She spent a few years living primarily in her natal village, taking care of her aged mother, but when her mother died family differences in the household drove her to the apartment. Although her ex-husband Manuel gives her

Virginia with anthropologist on the path leading to her family home in a northern Portuguese village. [Photo by Caroline Brettell]

some money each month, it is not enough to get by. Recently Virginia has taken a job caring for an elderly woman five afternoons a week.

Virginia's life has been shaped both by migration and emigration, her own and that of others close to her, to the urban centers of Portugal, northern Europe, and South America. While her life story is uniquely her own, it also reflects many aspects of the roles and experiences of migrant and immigrant women more generally.

In 1974 two American anthropologists, Michelle Rosaldo and Louise Lamphere published a book titled *Woman, Culture and Society*. This book brought gender as an analytic concept into the mainstream of anthropology. Two years later the journal

Anthropological Quarterly published a special issue that dealt with the topic of "Women and Migration" (Buechler 1976). For the first time the presence of women in migration flows was recognized and considered in a systematic fashion. Prior to this time, in anthropology as in other social science disciplines, there was a rather pervasive assumption that the migrant, and particularly the international migrant, was a young male who left his homeland for economic reasons. This assumption has persisted well into the 1980s despite the fact that some migration streams—particularly those to the United States—have been dominated by women in recent years (Houstoun, Kramer, and Barrett 1984).[2]

In all of these studies, women are not only portrayed as actors rather than passive followers in the migration process—equally affected by the forces of capitalism, colonialism, or socialism; they are also described as central to the networks of exchange of people, goods, services, and information by which urban immigrant communities function and survive. There is an emphasis on how women themselves understand their lives and the challenges posed by migration; how women's experiences of emigration might differ from those of men; and how geographical mobility, both within and across national boundaries, might alter not only the culturally rooted understandings of what it means to be a woman but also various other aspects of culture that individuals and families bring with them as they migrate or emigrate.

It is some of these issues that I discuss here, drawing on the lives and experiences of Portuguese immigrant women like Virginia who have emigrated to a number of different receiving societies. My discussion centers on a few questions: Are the decisions of women to emigrate any different from those of men? How are women incorporated into the urban labor force in the country of immigration? What is the impact of salaried employment on family roles? Are immigrant women politicized and, if so, how? Do men and women differ in their desire to return to the country of origin?

The Decision to Emigrate

Traditionally it has been assumed that a man decided to emigrate and that women and children would either follow afterward or remain in the sending country. In the history of Portuguese emigration this is true to some extent. Familial emigration tends to follow a period of emigration heavily dominated by men. And yet, does the fact that women follow men mean that women are only passively involved in the decision to emigrate? The answer to this question must be no because it is inappropriate to study the process of emigration, and particularly the decision to emigrate at the level of the individual. No matter who departs, such decisions are generally collective ones taken by the members of a household. For the most part, wives are fully involved as partners in a domestic enterprise. Not only does the family as a unit decide whether to emigrate, who will emigrate, and for how long, but also what resources will be spent on the process and what money earned in the city or abroad will be sent back.

Recent emigration streams reveal that many women often get jobs abroad prior to their husbands and are, therefore, the first to emigrate. This is the case among Turkish women in Germany and for Portuguese women in London (Giles 1991). Furthermore, not all women who are involved in emigration are married. Single women like Virginia often have some of the best opportunities for employment in domestic service in the receiving societies.

The overriding factor leading to a decision to emigrate is economic. And yet, when we delve deeper into the personal stories of female emigrants, especially those who are single, we find that often they are also emigrating to join a family member. Klimt (1992:86) quotes one Portuguese woman in Hamburg, Germany, who claimed she "emigrated thinking not only of money, but of the longing and desire to be with [her] sister." Indeed, Klimt found that Portuguese women in Germany, whether single or married, tended to emphasize the familial rather than the material motives even though they worked for and contributed equally to the new house built in Portugal. In Virginia's case it was the need to support herself and her son that sent her to Lisbon, and the request of her sister that took her to Paris.

Other single women decide to emigrate because they want to change their lives; they are looking for a life different from the one to which they are destined in their home village. In many cases, it is not poverty that motivates emigration but an active effort to improve one's life. In Paris, I met several Portuguese women like Virginia who were no longer young, who were not directly attached to a man, and who wanted to earn money so that they could settle themselves comfortably in their waning years. Some of these women, like Virginia, have now returned to Portugal and have set themselves up in small apartments in provincial towns throughout the country. They have independence and financial security and do not have to continue in the back-breaking life of cultivating the fields.

Gender and Labor Force Participation

The great majority of immigrant women, no matter from what country they come or to what country they emigrate, become part of the urban labor force.

Portuguese women in France have shown a high level of employment. More than half of Portuguese women in France over age fifteen are actively employed. Like immigrant men, immigrant women are occupationally concentrated. In France, the majority of first generation Portuguese immigrant women found work as private domestics, cleaning ladies, or *concierges*. Employment for Portuguese immigrant women has often been linked to housing; consequently, women could combine their productive and reproductive roles. In more recent times, employment patterns have changed and more women are working in the secondary sector of the economy—in manufacturing. It is also true that the generation of Portuguese born in France have a different employment experience—they are citizens who are bilingual and many new opportunities are open to them. Whereas twenty years ago you would not have found a Portuguese taxi driver in Paris, today it is common; and women can be found in a range of civil service positions.

Portuguese women in London have moved into the domestic service sector of the economy. Forty-three percent of the Portuguese women interviewed by Giles (1992) were employed as waitresses or cleaners in the hotel and catering trade; 18 percent were private domestic cleaners; and 18 percent were on the cleaning staff of hospitals. The remaining 21 percent either worked full time in their homes or were nurses, teachers, or hairdressers. Giles writes of the exploitation to which these women are exposed, particularly in the form of low wages and the fear of deportation. In addition, they frequently work in isolation and by the time they get home to face domestic work they are exhausted.

The high rate of employment among Portuguese immigrant women is equally characteristic of populations in the United States. Lamphere (1986) found that Portuguese men in Rhode Island were more likely to encourage their wives to work than Colombian men who thought that having a wife who worked cast doubts on their role as the male provider. Portuguese men thought that what their wives could earn was necessary to the survival of the household. In Rhode Island, some Portuguese women work as domestics; but greater numbers are employed in the garment industry. Lamphere's study encompasses an historical approach; she argues that in the past the women working in the textile mills were the daughters of French-Canadian, Irish, English, and Polish immigrants. Today these working daughters have been replaced by the working wives of Portuguese and Colombian immigrants.

Gender, Work, and Family

How does this high rate of employment affect gender roles within the household and family? While many immigrant women, like gainfully employed women in general, are as exposed to the so-called "second shift" or "double-day," most research documents a definite change in the division of labor and gender relations within the household by comparison with the sending society.

Among first-generation Portuguese immigrant families in France, the absence of kin networks, combined with the fact that many couples left children with maternal grandparents in Portugal, resulted in a greater sharing of roles between husband and wife. Among couples with co-resident children, women worked as concierges or did occasional cleaning, and in these cases husbands participated less in domestic chores. In both cases, husbands and wives spent more leisure time together in France—a definite change from Portugal. Men were deprived of the kind of male public space that exists in the village squares of northern Portugal.

In her work among Portuguese immigrant women in Montreal, Canada, Meintel (1987) found that Portuguese women with young children tend to turn to work as hourly cleaning women or to home piecework because the conditions of work are both more flexible and less stressful. This is a strategy that allows for the combination of productive and reproductive roles. Meintel observes, however, that such an option is possible only if these women are in stable marital relationships with partners who earn a good income. Piecework and hourly cleaning are not excessively lucrative!

Among Portuguese women in Rhode Island (Lamphere 1987) a somewhat different option has been pursued. Given the constraints of the local economy, wives and mothers are forced into the productive sphere of waged work in textile factories. As a result, reproductive labor within the household is reallocated and husbands take on many household chores that are normally defined as female tasks. In addition, husbands and wives work different shifts in order to accommodate child care. As in France, waged employment for Portuguese immigrant women in Rhode Island has also had the effect of drawing nuclear families closer together, while ties to extended families and friends have become less important.

In Hamburg, Germany, Klimt (1992) has found that Portuguese women face for the first time the demands of balancing shift work with caring for the family. They are helped by husbands who understand the value of teamwork and actively participate in doing household chores, grocery shopping, cooking, and child care. Klimt documents the judgment passed by Portuguese immigrant women on arrogant husbands "who did not participate in housework; [on] weak-willed wives who let them get away with it; [on] women who were *escravas* (slaves) and had to ask their husbands permission to make purchases or leave the house; and also [on] wives who controlled the finances and never allowed husbands adequate spending money" (Klimt 1992:202–203). It should be noted that these Portuguese women in Germany differ from their counterparts in Montreal, Canada. The Montreal Portuguese women studied by Meintel hold on to the belief that the male should remain the head of the household and few of them leave the house without consulting or asking the permission of their husbands.

Women's Politicization and Encounters with "The Other"

There is very little research on the political activity of immigrant women in general and of Portuguese immigrant women in particular. It seems that it takes time for political consciousness to emerge. Immigrant women have very little time for anything beyond their work and their domestic chores. What leisure time they enjoy is spent with family or friends.

Where there is evidence of political activity it has generally emerged from a problem that immediately affects their working or domestic lives. Wenona Giles (1991, 1992) has described labor disputes in the London hotel and catering industry in which Portuguese immigrant women took part. These women were also involved in a six-year struggle to protest poor housing conditions. The women attended meetings with the Housing Council, an activity that required them to take off time from work or rearrange their schedule. Interestingly, Giles observes that the involvement of women in a protest movement was quite different from what they claim would have happened in Portugal—men would have attended the meetings. The implication is that the situation can be different abroad such that the kind of public activities representing the interests of the household that would have been the purview of men in Portugal are the responsibility of women once abroad. However

Giles also notes that the movement that these Portuguese immigrant women initiated soon became bureaucratized and progressively they lost control and became more silent.

The strategies of resistance described by Lamphere (1985) are much more subtle. In her study of a New England apparel plant, she found some resentment between older (Italian, Irish, French-Canadian) and newer (Portuguese, Latin American) female immigrants. Most of it centered on accusations of "rate busting." The perception is that new immigrants work too fast and the piece rate is lowered such that all workers have to increase their output to make the same pay. However, despite these divisions and tensions, there is also a culture of resistance that crosses ethnic lines and that develops when unions base their organizational activities on the informal networks that are established among women who bring their social and familial roles to the workplace. Women humanize the work culture and this provides a powerful basis for collective action when confrontation with management is necessary.

Klimt (1992) has written about the encounter between social workers and Portuguese immigrant women and the varying concepts of gender, family, and "good citizenship" that each group holds. Her study focused on a Portuguese women's group in Hamburg that was organized by professional German social workers. Klimt draws our attention to an evolutionist model that underlies German attitudes embodied in the expectation that migrants will change from being an uneducated conservative peasantry to an enlightened and engaged urban proletariat. She tells us that German social science literature about foreign workers portrays peasant women as dominated by their menfolk, and excluded from familial decision making. In German eyes, migration (and, by extension, urbanization) makes immigrants more sophisticated. Alternatively, there is an image of immigrant women as exploited and oppressed. In Germany, both these images derive to a large extent from observations of Turkish families but are applied to all immigrants.

As a result of these images, the courses offered to immigrant women stress personal health and hygiene, cooking, and childrearing. They do not address issues such as union organizing, financial planning, or job training even though, at least in the case of Portuguese women in Germany, the large majority of women work in heavy industry or the service sector and manage or co-manage family finances. In other words, they are aimed at making immigrant women conscious of themselves as women, wives, mothers, and domestic consumers (p. 216). In addition they socialize immigrant women, Portuguese and others, to the German way of doing business—orderly meetings, not talking all at once, arriving on time.

Klimt notes that the Portuguese women with whom she worked attended these classes because they were fun—a break from their normal routine. However their goals were not those of their German instructors. They wanted to become *senhoras* (ladies) in Portugal. They did not want to become part of a more liberated and proletarian German working class. Portuguese immigrant women and the German social workers agreed that Portugal was backward. But for the Portuguese women to focus on homemaking, on feminine forms of leisure, and on family life was not a way to become more German, but to become better than the Portuguese women who had remained behind in the villages of Portugal. The women who were the subjects of Klimt's research "positioned themselves somewhere between Turkish women, whom they imagined to be totally submissive and powerless, and German women, whose life styles they thought of as unacceptably loose" (Klimt 1992:220).

Returning Home

Klimt's observation that Portuguese immigrant women in Germany assess themselves and formulate their goals in relation to the country they have left behind leads me to the final issue—the temporariness or permanence of emigration.

One of the reasons why I went to conduct research among Portuguese immigrants in France was because I wanted to study a population that had more opportunity to move back and forth between the country of emigration and the country of immigration. I was interested in the relationship between distance and the perception of permanence of emigration. I indeed found that the Portuguese I knew in France had a powerful return orientation which was essentially absent among the Portuguese I had previously worked with in Toronto, Canada, or Providence, Rhode Island.

This difference is also reflected among the Hamburg Portuguese families studied by Klimt. She writes about a couple named Adelina and José who framed their future in terms of a return to Portugal. They lived modestly in Germany in order to live well in Portugal. In fact there is an ethic of self-restraint and denial among the Portuguese of Hamburg. Any excessive consumerism abroad draws the criticism of compatriots.

Row of new houses built by Portuguese emigrants in their natal village with money earned in France, "casas franceses." [Photo by Caroline Brettell]

Adelina and José argued not about whether or not to return to Portugal but about when and under what circumstances. Their daughter felt the same way. But José has a sister and brother-in-law in New Jersey who have decided to settle permanently there. While Adelina and José have built a nice new house in their natal village, the couple in New Jersey have not and only return to visit each summer.

José and Adelina, like other Portuguese couples in Hamburg, act in unison to achieve their goal to return to Portugal and are equally involved in making it happen. The only gender difference occurs when children wish to remain abroad; in this case wives tend to argue for remaining longer in Germany to stay near children. However, even this position does not mean giving up the commitment to return to Portugal some day. It may mean separation from children, but in some sense this is the nature of the Portuguese family in a country that has experienced emigration for centuries.

In other contexts husbands and wives do not always share the same ideas about returning to Portugal. Among couples I studied in France, I found that the women were sometimes more reluctant to think about returning than were their husbands. To some extent this was a function of the kind of work they did. They were well integrated into French life as domestics and concierges while their spouses worked with other immigrants in a factory environment and were consequently more alienated from their host society.

Giles (1991), by contrast, found that among the Portuguese families living in London the women were more interested in returning to their homeland. There was a difference, however, between single and married women. The former enjoyed the social and economic independence of their life in London and were more reluctant to consider return to Portugal. Certainly the attitude with respect to returning to Portugal is affected by the attitudes of the host society toward immigrant groups, by work laws, by the susceptibility to exploitation and the fear of expulsion.

As Klimt (1992) has observed, the return orientation is a powerful mechanism that liberates migrants from the need to measure their worth in German terms. A Portuguese chambermaid in Germany can be a successful property owner with sophisticated tastes in Portugal. We can never say with certainty that all those immigrants who say they will return to Portugal and plan for it by building a house and buying land will do so. But what is important is that they operate with this future in mind.

Conclusion

In this article I have outlined some aspects of the experience of Portuguese immigrant women in a number of host societies. Those experiences can certainly be shaped by the particularities of the occupational structure and of immigration policy in the receiving country. This creates difference. But there are also experiences that Portuguese women, or even migrant and immigrant women in general, share no matter where they go. They share these experiences because they are women who must juggle the pressures of domestic life with those of their job. This juggling act is particularly difficult in an urban environment because work lives and home lives generally take place in separate spheres. In some cases women have found the kind of work that brings the domestic and wage-labor activities back together—home piecework or concierge, for example.

What is certain is that migration profoundly impacts both the public and private lives of women and that looking at this impact is as valid and as important as the study of the classic male migrant who has so long served as a prototype for all migrants.

258   Women are Migrants Too

Notes

[1] See Brettell (1982) for a more detailed discussion of Virginia's life as an emigrant.
[2] By the mid-1980s a new awareness of the role of women in migration led to the publication of numerous anthologies and case studies dealing particularly with female migration and immigration both in the past and at present. See, for example, Simon and Brettell 1986, Gabaccia 1992, Gilad 1989, Diner 1983, Ewen 1985, Weatherford 1986. For an analysis of the anthropology of immigrant women in particular see Brettell and deBerjeois (1992).

Surviving in the City
Coping Strategies of Female Migrants in Nairobi, Kenya

NICI NELSON

In this essay, anthropologist Nici Nelson examines the coping strategies of three female migrants to Nairobi, Kenya. All three women migrated to the urban area following the death of a husband or break-up of their marriages. They settled in a shanty town called Mathare Valley and in different ways became successful entrepreneurs. Through their life histories, Nelson traces the women's migration to Nairobi and their adaptation there, focusing on the strategies they used to establish themselves in the town environment. Some of the strategies, such as different forms of generating income from informal sector work, the use of investment and rotating credit associations, and the building of informal sector housing, are similar to strategies described by Eames and Goode in "Coping with Poverty." Similarly, the women migrants also develop forms of matri-focal linkages with mothers, sister, daughters, and nieces, in a fashion reminiscent of Carol Stack's description in "The Kindred of Viola Jackson" in Part Four.

The women's urban careers were especially successful because they moved from economic achievement in the informal economy to consolidating their gains in the formal economy. In learning how the women adjusted to a difficult urban environment, we gain insights into the strategies employed by the plurality of low-income, female, urban migrants who survive, raise their children, care for their female relatives, and hope for a better future in the cities of developing countries around the world.

Source: Article written expressly for *Urban Life*.

Women Migrating to Town

Until the mid-eighties, analyses of rural-urban migration in Africa failed to acknowledge women as independent players in the migration game (Brydon 1987). Women everywhere, not just in Africa, were assumed to migrate to town only in the wake of a male authority figure (Chant 1991). Women were not seen to have agency in their own lives but were viewed as perpetual dependents.

This article tells the stories of three women who migrated independently to Nairobi, Kenya: Mama Wambui, Mama Mumbi, and Njoki. I have known them since 1970.[1] In this article I wish to relate their urban life histories in order to illustrate the coping strategies they used to survive in a difficult urban environment. They all left the rural area and migrated to Nairobi alone at various times before and after Independence (1963). Though their reasons for coming to town were different, for all of them the move was an attempt to better their lives. This account will discuss the ways they sought to achieve this betterment.

The site of this ethnography was a shanty town on the edge of Nairobi, called Mathare Valley. In the 1970s when I began doing fieldwork in the area, it had a population of fifty thousand living in self-built mud and wattle houses with cardboard and tin roofs. Mathare Valley had been settled by migrants, mainly Gikuyu in the period just after Independence, after the Mau Mau Emergency was over. When I first started fieldwork in the area, it was remarkable for its large number of female-headed households (60 percent of households by my calculations). There were two types of housing. The first type was mud and wattle housing lower down the slopes of the Valley, built by those who had squatted illegally either on land belonging to Asians from nearby neighborhoods or government-gazetted land. The second type was so-called Company housing, built on legally purchased land by groups of local investors. The housing was of more permanent materials but still did not meet the municipal Building Regulations (and thus was illegal). However, there was a booming market for housing in the post-Independence era and Mathare Valley, because it was less than ideal for formal sector speculators to build on, was central enough to prove an attraction for informal sector builders.

While some of the men were casual or skilled laborers or even employed as low-level clerks, most of the inhabitants of the Valley, men and women, were involved in informal sector activities. The men were artisans of various types; the majority of women brewed *buzaa* (a home-brewed maize/millet beer) or engaged in sex work. Some women from time to time took employment as house servants or as bar girls. Their educational levels were too low to qualify them for anything else (Nelson 1979). As in many parts of the world, such women found employment in the informal sector.

These women had migrated to town alone, for a variety of reasons connected with barrenness, breakdown of marriage, poverty, and ambition (Nelson 1990). Living in this squatter community, they developed a number of individual and communal strategies which enabled them to survive in a difficult environment (Nelson 1978).

The women who arrived early in the history of Mathare's expansion (late '50s–early '60s) obtained plots of land on which they could build. I called these women "Old Timers." Many of these had already been in Nairobi for some years before this period and had honed their skills of urban survival. Those who arrived in the 1970s were too late to build and had to rent from Old Timers. I called these women "New Comers." Many of them were "quick studies" of older women and copied many of the strategies they observed had been successful for the older women. In the next section I shall give the urban case histories of three women in order to illustrate the different types of strategies employed, their interrelation, and what made them successful.

Urban Case Histories of Three Women

As much as possible, I want the lives of these women to speak for themselves. I will use their urban case histories, as they were told to me in focused and formal interviews as well as innumerable casual conversations and gossip sessions over cups of tea on cold, rainy mornings, and in the shade of the roof eaves in the airless, hot afternoons, drinking home-brew beer in their houses. The role of biography and life history has an ambiguous status in anthropology. It is, in the words of Davison (1989) a "difficult genre." Analyzing the life of an informant, whether it is in the form of a biography or case history (abstracted from numerous observations and conversations by the researcher) or a life history (an oral account of the informant transcribed wholly or partially complete in her/his own words) gives the ethnographer and the reader an illusion of rooting the discussion in reality. However, it is important to recognize that the case history/biography inevitably bears the imprint of the ethnographer who evaluates, orders, and interprets the information and creates the life. The lives represented here are in part my creation though I sincerely hope that I have dealt with them objectively and accurately.

The second problem with the use of case histories is that of representativeness. The three women I shall introduce in this section are representative in that they have utilized exactly the same coping strategies as their other sisters in Mathare Valley. They are not representative of all women in Mathare because they have operated them more successfully than many others did.

Mama Wambui

Wambui was definitely one of the original settlers of Mathare—an Old Timer. A handsome, vigorous old woman with a shaved head (in the old-fashioned Gikuyu manner), she wore the draped colored cloth over her cotton washdress in the manner of older rural women and her earlobe-holes were stretched through years of wearing heavy, bulky earrings. She was an exceedingly shrewd woman with a shrewish, and much-feared, tongue and an earthy sense of humor.

She lived in a rabbit warren of tiny, dilapidated, mud and wattle houses (seventeen in all) which she had built over the years. Some were rented and some were occupied by her three sons, two daughters-in-law, five grandchildren, and her blind sister.

Wambui was a very open person and enjoyed being interviewed. She was also one of the few older women willing to talk about sexual matters to a younger woman. Perhaps her part-time occupation of female circumcisor gave her such license. Conversations with her and her sister, Amina, gave me many fascinating insights into their early life in town as sex workers.

Wambui had been married very young to an old man with many wives. (By my calculations this must have been roughly around 1925 or 30—Wambui had no idea of her age and was vague about dates.) She was with him for several years. Unfortunately, he died while Wambui was pregnant with her first child, before she had established rights to any of his land. She was chased from the homestead by her co-wives and their grown sons. Pregnant, she returned to the *shamba* (farm) of her brothers where she lived with her child for several years. The son by her marriage died. She did not like it at home because her brothers resented her presence there. There was not enough land to support another farmer.

In the meantime her sister, Amina, who was also living at home after being divorced for barrenness, had met a Moslem in the nearby trading center and had run away to Nairobi with him, adopting a "Swahili" style of life there.[2] Wambui followed her to Nairobi (this would have been sometime before the war). The two of them were beautiful and greedy for money and life. Neither married again, but they lived together in Pumwani, Pangani, and Eastleigh—Amina as a muslim. In their own words, they "hunted men" together, and "made men cry for them" (see White 1990 for a historical study of this type of sex work). They brewed beer and practiced sex work of various kinds. Neither of them thought much of the future. Amina was childless, but Wambui bore four sons, one of whom was retarded. Then sometime after the war, Amina started to lose her sight (she must have been in her forties at this time) and began to suffer from vague ill health, depending more and more on her sisters for support (there were now four of them in town). Wambui had been involved in the Mau Mau activity during the Emergency though she was never anxious to reveal exactly how much and in what way. In any case, she and Amina were both detained during the Emergency between 1956 and 1958. After her release she returned to Eastleigh and eventually followed the advice of a man she was living with to build in Mathare Valley. At this point Wambui was in her late forties, roughly, and had grown, married sons who seemed to be very dependent on her, as was her now almost totally blind sister. She was much sobered by her detention and obviously felt the need for some security. She would undoubtedly have realized that she was approaching the age when she could no longer hope to live well on sex work. Investment in housing seemed a logical option.

Her "Town Husband" (as women locally called the men they lived with temporarily in town) lent her the money to build her first two units in Mathare (in this case I am using "unit" to mean one room. Locally a "room" was called a "house" because one or sometimes two families shared a room. I use "unit" to avoid confusion and ethnocentricity). She lived in one unit and rented out the second unit. She paid him back in the first year from the rent. Housing was such a good investment that one could realize one's investment in less than a year.

Wambui and her three sons then set about expanding her investments. With their help she built additional units as she managed to save money for materials from the rents from the initial units. In addition to renting rooms, with the help of her sons and daughters-in-law and later her grandchildren, she brewed *buzaa*, honey beer, and *changaa* (wholesale local gin). She also raised goats, cultivated land in marginal areas around the Valley, sold firewood, and operated as a female circumcisor.

She sent her sons to school but without much success. The eldest had low-paying casual work in some uncertain capacity in town. The second son had trained as a mechanic but drifted in and out of work, usually in the small informal-sector garages scattered on open ground near the center of town. He was rumored to deal in stolen goods. The third one had refused to attend school from an early age, and the last was mentally retarded and slept in the room with the goats.

Wambui belonged to a number of saving cooperatives. She was involved, in 1972, in a scandal about the liquidation of a large cooperative. Later, she and a couple friends took their share of the money (and if gossip was correct *more* than their share) and started a bar and butchery cooperative. Subsequently this cooperative business seemed to be run solely by her younger son and her co-owners grumbled in a disgruntled, vague sort of way that somehow they had been cheated. Wambui looked blank when asked about this point and mumbled something about them not being very good businesswomen and leaving all the hard work to her and her son.

Wambui was a member of her village KANU Committee, though not an important one. She was the head of a Gikuyu Women's Dance group who had often been asked to dance for various government officials as well as President Kenyatta at his country house. The members felt that they had been instrumental in influencing him on behalf of the people of Mathare. When they danced there they would "sing the troubles of the women of Mathare." Many other Mathare residents confirmed this view of their role in obtaining better treatment from the city council.

Wambui was a strong-minded and outspoken person. She made enemies with her abrasive tongue. She was not a person people sought out to settle disputes; on the contrary she was more likely to be at the center of controversy. She was energetic and always had an eye to the main chance. She was able to bully people to follow her lead. Those who complained would be shouted down by Wambui. Those who persisted in objecting might even be threatened by her strong, surly sons.

When I knew her she must have been in her mid-sixties and did not have any relations with men other than those of business or friendship. She claimed to be glad to be finished "with all that." Men were not trustworthy as lovers and husbands, and it was better to concentrate your energies on one's relatives and children. This Wambui did with great energy. She spent most of her time with her family—her natal family and her children. She also had two other unmarried sisters who lived, worked, and owned houses in Mathare. The sisters and their children cooperated in many social and economic ways. There was constant visiting, shared eating, and help with beer brewing and child care. Children were shuttled around from aunts to grandmother and back to their mothers. Wambui's various female relatives in Mathare (three sisters and four nieces) and her sons were all members of upwards of six land-buying societies and housing cooperatives which were purchasing land and properties in and around Nairobi. Elsewhere I have written about sister-clusters in Mathare (Nelson 1978) as a coping strategy of single women migrating to town.

In the allocation of plots and houses in New Mathare in 1975,[3] only Wambui in this sister-cluster received a plot (a site and service plot). She handed this plot over to her oldest sons to build on, live in, and rent. She remained for the most part in Old Mathare, where her economic base was, until her death in 1980. Ironically, she, who always seemed so healthy, predeceased her older sister who continued to "enjoy" ill health while living with another sister outside Nairobi. In the eighties this sister obtained a plot of agricultural land outside of Nairobi in one of various allocations of rural land for the urban poor and homeless. She lived there with various relatives: wife of one son, one unmarried daughter, assorted grandchildren and grandnieces and grandnephews, her sister, the now totally blind Amina, as well as Wambui's retarded son (who was now relegated to sleeping with and caring for the two cows). The other sister still lived in her one room in Old Mathare caring for her daughter's two children and trying to eke out a living variously selling vegetables or working as a house servant. When she worked as a house servant, she would send her grandchildren to stay with the rural-based sister.

Discussion of Wambui and Amina's Coping Strategies. Wambui, and to some degree her sister Amina (until she went blind), was a highly successful Mathare Old Timer. During her nearly thirty-five years of urban life she had shifted strategies when the need arose and her family/life cycle circumstances altered.

Amina's migration into town demonstrates a strategy described by Bujra for single women migrants. Bujra describes women coming into Pumwani in the 1930s. One of their coping strategies was to convert to Islam. For these unmarried women, cut off to a greater or lesser degree from their families (natal and affinal), the mosque provided a surrogate family and a "status" in the community. For single women in Kenyan urban areas, covering their head and fasting during Ramadan underlined their "respectability," even when they were discreetly carrying out sex work (Bujra 1975).

Wambui was a disenfranchised, young widow of an old polygamist, a difficult status as described by Potash (1986). She migrated to town to join her sister, Amina, who had gone before. Joining relatives is a common strategy for new migrants coming to town. A woman joining her sisters in town is not as commonly recognized a strategy as that of men joining their male relatives, though many of my Mathare informants had done just that. Four sisters came from Limuru and lived in Eastlands in the 1930s. They subsequently invested in housing units and moved to Mathare in the late 1950s–early 1960s. There they formed sister-clusters, cooperating in productive activities, child care, eating, and sharing resources. These sister-clusters were not uncommon in my experience in Mathare Valley and constituted another manifestation of the matrifocal emphasis in the ways Highland Bantu female rural-urban migrants manipulated the previous patrilineal kinship system.

The developing of matrifocal emphases in urban kinship formation is very evident in the coping strategies of female migrants to the city in many parts of the world. Kenyan women are no exception. What was very interesting about Wambui's matrifocal family was not only manifest in the fact that female relatives cooperated together, but also in the fact that Wambui was the head of a family of three able-bodied sons. It was Wambui who made family investment decisions and directed the labor, the earnings, and the consumption of her three sons and their families. This would never have been the case in the rural area, where an aged mother would have given over more and more of her land and cattle to the use of the wives of her sons. The operation of the house property complex in Central Province gave women great status as "head of a house," but it was a position of honor rather than real authority. It meant in practice that mothers as trustees of land on behalf of their sons deserved great respect but would never have expected to have been a direct authority figure over the economic lives of her sons in the same way as Wambui was.

In Kenya, before the twentieth century, women's sexuality was linked to the growth of the lineage by the mechanisms of bridewealth and marriage. Very early in the colonial era, women migrated to the city to escape from unsatisfactory marriages. They took control of their sexuality and learned to translate sexual services directly into cash income (White 1990). Wambui and her three sisters—when they were young and beautiful—all made what would seem to have been a good living from various forms of sex work. In addition, women formed closer, but still relatively temporary, forms of conjugal relations with male migrants separated from the rural wives and families by the prevailing mode of circular migration. These were referred to in Mathare Valley in the 1970s as Town *Bwana* (Town Husbands). It was one such Town Bwana who advised Wambui and lent her money to build two units of housing in the expanding shanty town, Mathare Valley.

Building informal sector, self-help housing is for incoming migrants a common form of coping strategy in most Third World cities, where the rapid growth rates have necessitated the rapid expansion of the built environment. In Kenya, as in most Third World cities, the state or the municipality cannot keep abreast of the demand for housing. As a result, the individual entrepreneur has the possibility of providing self-built housing for rental. The building of such informal-sector housing was a strategy to give the rural-urban migrant (male and female) a foothold in the city and an income.

In general, employment in the informal sector is part of the coping strategies of migrants arriving in the city. The informal sector is the low-investment, self-employed, easy-entry sector of the economy. African women migrating to towns in the twentieth century lack skills and education and find themselves at a severe disadvantage in the formal job market. Armed with skills from their reproductive/farm managerial activities in the rural area, many women successfully translate these skills into income-generating activities in the urban area. Women obtained employment as house servants and child-care workers. They cooked and sold food and provided sex (on a casual and commercial basis) for single male migrants. From growing food, they moved to trading in foodstuffs.

In Mathare Valley and other shanty towns in East Africa, women made an income brewing and selling beers of various kinds. This is an interesting cultural change in the transition from rural to urban cultural practice. In the rural areas, certainly in the precolonial social formations, beer brewing was entirely a male activity, connected with building/reinforcing male friendship network building and patron-client linkages (Clark 1980). Throughout the twentieth century, when beer became commercialized in Nairobi and other East African towns, it was women who made and sold it. Once beer became part of the cash economy and disconnected from the male structures of friendship and prestige, its provision seems to have become a logical extension of women's role as providers of food, services, and sex in the reproductive realm. This view is reinforced by the fact that the women who sold and still sell beer do so in their own homes in an atmosphere which men say is like the rural village. In addition, selling beer is closely connected with the selling of sex. (Alcohol and sex are commonly linked in urban leisure provision everywhere.) In Nairobi, in the thirties, Gikuyu women began to make a living selling honey beer (the Gikuyu form of alcoholic beverage similar to European mead) and eventually in the postwar era learned to brew Luo maize/millet beer. The reasons for this are obvious. It was easier and cheaper to obtain commercial grade maize and millet than honey (or its nearest substitute, sugar cane). Gikuyu male customers soon learned to appreciate the taste and the cheapness of buzaa. This swift adoption of a Western Province beer by brewers and drinkers of Central Province is a form of cultural transmission. This could only have occurred so rapidly in the cultural heterogeneity of the urban area. It was a piece of cultural transmission which benefited female migrants to the urban area in Kenya from its earliest days until the government pronouncement in 1983 which made such illegal brewing more difficult.

In looking at the strategies of Wambui, one can see several rural skills and income-generating strategies translated into an urban context as a coping strategy. One of these was the keeping of goats. In rural Kenya, livestock was a form of wealth which men and women accumulated. Men accumulated large stock (cows and camels), while women were restricted to small stock, such as goats. Both sexes accumulated stock as wealth. In Mathare, women continued to keep goats, but not so much to build up wealth as to generate income. In the urban area women and men were fully incorporated into the cash economy. This meant stock no longer represented wealth, only income. Goats were ideal because they ate trash and browsed at will. Women sold them to the local butcheries when they needed cash.

Women also continued to cultivate, but it was a form of urban cultivation, utilizing empty ground and such strips of land as the center strips or verges of roads. Some women could raise enough maize or beans to make a significant contribution to the family consumption. For other women, I think it was a form of anti-stress therapy, as gardening is for suburban middle classes in Europe and the United States. Women said they liked to cultivate because it reminded them of growing up in the village.

Wambui was a circumciser, hardly a common urban coping strategy. There were one or two rural migrants in the Mathare area who had translated what were called by Gikuyu themselves "the things of *zamani* (long ago)" into the urban environment. There were a couple "traditional" doctors or diviners and two circumcisers. Young women were circumcised in the urban area as well as the rural area and Wambui claimed to make a tidy little sum during that time of the year. The peculiarly urban slant of this rural-urban translation was that she had received training on how to be a "modern" circumciser at a local hospital. She used a safety razor instead of the old form of circumcising knife and bound the wounds of circumcised girls with sanitary towels instead of moss or rags. One could always tell when Wambui was off to work. She would march along the road holding a handful of sanitary towels which she would wave at me, usually shouting some slightly off-color suggestion that I might like to be circumcised myself in order to become a "real woman." Such sallies were always greeted with hilarity by other women, who knew Europeans disapproved of this old Gikuyu custom.

Another "thing of zamani" which was translated and transformed in this urban social practice were the so-called "traditional" dance groups. At one level this was a form of recreation which was becoming common in both rural and urban Kenya. No longer tied to the ritual cycles of the Gikuyu year, it has become an excuse to put on some plastic simulated-leather version of traditional dress, don the bead jewelry, and sing the songs of yesteryear. What was most interesting about the groups in Mathare was the fact that they often sang for politicians like President Kenyatta. When they did that, they made a point of singing about the "troubles of the women of Mathare" to the old tunes in the hope that the politician so entertained would be moved to act on their behalf. They were firmly convinced that on various occasions this strategy had worked to save Mathare people from harassment from the municipal authorities.

Mama Mumbi

Though an Old Timer, Mama M. was not a very old woman. She would never admit to any age, but I calculated that she was not more than forty-five. A plump, light-footed, pretty woman, her occasional flights of girlish high spirits did not entirely conceal her shrewd and ruthless businesswoman's mind. She held a high position in the KANU Committee of her area and was one of the most respected elders in her section of Mathare Valley. When I knew her, I calculated that she was also one of the richest women in Mathare.

What I know of her finances and details of her personal life was pieced together from intensive observation over an extended period. Mama M. was not very forthcoming on many personal issues and disliked the formal interview situation. I did not have the easy joking relationship with her that I had with Wambui.

Despite this, she was one of the people whose life I was involved with. We visited her mother in the rural area or attended *itega* (donation parties) held to help her friends and relatives. I was present when she settled quarrels, discussed personal and political issues, and drank at the local private club the political leaders set up for themselves.[4]

Mama M. was born in Limuru, one of two children. She led an active life, performing many of the chores a boy would normally be expected to do since her older brother had been sent to school. She herded goats and used to delight in telling how she could defeat the boys in their rough games. Though she was small for her age she made up for it in courage, speed, and cunning. She never went to school, a fact she often mourned. She had taught herself as an adult to read and write a little but used to say that had she had the opportunities of today's girls, she would have become president.

She married young and her husband was actively involved early on in the Mau Mau struggle. During the period of the Mau Mau, she moved back to her mother's farm in Limuru. The reason for the divorce was undoubtedly the fact that she had borne no children (the "Mama" title given her early on by the residents of Mathare was a courtesy title only). She always had a close relationship with her mother and brother. He had become a District Officer and, at the time of my research, he was posted in Rift Valley. He had given over the farm in Limuru to her, a very generous act unusual in a Gikuyu brother. It was a small and well-watered shamba. By the 1970s she had built a tin-roofed, concrete-block house for her mother and hired regular farm help to cultivate under the supervision of her mother. Her mother was as lively as a cricket and visited Mathare frequently, always taking away money and goods. When I left she was nagging Mama M. to build her a rain collection tank so she wouldn't have to carry water anymore.

Towards the end of the Emergency, Mama M. came to Nairobi. She was one of the lucky ones who had a relative already working for a European, and he obtained a job for her with a European family. She worked as a servant for a number of years and with her savings built a house in one of the Eastleigh shanties. At this time she met one of the men responsible for the opening up of Mathare and lived with him first in Eastleigh and then in Mathare. When he died in an automobile accident, she became the lover of another important local leader. This was during the period of the greatest expansion of housing stock in Mathare, and she was allocated a central, level site on which she built several substantial houses with tin roofs. She was also one of the leaders of the early village associations which raised money for the Meeting Hall and the Nursery School. She was granted a concession by the KANU Committee to wholesale bottled beer to the beer sellers in that part of the village. In the 1969 elections she was made a member of the Committee.

When I knew her in 1970–74, she was a wealthy woman by Mathare standards. She owned seven units in Old Mathare and had received an allocation of a new house in New Mathare. Through her influence, she had only lost four of her old houses in the process of tearing down after the allocation. She wholesaled bottled *Tusker* (locally manufactured Lager) to beer sellers in Mathare (the only person that did so in this section of Mathare). She also brewed and wholesaled buzaa to a circle of women clients. Probably due to her privileged political position she was never raided by the police and was known to hide the beer and equipment of clients of hers during police raids. She owned a maize meal wholesaling business, a firewood-selling business, and a small store. She was a member of the largest women's investment company in Mathare. She also belonged to various Harambee groups in Eastleigh, three successful land-buying associations, and claimed to have plots of land in Rift Valley and the Ngong hills which were farmed by hired labor. Her mother managed her father's shamba.

When I met her she was no longer the local leader's Town Wife. She now lived with a handsome man some ten years younger than she who was a police driver. He was definitely henpecked. He handed over his whole salary to her, and she banked it in her savings account and doled out spending money. People sneered at him behind his back for allowing her to control him. They parted company in 1980 and since then she has lived alone with two children she adopted in 1981.

Mama M. was unhappy with her childless state and tried to rectify her situation in a number of accepted ways. While I was doing my research she was fostering the daughter of a widowed friend of hers. In the early seventies she was sending the girl to typing courses in Eastleigh, and the girl performed household duties and helped her foster mother to retail buzaa. This girl did not fulfill Mama M.'s expectations. She did poorly on her courses, did not get a job, and eventually ran away to live with a man elsewhere in Mathare. In 1981, she adopted a young brother and sister of one and three years old respectively, from a widowed woman with too many children to care for. She obviously loves the role of mother and is anxious to educate her children well. The girl is quite bright and in 1990, Mama M. told me she hoped she would go to University. Mama M. has cut all economic and most social ties with Old Mathare. She only goes there for political meetings since she is still on the KANU Committee there. She now lives full time in New Mathare and manages her formal sector investments and businesses.

Discussion of Mama M.'s Coping Strategies.   Mama M. was a very successful Mathare migrant Old Timer, but one who utilized different coping strategies than Wambui had in the generation before her. Wambui had depended on her matrifocal extended family of sisters, nieces, and children, all co-resident in Mathare Valley and nearby neighborhoods, something Mama M. couldn't do because she had no sisters and no children. While Wambui had been a successful sex worker in her prime, she had (at her own admission) spent most of the money she earned in that period on daily consumption, clothes, and good times. She did not invest in business until she was in her forties.

Mama M. was divorced early for barrenness and concentrated early on a business career, so that by the time she was forty she was already a relatively wealthy woman. She seems not to have practiced casual sex work but had formed a limited number of long-term relationships with locally powerful men. She then used these men as patrons to assist her to invest in housing, to obtain franchises for certain lucrative businesses, and to gain entry into the political arena herself. By the time I knew her she was a patron herself and had become sexually and economically autonomous. The degree of her sexual autonomy is demonstrated in the fact that she had a younger lover whom she dominated.

She took advantage of various types of business activity and investment. The 1960s and 1970s were an excellent time for small entrepreneurs to make a reasonable living in the informal sector, and then to translate such success into investment in the formal sector. Beer brewing was illegal, but not regarded as a serious focus of police action during this period.[5] Profits from beer brewing could be translated into informal-sector housing. That in turn could be invested in legal housing. Both Wambui and Mama M. accomplished this when they received allocations of housing in New Mathare. In the late 1970s and early 1980s further opportunities for investment in low-income housing developments occurred in Dandora. In order to accept these allocations, the allocatees had to invest a substantial sum, either as a down payment on the mortgage for prebuilt houses, or to build the requisite concrete-block house on the site and service plot. In addition, in the 1970s and the 1980s there was a plentiful supply of rural land coming onto the market, and many Mathare residents joined land-buying companies and invested in rural land. They rarely chose to live on these farms but had them managed by hired labor or relatives.

Elsewhere, I have followed in detail the history of one rotating credit society for the period of 1970 to 1990 and traced its successful evolution into an investment cooperative. Mama M. was a member of this cooperative, among others. One of the reasons for its relative success in translating the earnings of these beer brewers and wholesalers into the formal-sector investment arena was the many opportunities for relatively small-scale investments which could be capitalized and built upon. In addition, there was relatively easy access to low-interest money to use for these investments. These small-scale, urban informal-sector entrepreneurs graduated from small-scale to larger-scale investments, consolidating their gains as they went, until they were able to cease operating in the informal sector altogether (Nelson 1995).

To ensure her security and care in her old age, Mama M. tried fostering a young girl. When that failed she adopted young children. It is her hope that when she is old enough to need caring for, these two children will be grown and can manage her investments and businesses.

Njoki

Njoki was a young woman who had only been in Mathare for three years when I met her. She had arrived after the moratorium on building in Mathare. She was definitely a New Comer, and she was not yet a successful entrepreneur. She was very much at the stage of establishing herself.

Njoki had married at eighteen and moved to her husband's parents' house where she lived for eight years. The marriage was happy at first because her husband had been there with her. After three years of marriage he had left and gone to Nairobi to look for a job. She stayed behind and found that she could not coexist peaceably with her parents-in-law. Her husband traveled to Kisumu for work and was away for many months at a time. She claimed that her parents-in-law were "cruel" but would not say more than that. After eight years of marriage she returned to her own parents, and when her husband made no effort to come and get her she considered herself divorced. She kept custody of the children, which was unusual, but her husband's parents were poor and had many sons living at home trying to eke out a living on a tiny plot. Though her husband provided nothing for the boys, he sometimes visited them.

Njoki lived with her brother for several years, while she worked in bars in the market town near her brother's farm. She was no doubt entering into a number of relationships of various kinds with the men she met there. Njoki was an attractive woman, intelligent, happy, and flirtatious. In Mathare she had a plethora of admirers; a fact which she capitalized on, constantly changing her lovers when it seemed advantageous.

In 1969 Njoki left her mother and brother in the rural area. She felt that Nairobi would be better for *biashara* (business) of various kinds than the small trading center near her home. She left the children with her mother and brother, remitting money to pay for food, school fees, and clothes. She came to Mathare and rented a room from a successful woman entrepreneur who became her patron in due course. She started brewing beer and through a combination of hard work and personality was a very high earner. The protection of her patron helped her to avoid arrest and high bribes to the police.

In 1973 her brother died and his widow claimed that the plot was not big enough to sustain the old mother and Njoki's children. By this time she had saved enough money to buy into a land-buying company to obtain a four-acre shamba near Lake Nakuru. She built a small house there for her mother and her two sons to live in. They farmed the dry, rather infertile shamba, obtaining in the first year enough maize and beans to feed them for ten months or so. Njoki visited them every month and brought money for school fees and foodstuffs which were cheaper in town.

Njoki was one of the most successful of the younger women brewers I knew in Mathare. She made K.sh. (Kenyan shillings) 500 a month from brewing. She had a bank account, opened for her with the help of one of her boyfriends who worked in a bank. (It was not easy for an illiterate woman to open a bank account in Kenya at that time.) Toward the end of my period of research she had formed a relationship with a man employed in a white-collar capacity. Njoki was learning how to read and write from him, because she said she would be a better businesswoman if she could keep proper records. This man, she said, had promised to "lend" her K.sh. 1,500 for a down payment on a house. She was looking for an area in a town outside of Nairobi where a concrete-block house could be built. She planned to rent it out for income and to stay in Mathare to brew beer.

Njoki belonged to one rotating credit society which had a relatively high weekly contribution of K.sh. 20. She was going to be sponsored to join one of the most prestigious of the women's associations in Village II as soon as she could save the K.sh. 1,500 for the "share." An older woman from whom she rented a room and regularly bought beer wholesale was her sponsor.

Sadly, I lost track of Njoki and never saw her after I left in 1974. However, I had news of her. I was told by her above-mentioned patron that she did build her four-room house in a small town, Ngong, and had moved there when beer brewing became increasingly difficult and decreasingly profitable in the early eighties (see footnote 5).

Discussion of Njoki's Coping Strategies. Njoki has been included as an example of a later arrival to Mathare. Her arrival and her adjustment to urban life shows the continuity in strategies between Wambui (arriving in the 1930s), Mama M. (arriving in the 1950s), and her own (having arrived in Mathare in 1969).

Njoki practiced another strategy for urban survival. It was not one used by Wambui and Mama M., but it was a very common coping strategy in Mathare. That was the fostering of her children outside of Nairobi, staying with her mother. In payment for this help, Njoki cared for her mother, finding her a shamba, building her a house, and providing money for school fees and extras.

In common with many urban migrants in Mathare Valley, Njoki took over the care of her mother. Njoki did this contingent on her mother fostering her children and managing her farm. Mama M. had no children, but while her mother was alive she managed the farm.

Njoki, like Mama M., while uneducated in her rural childhood, recognized that the more complicated economy of the urban area disprivileges those who are not part of literate culture. Realizing this, these two intelligent women set out to acquire such skills.

The Coping Strategies Compared

The urban case histories of these three women demonstrate the range of coping strategies employed by two women who by the 1970s had become relatively successful urban entrepreneurs (even graduating from the informal to the formal economy) and one who was, when I lost contact with her, still at the point of consolidating her status as a successful rural-urban migrant. What conclusions can one draw from the comparisons and contrasts? What can they tell us about the coping strategies of Nairobi women rural-urban migrants?

The comparisons are revealing. All these women are admittedly capable, independent, hard working, attractive, and intelligent. They have utilized their relationships with men to accumulate money, information, skills, or privileges. In the early days of the growth of Nairobi, up until the 1970s, there was a dearth of women. This was caused by historically shifting combinations of the following factors: a strong rural peasant agriculture with relatively little landlessness, colonial attitudes to family migration, circular migratory patterns with the split household, and lack of formal-sector employment opportunities for women in the city. Women lack the education to compete successfully with men in the formal economy. However, they can benefit from men's employment through sex work. Until the 1980s it was a lucrative form of self employment. In the 1980s it became increasingly a buyer's and not a seller's market. In addition, HIV/AIDS may have diminished the market for casual sex work.

The most lucrative source of income for these women in the twenty years after Independence was buzaa brewing. It was an easy field to enter, no expensive capital investment was needed (only access to a room for selling), and the profit margins were good. A hard-working brewer could earn twice or three times the minimum wage in a month. Sadly the advent of buzaa-brewing by capital-intensive, formal-sector companies has made such an activity more difficult and less profitable for current rural-urban migrants. New incoming rural-urban migrants sell hash or homemade gin. Where there are gaps in the market and opportunities, those in the informal sector will seek these out to exploit.

These women invested in a wide range of activities—companies, land, houses, and cooperative ventures—thus spreading their risks and maximizing their chances for success. Their capacity for accumulating surplus depended on a secure base of one or more rooms to rent, a fact which Njoki recognized when she was trying to find her way into the housing market. Housing was and still is a secure form of investment. In the early days of Nairobi's expansion, housing was cheap enough for a relatively low-income person to afford to build and which repaid itself in less than a year. This is still the case, though the expansion of formal sector low-income housing in Eastlands has in the 1980s somewhat undercut the market for informal-sector housing.

These women have at some time or other employed some or all of the strategies relating to their relatives. They have cared for their mothers, fostered children with their mothers, received help from brothers where possible, lived in close conjunction with sisters in Mathare or other neighborhoods of Nairobi, and have seen part of a successful old age as lying in the education of their children. They have all educated (or tried to educate) their children or adopted or fostered children if they didn't have any of their own. Their children's labor, both as youngsters and later as adults, contributes to these women's domestic economy—Njoki's sons worked their grandmother's fields, Wambui's sons mended her houses, Mama M.'s foster daughter did housework and sold buzaa. Where possible Mathare women built matrifocal families which contributed to their coping capability.

All three women were active joiners and used women's organizations and other associations as part of their strategies. Some women (as in Wambui's case) join restructured "traditional-style" dance groups which are used as propaganda weapons in their struggle for urban survival. All three had a large network of friends that they called upon in times of need. As the two older women advanced in age and their careers, they had established themselves as women's leaders in a variety of associations as well as establishing themselves at the center of a buzaa-brewing or house-rental network. They became women elders in this community, an interesting urban variant of an old Highland Bantu structure . . . which would never have admitted "Big Women" alongside "Big Men" to the status of elder or patron (Ross 1974). In the process, such successful women secured clients who could act as a base for political activity. The two older women had, in their time, been clients to other important male patrons before becoming patrons in their own right. Less successful women depend on such patrons for help.

These three women do not represent the norm. However, they have been selected because their urban case histories represent normative behavior. All the coping strategies they practiced were characteristic of thousands of other female migrants to Kenya's cities. They utilized them more successfully than most. For others, these strategies allowed survival in the urban area, though not the ultimate security of translating their economic activities from the informal to the formal sector.

Notes

[1] I carried out my original fieldwork in Mathare Valley between 1970 and 1974. It was a conventional participant observation study with informal interviews. I also conducted a series of structured, life-history interviews with eighty-nine selected informants.

[2] Janet Bujra, working in a neighboring area, Pumwani, in the late sixties, conducted oral history research among a number of successful female entrepreneurs in that area. One of the coping strategies she noted was joining the Islamic mosque and becoming a "Swahili" (the local designation for someone practicing the Islamic faith). For many women this was a way of achieving a higher status. They could discreetly carry out sex work, yet be accepted as "respectable" women as long as they covered their head, ate Swahili food, and fasted during Ramadan (1975).

[3] In the late 1960s the Nairobi City Council tried unsuccessfully to destroy Mathare Valley. There was a public outcry, the residents of Mathare Valley mobilized their contacts in the city and national hierarchies, and the Council gave up the idea of bulldozing the Valley. Instead they entered into a contract with the National Christian Council of Churches to build some low-income housing and to develop

a site and service scheme (an area divided into plots where the authorities lay out roads and services such as water and sewerage. Allocatees have to build a house to certain building standards). These plots and houses in so-called New Mathare were supposed to replace Old Mathare. The lucky allocatees were supposed to tear down their units in Old Mathare. This always seemed to me a faint hope, since there were only 250 units in New Mathare and there were thousands of house owners in Old Mathare. In the event, even the allocatees didn't tear down all their units.

4 She seemed to like and respect me and always welcomed me to her house in a very friendly manner—complaining if the pressure of work made it difficult for me to visit her daily. However, she always maintained a reserve and formality with me, and I have subsequently wondered if she preferred me to be in her house so that she could keep tabs on me. Perhaps she enjoyed the prestige of having a European "friend" she could show off on important occasions. Maybe she did genuinely like me but felt that her position as the most important woman leader in the village made it undignified for her to be interviewed in the same way as other women who were my informants. She preferred her role of gate keeper and was always helpful in introducing me to women and reassuring them that my research had her approval. Certainly in revisits over the intervening years she has always seemed to enjoy my coming to see her and while I was there would tell people present who didn't know me of "my research" in a way which made it clear that she assisted me in this capacity as gate keeper and not as an informant.

5 In the 1960s and 1970s, the brewing of African beer in the municipalities of Kenya remained illegal. Unlike Tanzania and Uganda, the Kenyans did not change the existing colonial legislation. However, the legislation was not very stringently enforced. The fines were low and the brewers rarely jailed. In 1983, the president made a decree which forbade the brewing of African liquors and beer. From that time the police and court pressure became almost insupportable. Fines went up tenfold, and brewers were often jailed. By 1990 many of the women who had previously been full-time brewers in Mathare had given it up in despair.

European Cyclical Migration and Economic Development
The Case of Southern Spain

ROBERT RHOADES

A much neglected aspect of migration has been the return flow of migrants from cities back to their rural homelands. Some scholars, who have argued that migration is beneficial to both the host and donor societies, claim that return migration has several important benefits for the migrants' rural homelands. First, workers may bring back valuable work skills and industrial experience that will upgrade the home labor force. Second, the migrants' foreign earnings may be used to establish innovative businesses, cooperatives, and farms that will contribute to the revitalization of the rural homeland. Rhoades raises serious doubts about this view in his ethnographic case study of return migrants in a southern Spanish village.

Migration and Development: A Debate

During Western Europe's twenty-year "economic miracle" (1955–1975), over ten million southern Europeans emigrated to the industrial world north of the Alps and Pyrenees. Lured by promises of higher wages, secure jobs, or simply the hope of escape from poverty, they left the impoverished Mediterranean basin and sought

Source: Article written expressly for *Urban Life*.

their fortunes mainly in the labor-deficient regions of Germany, Switzerland, and France. However, these migrations were not terminal, one-shot affairs but governmentally planned, circular movements of labor between Europe's rural fringe and its industrial core. Migrants generally perceived themselves as "target workers" who temporarily went abroad for the purpose of earning enough money to build a new life upon return to their homelands. Correspondingly, labor-recruiting nations and employers looked upon immigration as a temporary, "stop-gap" solution to domestic labor shortages and thus discouraged permanent settlement of alien workers. This dovetailing of individual and national desires has resulted in continuous voluntary and periodic pressured returns of large numbers of migrants since the earliest stages of the post-war migrations.

The systematic transfer of manpower from Mediterranean regions of high unemployment to labor-starved regions in the North initially seemed a timely answer to many of Europe's economic and political ills. Migration across national frontiers was seen as fostering the cultural mingling of diverse Europeans, a necessary step toward realizing the dream of a "United States of Europe." More importantly, however, southern European countries would receive through remittances the foreign currency needed to overcome balance of payments problems. Also, the return of migrants was optimistically projected as a potential force in the economic uplifting of southern Europe. In fact, officials of northern European governments proclaimed that the exchange of "workers for wages" constituted a special form of "development aid" (Rhoades 1978a). Returning migrants were expected to carry home modern work habits, progressive attitudes, industrial skills, and the necessary capital to rejuvenate their regions' stagnated economies. It was believed that returnees could form a new entrepreneurial class capable of establishing businesses, industries, and modern farms needed for Mediterranean development.

By the early 1970s, however, the development aid interpretation had come under serious question. Critics argued that social and economic "costs" associated with emigration overshadowed actual "benefits." In a reversal of thought, emigration was seen as a "form of development aid given by poor countries to rich countries" (Castles and Kosack 1973:8). Industrialists, they argued, were interested in maintaining high profits through recruitment of a ready-made work force willing to work at lower wages than nationals. Furthermore, during periods of recession and high unemployment, industrial nations could export their unemployment problems by sending foreigners home. Antagonists of the development aid perspective also correctly pointed out that recruiting countries only accepted physically and educationally qualified migrants with at least some urban-industrial experience. However, since foreigners filled lower-class, manual jobs no longer desired by northern Europeans, they received no opportunity to learn new skills. At the same time, the absence of a large proportion of their best workers negatively affected southern European agricultural and industrial productivity. Finally, critics argued that it is probably a "myth" that returning migrants invest in a manner conducive to their home communities' development.

Unfortunately, this important debate on migration's role in development has been carried out without information on the actual behavior of returnees and their impact on sending regions. Empirically, virtually nothing is known about how returnees are investing their savings or whether they are applying skills or ideas acquired abroad in an innovative way. However, controversies on this topic can only be resolved through a firsthand study of returnees in their home communities. The purpose of this essay, therefore, is to present the results of an in-depth study of cyclical migration and development in Spain's province of Granada. Although research was confined to one geographical region, the results are relevant to a worldwide debate over the problematic link between migration and development. At the heart of this debate is whether urban regions, via the process of rural-urban migration, exert a positive developmental impact on labor-exporting areas.

Return Migration: An Andalusian Dream

The movement of migrants back to their places of origin has been described in many terms: return migration, counterstream migration, reverse or homeward migration, and repatriation. Migrants at this stage, now called returnees or repatriates, intend to take up relatively permanent residence in their native lands for the indefinite future. Thus, the return home is not just for a brief holiday or to take care of pressing family business. Social and economic commitments will now again be physically anchored in the home community, not in some distant, alien place (see Gmelch 1980 and Rhoades 1979b for detailed discussions of return migration).

One Mediterranean region which has been strongly affected by return migration has been the Spanish province of Granada. For a quarter of a century, Granada's impoverished villages and towns have sent thousands of native sons and daughters on the northward journey. Most communities have lost one-third of their inhabitants since 1960, mainly young adults who have sought their fortunes in northern industrial Spain and as "guest workers" abroad. Despite this drastic drop in population, however, many villages exhibit an aura of prosperity in the face of general demographic and economic decay. The striking impact of migrant investments in their home communities can be seen everywhere: construction of new homes, renovation of old ones, appearance of new businesses, increase in modern farm machinery and automobiles, and the presence of durable goods. Those who support the "migration as development" thesis point to such outward changes as evidence of their position. Migrants are, it seems, returning and applying their urban-acquired aspirations, values, and earnings to the modernization of their communities.

Fates of Return: Failures, Swallows, and Germans

However, closer examination of communities and individual cases reveals that migration is not a monolithic force. There are clearly distinct types of migration streams flowing out of Granada, and each one generates its own return pattern. "Internal" migration to Barcelona, for example, and "external" migration to West Germany have been directed toward industrial employment. However, migrants to Barcelona rarely return permanently to the village while most international migrants intend to return after some years abroad. Most jobs in France and Switzerland have been seasonal and temporary, mainly for a three-month harvest or a six-month construction period. Migrants with these destinations use the village as a home base and return temporarily every year.

Individuals vary widely in their desire or ability to use different migration streams as economic strategies. Although the types overlap, international migrants can be classified as "failures," "swallows," and "Germans." "Failures" are known in Spanish as *los fracasados*, "those who have failed." These are returnees whose migration experience was short-lived and for whatever reason chose to return home after a few months abroad. Typically, "failures" were unable to adapt to the foreign culture or failed to accept separation from their home community. Frequently, they return home disillusioned with nothing to show from their journey abroad. The "return of failure" has no innovative impact on the village, and fracasados rapidly blend in with those who never emigrated (Cerase 1970:220).

José B., an unmarried twenty-eight-year-old day laborer who also cultivates his family's small fields, illustrates the case of a fracasado. In 1970, his brother-in-law secured him a job in a bolt manufacturing plant near Frankfurt. Although initially elated by the prospects of earning over ten times his village income, José experienced severe "culture shock" within two months of his arrival in Germany. He lived with his brother-in-law in a small, cramped room in company barracks where they also cooked meals on a hot plate. José's contract began in late November, the onset of the German winter. He found the Germans unfriendly, the food not to his taste, the language impossible, and the climate unbearable. By late January, José had had enough and, disillusioned, he walked away from his assembly-line post and returned forever to Granada. He arrived home with $575 in savings and a few electronic items purchased in Germany. Still today, he rarely talks of his migration experience.

"Swallows" are known in Spanish as *los golondrinas*, migrants who engage in planned, repeat migration on a seasonal basis. Most international golondrinas work in the French grape harvest or in construction in Switzerland. Like their feathered namesakes, "swallows" predictably depart and return by the seasons. Every year during the off-season, they may be active in the local economy. In the Andalusian case, men generally go alone to Switzerland while the French grape harvest frequently attracts complete families. The migratory "swallows" generate greater earnings than fracasados. Sometimes they save enough to renovate a house or purchase a parcel of land. However, their migration strategy is subsistence-oriented; that is, their aim is to earn enough to live on until the next work period. "Los golondrinas," villagers will tell you, "eat here in the village what they earn there."

Mañuel M. typifies the golondrina. In the village he farms two hectares, works at odd jobs, and owns a small bar, but every year he applies for a six-month contract to work in Swiss construction. For over a decade, Mañuel has traveled to the Spanish emigration branch office in Granada where he applies for a Swiss contract. Generally, he secures work with the same company from Geneva. During his absence, his wife and children take care of the farm and bar. Since this strategy generates income that will be used to support the family throughout the year, it holds limited potential for community development. The impact, therefore, of los golondrinas is only slightly more significant than that of los fracasados.

"The Germans" or *los alemanes*, as they are locally called, are long-term migrants returning from northern Europe. Village inhabitants consider industrial, intra-European migrants the migration "elite" since they generate the greatest physical impact on villages. Everyone knows the potential for rapid financial gain is enhanced by securing work in Germany or similar industrial positions in France, Holland, or Switzerland. Although males initially emigrate alone, the rest of the immediate family follows after a foothold is gained abroad. Frequently, all family members of age work. After several years abroad, los alemanes return with the intention of remaining in the village where they can live "semiretired" on their investments.

Moises V. is an *alemán* who spent twelve years in Germany. He and his wife, who worked abroad nine years, were able to save more than $40,000. Two of their three children were born there; all speak German better than Spanish. In 1973, Moises and his wife decided to bring their family home. During his annual vacation, he made arrangements to purchase the home of the village physician who had moved to the coast. Moises also acquired four hectares of land and a small tractor. Before leaving Germany, they purchased all furnishings needed for their new home. Throughout their migration experience, Moises and his wife planned and dreamed of their final homecoming. Before going to Germany, Moises was a *campesino* (peasant) who had no land and depended on local landlords for jobs or land to cultivate. Migration, however, was Moises's only chance to change this. As he put it:

> Fifteen years ago, this town was owned by four men. They wouldn't even greet me on the street. They even had a club where I couldn't go. One of them lived here in this house. It's mine now. Everyone knows who Moises V. is. There is no finer house nor furnishings in this village than mine. I owe everything to Germany.

In Moises's community, as in many others, the alemanes are largely responsible for the village construction booms, growing bank deposits, presence of modern consumer goods, and the general appearance of village prosperity. If there is any hope for development through migration, it must come from this class of returnees. The remainder of this paper, therefore, will focus specifically on village-level activities of returned "Germans."

Returnee Investment

The volume of capital sent home by Andalusian migrants has been staggering. If these funds were properly invested in employment-generating enterprises or in economically sound businesses or farms, fundamental changes could come to Andalusia. Migrant remittances from northern Europe have been so massive in recent years that new banks have opened in many small communities. In 1972 alone, the 179,000 Spanish migrants in West Germany sent or brought home German marks worth almost one billion U. S. dollars (Bundesanstalt für Arbeit 1973). In one village of 1,500 residents, migrants sent home $6 million by 1976. A study of the same village indicated that migrants saved an average of $6,000 each, although a few families saved over $40,000. These earnings are set aside for specific types of investments in a variety of undertakings. The main types of investments are: (1) housing, home furnishings, and durable goods; (2) small-scale businesses (bars, shops, grocery stores); and (3) agriculture.

Symbols of Success: Houses, Furniture, and Durable Goods

A desire to improve housing ranks as a major motivation for emigration, especially among married migrants. This is accomplished by restoring the family home, constructing a new one, or renovating an older, purchased home. Often, migrants begin the construction of their post-emigration residence early in the migration cycle, with the wife or other family members returning to supervise the construction project. It is not unusual for migrants to miscalculate costs and face the need to re-emigrate to earn funds to finish their building project. Half-finished migrant houses with grass and weeds growing around are not uncommon sights in Granada. However, the desire for housing has created temporary local employment for those left behind.

The migration-stimulated housing boom has altered significantly village settlement patterns in many communities. The physical concentration of returnees' homes in villages has been labeled *el centro alemán* (the German Center) by locals. In one village on the plains north of the Sierra Nevada mountains, this shift has been especially dramatic. Prior to migration to Germany, most workers lived in poor housing or caves situated on the village fringe. In 1966, more than one-fifth of the village populace lived in caves; by 1976, however, this percentage had fallen to 8 percent. Since caves symbolize lower status to community members, a central element of return migrant ideology centers on changing residence within the village. Thus, the exodus has been toward the lower barrios along the main village thoroughfare. In this el centro alemán, which is a kilometer-long physical concentration of new migrant houses, shops, and bar-restaurants, real estate values have increased over 1000 percent in ten years.

"German" returnees not only come home wealthy by local standards, they display this wealth through conspicuous consumption of luxury goods acquired abroad. The return lifestyle is distinguished by a characteristic type of home furnishings, goods consumption, and clothing. The German flavor is very strong. Symbols of migration success always include plush furniture, televisions, chandeliers, German tourist wall plaques, ashtrays, and similar paraphernalia. Many migrant households contain wall-long glass cabinets which proudly display German beer steins and glass articles as well as built-in bars stocked with a wide array of liquors. It is no exaggeration to classify many returnees as Germanophiles in terms of consumption. They always bring back their limit of consumer goods on annual trips and upon their final return. Electronic gadgets and appliances are especially desirable.

Villages influenced by heavy return migration from industrial Europe show outward signs of social transformation. Today, former campesinos (peasants) or *jornaleros* (day laborers) who emigrated and returned with solid savings live in the most modern houses, frequently next door to former landlords or professionals. However, the old establishment finds it extremely difficult to keep up with the consumption habits of returnees. Moises V., the alemán returnee mentioned above, brought his entire household furnishings—including bathtub and doorknobs—to make sure there would be no village residence better decorated than his.

Migrant Businesses

After returnees have satisfied their desires for improved housing and living conditions, they put their energy and remaining savings into some local enterprise. The majority buy a parcel of land to farm, but a number try their hand at a small business. The primary goal in setting up a private enterprise is to live in a semiretired state. Returnees do not plan, initially at least, to take up wage labor in the fields. Instead of "working like Negroes" (*trabajando como negros*), as they claim was the case before, they now live "on their own account" (*por su cuenta*). Returnees with small businesses describe their aspirations in terms of "being independent," "no longer a slave," or "to be one's own boss." As a result, very few actually work in occupations held in Germany since it would mean they would have to become laborers again in Spanish cities. Indeed, many skilled workers (mechanics, carpenters, welders, masons) do not market their skills upon return. Instead, they attempt to live from various investments (Rhoades 1978a: 142–143).

Returnees are amazingly predictable in the kinds of businesses they establish: bar-restaurant combinations, grocery stores, shops, and vehicle hire. Investments center primarily on undertakings that are manageable on a family scale. This has caused the number of bars, for example, in one village to rise from three to nine in ten years. Eight of these bars are owned by returnees. The same village, with a declining population and only slightly over fifteen hundred inhabitants, now contains six grocery stores, one supermarket, and six bread shops. Most of these enterprises were recently added by migrants, and there is evidence that as more return from Germany, the growth of small businesses will continue.

Returnees are not adventurous in investing and are unwilling to gamble savings in risky financial schemes. Even though migrant families frequently return with considerable amounts of capital, opportunity for investment in the village is severely limited. Furthermore, in a few cases, entrenched middle-class entrepreneurs and authorities have conspired to refuse business permits to returnees. The traditional business elite has not departed in the wake of the unexpected competition. They simply sold their shops to returnees and opened more profitable stores, selling modern appliances and furniture to meet returned migrant consumption needs.

Migrant Farming Enterprises: A Questionable Future

The purchase of agricultural land is seen by many migrants as necessary for long-term security and a symbolic ingredient of post-emigration lifestyle. Demand for small cultivable parcels has created strong inflationary pressures in land values. According to local bankers in one village, quality irrigated land now sells for $14,000 to $15,000 per acre while dry land may cost up to $6,000 per acre. Interest in land is due in part to a lack of alternative investment opportunities in the village and returnees' general distrust of risky investment schemes. "Land," the migrants declare, "will always be there, come war, famine, or depression." Land is purchased from landlords who have capitalized on the land-hungry mood of returnees to reap handsome profits. In general, however, returnees are not concerned with modernizing newly acquired parcels as much as continuing with traditional patterns of land use. For a variety of reasons, parcels may not always be intensively cultivated. Often crops or fruit are not worth harvesting due to low prices or lack of cheap labor. Farming alone can no longer support a family and maintain the standard of living migrants have grown accustomed to in northern Europe. These who attempt to rely strictly on small-scale agricultural investments often must re-emigrate (Rhoades 1979a:65–69).

A number of returnees have invested heavily in modern farm machinery. In one community, for example, the number of tractors rose from eighteen to forty-five between 1969 and 1976, the years corresponding to heaviest return from Germany. On the plain of Guadix, north of the Sierra Nevada range, several migrants purchased large John Deere tractors for $11,000 each. These large machines are built for deep-plowing or wide-sweeping operations customary on the American Great Plains, not for the shallow-soil cultivation practiced in the area. Since most former migrants do not have sufficient land to justify ownership of a tractor, they attempt to hire out the machine and labor. Unfortunately, demand for tractor time is restricted to planting and harvest seasons. Furthermore, unplanned expenses related to repairs, maintenance, attachments and high fuel costs have sharply diminished their profitability. Tractor owners also admit there are "too many tractors for so little land" and that a saturation point has been reached. Also, the increase in farm machinery is reducing the availability of manual jobs in agriculture. Ironically, return migration investments contribute to the need for more out-migration among the laboring class.

Post-Return Lifestyles in Social Context

Throughout the long and lonely migrancy period, the typical Spanish migrant yearns to return to his cultural roots. Nostalgia is a prime mover in directing the migrant homeward. If a worker departed for Germany during his twenties or later, the village remains his main social frame of reference while abroad. The desire to emigrate and return a Spanish "Horatio Alger" success is an impelling image. In terms of ideology, the migrant is Spain's modern conquistador whose "cities of gold" are not in the Americas but in the factories along the Ruhr, Rhine, and Saar regions of northern Europe. And his mission, like that of the ancestral conquistador, is to acquire his fortune abroad, and return to bask in the praise of his countrymen. However, only in the context of his village—not among strangers—can he be a proud entrepreneur, landlord, or homeowner. It is not difficult to imagine the emotions of a peasant of humble origins who is now able to return triumphantly to the place that formerly exploited and humiliated him.

Another gauge of the philosophical orientation of returnees is found in the results of the first political elections held since the Spanish Civil War. During the 1977 campaign, emigration was the central political issue for all parties in Granada. Posters and handbills from the left, center, and right proclaimed "stop emigration" as a key slogan. Returnees, however, often were suspected of leaning toward the left in political and labor matters. This image was not helped by a few former migrants who ran for public office on the Communist ticket. After the elections, one of the "folk explanations" why a given village voted Socialist or Communist was that "too many migrants live there" (Rhoades 1979a:69). Especially among the middle and upper classes, a fear was prevalent that emigrants had become "men of ideas" and thus overly critical of the social status quo. This was not true, however, of the alemanes. Election results demonstrated that communities tied closely to Germany for jobs tended to vote for moderate parties. Successful returnees do not have radical change on their minds but are voices of moderation in Spain's post-Franco political experiment. Bitterness, however, can be found in many parts of Andalusia, especially in the communities characterized by the golondrina pattern of seasonal out-migration. Communities lacking a migration outlet or those facing constant uncertainty in the fight for seasonal contracts in France or Switzerland tend to be antagonistic in political matters. The alemanes, however, are voices of political and cultural moderation. They are not interested in risking loss of their new status with an uncertain political system.

An Assessment

What conclusions germane to the debate over migration and development can be drawn from this ethnographic study of Andalusian returnees? Outwardly, many sending communities verify the thesis that circular migration is conducive to economic development. The improvement in income, material life, housing, and the growth of a small business sector seem to testify to the notion that migration is a positive force which integrates peasant communities into national economies. Since the migrations began, unemployment has actually decreased in some communities, agriculture has been mechanized, and rural credit problems partially overcome. From all appearances, migration has allowed rural populations to "share the fruits of development."

However, serious doubts can be raised as to the permanence of these migration-induced changes. The centro alemán can be compared to a "stage prop" which will crumble as soon as the migration drama reaches its final act. As special "worker suburbs" of West German industry located a thousand miles away in Spanish villages, the prosperity of the "German Centers" depends upon the continuing availability of jobs in northern Europe. However, in 1973 Germany abruptly closed its doors to new migrants, and other industrial nations have pursued similar policies. If migrant investments fail, as many have, returnees will not be able to repeat their international migration experience. Most returnees are relatively young men and women in their forties, and it is doubtful that their investments will last the rest of their lives. Even if they "semi-retire" with a restricted standard of living, their children will be forced to seek work outside the region.

Returnees may construct new homes and fill them with modern furnishings, but such investments do not create resources or conditions which will guarantee long-run prosperity. Returnees invest in small-scale, highly competitive businesses located in depressed regions which continue to lose population. Commercial agriculture or agrarian innovations are not a primary concern of former migrants. Most consumer items purchased by migrants are low quality, mass-produced goods which will deteriorate rapidly in value. Given local wages, such goods cannot be easily replaced. Migrant families may enjoy at least short-term social mobility, higher incomes, and improved conveniences, but outside the "glitter" of their homes, the stark village reality continues. Rural communities may have had a new "facelifting" by returnees, but the local infrastructure remains largely unaltered and no new employment opportunities have been created through migrant actions. In other words, the changes brought by migration are only "skin-deep"; they do not represent fundamental structural changes in the economy.

Returning to the Returnees: Impact of Migration after Ten Years

Exactly a decade has passed since I lived in Andalusia and conducted migration research. My return to the villages in 1987 was cause of great celebration and endless hours of discussion about my own fortunes and those of my migrant friends since I last saw them. The massive return of migrants was only beginning in 1976 and 1977 when I set forth my hypothesis on migration and change. Today, the former migrants look back nostalgically on those days as *la buena época de emigración* (the great age of emigration). As

Spaniards returned home from Northern Europe, they were not replaced by others. The *migration drama* about which I wrote had indeed reached its final act. Now, time was on my side. Ten years are sufficient to determine if the changes brought about by migration were, as I argued, *only skin deep*.

Both returned migrants and government statistics will tell you that the economy of Spain and Andalusia has deteriorated over the past decade. Spain's unemployment rate climbed from 5.2 percent in 1977 to 16.3 percent by 1982. Andalusia's unemployment rate shot up threefold, from 7 percent in 1977 to over 21 percent in 1982. These increases are due to many factors, including the drying up of the emigration outlet. The Spanish population continued to grow vigorously, while, from 1973 to 1982, an actual decrease in the number of available jobs occurred (Lagares Calvo 1982).

Within the migrant-sending areas, conditions got even worse. Populations of the villages continued to fall another 10 to 15 percent. The Socialist party, which the German returnees initially rebuffed, came to power and won the migrant vote. Unemployment reached crisis proportions, and the governments of Andalusia and Extremadura instituted a rural unemployment compensation system, whereby the government pays up to 180 days of unemployment. In the villages I had studied, this welfare system replaced migration as the main source of income for the rural populace. The *migration as development* thesis obviously had not worked out as European planners had hoped.

Despite negative statistics and the pessimistic views of my migrant friends, however, those villages which had sent migrants to industrial Europe continued to show an outward appearance of prosperity, which puzzled me. In fact, one of my main research villages—Alcudia—continued to enjoy the growth of small businesses and new homes even as the population fell. Here, my *stage prop* had not fallen as predicted, but had, in fact, improved. Since 1977, the number of restaurants in this village of thirteen hundred inhabitants increased from nine to thirteen, the number of supermarkets from one to two. In addition, two new discotheques and four new hairdresser shops opened for business. The centro alemán consisted of two to three rows of new, two-story homes, along the main road. The owners, all returned migrants, were now in their forties and early fifties.

Nearby villages that had sent migrants to the seasonal French harvests or to temporary Swiss construction sites had not fared so well. They continued to see a decrease in population, with no compensation in new construction or small businesses. I was reminded of the *green revolution* debates. Migration had increased inequities between the more prosperous communities (German-linked) and the poorer ones (seasonally French- or Swiss-linked).

I was wrong on another point. There may have been no fundamental economic structural changes in the migrant-sending regions, but I sensed fundamental structural changes in the minds of the Andalusian migrants. Unlike earlier ages of emigration, when their Andalusian ancestors went to the New World and rarely returned permanently, the European migrant did come home to stay. Women and young people, especially, are now aware of alternatives. The village, for most, still remains their base of operation, but they are knowledgeable of the European urban core. For a livelihood, returnees combine diverse strategies, including farming, seasonal migration for tourism, small businesses, and unemployment compensation. I admire now, like I did not in 1977, their tenacity and creativity in coping with an economically difficult situation and in managing to somehow come out on top, at least spiritually.

Reflections of an Urban Anthropologist

WALTER P. ZENNER

One goal of scholarship and scientific inquiry is an increased understanding of the place of humanity in the universe. Such understanding is always incomplete. In this essay, one of the editors reflects on his ethnographic fieldwork and personal experiences and their contribution to the larger goal.

Thoughts on a Day in Ma'aruf

It was a glorious, sunny February day in Ma'aruf, an Arab village in the mountains of Galilee. After the cold, rainy winter months, one sensed the coming of spring. The hills were covered with green, and there were white blossoms on the almond trees and red anemones in the fields. I went to my friend's house, as I did whenever I visited this village. He served me coffee in the traditional way, first a cup of bitter coffee—the ritual sign of hospitality—and then a cup of sweet Turkish coffee. We talked about the latest news in the village and the world. For a moment I felt like the nineteenth-century traveler who sensed an "immovable East," barely changed from biblical times.

Then we went out on his terrace, and my gaze wandered to the villagers in the streets. Boys were playing. Men in a truck from the Gaza Strip were selling cheap trinkets and pottery, mostly imports from Hong Kong and Taiwan. Women were going to the bakery to buy bread. Men were returning from work in the city.

Fifty years ago, this village had five hundred inhabitants, almost all of them engaged in agriculture. Today there are ten times that number and 80 percent of the men work outside the village, either in factories or in various kinds of government jobs. There is even a small factory in the village itself employing young girls and women to make nylon stockings. Fifty years ago, the villagers grew most of their own food, importing only rice, coffee, and sugar. Today they grow a few cash crops, such as watermelons, tomatoes, and plums, for the market in Haifa, the nearest city, but they also import much food. Fifty years ago, it took several hours to reach the city by foot or donkey. Today taxis and buses go back and forth all day. Most villagers have radios and television sets, and they receive world news from the Israeli radio or from Lebanon, Egypt, or Jordan. They watch the television commentaries of the editor of Egypt's leading paper and listen regularly to the B.B.C.

Fifty years ago, the villagers' life span was short, and the infant mortality rate was high—many babies lived only a few days. Today the women have their babies in hospitals and mortality rates have plummeted. The villagers worry now about the way in which their young people are straying from the traditional ways of life. Many old people receive social security benefits, unknown a generation ago. Fifty years ago, Ma'aruf was a village much as it had been for five hundred years—near a city, yet still far away. Today it is but a suburb of Haifa, a sprawling, industrial city, a port of trade with the four corners of the modern world.

As we sat on his terrace, my Ma'aruf friend asked me for advice about his son and daughter. Should his son study art or go to work in a factory? Should his daughter, who had done well in school, go to the university, where she might encounter strange men? I wanted to help him, but what advice could I give? Did I know more about the future than he did? The changes which were engulfing this five-hundred-year-old village in the Galilee mountains were also swirling about my own life.

Unlike my friend in Ma'aruf, whose family had lived in that village in Galilee for half a millennium, I was a wanderer. My family, too, had lived in one place for a long time—a small town in southern Germany. Records showed Zenners living there 300 years ago. Probably the Zenner family had lived in Franconia for centuries, perhaps a thousand years. After World War I, however, my father sought his fortune in the city of Nürnberg. Then, like many other European Jews, my family fled from the Nazi regime. Those who stayed behind were murdered. Of the many Jewish communities, often centuries old, that existed in Europe and the Middle East in 1800, only a few remain today. The Jewish experience under Hitler was, of course, exceptional. But the breakup or transformation of traditional communities and cultural patterns is a phenomenon that has been accelerating for more than a century.

Since the Industrial Revolution in the early nineteenth century, all sorts of peoples have been on the move—as immigrants to new countries, as peasants seeking jobs in cities, as refugees from famine, persecution, and genocide. Arabs, Chinese, Vietnamese, Hindus and South Asians, Muslims, Amerindians, Ibos, Gypsies, Irish, Scots, Welsh, English, French, Italians, Serbs, and many others have joined these streams of humanity leaving their family homes, and often their homelands, for other places. These migrations have reflected changes in technology, in political organization, and in the world economy. As many of these peoples became urban dwellers, some for the first time in their historical experience, the cities themselves were changing in fundamental ways. Now the people of Ma'aruf were joining this movement. Some were working in far-off places, others had become daily commuters, still others were studying abroad. In other Arab villages, people had been uprooted in the past forty years by wars, land expropriation, and poverty.

On a Visit to Los Angeles

A few years after this visit to Ma'aruf, I attended a conference in Los Angeles. When it ended, I stayed another day to see some friends who lived there, whom I had not seen for thirteen years. We had all been living in Chicago then; now my home was in the Northeast and theirs in southern California.

I had known Renee since we were in sixth grade. We had gone to high school and summer camp together. Ernie, her husband, had been my camp counselor. After going away to school, we three had returned to Chicago. Now we were far apart. In Albany, where I live, there are very few people who knew me before I was a college professor and married. Almost no one knew my family before we moved there. One day, when my wife and I were going out and leaving our young daughter with a baby sitter, we realized that if something happened to us, neither the sitter nor our neighbors would know our next of kin. Since then we have made some friends with whom we have become close; yet the feeling is not quite the same with them as with those who have known me since childhood or since college.

For Ernie and Renee, however, it is different. Ernie has two brothers in Los Angeles. There is also a whole colony of ex-Chicago

Jews in the city, and one meets old friends from the West Side or the North Side. Even though my friends now live like Californians—enjoying jogging and eating organic foods—they have many links with their past.

In the Los Angeles smog, I suddenly remembered the sunny day in Ma'aruf and realized how close that place is to the clouds of industrial smoke over Haifa Bay. Whether in Los Angeles or Albany with strangers and new acquaintances or in Ma'aruf, surrounded by lifelong friends, enemies, and kin (who often are all rolled into one), we all face the unknown. The great forces of the world in the twentieth century have swept all of us up, and we must find others to help and support us. In this world, we seek the shelter of small groups to give us some protection from life's storms. Now we are all city folk who must find new havens.

Part Four

Urban Family, Kinship, and Interpersonal Relations

When people discuss the family they often speak in inexact terms. The group of people who claim a close relationship in terms of descent and marriage is often seen as the same as those people who share a place of residence (household, home). People may share a home, but not feel the kind of commitment with which we associate family, as in the case of college roommates. The two concepts overlap. Still, when people today speak about "nontraditional families," much of the time they are talking about households that include people who are not necessarily kin. Examples are a single parent, his or her children, and a lover who share a house; children living together with relatives who are not their parents; or students living together in an apartment. Such compound households have always existed for a wide variety of reasons, including celibacy, divorce, widowhood, disease, and the like. The heroine of *Anne of Green Gables*, who lived with Marilla, a spinster, and her bachelor brother, exemplifies this. Whether more households of this type exist in contemporary cities than in rural areas or other periods requires further research.

Many theorists from different schools (e.g., the followers of Karl Marx and Louis Wirth) see urbanization and industrialization leading to the decreasing importance of household functions and the weakening of the family. They write that urban life tends to sever ties between the nuclear family (parents and unmarried children) and its extended kinfolk (parents of adult children, their siblings' children, uncles, aunts, cousins). This weakening in urban settings is due to the fact that the tasks that the family performs for its members are limited to early childhood and elder care, eating, sleeping, and emotional support and expression for nuclear family members. Except for the last named, the site for such activities is the home.

Other functions carried out by the family in a rural context, they argue, are taken away from the family in the city. They are transferred to other institutions. Credit, for example, is provided by banks rather than by relatives. The workplace is outside of the home, and employment is found through impersonal agencies and advertisements, rather than through family and friends. Child-care centers and the schools take an increasingly important share of childrearing, while hospitals, public welfare departments, senior citizen centers, and old-age homes are more significant than family and kin in the care of the ill, the needy, and the aged. Sex, too, is often found outside of marriage and may be quite impersonal. This picture of the family fits in quite well with the Wirthian theory of urbanism as a source of isolation and loneliness (Wirth, "Urbanism as a Way of Life"; C.C. Harris 1970).

Much of the criticism of the Wirthian theory comes from studies which have shown that family ties of urbanites are often strong and that connections with extended kin survive in urban settings. Several aspects of this critique will be stressed in this essay and in the articles that follow. The first is that urbanization and industrialization, even in the West, do not necessarily reduce familial ties to those of the nuclear family. The second is that non-Western family types persist in modern cities in the Third World, even though these cities are affected by westernization and urbanization. The third is that economic function and social status are stronger influences than urbanism on the form of the family and on relationships between nuclear families and their kin.

The Urban Family and Industrialization

Anthropologists and historians have made a major contribution to theories of urbanism by pointing out that the association between urbanism and attenuated families is by no means simple. They have shown that the rosy picture of people living in extended family households in preindustrial societies was, to a large degree, a wishful idealization. These "history of the family" scholars have shown how important nonfamilial institutions like the wet nurse were for preindustrial urban people. They also have revealed the extent to which illegitimacy, prostitution, child abuse and neglect, and dissolution of families existed before modernization. It turns out that the nuclear family household, often truncated, was quite common in premodern Europe (Ranum and Forster 1976; Stone 1977; Laslett 1972).

During and after the Industrial Revolution many changes took place in the Western family, both in the working class and in the middle and upper strata. The forms and functions of the family and kinship changed during different stages of industrialization and the rural-urban migration which accompanied it. Michael Young and Peter Willmott (1973) describe three stages in the transformation of the English family from its preindustrial past to its contemporary form. The stages are: (1) the family as unit of production; (2) disruption of this unit and transition to the family as unit of consumption; and (3) the symmetrical family as a unit of consumption. In the first stage, the household is the site of production in both agriculture and handicrafts. All family members engage in productive activities. Among urban craftsmen, the workshop is part of the home. The movement from working for oneself or one's family in a small workshop to being a wage laborer in a large factory, managed by strangers, is associated with the growth of cities during the Industrial Revolution.

The second stage, the transition from the domestic system to the factory system, was still incomplete in the nineteenth century. In some trades, like bootmaking and tailoring, craftsmen still needed to employ their wives. But generally the productive functions of the family were lost, and as factories and other specialized workplaces replaced the family as units of production, schools took over educational tasks. While many women did work in factories, during their childbearing and rearing years they were often confined to their homes, completely dependent on their husbands for support. The financial resources of the working-class family were especially strained during these years because children needed to be supported and often did not contribute to the family income. The battering and abuse of women and children by men, who were themselves oppressed in the factories; desertion of families; and the use of the pub or tavern for recreation and escape were common features of working-class life. Aspects of this second stage in the transformation of the family have persisted in England and other parts of the Western world well into the latter half of the twentieth century, such as the docker families described by Young and Willmott (1957).

Family disruption of the type that occurred during the Industrial Revolution continues in Western Europe and North America, particularly among poor migrants, although migration may strengthen other kin ties. Susan Keefe's comparison of Anglo and Mexican-American families in California disagrees with those who argue that extended kin ties wither away in modern industrial societies (Keefe, "The Myth of the Declining Family"; Rhoades, "European Cyclical Migration"; and G. Gmelch, "West Indian Life"). Sometimes only husbands or wives can go to the city, and some of the children may be left behind. The migration of West Indians described by George Gmelch (1992), for example, often required that parents leave some or all of their children, as well as spouses, behind in the Caribbean (see Gmelch, "A West Indian Life").

In addition to the disruption of kin ties, the family is also affected by the housing market in cities. The family may be forced to reside in a furnished one-room apartment; continued contact with their families of origin in the rural countryside or in another country is difficult. "On the other hand," notes A. Vieille (1954) in a study of working-class families in the Paris area, "the extreme overcrowding of tenants, cooped up in rooms which are too small, and the common facilities for water, washing, and so on bring neighbors into some degree of close contact with the life of the family." This kind of life with strangers, however, is usually transitory. Most people continue to rely on family and kin for assistance, even among the urban poor, as described by Carol Stack in "The Kindred of Viola Jackson."

The emergence of the symmetrical or companionate family represents the third stage, according to Willmott and Young. The adjective "symmetrical" implies that husband and wife are involved in the same kinds of activity and share both "breadwinning" and homemaking. The term "companionate" suggests that relationships are based on emotional needs, rather than being forced on adult children by their parents. The terms imply a utopian ideal which has not been achieved anywhere. Still, families striving for such goals first arose in the British and North American middle classes in the nineteenth century. They are marked by a decrease in births, a rise in the educational level of women, and less segregation of gender roles. For example, more wives are employed and husbands increasingly help with households, although in practice the burden of housework has still fallen on women. The use of labor-saving devices in the home permits more time for outside activities, plus it engenders a desire for more income to buy more devices.

Young and Willmott's delineation of stages, however, cannot be applied mechanically to societies, even within the Euro-American industrialized sphere. This type of household may only exist in a segment of the middle class. It certainly was not characteristic of the working-class families of East London, studied by Young and Willmott in the 1950s.

Whether or not development toward a symmetrical family can be at all applied to the world outside of western Europe and North America is arguable. Middle-class women in Guatemala City, whether or not they work outside the home, bear the full responsibility for child care and housekeeping, unless they hire servants to do these tasks (Bossen, "Wives and Servants"). Kenneth Little (1973) has claimed that urban African women have achieved a large measure of liberation from the constraints of the traditional culture by their migration to towns. Still, elements of traditional kinship perceptions persist in Africa and elsewhere.

William Jankowiak's article ("Urban Chinese") also shows how people in another society deal with change in their family lives in an urban context. His work was done in a province of the People's Republic of China. China has an ancient urban tradition, but this tradition has been challenged by political and economic pressure from the outside and by intense ideological conflict within China. The Communist state has sought to transform families and individuals by enforcing a wide variety of laws, including one that restricts married couples to having just one child. With these new rules on top of what adult Chinese had learned under the "old regime," confusion over proper ways for men and women to behave has arisen. For North Americans such bewilderment over gender roles as well as conflicts over childrearing, feminism, and "family values" are a familiar part of our lives.

Socioeconomic Status and Extended Kin

Economic status in both preindustrial and industrial cities has been an important factor in determining the character of family life. The usual picture of modern urban society as one in which the family's functions have been reduced to those of child care and consumption has been challenged by studies that demonstrate the importance of extended kinship ties in economic activity (e.g., the family firms and kin networks described in Zenner, "Transnational Web").

Kinship ties in both preindustrial and industrial societies are most ramified among the political and economic elites. These groups have powerful kin networks; consider, for example, European nobility and royalty. All the royal families of Europe intermarried (Fleming 1973). The emergent ruling classes of modern colonial and industrial societies show similar patterns. In Brazil, Argentina, Chile, the United States, and Britain, the rise of merchants and landowners to key positions in society often coincided with marriages to members of an older elite. While some of these elites were rural in origin, they often maintained homes in large urban centers where their wealth could be transformed into political office, like the aristocracy before them (e.g., Balmori and Oppenheimer 1979; Lewin 1979). Today these elites tend to be multinational. For instance, Grace Kelly, a Philadelphia heiress and movie star, married the prince of Monaco; her daughter has married a French millionaire. Jacqueline Bouvier was married first to John F. Kennedy and later to Greek shipping tycoon Aristotle Onassis. She also has affinal ties with the Auchincloss family, which is in turn kin to the Roosevelt family.

The economic functions of family and kin are weakest among the isolated urban poor and among impoverished recent migrants to the city. But even among these, as Stack, and Eames and Goode ("Coping with Poverty") show, there is a substantial amount of mutual aid provided by kin and friends.

The poor may also rely on assistance from unrelated neighbors and friends. The complex household of the protagonist in *Madame Rosa*, an Academy Award-winning film, is one example. Madame Rosa was an ex-prostitute who in her old age fostered the illegitimate children of other prostitutes as well as an assortment of other abandoned children. She would fit in well in the furnished rooms of French working-class families studied by Vieille (1954), which was discussed earlier. This is a world where people must often find friends, for many have no relatives to whom they can turn for help.

In modern welfare states, bureaucrats interfere in the family lives of the poor more than in other classes of people. In the United States, receipt of welfare is contingent on the absence of an employable male in the household, which encourages husbands to desert their wives and children or not marry the women with whom they have children. Nevertheless, as Stack (1974; and "The Kindred of Viola Jackson") shows, the support of the poor by the state is often inadequate and the maintenance of extensive networks of kin and friends is still necessary. Bureaucratic intervention thus changes both the roles of men and women in the family, as well as the structure of the household itself. Governmental action—whether with regard to welfare assistance, protection of children against abuse, or education—affects the poor more than other classes and can transform the family. Whether even well-intentioned intervention by governmental agencies benefits the poor and others is a subject about which there is considerable debate (also see Orent 1977; Handelman and Shamgar-Handelman 1978).

In the middle-status groups, the situation differs. The usual sociological stereotype is that the strong conjugal family with only weak links to extended kin is typical of the middle class. That is where one would expect to find the symmetrical or companionate family which is essentially a unit of consumption, not production. Here again, sociologists and anthropologists have found that middle-class families in countries like Great Britain and the United States often have strong bonds with their extended kin. It is common for grandparents to provide their grandchildren with riding lessons and other expensive amenities which the parents of these children could not pay for on their own (C. A. Bell 1968). Many Jews of East European origin in New York City often are involved in clubs organized on the basis of kinship, such as cousins (Mitchell 1978). Small businesses are often organized as family firms (Leichter and Mitchell 1967). Thus, even people in a large metropolis may be highly involved with their kin. Not surprisingly, we find that the involvement of family in business has been quite common, even though it may entangle the business with the emotional tensions of kin ties (see Zenner, "The Transnational Web of Syrian-Jewish Relations").

While the modern, educated middle classes in India and Africa appear to adopt a European style in their lifeways, this emulation of the West is only partial. For instance, in the small Indian town near New Delhi described by Sylvia Vatuk (1974), urbanization/modernization has had little impact on family life. Marriages even among the Western-educated are still arranged, and marrying outside one's caste is still forbidden. Recent rural migrants continue to participate in the joint ownership of rural property which they and their kin share. Ties with distant kin are maintained and the interests of the extended kin group are still considered to outweigh the desires of individual members. Married children who establish new households in the city are expected to care for and take in elderly parents (Vatuk 1972). Among Indian and Pakistani immigrants to the United States, many parents still try to arrange marriages for their children, although many of the children have opportunities to resist their parents' wishes, such as going to college.

In Africa and elsewhere, polygynous households where there is more than one wife per husband continue to exist. In some African cities, men who are Western educated still wish to use their achievement by modern standards to reach the traditional goal of maintaining a polygynous household. For some women who work outside the home, polygyny may resolve the problem of child care while they work. These examples show how modern, often European-educated, Africans still use traditional patterns for expressing themselves and for finding solutions to urban problems. (Clignet and Sween 1974).

Middle-class Japanese also maintain structured ties with kinfolk who live in other households. Even the salaried employees of large corporations who live in Tokyo suburbs frequently live near their parents. It is quite common for children to be assigned to stay with a particular grandparent. The child may bathe his grandparent and the grandparent will play with the child. The relationship may be quite intimate. Such children are grief-stricken when their grandparents die (Vogel 1967). Intimate emotional and economic relationships between extended kin are not incompatible with modern urban life, either in the West or in non-Western cultures. In fact, the sociability and mutual aid that urban people find in the family and among extended kin are as effective as what they would find outside the bosom of the kindred. Urban society provides alternatives to kinship ties, but it does not destroy them.

The Range of Interpersonal Ties
with Kin and Non-kin

Despite the emphasis anthropologists have given to kinship, many individuals have relatively weak ties to their kin. Many only call, write, or visit their parents or mature siblings on rare occasions, such as Christmas, Passover, or Ramadan. Though some studies stress the perpetuation of closely knit small groups and stable neighborhoods, connections between many individuals are indeed of a temporary nature. Weak ties with some people did, of course, occur in premodern times. Certainly traders and other itinerants in preindustrial societies had such loose ties with their clientele, but loose ties are more common in this day of the large corporation. In many communities where heads of families are employed by the armed forces or a large corporation, people become accustomed to the fact that some families are here today and gone next year. In some areas of work, like government service, what one knows is as important as who one knows. The prospective worker seeks to impress management with his or her competency rather than prevailing on friends and acquaintances who are obliged to perform favors (Wolfe 1974; Jacobson 1975). Yet emotional friendship ties may become entangled with the presumably "objective," "universalistic" criteria of such rational bureaucracies, as they do in small family businesses. Such entanglements, especially when they involve hiring and firing, are the stuff that executive-suite dramas, situation comedies, and soap operas (e.g., "Melrose Place," "Murphy Brown") are made of.

The strategies that one employs successfully in the corporate bureaucratic world differ from those of such settings as family firms and political machines, where one's personal relationship to the boss is equally or more important than one's technical competence. In the corporate world, an individual who wishes to succeed may find his or her chances are better by having several wide-ranging networks of acquaintances (as opposed to friends) who provide that person with information about jobs, grants, and other opportunities for advancement, rather than investing time and emotion in being an active member of an intimate group. The investment in "inbred" group memberships may tie the individual down to a specific job or get one stuck in an unsatisfactory situation (Granovetter 1973).

At the same time, those who are mobile and who have few relatives near home may reproduce friendship circles, which replace the absence of relatives in the vicinity. For example, in the late 1950s, in a suburb of a northeastern American city, an eight-year-old girl reported to her parents—who came from New York City—

that there was one other Jewish girl in her class. The girl's parents were delighted and contacted the other couple. Together the two couples placed an ad in the neighborhood paper, suggesting a meeting of a "Fairville Jewish Club." Other couples in the essentially Gentile suburb responded, and a Jewish club that lasted on and off for nearly fifteen years was founded. The content of the meetings was not particularly Jewish, but the format of meetings—revolving around some kind of meal—resembled that of other Jewish organizations, including the New York City cousin clubs. Friendships formed in that organization have continued long after the dissolution of the club itself (Zenner 1978).

A similar "reproduction" of kin-like groups occurs in child-care cooperatives and car pools, which have been studied in Great Britain and North America. Sometimes groups of parents that start to share such functions, otherwise carried out by kin, end up as friendship groups that maintain patterns of cooperation even when some move out of the neighborhood and new people move in (Cohen 1974; Coombs 1973). Adults who meet through their children's involvement in Little League or similar activities or people who belong to churches and synagogues may develop similar friendships. Thus, while many interpersonal relations in the modern urban society are temporary, patterns of cooperation have emerged to fill gaps left by the absence of extended kin and durable friendships.

So far, gender relations as such have been underplayed in our discussion. Yet it is obvious that whether or not occupations and household tasks are segregated into male and female roles, gender is crucial to our understanding of familial and extrafamilial relationships.

Urban settings also have been the scenes for substitutes for certain familial relations. Extramarital sex for hire is but one example of such specialization. It may supplement sex between husband and wife or it may be the main sexual outlet for some urbanites. Other examples include such nurturing and healing institutions as schools, hospitals, hospices, nursing homes, and convents. While convents in particular may be associated with rural settings, they represent specialization which grew up in cities. Such settings do involve an intensification of interpersonal ties comparable to the family. Prostitution, on the other hand, can be used as a metaphor for the kind of urbanism described by Wirth, marked by casual contact involving payment for services rendered. In both fictional and ethnographic accounts dealing with prostitution, however, we find the human need for intimacy finding expression (E. Cohen, 1984).

Several of the articles (Keefe, Stack) in this section demonstrate the persistence and importance of intimate ties between the individual and kin outside of the nuclear family. Jankowiak's article shows how men and women in China deal with changing definitions of gender roles. Bossen's article deals with the interaction between unrelated women in a single household. All of these articles explicitly show how the family in the urban setting is part and parcel of larger social systems and how that larger world produces tensions within the family.

Walter P. Zenner

The Myth of the Declining Family

Extended Family Ties Among Urban Mexican-Americans and Anglo-Americans

SUSAN EMLEY KEEFE

Traditionally, it was assumed that nuclear family systems arise with urbanism due to increased geographic and socioeconomic mobility and to the extended family's loss of economic function. Substantial evidence supports the thesis that extended family ties persist among urban Mexican-Americans and Anglo-Americans in southern California. The two ethnic groups differ in reference to the geographic distribution of kin, Chicanos having local kin groups in contrast to the dispersed kin networks of Anglo-Americans, but, for members of both ethnic groups, the extended family endures and contributes in positive ways to ethnic adaptation to urban life.

It used to be thought that families living in modern cities had little contact with their relatives. This idea was suggested when people compared the apparent individualism of their own family lives with their fondly held, though often misguided, images of the "good old days." During the past two decades, there has been much careful research on kinship ties, and the general findings of these studies are (1) that kinship ties are extremely important in contemporary urban society and (2) that the existence of a vital, all-embracing extended family of the "good old days" was mostly a myth. (Caplow et al. 1982:195)

Source: Article written expressly for *Urban Life.*

The theory that urbanization leads to extended-family breakdown has a long history in the social sciences. As Caplow et al. (1982) point out, the theory assumes that kinship organization in cities changes from an extended family system to a more isolated, nuclear family system and, furthermore, that urbanization is the cause of this change. The theory has its roots in the nineteenth century with the development of more sophisticated comparative and evolutionary social theories. For example, in his book *Ancient Law*, Henry Maine argued that, as societies become more complex, there is an evolutionary shift from kinship status to contract status:

> The movement of progressive societies has been uniform in one respect. Through all its course it has been distinguished by the gradual dissolution of family dependency and the growth of individual obligation in its place. The Individual is steadily substituted for the Family, as the unit of which civil laws take account (Maine 1861:168).

Other nineteenth-century scholars, including Émile Durkheim, Ferdinand Tönnies, and Max Weber, agreed in general that urbanism is associated with increasing individualism, growing alienation in a mass society, greater geographic and socioeconomic mobility, and the loss of a sense of community. More recent neoevolutionists, such as Elman Service (1967), continue the argument that, in comparison to primitive societies where kinship is the most significant organizing principle, urban, state-level societies have other means of organizing public life, and kinship tends to be confined to the private sphere.

Early twentieth-century sociologists and anthropologists adapted these theories to the contemporary process of urbanization and to the associated process of industrialization. Contrasting urban society with rural, preindustrial society, Talcott Parsons (1943), Robert Redfield (1941), Ralph Linton (1949), and, most especially, Louis Wirth (1938), as well as others in the *Chicago School* associated urban life with the weakening of bonds of kinship (Wirth) and the "isolation of the nuclear family" (Parsons). In addition to citing the increasing importance of individualism in urban societies as a factor in the decline of the kin group, these theorists emphasized the extended family's loss of significant economic and social functions. In urban, industrial societies, the family is no longer the unit of economic production; moreover, the labor market's demand for workforce mobility results in migration and dissolution of local kin groups. With increased socioeconomic mobility and an emphasis on individual achieved status, the ascribed status of kinship and the associated resources of inheritance and a family name and reputation become less important. The extended family may survive, but it functions more in affective than in instrumental ways (although it is generally argued that it may remain economically functional among the poor who rely on kin for mutual aid). The extended kin group remains significant in urban societies, it is argued, primarily due to emotional bonds of attachment and to the socializing patterns they produce. Finally, according to this school of thought, due to the presumed fragility of affective, noneconomically based bonds, the frequency of visiting such kin is relatively insignificant.

The theory of the declining urban extended family continues to be perpetuated by some more contemporary social scientists (Goode 1963, 1966; Harris 1969; Smelser 1966) and is reported in textbooks read by new generations of social scientists. Moreover, as Caplow et al. (1982) note, it is a theory held, for the most part, by the general population. Perhaps this is one of the reasons why the theory persists despite the convincing evidence to the contrary amassed by researchers over the last thirty years.

Oscar Lewis (1965) is perhaps best known for proposing that urbanization and industrialization are compatible with extended family bonds when he found "urbanization without breakdown" in Mexico City. In fact, cross-cultural studies find the retention of extended family ties in urban areas around the globe: in India (Vatuk 1972), the Philippines (Jacobson 1970), West Africa (Aldous 1962), Brazil (Wagley 1964), Yugoslavia (Hammel and Yarbrough 1973), Canada (Garigue 1956), and England (Young and Willmott 1957), as well as elsewhere. Work with many urban-American ethnic minority groups, including Italian-Americans (Palisi 1966), Jewish-Americans (Winch, Greer, and Blumberg 1967), Puerto Rican–Americans (Garrison 1972), and Japanese- and Chinese-Americans (Light 1972) also indicates the existence of local kinship ties which involve significant levels of visiting and mutual exchange of goods and services. Furthermore, urban-dwelling, mainstream Anglo-Americans are by no means cut off from their extended family ties. As Sussman (1959), Sussman and Burchinal (1962), Litwak (1960a, 1960b), Adams (1968), and Greer (1956) have demonstrated, Anglo-Americans maintain a *modified extended family*, in which kin ties remain important in affective and instrumental ways despite geographic mobility. Of course, considerable variation in the precise nature of kinship organization exists among these separate cultural groups, but, clearly, urbanism does not necessarily result in the extinction of extended family networks. In Barbados, as Greenfield (1961) points out, a nuclear family system can also arise in nonurban situations, further calling into question any proposed causal relationship between urbanism and nuclear family organization.

This study examines the extended family ties of urban Mexican-Americans[1] and Anglo-Americans in southern California. The findings are based on research conducted in three towns where Chicanos make up a large segment of the population: Santa Barbara, Santa Paula, and Oxnard.[2] Data were collected by means of two large-scale surveys of several hundred respondents and a series of in-depth interviews with a small number of informants. In addition to the expected cultural differences between the Mexican-Americans and Anglo-Americans interviewed, significant differences in socioeconomic status are evident between the two ethnic groups: most of the Mexican-Americans come from blue-collar households and have not completed high school, while most of the Anglo-Americans live in white-collar households and have completed one or more years of college. Within the Chicano sample itself, there is considerable heterogeneity. Generation accounts for much of the variation by class and culture within the ethnic group, particularly for the contrast between immigrants from Mexico and the more acculturated and assimilated second- or third-generation Mexican-Americans.

Consistent with early social science theory, research on Mexican-Americans has more often than not asserted that the traditional Mexican-American extended family is disappearing with urbanization and acculturation (Alvirez and Bean 1976; Grebler, Moore, and Guzman 1970). Nevertheless, it is also suggested that, in comparison with the Anglo-American nuclear family system, Chicano family ties remain stronger (Gonzalez 1969; Madsen 1964); yet, few studies have actually collected kinship data on both Anglos and Chicanos. Analysis of the data on kin ties from the author's research indicates both ethnic groups retain considerable extended familism; however, there are important ethnic differences in extended family structure and the cultural values associated with familism. In the following section, the extended family systems found in these two urban ethnic groups are described, and representative case studies are presented to illustrate the differences between them.

Mexican-American and Anglo-American Extended Families

Many similarities actually exist between Mexican-American and Anglo-American kinship patterns. Both are founded on the bilateral kindred and affinal extensions. The nuclear family is the basic and most significant familial unit and normally constitutes the household. Relatives in the kindred sometimes interact as a social group and are often relied upon for assistance in times of need. Likewise, members of both ethnic groups remain in frequent contact with relatives who live nearby. Moreover, the distinction between more important, primary kin (parents, siblings, and children) and less important, secondary kin applies in both ethnic groups.

Distinctive for Chicanos is the inclusion in the extended family of fictive kin (*compadres*) ritualized through religious, and sometimes secular, ceremonies. Baptismal compadres take on special obligations, especially the willingness to assume parenthood of their godchildren, if necessary. As godparents of a child, compadres or co-parents have a special link with the real parents of the child and are typically close friends or relatives. Fictive kin often fill the same role as real kin in the Chicano extended family; they are accorded the same attention and affection and render mutual aid when it is needed. The tendency to choose relatives as compadres increases with each generation among Mexican-Americans, however, so that the ethnic distinction of having kin who are only fictive is perhaps less significant than has sometimes been portrayed by researchers.

The analysis of family data from the author's research reveals that the distinctiveness between Anglo-Americans and Mexican-Americans emerges more in the comparison of interaction and exchange with real, as opposed to fictive, kin. Moreover, there are significant differences in family organization between immigrant Mexicans and later generations of Chicanos. Finally, consideration of kin *and* non-kin social ties leads to a more comprehensive and realistic comparison of the more kin-isolated lives of Anglos versus the kin-dominated lives of Chicanos.

Turning first to a consideration of kin living in town, Mexican-Americans are much more likely to have relatives in town than are Anglos. Less than half (46 percent) of the Anglos are related by blood or marriage to other households in town, while 86 percent of the foreign-born and 94 percent of the native-born (second and third generation) Mexican-Americans have nearby relatives. Chicanos are also related to larger numbers of households in town than Anglos, although there is a significant difference between native- and foreign-born Mexican-Americans. The second and third generations have an average of seventeen and fifteen related households in town respectively, while the first generation averages only about five related households. The Anglos, in comparison, have an average of only three and a half related households in town.

Anglos and Chicanos are both likely to visit with their relatives in town, but Chicanos visit more kin and more often than the Anglos. Ninety percent or more of the Anglos and three Mexican generations with nearby relatives visit at least one related household weekly. However, Chicanos are more likely to visit households daily; 37 percent of the first generation, 52 percent of the second generation, and 54 percent of the third generation visit at least one household daily compared to 26 percent of the Anglos. Numbers of kin visited fall into a similar pattern. Anglos with kin in town visit an average of two households a week while immigrant Mexicans visit an average of three and native-born Mexican-Americans visit an average of four.

Exchange of aid with kin is characteristic of both ethnic groups, but native-born Chicanos far surpass both Anglos and immigrant Mexicans in frequency and variety of exchange. Over 40 percent of the second and third generations have given all six types of aid inquired about to relatives in town in the last year and have received three to four types of aid. In contrast, 41 percent or more of the Anglos and immigrant Mexicans have given only two types of aid and received only one type of aid.

In summary, Anglos are unlikely to have a local kin group. If they have relatives in town, they are few in number. However small the local kin group is, Anglos nevertheless visit their kin frequently and exchange goods and services with them. First generation Mexican-Americans have slightly larger local kin networks than Anglos and visit these kin somewhat more frequently; their exchange of aid, on the other hand, is somewhat less frequent than for Anglos. The native-born Chicanos, in contrast, have the largest local extended families. Moreover, they visit with more kin and exchange aid more frequently than either the Anglos or immigrant Mexicans.

Analysis of family organization by kin type rather than residence yields another perspective on ethnic differences. First, considering relations with primary kin (parents, siblings, and children), all three generations of Mexican-Americans, as well as the Anglo-Americans, maintain contact with the overwhelming majority of their primary kin. In addition, goods and services are exchanged with the majority of primary kin, although this is more characteristic of the native-born Chicanos. All three Mexican-American generations have more primary kin in town than the Anglos; however, the majority of both the Anglos' and Mexican immigrants' primary kin live outside the local area. This affects the frequency of visiting primary kin. The native-born Chicanos see the majority of their primary kin at least weekly while the Anglos and immigrant Mexicans do not.

These Mexican-American children growing up in public housing in a southern California city are establishing ties with kin which will become their primary means of social adaptation to city life. (Photo by Kathryn J. Lindholm]

While primary kin form the core of the individual's extended family in both ethnic groups, secondary kin tend to dominate numerically as local relatives and in the individual's network of interaction and exchange. Because native-born Chicanos recognize more secondary kin than Anglos or immigrant Mexicans and are more likely to have secondary kin nearby, their local extended families tend to be much larger. Anglos (5 percent) are least likely to have local secondary kin and have the smallest average number of secondary kin (2.1) in town. The tendency to have locally residing, secondary kin increases from generation to generation among the Mexican-Americans; while immigrant Mexicans have an average of 7.3 secondary relatives in town, the second generation averages 22.7, and the third generation averages 32.7 secondary kin in town. Interaction with secondary kin is much less common than with primary kin among all groups, but it is least common among Anglos who visit with only 12 percent of their secondary kin regardless of place of residence, compared to the three Mexican-American generations, who see 35 percent or more of their secondary kin regularly. Exchange of goods and services with secondary kin is infrequent among all groups.

In sum, the native-born Mexican-Americans have far and away the largest, most integrated extended families. The native-born Chicanos count more relatives than the Anglos or immigrants and interact and exchange aid with more relatives. While the first-generation Mexicans have much smaller kin networks, the networks are relatively well integrated through visiting and mutual aid. Anglos count a good many relatives, but the number included in interaction and exchange is comparatively small. Anglos have an average of only twelve relatives with whom they visit, less than half the number visited by first-generation Mexicans and less than one-third the number seen by the native-born. The Anglos also exchange aid with the smallest number of kin (eight) compared to between thirteen and nineteen for Mexican-Americans depending on generation. Thus, not only are Anglos less likely to have a local kin network than Chicanos, but also their full kin network is smaller and more selective than the Chicanos' kin network. Apparently, kinship as a social system is less important for Anglo-Americans.

Among Mexican-Americans, on the other hand, the kin group grows stronger and more localized with each generation. The first-generation immigrants tend to locate in urban areas where they have secondary kin, but most of their relatives remain in Mexico. Once settled, they generally establish small, but well-integrated, local extended families, primarily through their married children. Second-generation Mexican-Americans thus inherit a fairly large local kin group made up of their parents, siblings, and perhaps more distant kin, which is extended through their own spouse and offspring as well as the spouses and offspring of their siblings. The third generation, which is likely to remain residing locally, has a vast number of nearby kin, although they tend to confine the greater part of their interaction to their primary kin—parents, siblings, and children.

This process in which the later, and better-off, generations become more familistic calls into question the idea that Mexican-American extended familism is tied to poverty and the search for resources outside the nuclear family (Alvirez and Bean 1976; Grebler, Moore, and Guzman 1970). Research with other groups indicates that the urban poor are likely to have relatives who are equally as poor and have few resources to exchange. Furthermore, social agencies are designed to meet many of the needs of the poor, and, although many needs certainly go unmet, the agencies nevertheless offer tremendous resources of which a number of the poor take advantage (Jacobson 1970; Wagley 1964). Instead of the lower class, therefore, it is the urban middle and upper classes whose members have resources to spare where the tradition of extended familism flourishes.

The primary difference between the extended families of the two ethnic groups, then, involves the nature of their geographical proximity. Chicanos tend to have a *traditional* extended family, defined as a localized kin group consisting of a number of related households whose members interact together frequently and exchange mutual aid (Keefe 1979:352). Anglo-Americans, on the other hand, tend to have a *modified*, or what I have referred to as a widespread, extended family, in which ties with relatives, especially primary kin, are maintained despite geographic distances separating kin. This difference in extended family structure comes about because of a difference in geographic mobility. Anglos are more mobile than Chicanos, tend to live near few relatives, and consequently visit kin infrequently. Contact may be more frequent by mail or by telephone, however, particularly between primary kin (Keefe and Padilla 1987). Immigration, of course, affects the kin group of foreign-born Mexican-Americans, but among native-born Chicanos, residential stability is a common trait; 32 percent of the second generation and 43 percent of the third generation in the study were born in the city in which they were interviewed (compared to only 4 percent of the Anglos). This difference in geographic proximity leads to several related differences in extended family structure. While members of both ethnic groups maintain contact with most of their primary kin, Chicanos see their primary kin and exchange goods and services with them more frequently due to their proximity. Secondary kin are less important for both Mexican-Americans and Anglo-Americans, but, due to the fact that Anglos are extremely unlikely to have locally residing secondary kin, interaction and exchange with secondary kin is much less frequent for Anglos. Finally, the relative lack of local kin in general among Anglo-Americans means that most of their social network is made up of non-kin (friends, neighbors, coworkers, etc.) compared to the kin-dominated social networks of Chicanos. While 89 percent of the Anglos' social contacts in town are non-kin, only about half (52 percent) of the first generations', 41 percent of the second generations', and 24 percent of the third generation Mexican-Americans' social network is made up of non-kin.

Family Case Studies

In order to fully appreciate the ethnic differences described previously, three case studies are presented in this section representing aspects of immigrant Mexican, native-born Chicano, and Anglo-American family organization. It should be emphasized that each case study represents the life of an individual whose story is unique from every other individual in their ethnic group. Yet, in these case studies we also find a pattern of family organization which, in its broad outline, fits that of the ethnic group at large. It is this pattern which is of primary interest here; the details of the individuals' lives add interest and demonstrate some of the possibilities in variation within the group.

Carmen Muñoz: A Mexican Immigrant

Carmen Muñoz is a fifty-four-year-old housewife with seven children. She was born in Hermosillo in the state of Sonora, Mexico, and has been in the United States for twenty-two years, living mostly in Santa Barbara. Carmen left most of her family in Mexico, and, since she has not traveled back since migrating to the United States, her ties with kin there are negligible. Both of her parents are dead. One of her sisters is living in San Diego and the other is in Tijuana, a Mexican border town. Her brother just recently moved back to Mexico after having lived in southern California. She sees her siblings only rarely now, as she lives in Santa Barbara, but her sister in San Diego helped Carmen when she originally migrated to the United States. Carmen cannot remember many of her other relatives and old friends that are still living in Mexico, having lost contact with them long ago. Her second husband, Miguel, has many relatives in Mexico, including his mother and siblings, and his ties are much stronger to kin in Mexico than are Carmen's. Miguel's mother came to live with them for several years but then moved back to Mexico. Carmen has met few of Miguel's other Mexican relatives and does not feel close to any of them.

Carmen and her first husband chose *padrinos* (godparents) for all of their children when they were living in Mexico, and she sees some of them occasionally on their rare visits to the United States, but, basically, she no longer has contact with those compadres. She does, however, have compadres in town, her youngest child's baptismal padrinos, and she sees them regularly.

Carmen's close social network consists primarily of her children and her children's families. She sees her five married children almost daily and has a high level of exchange of goods and services with them. For example, several times when she became critically ill, her sons or daughters would accompany her and her husband to the emergency room. When one of her daughters was hospitalized, Carmen spent most of her time at the hospital. Presently, another daughter is having financial difficulties and Carmen has taken in all four grandchildren for a while to alleviate some of the burden. Carmen's children often give her rides to the market, to church, and take her on other errands, as she does not drive and Miguel often works the night shift, sleeping during the day. This type of exchange appears to be limited to her children. Although she knows a few of her neighbors, she does not exchange favors, advice, child care, or money with them. Her exchange with her compadres in town is also minimal. There is no one in town whom Carmen considers to be a close friend.

Anna Fuentes: A Native-Born Chicana

Twenty-three-year-old Anna Fuentes is a second-generation Chicana, born in Santa Barbara. Anna and her husband, Ruben, were married immediately following her graduation from high school, and, while they are looking forward to it, they do not have children yet. As a native Santa Barbaran, Anna has a large local kinship network and very close relations with her primary kin. Specifically, Anna has her parents, one sister and one brother living in town, while a second brother lives in nearby Oxnard. Ruben has nine siblings, only one of whom does not live in town. Anna estimates that she and Ruben have about forty other relatives in town, and, of these, they see ten at least monthly. Anna usually takes her mother shopping every Saturday, and, on Sunday, she and Ruben have dinner at her parents' house. Every Monday night, Anna and Ruben have dinner at his parents' house. These immediate kin are the only individuals who Anna and Ruben are sure to see socially several times a week. Frequency of contact diminishes rapidly outside of the immediate families, as Anna sees her closest first cousin, on the average, only once a month and her aunts and other cousins perhaps two or three times each year.

Anna tends to be self-reliant and rarely asks for help from others, but, in time of trouble, she says she would rely on her primary kin. On the other hand, she recalls that she has been of service to several relatives in the past year. For example, her mother and sister confide in her about their problems, and several other relatives have also come to Anna for advice about their personal problems. Furthermore, Anna has loaned some money to one of her sisters-in-law, and she has helped her parents with household chores, as well as such tasks as preparing tamales for a party.

Anna feels very close to her family; they are the most important people in her life. She and Ruben have friends, but they are secondary to their relatives. Ruben and Anna have six good friends, all Mexican-Americans. Four of these are compadres, as Anna and Ruben are padrinos to their children. Anna sees her friends regularly and sometimes has invited them over with her relatives. For example, the one large party she had during the year of interviews was a barbecue with family and friends celebrating her and Ruben's fifth wedding anniversary. Anna does not generally exchange goods or services with friends, preferring when necessary to rely on family.

Amy Cooper: An Anglo-American

Amy Cooper is a thirty-one-year-old mother of two young children. Amy met her husband, Donald, in Santa Barbara, where they have lived for the last eleven years.

Amy has only one relative living in town, Donald's cousin, who they see every month or so and have helped out financially on occasion. She mainly socializes with four female friends whom she has known for ten years or more. Amy not only gets together with each of her friends several times a week, but also talks to them on the telephone frequently. Most of these friends have small children as well, and they often take them to the beach or to the pool together. Amy and her girlfriends talk about shared problems concerning marital difficulties, disciplinary problems with children, worries about sick relatives, and so on. They also help each other out with baby-sitting, housecleaning, and small loans of money. Amy is also friends with a neighbor at her apartment building, and they often exchange child care or borrow small items when necessary.

Amy feels very close to her parents, but, because they live elsewhere in California (Fontana), she cannot see them as often as she would like. Still, she manages to visit with them monthly, sometimes at their home and sometimes at hers. During the interviews, Amy's mother came to stay for several days, and they talked at length about the children, Amy's grandmother's illness, her father's drinking problem, and the stress of her mother's job. Amy often takes her problems to her mother for advice, because "she cares about my life and the children." The Coopers seem to have continual financial problems due to Donald's low income in his occupation as a musician and music teacher, and Amy's parents have loaned them money several times beginning when they were first married. Amy's only brother lives in Manhattan Beach, California, and they remain in frequent contact often meeting at her parent's home. Amy worries about his wife, who has had some disturbing psychological problems. Clearly, Amy's primary kin are important to her, and she works to maintain close contact with them. Nevertheless, she has not felt it necessary to move back to the Los Angeles area, content to have her social contact with primary kin remain periodic.

Amy has several other relatives she cares about, mostly on her side of the family, including her grandparents and an aunt. Donald's mother is the only in-law she interacts with much (aside from his cousin in town), since he has no siblings and his father is dead. These relatives also live elsewhere in southern California, limiting social interaction with them, although mutual aid, especially when visiting in each other's homes, is offered.

Cultural Definitions of *Close* Family Ties

As the case studies demonstrate, familism in the traditional sense of interacting with a large, local kin group is a pervasive Mexican-American trait irrespective of level of acculturation. Those who immigrate to the United States must leave their relatives in Mexico; thus, their interaction with them obviously declines. They tend to remain emotionally close to their parents and those siblings left behind, however, and any relatives who happen to live in town become important. As the immigrants grow older, time and energy is invested in maintaining a primary kin network like Carmen's, which is based on adult children and their families. Non-kin, including friends, neighbors, and coworkers, on the other hand, never come to figure significantly in their social lives.

For the native-born, the extended kin group becomes large and cohesive. Most significant are the primary kin: parents, siblings, and adult children. Friends and other non-kin are likely to be integrated into the native-borns' social networks but never to the exclusion of relatives. For most native-borns, like Anna Fuentes, the kin group is the core of their social life. Familism as a cultural trait is thus nurtured by the first generation only to come into full bloom in later generations due to geographic stability.

As suggested elsewhere (Keefe 1984), Anglo-Americans also maintain a preference for *close* extended family ties; what differs is the ethnic definition of closeness. Mexican-Americans and Anglo-Americans share many interpretations of *closeness*, such as the expression of love and affection between kin, evidence of trust and respect among family members, sharing life experiences as a family, and knowing family members are there if needed. Chicanos differ, however, on one fundamental aspect in defining *closeness*: the need for the consistent presence of family members. Chicanos value the physical presence of family members while Anglos are satisfied with intermittent meetings with kin supplemented by telephone calls and letters. For Mexican-Americans, it is important to see relatives regularly face-to-face, to embrace, to touch, and to simply be with one another, sharing the minor joys and sorrows of daily life. For Anglos, these experiences are integral to nuclear family life but less important with regard to extended family ties. Anglos also feel comfortable having friends function in these roles, while Chicanos reserve them primarily for kin. As Adams (1970) has pointed out, friends and relatives can be interchangeable for Anglo-Americans with regard to social visiting and minor kinds of mutual aid.

Geographic proximity, in other words, is not the basis for the Anglo-American conception of *closeness* in kin ties. In fact, there are many aspects of close family relations that can be unaffected by the physical presence or absence of kin: carrying a family identity as part of a personal identity, talking or worrying about family members, and experiencing a psychological feeling of well-being stemming from family members' support. Other aspects can be fulfilled with the intermittent physical presence of kin, including being present during holidays and in times of crisis. Amy Cooper is really somewhat atypical of our sample of Anglo-Americans in that all of her primary kin live in California. Most of the Anglos in the study were born outside of California and have at least some of their primary kin living in other states, which makes them even more inaccessible.

In conclusion, early social theorists, looking at American society in general, were correct in their description of urban life as being less kin-based. This is true insofar as it concerns the face-to-face social communities of the Anglo-American majority, but it is wrong to conclude that this ethnic trait is an urban trait. In many contemporary, urban societies and urban-dwelling ethnic groups, such as Mexican-Americans, extended kinship dominates social life. Moreover, it does not follow that Anglo-Americans lack kin ties because, in fact, Anglos have significant extended-family ties which can be activated immediately and intensely in times of need (Sussman 1965). In rethinking the relationship between urbanism and kinship organization, much remains to be done in describing the extent of cross-cultural variation and potential explanations for that variation. Furthermore, it would appear that focusing on the social lives of individuals, rather than on apparent social communities, would be a better technique to use in future research on the question. In any case, it is clear that the extended family survives in cities and contributes in positive ways to ethnic adaptation to urban life.

Notes

[1] The terms *Chicano* and *Mexican-American* are used interchangeably in this paper to refer to the entire ethnic group of Mexican descent in the United States. Modified versions of these terms are used to discuss subsegments of the ethnic group (e.g., immigrant Mexicans, native-born Chicanos). The term *Anglo-Americans* is used to refer to white Americans of European descent. Considerable cultural and socioeconomic diversity, which affects family organization, obviously exists within the Anglo-American ethnic group. My research, however, indicates that Chicano, versus Anglo, ethnicity is the most significant factor affecting extended family organization within the population sampled.

[2] The author expresses appreciation to the National Institute of Mental Health which provided funding for this research (Center for Minority Group Mental Health Programs, Grant number MH26099, Principal Investigator: Amado M. Padilla). The first survey randomly sampled residents in three selected census tracts in each of the three cities; the final sample included 666 Chicanos and 340 Anglo-Americans. In the second survey, which produced a sample of 381 Chicanos and 163 Anglo-Americans, respondents who indicated willingness were reinterviewed. For the second set of interviews, a much longer questionnaire was used. In-depth case studies were subsequently done of twenty-four Chicanos and twenty-two Anglos. Cases were selected randomly to cover a stratified range of cultural, socioeconomic, and family organization categories. Further description of the research design and findings can be found in Keefe and Padilla (1987).

The Kindred of Viola Jackson

Residence and Family Organization of an Urban Black American Family

CAROL B. STACK

A common stereotype of the family life of the urban poor is that it is disorganized. Parallel to this image is the portrayal of the black family as one which is centered around a grandmother, her daughters, and her daughters' young children. The prevalence of such a fatherless household has been variously seen as a retention of African culture, as a product of slavery, and as one of the outcomes of urbanization and certain welfare policies. It is often viewed as something that is pathological. Stack, in this article, challenges these portraits. She points out that the idea of "matrifocality" cannot fully describe or explain the variety of strategies by which North American blacks have adapted to the situation of urban poverty. Rather than stressing concepts like household and kin group, she uses dynamic or process concepts like "adaptive strategy" and "alignment." It will be useful to compare her description of the urban black kindred with Oscar Lewis's view of "The Culture of Poverty."

Introduction

Concepts can become so widely accepted and seem so obvious that they block the way to further understanding. Descriptions of black

Source: Reprinted with permission of The Free Press, a Division of Macmillan, Inc. from *Afro-American Anthropology: Contemporary Perspectives*, edited by Norman E. Whitten, Jr. and John F. Szwed. Copyright © 1970 by The Free Press.

American domestic life (Frazier 1939; Drake and Cayton 1945; Abrahams 1964; Moynihan 1965; Rainwater 1966a) are almost always couched in terms of the nuclear family and in terms of the fashionable notion of a matrifocal complex. But in many societies the nuclear family is not always a unit of domestic cooperation, and the "universal functions" of family life can be provided by other social units (Spiro 1954; Gough 1959; Levy and Fallers 1959; Reiss 1965). And matrifocal thinking, while it may bring out the importance of women in family life, fails to account for the great variety of domestic strategies one can find on the scene in urban black America. The following study suggests that if we shed concepts such as matrifocality we can see that black Americans have evolved a repertoire of domestic units that serve as flexible adaptive strategies for coping with the everyday human demands of ghetto life.

In the fall of 1966 I began to investigate black family organization in midwestern cities. I concentrated upon one domestic family unit—the household of Viola and Leo Jackson—and their network of kin, which proved to number over 100 persons.[1] My immediate aim was to discover when and why each of these people had changed residence, and what kind of domestic unit they joined during the half-century since they had begun moving north from Arkansas.

The data show that during the process of migration and the adjustment of individuals to urban living, clusters of kin align together for various domestic purposes. It soon became clear that matrifocal thinking provided little insight into the organization of domestic units of cooperation, for example, those groups of kin and non-kin which carry out domestic functions but do not always reside together (Bender 1967). In certain situations such as the death or desertion of a parent, the loss of a job, or in the process of migration it was found that an individual almost always changed residence. But matrifocality proved to be a poor predictor of the kind of domestic unit the individual might subsequently enter. Among Mrs. Jackson's kin one can find various assortments of adults and children cooperating in domestic units: children living with relatives other than their parents, and also clusters of kin (often involving the father) who do not reside together but who provide some of the domestic functions for a mother-and-child unit in another location. Not only does matrifocal thinking fail here, but also little or nothing in the current writing on black American family life helps deal with questions such as the following that arise when we examine Mrs. Jackson's kin: Which relatives can a person expect will help him or her? Which relatives will care for parentless or abandoned children? And who will look after the ill and elderly? I will discuss these questions, and the challenge that Mrs. Jackson's kin and their lifeways put to our powers of explanation. First, however, I will deal briefly with the nature of matrifocal thinking.

The Matrifocal Complex

Matrifocality has become a popular replacement for the discarded nineteenth-century concept of matriarchy. Some would argue that matrifocality is more sophisticated, but I suggest that it is no more useful than matriarchy for characterizing urban Negro households.

When the rules for reckoning kinship are not explicit, then it is difficult to determine the basis upon which households are formed. As so, as M. G. Smith (1962:7) has pointed out, by necessity the anthropologist then must rely on data on household composition. It is in this context that the term "matrifocality" is most widely used. However, it also has been used to refer to at least three units of information: (1) the composition of a household, (2) the type of kinship bond linking its members, and (3) the relationship between males and females in the household. In fact, matrifocality tells us little about the actual composition of the household, and the relational link upon which the household is formed. Schneider (1961) points out that in the past the terms "matrilocal marriage" and "matriliny" were used interchangeably (see Bachofen 1861) and that the matriarchal complex referred to a household which did not include the husband or father. Both González (1965) and Smith (1962) use matrifocality to refer to the composition of households. These and similar formulations ignore the developmental history of domestic groups (Goody 1958). In addition, they supply no information on the age and circumstances in which individuals join households, the alternatives open to them, the relational links they have with other members, or who the members are. *Matrifocality is not a residence rule, and in particular, it is not a rule for post-marital residence.* Residence, one of the dynamics of social organization, can be understood only if the basis for the active formation of households is known.

A further complication is that notions such as matrifocality, maternal family (C. King 1945), and matriarchy inadvertently are associated with unilineal descent. It was Bachofen's contention (1861) that matriliny (descent through women) and matriarchy (rule by women) were but two aspects of the same institution (Schneider 1961; Lowie 1947). This claim had to be discarded when observers failed to find any generalized authority of women over men in matrilineal societies. This controversy is well known. What is less widely appreciated is that there is a close parallel between matriarchal and matrifocal thinking, in that both imply descent through women. For example, M. G. Smith (1962) defines Caribbean matrifocal households as ones which are composed of blood-related women plus all their unmarried children. González (1965:1542) defines consanguineal households in terms of the type of kinship bond linking adult men and women in the households such that no two members are bound together in an affinal relationship. She suggests that consanguineal households may also be matrifocal (1965:1548) and that there is evidence that consanguineal households exist among lower-class Negro American groups (DuBois 1908; Frazier 1939; C. King 1945). The tentative classification that emerges from studies of black American households as consanguineal or as both consanguineal and matrifocal is confusing. In this confusion the use of the notion of matrifocality roughly coincides with Schneider's (1961:3) definition of matrilineal descent units in which he states that the "individual's initial relationship is to his mother and through her to other kinsmen, both male and female, but continuing only through females." *Matrifocality is not necessarily a correlate of matrilineal descent, nor does it imply a structure for linking families in the same community.*

The term "matrifocality" may have value as an indication of the woman's role within the domestic group, but it tells us little about authority, decision making, and male-female relationships within the household, among extended kin, and in the community. Used in this context to refer to a dominant female role, and as a designate of residence classification, reference to the matrifocal household may lead to confusion between residence and role behavior. Analysis of role relationships and interactional patterns that is limited to their classification as matrifocal is at best uninteresting. The role organization of urban Negro households exists in a dynamic system which can be illustrated by the life histories of individuals in households as they adapt to the urban environment. This adaptation comes out dramatically when one examines Viola Jackson's kin and their many ways of forming a domestic unit.

Frequently, discussions of matrifocality and consanguineal households ignore crucial aspects of family organization. Some of the matrifocal thinkers seem to assume that children derive nothing of sociological importance from their father, that households are equivalent to the nuclear family, and that resident husband-fathers are marginal members of their own homes (M. G. Smith 1957).

A look at Viola Jackson's kindred raises doubts about many of these assumptions.

Urban Family Organization

Clusters of Kin

The past fifty years have witnessed a massive migration of rural, southern blacks to urban centers in the United States. The kindred of Viola Jackson are a part of this movement. Ninety-six of them left the South between 1916 and 1967. Some of them first moved from rural Arkansas to live and work harvesting fruit in areas around Grand Rapids and Benton Harbor, Michigan, and Racine, Wisconsin; eventually they settled in the urban North. Two major patterns emerge from their life histories: (1) relatives tend to cluster in the same areas during similar periods; and (2) the most frequent and consistent alignment and cooperation appears to occur between siblings.

During the process of moving, Viola Jackson's kin maintained communication with relatives in the South. They frequently moved back to the South for short periods, or from Chicago and other midwestern cities to fruit harvesting areas on a seasonal basis. Therefore it is difficult to separate the data in terms of phases such as "migration" and subsequent "urban adaptation." During some seasons busloads of rural blacks were brought to the North to harvest fruit. Many families worked their way back South only to repeat the process in order to avoid the poverty and unemployment there. This circulatory migration mainly involved the younger families and individuals.

Frequently, migrant workers follow their relatives and large urban neighborhoods reflect the geographical boundaries of the hinterland. Once these facts are established it is important to find out who made the original move, his age at the time of the move, which relatives joined one another to form households, and the context of each move.

Between 1916 and 1967 Mrs. Jackson's kin lived in five states, and groups of 10 to 15 individuals tended to cluster in the same areas during the same time periods. An example of this can be seen in table 1, which shows where Viola's mother and siblings were living during that time period.

The basis for the active formation of households during migration and urban settlement can only be understood if material developing out of life histories is related to the realities of kinship and non-kinship factors. During this period of migratory wage labor in the

Table 1 Residence and Kin Clusters

AREA AND TIME PERIOD	EGO'S MOTHER (MAGNOLIA)	EGO (VIOLA)	B	S	S	S	B
Arkansas							
1916–1917	X	X	X				
Arkansas							
1928–1944	X	X		X	X	X	X
Blythe, Calif.							
1927–1928	X	X	X				
Grand Rapids, Mich.							
1944–1946		X		X			
Benton Harbor, Mich.							
1946–1948		X	X	X			X
Racine, Wisc.							
1947–1948		X		X			X
Decatur, Ark.							
1948–1952	X	X			X		X
Chicago, Ill.							
1950–1953				X			
Champaign, Ill.							
1952–1954	X	X	X				
Gary, Ind.							
1954–1955				X			
Champaign, Ill.							
1955–1967	X	X	X		X	X	X
Chicago Heights, Ill.							
1959–1967				X			
Chicago, Ill.							
1965–1967				X			

young adult's life, the data show that the strongest alignment is of cooperation and mutual aid among siblings of both sexes (after the age of thirteen). Siblings left the South together, or shortly followed one another, for seasonal jobs. They often lived together in the North with their dependents and spouses, or lived near one another, providing mutual aid such as cooking and child care.

Domestic Arrangements

Case 1

In 1945 *C* left her husband and daughter in the South with his parents and moved to Racine, Wisconsin, to harvest fruit. At the same time *C*'s brother's wife died leaving him, *J*, with two young sons. *J* decided to move north and join *C* in Racine. He and his two sons took a bus to Racine where he got a job in a catsup factory. The company furnished trailers which *C* and *J* placed next to each other. *C* cooked for *J* and his two sons and cared for the children. They were cooperating as a single domestic unit. This situation continued for about a year and a half and then they all returned to the South.

Case 2

By 1946 Viola and Leo had four children and Leo was picking cotton. They were anxious to leave the South in order to find better wages and living conditions. Viola, Leo, and their children joined a busload of people and moved to join Viola's brother, *L*, in Benton Harbor, Michigan. In Benton Harbor all the adults and the older children worked harvesting fruit. At the same time Leo's twin brother and Viola's brother, *J*, and his two sons moved to Benton Harbor. Leo's twin brother moved into Viola's and Leo's household. *J* and his sons moved into the household of *J*'s brother, *L*, and *L*'s wife.

Case 3

In 1948 *C* decided to move north again. This time she took her daughter with her. She moved to Benton Harbor where Viola and her family, their two brothers, *L* and *J*, and Leo's twin brother were all living. *C* and *J* and their children began cooperating as a single domestic unit as they had in Racine.

The pattern described above of cooperation and mutual aid among siblings becomes even more apparent as these individuals move to urban areas. Sibling alignment in the urban context will be discussed in the next section.

Sibling Alignment and Kin Cooperation in Urban Areas

Understanding residence and family organization for people whose economic situation is constantly changing, and who therefore frequently change households, is not easy. Aside from the common observations of household composition based upon where people sleep, there are many other important patterns to be observed, such as which situations lead to a change in residence, which adults share households, and with which adult relatives are children frequently living.

One pattern, a continuation of a pattern formed during the early stages of migratory labor, is the cooperative alignment of siblings. By the time the majority of Viola Jackson's relatives had established permanent residence and jobs in the North, there were numerous examples of siblings forming co-residential and/or domestic units of cooperation. These sibling-based units, apparently motivated by situations such as death, sickness, desertion, abandonment, and unemployment, most often focused around the need for child-care arrangements. Here are two examples:

Sister/Brother

In 1956 Viola and Leo were living in Champaign, Illinois. Viola's brother, *J*, took the train from the South to visit them. After the visit he decided to move to Champaign with his two sons and look for work. *J* rented a house near Viola's and got a construction job. When he brought his sons to Champaign Viola cooked for them and cared for them during the day.

Sister/Sister

In 1959 Viola's sister, *E*, was suffering from a nervous breakdown. *E*'s husband took their four youngest children to his mother in Arkansas. *E*'s sister, *C*, was living in Chicago and she cared for *E*'s oldest daughter. After *E*'s husband deserted her, *E*'s twin sister, *M*, moved into *E*'s house. The household was composed of *E*, her oldest daughter who had been in Chicago, *M*, and *M*'s two youngest daughters.

These alignments may be largely attributed to adaptation to urban socioeconomic conditions. One such urban pattern is a minimum of emphasis on the inheritance of property. For obvious social and economic reasons, poor and highly mobile urban apartment dwellers do not develop strong ties to a homestead or a particular piece of land, even though they may express strong regional and even neighborhood loyalty or identification. This contrasts with the rural South and Young's and Willmott's (1957) observations that apartments in Bethnal Green were kept in the family. The high frequency of moving from one apartment to another in economically depressed urban areas is related to the degree of overcrowding, the shortage of apartments, urban renewal, and the changing employment situation. Another situation causing these alignments to form is the arrival of a new migrant to the urban area wherein he lives with siblings. With time, if he successfully establishes himself in a job in the urban area he may move out of his sibling's household.

Crisis Situations and the Residence of Children

It has already been pointed out that migration, unemployment, sickness, and desertion by necessity often lead to a change in residence. Most often these changes are closely related to the need for child-care arrangements. The choices and expectations involved in placing children in a relative's home largely focus around which adult female relatives are available. In selecting the specific relative, the following criteria are considered: the geographical locations of these adult female relatives; their source of financial support, their age, their marital status, the composition of their household, and the ability of the people making the decision to get along with these females. At the same time, due to the flexibility and mobility of urban individuals, decisions frequently center around the relational link the child has with female members of a particular household. This means that the distance and location of a household, for example, are not a great deterrent, and that in fact the economic, distance, and other decisions are made after the kin criteria are met.

Children in the extended kin network of Viola Jackson frequently live with relatives other than their biological parents. The child-female links which most often are the basis of new or expanded households are clearly those links with close adult females such as the child's mother, mother's mother, mother's sister, mother's brother's wife, father's mother, father's sister, father's brother's wife.

Here are some examples.

Relational Link	Domestic Unit
Mother	Viola's brother married his first wife when he was sixteen. When *she* left him, she kept her daughter.
Mother's mother	Viola's sister, *M*, never was able to care for her children. In between husbands, her mother kept her two oldest children, and after *M*'s death, her mother kept all three of the children. Her brother offered to keep the oldest girl.

Mother's mother	Viola's daughter (age twenty) was living at home and gave birth to a son. The daughter and her son remained in the Jackson household. The daughter expressed the desire to set up a separate household.
Mother's sister	*M* moved to Chicago into her sister's household. The household consisted of the two sisters and four of their children.
Father's mother	Viola's sister, *E*, had four daughters and one son. When *E* was suffering from a nervous breakdown her husband took three daughters and his son to live with his mother in Arkansas. After his wife's death he also took the oldest daughter to his mother's household in Arkansas.
Father's mother	When Viola's younger sister, *C*, left her husband in order to harvest fruit in Wisconsin she left her two daughters with his mother in Arkansas.
Father's sister	When Viola's brother's wife died, he decided to raise his two sons himself. He kept the two boys and never remarried. His residence has consistently been close to one or another of his sisters who have fed and cared for his two sons.

These examples do indeed indicate the important role of the black female. But the difference between matrifocal thinking and thinking about household composition in terms of where children live is that the latter can bring to light the dynamics of household formation, and the criteria, rules, and decisions that the process entails.

The summaries of the social context in which children changed households indicates which adult female relatives are frequently called upon for service. The alignment and cooperation between siblings, such as mother's sister and father's sister, has already been noted. This has been underestimated by workers who select the grandmother household (especially mother's mother) as the only significant domestic unit. It must be noted that the crucial role which paternal as well as maternal grandmothers assume in socialization is a frequent, but definitely not a unique, alternative.

Since social scientists have stressed the existence of female-centered, woman-headed, matrifocal black families, it is of particular interest to look at the formation of grandmother households in Viola's kin. Here is a summary of the households in which Viola's mother, Magnolia, has lived.

Magnolia

Age	Content of Domestic Unit or Household
60	In 1958 Magnolia's second husband died and she was left alone with her daughter's (*M*) two oldest children. Viola sent her two oldest sons to care for Magnolia and the two children.
62	In 1960 Magnolia moved to Champaign and joined the household of her twin daughters, *E* and *M*, bringing *M*'s children with her.
65	After *E*'s death, Magnolia and her daughter moved to Danville, Illinois, with *M*'s two children, whom Magnolia raised in the South, and *M*'s two youngest children.
67	After *M*'s death, Magnolia joined her daughter Viola's household for a short time.
67	Soon afterward, Viola and her husband rented a nearby house for Magnolia and the four grandchildren. Magnolia is on welfare, cares for the four children, and constantly receives help from the Jacksons and from her children living in Chicago.

When a grandmother household is characterized as matrifocal we get little insight into the dynamics of its formation. At best, it suggests a mother hen who gathers her chicks about her. After age sixty, Magnolia's residence was determined by her children, who decided to bring her to the urban North to care for her. Her move North was prompted by her children's concern for her health and well-being.

We find that Magnolia has frequently shared households with her children and grandchildren. In fact, she has consistently moved to join her daughter's households to be cared for, or to care for her grandchildren. Instead of simply gathering her flock, each move and new household in which Magnolia lived after age sixty was formed on a different basis.

By the time Magnolia was elderly she was living in the urban North in a grandmother household caring for her grandchildren. This was the result of the illness and subsequent death of one of her daughters. At this time a house was rented and maintained for Magnolia and the four grandchildren by Viola and her husband, Leo. The rented house was one block from Viola's home and the two households functioned primarily as a single domestic unit of cooperation. The cluster of relatives consisted of four generations: Magnolia, the four grandchildren, Viola and Leo Jackson, ten of their children, and their grandchild, the son of Viola Jackson's oldest daughter.

This four-generational kin cluster is not a co-residential unit, but a domestic unit of cooperation. The main source of financial support consisted of Leo's seasonal construction work, welfare payments to both Magnolia and Viola's daughter (for her son), and the part-time jobs of some of the teenage children. These individuals used Viola's house as home base where they shared the evening meal, cared for all the small children, and exchanged special skills and services. Frequently, Viola's brother (whose wife had died) ate with the group and participated in the exchange of money, food, care for the sick, and household duties. The exchange of clothes, appliances, and services in crisis situations extended beyond this kin cluster to relatives in Chicago and St. Louis. This group is an example of an urban kinship-based domestic unit which formed to handle the basic family functions.

Concluding Remarks

The examples from the preceding sections support the suggestion that domestic functions are carried out for urban blacks by clusters of kin who may or may not reside together. Individuals who are members of households and domestic units of cooperation align to provide the basic functions often attributed to nuclear family units. The flexibility of the blacks' adaptation to the daily social and economic problems of urban living is evidenced in these kinship-based units which form to handle the daily demands of urban life. In particular, new or expanded households and/or domestic units are created to care for children. The basis of these cooperative units is co-generational sibling alignment, the domestic cooperation of close adult females, and the exchange of goods and services between the male and female relatives of these females. To conclude, it is suggested that these households and domestic units provide the assurance that all the children will be cared for.

Note

[1] Names throughout the paper are pseudonyms.

The author would like to thank Professors E. Bruner, D. Shimkin, F. K. Lehman, D. Plath, and O. Lewis, and Mr. W. Ringle, for their interest in this work and helpful comments.

Urban Chinese
Family Life in a Communist Society

WILLIAM JANKOWIAK

William Jankowiak did his field research in the city of Huhhot in the Chinese province of Inner Mongolia. The people of Huhhot faced the challenge of following laws and regulations that transformed the nature of their obligations to their parents, their children, and their spouses. Even the expectations that husbands and wives had of each other changed as the state strongly discouraged couples from having more than one child. People who had grown up expecting to have many children and to live in a circle of kin now found themselves with only one adult child. Men and women faced other challenges, as women began to work outside the home, while bearing a double burden of housework and child care and their jobs. Gender antagonism continued as it had in the past, but in a new setting.

The obligation that the Chinese feel to assist their relatives is much stronger than what we find in the United States, but how this will work itself out in a China with small families is not yet clear. With a single child, the urban Chinese family today is in form more like urban families elsewhere, but the way they function is not necessarily the same, as Jankowiak shows us.

Ever since the Chinese state unified the populace five thousand years ago, scholars have referred to the cultural patterns that constitute China's cultural essence as "the Chinese way of life." These cultural patterns consist of a standardized written language,

Source: Article written expressly for *Urban Life*.

In China the success of a man's life often is determined by his ability to reproduce himself through time. To die with grandsons alive and well is regarded as a time of joyful sorrow. The photo reveals two grandsons, wearing both the colors of mourning (white) and happiness (red), leading a funeral procession down a city street carrying a tree that symbolizes family prosperity. [Photo by William Jankowiak]

a patrilineal (i.e., father's side) descent system, a patrilocal (i.e., father's locality) residence rule, and a social order organized around the principle of hierarchy and meritocracy (see Pasternak and Salaff 1993). The "Chinese way" is a popular image frequently evoked by both Chinese and some foreign scholars to account for the continuities and uniformities found in Chinese behavior. Although this image retains some utility when discussing rural Chinese cultural beliefs and behaviors, it no longer is an accurate portrait of urban Chinese life in the People's Republic of China.

In this chapter I will examine the impact of urbanization and socialist policies on men and women's interest, commitment, and daily involvement in family activities in Huhhot, the capital of Inner

Mongolia Autonomous Region, People's republic of China. Ethnographic data was collected during two field seasons between 1981 and 1983, and in 1987 for a total of thirty months.[1] My research explored what the Chinese meant by kinship and family, dispute management and mediation, power and authority, ethics, gender and sexuality, ethnicity and individuality, and so forth. I wanted to understand the thoughts, values, and ambitions of the Huhhotians. I especially wanted to know what they privately and publicly desired, were ashamed of, and yearned to accomplish (see Jankowiak 1993). By striking a balance between these often competing domains of interaction, I hope to reveal the significance of the new cultural patterns present within the contemporary urban Chinese family.

The Rural and Urban Chinese Family

Throughout much of Chinese history, the family was organized around a cosmology of filial piety that encouraged total obedience, respect, and loyalty by the junior generation toward the senior generation (Freeman 1965; Wolf 1982). This cosmology was sustained through the prevalence of the "big family"—family compounds with several generations and a number of related marital couples living together (Whyte and Parish 1984:153). The head of the family was the father, who controlled the distribution of the family inheritance. His wife, who was initially seen as an outsider, was assigned lower status in her husband's family.

If kinship is of paramount importance in rural China, it is viewed as a mixed blessing in Huhhot. It is as much a potential burden as a potential benefit or a familial necessity. Parents, children, siblings, and other kin tend to work at different kinds of jobs, developing individual skills and, thus, unconnected networks of job-related friends. As a result, the dependence upon one's kin is greatly reduced in favor of increasing reliance on friends in the workplace. In fact, upwardly mobile kin often deliberately cut ties of blood which bind them to their more economically humble relatives.

This change requires that the Chinese pursue a broad-based strategy of social interaction that includes both kin and non-kin. One insightful informant, when asked to make a distinction between kin and friends, acknowledged that "friends are for mundane matters, family is for ritual affairs." A twenty-eight-year-old female informant poignantly observed that "We hide from our cousins but not our friends."

The urban Chinese family is organized primarily into two different forms: nuclear and stem. While the nuclear family is the preferred form of family arrangement, most Chinese, at one time or another, will enter into some form of stem family arrangement (i.e., a family with a married couple, children, and another relative, usually a parent). The rural ideal of the joint or "big family" (Cohen 1976) as the preferred family organization no longer exists in urban China or, if it does, it exists in small numbers. Today, only at times of a major rite or life-crisis (e.g., marriage, death, or serious illness) will all siblings and their children congregate. Although the range of kinship bonds is shrinking, the value attributed to marriage and family life has never waned. People continue to think of the family as the dominant metaphor by which to assist and evaluate another's progress through life.

Although the age hierarchy continues to be a vital part of daily life in rural China, its significance in the city has softened. Unlike their rural counterparts, married couples, in setting up a household, start by forming a nuclear family. Later, upon the death of one of their parents, the family structure changes to incorporate the living parent. This re-incorporation, however, does not lead to the elderly parent becoming the head of the family.

While an elderly parent on ceremonial occasions is referred to as the head of the family, and given the seat of honor whenever a photograph is taken or a special dinner is cooked, the fact is that the elderly parent is perceived to be an important but, nonetheless, burdensome duty.

Every elderly person I talked with lamented that, although his or her physical needs were taken care of, they still did not receive the respect they desired or felt they deserved. Some elderly even talked as if their children had abandoned them. Significantly, fathers complained more often than mothers about the loss of their children's active attention and freely given respect.

Observations of elderly parent and offspring interaction found that mothers were, in fact, treated with greater tenderness, attention, and respect than fathers. (For example, they were more often asked for their opinion and their views were listened to.) Obviously, mothers, and not fathers, are able to draw upon the strong, intimate child-parent bonds which they established and maintained throughout their life span. Without property and other "resources of power," fathers who took little or no interest in their children's development are unable to command their adult children and, therefore, receive only a ritualistic admission of deference and a nominal articulation of love.

The Urban Domestic Sphere:
The Meaning of Marriage

Unlike in the countryside, there is in the city an increasingly wide range of responses to the meaning of marriage and family life. As a rule, if a couple loved one another, they repeatedly strove to maintain mutual consideration. Thus, for example, marriage, in the words of one female, should be "a bond between equals who do not keep secrets and who enjoy one another's company. They should prefer to do everything together."

For the most part, men shared similar expectations of marriage. For example, a male forty-two-year-old told me that after "marriage you should eat together, go to the movies together and always strive to be an ideal couple." A middle-aged man, who was recently divorced, told me that although his "wife was not a good person, in the best marriages there were no secrets." Consideration and mutual respect are values used by spouses and outsiders to evaluate the quality and success of a marriage. They are not gender-specific traits.

A Chinese man, for example, told me that "if you want to go out at night, but notice that your wife becomes upset, you must stay home and keep her company." Another man who studied English and Esperanto in his spare time admitted that he preferred on Sunday to study all day, but he noticed that his wife became increasingly quiet and "despondent," so he gave up the practice. He noted that "it is important to be considerate to your wife. That is why every Sunday we go to the park for a walk." Though not every man interviewed responded with similar sensitivity, a wife's wishes are given great sway in how a husband will spend his free time. Sacrifice and compromise are not constitutionally foreign to either spouse.

Still, tensions exist. Many men argued that they did other things for their wives, and it was inconvenient of their wives to demand that they cease what one male worker called "having fun." Some worker families made a simple adjustment or compromise: together they visited other couples and then separated into unisexual groups to "discuss things." Other families, especially those recently married, often continued to independently visit their friends.

While it is difficult to determine the degree to which any marriage is truly happy, it is noteworthy that both rural and urban Chinese spend time assessing one another's marriages and evaluating them in terms of assumed and perceived states of happiness and unhappiness. In the urban centers this assessment, however, is more

Family photographs represent one of the primary means by which the Chinese remember living and deceased family members. In every rural and most working-class urban homes, the family photo album is proudly displayed on the living room wall. In college educated homes, however, family photos are stored in a photo album that is shown only upon request. [Photo by William Jankowiak]

frequent and focused. From daily conversations it is obvious that younger urbanites have increased expectations and demands for emotional satisfaction within marriage. It was not uncommon for the Chinese to speculate on the frequency with which happiness is achieved. For example, a thirty-seven-year-old female worker told me, referring to her friends and neighbors, that "maybe 2 percent of the marriages I know of are very happy, 80 percent are okay and the remaining 18 percent are terrible." A male government official noted that "In America 50 percent of the marriages end in divorce. In China 50 percent of the marriages are unhappy." It is difficult to assess the representatives of these opinions. Of the seventy Chinese families that I knew reasonably well, I estimate (based on the presences or absences of interpersonal friction and strife) that 48 families, or 56 percent, had satisfactory marriages, while 21, or 44 percent, were unsatisfactory. In short, the percentages are not always exact, but the patterns generally are. It is important to remember that marriage in China, as in America, goes through cycles of adjustment in expectations and pressures and, therefore, unsatisfactory marriages often, in time, become more satisfying and even develop into a love of deep attachment (Goode 1963).

Those couples who enjoyed one another's company and accommodated, if not actually enjoyed, their spouse's personality style and individual quirks seem to have the more satisfactory marriages. A common means of communicating this is for one spouse to ask the other spouse to interpret his or her dreams, a request that is treated very seriously. The request is an invitation to subjective intimacy. Dreams are but one means used to convey anxieties and intimate moments.

Marital Satisfaction and Sexuality

Sexuality is another *means* by which affection is *expressed* and *withheld*, and intimacy given or denied. Although I did not study sexual behavior in the countryside, my analysis of urban behavior found that women generally controlled the frequency of intercourse in marriage. If a wife felt that the marriage was good, she would more than amicably acquiesce to her husband's advances; if not, these advances were rejected directly or with "various excuses." The latter was especially true if a woman did not like her husband.

Rather than focus on the husband, urban wives, much like their rural counterparts, focused attention on their child and sought companionship outside the marriage with friends. A man, for example, who had just become a father observed that "after the child comes, the wife plays with it, and not with the husband." Another man admitted that after a child arrives men associate with male friends, adding that "the lovers are no longer deeply committed to one another, they are committed only to the child." Even if a woman truly loves her husband, the two roles seldom are easily blended and integrated.

If a woman loves her husband, she will strive to maintain his interest and involvement. A thirty-one-year-old woman, for example, confided to me that "after I had given birth I no longer cared for him (her husband) as I had before. The only reason I continue to have sex with him is because he is a good man and I like giving him nice things." The ability of women to control sexual frequency is vividly revealed in the comment of a thirty-seven-year-old male who asserted quite strongly that it is common to hear wives teasing about and even, at times, threatening "to withhold sex if their husband failed to perform some household task." When women do not like their husbands, it is common for them to reduce the frequency of sexual intercourse. A forty-three-year-old man admitted, for example, that "my wife did not like sex before we had a child. Afterwards she did not like me, so we stopped having sex."

Chinese sexual techniques, as in other state-level societies, vary by social class. For the most part, educated men are aware that women's sexual arousal differs from their own and stress the importance of foreplay as the primary means for stimulating their wives to orgasm (*kuaigan*). Independent interviews with their wives found, however, that husbands were not generally successful in satisfying their wives. Educated women told my female research assistant and, on a separate occasion, repeated to me, that their husbands were sexually too demanding and, thus, they did not really enjoy sex.

Among the educated strata, those men who believed that marriage should be based on emotional and spiritual compatibility often became upset over their wives' not reaching an orgasm. This was vividly demonstrated to me when one informant lamented that "nothing he did" aroused his wife and, hence, he felt personally responsible for his wife's inability to reach an orgasm. In exasperation, he did the unexpected: he turned to his friends for advice. They told him to kiss her breasts and to talk to her; some suggested that he show her some pornographic pictures (easily obtainable in the city's underground market). Unfortunately, their suggestions did not lead to any noticeable changes. Unlike workers, peasants, and herders, some members of the city's educated population are concerned with a new notion of eroticism, one that assumes women should also enjoy the sex act in and of itself. This is a truly new idea. In Imperial China, the primary motive behind an educated man's interest in stimulating his lover was the belief that an aroused and satisfied woman could transfer *yin*, the female essence, to her male lover. In Huhhot, not one informant believed this. The growing concern of some educated men with their wives' sexual satisfaction is consistent with other studies (Kinsey, Pomeroy, and Martin 1953) on human sexuality, which found the scope and intensity of a person's erotic experimentation was associated with their level of education. For example, almost half of my sample of educated men (n = seven of sixteen) admitted that their wives or lovers performed fellatio on them; however, among the city's working class, no one reported engaging in fellatio.

Domestic Power: Men's and Women's Complaints

Marriage and the formation of a family continue to be major transition phases in Chinese life. In the countryside, marriage involves separation of a woman from her natal family and subsequent incorporation into her husband's family. But prior to and after marriage, women are instructed to obey their mother-in-law and husband. The emphasis is on obedience and deference. A newly married woman is reminded that, in time, she will gain power and place within her new family and, thereby, establish her own authority and independence. In an attempt to achieve power women must rely on deception and guile, whereas men, secure within their natal family, do not hesitate in openly expressing their opinions and demands. In effect, the prevailing view in the countryside is that women can only gradually, over the course of a lifetime, expand their authority in the family.

In urban China the *gradual* expansion of women's influence within the home has been aided by the institutionalization of neolocal residence, bilateral descent, and equal work opportunity for men and women. These new realities have enabled contemporary women to achieve a sphere of power and domestic independence faster than had been the case in their mother's generation.

Chinese men and women are highly cognizant of the fact that domestic relations are radically different from those found in the countryside. They also believe that in other times and in different social contexts men had more power and control within the family. It is an idealization, however, that was far from true even in Imperial China. Patterson found that the "theme of a powerful woman and the henpecked husband is an almost obsessive theme in Chinese literature" (1982:325), a finding that suggests, at the very least, men were responding negatively to the strength and domination of women in a clearly tension-filled spousal relationship. Be that as it may, China's men believe that, in the past, husbands had an easier time controlling their wives than they do today. Furthermore, although no one in my sample believed that it is proper or correct for a wife to be dominant within the family, everyone agreed that it is typically the case. One man remarked that "in the past the mother-in-law was fearsome, now the wife is fearsome." The frequency in which this expression is invoked suggests that males are more ambivalent and less secure than in the past with their position within the family and society. Although Chinese men, particularly the uneducated, believe that female domestic power is both authentic and onerous, they have little power to effect change. Men are keenly aware, for example, that women's self-presentation style shifts depending on the social context. For example, whereas a woman prefers to speak softly on a date, once married, she is just as likely to shout commands at both her child and husband. A male worker of mild temperament accustomed to listening to his wife issue pronouncements turned to me one day and, matter of factly, said "women shout a lot. It's their way. We just have to accept it." Women, for the most part, are not sympathetic to their husband's disappointment.

It is not that uncommon, for example, for an angry wife to yell at her husband when he leaves the house, thereby communicating to her neighbors her preeminence and authority within the family. In this way, the "henpecked" jokes manifest a deeper underlying but unspoken uneasiness men have toward their position and duties in the domestic sphere.

Because women are indeed saddled with the double burden of working and handling domestic chores and child care, they often feel overworked, exhausted, and numbed by their duties (Whyte and Parish 1984; Wolf 1985; Honig and Hershatter 1988). From this evidence, some scholars have inferred, by omission, that men's lives are without difficulties and are easier than women's. In Huhhot many men are not so sure. In 1987, in fact, men frequently joked in small clusters about the advantages of being a woman. They note that everyone "cared for" and "helped" women. In addition, men believe that, regardless of the rhetoric, it is more their responsibility, and not their wives', to achieve a promotion, increase household income, and expand personal connections. It is a responsibility, an expectation, that they find demanding and seriously. Failure to perform satisfactorily often results in their wives complaining that their husbands "let the family down." It is a complaint that men do not want to hear because it is perceived as a stigma attacking the core of their gender identity.

Although most Chinese wives *do not* habitually lament and describe their husbands' shortcomings, a husband's underachievements are noted and commented upon. Typically, Chinese women expect their men to demonstrate clear competence in their work and provide some demonstration or evidence of worldly ambition and the likelihood of future success. In this way women continuously assess men's and, in particular, their husbands' performance, achievement, and relative social standing vis-à-vis other men in the prevailing social hierarchy.

In turn, men feel compelled to maintain a posture that most will never actually achieve: becoming an important and influential person. Not surprisingly, the striving for "success," with its accompanying emphasis on symbolically indicating that it is within one's grasp, can promote an uncertainty that is sometimes acute. For example, one man told me that he never would get married because his father was "not important" and he had no important relations to help out. Ambitious women, in particular, expect and demand more things from their husbands and often become extremely disappointed with their failure to deliver. Both men and women are equally demanding but, because they desire different things from one another, they often become disinterested, critical, or unresponsive when their demands are not recognized or, at least, partially meet.

Daughter-in-Law, Mother-in-Law, and New Family Interaction

In the countryside, a woman, especially if she has married outside her village, seldom returns to her parents' home. It is assumed that she will assume a new identity and that, regardless of personal feelings, will strive to identify with and support the interest of her new family. In the city this is no longer the norm. Women regularly, often with their husbands, visit their mother's family. This is new. The factors that contribute to a woman's success in shifting her husband's allegiance, at least in the early years of the marriage, are the absence of a patrilocal residence rule, her new-found financial independence, and a husband's emotional dependency on his wife.

The most significant event to alter a wife's kin orientation is childbirth. It is an event that fundamentally alters the social roles which form the nuclear family. The young wife, who dutifully had followed the patrilineal custom of regularly visiting her husband's family will, after the birth of the child, look to her mother for advice, emotional support, and free child care. If her mother is retired or has remained a full-time housewife, she will in turn assist her daughter and help raise the grandchild.

In an effort to prevent the loss of their sons, Chinese mothers today, in a dramatic break with traditional norms, tend to cater to their daughters-in-law. Indeed, most mothers-in-law treat their daughters-in-law as honored guests whenever they visit. One fifty-four-year-old mother pointed out to me that she treated her daughter-in-law with extra special attention because she did not want to lose her son and become a forgotten mother. She added

> Whenever she drops over, I give her special things and even if she wants to help out, I always praise her and thank her. You see China has changed. I'm afraid if she doesn't feel comfortable in her husband's home she will stop accompanying him and, in time, I will lose my son to her family. [long pause] Do you know that in China daughters follow their mothers; husbands follow their wives?

Another elderly woman bitterly and continually complained that her son loved his wife more than his own mother because "men love sex more than their own mothers."

Further evidence that the dwindling homage paid to mothers-in-law extends beyond Huhhot can be found in television programs that focus on the plight of the "ill-treated mother-in-law." I saw three such television programs while in the field. It is becoming a common sour chord in urban, but not rural, Chinese culture.

Parent–Child Relations

The Mother-Child Bond

One of the primary means whereby rural Chinese women attempt to secure and protect themselves from a hostile mother-in-law and often unsympathetic husband is to foster an intense emotional dependency with her children so that, once grown, they will take care of her (Wolf 1972). In Margery Wolf's study of contemporary urban life in the People's Republic of China (PRC), she observed that recent socialist changes no longer make it necessary for women to foster this type of parent-child dependency. She adds that:

> The uterine family has disappeared because the need for it has disappeared. Urban women do not express the same degree of anxiety about their old age that they used to. Young women work and expect pensions, older women who do not have pensions are assured by the government that they are cared for. (1985:207)

I found that the parent-child dependency had not disappeared. It is persistent, however, for a different reason: the continuing preference and habit to cultivate bonds of intense emotional dependency. Mothers continue to exercise tremendous psychological control over their offspring. In fact, the mother-child relationship is the most admired and revered parent-child dyad. It is the mother who is the primary educator of very young children. Of all family dyads, the mother-child bond is by far the most emotional, enduring, and psychologically pleasing. Middle-aged informants frequently confided to me that their emotional involvement with their mothers remained remarkably strong after their marriage and throughout their adult lives.

Although the Chinese respect their fathers, they adore their mothers. It is culturally understood and accepted that a son or daughter will exchange, at some point, harsh words with one's father, but it is considered bad and regrettable form that this would happen with one's mother. The intensity of the emotional adoration was expressed to me by several Huhhotian college students in their twenties, who allowed me to read sections of their diaries. One twenty-three-year-old female told me that

> Since I came to this city, I've missed my family, especially my mother. I cried while I read my mother's letter. I often dream of my family and getting together to eat dinner and watch television or go to the movies. I often say to myself, "You aren't a child; you're a grown-up." I do not know why I cannot overcome my weakness. Maybe my mother gave me too much love.

A nineteen-year-old student who was suffering from a cold acknowledged that

> I think of my dear mother. If she was here, she could cook delicious food for me and comfort me. But here five thousand miles away from home, who could be as dear as my mother?

Finally, a twenty-one-year-old male student recorded rather bleakly in his diary

> another Sunday of loneliness and restlessness. I'd rather be a bird, then I could fly back home and see my mother.

Adoration is probably not too strong a word to describe the emotional connections above. In this respect and many others, the Chinese mother is the glue that binds the family together. She is the center of the communication network. Through visits she becomes the focal point for news and a pivot for influencing various kin opinions and actions.

For reasons other than simple fear of a vengeful mother-in-law or hostile spouse, the emotional bonds between mother and child formed during infancy and the early childhood years are never relinquished. These bonds are sustained, in large part, through a Chinese tradition which promotes and legitimizes intense life-long emotional dependency between mother and child (Solomon 1971; Pye 1985). It is a bond that is idealized in literature and in conversation as a celebration of harmony, remembrance, and enduring love. Moreover, the intensity of its expression signifies to everyone the continued importance, influence, and power of the Chinese woman.

The Father-Child Bond

Throughout Chinese history, fathers, in both rural and urban settings, believed that their role, as a counterpoint to the role of

Voluntary associations are part of almost every culture. In China, however, the state is fearful of anti-government activities and discourages the formation of voluntary associations. One exception is playing cards, which is regarded as a harmless form of public entertainment men enjoy on their way home from work. [Photo by William Jankowiak]

mothers, was to *not* encourage or tolerate emotional indulgence to promote that dependency. They assumed instead the role of a stern disciplinarian (Fei 1939; Ho 1987; Wilson 1974). Chinese fathers were not, however, without compassion or love for their children. Most Chinese fathers, in fact, felt a warm, deep sentiment toward their children though the articulation of that sentiment was restrained by their traditional parenting role and its expectations (Solomon 1971). In some cases, a father supplied strict discipline as a complement to the mother's overindulgence. Or, at least, a balance was to be reached between a mother's understanding and a father's demands. Solomon quotes a Qing dynasty scholar-official who wrote that a "father loved his child with all his heart, but he would not express it" (Solomon 1971:60). It was a posture that sometimes produced resentment and acute anxiety for the child in later life (Solomon 1971:39–61). Nonetheless, a cultural ethos emerged which justified different parenting postures: the father facilitated a child's entry into the outside world, whereas the mother provided a secure and loving environment within the home. It was assumed that these roles were inevitable and unchangeable. Moreover, it also was assumed this sexual division in parenting roles contributed to producing a more responsible and ethical person overall.

The Emergent Urban Father-Child Relationship

The traditional Chinese conception of the parenting process is similar to the American 1950s typology which posits that, within the domestic sphere, men perform an instrumental or competence-directed role, whereas women perform the more expressive or empathetic role. This typology is an accurate representation of how the Chinese peasant views parent-child relations. It is also strikingly similar to the parenting style found in Taiwan (Ho 1987). However, in contemporary urban China, the emergency of new opportunities, in a socialist milieu, has fostered a supportive environment for the expression of warmer sentiments and closer interaction between father and child. This expression is a result of a new attitude readily found in casual conversation and reflective comments, and stresses the importance of intimate father-child interaction. As such it challenges the traditional father-child role, a role and style of interaction that was, in fact, seen by the previous generations' fathers as no longer satisfying or necessary.

There are three factors which contribute to the increasing intimacy of father-child interaction in both public and private settings. First, over 80 percent of women between twenty-six and forty-six years old work—a fact that compels even the most reluctant father to become more involved in caretaking activities. Second, the economy of domestic space, or the typically small, one-room apartment, places the father in constant and close proximity to his child, thereby enabling more intimate parent-child interaction. Third, a new folk notion promoting fatherly involvement has emerged within many households.

Father-Daughter Love

The core of Chinese kinship ideology has been the father-son relationship (Hsu 1967). The homage to that relationship and the patrilineal tradition which spawned it continues to be expressed in a variety of social settings. Publicly the Chinese speak continually about the importance of "having a son," an obsession so acute that whenever people ask a pregnant woman about the expected delivery date, they seldom use the gender-neutral word "child" but, instead, use the word "son" as the generic term for the fetus. Hence, they ask "when are you going to have your son?" The obsession is so complete that everyone interviewed on the topic publicly hoped for a son. However, my research assistant found in private interviews with the college-educated women that half of them wanted a daughter, a fact which suggests that women's public comments are more a social form than an accurate expression of personal conviction. At least among the college-educated, it also suggests that the linguistic terminology used to speak of pregnancy might be more a residue of tradition than true evidence of a continued preference for a son.

Although the urban Chinese continue to publicly value sons over daughters, I found that parents were also very happy with the birth of daughters. As previously shown in the section on mother-in-law and daughter-in-law relationships, sons are increasingly regarded as unreliable in fulfilling family obligations. They are seen as easily lost to their wife and her family, while daughters are thought of as more considerate and faithful in continuing to visit their natal home. Sons are viewed as less of an asset than before. Chinese fathers also indicated they were more demanding with their son than their daughter. They interacted with their daughters more openly, more warmly, and less critically. Moreover, fathers tended to speak less harshly to their daughters. Whenever fathers discussed their children, it was common to stress "how wonderful little girls are." This is a new occurrence and, as such, it constitutes an enormous shift in a patrilineal tradition which valued sons and grandsons over daughters and granddaughters.

The socialist transformation of cultural meanings has had a corresponding impact on urban men's conception of themselves as husbands and fathers. Young fathers continue to assume a firm and somewhat formal posture toward their sons, while paradoxically insisting they did not want to be as formal and reserved as their fathers had been with them. In China, I often heard a man insist (much as in traditional China) that, while he "loved his father, he did not like him." Younger Chinese males felt strongly that it was improper for a child to grow up and not like his or her father. Although contemporary Chinese fathers wish to become close friends with their children, as opposed to striking the more traditional note of a stern moral authority ever ready to criticize shortcomings, they remain uncertain and confused as to how to express this wish. Warmth and immediacy of affection are not easily achieved. It is easier for a father to accomplish this with a daughter than with a son. Significantly, fathers are more ambivalent than mothers in balancing their obligations as both spouse and parent.

This ambivalence was profoundly articulated by many college-educated fathers who voiced concern that their children loved their mothers more than them. Although the male desire to become more emotionally involved is far from achieved, it is a desire frequently heard in intimate conversation among close friends. As such, it has enormous implications for the quality of future urban parent-child relations and the development of a new Chinese person.

Conclusion

Not only has the socialist transformation of China's urban infrastructure stimulated the re-evaluation of customary kinship obligations, it also has resulted in a re-evaluation of the conjugal expectations and parenting duties. The transformation has not, however, eliminated gender antagonism—only the style in which it is expressed. Previously muted through habit and the pragmatics of patrilocal politics, women's yearnings, opinions, and demands have forcefully emerged to reshape the politics of family management.

The new "resources of power" have enabled *urban* women to initiate divorce, organize the Sunday visiting schedule to favor their natal family over their husband's, control the frequency of sexual intercourse, participate in romantic affairs, effectively ignore an overbearing mother-in-law or husband, and, at the same time, retain a greater hold than their husband's over their children's love and loyalty. They are also now better able to balance their spouse's expectation and demand for greater intimacy with the desires and obligations necessitated by childrearing. Given access to these new-found "resources of power," women have achieved, within the domestic sphere, a greater degree of female independence and autonomy than in any previous time in Chinese history.

On the other hand, urban men, who are employed in a socialist organized work enterprise, are confused by the transformation of the social organization, which has undermined their place within the Chinese social order. They are inclined to speculate that women have an easier life when compared to the full weight of male social responsibilities. Among intellectuals, self-doubt has been further experienced regarding the father's role in the parenting process. Exacerbating this uncertainty is the re-evaluation of the importance and value of daughters. This shift in public sentiment—that a daughter makes just as good, and, in many instances, a better child than a son—cuts across every social class and constitutes the emergence of a new urban consensus, carrying enormous implications for the meaning of marriage, family, and gender relations within urban Chinese society.

Note

[1] The material that forms much of this research was collected in Huhhot, the capital of Inner Mongolia Autonomous Region, People's Republic of China between 1981 and 1983 and again in 1987 for a period of two and a half years. Partial funding for the research was provided by the University of California General Research Grant, Sigma Xi, and CSCPRC, National Academy of Sciences. I am grateful to the following scholars for their advice, encouragement, and thoughtful suggestions: Chris Atwood, Jim Bell, George Gmelch, Tom Paladino, and Walter Zenner.

The sample for much of my data was the total universe of three hundred households and the public sphere in which I conducted scanning and focus sampling on a variety of topics and behaviors. (These topics and behaviors included bicycle accidents, sex differences in use of public streets, incidents of sexual harassment, mate selection criteria, domestic power relations, traditional and socialist mortuary rites, and market interactions.) After I conducted a broad preliminary survey, I found it more fruitful to cultivate long-term relationships with a smaller group of friends. Most interviews were conducted in Mandarin except for those students who wanted to practice English. I interviewed two hundred students, a third of whom were Mongolians. In general, most of my information came from observation and unguided interviews.

The specific methods used in recording information on Huhhotian sexuality varied according to locality, concerns of privacy, and the informant's personality. I used two lines of inquiry: First, I would introduce the topic by asking about the marital satisfaction of mutual friends, which stimulates speculation on the quality of their relationships and sexual behaviors. Once the topic of sexuality was raised, it was a relatively simple transition to ask more direct personal questions about one's own sexual behaviors. Second, on the advice of a key informant and good friend, I openly discussed specific sexual practices or problems that I myself was having with my "wife." I found this gambit extremely productive. Informants appreciated that I had freely shared with them a personal problem or experience and usually reciprocated by offering their own observations and opinions about certain forms of sexuality, perceived male-female drives, and, most importantly, their own sexual behavior. The first time I tried this approach a number of women and some men balked; however, I took the same approach so often, in a variety of settings, that women and men became accustomed to speaking frankly about sexuality in front of me. Nonetheless, whenever my informants' responses began to sound similar, I assumed I was no longer obtaining strictly personal data but rather generalized cultural accounts. This usually happened whenever I solicited information about the frequency of sexual intercourse. My survey of sexuality in Huhhot must be seen as an exploratory study; any conclusion drawn from it and applied to other areas of China must be viewed with caution.

Wives and Servants
Women in Middle-Class Households, Guatemala City

LAUREL BOSSEN

While most of the articles in Part Four have touched on the domestic roles of women, few have related their roles within the home to their contribution to the general economy. Bossen tackles this relationship in an article in which she shows how middle-class women in a Latin American city employ poor women in their households. She shows where the roles of the two classes of women overlap and where they are distinct. In this situation there are many underlying tensions. As Bossen points out, the kind of affluence which allows these privileged women to afford domestic servants is related to the poverty of those who become domestics. The women about whom Bossen writes are not extremely wealthy, for most women of the upper class would not work outside the home; yet even the middle class in Guatemala City and many other Third World cities can still afford to hire domestic servants.

Introduction

The contemporary urban middle-class household of Western society is generally portrayed as a nuclear family that has abandoned many of the traditional tasks associated with rural households. Production is typically removed from the home to large enterprises where there is little need to rely on extended family ties to expand the labor force. The husband becomes the principal money earner working outside

Source: Article written expressly for *Urban Life.*

the home, while the wife adjusts to a diminished work role in the home combined with continued responsibility for domestic services and child care. The shrinking of domestic work is encouraged by modern technology which reduces the labor input in a wide range of traditional goods and services that were once produced in the home.

While this model fits the North American experience, there is a noticeable difference in the middle-class household of urban Latin America where the gap between rich and poor, urban and rural society is more extreme. In Latin America, high rates of unemployment, the low cost of unskilled domestic labor, and the relative scarcity of labor-saving appliances combine to produce an urban middle-class household that typically includes one or more young female servants as additional residents and participants in household activities. Indeed, the literature indicates that a large part of the surplus female population found in Latin American cities is the result of a general influx of young, single women from poor rural areas who seek work in domestic services (Boserup 1970; Jelin 1977; Chinchilla 1977; Hollandar 1977; Smith 1973).

In the cities, young women who lack specialized job skills are absorbed into middle-class households where they share the labor of middle-class women as housekeepers. Their domestic tasks require that they spend most of their time *with* the family, but they are not *of* the family; they are not kin. Nonetheless, the continuous presence of domestic servants in the home implies an intimate relationship and means that, if they remain for a long time, they may be treated as members of the family in certain limited ways. If they are liked and trusted, they may be treated "like a daughter" and respond with the feeling that their employer is "like a mother." Moreover, they typically play the role of a surrogate mother within the household, caring for the young children when their mother goes out. The fact that many domestic servants are young women with few family ties in the city, or come from urban families that have been splintered by the pressures of poverty means that they may be particularly receptive to such partial incorporation. At the same time, a high degree of distrust and tension can develop between the middle-class woman and the domestic employee. Of course, the young maidservants occupy an inferior status economically, legally, and socially within the household that employs them. They may be seen as "resident aliens." Within their place of employment and residence, the middle-class household, legitimate kinship claims (and the servant's lack of them) define economic and social rewards.

In this discussion, I compare the position of middle-class wives and their servants—two sets of women who work for, live within, and depend on middle-class households in Guatemala City. By comparing the economic and social roles of these women who live and work side by side, I hope to illustrate how domestic roles articulate with kinship and class relations. First, I show how the work roles of wife and servant are interwoven within urban middle-class households, and then I consider the way the legitimate kinship ties of the wife serve to define her economic and social position, and contribute to the stability of class-stratified urban society.

The Middle-Class Community

Villa Rosa is a modern middle-class neighborhood in Guatemala City with slightly more than four thousand residents.[1] The houses are relatively homogeneous, suburban-style homes, around fifteen years old, with electricity, modern plumbing, six to eight rooms, gardens, and driveways. In 1974, these houses were generally worth from $12,000 to $18,000. Consistent with the larger Latin American pattern of urbanization (Boserup 1970), the census data for this area show a remarkable surplus of women: 142 females per 100 males! This compares to 111 females per 100 males for Guatemala City as a whole (Guatemala 1974:25). There are two main reasons for the more extreme sexual imbalance found in Villa Rosa. First, while middle-class men's occupations are sometimes based in rural areas or provincial centers, their female kin and children tend to reside in the capital city where they can profit from the greater concentration of cultural, educational, and occupational opportunities. Second, female domestic employees are a significant fraction of the resident population in middle-class neighborhoods. Census and survey samples show that resident female domestic employees comprise just under 11 percent of the total population in Villa Rosa. Roughly 60 percent of the households employ them. Indeed, they are considered a normal feature of the middle-class household. These live-in domestic workers are further supplemented by day-workers who commute from neighboring working-class districts and shantytowns, and who are not counted among the resident population.

The Economic Role of Wives
and Servants in the Family

In Villa Rosa as in most of Latin America, housework is defined as women's work. Male participation is considered rare and abnormal.

Housework is performed both by unpaid family members, and by domestic employees drawn from the rural and urban working classes. In comparing the roles of wives and servants in Villa Rosa, we cannot fail to note the inconsistency of conventional social definitions of work whereby women who work in someone else's home are considered to be economically active, while women who work in their own homes are considered to be fulfilling family obligations, but not "working." In Villa Rosa, approximately half of the wives and daughters of middle-class households earn regular cash incomes.[2] Yet a substantial proportion of the women stay home and dedicate themselves to domestic tasks. Combining the percentage of women who stay home with that of women who are introduced into the home as servants, it is evident that this neighborhood consumes a high level of personal domestic services. Approximately one out of every four to five residents (19–25 percent of the *total* population) is involved in domestic upkeep.[3]

The presence of domestic servants in more than half of all Villa Rosa households is related to a variety of factors, but does not appear to be closely linked to outside employment by the wife. Households that lack domestic employees are generally characterized by one or more of the following features: the lack of young children, the lack of outside employment by the wife, and the presence of another adult female relative with at least some time available for housework. That is, they seem to have less work per woman (as indicated, say, by a low ratio of men and children to adult women), or a tight household budget. For instance, in a nuclear family lacking young children, housework was shared by a working mother and three daughters attending high school and university. With four capable females, they felt it would be unnecessary to hire a maid even though they could afford it. In households that have domestic employees, there may or may not be a high ratio of domestic consumers per woman. The ability to pay seems to be the key factor, whether the services are marginal or central to the well-being of the household.

Housework in Villa Rosa includes a variety of familiar tasks: washing and ironing clothes, buying food and household articles, cooking, washing dishes, general housecleaning, and child care. As part of their middle-class standard of living, residents of Villa Rosa consume more elaborate meals, fashionable clothing, and home furnishings than most Guatemalans. These consumption patterns entail extra time and effort for the housekeeper. In Villa Rosa, housekeeping is obviously facilitated by some forms of modern labor-saving technology such as stoves and running water for cooking and cleaning, ready-to-wear clothes, and the availability of stores, supermarkets, and processed foods. At the same time, the fast-food industry has not yet transformed daily dining patterns. In many of the households I visited, the husband and children return each day during the two-hour lunchbreak for a home-cooked meal together. In addition to family meal preparation, hand laundry and ironing are time-consuming tasks. Laundromats are scarce, and the few who own washing machines complain that they have broken down and cannot be serviced. Thus, the household of Villa Rosa remains a place of labor-intensive service work, much of it manual.

The economic roles of housewives and servants involve considerable overlap, but have some important differences. To understand their interrelationship, we must consider their social characteristics, the division of labor between them, and the division of rewards for their contribution to the household. Among middle-class women, we find that kinswomen of any age may be involved in housework. They may be unmarried daughters, young wives, or older women and grandmothers. Their educational levels are high, averaging around nine years for all adult women. In contrast, the domestic servant is typically young (average age of twenty-one), single, and averages only 1.9 years of schooling. As indicated by their youth, most domestic employees do not stay long. In the course of my interviews, I found that a number of households were looking for replacements for employees who had left or been dismissed.

The role of the domestic employee is to perform or assist in the housework for which the middle-class woman is held responsible. In most cases, the middle-class woman supervises or herself performs some of the housework despite the presence of domestic employees. In the few cases where the middle-class woman has very little spare time, she may relegate nearly all of the housework and child care to one or more domestic employees. There is a division of labor which tends to occur between middle-class women and domestic employees, but it is by no means rigid. The middle-class woman normally wants to maintain control over childrearing, spending, and food preparation. The employees are assigned to the more monotonous and less responsible tasks of washing clothes, ironing, sweeping, mopping, errands, and washing dishes. If the employee is trusted, she is given greater responsibility in shopping, cooking and child care.

In housekeeping, the economic roles of the middle-class woman and the domestic servant may alternate. If an employee has just quit or been dismissed, or if a family cannot afford one, the middle-class woman will assume the manual tasks of preparing and serving food, and cleaning up after other members of the household. Unlike the occupational roles of middle-class men vis-à-vis lower-class men, the distinction between intellectual and manual labor is not readily applied to women doing housework. This may cause some real discomfort to middle-class women, as in the following case:

> Francesca lives with her husband, two adult sons, a divorced daughter and her young grandson. Although four adults are working outside the home, Francesca finds her access to cash is inadequate. She desperately craves an outside job to increase her personal income, but is unable to find one that is commensurate with middle-class status. Meanwhile, she is expected to provide housekeeping services for the four working adults and grandchild. Her daughter in particular depends on her for child care and pays Francesca $20 monthly, exactly the average income of domestic employees. Francesca bitterly complains: "They treat me as if I were a servant in the house, only without a salary. At times I despair. Closed-up in the house, it is very depressing. One wants to leave running."

Francesca's comparison with servant status illustrates that the boundary between women of different classes is not clearly expressed in the housework they perform. On the one hand, this could foster certain shared interests between women who, as women, must work in the same milieu regardless of class background. On the other hand, there are obvious tensions, for despite any similarity of actual work roles and economic dependency on the same household funds, the rewards for wives and servants are of a different order, expressing their unequal positions.

The servant is paid a wage—by day, week, or month—whereas the wife receives a "share" of the family estate. More specifically, the average servant in Villa Rosa works for a very low wage, roughly $20 per month, plus room and board. She works without a contract, and is on call for long hours, morning through evening, without formal provisions for holidays, sick leave, pension, or maternity leave. Upon dismissal, she loses not only her wage, but her whole "situation," her temporary home.

In contrast, middle-class wives and kinswomen receive much greater rewards in cash and kind. The wife's rewards are not explicitly settled as to amount or percentage of the husband's income; she depends on the fortunes of her husband's economic ventures and upon his personal discretion in allocating income to her for household maintenance. Interviews with wives in Villa Rosa revealed a wide range of budget variation by which the wife may receive from less than one-fourth to nearly all of her husband's pay, where male earnings averaged $328 per month. Rigorous comparison with the wage of the domestic employee is impossible for the budget of the middle-class woman is clearly not the same as a wage. Much of the money is spent on collective needs for food, clothing, household articles, and the children's education. But having the means to feed, clothe, and educate one's children is *part* of a higher standard of living. Unlike the servant, the wife is guaranteed not only her own maintenance, but that of her children. Even if she may not get regular holidays or "time off," she cannot be summarily dismissed from her "job" or from the marital estate, the home. In contrast, the low wages and working conditions of domestic servants are not compatible with raising children of their own. In this context, it is clear that the economic rewards of the middle-class woman are at least several times greater than those received by the domestic employee who shares the same work.

The similarity and proximity of their work, and the disparity of rewards between the wives and servants of the middle class would be expected to produce invidious comparisons and tensions. This occurs on two levels. First, the wives of Villa Rosa appear to share a generalized distrust of domestic employees as representatives of the poor classes. In discussions among middle-class women, the problems of finding "trustworthy" domestic servants, and the inconveniences of dismissing those who were thought to be pilfering, immoral, or unreliable workers frequently arise as topics of animated conversation. One housewife who had fired three young women within several months was frustrated because she could not find an adequate replacement. With four teenaged children for whom she was shopping, cooking, and maintaining stylish clothes, she felt she needed domestic help, but always found it difficult to find young women of "good character." Servants, on the other hand, recount work experiences in which they claim employers withheld pay, skimped on food, falsely accused them of theft, docked their meager wages for the cost of lost or broken items, or fired them without giving notice or full pay.

A second level of tension seems related to the fact that cheap domestic labor, while it lightens the workload, obviously has implications regarding the perceived economic value of the housewife. The middle-class housewife knows that most of her daily work is unskilled, and that there are scores of lower-class women willing to perform the same work for less pay. This tends to devalue the tasks of housekeeping. The cash value of housework is so low that for the same budget money a husband could hire three to four live-in employees to replace the economic services of the middle-class housewife. Alternately, the middle-class woman who desires to increase her personal spending money from the household budget knows that by dismissing the maid and doing all the housework herself, she only gains about $20 per month. The low market value of housekeeping undoubtedly creates a certain economic uneasiness for the middle-class housekeeper, particularly in a society where the accepted rationale for differential economic rewards is linked to differences in occupational role.

In this situation we would expect the middle-class woman to try to differentiate her domestic contribution from that of her servant.[4] Clearly, little training is involved in washing clothes, ironing, and mopping floors. The middle-class woman does not claim superiority in these areas. Instead, she may attempt to excel in new kinds of housekeeping skills that emphasize and reinforce superior class status for the household. Thus she dabbles in gourmet cooking, fancy needlework and crafts to beautify the home, interior decorating, home tutoring of the children, and so forth. By these activities, still outside the market economy, the middle-class woman seeks to demonstrate that her value to the household cannot be matched by the lower-class domestic employee. Overall, such efforts appear to be rather weak and unconvincing in terms of their direct economic worth. It must be remembered that the link between such housework and the productive process of the modern economy is indirect. Capitalist production is removed from the home and even from the neighborhood. In housework, increased output of services does not result in increased cash income. Maintenance and reproduction of the population is still an essential form of work, but in Villa Rosa it is confused with a range of services and consumption that go beyond economic maintenance and extend into the realm of conspicuous consumption of luxuries— activities which are not usually considered "work." Given the inequality of rewards for work of seemingly equal value, we now look more closely at the role of kinship as it relates to social and economic inequality in these middle-class homes.

The Role of Legitimate Kinship

In modern urban society, home and family remain crucial for social reproduction. Broadly defined, social reproduction encompasses three types of activity: (1) the daily feeding and maintenance of the labor force which restores the capacity of employed workers from day to day; (2) the reproduction of the society through caring for children and raising the next generation of productive people; and (3) the reproduction of the class structure. This third aspect involves a means of identifying, training, and channeling children to fulfill different hierarchical positions in society with minimal disruption as they assume their adult roles.

Within the urban middle-class households of Villa Rosa, domestic servants participate in the first and second types of middle-class social reproduction. They perform household maintenance and provide child care in middle-class homes. But servants are not permitted to engage in the third type. Lacking previous kin ties to the middle class and formal marriage to middle-class men, they are debarred from reproduction of the privileged class. While some may take the view that this type of social reproduction is largely a passive role, others such as Papanek (1979) have suggested that it does involve goal-directed activity which brings real economic rewards. She labels this form of unrecognized work "status production." I would suggest that much of this status production work takes place in the idiom of family and kinship roles in the middle class. Clearly, the most important factor that conditions a middle-class housewife's reward is not her overt work role (which is shared with servants) but her kinship role as defined by her marriage. The kinship role of middle-class women is the basis for the reproduction of the class structure. The marriage contract is the means by which she is able to claim a share of her husband's income. It is not surprising that some 90 percent of the marital unions in Villa Rosa are legally contracted rather than common-law (the form that predominates among low-income populations).

By virtue of the marriage tie, it might be proposed that the wife provides additional sexual and childbearing services, which are outside the province of servants. However, I would maintain that it is neither sex nor reproduction per se that distinguishes the wife's contribution. Regarding sex, few would realistically claim that the wife is the only woman to provide sexual services to the middle-class man. Certainly the women of Villa Rosa do not claim this. Other women, including servants, are often enlisted and may even have children by middle-class men. But under these circumstances, the servant, unlike the wife, risks loss of employment and material support for the resulting offspring who are "unrecognized," that is, illegitimate. The resident servant lacks a license to produce middle-class children, and she is generally not permitted to raise lower-class children within a middle-class household. Even though the servant's work role may replicate that of the middle-class wife, it is only the wife who holds the right to bear and raise middle-class children in Villa Rosa and receive greater rewards in the name of (middle-class) motherhood.

The children of servants and ex-servants are not seen in Villa Rosa, for they are raised in the working-class districts and shantytowns of the city or in the rural villages from which the servants migrated. Thus Julia, a young woman of twenty-one who had worked for five years in the home of Augusta in Villa Rosa, and who had been loved "like a daughter" by her employer during those years, would sadly depart to raise a family in one of the poorer zones of the city; while Margarita, a twenty-four-year-old single mother leaves her three children with her own poor mother in the shantytown in order to earn a meager salary of $18 per month in Villa Rosa.

Although servants help to care for middle-class children, it is precisely in the area of motherhood that the middle-class women of Villa Rosa most jealously guard their control. This goes beyond the general rule that domestic servants be childless (see Arizpe 1975, 1977) or able to leave their children with someone else. It includes an active kinship role for the middle-class woman, an emphasis on "mothering" which socializes her children for a privileged position in a class society. It is just this contribution which middle-class women emphasize as uniquely important to them. Many women express concern about the harm that may come to their children if they should decide to work outside the home. A typical expression of their concern is as follows:

> Children cannot be left in the charge of servants. They will not learn well. They will acquire the vocabulary of servants. A woman should not work until her children are well formed. The love of a mother is indispensable. . . . Mother's love is special. It offers much security and affection. Others do not care for your child in the same way.

Although there are working middle-class women with children, these women still stress their personal role in instilling cultural values and in supervising the social development of their children.

The problem of establishing children's pedigrees as opposed to illegitimacy is one that affects middle-class men and women differently. Men are free to deny affiliations to children produced with lower-class women provided they do not marry them. The fact that some biological offspring lack fathers to sponsor their entry into the privileged classes need not affect a middle-class man personally provided that he has the economic means to maintain himself independently at the appropriate standard of living. In contrast, women are not able to deny the act of maternity, for it is so obvious. A middle-class woman who produces children without a certificate (legal marriage) of fatherhood from a man with the social status and wealth to maintain her class position risks the loss of membership in that class. Middle-class women must be able socially to "prove" the paternity of their children in order to maintain their class privilege. Social proof generally consists of a marriage contract and the absence of any evidence or insinuation of independent interaction with males other than a woman's kin or husband. She must be above suspicion. Legal, monogamous marriage is the means by which parents of middle- or upper-socioeconomic status establish the right of their children to inherit their class status and privileges. The emphasis on the social aspects of motherhood may be seen as a complementary social function which can be used by women to reinforce their class position. In Villa Rosa, women's economic contribution even if they work outside the home is generally inadequate to support middle-class status. Thus they emphasize their ability to provide legitimate children with the cultural values and social graces which women of other classes generally lack the means to cultivate.

Conclusion

In comparing the economic and social roles of the two classes of women that reside in the households of Villa Rosa, I have shown that the domestic services they provide are similar. Superficially, they perform the same kinds of tasks in their day-to-day routines, the one substituting for the other in work, if not in reward. The major difference is that the middle-class wife is officially designated to provide regular sexual and socialization services within the household, while the servant may only do so on an informal, illicit, or impermanent basis. Another difference is that the middle-class woman may dispense a significant share of the household operating fund, while the domestic employee is rarely trusted with more than the grocery money, carefully itemized.

Beyond the similarities in the housework they perform, in the final analysis they are not involved in the same kinds of production, or work. The domestic employee produces services that are consumed immediately and are privately valued by the family that employs her. By virtue of the fact that she is non-kin and receives a cash wage for the work, her labor and her reward are defined as social. She is recorded "economically active" in the census, and her earnings are counted in the GNP. In contrast, the middle-class wife is not considered to be "economically active" when she provides domestic services for which she is not "paid." Her reward is privately determined within the family; it does not correspond to any going wage rate in the labor market. However, the middle-class wife does, in a sense, produce a "product" that is ultimately realized in a wider social context. She produces legitimate children who are prepared to assume public roles as the next generation of the middle class. Her domestic role as mother has a recognizable social value for the power structure, since it is the means to reproduce the system of class divisions. It is also her means to maintain her class advantage.

A final question that necessarily arises regarding the roles of the domestic servant and the employer in middle-class households is whether the middle-class woman exploits her employee. Jelin (1976:144), writing of domestic employees in Brazil, has asked, "To what degree, in capitalist societies, does the 'liberation' that upper-strata women attain through getting jobs also entail the exploitation of lower-strata women?" There are several sides to this question. On the one hand, it cannot be denied that domestic employees are exploited. Their rewards are set at a minimal subsistence level, clustering at the bottom of the urban wage scale, and generally considered insufficient to support reproduction. The average wage is so low that it is impossible for most domestic employees to accumulate any savings after meeting their personal clothing and health expenses. Servants frequently complain that they are unable to acquire any assets to safeguard against the day they lose their job. On the other hand, if we assume that modern technology will soon provide alternatives to the employment of domestic labor (laundromats and fast-food services are currently expanding in Guatemala City), then domestic employment may suffer a great drop, much as it has in advanced industrial countries such as the U.S. and Canada relative to the turn of the century (Ryan 1975, Leslie 1974). Vast numbers of rural and urban women will lose their principal alternative to unemployment. If this occurs, the condition of working-class women will probably deteriorate even further, while middle-class women will be free of accusations of exploiting their servants. They will no longer have to cope with anxieties about hiring trustworthy servants to join their households. At that point, the individualistic features of domestic exploitation will fade to reveal a more generalized macroeconomic condition wherein still larger sectors of the population are unemployed and lacking any means of livelihood. If such labor substitution by capital-intensive services takes place in the domestic sphere, the urban middle-class household will probably move one step closer to the North American model by giving up the domestic employee, while the displaced servant class—no longer cloistered in middle-class homes—may begin to struggle for social solutions to their problems of unemployment and poverty.

Notes

1 Villa Rosa, the name of the community, and personal names used are pseudonyms.This discussion is based on research that was conducted in Guatemala City in 1975, supported by a doctoral research fellowship from the Organization of American States.

2 While census figures give 38 percent, my own survey data show 57 percent of the women earn some outside cash income.

3 This calculation includes live-in domestics and full-time housewives but not middle-class women who work outside the home part time or lower-class women who work on a day basis. These would add to the numbers involved in housework in Villa Rosa.

4 If paid employment commensurate with the status and income of middle-class males were available, it could be assumed that the middle-class women would become more active in the market economy. However, such employment opportunities are rare for the women of Villa Rosa (see Bossen 1978).

Part Five

Urban Class and Ethnicity

Wirth defines the city as "a relatively large, dense and permanent settlement of socially heterogeneous individuals." The heterogeneity that Wirth refers to includes the different backgrounds of people who live in cities, the many occupational specialties by which people make their livings, and the system of rewards by which some live grandly while others may starve. While the people of the countryside are not completely homogeneous, the degree of heterogeneity in large cities is much higher.

The concepts of "class" and "ethnicity" have been developed by social scientists to understand heterogeneity within a society. The way in which these terms have been used by social scientists will be examined in this essay. I will then proceed to discuss the role of political and economic conflict in perpetuating urban diversity, the relationship of ethnicity and culture to personal expression, and the development of a common "ethnic" identity by all people in a city. The aim is to clarify the usage of class and ethnicity and to stress some related themes.

Class and Ethnicity—Two Overlapping Concepts

When social scientists construct abstract models of social systems, they generally assume that some division of labor in society is necessary. All human societies have divided certain tasks, at the very least along the lines of age and sex. For example, only women can bear children and lactate; young children and the elderly are generally weaker than ages in between. As societies become more complex, so does the division of labor. The degree to which simple societies, like those of hunters and gatherers, are or were stratified is a matter of controversy, but certainly many horticultural, agrarian, and preindustrial urban social systems were at least somewhat stratified. They gave lesser and greater awards of power and prestige to individuals on the basis of the social position they occupied and the function they presumably fulfilled.

In stratified societies, people are unequal in the goods they own, the control they command over their goods and lives, the material and symbolic rewards which others accord them, and their access to strategic power within the society. In such societies, people are often grouped together with those who have similar power and prestige. We often set up ideal types or construct perfect models of societies. In one type, individuals' status groupings are determined at birth and people within the society cannot change their status during their lifetimes. Often such a society is called a "caste society," although the Indian caste system is much more complicated than such a simple description would suggest. Another type is the "open class society." In an open class society, while individuals are born into a status grouping or class, they may rise or fall in class affiliation. So far, we have talked about social position, power, wealth, and class without mentioning race, religion, national origin, or other components which we think of in relationship to ethnicity.

If people can change their social position, the fact that X once had a higher rank or Y had a humble birth will be remembered. Thus, there is a disparity between the status that a person acquired at birth, one's ascribed status, and the status he or she has achieved. In addition, if we assume migration, religious diversification, racial differences, and the presence of different speech communities in one place, we are dealing with the kind of cultural diversity and multiplicity of self-identities that we have come to call "ethnicity." In a perfect closed-caste society, ethnicity and class would be identical, but they are not in the complex societies that we encounter everywhere in modern times (Parsons 1951, 1975).

Parsons (1951) sees both social classes and ethnic groups as sets or aggregates of families and extended kinship units. He defines social classes by status in a stratified society, while ethnic groups are defined on the basis of descent either from a common ancestor or from "ancestors who all belonged to the same categorized ethnic group." (An alternative definition of ethnic groups stresses similar themes: An ethnic group can be defined as a "group of people who claim a common origin and who share a sense of a common fate.") In an open class system, where people may change status, the two would often not be identical. For instance, in India one can find members of a low "untouchable" caste who are wealthy and powerful and can be considered members of a ruling elite.

Because of this discrepancy between the status into which one was born and the status one has attained, individuals face conflicting claims on their loyalties and groups (whether based on class or ethnicity) and may face internal divisions. Because ethnic loyalties, including those grounded in race and sect, are acquired through early socialization, they are sometimes called "primordial" by social scientists (Geertz 1973). Such sentiments are seen as divisive in new nations which seek to unite peoples from a diversity of backgrounds (e.g., Yugoslavia, Canada, Rwanda, the United

States) and as irrational by those who see political struggles resting upon the present circumstances of different classes.

Ethnic groups are groups that appear in a situation where there are other ethnic entities. The various waves of migration from different places and religious schisms are among the factors that create ethnic diversity. The concepts of class and ethnicity overlap.

This intersection of class and ethnicity can be illustrated by looking at one occupational group, dockworkers. Dockworkers (also called longshoremen) in many ports around the world were known for their remarkable similarities, such as their solidarity, which arose from having cohesive unions. This has been reinforced by the common ethnic/national origins of the dockers in particular cities (e.g., San Francisco, New York City, Haifa and Ashdod in Israel). This common background often resulted from a "founder's effect"; that is, early migrants from a certain locality entered a particular occupation and encouraged their compatriots who followed them in the city to do the same. This, in turn, may be the product of a "balkanized" or split-labor market.

A split-labor market is one where workers who are classified as belonging to one category (ethnic, racial, religious, or sexual) are channeled into one kind of job. Usually those belonging to one category get more skilled jobs and are paid more, while those who are stigmatized are given jobs paying less. For instance, the West Indian migrants in Britain studied by George Gmelch found jobs on London buses and with the British Rail services. The lower-class domestic servants discussed by Bossen ("Wives and Servants") are a good example of such a segment of a split-labor market. The "pink-collar" jobs, such as beautician, typist, or even elementary-school teacher and social worker, which typify female employment in the United States, are another. So are "illegal aliens" in the United States, who often take low-paying jobs requiring little training. The existence of a group of workers who accept difficult working conditions and less pay than other workers depresses working conditions for all and is often the cause of ethnic antagonisms (Bonacich 1972). On an interpersonal level, Bourgois ("Office Work and the Crack Alternative") illustrates such tension in his description of legitimate jobs held by Hispanic youth in New York, prior to their careers as drug dealers.

Generally members of ethnic groups share common rules of behavior and a common set of symbols, which are sometimes termed a "subculture." Some subcultures, however, may be based on a principle other than common origin, such as occupational subcultures or those based on sexual orientation. The distinctive ways of life of celibate religious orders, longshoremen and stevedores, entertainers, and the "gay lifestyle" are examples of such "non-ethnic" subcultures.

"Subculture" as behavioral patterns may mark social classes as well as ethnic groups. Perhaps no subculture has received as much attention from social scientists as the "culture of poverty" as described by Oscar Lewis. Lewis ("The Culture of Poverty") set out to delineate patterns of behavior shared by a whole class of people, the urban poor. It should be noted that Lewis claimed that only 20 percent of the poor actually developed a culture of poverty—that is, persistent and often self-perpetuating cycles of behaviors that were difficult for them to shake, even when conditions permitted. For instance, poor individuals addicted to drugs would find it difficult to keep well-paying jobs, even when they became available in good times.

Lewis's concept of the culture of poverty was an attempt to develop a model of the behavior of the poor in a variety of cultural settings. No concept in urban anthropology has provoked more controversy and filled more journal pages with criticism and debate. The controversy has overspilled the boundaries of anthropology and has been much discussed by other social scientists and professionals concerned with the poor. This concept will be discussed here in some detail, because of the importance of discussions of the causes of poverty in current debates about welfare reform (Eames and Goode, "Coping with Poverty," "An Anthropological Critique"; K. Newman 1992).

While the academic debate no longer revolves around the concept of the culture of poverty, the issues raised by the controversy remain important ones. Today the term "underclass" is used to define people who seem permanently enmeshed in conditions of impoverishment. Moreover, the number of people living below the poverty line in many industrial and developing nations continues to grow.

In brief, Lewis's culture of poverty is a distinct (and self-perpetuating) way of life that develops among the lowest strata in capitalistic societies in response to economic deprivation and inequality. Lewis identifies some seventy traits that he considers characteristic of this subculture of American society.

According to Lewis, the culture of poverty represents "both an adaptation and a reaction of the poor to their marginal position in a class-stratified, highly individuated, capitalistic society." It represents an effort to "cope with feelings of helplessness and despair that arise from the realization by the poor of the improbability of their achieving success in terms of the prevailing values and goals." Contrary to what Lewis clearly hoped for, his culturalist approach shows simply that efforts to provide better economic opportunities and housing for the poor will achieve little in terms of improving their lifeways, which are learned at an early age (Eames 1976).

The views of Lewis have been severely criticized by Charles Valentine (1968), Carol Stack (1975 and "The Kindred of Viola Jackson"), and others who offer a structuralist, as opposed to a culturalist, explanation of poverty behavior. They argue that the behavior of the poor is determined by economic conditions established by the larger society, and that those values and behaviors of the poor that are different from those of the dominant classes are the result of their inability to achieve the higher goals defined by society because of their disadvantaged position.

The structuralist interpretation can be seen in several of the essays in this part. Eames and Goode examine the economic adaptations of the poor. The similarities they find in the responses of the poor to low and sporadic income in a wide range of cultural settings support the view that the behavior of the poor is directly "linked to economic social conditions rather than a cognitive or value-based cultural framework."

It should be noted that poverty and affluence and ethnic diversity are not limited to urban areas, as both Lewis and his critics realized. What does, however, appear in urban areas is the close juxtaposition of rich and poor, as well as large numbers of people from many different regional, racial, and religious backgrounds. This is particularly apparent in commercial areas. This is what gives urban heterogeneity its special character, although conflicts along class and ethnic lines can be either urban or rural.

Political and Economic Conflict

Much of the work on class and ethnicity is concerned with political and economic conflict. This is explicit in some of the following articles and implicit in them all. As Fischer (1972, 1975b) suggests in his subcultural theory, the city intensifies subcultures by bringing more people into them. By bringing peoples bearing different subcultures into one place and "rewarding" some and "punishing" others, the city sharpens conflict and heightens class and ethnic antagonism.

Split-labor markets tend to make ethnic and class lines coincide. For instance, in the United States more white males work as skilled workers than do Hispanics or blacks; thus as the economic interests of the white workers differ markedly from those of the minority employees, they can be seen as reflecting separate class interests. Yet they also become ethnic conflicts, since the skilled workers belong to one ethnic category and the unskilled to another. This can be seen in the relations between West Indians and white English laborers in Britain or between Turkish and Spanish migrants and Germans in Germany (Rhoades, "European Cyclical Migration"; Gmelch, "A West Indian Life").

Split-labor markets are only one aspect of economic specialization along ethnic lines. One may also find ethnic specialization in certain trades, such as small businesses opened by minorities like Jews, Lebanese, Chinese, and Greeks (Zenner, "Transnational Web of Syrian-Jewish Relations"). As Zenner points out, such ethnic groups have connections that go beyond the locality in which they live. In fact, economic connections in all cities today are global. Not only migrants, but the flow of goods and services are multinational. For example, if one looks at the labels in clothing today, one finds that much of our clothing comes from countries like China, Sri Lanka, India, and Turkey.

In some trades and industries, there is a cleavage within the ethnic group. In the late nineteenth and early twentieth centuries, for example, many of the factories producing ready-to-wear garments in New York City and elsewhere were owned by Jews. With the mass immigration to the United States from Eastern Europe, penniless Jewish immigrants were employed by these factory owners, often under trying conditions. The Jewish garment workers in New York City organized some militant unions, and the Jewish community was rent by a fierce class struggle (Howe 1976).

While much of our attention is focused on the class and ethnic consciousness of the workers and the disadvantaged, it is important to note that the privileged are often better organized than their less affluent counterparts. Abner Cohen's example of how "the City," the financial district in London, is organized is a case in point (1974b). The fact that the most privileged people in any society comprise a relatively small group who may belong to a small set of families, go to the same schools, and belong to the same clubs makes informal organization of such a class much easier.

William Domhoff has suggested that such upper-class solidarity may appear even in a large country like the United States. In his book, "The Bohemian Grove and Other Retreats: A Study in Ruling Class Cohesiveness" (1974), he describes some exclusive encampments where rich and powerful men from all over the country come together for a week or so of recreation. Corporation executives and high government officials (including presidents and governors) live and play together. Among their guests are leading entertainers. Such camps are not meetings of a conspiratorial elite, but they do establish a sense of camaraderie (Domhoff 1974). While gatherings like these may not unite the men for political action, it certainly establishes a framework of mutual understanding and accommodation. Cohen's stress on the informal and often invisible organization of ethnic groups and classes is well-illustrated in this instance.

By contrast with the elite, the middle and lower classes are aggregates or categories rather than well-organized interest groups. Those who are well organized have coalesced around such groups as trade unions or certain ethnic organizations. Still, the interests of groups—both urban and rural—who are of lower and middle status in modern societies are usually mediated by other individuals who represent these groups. Sometimes these individuals are elected officials, while at other times they are persons of fairly high status who are linked to the powerful elite. Owen Lynch ("A South Indian Caste"), in his description of Adi-Dravida participation in political parties, has suggested how members of that caste advance their interests through politicians who belong to particular parties. The Adi-Dravidas have identities, each of which can be used for political mobilization along ethnic lines. First of all, they are south Indians, speaking a distinctive language, in western India. Secondly, they are members of a caste-group which is considered "outcaste" by many Hindus. Politicians stressing each of these identities have vied for the Adi-Dravida vote. Different political leaders also can offer patronage to the Adi-Dravidas and other such groups, if they are elected to office. While Lynch's article concentrates on the Adi-Dravidas as a whole, Kathleen Logan ("Urban Women as Political Activists") discusses political action from the viewpoint of leaders and activists.

So far in this essay, gender has not been discussed, although it has in previous sections. In her essay on political activism among urban women, Logan aptly points out the differences between middle-class and working-class women. In an earlier essay, Logan (1988) pointed out that in many places, mobilization, as in the case of union organizing, for one's interest in the workplace is inhibited. This has certainly been true of Latin America, but the decline of trade union power in the United States and western Europe in recent years shows that this is not limited to the Third World. Logan suggests that the failure of workplace movements has heightened the importance of residentially based mobilization in which many women participate. Middle-class and elite women, on the other hand, have utilized civic associations (e.g., the League of Women Voters in the U.S.) and traditional political parties. The question Logan asks in her essay is, "What difference does this increased political participation by women make for those problems which affect women more than men?''

Philippe Bourgois (''Office Work and the Crack Alternative'') deals with the intersection of gender with class and ethnicity, too. As already noted, he does so on the interpersonal level. He suggests that many working-class males, especially those belonging to minorities, feel somehow dishonored (disrespected) when subordinated to women. While his article gives us the perceptions of these men in a North American city, he is dealing with questions with wider political ramifications. Janet Abu-Lughod's article on Arabic-Islamic cities deals with a society where such notions of male honor and male control of women's sexuality, combined with religious strictures, are part of a system involving sexual segregation.

Ethnicity and Cultural Content

While ethnicity is not only an instrument to gain political clout or to provide the group with economic resources, this is the emphasis we find in this section. The symbols that unite a group are more than weapons in its struggle with others. The symbols have meanings of their own which transcend interethnic and interclass conflict.

Let us use the Carnival (Mardi Gras) celebration as an example of ceremonies that show how symbols are used to unite communities and/or provide symbolic arenas for interclass and interethnic conflicts. Gonzalez (1970) analyzes the Carnival in a city in the Dominican Republic in terms of how it mirrors social and economic differences. But there are more universal meanings expressed in Carnival. The Carnival inaugurates Lent, a period of austerity. Yet the license of Carnival contrasts sharply with the fasting which traditional Christians practice during this six-week period. In the Dominican city studied by Gonzalez, both upper- and lower-class people wear costumes, but the differences between the classes are marked. Different groups fight mock battles during this period. While many different groups of people who have immigrated to the Dominican Republic have joined in Carnival celebrations, generally North Americans, Chinese, Jews, and Lebanese have not, thus marking their feelings of separation from the larger community.

In dealing with the choice of symbols and identities, advantages to be gained in a conflict may play a role, but the other factors may have weight as well. For instance, the different identities of the Adi-Dravidas, described by Lynch, will bring different symbols to the forefront. Whether one of the political parties vying for the Adi-Dravida vote, the DMK, is a "political group with para-ethnic functions" or an "ethnic group with para-political functions" may vary with context; what is clear is that the two are bound into one package. The immigrant may find satisfaction by being with other Tamil-speakers, whether or not this is advantageous in a material way, as well as sharing political and economic interests with them. It is similar for Syrian Jews who seek each other's company, both for economic and for ethno-religious reasons.

Just as ethnic and class symbols may have meanings beyond those of economic and political conflict, so aesthetic expression may have political consequences. This point is made very ably by Barbara Kirshenblatt-Gimblett ("Ordinary People/Everyday Life"). For instance, she points out that alternate-side-of-the-street parking regulations in New York are relaxed on certain Jewish festivals, because Orthodox Jews are not allowed to drive on these holy days. Even though Catholics and other religious groups do not share such prohibitions, they have demanded a similar relaxation of parking rules on their holidays. While she discusses this primarily with regard to urban celebrations, there is a very complicated field of inquiry in dealing with aesthetic expression and entertainment in a complex urban society.

The question of power is not merely a conflict between elite culture and that of the lower classes. After all, wealthy people control the mass media, which generally promulgate tastes for rock music more than they do for opera or chamber music. In addition, symbols that mark a particular ethnic or religious group publicly may not be what is most significant in terms of the group's own traditions. Thus, Chanukkah is much more visible to American Gentiles, even though it is a relatively minor celebration tradition-ally, while Jews may find greater significance in observance of the Day of Atonement in the synagogue or Passover at home.

Similarly, the satisfactions and dissatisfactions of ethnic group membership cannot be reduced to the role which they play in competition with others.

Culture, Structure, and Strategy

The articles in Part Five, as well as other sections of this book, touch on basic issues in anthropology and the social sciences, beyond urban studies. These are questions which relate to our picture of human nature. There are two major thrusts in anthropology concerning the role of culture. One is that human beings are basically realistic and rational in aiming to remain alive, healthy, and comfortable. The other is that various forces, especially culture in the form of early childhood learning, can so shape human behavior that humans will not respond realistically to social and environmental conditions.

The "culturalist" notion of a self-perpetuating culture of poverty implies the latter idea. The structuralists who stress the adaptive nature of the behavior of the poor take the former viewpoint (Eames and Goode, "Coping With Poverty"). The emphasis on strategy, whether strategies for survival as in this article or for political mobilization (see Lynch and Logan), also implies realism and rationality. This is also implicit in the articles by Nelson and Brettell (Part Three), Bourgois, and Zenner.

A related issue is the need to define the boundaries of a subculture in a world in which all institutions and societies on the globe are interconnected. This came out in the discussion of the culture of poverty. It is not only poverty which is not exclusively an urban problem, but also affluence and entrepreneurship. Defining subcultures, whether of poverty or of dockers or of Syrian Jews or of IBM, is thus a difficult task.

The problem of defining culture has perplexed anthropologists for a long time. As used in the essays here, it includes norms and values which are viewed by the subjects involved as good, as well as the practices of the people themselves. Some authors stress the norms, while others emphasize practice. Lewis, for instance, seems more interested in the practices of the poor, not in what they give lip service to. Those who stress strategies and the influence of the system on people in cities also seem much more concerned with actual practice, rather than the norms, symbols, and values of the people. The discussion of urban class and ethnicity has brought us face to face with basic issues in the social sciences.

Walter P. Zenner

Coping with Poverty
A Cross-Cultural View of the Behavior of the Poor

EDWIN EAMES and JUDITH GOODE

Whatever the causes of poverty, the poor must develop strategies to cope with low, sporadic income and inadequate resources. In this selection, Eames and Goode examine the adaptive techniques developed by poor people in industrialized societies. The comparative framework they use reveals many similarities in the behavioral responses of the poor despite their different cultural backgrounds. This framework suggests that many behaviors of the poor develop in response to a set of economic and social conditions rather than from a cultural or cognitive origin. (Note the similarity of some of the strategies described here, particularly the role of urban kin groups in providing support, with the group-oriented strategies described among urban migrants in Part Two.)

Much of the literature dealing with the behavior of the poor in modern capitalist societies attempts to develop a psychological or cognitive understanding of the values of the poor. Individuals, as well as the motives and values underlying their behavior, are frequently used as a basic focus of analysis. To the extent that this emphasis is maintained, the behavior of the poor is often seen as dysfunctional and irrational, and the larger issue of the adaptiveness of common response patterns is obscured. It is these common response patterns that we refer to as coping mechanisms. In the

Source: Adapted from Edwin Eames, Judith Granich Goode, "Coping Responses of the Urban Poor," *Urban Poverty in a Cross-Cultural Context.*

following discussion we will emphasize shared patterns of coping responses found among poor people in industrial societies in as wide and varied cultural settings as possible.

From our perspective, many aspects of the behavior of the poor can be seen as direct responses to the conditions of poverty. Poverty in capitalist-industrial societies is defined by inadequate access to material resources. This means that the poor not only have no accumulated wealth and low cash incomes but their income is sporadic, intermittent, and uncertain. Those in poverty are those located in the bottom sectors of the job market, where they not only receive minimal rewards for their work but are in positions where the sources of income are frequently cut off. They work in jobs that may often disappear as the needs of the economy change. In addition, their jobs are frequently so menial—lacking the protection of labor laws, unions, and social security and lacking in mobility potential—that there is an expected high turnover rate. This is the result of the employer's expectations of turnover, the resultant short-term exploitation of the worker, and the employee's perception of a dead-end situation. Many of these jobs are character-ized by heavy labor investment or short-term contracts (day labor). Others involve work in illicit activities or begging, scavenging used goods, or selling minute quantities of goods or services.

Whatever the sources of cash, a variety of similar conservation techniques and strategies has been developed by poor people all over the world to manage this limited and insecure income. One way of conserving resources and adding to them is the development of alternatives to the formal retailing, savings, credit, and insurance institutions in society. These involve informal, small-scale networks to distribute new goods and services, major mechanisms to recycle secondhand goods, or the use of swapping or direct exchanges of goods. Capital is saved by storing it in goods that can be sold or pawned. Insurance is provided by kin and quasi-kin networks and social and economic support systems. The very practices that make survival possible are often viewed by the middle class as indulgent and irrational behaviors perpetuating poverty.

Everyday Needs

Food

Basic survival needs include food, shelter, and clothing. One of the characteristics of the diets of the poor is that they are composed of basic staples that are high in starch content, such as rice, maize, or potatoes (depending on geographic area and cultural traditions). In relation to other foodstuffs available, these items are inexpensive and high in caloric content to meet energy needs. On the other hand protein sources such as meat and dairy products are very expensive and would not provide adequate caloric intake if the amount of money invested in carbohydrates were invested in them. In such circumstances, it is common to find people who raise a few chickens or hogs to sell for profit so that they can convert the income into carbohydrates. In Oscar Lewis's account of the Sanchez family, Jesus Sanchez occasionally raises hogs, not for consumption but for sale. It is economically rational to do this although dieticians observing these activities might be disconcerted by what appears to be ignorant nutritional behavior (Lewis 1961).

A common characteristic of cash-conserving behavior is the purchase of small quantities of foods at frequent intervals (often on a meal-by-meal basis). In part, this is the result of the lack of storage facilities (refrigerators, freezers, pantry space) available to those with poverty incomes as well as the nature of the cash flow for this population. Frequently one finds tiny stores maintained in households in low-income areas in which it is possible to buy shortening by the tablespoon (Lewis 1965). This enables the vendor to earn cash income and the purchaser to obtain a necessary foodstuff that he or she could not afford in larger quantities in the formal retail market.

The descriptions of squatter settlements are filled with examples of parts of homes being used to store small inventories of foodstuffs for sale. Roberts (1973) found more than 75 percent of the homes in one such settlement in Guatemala City to be engaged in some petty enterprise. Most of them were involved in selling household necessities: food, sewing equipment, and fuel. Occasionally residential entrepreneurs will go to the central market daily and then sell small amounts of food and kerosene door to door in their neighborhoods. They are limited to what they can carry and thus sell minuscule quantities—a cup of kerosene, for example.

There are many examples of what Raum (1969) calls the "common mess" in the literature. Often males who are between wives or supporting their families left behind in the countryside practice pooling their money for joint purchase of food and communal preparation. Other variations of this form of economic efficiency are the feeding patterns that occur when members of several households (especially children) are customarily fed by one female in her household. Perhaps they are best described in the work of Carol Stack (1974) who studies domestic cooperation between black poverty families in the United States.

Another variation of this technique can be seen in household food exchanged when several cooks cook more than is necessary for their family and then exchange the surplus. Such cash pooling and bulk purchasing tends to be less expensive, and common preparation conserves fuel, labor, and time.

It has frequently been noted that poor people often avoid the cooking of food in their own household units. There is a pattern of purchasing cooked or prepared foods from vendors (street vendors in Asia and Latin America, take-out and fast food restaurants in the United States). Rather than wasting cash resources, this can be seen as a conservative measure since the appliance and fuel costs involved in cooking can often outweigh the cost of buying from vendors, who are in a sense engaged in communal preparation. Another reason for reliance upon food vendors is that the time requirements of the marginal jobs and the supplementary conserving and scavenging activities may make the schedules of different household members so diverse as to preclude their eating together. Thus, working intermittently, at odd hours, and trying to juggle the work schedules of various household members may work against common mealtimes as well as time for the preparation of food. However, in spite of the adaptive nature of street snacking, it is often condemned by outsiders as a symptom of laziness and ignorance.

Housing

A basic strategy related to housing is the development of high-density occupation. When several families or individuals share a given residential unit, this can decrease their housing expense. Housing under these conditions may be rented by the group of families or individuals. Often, one family rents an apartment from a landlord but then takes in other families as boarders to augment its income. In Singapore, for example, a family of five cooking, eating, and sleeping in a tiny cubicle manages to augment its cash by renting upper and lower berths in its already constrained living space (Kaye 1966).

Among the poor, renting is almost a necessity due to capital limitations, and the rental housing market for low-income populations consists of units invariably congested and substandard. Such inadequate housing is still highly priced since profit-oriented landlords require as high a return as possible in a high-risk market.

The only exception to renting is the widespread occurrence of occupant-built housing or sweat equity rehabilitation throughout

People gather around a hand pump on a sidewalk in Calcutta to wash and drink. The city's streets are home to hundreds of thousands of residents. [Photo by Barbara Walton, AP/Wide World Photos]

the world. In these cases, home ownership is achieved by taking over vacant land or vacant buildings and establishing rights to them through the investment of time and labor. Such irregular settlements of new housing are found everywhere today. In the United States, government policies have recently fostered urban homesteading to recycle and rehabilitate older housing units. These programs are intended to develop a variety of housing for the poor, who can achieve the capital assets of a home through minimal investment of cash but heavy investment of time and labor. Unfortunately, these programs up until now have been used predominantly by the nonpoor.

In much of Latin America, the Middle East, and Asia, the spontaneous community of squatters has been very common. Such communities have been studied by a number of anthropologists and some common features have been noted. For squatting to be successful, some degree of organization is necessary in taking over and retaining land that was not formally purchased. As Mangin (1967) noted for Peru, squatters are rarely the most recent immigrants to the city. Contacts and urban experience are necessary for inclusion in the initial squatting attempt. When successful, squatter settlements provide a whole new pattern of housing and housing costs for the poor. Squatters avoid the initial costs of home purchase they would incur in the formal housing market. They also avoid the inevitable monthly payment involved in renting a substandard unit. Instead they intermittently invest cash in building materials and labor in construction. For those with sporadic employment, such labor time is often available.

Municipalities have recognized that such occupant-built housing settlements are cheaper housing solutions than governments can provide. They often develop procedures to legitimize the settlement, create legal land tenure, and provide municipal services to these communities. Community-wide legitimization usually requires a cash outlay in the form of taxes or a labor investment in the communal construction of some public facilities like roads, sewers, and water systems. Thus, housing expenses do increase but the self-built house in such an approved settlement becomes a capital asset which can appreciate over time. As an indication of the significance of squatting, 62 percent of the households in Lima, Peru; 45 percent in Ankara, Turkey; and over 33 percent in Karachi, Pakistan; Manila, the Philippines; and Caracas, Venezuela, are located in such settlements (Abrams 1964).

Clothing

As Michael Harrington noted, America's poor are among the best-dressed poor in the world. In part this is the result of readily available, cheap, and mass-produced clothing. In addition, for clothing probably more than for any other item of consumption, the secondhand market allows the maintenance of the outward manifestation of adequacy. The utilization of secondhand goods conserves cash in two ways. One can buy used goods with minimum outlay and one can later raise cash by selling. In Japan, secondhand clothes hawkers are prominent around urban markets (Caldarola 1968). The wife of Jesus Sanchez was a vendor in the secondhand market in Mexico City (Lewis 1961). In the United States, Goodwill and the Salvation Army are manifestations of this institution.

Used goods can also be acquired directly without the need for cash. Carolina Maria de Jesus, a scavenger in São Paulo, Brazil, notes that she, like most scavengers, acquires shoes and clothing for her family as she rummages through trash and garbage (de Jesus 1962). Secondhand clothing is also distributed by formal charities. In a study of household budgets of the poor in Hong Kong,

families often stated that they paid no money for clothes since they received altered clothes from a charity (*Journal of the Hong Kong Institute of Social Research* 1965). A typical source of used clothing is one's patron or employer. According to an eighteenth-century European social commentator, it is an obligation of an employer to a domestic servant to give ". . . from time to time some part of your wardrobe or cast-off clothing" (Taylor 1968:570). Pauw (1963) describes the frequent payments in goods to domestic servants in South Africa, and this is a typical pattern for day workers in the United States.

Another common informal market for clothing and household goods is the marketplace for stolen goods. Such thieves' markets are described as occurring all over the world. Patch mentions that in Lima, Peru, the thieves' market also redistributes the belongings of the recently deceased. Such goods are tainted by their association with death. However, they are bought and sold by the poor (Patch 1967).

Extraordinary Capital Needs

Investment and Savings

Unlike the daily requirements of food, clothing, and housing, there are extraordinary expenses that occur at different stages in the life cycle or in crisis events, which require large cash outlays. Once again, the shared patterns of the poor can be seen as an adaptive response based upon the need to conserve limited and intermittent cash resources. This point can be seen in the tendency to invest some resources in large appliances and household furnishings, which can readily be converted into cash. As Lewis and Leeds point out for poor households in Mexico and Brazil, the purchase of television sets, blenders, and other appliances is not simply an extravagant attempt at conspicuous consumption, but is an investment in items that can be pawned in times of emergency (Lewis 1969, Leeds 1971). Obviously, they must be purchased in times of relative affluence. Thus the cycle of relative prosperity and crisis/impoverishment within the condition of poverty is tempered by this modified savings for emergencies. Even bedding (mattresses, pillows, headboards) can be viewed within this framework since it

◀ A second-hand clothing market in Dublin, Ireland.
[Photo by Pat Langan]

involves pawnable items often purchased at the time of a wedding, when relatives pool resources to help establish a new household.

Because of their economic position, the poor rarely have access to large sums of money. Nevertheless, they have developed techniques to raise large sums for emergencies. These techniques are strikingly similar all over the world. Lotteries, both legal and illegal, are found throughout the world. Since the poor can only afford partial tickets, the winnings are only small windfalls. However, they are often used for the few large purchases made in a lifetime. Marta Sanchez recalls that her father used two minor lottery winnings to buy a radio and a large metal bed (Lewis 1961). Both of these items were potentially pawnable. Thus the purchase of capital goods is a major technique for saving or storing cash windfalls for the future.

Less formally organized institutions for credit also exist. One major type is the informal credit association. One example of such an association is the *ooi* in Hong Kong. The fixed membership in this group pays a small monthly fee. Any member may borrow from the pool in times of crisis (*Journal of the Hong Kong Institute of Social Research* 1965). In Kampala, Uganda, rotating credit associations are found. Again each member contributes monthly, but in this case the monthly fund is lent to each member in rotation, enabling him to make a major purchase (Gutkind 1967). In Mexico City, such groups are called *tandas* and pooled money is distributed by drawing lots (Lewis 1965). Leeds (1971) found that groups of workmates in Brazil developed informal credit pools called *vaquinas* and *caixinhas*. (Literally "little cows" and "little boxes," these words resemble the English "kitty.") Raum (1969) also discovered a varied number of different groupings all designed to "maximize small monthly resources."

Government policies often provide other ways in which a lump sum of capital can be acquired. Peattie (1967) describes the way the residents of one squatter settlement in Venezuela use their severance pay (required by labor laws) as lump sums of capital to be saved or invested. Other examples of similar perceptions and usages of government-provided lump sums are tax rebates and compensation for injury. Such money can be used for major purchases or coping with crises.

Crises

Savings in the forms discussed above are frequently exhausted by crises which take place. Medical emergencies occur particularly during the heavy childbearing years in a family and during old age. Illness has a dual consequence. Medical costs can quickly exhaust savings. In addition, for those employed in the informal sector of the economy, jobs rarely include sick leave or unemployment compensation. In fact, illness is frequently used as an excuse for firing an individual and loss of both current and future income often results.

Another type of crisis frequently faced by this population is conflict with governmental authorities (legal emergencies). Squatters are frequently confronted with the specter of loss of land and housing. They are open to a variety of governmental actions which may threaten the property rights acquired through sweat equity. Adolescent males are often involved in antisocial behavior and harassed and arrested by police authorities. In all of these crises, expenditures for lawyers, bail, and legal documents place a burden upon those already faced with the need to survive on a daily basis.

These as well as a whole variety of other crises force many of the poor to borrow cash from usurers rather than from the banks and legitimate credit institutions that frequently reject them. When money is borrowed from a usurer who demands illegally high interest rates, repayment can become a crisis. Illegal mechanisms of store credit such as those described by Caplovitz (1963) are further examples of usury. Installment buying by the poor can work for and against the buyer. On the one hand, such credit provides the opportunity to obtain the electric appliances which can function as savings. On the other hand, it often commits the buyer to exorbitant payments. With sporadic income, payments are frequently missed with the resulting loss of the item itself or large penalties exacted.

Mutual Support Networks

For many of those in poverty, the source of much cash, goods, services, and social support is a network of extended kin and close friends who behave like kin. Although these kin usually face the same conditions, their collective support becomes an essential element in survival. Crises that affect one household unit at a given point in time may be offset through the help of households linked by kinship or fictive kinship. These units are not likely to have medical or legal emergencies at the same time.

Child care can also be provided by members of an extended kin network to permit mothers to work. This is easiest when kin reside together or in close proximity to one another. In other situations, children are given to other families for months or years to be raised. This frees more members of individual nuclear family units to participate in activities outside the home to generate income.

Mutual aid in emergencies and child care are but two examples of the aid that can be provided by kin. In addition, much of the feeding, housing, and clothing of individuals necessary for survival depends on the strong ties of kinship. Carol Stack has described the household of Viola Jackson, one of her informants, as the central household in a dispersed cooperating kinship network. As economic opportunities in Viola's area expanded, many kin from other areas joined her and became part of the household, contributing to income and sharing in food and shelter. Her brother and his household were located within walking distance. They ate in Viola's house and contributed to its support ("The Kindred of Viola Jackson"). These kinds of cooperative domestic networks are found throughout the world. Peattie describes them in Venezuela, and Lomnitz describes them in Mexico (1974).

A major investment of the poor is in an extended social support system which becomes the ultimate basis of economic and social security. When one is in difficulty, one may withdraw economic or social capital from this kinship bank. On the other hand, when one has periods of relative affluence or windfalls, one must invest in the kinship network. Stack (1970, 1974) has described how important it is to constantly borrow and trade within the network even if one does not need anything. It is necessary to keep the ties strong and the channels of giving and taking open. The network of mutual support which is critical to the survival of the poor is frequently criticized by social analysts. They claim that such commitment to the network prevents an individual or household from moving out of poverty since all "surplus" is redistributed among members of the network. However, it is this basic support mechanism that keeps most of the poor from succumbing to the most deleterious effects of material deprivation. Most attempts to change one's economic position require severing these ties. As a result, such mobility attempts are risky in both the social and economic sense.

Dominant Class Conceptions of the Behavior of the Poor

A commonly held view of the behavior of the poor is that they lack the ability to defer immediate gratification of basic urges. This view gets translated into three major domains: money, sex, and violence.

Several commentators have indicated that such stereotypes have no basis in fact; that the real behavior of the poor is being contrasted to the ideal behavior of the middle class which is perhaps more circumspect about its behavior (Miller, Reissman, and Seagull 1965).

The poor are frequently castigated for their inability to save, their consumption of useless status items and costly snack foods, and squandering their limited resources. What we have tried to demonstrate in the previous discussion is that many of the specific behaviors that might appear to be irrational consumption practices are rational indeed within the economic resource setting in which the poor are located.

A widely held view is that poor people are sexually promiscuous, have a pattern of early initiation into sex, and are unable to maintain a long-term marital union based upon monogamous mating. There is indeed a high level of consensual (common-law) and extralegal unions among poor people all over the world. This is partly related to the economic expenditures required by church and state in the establishment of marriage. In addition, the legal expenditures of dissolution are often greater than those of marriage. Such avoidance patterns conserve scarce resources. Conditions which become important factors in the instability of both mating and marriage are primarily economic. Although a household unit might try to place all of its members in the job market, conditions of the labor market may make this impossible. The market for women as domestics makes it frequently the case that the woman is more viable in the informal labor market. Frequently, where welfare systems exist, they specifically discourage stable married pairs as eligible, thus encouraging mother-child households.

Within the conjugal family unit, women are usually responsible for the care and well-being of infants and young children. Therefore, adult men who are not significantly contributing to the income of a household are liabilities to the household rather than advantages. For these economic and social reasons, the household unit centers around the mother-child bond. When such families dissolve marriage ties, it is almost always the women who remain responsible for the children. Knowing this, women play an important role in decisions about entering into formal marriage or breaking up marital ties. Very often, women prefer to rely more on their own kin for mutual support than on a spouse who may become a financial liability. This leads to a high frequency of female-headed households consisting of women and their female kin (sisters and mothers) and their children. Marvin Harris (1971:367) points out, "Like all domestic arrangements, the matrifocal family arises under specific and known material conditions and represents an adaptive achievement that is no more or less 'pathological' than any other family form.'' Such conditions include a general lack of access to strategic resources, with women and men in equal positions in a labor market where single incomes are insufficient to support a family. He points out that while everyone strives for a traditional union, men often prefer temporary unions because they realize their inability to support their families. Women who have the backing of a kinship support unit may also prefer a temporary union to the danger of a permanent male freeloader. Studies in low-income communities in Tokyo, Rio de Janeiro, Guatemala City, Mexico City, Ciudad Guayana (Venezuela), Johannesburg, and Witwatersrand (South Africa) all document the high incidence of informal unions in these settings (Southall 1970; de Vos and Wagatsuma 1966; Taira 1968; Peattie 1967; Pearse 1961; Roberts 1970; Whiteford 1964; Phillips 1956; Verster 1967).

Informants' statements seem to indicate that these relationships are seen as allowing for flexibility in situations of financial insecurity. One favela dweller in Rio de Janeiro says about a husband: "I don't have one, I don't want one." She says that married women work terribly hard and their husbands ". . . remain home under the blankets. Some because they can't find jobs, others because they are sick, others because they are drunk" (de Jesus 1962). Marris (1961) encountered a high incidence of broken marriages in Lagos and found people directly linked them to financial situations. Mañuel Sanchez articulately states his view of the relationship between one's economic situation and marriage:

> There is also the matter of being poor. If one begins to examine what a marriage comes to, a poor man realizes he doesn't have enough money for a wedding. Then he decides to live this way, without it, see? He just takes the woman, the way I did with Paula. Besides, a poor man has nothing to leave his children, so there is no need to protect them legally. If I had a million pesos, or a house, or a bank account or some material goods, I would have a civil marriage right away to legalize my children as my legitimate heirs. But people in my class have nothing. That is why I say, "As long as I know these are my children, I don't care what the world thinks." . . . And the majority of women here don't expect weddings, even they believe that the sweetheart leads a better life than the wife (Lewis 1961: 59).

Thus, ties based on marriage (the conjugal bond) may be weak, but ties to consanguine (blood) kin of the mother are quite strong. This is the very network that is the core of the mutual support mechanism discussed above.

Male Adolescent Antisocial Behavior

In addition to alleged sexual promiscuity, the poor are viewed as prone to violence. In particular, this kind of behavior is associated with male adolescents. This behavior is indeed found in strikingly similar manifestations throughout the world. An obvious "tough" lifestyle is frequently found among poor urban adolescents, related to the nature of their difficulties in entering the labor force in industrial society. These groups share dress, language, and recreational patterns involving drinking, physical contests, and gambling. Casual illicit activities and challenges to authority are frequent. Such varied groups as the *tsotsi* among young men in South Africa described by Pauw (1963), the *hampones* in Lima, Peru, the gangs (*gallades* and *colleras*) described by Patch (1967), the street gangs in Tokyo described by Caldarola (1968), the gang of Mañuel Sanchez in Mexico City (Lewis 1961), and the street-corner men described by Hannerz (1970) and Liebow (1967) in the United States are remarkably alike in lifestyle.

These young adult males face a labor market that is worse for them than for their adult counterparts. While marginal occupations such as delivery boy, errand boy, and shoeshine boy exist as niches for the young, those between early teens and early twenties are viewed as unreliable. This group has particular difficulty entering even those monotonous dead-end jobs possible for the unskilled. They view these jobs as dull and boring and are viewed with mistrust by their employers. Some of the violence is also associated with a broad range of illicit activities developed to generate income. These would include petty theft, sale of narcotics, pimping, and dealing in illegal lotteries.

As one goes through this life-cycle stage, there are two paths which usually develop. If a male marries and becomes a family man, he then is viewed as reliable and is pressured to produce income. An example of the shift in one's behavior and friends when this transition is made can be found in the article "From Hell Raiser to Family Man" (Hill 1974), which describes the process in an American Indian group. The other path is to become a professional criminal. Success as a family man is extremely difficult in poverty circumstances, but success as a criminal involves social and physical risks. Often those who fail to become steady, good providers in marriage move in and out of short-term male networks and male boarding house areas throughout their lifetimes. The street-corner men in the United States described in *Tally's Corner* (Liebow 1967) and *Soulside* (Hannerz 1970) have their counterparts in cities all over the world.

Conclusions

A basic characteristic of the behavior of the poor is the similarity of behavioral strategies that have been developed to cope with poverty conditions. An essential element of the poverty situation is low, sporadic income in an industrially based economy. Given such societal conditions, the poor have developed a variety of techniques to survive despite limited resources.

Survival in this lowest and most insecure economic niche is managed through a variety of mechanisms. These include resource conservation, informal savings and credit mechanisms, alternative consumption outlets, and most significantly the support of kin-based networks. Movement out of poverty usually involves the risk of cutting oneself off from one's social obligations to, and potential support from, kin.

There are several generally held attitudes about the behavior of the poor. A fundamental view is that poor people are unable or unwilling to defer immediate gratification for future rewards. Three related areas—money, sex, and violence—have been seen as areas of self-indulgence. In all three areas we have linked the behavior of the poor to economic and social conditions rather than a cognitive or value-based cultural framework. Once again, the general cross-cultural similarity in the behavior of poor people in many parts of the world is striking. One can only conclude that poverty in any industrialized cultural setting results in a set of similar behavioral responses which are the basic tools for survival for the urban poor all over the world.

The Culture of Poverty

OSCAR LEWIS

This selection by Oscar Lewis is probably the most widely cited article ever written on poverty. Lewis first mentioned the "subculture of poverty" (later shortened to "culture") in his book Five Families *(1959), describing the daily lives of five Mexico City households. The concept appears again in his* Children of Sanchez *(1961), and later in its fully developed form in the introduction to* La Vida: A Puerto Rican Family in the Culture of Poverty *(1966), and in an article in* Scientific American *in 1965.*

Through the "culture of poverty" Lewis attempts to show that poverty is not just a matter of economic deprivation but that it also involves behavioral and personality traits. Once people adapt to poverty, attitudes and behaviors that initially developed in response to economic deprivation are passed on to subsequent generations through socialization. The implication that poverty is cultural has been severely criticized, as is discussed in the introduction to Part Five and in the Goode and Eames essay ("An Anthropological Critique of the Culture of Poverty").

Although a great deal has been written about poverty and the poor, the concept of a culture of poverty is relatively new. I first suggested it in 1959 in my book *Five Families: Mexican Case Studies in the Culture of Poverty.* The phrase is a catchy one and has become widely used and misused. Michael Harrington used it extensively in his book *The Other America*, which played an important role in sparking the national anti-poverty program in the United States.

However, he used it in a somewhat broader and less technical sense than I had intended. I shall try to define it more precisely as a conceptual model, with special emphasis upon the distinction between poverty and the culture of poverty. The absence of intensive anthropological studies of poor families from a wide variety of national and cultural contexts, and especially from the socialist countries, is a serious handicap in formulating valid cross-cultural regularities. The model presented here is therefore provisional and subject to modification as new studies become available.

Throughout recorded history, in literature, in proverbs, and in popular sayings, we find two opposite evaluations of the nature of the poor. Some characterize the poor as blessed, virtuous, upright, serene, independent, honest, kind, and happy. Others characterize them as evil, mean, violent, sordid, and criminal. These contradictory and confusing evaluations are also reflected in the in-fighting that is going on in the current war against poverty. Some stress the great potential of the poor for self-help, leadership, and community organization, while others point to the sometimes irreversible, destructive effect of poverty upon individual character, and therefore emphasize the need for guidance and control to remain in the hands of the middle class, which presumably has better mental health.

These opposing views reflect a political power struggle between competing groups. However, some of the confusion results from the failure to distinguish between poverty per se and the culture of poverty and the tendency to focus upon the individual personality rather than upon the group—that is, the family and the slum community.

As an anthropologist I have tried to understand poverty and its associated traits as a culture or, more accurately, as a subculture with its own structure and rationale, as a way of life which is passed down from generation to generation along family lines. This view directs attention to the fact that the culture of poverty in modern nations is not only a matter of economic deprivation, of disorganization, or of the absence of something. It is also something positive and provides some rewards without which the poor could hardly carry on.

Elsewhere I have suggested that the culture of poverty transcends regional, rural-urban, and national differences and shows remarkable similarities in family structure, interpersonal relations, time orientation, value systems, and spending patterns. These cross-national similarities are examples of independent invention and convergence. They are common adaptations to common problems.

The culture of poverty can come into being in a variety of

historical contexts. However, it tends to grow and flourish in societies with the following set of conditions: (1) a cash economy, wage labor, and production for profit; (2) a persistently high rate of unemployment and underemployment for unskilled labor; (3) low wages; (4) the failure to provide social, political, and economic organization, either on a voluntary basis or by government imposition, for the low-income population; (5) the existence of a bilateral kinship system rather than a unilateral one; and finally, (6) the existence of a set of values in the dominant class that stresses the accumulation of wealth and property, the possibility of upward mobility and thrift, and explains low economic status as the result of personal inadequacy or inferiority.

The way of life which develops among some of the poor under these conditions is the culture of poverty. It can best be studied in urban or rural slums and can be described in terms of some seventy interrelated social, economic, and psychological traits. However, the number of traits and the relationships between them may vary from society to society and from family to family. For example, in a highly literate society, illiteracy may be more diagnostic of the culture of poverty than in a society where illiteracy is widespread and where even the well-to-do may be illiterate, as in some Mexican peasant villages before the revolution.

The culture of poverty is both an adaptation and a reaction of the poor to their marginal position in a class-stratified, highly individuated, capitalistic society. It represents an effort to cope with feelings of hopelessness and despair which develop from the realization of the improbability of achieving success in terms of the values and goals of the larger society. Indeed, many of the traits of the culture of poverty can be viewed as attempts at local solutions for problems not met by existing institutions and agencies because the people are not eligible for them, cannot afford them, or are ignorant or suspicious of them. For example, unable to obtain credit from banks, they are thrown upon their own resources and organize informal credit devices without interest.

The culture of poverty, however, is not only an adaptation to a set of objective conditions of the larger society. Once it comes into existence it tends to perpetuate itself from generation to generation because of its effect on the children. By the time slum children are age six or seven they have usually absorbed the basic values and attitudes of their subculture and are not psychologically geared to take full advantage of changing conditions or increased opportunities which may occur in their lifetime.

Most frequently the culture of poverty develops when a stratified social and economic system is breaking down or is being replaced by another, as in the case of the transition from feudalism to capitalism or during periods of rapid technological change. Often it results from imperial conquest in which the native social and economic structure is smashed and the natives are maintained in a servile colonial status, sometimes for many generations. It can also occur in the process of detribalization, such as that now going on in Africa.

The most likely candidates for the culture of poverty are the people who come from the lower strata of a rapidly changing society and are already partially alienated from it. Thus landless rural workers who migrate to the cities can be expected to develop a culture of poverty much more readily than migrants from stable peasant villages with a well-organized traditional culture. In this connection there is a striking contrast between Latin America, where the rural population long ago made the transition from a tribal to a peasant society, and Africa, which is still close to its tribal heritage. The more corporate nature of many of the African tribal societies, in contrast to Latin American rural communities, and the persistence of village ties tend to inhibit or delay the formation of a full-blown culture of poverty in many of the African towns and cities. The special conditions of apartheid in South Africa, where the migrants are segregated into separate "locations" and do not enjoy freedom of movement, create special problems. Here the institutionalization of repression and discrimination tends to develop a greater sense of identity and group consciousness.

The culture of poverty can be studied from various points of view: the relationship between the subculture and the larger society; the nature of the slum community; the nature of the family; and the attitudes, values, and character structure of the individual.

1. The lack of effective participation and integration of the poor in the major institutions of the larger society is one of the crucial characteristics of the culture of poverty. This is a complex matter and results from a variety of factors which may include lack of economic resources, segregation and discrimination, fear, suspicion or apathy, and the development of local solutions for problems. However, "participation" in some of the institutions of the larger society—for example, in the jails, the army, and the public relief system—does not per se eliminate the traits of the culture of poverty. In the case of a relief system which barely keeps people alive, both the basic poverty and the sense of hopelessness are perpetuated rather than eliminated.

Low wages, chronic unemployment and underemployment lead to low income, lack of property ownership, absence of savings, absence of food reserves in the home, and a chronic shortage of cash. These conditions reduce the possibility of effective participation in the larger economic system. And as a response to these conditions we find in the culture of poverty a high incidence of pawning of personal goods, borrowing from local moneylenders at usurious rates of interest, spontaneous informal credit devices organized by neighbors, the use of second-hand clothing and furniture, and the pattern of frequent buying of small quantities of food many times a day as the need arises.

People with a culture of poverty produce very little wealth and receive very little in return. They have a low level of literacy and education, usually do not belong to labor unions, are not members of political parties, generally do not participate in the national welfare agencies, and make very little use of banks, hospitals, department stores, museums, or art galleries. They have a critical attitude toward some of the basic institutions of the dominant classes, hatred of the police, mistrust of government and those in high position, and a cynicism which extends even to the church. This gives the culture of poverty a high potential for protest and for being used in political movements aimed against the existing social order.

People with a culture of poverty are aware of middle-class values, talk about them and even claim some of them as their own, but on the whole they do not live by them. Thus it is important to distinguish between what they say and what they do. For example, many will tell you that marriage by law, by the church, or by both, is the ideal form of marriage, but few will marry. To men who have no steady jobs or other sources of income, who do not own property and have no wealth to pass on to their children, who are present-time oriented and who want to avoid the expense and legal difficulties involved in formal marriage and divorce, free union or consensual marriage makes a lot of sense. Women will often turn down offers of marriage because they feel it ties them down to men who are immature, punishing, and generally unreliable. Women feel that consensual union gives them a better break; it gives them some of the freedom and flexibility that men have. By not giving the fathers of their children legal status as husbands, the women have a stronger claim on their children if they decide to leave their men. It also gives women exclusive rights to a house or any other property they may own.

2. When we look at the culture of poverty on the local community level, we find poor housing conditions, crowding, gregariousness, but above all a minimum of organization beyond the level of the nuclear and extended family. Occasionally there are informal, temporary groupings or voluntary associations within slums. The

existence of neighborhood gangs which cut across slum settlements represents a considerable advance beyond the zero point of the continuum that I have in mind. Indeed, it is the low level of organization that gives the culture of poverty its marginal and anachronistic quality in our highly complex, specialized, organized society. Most primitive peoples have achieved a higher level of sociocultural organization than our modern urban slum dwellers.

In spite of the generally low level of organization, there may be a sense of community and esprit de corps in urban slums and in slum neighborhoods. This can vary within a single city, or from region to region or country to country. The major factors influencing this variation are the size of the slum, its location and physical characteristics, length of residence, incidence of home and land-ownership (versus squatter rights), rentals, ethnicity, kinship ties, and freedom or lack of freedom of movement. When slums are separated from the surrounding area by enclosing walls or other physical barriers, when rents are low and fixed and stability of residence is great (twenty or thirty years), when the population constitutes a distinct ethnic, racial, or language group, is bound by ties of kinship or *compadrazgo*, and when there are some internal voluntary associations, then the sense of local community approaches that of a village community. In many cases this combination of favorable conditions does not exist. However, even where internal organization and esprit de corps are at a bare minimum and people move around a great deal, a sense of territoriality develops which sets off the slum neighborhoods from the rest of the city. In Mexico City and San Juan this sense of territoriality results from the unavailability of low-income housing outside the slum areas. In South Africa the sense of territoriality grows out of the segregation enforced by the government, which confines the rural migrants to specific locations.

3. On the family level the major traits of the culture of poverty are the absence of childhood as a specially prolonged and protected stage in the life cycle, early initiation into sex, free unions or consensual marriages, a relatively high incidence of the abandonment of wives and children, a trend toward female- or mother-centered families and consequently a much greater knowledge of maternal relatives, a strong predisposition to authoritarianism, lack of privacy, verbal emphasis upon family solidarity which is only rarely achieved because of sibling rivalry, and competition for limited goods and maternal affection.

4. On the level of the individual the major characteristics are a strong feeling of marginality, of helplessness, of dependence and of inferiority. I found this to be true of slum dwellers in Mexico City

and San Juan among families who do not constitute a distinct
ethnic or racial group and who do not suffer from racial discrimination. In the United States, of course, the culture of poverty of the
Negroes has the additional disadvantage of racial discrimination,
but as I have already suggested, this additional disadvantage
contains a great potential for revolutionary protest and organization
which seems to be absent in the slums of Mexico City or among
the poor whites in the South.

Other traits include a high incidence of maternal deprivation, of
orality, of weak ego structure, confusion of sexual identification,
a lack of impulse control, a strong present-time orientation with
relatively little ability to defer gratification and to plan for the future,
a sense of resignation and fatalism, a widespread belief in male
superiority, and a high tolerance for psychological pathology of all
sorts.

People with a culture of poverty are provincial and locally oriented
and have very little sense of history. They know only their own
troubles, their own local conditions, their own neighborhood, their
own way of life. Usually they do not have the knowledge, the vision,
or the ideology to see the similarities between their problems and
those of their counterparts elsewhere in the world. They are not
class-conscious, although they are very sensitive indeed to status
distinctions.

When the poor become class-conscious or active members of
trade-union organizations, or when they adopt an internationalist
outlook on the world, they are no longer part of the culture of
poverty, although they may still be desperately poor. Any movement, be it religious, pacifist, or revolutionary, that organizes and
gives hope to the poor and effectively promotes solidarity and a
sense of identification with larger groups destroys the psychological
and social core of the culture of poverty. In this connection, I suspect
that the civil rights movement among the Negroes in the United
States has done more to improve their self-image and self-respect
than have their economic advances, although, without doubt, the
two are mutually reinforcing.

The distinction between poverty and the culture of poverty is
basic to the model described here. There are degrees of poverty and
many kinds of poor people. The culture of poverty refers to one way
of life shared by poor people in given historical and social contexts.
The economic traits which I have listed for the culture of poverty
are necessary but not sufficient to define the phenomena I have in
mind. There are a number of historical examples of very poor segments of the population that do not have a way of life that I would

describe as a subculture of poverty. Here I should like to give four examples:

1. Many of the primitive or preliterate peoples studied by anthropologists suffer from dire poverty which is the result of poor technology and/or poor natural resources, or of both, but they do not have the traits of the subculture of poverty. Indeed, they do not constitute a subculture because their societies are not highly stratified. In spite of their poverty they have a relatively integrated, satisfying, and self-sufficient culture. Even the simplest food-gathering and hunting tribes have a considerable amount of organization, bands and band chiefs, tribal councils, and local self-government—traits which are not found in the culture of poverty.

2. In India the lower castes (the Chamars, the leather workers, and the Bhangis, the sweepers) may be desperately poor, both in the villages and in the cities, but most of them are integrated into the larger society and have their own *panchayat* organizations (a formal organization designed to provide caste leadership) which cut across village lines and give them a considerable amount of power. (It may be that in the slums of Calcutta and Bombay an incipient culture of poverty is developing. It would be highly desirable to do family studies there as a crucial test of the culture-of-poverty hypothesis.) In addition to the caste system, which gives individuals a sense of identity and belonging, there is still another factor, the clan system. Wherever there are unilateral kinship systems or clans one would not expect to find the culture of poverty, because a clan system gives people a sense of belonging to a corporate body with a history and a life of its own, thereby providing a sense of continuity, a sense of a past and of a future.

3. The Jews of eastern Europe were very poor, but they did not have many of the traits of the culture of poverty because of their tradition of literacy, the great value placed upon learning, the organization of the community around the rabbi, the proliferation of local voluntary associations, and their religion, which taught that they were the chosen people.

4. My fourth example is speculative and relates to socialism. On the basis of my limited experience in one socialist country—Cuba—and on the basis of my reading, I am inclined to believe that the culture of poverty does not exist in the socialist countries. I first went to Cuba in 1947 as a visiting professor for the State Department. At that time I began a study of a sugar plantation in Melena del Sur and of a slum in Havana. After the Castro Revolution I made my second trip to Cuba as a correspondent for a major magazine, and I revisited the same slum and some of the same families. The physical aspect of the slum had changed very little,

except for a beautiful new nursery school. It was clear that the people were still desperately poor, but I found much less of the despair, apathy, and hopelessness that are so diagnostic of urban slums in the culture of poverty. [The slum dwellers] expressed great confidence in their leaders and hope for a better life in the future. The slum itself was now highly organized, with block committees, educational committees, party committees. The people had a new sense of power and importance. They were armed and were given a doctrine which glorified the lower class as the hope of humanity. (I was told by one Cuban official that they had practically eliminated delinquency by giving arms to the delinquents!)

It is my impression that the Castro regime—unlike Marx and Engels—did not write off the so-called lumpen proletariat as an inherently reactionary and anti-revolutionary force, but rather saw its revolutionary potential and tried to utilize it. In this connection, Frantz Fanon makes a similar evaluation of the role of the lumpen proletariat based upon his experience in the Algerian struggle for independence. He wrote:

> It is within this mass of humanity, this people of the shanty towns, at the core of the lumpen proletariat, that the rebellion will find its urban spearhead. For the lumpen proletariat, that horde of starving men, uprooted from their tribe and from their clan, constitutes one of the most spontaneous and most radically revolutionary forces of a colonized people.

My own studies of the urban poor in the slums of San Juan do not support the generalizations of Fanon. I have found very little revolutionary spirit or radical ideology among low-income Puerto Ricans. On the contrary, most of the families I studied were quite conservative politically, and about half of them were in favor of the Republican Statehood Party. It seems to me that the revolutionary potential of people with a culture of poverty will vary considerably according to the national context and the particular historical circumstances. In a country like Algeria which was fighting for its independence, the lumpen proletariat was drawn into the struggle and became a vital force. However, in countries like Puerto Rico, in which the movement for independence has very little mass support, and in countries like Mexico which achieved their independence a long time ago and are now in their postrevolutionary period, the lumpen proletariat is not a leading source of rebellion or of revolutionary spirit.

In effect, we find that in primitive societies and in caste societies, the culture of poverty does not develop. In socialist, fascist, and in highly developed capitalist societies with a welfare state, the culture of poverty flourishes in, and is generic to, the early free-enterprise stage of capitalism and . . . is also endemic in colonialism.

It is important to distinguish between different profiles in the subculture of poverty depending upon the national context in which these subcultures are found. If we think of the culture of poverty primarily in terms of the factor of integration in the larger society and a sense of identification with the great tradition of that society, or with a new emerging revolutionary tradition, then we will not be surprised that some slum dwellers with a lower per capita income may have moved farther away from the core characteristics of the culture of poverty than others with a higher per capita income. For example, Puerto Rico has a much higher per capita income than Mexico, yet Mexicans have a deeper sense of identity.

I have listed fatalism and a low level of aspiration as one of the key traits for the subculture of poverty. Here too, however, the national context makes a big difference. Certainly the level of aspiration of even the poorest sector of the population in a country like the United States with its traditional ideology of upward mobility and democracy is much higher than in more backward countries like Ecuador and Peru, where both the ideology and the actual possibilities of upward mobility are extremely limited and where authoritarian values still persist in both the urban and rural milieus.

Because of the advanced technology, high level of literacy, the development of mass media, and the relatively high aspiration level of all sectors of the population, especially when compared with underdeveloped nations, I believe that although there is still a great deal of poverty in the United States (estimates range from thirty to fifty million people), there is relatively little of what I would call the culture of poverty. My rough guess would be that only about 20 percent of the population below the poverty line (between six and ten million people) in the United States have characteristics which would justify classifying their way of life as that of a culture of poverty. Probably the largest sector within this group would consist of very low-income Negroes, Mexicans, Puerto Ricans, American Indians, and Southern poor whites. The relatively small number of people in the United States with a culture of poverty is a positive factor because it is much more difficult to eliminate the culture of poverty than to eliminate poverty per se.

Middle-class people, and this would certainly include most social scientists, tend to concentrate on the negative aspects of the culture of poverty. They tend to associate negative valences [with] such traits as present-time orientation and concrete versus abstract orientation. I do not intend to idealize or romanticize the culture of poverty. As someone has said, "It is easier to praise poverty than to live in it"; yet some of the positive aspects which may flow from these traits must not be overlooked. Living in the present may develop a capacity for spontaneity and adventure, for the enjoyment of the sensual, the indulgence of impulse, which is often blunted in the middle-class, future-oriented man. Perhaps it is this reality of the moment which the existentialist writers are so desperately trying to recapture but which the culture of poverty experiences as natural, everyday phenomena. The frequent use of violence certainly provides a ready outlet for hostility so that people in the culture of poverty suffer less from repression than does the middle class.

In the traditional view, anthropologists have said that culture provides human beings with a design for living, with a ready-made set of solutions for human problems so that individuals don't have to begin all over again each generation. That is, the core of culture is its positive adaptive function. I, too, have called attention to some of the adaptive mechanisms in the culture of poverty—for example, the low aspiration level helps to reduce frustration, the legitimization of short-range hedonism makes possible spontaneity and enjoyment. However, on the whole it seems to me that it is a relatively thin culture. There is a great deal of pathos, suffering, and emptiness among those who live in the culture of poverty. It does not provide much support or long-range satisfaction and its encouragement of mistrust tends to magnify helplessness and isolation. Indeed, the poverty of culture is one of the crucial aspects of the culture of poverty.

The concept of the culture of poverty provides a high level of generalization, which, hopefully, will unify and explain a number of phenomena viewed as distinctive characteristics of racial, national, or regional groups. For example, matrifocality, a high incidence of consensual unions, and a high percentage of households headed by women, which have been thought to be distinctive of Caribbean family organization or of Negro family life in the U.S.A., turn out to be traits of the culture of poverty and are found among diverse peoples in many parts of the world and among peoples who have had no history of slavery.

The concept of a cross-societal subculture of poverty enables us to see that many of the problems we think of as distinctively our own or distinctively Negro problems (or that of any other special racial or ethnic group) also exist in countries where there are no distinct ethnic minority groups. This suggests that the elimination of physical poverty per se may not be enough to eliminate the culture of poverty which is a whole way of life.

What is the future of the culture of poverty? In considering this question, one must distinguish between those countries in which it represents a relatively small segment of the population and those in which it constitutes a very large one. Obviously the solutions will differ in these two situations. In the United States, the major solution proposed by planners and social workers in dealing with multiple-problem families and the so-called hard core of poverty has been to attempt slowly to raise their level of living and to incorporate them into the middle class. Wherever possible, there has been some reliance upon psychiatric treatment.

In the underdeveloped countries, however, where great masses of people live in the culture of poverty, a social-work solution does not seem feasible. Because of the magnitude of the problem, psychiatrists can hardly begin to cope with it. They have all they can do to care for their own growing middle class. In these countries the people with a culture of poverty may seek a more revolutionary solution. By creating basic structural changes in society, by redistributing wealth, by organizing the poor and giving them a sense of belonging, of power, and of leadership, revolutions frequently succeed in abolishing some of the basic characteristics of the culture of poverty even when they do not succeed in abolishing poverty itself.

An Anthropological Critique of the Culture of Poverty

JUDITH GOODE and EDWIN EAMES

In this essay, Judith Goode and Edwin Eames relate their criticism of Lewis's concept of "the culture of poverty" to current debates about how to reform the welfare system and deal with poverty in American society. First, analyzing the culture of poverty model and its conceptual flaws, they proceed to tackle contemporary discussion of the urban "underclass" and conservative explanations for why the poor remain poor. In all of these formulations, including Lewis's model, Judith Goode and Edwin Eames show that poor people are seen as being essentially different from more successful people in some basic fashion, whether genetic or psychological. Thus they need to be treated differently from "normal" middle-class people. Goode and Eames themselves view poor people as victims of flaws in the body social. Poor people's ways of life, as Eames and Goode elaborate in "Coping with Poverty," are realistic adaptations to bad situations, rather than due to personal failings.

Carol Stack's article, "The Kindred of Viola Jackson," George Gmelch's "A West Indian Life," and David Epstein's "Squatter Settlements" also suggest that people, whether poor or better off, adapt reasonably to the set of circumstances that they face.

The issue of the culture of poverty, the development of the concept, its potential as an explanatory device, and its policy implications,

Source: Article written expressly for *Urban Life*.

particularly in American society, all received considerable critical attention in anthropology in the late 1960s and 1970s.

In the history of anthropology, the 1960s marked significant shifts in theory and practice. These included the way culture was defined and interpreted as well as a critical concern with the ethics, social responsibility, and policy implications of research. Oscar Lewis's culture of poverty concept was conceived and presented in an earlier traditional voice. It appeared during the watershed period just in time to become a classic example of what not to do.

The development of the culture of poverty concept is intimately linked to the work of Oscar Lewis. The criticisms of the culture of poverty concept dealt with only one aspect of Lewis's work. His total life's work included many significant contributions, including peasant village studies using innovative data-collecting techniques and further innovations in his studies of slum residents. He was a pioneer in the development of the intensive focus on the family unit in the city, and his development of the method of portraying the "typical day" and the life cycles of individuals did much to accentuate the humanistic emphasis of anthropology. His informants were portrayed as real people, and Lewis has received kudos for his incisive biographical portrayals. However, the repercussions of his culture of poverty concept often seem to overshadow the positive contributions of his career.

Lewis began his career by attacking Redfield's folk society and folk-urban dichotomy; he continued by doing ethnographic studies in Mexico City which initially emphasized strong persistence of organization (family, compadrazgo, religion), only later to shift to an almost exclusive concern with the Mexican and Puerto Rican underclasses. These studies culminated in the development of the culture of poverty concept, in which he described the families he studied in terms of their disorganization and pathologies.

Lewis thus became the target of attack in much the same way that Redfield was earlier, when Lewis led the attack. Beginning his career by attacking overgeneralized and weakly documented concepts, Lewis ended his career being attacked for the same reasons.

Lewis's work showed glimpses of newer perspectives, but he failed to consistently use them. In this chapter, we will review the initial anthropological response to Oscar Lewis's culture of poverty concept which played a major role in the development of urban anthropology since it was roundly criticized. The critique stimulated many important ethnographic analyses which refuted its basic premises. We will also explore the reemergence of the culture of poverty ideology in the United States and the strong rebuttal of it by social scientists using structural explanations. Finally, we will point out the way in which the linkage between structure and culture can and should be further explored using ethnography and contemporary anthropological views of culture.

We argue that the belief in the "culture of poverty" is itself an aspect of the "culture" or ideology of industrial capitalism. It justifies the existing social order with its significant inequality in resources. In one form or another, it had been expressed since the seventeenth-century Elizabethan Poor Laws (Piven and Cloward 1971, Eames and Goode 1973). Michael Katz (1989) has provided an excellent social history of this ideological belief in America up to the present.

The 1980s reemergence of social science writings about the culture of poverty used the new label "underclass." The ideas are still echoed daily on editorial pages and in news magazines. They indicate the degree to which Lewis's work merely legitimized as "scientific" an idea which was deeply embedded in modern European and American thought, that poor people had moral flaws which inhibited their escape from poverty. As Hylan Lewis said during the first wave of critiques, "Like the idea of race, the idea of a culture of poverty is an idea that people believe, want to believe and perhaps need to believe . . . [it] has significant bearing on the . . . pressures and proposals for political and social reorganization of American society that are based on the imperatives of class and race." (1971:347).

The Culture of Poverty Concept

Lewis suggests that the culture of poverty is an integrated set of values, norms, and behaviors characteristic of some of those who live in poverty conditions. He also claims that there are some seventy traits that are diagnostic of those in the culture of poverty. These are subdivided into four subcategories: the nature of integration with the larger society, the nature of the slum community, the nature of the family, and the nature of the individual personality.

Under the category labelled relationship to the larger society, Lewis notes the general lack of participation in the institutions of the larger society. It should be apparent that lack of organization or evidence of disorganization is found at all four levels in the culture of poverty. Lewis suggests that the culture of poverty, once it comes into existence, tends to be perpetuated through time, regardless of changes in the circumstances of the people. He views it as a subculture that is transmitted intergenerationally. He indicates that by the time a child is six or seven, he or she has been irreversibly molded into the culture of poverty. Thus, an individual raised in the culture of poverty is viewed as unable to take advantage of changing circumstances.

Lewis's concept lacks the perspective of cultural relativism, a conceptual tool which is one of the strengths of anthropology. His ethnocentrism shows in his description of the culture of poverty as a thin culture and his equation of the culture of poverty with a "poverty of culture." The latter may indeed be a catchy phrase and a neat linguistic aphorism, but it demonstrates an attitude toward a particular segment of society that is pejorative. This attitude carries over into the discussion of traits, many of which Lewis describes as "lack of _____" rather than describing what is present. It is obvious that Lewis is working from a framework of middle-class notions of what should exist.

Lewis suggests that those in the culture of poverty lack organization, but he subsequently notes their ability to develop informal credit groups and mutual aid mechanisms. He obviously views organization from a middle-class vantage point, which assumes that only formal structures with official goals are "organized." We have mentioned [elsewhere] that one strength of urban anthropology is its ability to uncover informal structures and networks that have no labels and titles. It is obvious from Lewis's own data that much informal organization does exist, without formal names, officers, or archives.

A major critique of Lewis's work was that the data did not fit the model. In a recent analysis, Susan Rigdon calls into question such severe analytical shortcomings as she calls the culture of poverty concept, "a kind of Watts Tower of ideas, dramatic in effect but structurally unsound . . . The publication of the trait list was the nadir of a career filled with outstanding work" (1988:177). Often praised for the humanistic approach, which described the lives of the poor as struggles to survive in demeaning circumstances, the codified formula of the "culture" reduced these complex lives to a mechanical trait list.

Lewis's concept was derived from his original fieldwork in Mexico City. Lewis contends that in his later study of Puerto Rican slum life, he was testing the validity of the concept in a different cultural setting. However, it does not appear from the work in San Juan that the model developed earlier was actually tested in the field situation. What seems to have happened is that Lewis undertook the study in San Juan with a preconceived notion of what he would find and then selected from the available research material those segments that substantiated his original formulation. This point is apparent in the La Vida volume, where we note a significant discontinuity between the introduction to the volume, where the concept is outlined, and the rest of the volume, where the data are presented. Rarely do we find in this volume an interplay between theoretical formulation and empirically derived data, which could serve to sharpen the theoretical focus and aid in the interpretation of empirical data.

This disassociation between formulation and data is the basis of Valentine's critique of Lewis (1968). By selecting from the mass of data presented in the body of the La Vida volume, Valentine is able to demonstrate repeatedly areas in which the behaviors of members of the Rios family completely contradicts the culture of poverty trait list. These obvious contradictions remain unexplored and unexplained by Lewis and thus become a basic issue related to the validity of the concept.

Since Lewis relied mostly on interviews with members of one family in his Puerto Rican work rather than observing everyday life in the community, he had no opportunity to examine the nature of formal and informal community organization. Finally, the very family he selected was admittedly atypical and he did not present any information about the range of behavior in their community.

In response to Lewis, some urban ethnographers did analyses which directly countered his generalizations. The work of Stack (1974) and Lomnitz (1977) revealed the cultural logic and practice of large extended family support networks. Studies of squatter settlements by Leeds (1971), Roberts (1973), Peattie (1968), Uzzell (1975), and Safa (1974) illustrated the processes of community organization. Liebow (1967) and Valentine (1978) illustrated the ways in which the peripheral labor market limited people's choices and the cultural practices that emerged in response. Hannerz (1970) and Peattie (1968) showed the tremendous variability in responses within low-income communities showing that there were many pathways to survival and no simple shared culture.

In the late 1960s, there was a heightened concern among anthropologists about ethics and social responsibility. There was a rising awareness of how anthropological research had been misused in the past and could be misused again by powerful states and interests (Berreman, Gjessing, and Gough 1968; Lewis 1973). Much was written about our obligations to the people we studied and the avoidance of misapplication of anthropological research to public policy. Lewis was criticized for the policy implications of his concept. While he recognized the stigma and marginal position of poor people in industrial capitalism, he located the fundamental problem in their learned behavior and values which needed to be fixed.

This poorly conceived "culture" or way of life was then disseminated widely to middle-class Americans in journals such as *Scientific American* where it served to legitimize a preexisting tendency to "blame the victim." When he popularly disseminated an untested hypothesis, which was then generalized to the total capitalist-industrial world, Lewis acted contrary to the standards for concern about the uses and possible misuses of anthropological studies.

Culture Versus Structure

Since Lewis wrote, the concept of culture has been reshaped in anthropology. The concept was originally developed in the study of small, presumably isolated populations. Culture was objectified as a real thing (a list of traits or rules), a superorganic structure which determined behavior. The contemporary view sees culture more as process. Systems of local cultural practices and meaning are constrained by the structural conditions of life. The central paradigm of urban anthropology is often referred to as "macro-micro," an analysis of how the larger political, economic, and ideological macrostructure shapes people's choices.

Yet, this view of culture does not see people as passive victims of constraints but as resourceful, active agents creating meaningful lives within limited possibilities. Ethnography of the urban poor enables us to see up close how people struggle to make the best choices under dreadful conditions. They create strategies to cope and find meaning in their lives. Given this view of culture as a dialectical process, there is potential for change. Practices and meanings are constantly being negotiated, and reconstructed as conditions change.

Lewis's greatest flaws were his lack of clarity in dealing with culture and structure and his ultimate choice of a determinative superorganic cultural model. He clearly identified structure when he said

> The culture of poverty is both an adaptation and a reaction of the poor to their marginal position in a class stratified, highly individuated, capitalistic society. It represents an effort to cope with feelings of hopelessness and despair which develop from the realization of the improbability of achieving success in terms of the values and goals of the larger society.

Lewis recognized that his culture was a response to both economic scarcity and concentrated social stigma for those at the bottom in capitalist societies. But, he was confused about what was part of the constraining political economic structure and its attendant ideology of denigration and what was the cultural response under conditions of limited choice. For example, he includes as equivalent traits: high rates of under- and unemployment; low wages when employed; lack of savings; frequent purchase of small quantities of food; borrowing at usurious rates; small-scale informal credit mechanisms; and the use of second-hand goods. While the first three are clearly part of the structural conditions, the others are shared cultural practices.

Lewis glimpsed the importance of the dynamic relationship between culture and structure, but he never worked it out. In his work he ultimately gave priority to a culture, which once set in motion by material conditions, had determinative priority through carbon copy intergenerational reproduction. He never realized that his own words could be used to further marginalize the poor. In his humanistic narratives of real lives, people were depicted as active agents, but in the codification of the "culture of poverty," their personalities, families, and organizational capacities were weak and broken.

U.S. Policy

The contemporary debate on the underclass in America is really a continuation of the debate between cultural and structural explanations of poverty (Marks 1991). Yet it is the relationship between the two that is really the heart of the issue. Lewis's concept is still evoked in the contemporary discussion of the underclass as it was in the War on Poverty in the 1960s.

Ironically, Lewis was mostly directing his work to a concern with poverty in the Third World. He was not specifically interested in poverty in the United States. While he promoted radical social change through the political mobilization of the poor in the developing world, he casually distinguished the United States situation both in terms of its severity and policy treatment. He seemed unaware of the uneven economic development of regions and economic sectors in this country or of institutional racism. He advocated a social service solution in the United States which would change the behavior and values of the poor.

Ultimately, his concept had more influence on United States policy than elsewhere. His work, along with the work of others such as the Moynihan report on the Black family (1965) and psychological research "proving" that the poor could not defer

412   An Anthropological Critique

gratification (1968), served to justify an emphasis on programs which worked on the "culture" of the poor, and deflected attention from issues of redistribution. Ingrained in the job readiness, head start, and community action programs was the emphasis on changing the attitudes and beliefs of the poor rather than the structural change that would involve job creation, job placement, improving the quality of schools in poor neighborhoods, or making the larger political system more accessible.

Since 1965, poverty has continued to increase (*Newsweek* 1993). While poverty in rural areas and among white populations has experienced a major increase, the national debate focuses on the inner-city minority poor often referred to as the underclass.

Structural explanations of the increase in poverty play a major role in the discussions of the underclass (Jencks and Peterson 1991, Katz 1993, Axinn and Stern 1988, Sassen 1988). Major transformations of labor markets stem from several interrelated processes. These include global economic integration, automation, suburbanization of economic activities, deindustrialization, and the restructured service economy with part-time, high-turnover, no-benefit jobs. At the same time, Reagan tax policy is now being analyzed as a massive economic redistribution shifting more wealth to the top and widening the gap between top and bottom (Phillips 1990, Bartlett and Steele 1992).

One of the best known structuralist arguments was made in Wilson's *The Truly Disadvantaged* (1987). Wilson describes the effects of major structural shifts in the global economy since the 1970s on labor force dynamics, which have worsened job opportunities for the inner-city poor. He sees the flight of middle-class African Americans from the ghetto after affirmative action as leading to increased isolation, a concentration of the very poor, a weakening of local institutions, and an increase in social pathology such as teenage pregnancy, drugs, and violence.

While Wilson uses statistics to stress structure both in explaining poverty and offering solutions that require redistribution, he inadvertently reinforces mainstream ideas of cultural pathology among the ghetto poor. As Newman (1992) has pointed out, his picture of pathology is not substantiated by ethnographic analyses of the lives of the poor. Such work would not only show that some of his assumptions about the levels and uniformity of structurally induced pathology are not true but could demonstrate the mechanisms through which structure influences cultural practice.

During the Reagan years, cultural explanations of poverty were rampant, especially those that argued that anti-poverty programs themselves had reinforced the culture of poverty. Murray, in his book *Losing Ground* (1984), ignores economic shifts and blames poverty on the war on poverty, which destroyed the ethics of family and work among the poor by creating welfare dependency. He calls for government policies which force people to work to restore those ethics. This is very reminiscent of the workhouse ideology in eighteenth-century England, which attempted to eradicate the moral flaws of the poor by making them work. Gilder (1991), one of the now discredited supply-side economists writes that poverty is caused by poor people's straying from the only way out of poverty which is "work, family and faith." According to Gilder, the poor must work harder than others to arrive at a better position in society, but they will do so if they make the effort. According to Mead, "In the absence of prohibitive barriers to employment, the question of the personality of the poor emerges as the key to understanding and overcoming poverty" (1992:133). This assertion of the absence of structural barriers to employment belies all serious labor market analysis, which reveals the steep decline of stable, full-time jobs with benefits that can support a family. The policy implications of Gilder, Murray, and Mead involve no change in the structure and echo Social Darwinism. Only a good dose of hard work is needed to knock the bad values out of the poor. If their moral flaws and weak characters do not fit them for survival, so be it.

The welfare dependency theorists ignore the fact that welfare benefits themselves are inadequate to support a family at the poverty line. Much research has demonstrated that the poor want to work, the average length of time on welfare is short, and the cost of dishonesty in the system is attributed more to those who provide housing, health, and other services than to the recipients (Axinn and Stern 1988).

As analysts fight over the relative importance of structure or culture in explaining poverty, journalists provide images of the lives of the underclass. These descriptions of remorseless, violent teenagers; clever, entrepreneurial drug dealers; and welfare mothers as passive victims are implied to exotic, sensationalized "cultures." There is little explanation about the links between structural constraints and ideas and actions. Newman (1992) and Marks (1991) argue that what is needed is more urban ethnography to explicate the relationship between structure and cultural practices.

The urban ethnographic work of Sharff and Susser demonstrates how a close-up view of how poor families live shows the active way in which men, women, and children respond to the very limited possibilities available to them. Both writers focus on the intensive concerns about the future of their children which motivates the strategies and practices of the families.

Sharff (1987) describes the opportunity structure of one low-income neighborhood through the work experience of 133 families over one year. These households were characterized by underemployment. Work was available only in peripheral labor markets characterized as sporadic and low paying. Few were able to work continuously. Layoffs and seasonality characterized many jobs. Some menial but steady jobs required five-hour daily commutes but did not tolerate lateness or absence. Many households depended on the work of their children in government-funded summer job programs to tide them over for the year. With this job market, interhousehold sharing and work in the irregular (illegal) underground economy—involving street mechanics and home-based production and sale of drugs—as well as welfare were necessities. In such a way, shared practices were created in the neighborhood to cope with the limited opportunities.

The ethnographic work of Susser and Kreniske (1987) uses case studies of welfare recipients unable to obtain stable, adequately paying jobs and demonstrates how the practices of the welfare bureaucracy force subversion by those who must depend on it. She demonstrates how the only rational response of recipients in many situations is to hide information and become vulnerable to charges of fraud. This opens them up to exploitation by landlords who threaten to inform on them, sometimes using false information. A whole sector of welfare housing has developed in response to welfare rent payments. Landlords are able to charge more for substandard housing. Because most of the housing market rejected welfare families, they were a captive population for welfare housing.

Family Values

One of the best examples of the ethnographic examination of the specific links between structure and culture lies in the domain of the family. In cross-cultural studies of the family, residential composition and child-care patterns have long been seen as adaptive to economic constraints (See Eames and Goode, this volume). There are many forms of family in the United States that fulfill domestic functions. Carol Stack (1974) demonstrated that the multigenerational core networks of African American women she found in a midwestern urban community were related to, but not the same as, preexisting forms adapted to life in the rural South and readapted to the participation in unstable urban industrial labor markets. Rhoda Halperin (1990) demonstrates how the "Kentucky way," a pattern of family and kin relations developed in a rural

Kentucky farming era has been modified for adapting to low and sporadic income on the margins of industrial capitalism in Appalachia. The message from these studies is clear. Family styles are shaped by the structure. In conditions of unstable, low-income employment, nuclear families are often less significant components in larger sharing networks.

Today, the association between poverty and family is popularly assumed to be the reverse. Family pathology is seen as the root cause of poverty. The correlation between poverty and female-headed households is used to imply that such non-nuclear households are pathological and perpetuate poverty rather than seeing them as coping structures adapting to the labor market. We know that employment practices and the absence of child-care policy has placed stress on domestic roles across the class spectrum (Jencks 1988). We need policies to relieve these pressures. However, promoting "family values" and uniform nuclear families is misguided without structural change.

Hopelessness and Despair

Lewis implied that being poor in industrial capitalism created hopelessness and despair. If the belief in a culture of poverty is embedded in the dominant ideology of industrial capitalism, then the contempt for those at the bottom must have an effect on cultural practices and meaning. Recent trends toward a greater gap between rich and poor occurring in global cities (Sassen 1992) coupled with the media emphasis on hyper-mass consumption have added to this complex dynamic.

Recent ethnographic studies show how powerless peoples react to their position by creating subcultures that both mirror and resist dominant ideology rather than as broken, passive, marginalized victims. They tie the emergence of such resistance to an experience-based understanding of labor market opportunities and power structures rather than individual pathology.

One example is *Learning to Labor* by Paul Willis (1992). He spent a year doing ethnography (participant observation, informal group discussions, and interviews) in a school for low-income working-class boys in the industrial midlands of England. Through his careful analysis of the boys' own words, he demonstrates the formation of an oppositional culture in response to the middle-class achievement message of the school. While the school preached the value of education, the boys' experience with their family class position and their understanding of class in British society contradicted this message. He carefully analyzes the logic of their culture of resistance as a creative way to achieve personal validation, specialness, and subjective elevation in a world that demeans them. Rather than being pathological individuals or culturally deprived, they are keenly perceptive of their world. They create a culture which rejects many dominant values but is itself, a reflection of the competitive individualism of the society.

Philippe Bourgois (1989), working with Puerto Rican drug dealers, also finds a countercultural value system, which parodies the ideology of the dominant society in its goals of moving up career ladders and excessive material consumption. He links the street culture to the boys' experiences with work. Their job experiences in the mainstream economy were in the high-risk, high-turnover, low-paying segment of the peripheral labor market and included the common characteristics of physical difficulty, danger, and dirt. Again, he uses their words and insights, which link their social position to their cultural practices, which offer meaning and validation.

Dwight Conquergood, working with gangs in Chicago, through his film, *The Heart Broken in Two* (Siegel and Conquergood 1990), demonstrated the extraordinary insights of these boys about the limits of their lives and the creativity that accompanies their attempts to construct meaning. His analysis ends with the statement that only a steady paycheck had the power to replace their lifestyle. Elijah Anderson (1990) describes the worsening of life conditions in a poor neighborhood over the last two decades. He directly links the change in the nature of street culture to deindustrialization and the loss of stable jobs.

It is important to note that in all these studies, the authors demonstrate that in the respective setting, the alternative culture of resistance *is not dominant*. In other words, in the working-class school, there are many straight boys who don't break the rules. In Bourgois's neighborhood, there are many who are not part of the street. It is important to remember that in spite of the dominant image of low-income neighborhoods, such countercultural practices are just one type of response.

In all these studies, while the cultures of resistance are seen as ultimately self-destructive, the processes that shape them, the systems of power and exploitation, leave few other opportunities for cultural fulfillment. These studies show the relationship between structure that constrains possibilities and the cultural constructions that emerge within these limits. For any real change, it is these limits that must be addressed significantly in policy. Simply working on the systems of meaning without addressing the conditions from which they derive will not work.

There are still more relationships to explore. Especially important are the cultural practices and systems of meaning of employers, landlords, welfare workers, and others. How are they formed within the institutions that interact with the poor? Ethnographers are in the best position to do the careful and systematic demonstration of the dialectic between structure and culture both on the street and in institutional settings. Lewis's mistakes have been a useful catalyst for using the macro-micro perspective in an important way.

We would like to thank Richard J. Malloy, S.J., a doctoral candidate at Temple University, for his crucial insights about the reiterations of the culture of poverty debate.

Office Work and the Crack Alternative Among Puerto Rican Drug Dealers in East Harlem

PHILIPPE BOURGOIS

In this essay, Philippe Bourgois shows that those who become drug dealers do so for a variety of reasons. One has to do with the quality of work which they find in the legitimate sector of the economy. Drug dealers, as he shows, have had legal jobs, but they find their relationships with their superiors in these jobs unsatisfactory. In the incidents described here, the young Puerto Ricans felt unable to use the ways of behaving that they had learned in El Barrio in mainstream jobs, both because of their Latino heritage and because of the differences between the street culture and that of the office and factory.

Gender, class, and ethnic and racial identity, all play a role in the antagonism felt by Caesar and Primo toward their immediate superiors. Here, as in Sally Engle Merry's article "Urban Danger," conflict occurs on the borders of different ethnic groups. Both the office and the street are arenas for these conflicts. Barbara Kirshenblatt-Gimblett ("Ordinary People/Everyday Life") shows positive aspects of the interaction of subcultures in New York City, while Philippe Bourgois emphasizes that the structure of power and conflict can lead to self-destruction.

Source: Article written expressly for *Urban Life*.

East Harlem child biking through a block of abandoned buildings. [Photo by Philippe Bourgois]

For a total of approximately three and a half years during the late 1980s and early 1990s, I lived with my wife and young son in an irregularly heated, rat-filled tenement in East Harlem, New York. This two-hundred-square-block neighborhood—better known locally as *El Barrio* or Spanish Harlem—is visibly impoverished yet it is located in the heart of New York, the richest city in the Western Hemisphere. It is literally a stone's throw from multimillion-dollar condominiums. Although one in three families survived on some form of public assistance in 1990, the majority of El Barrio's 110,600 Puerto Rican and African American residents fall into the ranks of the working poor.[1] They eke out an uneasy subsistence in entry-level service and manufacturing jobs in one of the most expensive cities in the world.

The public sector (e.g., the police, social welfare agencies, the Sanitation Department) have broken down in El Barrio and do not function effectively. This has caused the legally employed residents of the neighborhood to lose control of their streets and public spaces to the drug economy. My tenement's block was not atypical and within a few hundred yards' radius I could obtain heroin, crack, powder cocaine, hypodermic needles, methadone, Valium, angel dust,[2] marijuana, mescaline, bootleg alcohol, and tobacco. Within two hundred feet of my stoop there were three competing crack houses selling vials at two, three, and five dollars. Several doctors operated "pill mills" on the blocks around me, writing prescriptions for opiates and barbiturates upon demand. In the projects within view of my living-room window, the Housing Authority police arrested a fifty-five-year-old mother and her twenty-two-year-old daughter while they were "bagging" twenty-two pounds of cocaine into ten-dollar quarter-gram "jumbo" vials of adulterated product worth over a million dollars on the streets. The police found twenty-five thousand dollars in cash in small-denomination bills in this same apartment.[3] In other words, there are millions of dollars' worth of business going on directly in front of the youths growing up in East Harlem tenements and housing projects. Why should these young men and women take the subway downtown to work minimum-wage jobs—or even double minimum-wage jobs—in downtown offices when they can usually earn more, at least in the short run, by selling drugs on the street corner in front of their apartment or school yard?

This dynamic underground economy is predicated on violence and substance abuse. It has spawned what I call a "street culture" of resistance and self-destruction. The central concern of my study is the relationship of street culture to the worlds of work accessible to street dealers—that is, the legal and illegal labor markets that employ them and give meaning to their lives. I hope to show the local-level implications of the global-level restructuring of the U.S. economy away from factory production and toward services. In the process, I have recorded the words and experiences of some unrepentant victims who are part of a network of some twenty-five street-level crack dealers operating on and around my block. To summarize, I am arguing that the transformation from manufacturing to service employment—especially in the professional office work setting—is much more culturally disruptive than the already revealing statistics on reductions in income, employment, unionization, and worker's benefits would indicate. Low-level service sector employment engenders a humiliating ideological—or cultural—confrontation between a powerful corps of white office executives and their assistants versus a younger generation of poorly educated, alienated, "colored" workers. It also often takes the form of a sharply polarized confrontation over gender roles.

Shattered Working-Class Dreams

All the crack dealers and addicts whom I have interviewed had worked at one or more legal jobs in their early youth. In fact, most entered the labor market at a younger age than the typical American. Before they were twelve years old they were bagging groceries at the supermarket for tips, stocking beers off-the-books in local *bodegas*, or shining shoes. For example, Primo, the night manager at a video game arcade that sells five-dollar vials of crack on the block where I lived, pursued a traditional working-class dream in his early adolescence. With the support of his extended kin who were all immersed in a working-class "common sense," he dropped out of junior high school to work in a local garment factory:

> I was like fourteen or fifteen playing hooky and pressing dresses and whatever they were making on the steamer. They was cheap, cheap clothes.

> My mother's sister was working there first and then her son, my cousin Willie—the one who's in jail now—was the one they hired first, because his mother agreed: "If you don't want to go to school, you gotta work."

> So I started hanging out with him. I wasn't planning on working in the factory. I was supposed to be in school; but it just sort of happened.

Ironically, young Primo actually became the agent who physically moved the factory out of the inner city. In the process, he became merely one more of the 445,900 manufacturing workers in New York City who lost their jobs as factory employment dropped 50 percent from 1963 to 1983 (Romo and Schwartz 1993).

Almost all the crack dealers had similar tales of former factory jobs. For poor adolescents, the decision to drop out of school and become a marginal factory worker is attractive. It provides the employed youth with access to the childhood "necessities"—sneakers, basketballs, store-bought snacks—that sixteen-year-olds who stay in school cannot afford. In the descriptions of their first forays into legal factory-based employment, one hears clearly the extent to which they, and their families, subscribed to mainstream working-class ideologies about the dignity of engaging in "hard work" rather than education.

Had these enterprising, early-adolescent workers from El Barrio not been confined to the weakest sector of manufacturing in a period of rapid job loss, their teenage working-class dreams might have stabilized. Instead, upon reaching their mid-twenties, they discovered themselves to be unemployable high school dropouts. This painful realization of social marginalization expresses itself across a generational divide. The parents and grandparents of the dealers continue to maintain working-class values of honesty and hard work which conflict violently with the reality of their children's immersion in street culture. They are constantly accused of slothfulness by their mothers and even by friends who have managed to maintain legal jobs. They do not have a regional perspective on the dearth of adequate entry-level jobs available to "functional illiterates" in New York, and they begin to suspect that they might indeed be "vago bons [lazy bums]" who do not *want* to work hard and cannot help themselves. Confused, they take refuge in an alternative search for career, meaning, and ecstasy in substance abuse.

Formerly, when most entry-level jobs were found in factories, the contradiction between an oppositional street culture and traditional working-class, masculine, shop-floor culture was less pronounced—especially when the work site was protected by a union. Factories are inevitably rife with confrontational hierarchies. Nevertheless, on the shop-floor, surrounded by older union workers, high school dropouts who are well versed in the latest and toughest street culture styles function effectively. In the factory, being tough and violently macho has high cultural value; a certain degree of opposition to the foreman and the "bossman" is expected and is considered appropriate.

In contrast, this same oppositional street-identity is nonfunctional in the professional office worker service sector that has burgeoned in New York's high-finance-driven economy. It does not allow for the humble, obedient, social interaction—often across gender lines—that professional office workers routinely impose on their subordinates. A qualitative change has occurred, therefore, in the tenor of social interaction in office-based employment. Workers in a mail room or behind a photocopy machine cannot publicly maintain their cultural autonomy. Most concretely, they have no union; more subtly, there are few fellow workers surrounding them to insulate them and to provide them with a culturally based sense of class solidarity.[4] Instead they are besieged by supervisors and bosses from an alien, hostile, and obviously dominant culture who ridicule street culture. Workers like Primo appear inarticulate to their professional supervisors when they try to imitate the language of power in the workplace and instead stumble pathetically over the enunciation of unfamiliar words. They cannot decipher the hastily scribbled instructions—rife with mysterious abbreviations—that are left for them by harried office managers. The "common sense" of white-collar work is foreign to them; they do not, for example, understand the logic for filing triplicate copies of memos or for post-dating invoices. When they attempt to improvise or show initiative they fail miserably and instead appear inefficient, or even hostile, for failing to follow "clearly specified" instructions.

Their "social skills" are even more inadequate than their limited professional capacities. They do not know how to look at their fellow co-service workers, let alone their supervisors, without intimidating them. They cannot walk down the hallway to the water fountain without unconsciously swaying their shoulders aggressively as if patrolling their home turf. Gender barriers are an even more culturally charged realm. They are repeatedly reprimanded for harassing female co-workers.

The cultural clash between white "yuppie" power and inner-city "scrambling jive" in the service sector is much more than a superficial question of style. It is about access to power. Service workers who are incapable of obeying the rules of interpersonal interaction dictated by professional office culture will never be upwardly mobile. Their supervisors will think they are dumb or have a "bad attitude." Once again, a gender dynamic exacerbates the confusion and sense of insult experienced by young, male inner-city employees because most supervisors in the lowest reaches of the service sector are women. Street culture does not allow males to be subordinate across gender lines.

"Gettin' Dissed"

On the street, the trauma of experiencing a threat to one's personal dignity has been frozen linguistically in the commonly used phrase "to diss," which is short for "to disrespect." Significantly, one generation ago ethnographers working in rural Puerto Rico specifically noted the importance of the traditional Puerto Rican concept of *respeto* in mediating labor relations:

> The good owner "respects" (*respeta*) the laborer . . . It is probably to the interest of the landowner to make concessions to his best workers, to deal with them on a respect basis, and to enmesh them in a network of mutual obligations. (Wolf 1956:235; see also Lauria 1964; Totti 1986)

Puerto Rican street-dealers do not find respect in the entry-level service sector jobs that have increased two-fold in New York's economy since the 1950s. On the contrary, they "get dissed" in the new jobs that are available to them. Primo, for example, remembers the humiliation of his former work experiences as an "office boy," and he speaks of them in a race- and gender-charged idiom:

> I had a prejudiced boss. She was a fucking "ho'," Gloria. She was white. Her name was Christian. No, not Christian, Kirschman. I don't know if she was Jewish or not. When she was talking to people she would say, "He's illiterate."
>
> So what I did one day was, I just looked up the word, "illiterate," in the dictionary and I saw that she's saying to her associates that I'm stupid or something!
>
> Well, I am illiterate anyway.

The most profound dimension of Primo's humiliation was being obliged to look up in the dictionary the word used to insult him. In contrast, in the underground economy, he is sheltered from this kind of threat:

> Rocky [the crack house franchise owner] he would never disrespect me that way. He wouldn't tell me that because he's illiterate too. Plus I've got more education than him. I got a GED.

Reflecting on the period he spent as a knife-wielding mugger on the street, Primo could not contrast more dramatically with his vulnerabilities to humiliation in a low-level service-sector job.

> I was with Rico and his girl, Daisy. We saw this Mexican . . . He was just probably drunk. I grabbed him by the back of the neck, and put my 007 [knife] in his back [grabbing me in a half-nelson from behind]. Right here [jabbing my lower back]. And I was jigging him *HARD* [grinning for emphasis at his girlfriend, who was listening, rapt with attention]!
>
> I said: "*No te mueve cabron o te voy a picar como un pernil* [Don't move mother-fucker or I'll stick you like a roast pork]" [Chuckling with his girlfriend]. Yeah, yeah, like how you stab a pork shoulder when you want to put all the flavoring in the holes.
>
> I wasn't playing, either, I was serious. I would have jigged him. And I'd regret it later, but I was looking at that gold ring he had [more chuckling].
>
> The Mexican panicked. So I put him to the floor, poking him hard, and Daisy started searching him.
>
> I said, "Yo, take that asshole's fucking ring too!"
>
> After she took the ring we broke out. We sold the ring and then we cut out on Daisy. We left her in the park, she didn't get even a cent. She helped for nothing [More chuckling].

Primo excels in the street's underground economy. His very persona inspires fear and respect. In contrast, in order to succeed in his former office job, Primo would have had to self-consciously alter his street identity and mimic the professional cultural style that office managers require of their subordinates and colleagues.

Primo refused to accept his boss's insults and he was unable to imitate her interactional styles. He was doomed, consequently, to a marginal position behind a photocopy machine or at the mail meter. Behavior considered appropriate in street culture is considered dysfunctional in office settings. In other words, job requirements in the service sector are largely cultural style and this conjugates powerfully with racism.

> I wouldn't have mind that she said I was illiterate. What bothered me was that when she called on the telephone, she wouldn't want me to answer even if my supervisor who was the receptionist was not there. [Note how Primo is so low in the office hierarchy that his immediate supervisor is a receptionist.]

> When she hears my voice it sounds like she's going to get a heart attack. She'd go, "Why are you answering the phones?"

> That bitch just didn't like my Puerto Rican accent.

Primo's manner of resisting this insult to his cultural dignity exacerbated his marginal position in the labor hierarchy:

> And then, when I did pick up the phone, I used to just sound *Porta'rrrican* on purpose.

In contrast to the old factory sweatshop positions, these just-above-minimum-wage office jobs require intense interpersonal contact with the middle and upper-middle classes. Close contact across class lines and the absence of a working-class autonomous space for eight hours a day in the office can be a claustrophobic experience for an otherwise ambitious, energetic, young, inner-city worker.

Caesar, who worked for Primo as look-out and bodyguard at the crack house, interpreted this requirement to obey white, middle-class norms as an affront to his dignity that specifically challenged his definition of masculinity:

> I had a few jobs like that [referring to Primo's "telephone diss"] where you gotta take a lot of shit from bitches and be a wimp.

> I didn't like it but I kept on working, because "Fuck it!" you don't want to fuck up the relationship. So you just be a punk [shrugging his shoulders dejectedly].

One alternative for surviving at a workplace that does not tolerate a street-based cultural identity is to become bicultural: to play politely by "the white woman's" rules downtown only to come home and revert to street culture within the safety of one's tenement or housing project at night. Tens of thousands of East Harlem residents manage this tightrope, but it often engenders accusations of betrayal and internalized racism on the part of neighbors and childhood friends who do not have—or do not want—these bicultural skills.

This is the case, for example, of Ray, a rival crack dealer whose tough street demeanor conflates with his black skin to "disqualify" him from legal office work. He quit a "nickel-and-dime messenger job downtown" in order to sell crack full time in his project stairway shortly after a white woman fled from him shrieking down the hallway of a high-rise office building. Ray and the terrified woman had ridden the elevator together, and, coincidentally, Ray had stepped off on the same floor as her to make a delivery. Worse yet, Ray had been trying to act like a "debonair male" and suspected the contradiction between his inadequate appearance and his chivalric intentions was responsible for the woman's terror:

> You know how you let a woman go off the elevator first? Well that's what I did to her but I may have looked a little shabby on the ends. Sometime my hair not combed. You know. So I could look a little sloppy to her maybe when I let her off first.

What Ray did not quite admit until I probed further is that he too had been intimidated by the lone white woman. He had been so disoriented by her taboo, unsupervised proximity that he had forgotten to press the elevator button when he originally stepped on after her:

> She went in the elevator first but then she just waits there to see what floor I press. She's playing like she don't know what floor she wants to go to because she wants to wait for me to press my floor. And I'm standing there and I forgot to press the button. I'm thinking about something else—I don't know what was the matter with me. And she's thinking like, "He's not pressing the button; I guess he's following me!"

As a crack dealer, Ray no longer has to confront this kind of confusing humiliation. Instead, he can righteously condemn his "successful" neighbors who work downtown for being ashamed of who they were born to be:

> When you see someone go downtown and get a good job, if they be Puerto Rican, you see them fix up their hair and put some contact lens in their eyes. Then they fit in. And they do it! I seen it.

> They turn-overs. They people who want to be white. Man, if you call them in Spanish, it wind up a problem.

> When they get nice jobs like that, all of a sudden, you know, they start talking proper.

Self-portrait spraypainted by an East Harlem crack dealer to mark his sales point. [Photo by Philippe Bourgois]

Self-Destructive Resistance

During the 1980s, the real value of the minimum wage for legally employed workers declined by one-third. At the same time, social services were cut. The Federal Government, for example, decreased the proportion of its contribution to New York City's budget by over 50 percent (Berlin 1991:10; Rosenbaum 1989:A1). The breakdown of the inner city's public sector is no longer an economic threat to the expansion of New York's economy because the native-born labor force it shelters is increasingly irrelevant.

New immigrants arrive every day, and they are fully prepared to work hard for low wages under unsavory conditions. Like the parents and grandparents of Primo and Caesar, many of New York's newest immigrants are from isolated rural communities or squalid shanty towns where meat is eaten only once a week and there is no running water or electricity. Half a century ago Primo's mother fled precisely the same living conditions these new immigrants are only just struggling to escape. Her reminiscences about childhood in her natal village reveal the time warp of improved material conditions, cultural dislocation, and crushed working-class dreams that is propelling her second-generation son into a destructive street culture:

> I loved that life in Puerto Rico, because it was a healthy, healthy, healthy life.
>
> We always ate because my father always had work, and in those days the custom was to have a garden in your patio to grow food and everything that you ate.
>
> We only ate meat on Sundays because everything was cultivated on the same little parcel of land. We didn't have a refrigerator, so we ate *bacalao*, [salted codfish] which can stay outside and a meat that they call *carne de vieja* [shredded beef], and sardines from a can. But thanks to God, we never felt hunger. My mother made a lot of cornflour.
>
> Some people have done better by coming here, but many people haven't. Even people from my barrio, who came trying to find a better life [*buen anbiente*] just found disaster. Married couples right from my neighborhood came only to have the husband run off with another woman.
>
> In those days in Puerto Rico, when we were in poverty, life was better. Everyone will tell you life was healthier and you could trust people. Now you can't trust anybody.
>
> What I like best was that we kept all our traditions . . . our feasts. In my village, everyone was either an Uncle or an Aunt. And when you walked by someone older, you had to ask for their blessing. It was respect. There was a lot of respect in those days [original quote in Spanish].

The Jewish and Italian-American white workers that Primo's mother replaced a generation ago when she came to New York City in hope of building a better future for her children were largely absorbed into an expanding economy that allowed them to be upwardly mobile. New York's economy always suffered periodic fluctuations, such as during the Great Depression, but those difficult periods were always temporary. The overall trend was one of economic growth. Primo's generation has not been so lucky. The contemporary economy does not particularly need them, and ethnic discrimination and cultural barriers overwhelm them whenever they attempt to work legally and seek service-sector jobs. Worse yet, an extraordinarily dynamic underground drug economy beckons them.

Rather than bemoaning the structural adjustment which is destroying their capacity to survive on legal wages, street-bound Puerto Rican youths celebrate their "decision" to bank on the underground economy and to cultivate their street identities. Caesar and Primo repeatedly assert their pride in their street careers. For example, one Saturday night after they finished their midnight shift at the crack house, I accompanied them on their way to purchase "*El Sapo Verde*" [The Green Toad], a twenty-dollar bag of powder cocaine sold by a new company three blocks away. While waiting for Primo and Caesar to be "served" by the coke seller a few yards away I engaged three undocumented Mexican men drinking beer on a neighboring stoop in a conversation about finding work in New York. One of the new immigrants was already earning five hundred dollars a week fixing deep-fat-fry machines. He had a straightforward racist explanation for why Caesar—who was standing next to me—was "unemployed":

> OK, OK I'll explain it to you in one word: Because the Puerto Ricans are brutes! [Pointing at Caesar] Brutes! Do you understand?
>
> Puerto Ricans like to make easy money. They like to leech off of other people. But not us Mexicans! No way! We like to work for our money. We don't steal. We came here to work and that's all [original quote in Spanish].

Instead of physically assaulting the employed immigrant for insulting him, Caesar embraced the racist tirade, ironically turning it into the basis for a new, generational-based, "American-born," urban cultural pride. In fact, in his response, he ridicules what he interprets to be the hillbilly naivete of the Mexicans who still believe in the "American Dream." He spoke slowly in street-English as if to mark sarcastically the contrast between his "savvy" Nuyorican (New York-born Puerto Rican) identity versus the limited English proficiency of his detractor:

> That's right, m'a man! We is real vermin lunatics that sell drugs. We don't want no part of society. "Fight the Power!"[5]
>
> What do we wanna be working for? We rather live off the system. Gain weight, lay women.

When we was younger, we used to break our asses too [Gesturing towards the Mexican men who were straining to understand his English]. I had all kinds of stupid jobs too . . . advertising agencies . . . computers.

But not no more! Now we're in a rebellious stage. We rather evade taxes, make quick money, and just survive. But we're not satisfied with that either. Ha!

Conclusion: Ethnography and Oppression

The underground economy and the social relations thriving off of it are best understood as modes of resistance to subordination in the service sector of the new U.S. economy. This resistance, however, results in individual self-destruction and wider community devastation through substance abuse and violence. This complex and contradictory dynamic whereby resistance leads to self-destruction in the inner city is difficult to convey to readers in a clear and responsible manner. Mainstream society's "common sense" understanding of social stratification around ethnicity and class assumes the existence of racial hierarchies and blames individual victims for their failures. This makes it difficult to present ethnographic data from inner-city streets without falling prey to a "pornography of violence" or a racist voyeurism.

The public is not persuaded by a structural economic understanding of Caesar and Primo's "self-destruction." Even the victims themselves psychologize their unsatisfactory lives. Similarly, politicians and, more broadly, public policy ignore the fundamental structural economic facts of marginalization in America. Instead the first priority of Federal and local social "welfare" agencies is to change the psychological—or at best the "cultural"—orientations of misguided individuals (Katz 1989). U.S. politicians furiously debate family values while multinational corporations establish global free-trade zones and unionized factory employment in the U.S. continues to disappear as overseas sweatshops multiply. Social science researchers, meanwhile, have remained silent for the most part. They politely ignore the urgent social problems engulfing the urban United States. The few marginal academic publications that do address issues of poverty and racism are easily ignored by the media and mainstream society.

There is a theoretical and methodological basis for anthropology's reticence to confront devastating social misery in its front yard. Qualitative researchers prefer to avoid tackling taboo subjects such as personal violence, sexual abuse, addiction, alienation, self-destruction, etc., for fear of violating the tenets of cultural relativism and of contributing to popular racist stereotypes. Anthropology's cautious and often self-censored approaches to social marginalization have obfuscated an ethnographic understanding of the multifaceted dynamics of the experience of oppression, and, ironically, sometimes even serve to minimize the depths of human suffering involved. It is safer and easier to retreat into documenting the "poetics" of exotic "others." It remains to be seen whether anthropology is prepared to face the twenty-first century's challenges as poverty is increasingly concentrated into segregated metropolises.

Notes

1 According to the 1990 Census, in East Harlem 48.3 percent of males and 35.2 percent of females over sixteen were officially reported as employed—compared to a citywide average of 64.3 percent for men and 49 percent for women. Another 10.4 percent of the men and 5.7 percent of the women in East Harlem were actively looking for legal work (City of New York 1993). In El Barrio as a whole, 37 percent of all residents received some combination of Public Assistance, Supplemental Social Security Income, and/or Medicaid benefits.
2 Angel dust, known as PCP or "Zootie," is an animal tranquilizer that is sprinkled on mint leaves which are then smoked in joints. It was the national drug scourge of the mid-1970s and continues to be popular among the younger generation in El Barrio.
3 Both of these police actions were reported in the local print and television media, but I am withholding the cities to protect the anonymity of my street address.
4 Significantly there are sub-sectors of the service industry that are relatively unionized—such as hospital and custodial work—where there is a limited autonomous space for street culture and working-class resistance.
5 "Fight the Power" is a rap song composed in 1990 by the African-American group, Public Enemy.

The author would like to thank the following institutions for their support: The Harry Frank Guggenheim Foundation, The Russell Sage Foundation, The Social Science Research Council, The National Institute on Drug Abuse, The Wenner-Gren Foundation for Anthropological Research, The United States Bureau of the Census, the San Francisco Urban Institute, and San Francisco State University. Finally, this could not have been written without the typing of Harold Otto, Henry Ostendorf, and, most importantly, Charles Pearson.

The article is a revised and condensed version of material presented originally in the following two publications: 1) "From *Jíbaro* to Crack Dealer: Confronting Capitalism in Spanish Harlem." In *Articulating Hidden Histories: Anthropology, History, and the Influence of Eric R. Wolf*, pp. 125–141, eds. Jane Schneider and Rayna Rapp. Berkeley: University of California Press. 1995. 2) "The Political Economy of Resistance and Self-Destruction in the Crack Economy: An Ethnographic Perspective." In *Annals of the New York Academy of Science*, Vol. 749, pp. 23–44, 1995.

A South Indian Caste in a Bombay Slum

OWEN M. LYNCH

*Indian society is divided along regional, linguistic, sectarian,
and caste lines. A "caste" in India is a group of people who
become members of the group at birth through biological
descent from other members who share a common name for
the group, and who generally do not marry outside the group.
There is a ranking of different castes in terms of power,
prestige, and ritual purity. Members of lower castes, especially
"untouchables," can pollute members of higher castes through
contact. This overly simple explanation of caste in India can
help explain one of the several identities borne by the Adi-
Dravidas, who are a low-ranking caste from southern India and
who have migrated to the metropolis of Bombay in West India.
In that city, different political parties compete for their votes.
One party calls on them to identify as "untouchables,"
members of the lowest-ranking caste, on an all-India basis;
another party bids them to remember their south Indian roots.
The way in which the Adi-Dravidas define themselves
politically is thus related both to their position in Bombay as
rural migrants from another region and to their caste.*

Shantinagar,[1] a pseudonym, has a reputation for being one of the
worst—if not the worst—slums in Bombay, India. It is inhabited
mainly by squatters from all parts of India. Much of the land is
swampy but the squatters are slowly filling it in as their settlements
creep across vacant space. Low-lying land is often flooded with
black, swampy, garbage-laden water during the monsoon season.

Source: Article written expressly for *Urban Life*.

A view of Shantinagar with upper-middle-class neighborhood in background. [Photo by Owen M. Lynch]

Perhaps this location helped make Shantinagar notoriously famous for the steaming stills that produced the bootleg liquor wetting many a thirsty tongue in Bombay.

One of the first things that hits the eye, when setting foot in Shantinagar and other places like it in Bombay, is the flags of many political parties waving conspicuously in the wind. Picketed here and there are the red and black of the Dravidian Progressive Federation (hereafter DMK), the blue and white of the Republican Party (hereafter RPI), the orange and green of the Congress Party, the red of the Shiv Sena, and the green of the Muslim League. What does this mean? Are these flags just for show or are they signs of real political life, activity, involvement, and consciousness?

In this paper a partial answer to these questions will be given by looking at them within the context of one of the communities, the Adi-Dravidas, who live in Shantinagar. The Adi-Dravidas of

Shantinagar are highly politicized and easily mobilized for political ends, issues, and symbols. They are politically conscious, aware, and involved. The first purpose of this paper is, then, to describe political life and its extent among these Adi-Dravidas. The second purpose is to explain their high level of political mobilization in terms of an ongoing process which maintains it.

Who Are the Adi-Dravidas?

Adi-Dravidas are a Tamil-speaking untouchable caste from Tamilnadu state in India. In Tamilnadu they are also known as *Paraiyan*, a name supposedly derived from the Tamil word *parai* for drum and from the association of this caste with drumming at village ceremonies and festivals (Thurston 1909:77). None of the Bombay Adi-Dravidas like the name Paraiyan and only reluctantly admit to it. Adi-Dravida is, however, a more acceptable name, although it is also a name which they show some reluctance to use. Adi means first and Dravida means settler in south India. The Adi-Dravidas claim to be the indigenous people of south India—those who were in India long before the Aryans, Brahmans, and Indic-speaking people invaded and conquered much of what is north India today. Sub-caste differences among Adi-Dravidas have for most purposes been eliminated, although there are occasional rumors of trouble over this. Although both Christians and Hindus are in the community, interfaith marriages take place without much difficulty.

Adi-Dravidas began migrating to Bombay about one hundred years ago. They came to work in Shantinagar's tanneries, which at that time were well outside the city's main settlement. To this day almost all Adi-Dravidas come from the same district of Tinnevelly in the south of Tamilnadu state.

The Adi-Dravida population in Shantinagar continues to increase with new migrants coming all the time. Today's migrants, however, are more sophisticated than the pioneer arrivals. Literacy is high and many, both male and female, read and write. Seventy percent (N 42) of male respondents were literate, using a fourth standard or better education as a criterion of literacy. Work in the tanneries has decreased and today Adi-Dravidas work in various occupations throughout Bombay. Eighteen percent (N 11) of respondents worked as dock laborers; 58 percent (N 35) as factory workers; and 23 percent (N 14) worked in various jobs such as truck driver, small shop owner, etc. Participation in unions is, moreover, relatively high with 63 percent (N 38) of respondents claiming union membership and 87 percent (N 33) of these reporting interest in union activities.

Mobilization

On the whole, Adi-Dravida political life in Shantinagar is divided between two parties, the DMK and the RPI. The DMK is a regional party that originated and remains primarily in Tamilnadu state. At the time of study, the DMK had almost complete control of Tamilnadu state government and had won enough seats in parliament for Madame Gandhi and the Congress party to take note and consideration of it.

The DMK was founded in Shantinagar about 1950. Today there are fourteen branches for all of Bombay city. Shantinagar is one of these branches. The Bombay general office and the Shantinagar branch office are one and the same. The meeting house is on a small side street off the main road of Shantinagar and is called, appropriately enough, Dravidian House.

The Shantinagar branch office has ten units of the party in various Adi-Dravida chawls or streets throughout the area. Although many of these units have meeting houses, not all are tightly organized and active; some are split by factional quarrels. The Shantinagar branch, however, is tightly organized under four men of the community who have respectable white-collar jobs elsewhere in Bombay.

What kind of political life do Adi-Dravidas of the DMK have in Shantinagar? First of all the DMK under its leaders can and does mobilize the entire community. The leaders have organizational skills and experience, as well as firsthand contacts with party members throughout the area. These contacts are constantly renewed by visits to the other branches and units, as well as by visits of members to Dravidian House. The ability of the leaders to mobilize the community depends to some extent upon the presence of external threat. Adi-Dravidas are south Indians, and in Bombay there is resentment against people from the south. Native Maharashtrians feel that the south Indians are taking away from them much needed jobs. This is one of the reasons for the rise of the Shiv Sena, a local party of Maharashtra state. Indeed, the Shiv Sena was at one time strongly anti-south Indian, though its overt expression of this theme was tempered at the time of study.

In 1968 when the Shiv Sena was particularly active, the DMK was the nucleus around which Adi-Dravidas gathered for protection. In one incident the police and the Adi-Dravidas of Shantinagar clashed; knives were drawn, and in the end a number of police were hurt and about thirty south Indians put in jail. An association was then formed called the South Indian Association in which the DMK leaders were particularly active. The Association sponsored a dance program in Bombay's Shanmukhananda Hall. Twenty-three thousand rupees were collected to hire lawyers for the imprisoned south Indians, all of whom were acquitted while the lawyers, all non-south Indians, were handsomely rewarded.

In 1967 the DMK was able to organize a number of meetings in which money was raised to support the electoral campaign of the DMK back in Madras state. It is reported that eighteen thousand rupees were raised and that Chief Minister Karunanidhi of Tamilnadu came to Shantinagar and delivered a speech.

The leaders of the DMK have also proven themselves within the community. Before the advent of the DMK there was a caste association of the Adi-Dravidas known as the Adi Dravida Mahajana Sangham (Adi-Dravida People's Society). This organization had come under the control of one man whose caste-oriented views did not accord with the broader political views of the DMK leaders and their own quest for leadership status. Through some sort of maneuvers, which they admit and which I could never definitely uncover, the DMK leaders were able to sidetrack the Sangham leader and reduce his organization to one virtually in name only.

More striking than these organizational and defensive activities, however, are the rallies and meetings that the DMK is continually running and sponsoring. These events are attended by large crowds of men and children who come to hear the politicians' speeches. Whether or not one attends, reports of what is said travel quickly and by the next day are subjects of analysis and critique.

During the 1971 elections to the central parliament, meetings of the various parties in Shantinagar, particularly among the Adi-Dravidas, were at a peak. Adi-Dravidas sponsored some events and attended many others of all parties. Before the elections, election lists were checked and potential voters contacted. On election day itself these lists were assiduously checked to get lazy voters and women to the polls. Techniques for voting twice or thrice were well known and relished as a form of political gamesmanship, so that some voted in the names of the dead or those no longer resident in Shantinagar. Children were also paid a few cents to go up and down the roads chanting slogans, to carry banners, ride on loud-speaker trucks, and distribute campaign literature. Socialization into politics is, then, very much a part of becoming an Adi-Dravida in Bombay.

Behind these activities there is a strong ideological pull from the DMK to which the Adi-Dravidas are drawn. The DMK is a sub-national party representing primarily the interests of the Tamil-speaking people of Tamilnadu state. For the Adi-Dravidas it is, then, a symbol of, as well as organizational contact with, their "native place," their home district, their linguistic roots and their Tamil culture. Adi-Dravidas are proud to be Dravidians and take pride in telling of the beauties of Tamil language and culture. This is all very important in Bombay where they are immigrants speaking a foreign tongue and possessing a foreign subculture. One informant explained this to me thus:

> We live in Maharashtra state; therefore, if we don't have the
> party, people will forget their language and culture. Moreover,
> it does no good if we become like Maharashtrians and learn
> Marathi and forget our motherland. Why? Because even then
> we are treated like south Indians and discriminated against.

Thus, the need for protective unity and organization strengthens pride in Tamil ethnicity and pleasure derived from Tamil language and culture. That need the party can and does satisfy not only by its activities and organization but also by day-to-day activities. In the party office and in various other places in Shantinagar, one can find reading rooms in which copies of Tamil newspapers and magazines are available. Political interest and contact are, thus, kept high.

Among the Adi-Dravidas there is some separation of class, as opposed to caste, issues. When asked the question, "Some say the government does not help the hutment-dwelling people because it is in control of the rich people, others say it is in control of the upper castes, what is your opinion?" 18 percent (N 11) replied the government was in control of the upper castes, 42 percent (N 25) replied the rich people, 17 percent (N 10) replied both, and 23 percent (N 14) replied neither. During the 1971 parliamentary elections no other issue generated more enthusiasm or discussion than Madame Gandhi's promise to eliminate poverty. That issue, as no other, generated a consciousness of kind that temporarily crossed caste, ethnic, and religious boundaries in Shantinagar.

The ideology of the DMK appeals to the Adi-Dravidas through its concern for the poorer classes, its anti-Brahman undertones, and its stress on egalitarianism. Adi-Dravidas are both poor and untouchable; the DMK promises to eliminate both poverty and untouchability. Given these anti-upper class and anti-upper caste feelings and their bitter resentment of discrimination, much of the DMK ideology and promises to put rice in every pot and a Brahman in every prison does appeal to the Adi-Dravidas. Yet in my interviews with them there was a definite uncertainty and ambiguity in their feelings about whether or not the DMK *really* was for them and was helping the untouchables in Madras state. Why then do they identify with the party and its goals? There are a number of reasons for this. First, identification with the party in Bombay provides a self in which they can take pride. In Bombay most Adi-Dravidas say, "We are free to go where we will and eat what we want. Nobody here pays any attention to our caste." It would be foolish for them to identify themselves in this city as untouchable and to add the stigma of untouchability to that of being south Indian.

Adi-Dravidas take an evident pleasure in identifying with, and being a part of, a winning and successful party such as the DMK has proved itself to be in Tamilnadu. They also take great pride in identifying with C. N. Annadurai, or Anna as he is called, the sainted founder of the party. Anna told them to be proud of their Tamil language and their Dravidian background. Anna, too, traveled overseas to America where he was for some time at Yale University. Now that he is dead, Anna is above question and has become the symbol par excellence around which they can unite. His origins are said to be poor and he was said to be for the poorer classes. Those who depart from what the Adi-Dravidas feel was Anna's message are not true followers of the DMK. Thus, it is not the party that may be at fault, it is only the leaders in it who may be at fault.

The final reason for identification with the DMK lies in the fact that the Adi-Dravidas in Bombay are an immigrant group, speaking a foreign language, and having customs different from those of the native Maharashtrians. In such a situation ethnicity becomes relevant both structurally and culturally when there is a struggle for scarce resources. The DMK is defined in not only structural but also cultural opposition to the Shiv Sena in Bombay through a clear enunciation and definition of the ethnic symbols of Dravidian culture, language, and society. This definition of the situation gives shape to the symbols and organizations selected to protect and enunciate the demands of foreign migrants versus local indigenes. Moreover, the DMK in Tamilnadu is a powerful party, which even Madame Gandhi must recognize. It is much more useful to link one's survival and one's struggle for existence and respectability in a hostile foreign environment to the DMK star with national influence than to a purely caste-based satellite with little organization or political clout such as the RPI. The sum and substance of the DMK in Shantinagar is that it is not an ethnic group with para-political functions; rather, it is a political group with para-ethnic functions.

Although the DMK is the dominant party among the Adi-Dravidas of Shantinagar, there is a significant minority party, the RPI. The RPI was founded in 1956 by the late Dr. B. R. Ambedkar, himself an untouchable, who became the first Minister for Law in

Adi-Dravida children in Shantinagar celebrate the birthday of Anna, founder of the DMK. [Photo by Owen M. Lynch]

independent India. The RPI is primarily of and for untouchables. In Shantinagar the RPI is not as well organized or as popular as the DMK. It does have meetings, officers, a small meeting house, and a series of public programs much like those of the DMK. The RPI, unlike the DMK, appeals to those who feel strongly the sting of untouchability. Republicans feel that the DMK has tricked the Adi-Dravidas and is really doing nothing for them.

In addition to their feeling that the DMK is really not doing anything for the untouchables and the Adi-Dravidas, the Republicans also have another reason for belonging to their party, and this is a more practical one. In their opinion their party is a national party, not a sub-national one as is the DMK. Moreover, the party has a following in the state of Maharashtra where it is supported by the Mahar caste, Ambedkar's own community. Republican party members have been elected to the Bombay Municipal Corporation. This is a very useful tie for squatters, such as the Adi-Dravidas, in Bombay. With some help from the RPI corporators, it is claimed, the Adi-Dravidas have been able to arrange to have water taps opened in their own chawls, though at

A main road in Shantinagar during the monsoon. [Photo by Owen M. Lynch]

their own expense. Getting water taps in a squatter area is a big problem since most of the people are there illegally. Electric connections have also been installed in many chawls through political connections, and, in 1970, the RPI through its municipal corporator was able to have ten street light posts installed. During the same year, a latrine for women was opened in one of the swampy fields so that the women would not have to use the open field. Unfortunately no arrangements for water or for sweepers to clean it out were made, so the women still use the open field and distillers use the latrine as a storehouse for the locally distilled moonshine.

The street lights and the latrine, as well as the electric connections, are a basis for public debate between the RPI and the DMK. Each claims to have accomplished these improvements and uses them to recruit Adi-Dravidas to their party.

Discussion and Conclusions

The Adi-Dravidas of Shantinagar are politically mobilized; they actively participate in local-level politics, are aware of political issues, and have a leadership with organizational skills. Political forms and symbols have also become the major framework upon which the organization of the community is hung. There are important linkages to the arena of higher-level structure and issues that are not localized and that integrate them into city, state, and national levels of political and social life. The analysis of political mobilization at the micro-level is important, then, because it provides some understanding of the kind and extent of change that is taking place in the urban areas of India. It also provides some understanding of what macro-level changes in political life and economy mean when they reach down into ongoing social life at the micro-level.

The major process maintaining this political mobilization is ethnic polarization. This is a process whereby under urban cultural and social constraints rural forms of caste organization are superseded by those of an ethnic form of organization. The phenomenon of ethnicity has largely been overlooked in India because it has been assumed that caste organization subsumes or substitutes for that of ethnicity. Yet there are reasons that negate such an assumption and which on closer inspection make ethnic forms of group organization particularly salient. Ethnicity has been defined as a situation in which:

> [T]he members of interest groups who cannot organize
> themselves formally will thus tend to make use, though largely
> unconsciously, of whatever cultural mechanisms are available
> in order to articulate the organization of their grouping. And it
> is here in such situations, that political ethnicity comes into
> being. (Cohen 1974a: xviii)

Ethnicity is, then, essentially a political phenomenon, and a form
"of interaction between cultural groups operating within common
social contexts" (Cohen 1974a: xv).

In the case of the Adi-Dravidas, caste organization has been
replaced by that of political party organization at the local level.
This is not surprising when a number of factors are considered.
First, in a large city such as Bombay, castes, but not the caste
system, exist. The caste system of rural India in which there is a
hierarchical arrangement of politically, religiously, economically,
and socially interdependent castes each with its own rights and
duties, functions, and customs does not exist in large heterogenous
cities of India. In such places the principles of social organization
are different, more complex, rationalized, and bureaucratic; here,
castes cannot and do not interact according to the traditional
principles of the rural caste system. Rather, the principles of caste
interaction are primarily political and *competitive*; the valency of
the system is political. (Similar arguments have been made by Fox
1967; Bailey 1963; and Leach 1960.) This fact has been quickened
by the advent of parliamentary politics and universal suffrage in
India.

Second, the Adi-Dravidas themselves are in many ways heterogenous. They come from different counties and villages in the
Tinnevelly district of Tamilnadu; they are of different religions—
Hindu, Protestant, and Catholic; they work at different jobs in
different parts of Bombay; there exist among them latent sub-caste
differences; they are mobile geographically as well as occupationally; and, as individuals in Bombay, they are freer from caste
restraints, control, and customs than in their native places. Given
such heterogeneity there are few traditional leaders and principles
of organization to which all give assent and respect. Some form of
organization and symbolism other than that of caste courts
(panchayats) and leaders is necessary to overcome and incorporate
this heterogeneity.

At first, it would seem that caste associations might arise in such
situations. But that overlooks the definition of the situation in which
the Adi-Dravidas of Bombay find themselves and the fact that the
Adi-Dravida Mahajana Sangham has been replaced by the DMK.
The Adi-Dravidas are immigrants and foreigners, as well as

culturally distinct in Bombay society. The DMK articulates the symbols, beliefs, and myths of Dravidian culture and separateness and provides the organizational structure within which they can unite as a group in Bombay. The roots of the DMK are in structural *conflict* over access to strategic resources and in cultural *opposition* to other groups, such as the Shiv Sena among the Maharashtrians, seeking those resources. In this sense the DMK and the Shiv Sena arise out of similar causes and out of similarly structured definitions of the situation. Caste associations cannot articulate or organize such a definition of the situation in which migration and ethnicity are paramount. That definition of the situation in Bombay also helps to explain why there is among Shantinagar's Adi-Dravidas great interest in, and support of, DMK politics back in Tamilnadu state. The DMK provides the myths and symbols of ethnic identity and organization in a way that other parties, such as the Congress, cannot and could not because of their all-India orientation and heritage. DMK success and strength in Tamilnadu is indirect support for local ethnicity in Bombay. The stronger the DMK is in Tamilnadu and in New Delhi, the more likely are ethnic demands for defense or help in Bombay to be heard and heeded.

Local-level parties, as ethnic phenomena, are also more salient than caste associations because they are symbolically caste-neutral but structurally allow caste interests to be aggregated and expressed. By the same token they are class-neutral but allow the class-based demands of an urban proletariat to be aggregated and expressed.

The RPI plays on the recessive themes of caste identity and untouchableness in Bombay. There is always the threat that those themes could become salient, and it is not easy for all Adi-Dravidas to suppress them completely. Those who define their situation in those terms are loyal to the RPI. The RPI is an organizational complement to the DMK because of its access to the Bombay Municipal Corporation.

The study of ethnicity in India has much to offer in terms of a general theory of ethnicity. First of all, it forces one to look to the definition of the situation that by and large determines the cultural form and symbols a group will select. This is to some extent overlooked by theorists of ethnicity such as Cohen (1974). Second, it shows that ethnicity can be expressed directly through political organization rather than through para-political organization. Finally, it suggests a different and intriguing approach to the dynamics of urban social structure in India. Such an approach pulls aside to some extent the now leaden sociological blinders of caste and casteism and asks us to look at India afresh. It suggests that similar processes, producing similar phenomena, are at work in India as in the USA, Nigeria, and elsewhere under the impact of national politics, industrialization, and worldwide interdependence of nation states. What is going on in India is a "civil politics of primordial compromise" (Geertz 1973:310) in which the conflicts between new identities and definitions of the situation are brought about by the very process of modernization itself. The problem, then, is not to destroy them but to domesticate them (Geertz 1973:277).

Epilogue

After the death of C. N. Annadurai, the DMK in Tamilnadu and Shantinagar split into two factions: the DMK and the AIADMK (All India Anna Dravidian Progressive Federation) led by the enormously popular film star M. G. Ramachandran (MGR) who claimed to inherit the mantle of Annadurai. Under MGR, AIADMK became and is the dominant faction. Shantinagar continues to be the scene of occasional riots and the Shiv Sena has become more powerful and more strident in its demands. In 1993 Bombay was racked by riots between Hindus and Muslims when Shantinagar was the scene of some of the most violent rioting and many were killed. Just how the Adi-Dravidas fared is not clear, but their need for ethnic identity, political organization, and united protection has never been greater.

Note

[1] The research for this paper was conducted for fourteen months during 1970 and 1971. It was generously supported by a grant from the American Council of Learned Societies and was supplemented by a fellowship from the American Institute of Indian Studies. The methods used included participant observation, interviews with leaders, and a questionnaire administered to sixty Adi-Dravidas in Anna chawl of Shantinagar. References to material on squatters in India may be found in Lynch (1979). A full study of ethnicity and identity change among urban untouchables may be found in Lynch (1969).

Urban Women as Political Activists
Mérida, Yucatán, Mexico

KATHLEEN LOGAN

Several articles in this collection have focused on the differences between men and women in the roles that they play in cities. Bourgois, for instance, has given his attention to men in how they related to women in an office situation ("Office Work and the Crack Alternative"). Other articles, such as the ones on migration by Brettell and Nelson, gave their attention to women. In this article, Kathleen Logan deals with the way in which women in the Mexican city of Mérida have "engendered" politics, that is, brought the concerns and interests' of women to the fore of political action.

As Kathleen Logan makes clear, "women" are not a uniform category. Rather, like men, they are divided along socioeconomic lines. Politically active working-class and middle-class women have different goals, and they rarely collaborate in political action. She shows this by contrasting middle-class reformers with working-class community organizers in Mérida.

For those who are unfamiliar with Mexican politics, the different roles of political parties may be unfamiliar. Since the 1920s, one political party, the Institutional Revolutionary Party (or PRI in its Spanish abbreviation) has held a monopoly of power. However, in recent elections, including the national election of 1994, it has been challenged on the left by the Democratic Revolutionary Party (PRD) and on the right by the National Action Party (PAN).

Source: Article written expressly for *Urban Life*.

Women in Mérida, Yucatán, Mexico have become known for their activism both as political partisans and as grassroots community organizers.[1] In the process of their engagement in politics, the women of Mérida have succeeded in engendering the politics of their city and state. Women's political participation, however, is divided along socioeconomic class lines. As a result, politically active working-class women and middle-class or elite women seldom work together toward the same goals. Consequently, the lack of unity among women forestalls the development of an agenda that could improve the lives of all women in the region.

The City as a Political Arena

During the past two decades many Mexicans have become dissatisfied with their nation's political and economic status quo. Consequently, increasingly greater numbers of Mexicans have become involved in reform efforts geared toward making their nation more politically and economically democratic. The reform efforts particularly focus upon bringing economic justice, holding honest elections, establishing a multiparty system and ending the decades-long dominance of the PRI (*Partido Revolucionario Institucional*), the party that has controlled the Mexican state since the early twentieth century.

One notable aspect of reform has been the entry of women into the once exclusively male domain of politics. While women in all parts of Mexico have become active politically, women in the southeastern state of Yucatán have taken an especially dynamic and central role. Mérida, the state capital and the region's largest city, has become the center for women's political activism.

As the state capital, Mérida is the center of governance and politics in Yucatán. It is the home of the state Congress, the Governor's office and the state bureaucracies as well as the Mayor's office and municipal offices. As the region's largest city, Mérida is also the economic hub of the state. The headquarters of the region's major corporations and professional and business organizations are here. In addition, Mérida is Yucatán's media and education center. The state's two universities are located in the city as are most of the state's technological institutes. The region's four daily newspapers and all of the major radio and television stations are based in Mérida.

Because of its position as the center of political, economic, and intellectual life in Yucatán, Mérida is the arena in which most of the political debate occurs and where most political actions originate. As a result, women in Mérida have considerable opportunity to be active politically and to make their influence felt. Middle-class and elite women of Mérida have become engaged politically in a variety of ways—as elected or appointed officials, candidates for office, political party activists, heads of state bureaucracies and leaders of urban civic associations.

The consequences of Mérida's urban growth also make the city a locale for women's activism. As is true of many cities in Latin America, Mérida's rapid urban growth is the result of rural-urban migration. As more and more rural migrants arrive, they find housing in the new residential working-class communities that ring the downtown area of Mérida. Often these communities lack elements of a public service infrastructure such as potable water, drainage, electricity, paved streets, sidewalks, or recreational areas. Consequently, the women of these communities become politically active by organizing campaigns in which they petition the government to supply the necessary services. In the case of these working-class women activists, the growth of the city itself provides the reason for their political engagement.

Women in Political Parties: Democratic Reform Efforts

During the period 1990–93 women were especially notable in their political presence. Women led the major state institutions during this time. Both the Governor of Yucatán and the Mayor of Mérida were women. The mayorships of four other municipalities, including two of the state's largest cities (Tizimin and Progreso), were also occupied by women. The Chief Justice of the State Supreme Court was a women as were two of the other four justices who served with her. That the posts of Governor, the Mayor, and the Chief Justice were occupied by women exemplified the success of individual women to rise within the structure of traditional political parties.

For the November 1993 elections, 23 percent of all the candidates running for office were women. The PAN (*Partido de Accion Nacional*, a right of center party and the major opposition to the PRI in Yucatán), nominated women as mayoral candidates for 20 of the 106 Yucatecan municipalities. The PAN nominees represent the largest number of women ever put forth for office by a political party in the state. That nearly a quarter of the candidates were women and that a major party put forth so many women for office demonstrates that political parties are beginning to recognize that women can be candidates and not simply behind the scenes support staff.

Certain other factors have also helped women gain political prominence.

Since until recently almost all elected officials were PRI and male, women as candidates for office, especially those from opposition parties, symbolically represent the greatest break from the politics of the past. Many observers think that the Mayor of Mérida, aside from her widely recognized talents as a public servant, was elected partly because as a woman and member of the leading opposition party in Yucatán (the PAN), she represented the most complete change offered voters.

In the eyes of many Yucatecans, women represent a political alternative not only because of their gender but also because of the gender-linked attributes women are believed to possess. Simply put, women are commonly thought to represent a higher moral authority.

And so, as public servants, women are expected to be more honest, trustworthy, and service oriented than men. As a result, when fraud, opportunism, and ineffectiveness are issues, women are likely to be sought as candidates to clean up government. Such has been the case in several Yucatecan towns where male mayors have either been removed from or voted out of office and replaced by women.

The PAN has been particularly active in seeking out women to run for local office in Yucatán. Local PAN activists say that the party has chosen women as candidates because they represent change and the hope for better government. But PAN members also report that sometimes it is easier to recruit women because men fear that if they run as opposition candidates, the PRI-dominated government will retaliate against them by threatening their jobs and businesses.

Sometimes the PRI has sought to nullify their opposition's "clean government" women candidates by putting women from their own party in office. Some Yucatecans believe that such a move by the PRI was in part responsible for the appointment of Governor Sauri to office as a counterpoint to the election of Ana Rosa Payan of the PAN to the Mayorship of Mérida. Such countermoves obviously also increase the number of women in public service.

There also seems to be a geometric effect in having women in public office. Once in power women serve as an inspiration and role model for other women to run for elected positions. As one woman mayoral candidate commented, "If there can be a woman as Governor of Yucatán than there can be a woman as Mayor of my town."

That women are becoming more integrated into partisan politics is also evident in the policy-making and leadership positions of the region's major parties. Women either head the party as in the case of the PAN or have central policy-making positions as with the PRI.

Women also have a conspicuous presence in the state bureaucracies of Yucatán. During 1990–93 there were over one hundred women at the managerial level in state agencies. Most of these women were appointed to their posts by the state's Governor. Although the Governor has declared herself an "anti-feminist" in several interviews, she, nonetheless, has appointed more women to head state bureaucracies than any other previous governor. Some of the women appointed to office by the Governor have, in turn, selected other women to serve with them in the state's bureaucracies.

It is important to note that this infusion of women into the politics of Yucatán represents an initial class of political actors. In nearly every case, the women are the first to occupy their particular post; only a very few of them are the second women to serve in a specific position. In addition, it is also important to recognize that while men still outnumber women in political positions and women still do not serve in proportion to their percentage of the population, Yucatecan women have succeeded in placing themselves at the center of politics and democratic reform in their state.

Women in Urban Civil Associations: Democratic Reform Efforts

Women's political activities for democratic reform in Yucatán extend far beyond their involvement in partisan politics. Women have also been instrumental in forming urban civil associations dedicated to democratic reform.

A group of young middle-class and elite women in Mérida together with a Roman Catholic priest have founded *Indignacion*, the first human rights organization in Yucatán. Indignacion investigates complaints of human rights violations and brings them to the attention of state authorities. The group also seeks redress of such violations by influencing public opinion via the local press. As the November 1993 elections approached, Indignacion also put public service announcements in the Mérida newspapers explaining basic voting rights.

In addition, several-score women in Mérida, primarily from the middle and elite classes, have formed the *Mujeres de Yucatán por la Democracia* (Yucatecan Women for Democracy), an urban civic association that focuses on democratic reform, particularly in regard

to honest and representative elections. The Mujeres de Yucatán por
la Democracia especially focuses on monitoring elections, public
education about democracy, and protesting human rights violations. For the fall 1993 elections, the Mujeres published a bilingual
(Maya and Spanish) pamphlet about citizen participation in
democracy.

Indignacion and Mujeres de Yucatán por la Democracia are
organizations that women have formed and where women lead. But
women are powerful in organizations that are headed by men as
well. The *Frente Civico Familiar* (Family Civic Front) and the
Movimiento Ciudadano por la Democracia (Citizen's Movement for
Democracy) are urban-based civil associations that seek democratic
reform. Like most groups dedicated to democratic reform, the FCF
and the MCD focus their demands on an end to manipulated vote
counts, single party dominance, and the overlapping identity of the
PRI with the Mexican government. Both groups have a male leadership but women are central to the activities and policy making of
the organizations.

Women are also important in groups that arise in the countryside
but which operate in Mérida as the seat of political power. One such
group is the *Frente Civico Yucateco 25 de junio* (Yucatecan Civic
Front of June 25th). The Frente protests against the state's agrarian
policies and the human rights violations that have occurred as a
consequence of these protests. From June 1992 until February
1994, the Frente has had an encampment in front of the Governor's
Palace in Mérida expressing its opposition to the state's agrarian
reform policies and also protesting the arrest of campesino leaders
involved in the June 25, 1992 demonstration against the state's
agrarian reform actions. While three individuals (one man and a
wife and husband team) provide the core of the Frente's leadership,
the woman is the president of the organization.

The women of the FCF, the MCD, Indignacion, and the Mujeres
de Yucatán por la Democracia represent the considerable activism
of middle-class and elite urban women in politics centered around
issues of democratic political reform. The activist women of the
Frente Civico Yucateco 25 de Junio, many of whom are low income
or working class, focus more on economic reform issues. The
women of the Frente thus have much in common with the women
who practice another kind of political activism in Mérida: campaigns
for public services.

Women as Community Organizers: Working-Class Women's Campaigns for Public Services

As important as middle-class and elite women have become in electoral politics and democratic reform efforts, women's political activism in Mérida has not been limited to these two kinds of political participation nor to activism by economically advantaged women. As in many urban areas of Latin America (Jelin 1990; Safa 1990), thousands of working-class women in the city have also become politically active primarily by organizing collectively to make claims on the government. As residents of the growing working-class communities surrounding the inner city of Mérida, they often lack basic public services such as potable water, drainage, electricity, paved streets, sidewalks, and recreation areas. Consequently, to get these services, working-class women mount campaigns to get the state to provide them.

In seeking these public services, women rely on time-honored mechanisms of protest and demand making such as forming clientalistic ties with politicians, staging public demonstrations, petitioning government officials and sending delegations to government offices.

Many of women's collective actions in Yucatán transpire under the umbrella of the Roman Catholic Church. As an institution, the Roman Catholic Church in Yucatán has not been much affected by contemporary transformations taking place within Catholicism. Neither the charisma nor theology of liberation movements, which have been so important in encouraging religiously based community activism in other parts of Latin America, have taken hold.

In Yucatán the Church remains steadfast in its traditional interpretation of its place in society. It does not see as its purpose to offer social criticism nor to encourage community activism. The Church instead stresses adherence to its dogma, observance of its rituals, and the importance of the spiritual in daily life.

Nonetheless, the Church, despite its traditional stance, does provide a base for community activism in low-income neighborhoods of Mérida primarily because of its social centrality and dominance as an institution in such areas. In most low-income neighborhoods of the city, the Church is not only the sole extra-community institution present but it also occupies a central position in the community social structure. The Church offers its parishioners traditional religious services, social activities, welfare, and self-improvement programs such as Alcoholics Anonymous.

Many Yucatecan women first become active in the Church in

time-honored ways such as serving as catechists, supporting the calendar of religious festivals, attending mass and rosary groups, and cleaning and decorating the church buildings. Because of the shortage of clergy, however, Catholic lay women have the opportunity to take more responsibility and leadership than they would otherwise. Particularly important for women are the rosary and Bible study groups. In many low-income neighborhoods in Mérida, dozens of groups with eight to ten members apiece come together each week to pray and discuss their faith. No clergy supervise these meetings.

The groups' discussions, however, seldom stay on purely religious topics. Family issues, especially alcoholism and family violence, and household concerns, such as rising prices and the lack of public services, become the central focuses of conversation. For women, these groups come to assume an importance in their lives beyond their initial spiritual purpose. As many women express it, the meetings give them a much appreciated break from their household and child care duties. The women consider the time spent in the rosary/discussion groups as time for themselves.

In their meetings, women begin to realize that they are not alone in having to confront alcoholism, increasing bus fares, or seasonal flooding because of faulty drainage. For many women, the local group meetings are their first experience with a public forum where their thoughts and ideas are taken seriously. For many, it is also their initial experience in reflecting critically upon the conditions in which they live. Since the local clergy exercise almost no oversight for (and, in fact, have little interest in) these weekly neighborhood meetings, women are free to structure them as they wish. Out of the weekly prayer and discussion groups grow many of the collective actions of the low-income women of Mérida.

In their claims making on the state, working-class women often engender their actions by using their status as housewives and mothers as the context in which to frame their requests. For example, a local community leader from one of Mérida's low-income neighborhoods petitioned the state for land for women in her community on which they could raise fruits and vegetables for their families' consumption or to sell in local markets. In her request for these garden plots, the activist emphasized the women's devotion to their families and their hard work as mothers. She was also careful to present herself as a humble grandmother making requests on her community's behalf. She did not mention her history as an organizer of the vendors in the downtown market of Mérida, also part of her identity as an activist but one that did not fit her carefully constructed image as a humble grandmother.

Mérida working-class community activists meet to discuss community problems and seek solutions. The woman in the center of the photo is their leader. [Photo by Kathleen Logan]

In another low-income community, women also engendered their petitioning of the state for public services by emphasizing their status as mothers; in this case, by making their requests through their children. When the Governor of Yucatán in the late 1980s came to a nearby community to inaugurate a new housing project, he was greeted by scores of children carrying placards describing the plight of their community without electricity, paved streets, or a drainage system. The women made certain that the children were dressed in their best clothes and that the youngest and most appealing children were at the front of the demonstration where they would not only catch the eye of the Governor but also the cameras of the news media assembled for the event.

After the demonstration for the Governor, the women of this community did get electricity for the areas of their community that had gone without it. Electricity was installed first because it is the easiest and least expensive public utility for the state to put in. The more expensive components of the public service infrastructure such as potable water, drainage, and paved streets were not placed in the community, although they were promised to it. Street paving particularly will have to await the installation of the pipes for water and drainage for to do otherwise would necessitate removing the pavement already in place.

Both of these claims-making actions on the state by the women from working-class neighborhoods were successful in part. In the first case, some forty women did get garden plots, which they held for several years. Unfortunately, the question of legal land ownership—often problematic in the expanding outer periphery of Mérida—arose. The land they held is now the likely construction site of a new middle-class residential subdivision.

The collective actions of the women from these two urban communities are examples of the kind of organizing efforts working-class women in Mérida have mounted. While their actions have not always yielded lasting results nor brought all of the benefits women desire, the material improvements women do get for their communities represent a betterment of their lives in, at least, some respects and constitute an important source of personal and political empowerment for the activists.

Engendering Politics in Yucatán

The mechanisms and motivations for women's political participation in Mérida are distinct along socioeconomic class lines. Women from the middle class and the elites are more likely to become active politically in partisan political parties or urban civic associations and organize themselves around political reform issues. Working-class women tend to be active politically as grass-roots organizers and form their activities around campaigns to get public services for their communities or to protest state economic policies. For middle-class and elite women, the re-structuring of Mexican democracy is their most important issue; for working-class women, it is the improvement of their economic status.

Working-class women are likely to organize their political actions around their status as mothers and housewives. When they make their demands that the government provide their communities with basic public services, working-class women voice their demands within the context of their rights and responsibilities as mothers. The working-class community activists of Mérida define motherhood to include collective organizing in the public arena as appropriate behavior congruent with the traditional definition of women as family and community caretakers. Their mode of political involvement as rooted in their notion of motherhood follows that of other working-class women community activists in Latin America (Alvarez 1989; Molyneux 1985; Kaplan 1982).

In contrast, middle-class and elite women are more likely to frame their political participation in terms of citizens demanding their rights within a democracy. As elected or appointed officials or as activists in urban civil associations, they do not engender their political actions in clear or overt ways. Middle-class and elite women do not directly call upon their status as mothers and housewives as a base for political activism as working-class women are likely to do.

Regardless of the source of women's motivation to be active politically, what is the nature of the nexus between women's political activism and the Yucatán state government? With women occupying prominent and powerful positions within the local state government does this indicate that there will be state-sponsored support for women and attention paid to women's issues?

For middle-class and elite women who are active in urban civil associations, their protests to the PRI-dominated state government for democratic reform puts them in opposition to the women who are PRI office holders. As a result, there has been little public dialogue indicating a link between them. For some urban civil associations in which women participate significantly (such as the FCF) there has been some dialogue with the PAN through women who are supporters of both. For the most part, however, middle-class and elite women who are active in urban civil associations choose to maintain their independence from all political parties in the state and the state government as well.

For working-class women their nexus with the state government and state office holders is quite different because to make their campaigns for services successful, they need to be linked with those individuals within the state government who control resources. For decades this has meant that activists needed to be linked to the PRI because the party dominated the power structure and controlled the distribution of state resources.

Consequently, working-class community activists have had little choice in where to turn for help. Simply, those communities with the most viable ties to the PRI were the most successful in garnering resources from the state. In Mérida, several neighborhoods have prevailed over other communities to get electricity, garden plots, and recreational facilities for themselves because of the neighborhoods' link to the PRI through certain women activists.

Throughout its history, when the PRI has had a project on women, it has focused upon women as they operate within a limited definition of the family and community. The party has not recognized any expansion of a definition of motherhood into an activist mode with women operating in the public arena such as the working-class women of Mérida have done (Logan 1990). The talents of these women seem to go unnoticed by the party and state officials. The best the community leaders can aspire to within the PRI power structure is to become grass-roots organizers for the party, positions where they will no doubt remain. A ceiling on their achievement seems to be in place because of gender and class biases against them.

Now, however, as Mexico evolves into a multiparty democracy the possibility exists that the state may not be exclusively dominated by the PRI.

The most likely alternative to the PRI in Yucatán is a regionally revitalized PAN. While it is difficult to predict the long range future of the PAN in Yucatán, the party has had some notable electoral success—its capturing the mayor's office of Mérida is the most obvious example. While the female mayor is not the first Panista mayor of Mérida (there was also a PAN mayor elected in 1967), she may be a harbinger of a PAN resurgence in the state. Her election indicates two noncontradictory trends: one, support for the PAN as an expression of popular discontent with the PRI and two, the possible emergence of the PAN as a true regional alternative to the PRI. For this reason, perhaps now working-class community activists will have to form alliances with PAN officials as well as PRI to improve their communities and economic status.

In the last several years, left of center parties such as the PRD (Partido de la Revolucion Democratica) and the PT (Partido de Trabajo) have entered the Yucatecan political arena. As political parties with a shorter history in Yucatán than the PAN, it is difficult to determine their potential political success, but they, like the PAN, may become regional political forces that will have resources to dispense to women activists involved in community campaigns for services.

Regardless of the political futures of the major political parties, however, how does having women in power affect the advancement of women generally in the region?

Having women in prominent political positions in Yucatán has not easily translated into a context helpful to women's activism nor to advances for women. Neither the Mayor nor the Governor has built her political career on women's issues. Neither has made women's concerns a part of her political agenda while in office. Neither has made attempts to form alliances with women activists of any socioeconomic class.

The absence of alliances between women in political office and community women activists of any socioeconomic class represents a missed opportunity to confront women's issues and improve the lives of Yucatecan women. The absence of linkages among women of different class backgrounds seems an opportunity lost.

In addition, it also seems unlikely that there will be state sponsored projects especially geared toward women. Efforts by female office holders to better the lives of women will most likely be incremental and based on improving conditions for all Yucatecans. Advances in education, health care, public services, and employment opportunities in the region will certainly benefit women even though they are not focused upon women as a distinct group.

Despite the lack of a women's agenda on the part of the female elected officials in Yucatán, there are some long-term benefits to having women active in electoral politics. The prominence of female politicians does create new socially accepted roles for women and provides role models for future generations of Yucatecan women. Also having women in public office may begin a trend of having more women elected or appointed to public office—and thus make women in state government less the exception and more the norm. Perhaps a space for women in public office has been opened in Yucatán.

The future of the women's political activism in Yucatán can take several alternative, and not necessarily mutually exclusive, paths.

First, working-class community activist women can continue to activate their networks of claims making whenever their communities have a particular need to be met and bring these needs to the attention of the state. The activists will persist in their community organizing as long as the material conditions of their lives remain as they are. Similarly, middle-class and elite women will likely continue to advocate for democratic reform until they see that it is achieved.

Second, if working-class women continue to meet regularly in small discussion groups such as they now do under the organizational umbrella of the Roman Catholic Church, they may develop a consciousness of their concerns, not only as housewives and mothers, but also as women. If this occurs, the chance of a popular feminism or a greater consciousness of gender subordination developing such as described as occurring elsewhere in Latin America is possible (Andreas 1985; Safa 1990). For a popular feminism to arise will depend very much on the changing consciousness of the activist women whose leadership first emerged in the neighborhood-based groups.

Similarly, middle-class and elite women, especially those who have used gender as a basis for their organizing (such as the Mujeres de Yucatán por la Democracia), may also begin to develop an enhanced gender consciousness. If so, they may create a feminist movement as other middle-class and elite women have done elsewhere in Mexico. Women who are elected or appointed to public office (almost always middle-class and elite women) may develop an agenda for women within the state bureaucracy.

Women's political activism in Yucatán has clearly placed women at the center of state government and of the movement for political reform. What women as political participants have not yet done is build alliances among women of different socioeconomic classes.

Note

¹ The research on middle-class and elite women's political participation was conducted during the summer of 1993 funded by a grant from the North-South Center at the University of Miami. Prof. Beatriz Castilla and Prof. Beatriz Torres of the Universidad Autonoma de Yucatán and Jane Morgan, graduate student in the doctoral program in Comparative Sociology at Florida International University were the other members of the research team on this project. The research on working-class women's community organizing was funded by a Fulbright Fellowship and a fellowship from the Organization of American States and was conducted by the author during 1985 and 1986.

The Transnational Web of Syrian-Jewish Relations

WALTER P. ZENNER

Some ethnic groups are international. Familial, kin, commercial, and charitable ties strengthen ethnic identity in a community which maintains itself in the cities of different countries throughout the world. Walter P. Zenner describes such networks in one group. He reminds us that ethnic diversity is not simply a lower-class phenomenon, but may also be found among middle- and even high-income populations. In fact, the relationship between commerce and finance and the city is quite close, since urban areas are the hubs of such activity. Zenner also suggests that assimilation is connected to the loosening of ethnic ties, particularly those that link the group member with the group's economic specialties or communal activities.

The Trading Minority

While urban anthropologists, in general, have concentrated attention on poor and working-class populations, considerable work has

Source: Article written expressly for *Urban Life*. Portions of this paper are excerpted from Walter P. Zenner, "International Networks of a Migrant Ethnic Group," which appeared in *Migration and Anthropology* (Seattle: The University of Washington Press for the American Ethnological Society, 1970, pp. 36–48). Published by permission of the American Ethnological Society.

also been done on the social lives of people in the middle and even upper strata of society. Just as poor, rural migrants and working-class people in cities maintain many ties with their kin, compatriots, and members of their own ethnic groups, so do the more affluent. The nature of such ties varies, depending on the types of economic activities in which members of the group engage, their historical and religious backgrounds, and the types of settings in which they are found.

One type of adaptation associated with ethnic groups that occupy a middle status in society has been referred to as the *middleman minority* or the *trading minority*. Trading minorities are ones in which a disproportionate number of ethnic group members work in commerce or are employed by others in their group who are so occupied. Before the rise of the modern, multinational corporation, the only way in which relationships of trust and credit could be enforced across international boundaries and over long distances was through common membership in a family or another community which could enforce discipline on its members living far away, such as a religious sect. Even today small firms continue to work over long distances using trusted members of the kin group or co-ethnics as firm representatives.

In the case of ethnic groups there are ties which bind beyond the family. Often religion, especially in the case of Europeans and Middle Easterners, plays a role providing a form of social cement between members of the group. These connections may give group members certain advantages such as giving them easier credit terms when making loans or providing employment. The value of group loyalty is not, however, always an advantage, since the group member must give up much in the way of personal autonomy, and the group itself may be fraught with internal conflict. For instance, a young man employed by his cousins in a small shop may have to work long hours and at lower wages in some cases than if he were employed in a corporately owned department store. In addition, the value of ethnicity should not be reduced to its economic worth. Adherence to a common religion, for example, also connects one's life to the divine and to life beyond one's own span on earth.

Intermediary minorities, even when many of their members live in rural areas, are generally tied to cities, since cities are the centers of commerce and finance. Cross-national groups in particular are concentrated in major metropolitan areas. The intricate web of relations of one such intermediary minority, that of Syrian Sephardic Jews, illustrates the role of ethnic identification in urban social adaptation.

The Syrian Sephardic Diaspora

A diaspora is an ethnic group whose members are scattered in different places within a country or throughout the world. The Jewish people who had already dispersed during the period of the Roman empire were the group to whom the label was first applied, but the word now pertains to many other peoples as well. Syrian Jewry is, itself, a product of the dispersion of Jews, and it has produced its own diaspora during the past century and a quarter.

Around 1800, the Jewish communities in the large Syrian cities of Aleppo and Damascus were composed of Jews whose ancestors had been in Southwest Asia since time immemorial, as well as the descendants of immigrants from Spain, Portugal, and Italy. Due to the fact that some of these Jews had a Spanish heritage, these Arabic-speaking communities were considered Sephardic, a word derived from a Hebrew term for the Iberian peninsula. In the nineteenth century, the occupations of Syrian Jews included craftsmen, rural peddlers, government contractors, and wholesale merchants.

The migration of Syrian Jewry occurred as a result of the economic shift in the world economy caused by European domination and industrialization and the opening of the Suez Canal, as well as a product of unrest within the Ottoman empire, of which Syria was a part. In the late nineteenth century, Syrian Jews immigrated to Beirut (Lebanon), Egypt, and Manchester (England). By World War I, they, alongside their neighbors belonging to other religions, were moving in substantial numbers to the Americas. Some, out of religious reasons, moved to the Holy City of Jerusalem at this time, presaging the larger immigration to Palestine/Israel after the First World War. Emigration from Syria continued from this period to the present. After World War I, international boundaries separated Aleppo and Damascus from some of their hinterlands. The rise of Arab nationalism and its conflict with Zionism (the movement which promoted the establishment of a Jewish state) made Jewish life in Syria quite difficult. By the 1950s when Jews were no longer allowed to leave, the vast majority of Syrian Jews lived outside of Syria. Small numbers thereafter have left either illegally or legally when governments loosened restrictions. Since 1992, the majority of the remaining Jews have left Syria.

In the cities and countries where they now lived, the immigrants and their descendants often maintained their separate Syrian-Jewish identities in varying degrees. In places with high concentrations of Aleppo and Damascus Jews, they formed congregations along former regional lines and strove to contract marriages within their own origin group. In places where numbers of Syrian Jews are small, they would meld into the local Jewish community, especially with others from the Mediterranean or Southwest Asia.

This analysis focuses on Syrian Jews in New York, Israel, and Manchester (England) with an emphasis on the international connections which bind the communities together and which stress their common ethnic origin. Those individuals within these communities who are involved in economic, communal, or familial activities on an international basis remain strongly identified with the Syrian-Jewish group, while those who lack such activity are more likely to have very loose ties to the group.

The data for this study was collected in New York between 1958 and 1960, and again in 1963; in Jerusalem in 1961, 1962, and 1993; and in Manchester in 1987.[1] Some material collected by Zerubavel and Esses (1987) and by Sutton (1988) also contributed to the conclusion reached in this study. For the most part, the Syrian Jews studied were born in or descended from individuals from the city of Aleppo in northern Syria and were therefore referred to as Aleppians or Halebis. Some were from Damascus, which is in southern Syria, and they were called either Damascenes or Shaamis (from the Arabic name for the city, esh-Shaam).

Uncovering the Network

Under scrutiny, Syrian Jews, whether in the United States, England, or Israel, exhibit an intertwining network of relationship between different communities. While engaged in a short study of Aleppo Jews in New York City in 1958, I met a visitor from Mexico, a female cousin in the first home that I had visited. One interviewee was married to a woman from Panama, an "import," in the then current slang. A man born in Brooklyn grew up in Manchester and lived in Colombia and Panama, before coming to live in New York. Another grew up in Central America and lived in Israel for a few years. There were also families with business connections in East Asia.

In the institutional sector of the different communities, one also found an international network in operation. Several rabbis and cantors had emigrated over the years from Israel and Syria. These continued to have close ties with other Syrian and Sephardic rabbis in Israel and elsewhere. In fieldwork in Israel I encountered rabbis who had served congregations in Latin America, Europe, and the United States before retiring to Jerusalem, as well as younger rabbis from Jerusalem visiting kin. In 1993, I heard of several such rabbis who regularly spend their summers in Israel. There were also contacts between Jews of Syrian origin in Israel and those abroad in support of institutions for both Syrian and other Middle Eastern Jews in Israel.

This material gives the impression that a significant segment of Syrian Jewry is extremely mobile, even over international boundaries. There has been no deep-seated inhibition against such mobility. The connections between different Syrian groups facilitate migrations and other contacts.

This point was given new emphasis in Manchester in 1987. In July of that year, I entered a Sephardic synagogue there. During a pause in the prayers, an elderly man told his neighbor that he had heard that morning on the radio about some political demonstrations in Panama, obviously revealing a personal interest in that part of the world. A few days earlier, I had interviewed another old but still active textile trader in his office and warehouse. When I asked him about his relatives overseas, he took out his address book and gave me addresses of sisters, brothers, and their children in various countries in South America, Europe, and Asia.

The delineation of waves of migration gives an indication of the general trend (such as out of Syria to the Americas or Israel) but does not reflect the back-and-forth patterns of migration. Immigrants who did not succeed returned to their former homes and the children of immigrants emigrated from the second home to another place. There are patterns which ordinary immigration statistics do not reveal. This becomes particularly confusing when one deals with a group like Syrian Jews in which a variety of citizenships and official nationalities are represented. Even in the eighteenth century, some Jews born and living in Syria held foreign passports. With the increasing interference of European powers in the Ottoman empire and with greater numbers of migrants, the practice increased.

Kinship and Commercial Networks

An important function of kinship among Syrian Jews is that it provides them with links to new economic and/or geographic situations. First it has been customary for one male member of a family to go to a certain country and to set up a store or other business. Then he sends for other kinsmen (brothers, nephews, cousins) to help him in his business. In the past, men who went to work abroad would send money to their families at home. Likewise, marriage may be involved in economic transactions.

Wealth in some places is still transferred at the time of a marriage in the form of a dowry. Men on occasion will marry relatively poorer women from Syria or Israel with practically no dowry.

These patterns can be illustrated by several examples. Ralph Ades was born in Manchester but brought up in Brooklyn where his father had a shop. On completing his schooling in New York, he joined a brother in business in Barranquilla (Colombia); then he moved to Panama City. After serving in the U.S. Navy in World War II, he married a cousin from Israel. Later after living in the United States, he returned to Latin America, where he worked with a brother who owned a factory.

Eddie Sitton's family also illustrates the operation of this network. Eddie's wife was born in Panama, but her father was born in Syria and her mother in Mexico. In an interview, Eddie reported how his own parents came to the United States:

WPZ: Could you tell me a little about your family? Are they Halebi?

ES: Yes, my grandfather on my father's side sent my oldest uncle to Alexandria (Egypt) to escape the (Turkish) army around the time of World War I. The Alexandria community supported refugees. Two uncles came to the United States. During the war my grandparents and my aunt died. My father was orphaned. The Red Cross contacted his brothers, who sent for him.

WPZ: What did he do in this country?

ES: He was a peddler (I learned he had lived in Chicago, where ES still has relatives).

WPZ: What did he sell?

ES: Dry goods.

WPZ: What about your mother's side?

ES: My grandfather on my mother's side went to Egypt. Cairo was a big cosmopolitan city compared to Aleppo, which then was a country town (by comparison!, WPZ). Then he came to America . . . It was too cold for him. Winters were colder then; they might have snow on Rosh Hashanah (the Jewish New Year, usually in September, WPZ). So he left for Panama and married. That's where my mother was born. My father went to Panama and married. I went to Mexico and married. . . .

WPZ: What about cousin marriage; is it common?

ES: There's nothing wrong with it.

WPZ: I know. I just wanted to know if it is common.

ES: Parents will encourage it, especially if the family is rich. *Yihus* (good family line) is the main reason. Money is secondary. My parents are second cousins; her (his mother's) sister is married to a cousin.

In this interview, Eddie Sitton did not indicate how he met his wife nor her relationship to him, although he did say that the marriage had not been arranged. In another incident, where a Mexican cousin was visiting a Brooklyn family, I was told that a match between her and a member of the household was under consideration.

The pattern of immigration to a place where one has relatives is very similar to the relationship between the wealthy merchants of Aleppo and Damascus and the poorer Jewish peddlers who sold the merchandise they had acquired on credit to peasants and nomads in rural areas (Zenner 1965). This can be seen in migration to Manchester.

In Manchester, which is one of the older communities in the modern diaspora, young Syrian Jews, from 1850 to World War I, established another link in the chain from wholesale merchants to peddlers and retail shopkeepers. They acted as shipping agents in Aleppo and other Middle Eastern commercial centers, sending cotton goods out from the mills of Lancashire. While the Manchester community was able to achieve a middle-class standing almost from its inception, the situation of Syrian Jews in the Americas was quite different, with the majority occupied as peddlers. Most of the descendants of these early immigrants are much more prosperous today. In the United States, Syrian Jews for a long time were specialized in the importing of household linens, lace, and infant ware. In more recent times, many have been importers of electronic equipment or have opened discount stores (Sutton 1979; Zenner 1982).

Small businessmen in the 1950s and 1960s would still ask relatives living abroad to join them as employees and junior partners. A young Israeli-born Syrian considered an offer from an older brother who was part-owner of a shop in New York. This brother was born in Argentina and had never lived in Israel. When he was grown up, he moved to New York City and opened a store in midtown Manhattan. In this case, the younger brother turned down the offer.

The position of Syrian Jews in Israel is somewhat unique. In some ways, Israel has become the impoverished homeland, especially since most Jews have left Syria and contact with those remaining is restricted. For a long time, Israel did not have the kind of commercial economy in which Syrian Jews have thrived, unlike the United States and Latin America. The kind of quick profit that could be obtained in a tourist area like New York's Times Square or various resort areas in the 1950s and 1960s could not be realized in Israel's more controlled economy. In addition, many of the Syrian Jews who immigrated to Israel came from those who were too poor to immigrate to the Americas. Since commerce was relatively unprofitable, many left this field for unskilled labor in some cases, and bureaucratic positions in others. Only some of the Syrian families in Israel continue to be involved actively in the commercial-kin network.

Those families that still maintain commercial ties include the families of merchants born in either Syria or Palestine but who made their fortunes abroad. For instance, Moise Kohen was born in Jerusalem. After World War I, he immigrated to Colombia and Panama where he was a shopkeeper for a number of years. After 1948, he returned to Jerusalem for religious reasons. His brother and his large family continue to live in Colombia. They write to each other frequently.

The Israeli-Syrian families with business and communal connections overseas continue to send members out of the country, at least for a number of years. In one family, five siblings immigrated to New York. One sister had already worked in New York. Then two brothers arrived and began to teach in Jewish day schools. One brother for a time also had a shop. While one sister returned to Israel, other family members remain active members of the Brooklyn Syrian community.

In addition to the Israelis, other Syrian Jews migrate to and sojourn in different parts of the diaspora, attracted by relatives who are living in that place, whether it is New York, Los Angeles, Mexico, or Manchester. In the New York metropolitan area one finds Jews of Syrian origin from Egypt, Lebanon, Manchester, and Latin America.

Migration between countries is only part of the picture. In the interview cited above, mention was made of movement from Chicago to New York City. One finds Syrian Jews following economic opportunities on a worldwide and countrywide basis. Some families move between Bogota, Panama, Cali, and Barranquilla or between Hong Kong, Manila, and New York. Others migrate between New York, Los Angeles, and Laredo (Texas). According to one rabbi in a congregation in New York, many families maintain a shop outside of New York until their children come of an age when they worry about giving them a Jewish education or marrying outside the community. Then they return to New York City. Some of the "out-of-towners" will spend their winters at resorts in Florida that are also used by New York Syrians.

The Communal Network

The network linking the various Syrian-Jewish communities is evident in the activities of the merchants, some of whom are communal leaders. The communal network has links with the larger Sephardic-Middle Eastern and general Jewish arenas of activity, as in the past. The network includes the flow of remittances which today go primarily from prosperous and wealthy Syrian Jews in the Americas and Western Europe to Israel and other Middle Eastern countries. Israel (previously both Syria and Jerusalem) provided rabbis to the scattered Syrian diaspora. In dealing with the flow of remittances and rabbis, the Syrian and general Sephardic networks overlap and will be discussed.

The remittance network has its roots in the old traditional system of sending contributions for the support of scholars and of the holy places in the Land of Israel. Much of this was related to traditional charities of the Middle Eastern Jews, such as support for the poor and needy (including orphans, widows, and brides without dowries) in the Syrian cities.

When the Syrian Jews emigrated, this loyalty to tradition was maintained. For instance, a beautiful synagogue, noted for its inlaid wooden Ark, was built in the Nahalat Zion quarter of West Jerusalem with money sent by the Ades family. This family, originally from Aleppo, was resident in Egypt at the beginning of the twentieth century, when the quarter and the synagogue were built. This synagogue was under the jurisdiction of a court of Aleppian rabbis. By the early 1960s, the synagogue had become somewhat run down, but it was restored by funds from Syrian Jews in the Americas in the late 1980s, and it now has a sign in English and Hebrew indicating it as a synagogue of the Aleppo Jews, even though most neighborhood congregants are not of that origin. In addition, it has become a site for Bar Mitzvahs of boys of Syrian origin from the United States.

In the 1930s an orphanage in Aleppo was supported by emigrés in the Americas. Through the 1970s, some Jewish schools in Syria, Iran, and Morocco were supported by funds from Syrian Jews in New York City.

In Jerusalem, a number of rabbis and merchants formed a *Committee of the Aleppian Community* after World War I. All three members were involved in general Sephardic and Jewish affairs, and the three went abroad on behalf of both the *particularistic and larger* communities. The main function of the Committee was to support the needy in the Aleppian group in Jerusalem. The heads of the Committee were self-appointed and the funds that they distributed were from Aleppians living abroad.

After the establishment of the State of Israel (1948) with its extensive welfare services, the need for private particularistic philanthropy lessened. In addition, the leadership of the Aleppian group had grown old and was not replaced. Several attempts to reorganize the committee failed. One cause of the failure was the fact that younger Israelis lacked the contacts with Aleppians abroad that the older leadership had. In addition, the younger men were more involved in general Israeli and Sephardic affairs. By 1962, the organization had largely atrophied, although some remittances were still channeled through it. A Women's Committee was active. This group composed of Aleppian women married to businessmen sold linen seconds at a bazaar. These seconds had been sent to them by a wealthy Syrian wholesaler and philanthropist in New York. Except for this, the Aleppian committee was nearly moribund.

The involvement of Syrian Jews in general Sephardic and Jewish activities is important for the flow of remittances. In Jerusalem and elsewhere in Israel, there are several institutions either founded by or receiving substantial support from overseas Syrian Jews. In most cases, the conduit for these funds is a local Syrian.

One institution which receives extensive Syrian-Jewish, as well as other Middle Eastern-Sephardic support, is the Porat-Yosef Yeshiva. This rabbinical academy was founded in the Old City of Jerusalem on the basis of a bequest from an Iraqi Jew living in India. After the fall of the Old City to the Jordanians in 1948, a new building was erected in West Jerusalem. After the Israeli conquest of the Old City in 1967, the old building was restored. The buildings contain many plaques which indicate the sources of the contributions made for this institution by non-Ashkenazic groups throughout the world. In addition to Syrians, others who have contributed have been Iraqis and Persians.

Smaller yeshivot have been founded as well with money from overseas Syrians but which serve Jews of Middle Eastern background in general. Yeshivot serving a variety of groups have flourished in recent years, especially after the Sephardic orthodox Shas party became part of various government coalitions and gained subsidies for such institutions. Several of these yeshivot were quite small and several tried to specialize. For instance, one was oriented toward those who served in rabbinical judicial bodies like the rabbinical courts recognized by the Israeli government, while another trained its students to preach.

A vocational school was built in a town near Tel Aviv with money from a North American Aleppian. This school was primarily for new immigrants, who in the 1960s were mainly from North Africa. The one who did on-the-ground organization in Israel was a well-known politician born in Aleppo. When the North American visited Israel, he ate at this political leader's home in a poor section of Tel Aviv. While the school was built for the larger community, the old Aleppo tie linked the philanthropist to the politicians.

Similar connections appear across a wide range of institutions. One finds the use of a particularistic link for getting funds for a wider public. In 1962, one young Syrian rabbi admitted that while he was himself uninterested in the Aleppian grouping per se, since Syrian Jews abroad wanted to give money specifically earmarked for Syrians, he had to look for needy Syrian boys to go to his yeshiva. This created a problem since Syrians are a small and relatively better-off group among the African and Asian Jews in Israel. They were more assimilated into the general Sephardic and Jewish populations than more recent immigrants like Moroccans. For people like this rabbi, the memory of Syrian origin is enhanced because of its importance to the Syrians abroad.

There are others for whom remembrance of the Syrian heritage has value in its own right. In the 1980s, a number of prominent Aleppian Jews in Israel did form a World Center for the Heritage of Aleppo Jewry. Even though these individuals were well integrated into Israeli life and held to a philosophy of ethnic integration rather than separation, they wanted to celebrate their specific heritage. As in the other cases, they reached out to the Syrian Sephardim abroad.

In addition to Israeli philanthropy, Syrians also contributed other institutions for Middle Eastern Jews. A leader of the Syrian community in New York was a chief supporter of Otsar HaTorah (literally the Torah fund or treasure), an orthodox Jewish school system for those living in Muslim countries and in France. The system was founded by a Polish rabbi who had worked with European refugees in Iran during the Second World War. The manner in which he reached the Syrian philanthropists is unclear, but the Polish rabbi had contacts in Jerusalem including Aleppian Jews.

The importance of the Aleppian rabbis and other religious specialists in this network cannot be overemphasized. Many of these rabbinic families had immigrated to Jerusalem prior to the First World War, but members of these families travelled back and forth to Syria and to various Syrian and other Middle Eastern communities overseas. The purpose of these journeys was to raise money for the sacred institutions in the Holy Land and also to provide religious services for Sephardic Jews abroad. It was not inconsistent for these purposes to go into business for oneself; hence, some of the rabbis established shops and other enterprises during their sojourns.

Some of the rabbis have lived in the diaspora for most of their careers, while others resided there for only short periods of time. Some who spent most of their careers in countries like Mexico have retired to Jerusalem. In turn, young rabbis from such families go overseas. In rabbinic households, there are frequent visitors from countries like Peru, Argentina, Great Britain, and the United States. Many of these visitors are either rabbis from these far-flung congregations or else simply family members. Sometimes Syrians in the diaspora will ask well-known old rabbis in Jerusalem (or elsewhere) for legal opinions or for talismans against some ailments.

In like manner, Aleppian rabbinical students from the Americas at Jerusalem yeshivot may be guests in rabbinic households and sometimes marry daughters of these families. Similarly, one finds such students in yeshivot in New York City. While those in this category are small, it adds an additional link to the chain of connections.

The congregations which rabbis of Syrian origin serve are not exclusively Syrian, though most are of Mediterranean or Middle Eastern origin. Neither are the rabbis and cantors in Syrian congregations in the Americas and elsewhere exclusively Syrian, but again most are of Afro-Asian origin. Among the Syrian Jews in Brooklyn in the late 1950s, one found a cantor of Iraqi origin, a school principal from Morocco, an Iraqi-Israeli cantor and a Yemenite-Israeli cantor. There were also several American-Ashkenazi rabbis of European origin, alongside the Syrian-born and Israeli-Syrian rabbis. The two cantors from Israel had studied liturgy with Syrian singers in Jerusalem.

In Manchester, the Syrian Jews were always part of a larger community of Mediterranean cotton traders, including Sephardim from Morocco to Iraq. Syrian Jews participated in the formation of all three Sephardic congregations in the city. While one of these synagogues was seen as more *oriental*, a term designating the Syrian and Iraqi Jews, Aleppians were active in all three. In the more oriental synagogue, however, the Aleppians were the leaders and remain so to this day. Still, it can be said that the Aleppians in Manchester have always been more integrated with other Sephardic Jews than in either New York City or Mexico City. In

1987, none of the rabbis in Manchester were of Syrian origin. The small size of the Sephardic enclave there and the lack of firm boundaries between the various origin-groups contributed to the differences between Manchester and New York.

Outside the Network

Withdrawal from the network takes a number of forms. Many Syrian Jews no longer enter traditional commercial occupations. Instead they become physicians, lawyers, or professors. This reduces their contacts with other members of the community, particularly among the Overseas Syrian Jews. For others, the change is more radical. For instance, one woman of Aleppian descent from Manchester married another English Jew who was a diplomat. Although they did not sever ties with the Jewish community, her husband's career made their social life one that was apart from other Jews, even when they were stationed in places with large numbers of Jews.

Ralph Sitt is an example of a Syrian Jew who has lived most of his life outside the Syrian-Jewish network. His father was one of the first Syrian Jews in New York City. Ralph's mother was an Ashkenazi woman from Manchester. He grew up in Harlem when it was a Jewish neighborhood, but not with a Syrian community. During the First World War, he joined the U.S. Army and rose to the rank of colonel. While stationed in Panama, he met and married a Gentile woman from Oklahoma, who converted to Judaism. After he left the army, he moved to Lima, Peru, where he opened a plastics factory. He has maintained membership in the Jewish community, although his autobiography does not indicate the degree of his commitment. His son married a Peruvian Catholic woman who did not convert to Judaism (Sutton 1988). While maintaining ties with his relatives and the Lima Jewish community, his relationship with Syrian Jews appears to be a distant one.

These cases can be contrasted with others. Several Israeli Aleppians were uninvolved and unconcerned with the particular Aleppian identity while in Israel, but when they moved to New York and settled in Syrian neighborhoods, they became quite active in such affairs. Another case is that of a Manchester Aleppian woman who married a Syrian Jew in the United States and lived most of her adult life among Syrian Jews. By way of contrast, two sisters born to an Aleppian family in a U.S. resort community went quite different ways. One married an Ashkenazi American Jew and moved to a small city, where she has little to do with Syrian Jews outside of her circle of relatives. The other, married to a Syrian Jewish merchant, lives in Brooklyn at the heart of the Syrian Sephardic community.

Conclusion

The delineation of transnational networks in a dispersed ethnic group is something that follows naturally from what has been written about migration. As with other intermediary minorities, the centers of activity are major commercial or religious centers. In fact, the migrations of Aleppian Jewry have followed the path of their trade from Aleppo to Manchester, New York, Buenos Aires, and elsewhere.

Some of the characteristics of the Syrian Jewish group, of course, may be particular to segments of the Jewish diaspora. The Jewish communities of Syria were themselves products of waves of migration and were always connected to Jewish communities elsewhere. Thus the daughter-communities of Aleppo Jewry are subentities within the Sephardic and Jewish dispersions. As such they reveal much about the social characteristics of transnational networks.

Note

¹ The research in New York and Jerusalem was supported at different times by Columbia University, the National Institute of Mental Health, and the Memorial Foundation for Jewish Culture. My work in Manchester was financed by a research grant from the Research Foundation of the State University of New York. This support is gratefully acknowledged. I am solely responsible for any errors. This article is a revised version of the one that appeared in the Second Edition of *Urban Life*.

Part Six

Urban Places and Spaces

Place and Planning

While it is obvious that cities are places, the way in which they are perceived varies among those who live there. Likewise, the city as a place may be transformed according to the plans of builders and designers; thus, a location may develop a different character according to the manner in which it was built. Homes may be open to those walking down a street through unhedged lawns and picture windows, or they may be shut off as private spaces surrounded by high walls or hedges and with latticed windows which face an inner court.

Towns and cities may center around markets, mosques, cathedrals, bathhouses, and other such buildings, or they may center around cafes, taverns, saloons, and the like. Streets may form a grid pattern, or they may wind along like a cow path. A city may be centered, as Washington is, with the Capitol building as a "pivot of the four quarters," the navel of the universe, making secular Washington resemble many sacred cities of the world (Wheatley 1971). Some cities have large open public spaces, such as plazas and parks, while others have almost no public spaces.

The differences between cities result from a complicated combination of factors. The mental image of what is appropriate combines with the availability of materials, the distribution of power, the ability of planners to convince political leaders to follow their designs, and the creativity of the masses in making the space provided for them their own. All of these are part of the "cultural construction of space and place" (Rotenberg and McDonogh 1993).

Conscious planning has created many cities. The Constantinople of Constantine, the Baghdad of the Abbasid caliph al-Mansur (d.775) and Saddam Hussein (see al-Khalaf/Makiyya 1991), the Washington of L'Enfant, and Brasília are examples of such designs (Epstein 1973; "Genesis and Function of Squatter Settlements"; Holston 1989). Urban planning on such a monumental scale serves to advertise the power of the political elite. Some suggest that urban planning implies a totalitarian imperative to control the lives of human beings completely. The exposure of such domineering trends is part of the critique of modernism by Rabinow (1989). The most extreme effort along these lines was the destruction of many villages by the Romanian dictator, Nicolae Ceacescu.

Ethnographies, however, focus on the way that ordinary and not-so-ordinary people either resist or otherwise transform the planners' visions. These points are well made by the contributors to this section, especially in regard to how even poor and powerless people have influenced the designs of planners and presidents. Epstein shows how Brasilia, a new capital for Brazil, was forced to tolerate squatters in spite of its original design, because there was an unforeseen need for poor workers in that new city of bureaucrats.

Epstein, Gans (1962), Peattie (1967), and others who have studied squatters, the homeless, and dwellers in deteriorating housing have pointed to the realistic manner in which these poor people, who often live in housing that is unseemly from a more affluent viewpoint, use the land on which they live. In some cases, these anthropologists have become advocates of such people to protect them from harassment and relocation by urban authorities (also see S. Gmelch, "An Urban Fieldwork Experience").

Barbara Kirshenblatt-Gimblett ("Ordinary People/Everyday Life") gives us insight into how ordinary New Yorkers utilize the space allotted to them. She contrasts what is done by these urban dwellers, as opposed to plans made for them by commercial developers on the one hand and governmental controls on the other. Some of her examples also show how these three forces interact, as with the case of alternate street parking regulations noted in "Urban Class and Ethnicity" (Part Five). She discusses the "Style Wars" as they are played out in New York City. "Hip hop" music is, at least, partly coopted by the mass media, while much energy is spent to suppress the painting of graffiti.

In a discussion of how local voluntary and quasi-voluntary organizations work, Theodore Bestor ("Forging Tradition") describes how residents in a Tokyo neighborhood maintain their own community and their definition of what that should entail in the face of the municipal government's efforts to impose another definition of community upon them. He shows how they use a local festival and similar activities to maintain the neighborhood's boundaries and, using the solidarity created by these activities, to resist governmental actions which go against local interests.

Janet Abu-Lughod ("Territoriality and Social Organization") shows both how various political and economic factors shaped the traditional Islamic city and how the Muslim religion influenced features of this kind of city. She is sensitive to the ways these patterns communicate certain meanings to inhabitants of Muslim cities. She opposes the view that there is an inherent plan for cities in Islamic lands, which can simply be imposed at any time period. The full article from which the selection has been excerpted is, in fact, a warning to modern Muslim city planners (Abu-Lughod 1987).

The City as a Focus of Identity

The city as a physical place may itself constitute an important source of identity for both present and former inhabitants. Sidney Waldron ("Within the Wall and Beyond") demonstrates this most clearly in relation to the old city of Harar, where the wall constitutes a boundary dividing those within from those without in terms of language and culture. It is an ethnic boundary, much as we might envision the ancient border separating the Jebusites of pre-Davidic Jerusalem from their Hebrew and Canaanite neighbors, for, as Waldron illustrates, the inhabitants of this city continue to identify as *ge-usu* even when they migrate to Addis Ababa.

In modern North American cities, which are inhabited by descendants or migrants from all over the world, the city may be a weaker focus of identity than in Harar, but it is not insignificant. Civic pride is often associated with loyalty to the local professional sports teams and with the name of the city itself. Bostonians are fierce Red Sox fans, and the New York Yankees draw supporters from a wide variety of ethnic groups. San Franciscans abhor the use of the term "Frisco," while Chicagoans can detect outsiders by the fact that they do not pronounce the city's name as *shikawgo* but as *shikaago* or even *tchikaago*. Like ethnic loyalty, such civic pride becomes much more marked when residents emigrate or otherwise come into contact with outsiders; thus, a small group of former Chicagoans may continue to root for the Cubs or for the White Sox after moving to Los Angeles or New York. The relatively recent phenomenon of civic loyalty in North American cities, as representative of a form of urban social cohesion, deserves serious study.

The appearance and location of a city is also of great significance to its residents, as well as to others. While the residents of different urban neighborhoods may use different cognitive maps of their city (e.g., a Puerto Rican may note the location of botanicas on New York City's Lower East Side and ignore the Jewish bookstores), certain features are shared by all such neighborhoods. Among these common features are those provided by the natural environment, although humans can transform these as well. Chicagoans, for instance, consider the lakefront to be of great significance, a view which is given added salience through Chicago's extensive park system that extends along the Lake Michigan shore. By contrast, the Chicago River is less marked in the consciousness of Chicagoans. In the center of Manchester, England, one may cross a bridge over a river and never realize the waterway is there because walls block one's view; hence, the communal focus is consciously placed elsewhere. This contrasts sharply with the way in which the

Seine flows through Paris, the Thames through London, or the Vlatava through Prague.

Neighborhoods

While urban anthropologists have studied workplaces, markets, and recreational sites, residential neighborhoods have been closest to the villages that were the sites of rural ethnography. Michael Whiteford ("Doing It") gives us a good picture of fieldwork in that kind of setting, as do several other selections. Residential neighborhoods are good sites for studying a wide variety of problems, as George Gmelch ("Urban Fieldwork") notes.

In previous sections of this book, we have discussed the effects of migration, wealth, power, prestige, and ethnicity on urban centers and the persons who inhabit them. In many ways, these aspects were discussed without reference to location, but location does matter. Both commercial areas and residential neighborhoods are still segregated, even if they are not entirely homogeneous.

Local-specific social networks are generated within urban neighborhoods, isolating them from other neighborhoods. For instance, people maintain some kind of relationship with neighbors in a suburb even when their closest kin or best friends live elsewhere. Children on a block play together, neighbors chat while weeding a garden or say hello while jogging. Neighbors whose property is adjacent often need to work out arrangements of how to deal with trees that do not recognize property lines.

In a similar manner, shopping malls—the epitome of the city/urban conglomeration created by the automobile—reveal this human tendency to build social networks. Despite the rapid turnover in sales staffs and in individual outlets, one finds social regularities present. The "mall rats" are the grandchildren of the kids who used to hang around corner drugstores and pool halls two generations ago. Just as many city dwellers used to go to the neighborhood business district, to Main Street in small towns, or downtown in big cities, so too the present generation visits the malls (Jacobs 1984).

Shopping areas, whether traditional markets, downtown areas, or contemporary malls, may be segregated on the basis of economic status and ethnic affiliation. They also may be places where individuals of differing heritages meet. Residential areas are generally more segregated by class and ethnicity. Both government policies and market forces (sometimes assisted by the actions of buyers and sellers) play a role in such segregation.

The word *ghetto* was first applied to urban quarters in Italy where Jews were compelled to live. They were created by the local government, in conjunction with the Roman Catholic Church. These areas had no Christian inhabitants, and they were isolated from the rest of the community each evening by virtue of a gate. Some ghettos in Italy, incidentally, displayed problems that appear in modern times such as overcrowding, the need for building more stories since land was scarce, and the neglect of housing because rents were controlled. In this instance, the motivation for segregation was religious, since Catholicism in that period required toleration of Jews, as long as their inferior status was clear.

Janet Abu-Lughod ("Territoriality and Social Organization") also shows how *defended neighborhoods* in the Middle East are products of political forces in which local inhabitants respond to the weakness of the government, as well as to religious injunctions. These quarters depend on a sense of common destiny shared by the inhabitants. This contrasts sharply with the isolation of highly mobile individuals in American suburban areas (see Zenner, "Reflections"). Still, observers have noted how quickly suburbanites can also develop the need to defend their common interests in the face of perceived danger.

In contemporary North America, the underlying patterns which lead to segregation along lines of socioeconomic status, ethnicity, age, marital status, and even sexual preference are more subtle. Sally Engle Merry, in her essay "Urban Danger," has touched on some aspects of these patterns in regard to renters in a public housing project. In her book, *Everything in Its Place* (1977), Constance Perin has shown the connections between the values of social mobility, safety versus danger and/or risk, and the way in which land zoning is carried out. Her study employed interviews with real estate developers, bankers, and others involved in the production of housing, as well as with those who rent and buy housing to illustrate how the desire to reduce risk to one's investment encourages racial and other forms of segregation, whether this is on the part of homeowners, bankers, or insurance companies. Perin's work, as well as the studies in this section, further emphasizes the role of location in determining community formation and in defining urban neighborhoods.

These studies of the uses of space in urban areas provide us with an arena to observe how market forces, state control, and folk improvisation intersect. Through them we can do research on fundamental problems in the social sciences. These, in turn, bear on crucial policy decisions of our day.

Walter P. Zenner

Within the Wall and Beyond
Ethnicity in Harar, Ethiopia

SIDNEY R. WALDRON

Sidney Waldron has written about a preindustrial walled city that has survived well into the late twentieth century. It is a city of the type that Gideon Sjoberg described in "The Pre-Industrial City." The distinction between "city" and "countryside" is marked by the existence of the wall. Waldron shows how the ethnic identity and self-image of the Hararis is shaped by the "wall." The ge usu' within the wall speak a different language than their neighbors outside. They also form an economic elite that has had power over their Oromo neighbors beyond the wall. While such a sharp physical division between city folk and rural folk is unusual in modern times, it was not so unusual historically. Ancient Jerusalem, before it was conquered by King David, was a city of Jebusites, a small ethnic group, living among Israelites. Phoenician, Greek, and Roman colonies in many places along the Mediterranean were urban colonies living among peoples who spoke different languages and practiced other cultures.

As Waldron points out, famine and civil war during the past thirty years have wrought revolutionary changes in Ethiopia. Many of the ge usu' have been forced to leave Harar, and Harari identity must adapt to life well beyond the wall.

Harar, Ethiopia, is a walled preindustrial city whose approximately twenty thousand inhabitants[1] speak a unique Semitic language and

Source: Article written expressly for *Urban Life*.

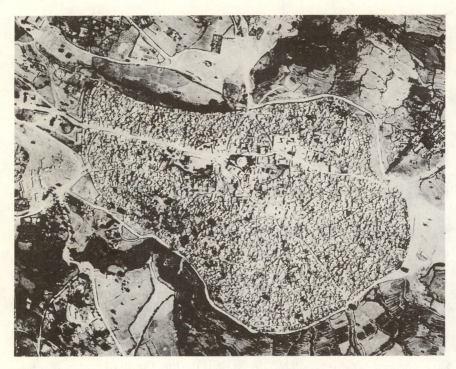

Aerial photograph of the walled city of Harar, Ethiopia, taken around 1960.

have an urban culture that is distinct from that of the surrounding peoples. Oral traditions state that the city's wall was built by Emir Nur, who ruled from 1552 to 1566. Since that time, Harar has retained its identity as an ethnic enclave although it has functioned as a vital market area for the surrounding peoples and as an important regional center of Islam. Located about halfway between the Red Sea and Addis Ababa, the capital of Ethiopia, Harar has long served as a trade link between inland Ethiopia and the outside world.

From the vantage point of Mount Hakim, the city of Harar resembles an island of houses in the midst of open country. In many ways, Harar is very much like an island, separated both physically and symbolically from its neighboring ethnic groups. The Harari call themselves *ge usu'*, "people of the city"; call their unique language *ge sinan*,[2] "the language of the city"; and call their way of life *ge 'ada*, "the customs of the city." Outside the city wall, they say, are *derga usu'*, "wild or uncultured people." The religion of the city, Islam, is its major cultural connection to many of the surrounding peoples.

For an anthropologist, such as myself, one of the most interesting phenomena of the city of Harar is the persistence of its ethnic group, the ge usu', who have maintained their identity despite at least four centuries of frequent and intense contacts with four other ethnic groups. These are the agricultural Oromo, who number some two hundred thousand in the area of Harar; the pastoral Somali, who are the dominant population in the arid regions; the small group of Argobba villagers; and, since the city's conquest and incorporation into Ethiopia in 1887, the highland Christian Amhara.

These outside groups are dealt with for economic, governmental, and many other vital reasons. This discussion will explore the means by which the Harari have maintained their distinct language and culture despite these contacts. Why have they not been absorbed by the surrounding Oromo, who outnumber them ten to one? Why haven't they become Somali, Argobba, or Amhara? Why, in fact, has Harar not become an ethnic melting pot?

Social Solidarity and Citizenship

The first insight into the integrity of the Harari comes from an appreciation of the internal solidarity of the city's society, the high value they place on their way of life, and some of the symbols they use to reinforce cultural self-awareness.

To the outsider, the city of Harar seems congested and maze-like in its complexity. To the ge usu', it is both home and sanctuary. When I first moved into the old city in 1962, I was oppressed by the crowded conditions. Noticing the wide open spaces outside the city, I asked many ge usu', "Why don't you move outside the wall?" The usual answer to this naive question was, "Because everything is inside."

The wall has ceased to be of defensive utility since the mid-nineteenth century. The gates did have an important economic function when Harar was an independent city-state. Each gate functioned as a customs station. Goods were taxed both as they entered and as they left the city (Paulitschke 1888:243). However, neither defense nor taxation explains the continuing importance of the wall. Now it must be viewed as the physical manifestation of the social boundaries that have preserved the Harari ethnic identity and which surround the Harari way of life.

Within the wall, the Harari ethnic group maintains its existence primarily by two means: (1) by defining and emphasizing the social duties of citizenship; and (2) by utilizing symbols of ethnic identity which enhance the consciousness of being Harari.

With few exceptions, the Harari ethnic group is endogamous. A ge usu' (Harari) is thus born of Harari parents. A Harari speaks ge sinan, the language of the city, as his or her mother tongue and uses only it within his or her own society, although he or she usually knows two or three other languages. Being born in the city and speaking its language would seem to be prerequisites enough for citizenship, but to fully qualify, an individual must participate in the city's three basic social institutions. These are *ahli*, the family network; *marinyet*, organized friendship; and *afocha*, community organization.

The family network links each person with dozens of other households spread throughout the city (Koehn and Waldron 1978:15–16). Each has a specific role which is defined for the individual by the kinship system. Unlike many other African societies, corporate kinship groups such as clans are not found in Harar, and unlike many other Muslim peoples, extended patrilineal systems of tracing relationships are not used here. Each person's family network overlaps other individuals' networks until the interconnections of families within the city are as numerous and intricate as the crossing of strands in a spider web. Each ge usu' is ultimately tied to every other ge usu', and closely related to a great many.

If kinship in the city establishes all-encompassing webs of relationships, each with its required form of behavior, friendship provides the ge usu' with a small closed group of confidants. Each ge usu' belongs to one and only one group of friends, made up of about five or six persons of the same sex. These are formed of playmates from one's neighborhood in early youth. Friends are seldom close relatives and perhaps never are brothers. The explanation for this is that status inequalities are built into all kinship roles, even those between elder and younger siblings. Friends are, above all, equals and thus should not be confused with relatives.

Friendship in Harar is extremely important in adolescence. Young men roam the streets with their friends, and share many of the experiences of maturation in each other's company. Indeed a friendship group sometimes seems to produce a shared responsibility orientation among its members, who are likely to develop a similar way of viewing the world around them.

Friendship groups convene at least once a week in the important institution of the *bercha*. A bercha is a calm and deliberative conversational session where friends discuss anything of mutual concern. Much of their conversation centers around the topics of their city, its place names, their legends, and the proper way of telling these in the language of the city. Awareness of the city's culture is thus heightened. Conversation is stimulated by the chewing of the leaves of *ch'at* (*Catha edulis*), called qat in Arabic. Ch'at, chewed in moderation, produces a mild euphoria and mental intensification. The bercha epitomizes the nature of friendship in Harar, a tranquil respite from the status considerations involved in the rest of Harari society, and a place where stories are told and advice is sought within the security of lifelong bonds of trust.

The afocha, a kind of communal organization, is the focus of social solidarity among the ge usu', however. In 1975, there were twenty-four men's afochas and fourteen women's afochas in Harar. Afochas are primarily concerned with weddings and funerals, but their inner workings are much more complex (Koehn and Waldron 1978). Afochas are made up of one's neighbors, for the most part, and are likely to include some of one's friends and some of one's relatives. Many friends and relatives will also belong to different afocha groups. The overlap of kinship, friendship, and afocha membership establishes a very high degree of social solidarity in Harar.

This social solidarity, which could also be called "interconnectedness," affects the ways in which the ge usu' behave toward one another. No one within the Harari ethnic group is a stranger, and there are no public acts that remain secrets from one's friends, relatives, or afocha mates. Thus a ge usu' is very careful about public behavior and how he or she treats other people of the city. Part of this consideration derives from a shared identity with them. But he or she also knows that if one should quarrel with another ge usu', or otherwise behave against the ethics of the city, one would become the subject of gossip, which would eventually reach everyone of concern to him or her.

Participation in the basic institutions of the city is the essence of Harari citizenship. The total amount of time spent in kinship, friendship, and afocha functions is extensive. However, the individual who attends to the city's social obligations also knows exactly what is going on inside the walled city. That individual has accurate and up-to-date information concerning market prices and political conditions, which is obtained in informal conversation at social events. From an overall social perspective, the result of this high degree of participation is an extremely tight-knit ethnic group, effectively closed to those not born in the city, which, in turn, helps explain the persistence of the Harari ethnic group.

Symbols of Identity

Underlying this tight-knit society is a conscious awareness of what it means to be a ge usu', a member of the city culture. Hundreds of local place names, coupled with their explanatory traditions, make the city a very meaningful place for the ge usu'. Although the city is bafflingly complex to the outsider, it is conceptually quite simple for the ge usu'. First of all, the city is divided into five quarters. Each of these quarters is further conceptually subdivided into neighborhoods. These neighborhoods are not merely spatial referents. Each has its tales and traditions which enhance the meaning of living in the city.

Usually, neighborhoods are named after *awach*, a category that includes Muslim saints, war heroes and learned men, and that translates directly as "fathers" in the sense of "fathers of the city." Perhaps fifty of the city's neighborhoods are named after awach. There are dozens more located throughout the city. (In fact, I recorded one hundred and fifty-six awach shrines in 1975.) Many of these awach are shrines of famous Muslim saints, which are celebrated in all-night ceremonies by the ge usu', wherein the life of Mohammed and praises to the saint are recited. Harar is thus a kind of holy city; to be a Harari is to live in it, in the constant presence of the awach. For the purposes of this discussion, that statement should be reversed: to live in the presence of the awach enhances the feeling of being a Harari.

The physical evidence of ethnic awareness is manifold in Harar. Even household architecture plays its role, since every feature of the traditional home has a pattern that is explained in terms of the past of the city. A good example is the explanation of the hard-packed red earth floor of traditional Harari homes. The red color of this specially prepared surface is said to represent the Harari blood spilled at the Battle of Ch'elenqo, where the city lost its independence forever to the forces of the Ethiopian Empire in 1887. Children are thus raised with the distinctiveness between ge usu' and other ethnic groups firmly entrenched as part of their surroundings.

Since its conquest, Harar has come into more and more intensive contact with outside groups, especially the Amhara, who comprised the dominant ethnic group of the Ethiopian Empire. The Harari seem to have made adjustments in the ethnic markers used to define themselves vis-à-vis the Amharas, who are Christians, as this contact increased. I can cite only a few examples here.

Richard Burton, who, in 1854, was the first European to visit Harar, reported the Harari to be virtual drunkards, in contradiction to the rules of Islam, which prohibit alcoholic beverages. "High and low," he said, "indulge freely in intoxicating drinks, beer, and mead" (Burton 1966:188). *Gohoy*, a kind of beer, used to be sold in the streets. However, a century later, the Harari do not tolerate the drinking of alcohol: Christians (Amhara) drink; Muslims (ge usu') do not. The ge usu' chew ch'at extensively; the Amhara eschew it. The ge usu' grow the world's most delicious coffee beans, in my opinion, but they seldom drink coffee—it is for Christians. They prefer imported tea, or drinks made from coffee leaves or husks.

One may react to these intensifications of the symbols that define group identity, whether one is Harari or Amhara, with distaste, seeing them as deplorable examples of bigotry and intolerance. Here, however, I am suggesting another perspective, that of a threatened ethnic group, trying against all odds to hold on to its identity, its culture, and its way of life.

Boundary Maintenance and Restrictions of Exchanges

Harari in-group solidarity, combined with the symbols of ethnic identity that define the people of the city as separate from all other peoples in the world, provides a strong basis for the maintenance of their ethnic identity. However, probably the most important social mechanisms with which the ge usu' have preserved their tiny culture while engaging in daily and important transactions with the surrounding and more numerous ethnic outsiders are those that are used in defining boundaries.

The perspective I have taken in analyzing Harari social boundary maintenance was developed independently of that of the great Norwegian anthropologist, Frederik Barth, but resulted in a remarkably similar conclusion. As Barth says,

> Stable interethnic relations presuppose . . . a structuring of interaction: a set of prescriptions governing situations of contact, and allowing for articulation in some sectors or domains of activity, and a set of proscriptions in other sectors, and thus insulating parts of the culture from confrontation and modification. (Barth 1969:16)

The way the people of Harar have held on to their identity is exactly by defining limits for the types of interactions permitted with the members of other ethnic groups. One may trade with an Oromo or an Amhara, but one may not marry a member of the

Street in Harar, 1963. Minaret of Jami Mosque in background was razed and replaced by a new structure in the 1980s.[Photo by Robert Embry]

outside group. One may engage in religious celebrations with other Muslims (and the Oromo, Somali, and Argobba are Muslim), but unless the fellow Muslims participate in the three basic social institutions of the city (kinship, friendship, and afocha), they are not Harari—they are still outsiders.

In categorizing the types of exchanges that are regulated by the ge usu', I have followed the suggestion of Claude Lévi-Strauss (1953:536). He suggests that the crucial exchanges in any society, which my focus restricts to interethnic exchanges, are of three types: (1) exchange of goods and services, or economic exchange; (2) exchange of personnel, (especially marriage, but also including adoption, and assimilation); and (3) exchange of information. One could probably consider biological exchange between groups, or gene flow, but data are lacking.

Sometimes anthropologists speak of social boundaries as if they were single clear-cut lines, as a circle on a map of ethnographic distributions. The approach I have used, however, produces three types of boundaries—each of which is measured as a frequency of interethnic transaction. However, as Barth has made clear, ethnic survival in contact situations is facilitated by forbidding some types of exchanges while permitting others.

The ethnographic details of Harari exchanges with each of the contingent ethnic groups are too complex to be presented here (see Waldron 1974:260–327). However, in the abstract, a pattern of boundary management by the ge usu' emerges, which has permitted the survival of their culture. Most important, here, is their restriction of the exchange of personnel across ethnic boundaries. Harari are permitted to marry only other Harari,[3] thus avoiding gradual dilution of their culture. Should a Harari marry a Christian, that person would be shunned and referred to as if he or she were dead.

If endogamy preserves the integrity of the population and its culture, its wealth and energy are derived from profitable economic exchanges with the surrounding groups. Of these, the Oromo have been historically the most important to Harar. Richard Burton described the Harar of one hundred years ago, saying, "Harar is essentially a commercial town: its citizens live . . . by systematically defrauding the Galla Bedouin (Oromo)" (Burton 1966:192). Although much has changed recently in the old system, the ge usu' traditionally profited in two ways from the surrounding Oromo peasants. First of all, they owned most of the farmland for miles around the city. This was cultivated by Oromo tenant farmers, who might be expected to yield as much as seventy percent of their crops to the Harari owner. Also, the Harari merchants profitably controlled the city's market, the sole source of regional specialties and imported goods for a vast area of this part of Africa. In a way, then, the Harari exploited the Oromo while forbidding marriage with them, and in this lay the secret of their duration and wealth.

The Harari also controlled the flow of information in and around the city, for they were and are multilingual. Most Harari are fluent in the Oromo language, for instance, although very few Oromo can speak the language of the city. The Harari merchants thus could manipulate prices on the spot, using ge sinan, the city language, as a kind of secret vehicle for price setting. Many Harari also speak Amharic, Somali, Arabic; many can speak English. Within the city the knowledge of markets and farms, of political and economic events is pooled within the population of ge usu'. It is shared in visits, in meetings of friends, relatives, and afocha. In a way, the system of information thus established is like a brokerage of strategic knowledge, and to become a member one must be a ge usu'.

Beyond the Wall: The Future of the Harari

The delicate balance of ethnic groups which has been discussed here has been altered irreparably by the events of the twentieth century. As I have indicated, the old farming economy of Harar was based on ethnic stratification: the Harari owned the land, and the much more numerous Oromo paid for the right to work it, often exorbitantly. Such exploitative forms of land tenure were widespread in Ethiopia before the revolution of 1974. Not surprisingly land reforms were one of the first and most necessary changes made by the new government. However, with these reforms, the traditional Harari economy was shattered, and the wealth of the city, which had permitted the ge usu' to spend long hours fulfilling social obligations, was gone forever.

In response to this and earlier economic changes, many Harari merchants had moved to the capital of Ethiopia by 1975. In 1977, when I last worked in Ethiopia, this population movement from the old city had become a virtual diaspora: there were more Harari living in Addis Ababa than in their old home city.

During the seventeen-year rule (1974–1991) of the socialist government of Mengistu Haile Mariam, all of Ethiopia suffered from famine, misrule, and economic collapse. Harar was no exception. Thousands of Harari left Ethiopia in search of a life worth living. "I never would have left Harar," a friend said, "if I thought there was any chance that there would be peace in Ethiopia within my lifetime." The diaspora now extended far beyond the boundaries of Ethiopia, with enclaves of Harari scattered throughout urban centers of the Muslim world and colonies of a few hundred in Toronto, Washington D.C., and Los Angeles. Some even settled in Sydney, Australia. Harari students-in-exile tried to maintain communications from the University of Moscow, Oxford University, Columbia, and UCLA, among many other temporary refuges.

One old friend spoke sadly of walking the back streets of Nairobi, Kenya, playing Harari songs on his tape recorder, hoping that someone would respond in ge sinan. In the early 1980s, there were perhaps one thousand Harari in Mogadishu, Somalia. "None of us are refugees," I was told, "We take care of each other." In cities like Jiddah, Saudi Arabia, where the Harari population was large enough, afocha organizations were reestablished in a conscious attempt to reconstitute a viable Harari culture. The Australian community had divided itself into five afocha organizations, which it named with nostalgic pride after the five old quarters of the city. By 1990, the word "diaspora" was incorporated into the Harari language.

The Harari in exile are trying to preserve their identity against all odds through nucleated settlements abroad, constant communications, and where possible, organized meetings to discuss community affairs and policy changes. In 1991, when a new government arose in Ethiopia, a massive meeting was convened in Toronto, one of the largest and strongest Harari enclaves, with over a hundred families. Over eight hundred Harari attended from all corners of the world, including a dozen honored old ladies flown in from the city of Harar itself. Members of the Toronto community told me all were guests among their Harari friends and relatives, and that the only two visitors who tried to stay in a hotel were somewhat forcefully relocated to Harari homes.

However, at lulls in the cultural programs where the old culture was celebrated, the problems of new times emerged. Parents were losing influence over their children, a chronic generational problem in all cultures, perhaps. But for the Harari, this implied cultural loss: would their children's children speak ge sinan? A letter from a young man in Texas, which appeared in the Toronto cultural newsletter, said that he felt alienated from other children because he spoke a strange language at home. Would Harari youth maturing in Western cities marry other Harari, or would their cultural heritage be dissipated? When I showed some slides of the gates and shrines that constitute the key landmarks of the old city, there was an enormous emotional response, but many of those in their teens or younger had never seen or experienced these symbols of Harari culture, only having heard of them from concerned parents. By the end of the 1991 meeting, the idea of returning to the desperate conditions of Ethiopia was in the air.

Judging from a two-day visit to the old city, which I was able to make in 1992, however, there may not be much of Harar's old urban culture waiting to welcome returnees. Outsiders have moved into the city, but, not having the experience of centuries of urban life to guide them, they do not have Harari skills in living in very close quarters, nor do they have the wealth necessary to preserve sanitary conditions, to keep buildings painted and decorated, and they are ignorant of the shrines and saints of the city. In high irony, the newcomers do not know what they have gained, while the Harari in exile lament what they have lost.[4]

Notes

[1] In this paper, I have used the term "Harari" interchangeably with the term of self-reference, ge usu' ("city person"). This use of Harari is somewhat misleading: (a) At present the old city, which is discussed here, contains some 20,000 persons. Of these, perhaps two-thirds were ge usu' in 1975, and the rest were Amhara and Somali. (b) Outside the old city is a proliferating new urban center at least equal in size to the old city. Ethnically, it is dominantly Amhara, with lesser numbers of Oromo, Gurage, and other Ethiopians. The term "Harari," which I have used in a restricted sense, could be used for any resident of the city of Harar, Ethiopia, population 45,000.

[2] Until recent years the Harari language, ge sinan, was restricted to the city walls. That is to say, one could walk through the Harari speech community in twenty minutes by walking through the city. It is a distinct Ethiopian Semitic language, akin to the national language of Ethiopia, Amharic, but not mutually intelligible with it.

[3] Important exceptions to this firm general rule are documented in the complete enthnographic description (Waldron 1974:270). For instance, sometimes a ge usu' man might marry an Oromo woman as a second wife. This would be seen as an economic and political stratagem by the ge usu', since, by doing this, he would be gaining a link with her village. He would never, however, bring this wife or any children back to Harar. They would be raised as Oromo.

[4] My research in Harar has been generously supported over the years. A Ford Foundation Foreign Area Research Fellowship sponsored the original work, 1962–64. In 1975 and 1977, research was supported by The Social Science Research Council, The State University of New York Research Foundation, and a Summer Stipend from the National Endowment for the Humanities.

Territoriality and Social Organization in Islamic Cities

JANET LIPPMAN ABU-LUGHOD

In many countries of Africa and Asia people are trying to preserve an authentic sense of self in the face of the changes wrought by industrial/capitalist developments. Many are searching within their inherited cultures for features that can be used today to keep a sense of their authentic collective identities. Among Muslim peoples, this effort has been applied to architecture and urban planning.

In the longer article from which this selection is taken, Janet L. Abu-Lughod has shown how the image of the Islamic city, which some contemporary planners in the Middle East are trying to use, was actually developed by Western scholars of Islamic cultures (Orientalists). Here she argues that this image ignores the social, political, and economic factors that gave rise to this type of city. She points out that Islam itself was a contributor but not the only cause of the kind of urban development that took place earlier. Islam contributed to spatial segregation between Muslims and non-Muslims by its laws and helped to create a situation in which males and females required a high degree of separation. In addition, the relative weakness of Islamic states gave the neighborhood greater power in the city than it would have under other

Source: Abridged from "The Islamic City: Historic Myth, Islamic Essence and Contemporary Relevance." *International Journal of Middle Eastern Studies* 19:155–176, 1987. Reprinted with permission of the author and Cambridge University Press.

circumstances. She argues that these reasons for the particular form of the traditional Islamic city are unlikely to be as important today as they were in medieval and early modern times.

In her article, Janet L. Abu-Lughod uses the term semiotics. Semiotics is the study of signs. By her analysis of the semiotics of space, the author shows how spatial arrangements showed the people in these cities appropriate ways to act.

What Created the "Traditional" City in the Islamic World?

At the present time of resurgence in Islamic beliefs, the question of the Islamic city has again come to the fore. In many parts of the Arab world, and especially in Saudi Arabia and the Gulf, urban planners with a new-found respect for the great achievements of the past are searching for ways to reproduce in today's cities some of the patterns of city building that have been identified by Western Orientalists as "Islamic."[1] However, these attempts conflate an "ideal" type based upon descriptions of (mostly) North African cities in the early twentieth century with a much more complex and dynamic reality.

A modest list of the forces that created the "traditional" Islamic city in the past would include: a particular terrain/climate; a technology of production, distribution, and transportation; a system of social organization; and a legal/political system which, in Islamic places and times, could vary considerably.

It is exceedingly hard to unpack this complex bundle to determine the extent to which Islam influenced any one of them at any point in time. We must dismiss climate/terrain entirely as being "Islamic," even though the Arab region in which this genre of city building was developed had a characteristic climate/terrain as well as an historic tradition that encouraged common solutions. We must also dismiss technology as being "Islamic," for there is nothing religious about pack animals, handicraft production, small-scale market arrangements, etc., any more than there is something religious about terrain and climate. Once one eliminates the influence of these factors, one is able to explore the social, political, and legal characteristics of Islam that shaped, but did not determine, the processes whereby Islamic cities were formed, transformed, and transformed again. These are the characteristics we explore in the rest of this article (also see Abu-Lughod 1983; 1984).

Let us begin with an extreme statement: namely, that the division of the Middle Eastern-North African city into a nested set of territories with clear markers and defended borders was not Islamic per se, but reflective of a social order that had much in common with other societies based upon the family writ large (tribalism, clans, and ethnicity). Fluctuations in the strength of the markers and the degree to which boundaries were defended were contingent more upon the state of law and order than on shifts in religious ideology. This is a clear indication that religion was not the sole determining variable.

However, to say that Islam was not the only cause of urban form is not to say that it was unimportant. On the contrary, it was a crucial contributing factor in shaping cities within its realms. It contributed in several important ways.

First, Muslim theocracies routinely made rough juridical distinctions among population classes on the basis of their relation to the Umma (community of Muslim believers) and thus the State. These distinctions were thus available in the repertoire of territoriality and could be translated into spatial segregation under certain conditions. Furthermore, the frequent inability of the state to transcend these communal cleavages and the laissez-faire attitude of the state toward civil society left important functions to other units of social organization, which strengthened them.[2] Since many of these functions (such as maintaining streets, water, and lighting; guarding turf; supervising and sanctioning behavior, etc.) were highly localized within small areas, and since many local areas were composed of socially related people, what we would call the neighborhood became a crucial building block of cities in the Arab world during medieval and even later times. It was therefore available in the repertoire of social responses, sometimes employed defensively by the residents themselves when law and order broke down, sometimes employed by the state as a way to control its subjects. Whether it was a mechanism for defense or a modality for control depended upon factors that were certainly not Islamic.

Second, by encouraging gender segregation, Islam created a set of architectural and spatial imperatives that had only a limited range of solutions. What Islam required was some way of dividing functions and places on the basis of gender and then of creating a visual screen between unrelated men and women. This structuring of space was different from what would have prevailed had freer mixing of males and females been the pattern. Such spatial divisions were a functional supplement to alternative patterns of person-marking (e.g., the veil or other types of clothing), which were also used but were often not fully satisfactory. Semiotics of space in the Islamic city gave warnings and helped persons perform their required duties while still observing avoidance norms.

And finally there was the Islamic legal system of property that governed rights and obligations vis-à-vis both other property owners and the state. Such customary laws and precedents set in motion a process whereby patterns of space were continually reproduced. Of primary importance were the pre-existing rights of individual or collective users of land and immovable property. Of secondary importance were the rights and responsibilities of proximate neighbors, which took priority over those of more distant neighbors. Then, finally, as a residual, there was the right of the collectivity or larger administrative unit. Under such circumstances, access to entrances took priority over major thoroughfares or the reservation of land for public purposes.

I would like here to speculate on these three themes, drawing upon evidence from both medieval and modern time periods. Even though this is hardly a scientific approach, on occasion scholars must be willing to engage in free association to generate hypotheses, which might be fruitfully explored, even though, and perhaps especially because, such hypotheses step beyond what is known.

Territoriality in the Arabo-Islamic City

One of the most striking features of the city in the Middle East and North Africa, certainly during medieval times but to some extent persisting feebly to this day in the older residential quarters, is its subdivision into smaller quarters whose approximate boundaries remain relatively constant over time and whose names continue to be employed as important referential terms, even when they do not appear on modern markers or street names, etc.

In contrast, in his study of neighborhoods in Chicago, Albert Hunter (1974) found that territorial names seldom persisted for even a generation, much less a hundred years, and there was widespread disagreement both as to the recognizability of many neighborhood designations and as to their geographic extent and borders. To some extent, the contrast between the persisting boundaries and nomenclature in Arabo-Islamic cities and the unclear and changing character of Chicago neighborhoods can be attributed to spatial design and markers.

Kevin Lynch (1960), in his brilliant book on urban form, *The Image of the City*, tried to probe, through mental mapping, the psychology of spatial borders and spatial concepts; he concluded, interestingly enough, that some quarters and cities are more imageable than others. There is no doubt in my mind that the historic quarters of Arab cities were built to be imageable in a way that gridiron-planned Chicago was not.

The design of the Arabo-Islamic city, with its convoluted paths, was *intended* to subdivide space into relatively permanent quarters. But a recognition of this fact simply begs the question. Medieval European towns were equally devoid of right angles and through streets; they also were subdivided into potentially organizable subpockets. Nevertheless, they are quite different in physical pattern and were quite different in social organization from the medieval Arab city.[3]

One must look for more than design to explain the signification of turf in the Arabo-Islamic city. One must look for a common creator of boundaries. There may be an overarching Islamic reason for the latter. Islamic property laws about differential responsibility to neighbors and control over accessways to dwellings may have been partially responsible for the typical cellular pattern found in residential quarters of medieval Islamic cities.[4] However, I see Islamic law as an adaptive mechanism for helping the society to achieve its goals, rather than as a deus ex machina determining them. Therefore, we must go behind the issue of how imageable cells of residence were created and maintained to explore why they were so typically the building block of urban society. This brings us, then, to the three hypotheses I would like to advance.

Turf and Juridical Classes

States that make juridical distinctions among residents lay the foundation for what can evolve into a system of spatial segregation. It is a necessary but, however, not a sufficient cause of residential apartheid. That is because social distance and physical distance are not necessarily the same thing. By social distance we mean the degree to which open egalitarian interaction is blocked, or rather the amount of work that must be done by two parties to overcome social barriers to intimacy. By physical distance we mean the degree to which physical contact is blocked by space or rather the amount of work which must be done to overcome spatial barriers to face-to-face contact. Clearly, we can all think of cases in which maximum social distance can coexist with minimal spatial segregation (master-valet, master-house slave) and, conversely, other cases where minimum social distance can be sustained over great physical distance (loved ones in other countries). Indeed, it is generally when lines of social distance become less marked that physical distance is intensified.

Medieval Islamic cities certainly did maintain the distinctions between juridical classes through social distance (as evidenced by sumptuary regulations, the semiotics of clothes, body postures, etc.), but spatial distance was not always a mechanism for maintaining social distance. On occasion, however, particularly during periods of tension, physical segregation was employed to intensify the social boundary markers.

For example, a juridically different category in most Middle Eastern theocracies consisted of the *dhimmis* (Christians, Jews, and Zoroastrians enjoying a special status of protection) who, where relevant, might be subclassified by specific faith or place of origin. Always there were rules governing their behavior and regulations concerning their collective responsibilities to the state. Often there were specific restrictions on the occupations open to them. Occasionally, there were rules specifying consumption patterns (whether they could ride horses or were confined to mules, and the like) and even permitted dress. But for the most part these regulations do not seem to have been viewed as oppressive. (When they became so, as for example during the reign of al-Hakim in Cairo, they occasioned great comment about the sanity of the ruler, indicating how great a deviation from normal they were.)

Residential segregation, however, was not invariable and was seldom involuntary. Voluntary concentrations were noted over and over again in urban histories, either in relation to certain economic functions (Coptic quarters near ports in Cairo) or to certain political advantages (Jewish quarters near the palace of the ruler). Such concentrations facilitated the exercise of self-rule in matters of personal status and helped, in the proximity-based city of the time, to gather the density required to support common special services and institutions. These common services and institutions, in turn, created markers for quarters that indicated to outsiders who was supposed to live there and indicated to insiders that they belonged there.

But there were certain times and places where the potential for physical segregation was translated into the creation of absolute segregation by juridical status. In Moroccan cities, for example, Jews were not segregated into "ghettos" until the nineteenth century. The promulgation of a new government regulation at that time was rationalized as being required for the safety of the Jewish population, and it was not enforced for long. The fact that it occasioned comment and required explanation is, in itself, evidence that it was unusual to require what was often chosen.

Clearly, the extent to which territorial distinctions were based upon juridical status varied from one part of the Arabo-Islamic world to another depending in part upon the statistical representation of dhimmis of various kinds. On the Peninsula this situation did not arise until the oil boom. Similarly, North Africa after the Almohads had no important Christian minority until the appearance of Europeans, and therefore the terms Christian and European were often interchangeable. A Western quarter was by definition a Christian quarter and vice versa (Munson 1983). This was not true for Egypt or the Fertile Crescent, where indigenous Christian minorities persisted throughout the Islamic period and continued to play an integral role in society. Jewish communities were found scattered throughout the Arab world, although usually concentrated within only certain parts of countries. Such concentrations were often linked to political conditions, as when Jews of Morocco moved to Mogador at the behest of the Sultan to handle the trade in his new port, or when Jews concentrated in the capital city to take advantage of royal protection.

The events in Lebanon over the past few decades have made me think a great deal about the conditions under which juridical status differences are likely to be translated into spatial segregation. It is clear that twenty years ago Beirut had a nuclei of predominantly Christian and predominantly Muslim quarters, which were the result of long-term voluntary sifting and sorting, but such modest segregation was far from complete. It is interesting to review some of the social science literature about Beirut at that period. Samir Khalaf and Per Kongstad (1975) indicated enormous mixing of persons of various religious persuasions as late as the 1970s in Hamra, a section of what was later to be called Muslim West Beirut, due to the civil war. Similarly, Fuad Khuri's anthropological study (1975) of the peaceful relations between a predominantly Muslim suburb of Beirut and its adjacent neighbor, a predominantly Christian suburb, stressed the intermixing of people and their coexistence. And yet, the civil war that erupted in 1975 began at the border between Fuad Khuri's two suburbs, and Hamra became an almost exclusively Muslim quarter in the course of the civil war and then the Israeli siege. It was not segregation that gave rise to intercommunal tensions; rather, it was tensions that gave rise to labels, which were then partially translated into reality, as population resifted and resorted itself to share a common fate. To the very end of the 1982 Israeli siege of Beirut, however, so-called Muslim West Beirut was never exclusively Muslim, as eyewitness accounts confirm.

Thinking over the present experience makes it possible to read back into history to try to fathom under what circumstances juridical status might have changed from a potential to a real cause of ethnic/religious segregation. It is clear that at times of outside threat when the state was weak, fragmentation was likely along the fault lines of society, which in Islamic states tend to lie along juridical status cleavages. When loyalty to the state is crucial, when defense becomes paramount, and when the state itself is under attack, one can expect segregation—either to protect or to control.

Economic threats may be as significant as military ones. The sectarian cleavages of Lebanese society were strongest in the late nineteenth century and appear to have been related to western commercial incursions (Fawaz 1983). The incursions of a commercial Europe into Moroccan economic life at the beginning of the nineteenth century seem to account for both the institution of Jewish ghettos in Fez and Rabat and the creation of Mogador as a largely Jewish commercial port.

The present experience also helps us to fathom how the transition might have taken place. Designation of a specific area as ethno-religious turf helps both to drive out others and to gather in persons of similar status. If, in addition, there are decrees or laws promulgated or if there are sanctions imposed, the segregation is intensified. (For example, after the ghetto in Rabat was established in 1807, guards were posted at the single entrance to the quarter to supervise entry and exit. The dual function of defense of inmates and control over them is clearly evident in the semiotics of space.)

Gender Segregation and the Arabo-Islamic City Form

The creation of male and female turf is perhaps the most important element of the structure of the Middle Eastern city contributed by Islam. It is important to remember, however, that the rules of turf were not only to establish physically distinctive regions; more important, they were to establish visually distinctive or insulated regions. The object was not only to prevent physical contact but to protect visual privacy. Line-of-sight distance, rather than physical distance, was the object of urban design. Thus, Islamic law regulated the placement of windows, the heights of adjacent buildings and the mutual responsibilities of neighbors toward one another in order to guard the visual privacy of women. Architecture assisted this process. Not only the devices of *mashribiyya* (lattice

Street in the older part of Rabat, Morocco. Note the narrowness of the street and the few windows visible. [Photo by Walter P. Zenner]

wood) screening but the layout of houses and even of quarters created the strangely asymmetrical reality that women could see men, but men could not see women, except those in certain relationships with them. Here is Lane-Poole's description of an Egyptian upper-class house in the early twentieth century:

> [As one enters the house there] is a passage, which bends sharply after the first yard or two, and bars any view into the interior from the open door. At the end of this passage we emerge into an open court. . . . Here is no sign of life; the doors are jealously closed, the windows shrouded. . . . We shall see nothing of the domestic life of the inhabitants; for the women's apartments are carefully shut off from the court. . . . The lower rooms, opening directly off the court are those into which a man may walk with

> impunity and no risk of meeting any of the women . . . [Another]
> door opens out of the court into the staircase leading to the harim
> rooms, and here no man but the master of the house dare
> penetrate. . . . When a man returns there he is in the bosom of
> his family, and it would need a very urgent affair to induce the
> doorkeeper to summon him down to anyone who called to see
> him. (Lane-Poole 1902:12–17)

But one need not take the testimony of a foreign observer to substantiate the universality of some of the principles. In the *aqsar* (castles) of southern Morocco, one can find the same bent entrances designed to create a visual blind spot. And urban building regulations were replete with requirements that the doors of buildings occupying opposite sides of the street must not face one another, another mechanism of visual control.

Similarly, within the dwelling the ideal was to segregate public from private space so that males could circulate without interfering with the movement and activities of females. Obviously, this was possible only, if at all, for the very wealthy, such as the household home that was described above. Compare Lane-Poole's account with the following description of elite housing in Jidda, Saudi Arabia, in the 1960s.

> A typical old house includes a wing for the men, usually on the
> first floor, with an access to the garden and to the ground floor
> balconies. In this part of the house the head of the household
> has his sleeping room, study, guest rooms, and sitting rooms.
> The second and third floors belong to the women; one is for daily
> living and another for receiving guests. (Altorki 1986:30)

For the poor, no such absolute segregation was possible. Rather, signs and codes helped regulate spatial symbiosis, often by rules that governed timing.

The most obvious semiotic of sexual segregation in the Islamic city was the sign used in front of the public bath to indicate ladies' day. Subtler signs governed other divisions of time and/or space, however. Take, for example, the zone just outside the houses that share a common accessway in a dead-end quarter. These are found in most parts of the Arab world, from the Fertile Crescent to Morocco. I have elsewhere termed this space *semi-private space*, a third category between public and private that is found infrequently in sex-integrated societies.[5]

The fact is that the ideal of separation between the sexes is best achieved by the wealthy who can afford to duplicate space and can afford the servant or slave girls who were never guarded from male sight or contact. Most poor women were less able to meet the ideal.

For them, the family writ large permitted the doing of tasks as well as the protection from strange males because the local neighborhood was an extension of the home and therefore the family. The blind alley or dead-end court street was such a device for achieving this compromise between the exigencies of life and the directives of female seclusion. Nawal Nadim has written very sensitively on this subject in her contemporary anthropological study of life in a poor *harah* (neighborhood) passageway in Cairo.

> A large number of activities take place in the harah [neighborhood] passage which in other parts of Cairo, or even during different historic stages of the harah, would be restricted to the physical setting of the dwelling. . . . [T]he manner and form of familiarity with which various intimate activities are carried out in the harah passage make it evident that the alley is actually considered by both sexes to be a private domain. Members of the two sexes in the harah treat each other with familiarity similar to that existing among members of the same family. Even outside the harah, any male resident is responsible for protecting any female member of his harah. He is further responsible for what she does, and he has the right to interfere in her activities if he finds them inappropriate. (Nadim 1975:174)

As one can see from this discussion, the family is simply written larger when it is impossible to achieve the physical and visual separation required between strangers. I am struck with the similarity of these rules in semi-private urban space to those that apply within an encampment of sedentarized bedouins (Lila Abu-Lughod 1986:1–35). It is clear that when densities are high and houses too small to contain the manifold activities women are supposed to do in them, the spillover space becomes appropriated as semi-private space, and co-residents who might inadvertently have visual access are appropriated into a fictive kinship relationship to neutralize danger. Dress is an important part of the semiotics of space. As Nadim notes, "clothing which is acceptable for a woman within the lodging is also acceptable in the harah" (Nadim 1975:180).

Nor is it only in Egypt that such adaptations take place. Elizabeth Fernea (1975) in her book on Marrakech, indicates that when women ran next door within the enclosed portion of their street, they did not cover themselves as fully as they would have, had they been going into public space. It was all in the family. Clearly, then, one of the reasons why the older pattern of city building has been maintained in many sections of Arabo-Islamic cities, even today, is that it is still well adapted to the complex demands for visual privacy for females.

Courtyard in the older part of Acre, Israel. The windows of the dwelling face the courtyard rather than the street. [Photo by Walter P. Zenner]

I am often struck, as I wander around Arab cities, with how easy it is to tell whether I am in public space or have blundered into semi-private space. I have often tried to identify the markers that indicate this. A sudden narrowing of the path, particularly if that narrowing has been exaggerated by the implanting of low stone posts or even a pile of bricks, is a sign of the shift, especially when the road widens again soon afterward. But even when the spatial semiotics are absent, the personal ones are present. There is the questioning look or the approach of someone wanting to help but clearly also wanting to know what you are doing there!

Institutions have been retained from earlier periods, one of which is the *nadorgi* (from *nadara*, to "sight") who, in Nadim's Cairo harah, was responsible not only for overseeing proper behavior between male and female harah residents but also for spotting strangers. As she describes it:

the nadorgi . . . is responsible for keeping an eye on those entering the harah and detecting their movements. He is usually someone whose shop or house is close to the entrance to the harah where he remains most of the time. Besides being a source of information concerning external movement into the harah, the nadorgi can provide equally valuable insights into the internal movements of the various harah residents. . . . Whenever illegal activities occur in the harah, and in most cases this is the smoking or trading of hashish, the role of the nadorgi becomes vital since he quickly warns of the entrance of outsiders into the harah. The nadorgi will approach the outsider under the pretense of wishing to help him find whomever he wants. This tactic serves two purposes: first, it detains the intruder and secondly, it provides the nadorgi with information about the outsider's destination and contact. (Nadim 1975:187–188)

We shall return to this point when we investigate the other function of the neighborhood in the Arabo-Islamic city, namely, defensive space.

The Neighborhood as a Key Element in Civil Society and the State

The final way in which Islam shaped the traditional Arabo-Islamic city was through neglect, ironic as that may seem. By failing to concern itself with matters of day-to-day maintenance, Islamic states often encouraged the vitality of other sub-state functional units. One of these was definitely the residential neighborhood.

The rather more rigid segregation between commercial and residential quarters in the classic Islamic city, as contrasted with the medieval European city, has been attributed to the need to separate private (i.e., female) from public (i.e., male) space. Whatever the cause, such segregation certainly did have important effects. It left to the residential areas a large measure of autonomy, since many of the public functionaries (the supervisors of the marketplaces or the supervisors of public morals) operated largely in the commercial sections of the city. Neighborhoods handled many of their internal functions on a more ad hoc basis, being unable to afford more commercialized services. For example, in the *aswaq* (markets), adjacent merchants might hire a guard, but in the neighborhoods more informal arrangements were likely. Having functions that could only be performed on a neighborhood-wide basis certainly strengthened cooperation within the district. It must also be acknowledged, however, that before the modern era, which emphasized the separation of population on the basis of class, the neighborhood often was composed of a leading family-household, surrounded by poorer families, which had a clientele relationship to the dominant household. In such cases, what we think of as municipal services were actually provided by the dominant household.

A second factor that strengthened the neighborhood was its role as protector. I would like to explore the issue of turf and defended neighborhoods because I find the literature produced by Orientalists on the role of *zu'ar* (militant), *futuwwa* (chivalrous society), etc., in the medieval Islamic city highly deficient in sociological sense. I have been struck over and over again with the fact that the traditional Arabo-Islamic city was designed to maximize what Newman has termed *defensible space*.

In the introduction to his book, *Defensible Space: Crime Prevention through Urban Design*, Oscar Newman (1972:2–3) writes that he is trying to find an architectural solution to the rising disorder in American cities. He claims:

> Architectural design can make evident by the physical layout that an area is the shared extension of the private realms of a group of individuals. For one group to be able to set the norms of behavior and the nature of activity possible within a particular place, it is necessary that it have clear, unquestionable control over what can occur there. Design can make is possible for both inhabitant and stranger to perceive that an area is under the undisputed influence of a particular group, that they dictate the activity taking place within it, and who its users are to be. This can be made so clearly evident that residents will not only feel confident, but that it is incumbent upon them to question the comings and goings of people to ensure the continued safety of the defined areas. Any intruder will be made to anticipate that his presence will be under question and open to challenge; so much so that a criminal can be deterred from even contemplating entry.
>
> *Defensible space* is a model for residential environments which inhibits [sic] crime by creating the physical expression of a social fabric that defends itself.

Certainly, what Newman has just described is the Arabo-Islamic semi-private quarter par excellence. But is the picture as benign as he has drawn it? Yes, the neighborhood defends itself—but perhaps it is defending its criminal activities or its warfare with the rest of society. Two non-benign parallels present themselves. These are boys' gangs and the militia turf in embattled Beirut during the civil war. Both offer a seamier view of the defensible space advocated by Newman.

Boys' gangs were certainly a feature of Arabo-Islamic cities in the past and continue to be present today. Concepts such as futuwwa and zu'ar may be given exotic meaning and significance by Orientalists, but to a sociologist they have a most familiar mien. We recognize the organization of local young males for the defense of their quarter—whether such organizations are called Latin Kings or Awlad al-Harah (literally, "the boys in the 'hood"). We recognize the gang leader, whether he is called Jeff Fort or Mohammed ibn Ali, and we recognize his role, whether he is called Doc or *Za'im* (Boss). Even the so-called codes of chivalry are to be found in boys' gangs.

Urban sociologist Gerald Suttles paralleled Newman's approach in his conceptualization of a "defended neighborhood" which he defined as a "residential group which seals itself off through the efforts of delinquent gangs, by restrictive covenants, by sharp boundaries, or by a forbidding reputation." He specifies the conditions under which defended neighborhoods become important in cities. (Here he is discussing places like Chicago, not Cairo, and yet the applicability is obvious):

> Granted the inability of formal procedures of social control to detect and forestall all or even most forms of urban disorder, some additional mechanisms seem necessary for the maintenance of order. Among the available mechanisms, a set of rules governing and restricting spatial movement seems a likely and highly effective means of preserving order. Such a set of rules has some fairly obvious advantages: it segregates groups that are otherwise likely to come into conflict; it restricts the range of association and decreases anonymity; it thrusts people together into a common network of social relations that overlap rather than diverge from one another. (Suttles 1972:2)

Residents are particularly likely to intensify their defense when the order in the outside society becomes weakened. Historically, in Arabo-Islamic cities, the neighborhood has been in a dialectical relationship to the external society. When central power was strong and when the city-wide hierarchical structure was working smoothly, agents of the central administration operated within the neighborhoods to provide information to the center and ensure conformance with central directives. This was certainly the case with the sheikh of the harah in Cairo at certain points, when he was essentially an informer for the police as well as for the *muhtasib* (inspector of morals). In his capacity as real estate expert, he acted to "steer" or supervise who should have access to vacant dwelling units in the quarter. Sometimes, the neighborhood was an administrative subset of the state. More often, however, the quarter played the opposite role, that of a defended neighborhood, particularly when chaos reigned. One reads, in the historical accounts of civil strife/invasions/street battles, the recurring phrase, "and people closed the gates to their harat" (pl. of harah). Alternatively, to gain control over the city, conquerors always had to destroy the gates to the harat, as Napoleon's forces did when they invaded Cairo.

One has only to think of Beirut during the recent civil war to have these phrases take on fuller meaning. During the height of disorder, virtually every block belonged to a different group or faction. Checkpoints blocked entry and exit to these defended territories. Often, barricades were constructed at the boundaries. The opposite side of defense was also evident. During the Israeli siege of 1982, neighborhood assistance was organized by block communities which allocated vacant apartments, oversaw the rationing of water use, and distributed food and medical relief as needed. One cannot resist reading back into history to evaluate some of the roles neighborhoods formerly played in the Arabo-Islamic city.[6]

Conclusions and a Note of Warning

Elsewhere we attempted to deconstruct Orientalist thinking about the Islamic city by showing not only that the idea itself was "created" on the basis of too few cases but, even worse, was a model of outcomes rather than one of processes. By that I mean that the goal was to generalize about a specific form of city at one long historic moment without unpacking the various causes of that particular outcome. That form was then equated with the Islamic city, regardless of whether there was anything particularly Islamic about the causes.

The reason it is important to criticize this approach is that in a number of Arab countries today planners are trying to recreate Islamic cities—but by means which are terribly inappropriate because they focus on outcomes, rather than processes. Such planners hope, by edict and ordinance, to preserve and to build anew cities on an Islamic pattern. It should be clear by now, however, why this approach is likely to fail.

Cities are processes, not products. The three Islamic elements that set in motion the processes that give rise to Islamic cities were: a distinction between the members of the Umma and outsiders, which led to juridical and spatial distinction by neighborhoods; the segregation of the sexes which gave rise to a particular solution to the question of spatial organization; and a legal system which, rather than imposing general regulations over land uses of various types in various places, left to the litigation of neighbors the detailed adjudication of mutual rights over space and use. These three factors were Islamic, per se.

However, in addition, the historic cities that developed in Arabo-Islamic lands in premodern times were deeply influenced by such non-Islamic factors as climate, terrain, technologies of construction, circulation, and production, as well as political variables such as the relation between rulers and the ruled, the general level of intercommunal strife, and fluctuations in the degree of internal and external security. Furthermore, the nature of any Islamic city at any point in time was the result not only of the contemporaneous nature of these variables but the inherited forms that took shape under earlier and different circumstances.

It is clear, then, that one does not have the capacity to recreate Islamic cities by edict. One has only the capacity to create conditions that might set in motion processes that, in the past, generated the forms of the traditional city in the Arabo-Islamic world. But it must be recognized that one cannot do that without being willing to live with the three conditions mentioned above, namely: (1) juridical distinctions between Muslims and/or citizens and outsiders; (2) segregation by gender and a virtually complete division of labor according to it; and (3) a fully decentralized and ex post facto system of land use and governmental regulation over space. In today's world, these three are considered retrogressive.

First, modern states accord basic rights and responsibilities in an egalitarian manner—at least in theory. Where distinctions are made on the basis of ascribed status they have attracted the criticism of the world. Hence, states such as pre-1994 South Africa, which made sharp juridical distinctions on the basis of color, or Israel and certain Muslim theocracies, which make similar distinctions on the basis of religion, are accused of using racist criteria. And contemporary societies that are organized on the basis of communal affiliations run the risk of fragmentation and strife, as occurred so tragically in Lebanon. Second, throughout the world there has been a trend toward increased equality between the sexes. Integration, not segregation, has been the ideal toward which most cultures are moving. Finally, modern municipal governments stress the provision of community facilities through a centralized system and stress the establishment of laws that apply to whole classes of places and uses, that is, zoning laws, building codes, street alignments, subdivision regulations, etc. Such regulations, as we have tried to show, are the antithesis of the assumptions and mechanisms of property law under Islamic legal approaches.

Therefore, none of the conditions still exist that would permit us to reconstruct Islamic cities by design. Only an essentialist view of the Islamic city, such as that held by earlier Orientalists, would allow one to even entertain such a notion.

That is not to say, however, that we could not build better cities in the contemporary Arabo-Islamic world if we paid closer attention to some of the true achievements of the past and if we learned from them. The historic Islamic city often achieved community, privacy, and beauty. It would be wise to seek these same goals, even though the old means are no longer available. But since cities are living processes rather than formalistic shells for living, they cannot be built by us. We can only encourage them to grow in the desired direction. Can we nurture neighborhoods that are supportive but not defensive? Can we foster privacy not for women alone but for households? Can we guard the rights of neighbors while still applying laws consistently? That is the task Arab city planners must set for themselves.

Notes

¹ Many of my reservations about the Islamic city have been triggered by discussions and conferences with Muslims from the Arabian Peninsula where, at present, the most serious and sincere efforts are being made to devise an operational definition of the Islamic city in order to build contemporary ones. Several students of mine from this area have forced me to think about this topic, if only because they were charged with studying how to do so. I acknowledge their contribution here.

² I would not necessarily attribute this to Islam, but I would note that such a pattern was all too often associated with its polities, for whatever reason.

³ Gideon Sjoberg (1960, but also see his articles above) has argued that Eastern and Western versions were quite similar due to their common level of technology. However, he ignores the fact that tribalism-ethnicity was seldom the organizing principle of spatial structure in Western medieval towns, nor was there as much separation between residence and business as there was in cities where gender segregation was the rule (i.e., in ancient Greece and in Islamdom).

⁴ Hakim (1986) argues this in convincing fashion, but he draws his empirical evidence almost exclusively from Tunis. I doubt that Islamic law can be the sole explanation, because the cellular structure of communities in that climate and culture region long predates the appearance of Islam, and the alternative to the "*harah, mahallah, humah*," etc. system found throughout the Fertile Crescent and North Africa, namely the tall *qasr* or apartment building found in Yemen, southern Morocco, and Saudi Arabia, is equally Islamic in being indigenously developed and suited to the cultural and geopolitical climate.

[5] See my article, "Contemporary Relevance of Islamic Planning Principles" (Abu-Lughod 1980). One should note, however, that this "privatization of public space" is not exclusively a phenomenon of the Arabo-Islamic or Middle Eastern city. In fact, I have taken this term from Lofland (1985) who uses it to describe how Americans develop proprietary interests in public space.

[6] Comparative studies are always valuable because they prevent us from jumping prematurely to the conclusion that our case is unique. In this connection, it is interesting to note the parallels from an entirely different case, Santo Domingo during the 1965 revolution. The social organization is graphically portrayed by a participant-observer, sociologist Jose Moreno (1970).

The Genesis and Function of Squatter Settlements in Brasília

DAVID EPSTEIN

Squatter settlements are found all over the world. Known variously as favelas *(Brazil),* barriadas *(Peru),* villas miserias *(Argentina),* colonias proletarias *(Mexico),* bidonvilles *(French-speaking Africa), and* bustees *(India), these settlements have one thing in common: they provide a place to live for poor people, many of them migrants to the city who cannot obtain any other form of housing. The internal characteristics of squatter settlements and their inhabitants have been the subject of much social science research. In this article David Epstein uses an historical-structuralist approach. He focuses on the interconnections between the poor and the dominant strata to explain the function of squatter settlements and why they persist despite government policy to the contrary. While the case of Brasília may seem peculiar to the Third World, recent reports about the shortage of affordable housing for workers in Colorado ski resorts shows that this problem can arise anywhere.*

Urban squatting is the fastest-growing, and one of the most wide-spread forms of settlement in Brazil and in many other countries in the underdeveloped sector of the capitalist world. Social scientists and public officials have often failed to take into account factors

Source: Reproduced by permission of the Society for Applied Anthropology from *The Anthropology of Urban Environments*, Monograph No. 11, 1972.

on the international and national levels which account for the existence of squatting in cities such as Brasília, the new "planned" capital of Brazil. The sources of this neglect also underlie many of the widespread misconceptions and mistakes in writing about urban poverty and worldwide underdevelopment in general.

In the case of Brasília, an understanding of the development of the squatter settlement component of the urban settlement pattern requires attention to the class, urban-rural, and regional disparities in the economy, and to the requirements for a low-wage labor in the face of low governmental priority for the housing and other needs of workers. Although planners and officials in Brasília inveigh against squatting, it is in fact a product of the same process of development that produced Brasília and in practice is tolerated and regulated by the same institutions that officially condemn it.

A squatter settlement in a city is an area where people build houses in violation of the formal legal rules about property rights, zoning, and type and quality of construction. Squatter settlements (or squatments) may be distinguished from slums in that most squatters (at least initially, and by their own, if not by official definition) own the houses they live in.[1] Large numbers of squatters, though by no means all of them, are members of the urban working class or the urban un- and underemployed, and large numbers of them, though again by no means all, live in housing of low prestige and durability. Slums, on the other hand, are inhabited mostly by renters, and the most common house types are the decayed town house and various types of tenements especially built for rental to the urban poor.

The Dualist Fallacy

One approach to squatter settlements is to regard them as fundamentally divorced from the city around them. When squatters are conceived of as in-migrants from rural areas regarded as the "traditional" sector of a dual society, the assumption of urban dualism follows naturally from the dualist image of the national society as a whole. Thus, just as Jacques Lambert (1959) argues that there are "two Brazils," a conclave of social workers in Brasília suggested that there are two Brasílias:

> The phenomenon of marginality which appears in the Latin American countries indicates the existence of a *dual urban social structure* and has in the economic factor one of the variables of its appearance.

> In addition to this economic variable, which assumes undeniable
> importance in the configuration of the situation of urban
> marginality, the concentration of marginalized groups in certain
> characteristic zones of urban space is observed [emphasis
> added]. (Lambert 1967:2)

While an effort is made to give this term a technical definition, or
at least usage, it should be noted that the Brazilian term *marginal*
is most often used in crime reporting to refer to individuals from
the lower-class, criminal milieu, such as pickpockets, illegal lottery
salesmen (*bicheiros*), pimps, and muggers. Use of the term, even
in a professional context, must evoke in most middle-class
Brazilians associations of the squatting phenomenon with crime,
violence, and social pathology in general, in correspondence with
their standard prejudices.[2]

Others argue that squatter settlements are in some sense rural,
either because of the alleged similarity of architectural forms to
those in rural areas or because of the supposed provenience and
associated social and cultural characteristics of their inhabitants
(Bonilla 1962).[3] Bastide suggests that the cultural assimilation of
foreigners in Brazilian cities is easier than that of rural migrants
who are ". . . bearers of a folk culture, because (a) internal migrations are family migrations . . . (and) (b) the rural family in the city
continues to 'socialize' its children according to rural models"
(Bastide 1964:76).

Building on the concept of subculture, Bastide goes on to suggest
that shantytowns are the locales of "microcultures" which are
sharply distinct from the urban milieu as a whole.

Other analysts are concerned with the effect on individual
personality of the allegedly rapid cultural change taking place in
rural-urban migration. Pye, for instance, suggests (and laments)
that the maladjustment and insecurity he believes associated with
such migration offer a threat to the national and international status
quo. This argument relies very heavily on a concept of social duality
similar to the arguments of the commentators already cited. States
Pye:

> Urbanization is . . . a profoundly disruptive process. In nearly
> all transitional societies the early emergence of urban centers
> has produced a *fundamental cleavage* between the worlds of
> the more modernized cities and the more traditional and village-
> based people. This *bifurcation of the social structure* is usually
> matched in the economic realm by the development of *dual
> economies*. In the psychological sphere the rapid transition from
> the compact and intimate world of the village to the highly

impersonal and anonymous world of the city can leave people
with deep personal insecurities.

Thus in a multitude of ways rapid urbanization can cause social,
economic, and psychological tensions which, translated into the
political realm, become sources of instability and obstacles to
rapid nation building [emphasis added]. (Pye 1963:84)

Lewis's concept of the *culture of poverty* is more carefully hedged
than any of the foregoing discussions, but it also emphasizes the
distinctiveness of its bearers from the larger society, rather than
the role they play in it. While on the one hand Lewis defines the
culture of poverty as a subculture and hence presumably a product
of Western capitalism, on the other hand he states:

It is a culture in the traditional anthropological sense in that it
provides human beings with a design for living, with a ready-
made set of solutions for human problems, and so serves a
significant adaptive function. (Lewis 1966:19)

The concept of the culture of poverty focuses attention on the
relative lack of organization and the isolation of its bearers. Yet
Lewis recognizes that many urban squatters may display a sense
of community untypical of the culture of poverty, especially when
the settlements are low-rent areas of stable residence, physically
and ethnically, racially or linguistically distinct from their surroundings (1966:23).

A synthesis of these outlooks would suggest that squatter
settlements, contrasting so sharply with the loci of oligarchic
traditionalism and the new Latin American consumerism (e.g., the
modern superblocks and monumental architecture of Brasília's
Pilot Plan), house people who, while they may or may not be bearers
of the culture of poverty, are isolated from modern Brazilian
national life and are rural, marginal, and maladjusted.[4] Fundamentally, these views suggest the squatters' living conditions and
their physical separation from the city derive from their failure to
pass from "traditional" rural ways to "modern" urban society, a
view evocative of the new unilinealism of the bourgeois liberal
development theorists such as W. W. Rostow and Cyril E. Black
(Rostow 1960; Black 1966).

The empirical basis for the pathologist-dualist viewpoint lies in
the blatant economic and social inequality which pervades every
phase of urban life in those cities where squatting exists. The
presence of this inequality is made painfully apparent by the
frequently close juxtaposition of shabby and foul-smelling squatments with luxury apartments, as in Rio de Janeiro, or with
monumental symbolic architecture, as in Brasília.

The policy implications of this view are equally clear—either eliminate these nests of social pathology and potential subversion by means of massive clearance and public housing projects or missionize their residents with community development and other professionally mediated forms of middle-class morality in order to integrate them into the modern sphere of the society. In fact, the writings of much of this school resemble the older religious missionary forms of colonialist humanitarianism, which translated the poverty and strange customs of the natives into a mandate to provide them as soon as possible with the blessings of clothing and Methodism. Today [1972] the Peace Corps tells its applicants that "the most basic contribution a Volunteer can make is to inject some sense of community, some inkling of latent power into a village or slum." This in spite of the fact that squatters have often successfully resisted repeated legal and forcible attempts to remove them and have developed complex networks of voluntary associations of various types!

In fact, both clearance (Safa 1964; Salmen 1969) and community development have been unsuccessful by almost any objective or subjective index. In part this failure is a consequence of the errors of individual programs and their executors, but only in part. It is also a product of the empirical and theoretical inadequacy of the pathologist-dualist position. There is little evidence that squatters are "folk" unable or unwilling to become "urban," or that they have failed to become integrated into the society, and much more evidence that it is the *form* of their integration that has resulted in the spectacular contrast between their lifeways and living conditions and those of their more affluent neighbors. It is not any lack of ties with the dominant sectors of the society that is the problem, but the kinds of ties that exist.

We may apply to dualist analyses of squatting the same criticism that may be made of dualist treatments of the relationship between the Northeast and the Paraiba Valley industrial region in Brazil, Indians and the larger societies of Mexico and Peru, and blacks and whites in the United States. Emphasis on the synchronic, internal characteristics that distinguish a subordinate (satellite, colonized) social group from the group that dominates it (the metropolis) may lead to neglect or even denial of the historic and continuing interconnections between the two groups, which gave rise to and sustain the disparity between them. From this first fallacy it is easy to move on to the assumption that the cure for the situation lies in the diffusion of certain characteristics from the dominant sector to the other or in the full integration of the dependent sector into the dominant. In fact, it is often at least arguable that the solution lies in transforming the nature of the already existing interconnection, or in eliminating the tie completely. To deemphasize the importance of the metropolis-satellite relationship, as the dualists do, is of course to obscure the possibility of such a revolutionary transformation.[5]

In contrast to the cruder imputations of the dualists, many writers emphasize the adaptive or even conservative characteristics of urban squatting. These writers describe a squatting cycle leading from the first tentative efforts to invade private or, more often, public land, to resistance to official challenges to their land tenure and, sometimes, to a high degree of stability as urban neighborhoods (Mangin 1963, 1964, 1965, 1967; Turner 1963). Some writers emphasize that except on the issue of land tenure, squatters tend to be politically centrist or even conservative (Bourricard 1964; Halperin 1963; Peattie, n.d.). Many anthropologists identify with squatters as with other informants and, in particular, look askance at uncritical schemes to "eradicate" squatting, establish public housing, and "reform" squatters (Safa 1964) and emphasize the relative satisfaction of the migrants with the squatment as opposed to their places of origin, especially when these are rural (Herrick 1966; Pastore 1968).

As a policy prescription, this view seemingly would imply a cautious attitude to mass clearance programs and would tend to suggest that public housing schemes (especially high-rise schemes and pay-as-you-go plans) fail to fulfill the needs of many squatters. Rather, where conditions permit, the indicated policy would seem to be one of granting land tenure free or at low cost and promoting improvements in such areas as water supply, electricity, and sewage. Some planners, as in Ciudad Guyana, a new industrial city in Venezuela (Rodwin, n.d.), have even favored regarding squatting as inevitable and setting aside areas where it can be permitted with relatively little disruption of the city plan.

Whatever the virtues of squatting as a strategy of survival or upward mobility, however, squatters continue at or near the bottom of a highly polarized urban social structure—if they are upwardly mobile, their ascent is a fairly shallow one. Even more accurate and less alarmist ethnographic data, if it is focused upon the characteristics of squatters and their settlements to the neglect of their position in the society as a whole and its development, takes the squatters' social position as a given and fails to come to grips with the roots of the problem.

Isolate and System

As anthropologists have moved from the study of the most primitive and small-scale of the social units comprising the underdeveloped sector of the global society to rural units in more developed parts of the society to the study of urban society, they have striven resolutely to retain two related attitudes. The first is to regard the unit under investigation, whether a tribe, a village, a neighborhood, a family, an individual, or a squatter settlement, as an isolate, a social organism, a largely self-sufficient entity. The second attitude has been characterized by Martin Nicholaus as keeping their "eyes . . . turned downwards, and their palms upwards" (Nicholaus 1968:9–10). In other words, they study the powerless under the auspices of the powerful, and the information they produce is much more readily available to the latter than to the former. This has been true in spite of the fact that many anthropologists have been sympathetic intermediaries between the rulers and the ruled (Gough 1968).

Without reducing anthropological works in general to the level of crude ideology, these two attitudes have tended to minimize the conflict of their holders with the dominant sectors of society. With a few exceptions (e.g., Leeds 1968), anthropologists have failed to provide much that is helpful to our understanding of elites or of national and international societies, except insofar as the isolates they study may be assumed to be representative.[6] In this sense anthropology has shared what Mills criticized in his *Sociological Imagination* as the "abstracted empiricist" retreat from the classical tradition of the social sciences.

The increased interest in cities on the part of anthropologists is to a degree a sign that some anthropologists are abandoning the traditional idealization of the exotic and the primitive.[7] Yet they have clung to emphasis upon the study of lower-class and lumpen elements studied as isolates by methods which resemble as closely as possible the methods used in primitive and peasant villages.

The facts of life in cities and the clear lack of demographic, social, and political equilibrium that are apparent on inspection, however, make the simple application of traditional research orientations untenable. Indeed, given a larger-than-local perspective it becomes apparent that the bulk of the ethnographic data we possess consists of "snapshots" (synchronic views) of primitives in the process of being peasantized, peasants in the process of being proletarized, and ruralities in the process of becoming urbanized,[8] whether through migration to cities or through the extension of formerly "urban" technology and institutions to the countryside. Most of the units traditionally studied by anthropologists as if they were microcosms are, in fact, subsegments of subsegments of a global system of social, and cultural relations established in the wake of the worldwide expansion of Western power. Even the nation-states themselves, in many cases, are specialized parts of this global underdevelopment system. The investigator who seeks to explain the forms taken by component units of this system ignores its existence and its specific forms at his peril; the applied social scientist who seeks to effect piecemeal change without considering how his efforts are conditioned by the requirements of the system and its component parts may be bitterly disappointed. The NATO intellectuals and their successors, who seek to explain the global disparities of wealth, power, and prestige as a consequence of the failure of "traditional" societies or "traditional" segments of dual societies to become "modernized," are at best neglectful of the structure and history of the underdevelopment system.

None of the foregoing should be interpreted as a suggestion that specific empirical studies are a waste of time and that all research should be directed toward the characteristics of the global society as a whole. It is rather to assert that such studies must be informed by some notion of what the underdevelopment system is all about and what it implies for the specific nation, region, or city and smaller social unit under examination.

The Case of Brasília

These rather broad assertions can only be exemplified within the limited scope of the present article or, indeed, even by far more extended discussion about a single city. In the late fifties, Brazil's federal government began to put into practice a century-old plan to build a new national capital in the savanna country (*cerrados*) of Southern Goiás state in the country's Central Plateau. The construction was guided by a plan written by Lúcio Costa, an eminent Brazilian architect-planner (1957:41–44). Approximately ten years after construction began in earnest, two-thirds of the population of the capital lived in areas whose urban ecology and architecture were in direct contradiction to the apartment-house superblocks proposed in the original plan. More than 15 percent of the population was housed in technically illegal squatter settlements and over 50 percent in satellite towns whose legality, while unquestioned, was granted in consequence of a last-ditch official effort to limit squatting to some degree. Many of the dwellings in the satellite towns were constructed of the same materials and have the same physical characteristics as those in squatter settlements.

The decision to construct Brasília in the face of the nation's scarce capital resources and the characteristics of the original plan reflected the character of the political and social stratification system of Brazil, in at least the following respects: (1) the monumentalist emphasis on dramatic architecture and broad vistas; (2) the favoring of automotive circulation in spite of the fact that cars remain a luxury for the vast majority of the Brazilian population; (3) the cursory attention paid to the needs and desires of the first residents (the construction workers) and to the lower-class residents in general; (4) the nondevelopmental, static, or skeletal character of the plan, expressed as a final output rather than a process of growth, which at all stages would involve human lives; (5) the necessity, given prevailing political practice in Brazil, of finishing the city according to plan within a three-year period (Kubitschek's presidential mandate) if it was not to be later abandoned; (6) the centralized character of the planning and execution processes themselves, with no provision for consultation or participation by any but upper-level technical and political personnel; and finally, (7) the division of the city into hierarchical sectors. The plan is thus false to the nature of social interaction in cities.[9] The general neglect of the social, in any serious sense, as opposed to the aesthetic and the symbolic, is one of the hallmarks of the plan and of Brazilian elite culture in general.

Squatting and Labor Supply

Building Brasília required large numbers of workers, who came from the poorest sections of Brazil, the Northeast (including Bahia), and the Center-West. According to various surveys conducted, from half to two-thirds of the residents of the largest squatter settlement in Brasília, the Social Security Invasion,[10] came from the Northeast of Bahia, and from one- to two-fifths from the Center-West States of Goiás and Minas Gerais.[11] Invariably the migrants themselves cite economic motivations as primary in their decision to move, although some comments in more extensive discussions indicate that many migrants were not unaffected by the more glamorous aspects of the Brasília experiment.

Just as the main strategic resource supplied by Africa in the slavery period was labor, today many underdeveloped regions of economies such as Brazil's have as a principal function the exportation of cheap labor. In Brazil this function is fulfilled by the

Northeast and to a lesser extent by some other rural areas, such as in Minas Gerais. The Northeast regularly disgorges migratory streams in accordance with the exigencies of the economy—to the Amazon if the revival of the rubber trade becomes necessary, to the industries of São Paulo, or to Brasília when a new capital is abuilding. Minas Gerais, a secondary source of such migrants, is also a case of the pattern of regional underdevelopment Frank calls "passive involution" (1967). To the extent that the conditions that underlie this exportation of human beings thereby serve the needs of the extant economic and political elites, serious doubts must arise as to the prospects for success of programs administered by these same elites with the declared intention of combating regional underdevelopment.

These considerations also apply to the urban squatter settlements, which serve as reception areas and places of residence for the migrants and some of their descendants and thus owe their existence to the distribution of wealth and power, which underlies the migratory process. Rather than viewing such settlements (with alarm or otherwise) as the products of an alleged failure to diffuse urban-industrial values to the rural-oriented lower class or as the pathological consequences of mismanagement or bad planning, we may consider the contribution they make to the provision of an economical solution to the supply of abundant, cheap labor for the urban economy, including not only the industrial sector, but also the largely labor-intensive service sector, which is such an important prop to the lifestyle of the upper and middle classes.

The squatments and to a considerable extent the satellite towns serve as reserves, at little cost to the employers, where large numbers of workers may be maintained; proximity to lines of transportation permits easy access to the work sites; high unemployment rates depress wages; domestic, service, and commercial work is available to diminish the effects of (and potential reactions against) this unemployment and ease the burdens of the middle and upper classes; official pressure permits the squatting to be confined to areas of low visibility to the outsider and at a distance from the middle-class zones sufficient to reduce casual contact between the classes; and the location, terrain, and settlement pattern are such as to facilitate military and police measures to repress or contain riot and rebellion should they arise. At the same time, the formal official condemnation of squatting as an evil to be eradicated permits the capital to maintain its symbolic "developmentist" associations in the eyes of the middle class.

On the other hand, from the viewpoint of the in-migrants, the relatively high economic rewards available in Brasília as opposed to the Northeast—especially its rural sector—as well as the generally higher level of public services (education, health, social security) provide the appearance of upward mobility. Squatting, by eliminating the need for payment of rent and property taxes, enhances the squatters' economic position and, in particular, provides a form of security in an unstable labor market characterized by frequent firings, late paychecks (due in part to the dependence of the construction industry on political decisions), and other insecurities. The physical form of the shack permits it to be expanded in accord with the changes in family size and unanticipated receipts of funds. In a society characterized by occupational multiplicity at all levels, the shack may also be used as a business asset: a store, a sewing business, rental of space for a store, or as a source of capital through its sale should the owner decide to move elsewhere.

It is impossible to estimate the numbers of migrants to Brasília who have left, but the rapid growth of the population confirms that a large number, and by all accounts of officials and squatters alike, the vast majority, remain in the new capital. As long as construction continues and the transfer of civil servants from Rio de Janeiro provides a basis for the service sector of the economy, the lower class retains an economic basis. In addition, the availability of public education of better-than-average quality and of medical clinics, such as those of the District Hospital, provides an incentive to remain, even in harder times—and those who have shacks need not concern themselves with paying rent. Women also find in domestic service and in small businesses, especially dress-making, that they can increase their income and improve their position vis-à-vis their husbands, and in several cases have successfully resisted the migratory urges of their spouses. Most squatters in Brasília, barring disaster or depression, want to stay, and a significant majority want to stay in the squatter settlement. Informants often supposed that the research was connected with the government and wanted to know if they would have any chance of obtaining legal title to their house lots.

Brasília's settlement pattern developed in response to conflicting pressures emanating from the official "planned" construction and from the housing needs of squatters. A tacit bargain was struck at Brasília between the work-hungry migrants and entrepreneurs and politicians. The workers were permitted access to undeveloped public land, readily available in the scantily populated, relatively flat areas of the new capital and to the waste materials from the construction process, such as the wooden forms used to mold the reinforced concrete employed in most of the monumental and residential apartment buildings. Another advantage provided by employers is truck transportation from the squatter settlements to the place of work. The marginal cost to the entrepreneurs of providing these advantages was nearly nil, and the advantage to them considerable in terms of permitting the large in-migration to continue and to improve their labor-supply situation. The squatters, on the other hand, possessed a limited bargaining power by virtue of the need for their presence in menial and service roles and of their potential for organized protest and disruption. For active protest to occur required (1) settlements containing large numbers, notably the Social Security Invasion, which in 1967 had over four thousand shacks, and (2) conditions of threat to the permanence of the settlement or some part of it.

Official and police action has had a regulatory function with respect to squatting rather than (except in occasional declarations of intent) constituting an effort to eliminate or to provide a viable alternative to it for the majority of squatters. Small squatments offering relatively slight prospects of resistance were removed from the centrally planned area housing the urban middle class to the larger and less centrally located Social Security Invasion. This squatment was the site of two efforts, backed by police force, aimed at removing squatters from privately owned land and from a highly visible position on one of the principal interurban motor routes into the city where their presence would detract from the symbolic and prestige functions of the new capital. While long-term financing for the purchase of publicly sponsored core housing and small agricultural resettlement schemes have been discussed, there is no realistic possibility that official policy toward squatting can do more than to specify its location to some degree and declare the intention to eradicate it.

Brasília's existence up to the present and the economic survival of its poor have in fact been largely dependent upon government expenditures, notably those connected with (1) the construction of the capital, which is continuing under the military dictatorship at a reduced rate, and (2) the salaries of the civil and military employees of the government. Industrial development has been quite restricted, and even agriculture has been limited by natural conditions, the lack of a regional plan, and the commercial manipulations of São Paulo interests concerned with maintaining control of the local markets. The growth of an urban population nearing the half-million mark, more orderly governmental administration by the military, and the completion of the railroad spur to Brasília (officially inaugurated in March 1967, but not in operation until a year later) may change this somewhat pessimistic picture and lead to some industrial employment to substitute for construction work as the city ages and to supplement jobs in the tertiary sector. Yet given the increasingly capital-intensive character of recent Latin American industrialization and the off-center location of Brasília in the Brazilian distribution network, the role of industrial employment is not likely to be great. The probable future decline in expenditures for new building may seriously injure the prospects of the majority of squatters and limit, if not actually reverse, the aggregate effects of migration on population growth in the lower class.

The official policy of the government in regard to squatting, furthermore, tends to discourage—although it does not prevent—the development of small enterprises, other than strictly commercial ones, and of more permanent types of buildings in general. By insistently proclaiming the illegality and eventual demise of the squatter settlements and denying public services such as street lighting, electricity, sewage, and a permanent water system, the government does not prevent the squatter settlement from growing (especially when it moves people into the place in its own trucks!), but it does suppress or deflect some internal entrepreneurial interest and prevent the gradual improvement of many homes beyond the wood-and-tarpaper stage, for which some squatters on occasion have the money and the skills. In the light of the difficult middle-run prospects for employment for squatters in Brasília and the lack of really viable alternate forms of settlement, the governmental policy seems to be somewhat short-sighted.

Thus, what recent in-migrants today see as at least a minimal improvement in their lives may not survive the eventual diminution of the rhythm of construction in the new capital. And in fact, throughout Latin America, current industrialization is largely capital-intensive. It may be that the urban under- and unemployed, when the marginal sense of improvement gained through in-migration and squatting in its initial stages is lost (for instance in the next, urban-born generation), will become a source of political unrest and challenge to the system as a whole (Petras 1969). The development of and prospects for such a challenge, like the genesis of urban poverty and its reflexes in urban ecology, can only be understood on the basis of systemic as well as local variables. Revolutionaries (and counterrevolutionaries) understand this point. Perhaps we can ask at least as much from academic social scientists.

Notes

[1] In Brazil, squatter settlements are known as *favelas, invasões, mocambos,* and (when over water, on stilts) *alagados.* Among other terms for them are *callampas* (Chile), *bidonvilles* (French), *barriadas* (Peru), and *gecekondu* (Turkey). In English, they are often referred to as *shantytowns,* but not all squatment structures are shanties, and not all urban, shanty agglomerations are squatter settlements.

[2] Norman Whitten and James Szwed (1968) use the concept of economic marginality in reference to intermittent or irregular income, a different usage from that dealt with here. Indeed, squatting not involving rent is adapted to marginality in this sense of the term. Use of the term *marginality* for this situation is confusing, however, to the extent that irregular income among sugar workers or urban squatters may be an aspect of their integration into the very heart of the functioning political economy, not of their isolation from it.

[3] Anthony and Elizabeth Leeds have effectively demolished this notion in their paper "Brazil and the Myth of Urban Rurality: Urban Experience, Work, and Values in 'Squatments' of Rio de Janeiro and Lima," presented in November 1967 at the Conference on Work and Urbanization in Modernizing Societies, St. Thomas, Virgin Islands.

[4] William Mangin (1967) suggests without elaboration that urban squatters are less alienated than central-city slum dwellers.

[5] This discussion incorporates many of the views of A. G. Frank (1967a, 1967b).

[6] See, for instance, one set of proposed criteria of representativity of Conrad Arensberg (1961).

[7] This is occurring only to a degree. In part, increased interest in the "urban" reflects the immediate social control and counterrevolutionary concerns of the rulers of American society, efficiently mediated through the academic marketplace, as in the case of the earlier success of "area studies" interests in the social sciences: Russia, China, Africa, Latin America, Southeast Asia. Suddenly we are confronted with poverty and urban studies.

[8] A paraphrase of a passage from Scott Cook (1968:259).

[9] For a conception of this interaction patterning from a planner's viewpoint, see Christopher Alexander (1966).

[10] *Invasão do I.A.P.I.* I.A.P.I. is the acronym for the former Industrial Workers' Social Security Institute, which sponsored the hospital behind which the "invasion," or squatting, began.

[11] Discussion of this data is to be found in "Planned and Spontaneous Urban Settlement in Brasília" (D. G. Epstein 1969).

Forging Tradition
Social Life and Identity in a Tokyo Neighborhood

THEODORE C. BESTOR

Before 1923, the area now occupied by Miyamoto-chô was a rural hamlet. Now it is part of central Tokyo. In this essay, Theodore Bestor explores what has made this a distinct, not distinctive, neighborhood and the activities which breathe life into this identity. He points out that the apparent venerability of the neighborhood itself is the result of instant traditions. Bestor thus gives us a Japanese expression of what Barbara Kirshenblatt-Gimblett discussed in "Ordinary People/Everyday Life."

From the moats of the Imperial Palace at Tokyo's center to the outermost fringes of the megalopolis, Tokyo[1] stretches in most directions at least fifty kilometers. The scale of the city seems overwhelming, and the streets provide no simple bearings. Tokyo is a labyrinth of highways, avenues, streets, alleys, and paths first laid down centuries ago when Edo (as Tokyo was known before 1868) was the castle town for the ruling Tokugawa shogunate (1603–1868).[2] Even today, modern highways and major thoroughfares still twist through the city along winding routes that originally were designed for the castle's defense or to link the castle town to villages that have long since vanished into the metropolitan sprawl. Off the main avenues, the back streets of central Tokyo are mazes lined with seemingly random assortments of high-rise office

Source: Article written expressly for *Urban Life*.

buildings, pockets of single-family dwellings, large apartment complexes, shopping districts, and small-scale factories.

To navigate the city, most residents depend on the highly efficient network of subways and commuter rail lines that thread throughout the city, and most Tokyoites' perceptions of space, distance, and proximity are based on mental maps that highlight the complex rail network and central Tokyo's several hundred stations rather than its traffic-choked thoroughfares. The ebb and flow of daily life is oriented around stations, many of them starting points for ganglia of narrow shopping streets that reach out into surrounding residential neighborhoods. Tokyoites tend to think of the city in terms of interlocking regions and places, rather than as points linked lineally across a geographic grid. The peculiarities of Tokyo's transportation system and the sense of place it engenders dovetail with other, social and cultural features of Tokyo's organization that resolve the enormous sprawling megalopolis into tiny, highly localized social arenas, the scale of which seems all out of proportion to the urban complex as a whole.

Urban Villages and Japanese Urbanism

Tokyoites are fond of referring to the city as a collection of villages, and many of the older, central sections of Tokyo are divided into well-defined neighborhoods that appear to validate this observation. These are not simply bureaucratic devices (such as postal districts or police precincts) that correspond only slightly with the social categories and groupings important in the daily lives of residents. Nor are such neighborhoods merely symbols of larger economic, social, or ethnic divisions within the city, such as a New Yorker might have in mind when referring to Wall Street, the West Village, or Williamsburg. Rather, these neighborhoods are geographically compact, spatially discrete, institutionally well-organized, and socially cohesive units that contain a few hundred to a few thousand residents.[3] Whether famous or not, each neighborhood possesses its own local identity and special characteristics, although in many cases only its residents know or particularly care about the details.

Since 1979 I have been carrying out research in an area of Tokyo I call Miyamoto-chô,[4] a small neighborhood that conforms to Japanese stereotypes of the "urban village"—a place where myriad organizations intertwine to form a highly cohesive, very localized social structure that directly affects many residents across a wide spectrum of their lives and livelihoods. Miyamoto-chô is a place where durable informal ties create a face-to-face community for many residents. It is a neighborhood in which local identity and cohesion—including symbolic and ritual expressions of the fundamental unity of Miyamoto-chô as a community—continue to be stressed, as residents work to reproduce the community in each succeeding generation.

By the standards of contemporary Tokyo, Miyamoto-chô is an ordinary place similar to hundreds of other neighborhoods that stretch in a wide arc to the north, east, and south of the city's center. No visible signs of social, economic, or cultural singularity set Miyamoto-chô apart from its surroundings. What makes Miyamoto-chô a separate social unit—distinct, yet not distinctive—from nearby neighborhoods are the crosscutting and overlapping institutions and relationships that define Miyamoto-chô as an entity and breathe life into this definition through the activities and interactions they promote. In part, this life is made possible by the neighborhood's cultivation of its own traditions, which creates an image of historical venerability for the neighborhood and its institutions even as it provides a cultural rationale for their existence and vitality.

Neighborhoods like Miyamoto-chô are common throughout Tokyo, but are especially characteristic of older, presumably more "traditional" areas, particularly *shitamachi* districts.[5] Shitamachi, sometimes translated "downtown," refers to the areas of central Tokyo that were once the old merchant quarters of preindustrial Edo, where communities of traders and craftspeople created a vibrant, plebeian urban culture outside and "beneath" the walls of the castle they served. Today the feudal regulations that created legal and social boundaries around occupational communities and upheld divisions of urban life into socially and geographically distinct estates or caste-like classes are long gone.[6] But central Tokyo still contains many districts with high proportions of locally self-employed merchants and craftspeople, and these continue to be considered shitamachi, whether or not they possess any real historical links with Edo's merchant quarters.

In the social and cultural geography of Tokyo, shitamachi is contrasted with *yamanote* (literally, "the foothills"), referring to the hilly western sections of the city that were home to the *samurai* warrior classes during the feudal period. Of course, samurai have vanished also, and today yamanote areas of Tokyo are stereotypically regarded as the province of the middle and upper-middle classes of *sarariiman* ("salarymen," i.e., white-collar workers) and their families. The contrast does not simply distinguish elite and non-elite classes, nor does it imply sharp segregation, for, in fact, Tokyo's residential patterns are quite heterogeneous in terms of wealth, education, and occupation. The distinction revolves in large

Tangle of small and large buildings illustrates the jumbled quality of urban space in central Tokyo. [Photo by Ted Bestor]

part around the character of community life and the traits of social interaction that are presumed to typify one part of Tokyo versus another. If shitamachi residents have an image of being open-hearted, informal, and outgoing (or, perhaps, meddlesome), yamanote residents are thought to value reserve, formality, and privacy (or, possibly, aloofness).

An important element of the shitamachi tradition is its perpetuation of strong, stable frameworks of neighborhood social life. Neighborhoods' formal institutions, their complex sets of interlocking ties among residents, and even their external relations with the municipal government are all suffused with sentiments of community solidarity and identity. In turn, these sentiments nurture the internal institutions and informal social frameworks of the neighborhood. In many cases this sense of local identity and autonomy is based on the manipulation, invention, and recombination of cultural patterns, symbols, and motifs to create an aura of stability and legitimacy based on what appears to be historical continuity. Amidst the fluidity of social life in the Tokyo megalopolis, a neighborhood's ability to sustain itself by claiming (or creating) a link with history and cultural tradition promotes a sense of secure identity not only for institutions but also for individuals.

In many ways, Miyamoto-chô epitomizes an old-fashioned shitamachi neighborhood where the weight of historical tradition alone appears to sustain community social structure and the values of communal identity, cohesion, and autonomy. The common metaphor of the "urban village" provides a ready explanation for how such neighborhoods are organized, and by stressing links to the past, the metaphor also offers an easy analysis of cause and effect that depends merely on historical inertia. The story could end there, and for many Japanese observers it does.

But on closer inspection, Miyamoto-chô's apparent retention of traditional patterns of community life is at best an illusion, for the neighborhood is descended neither from a rural hamlet nor from a community in the preindustrial city of Edo. It can lay no authentic claim to being part of the real shitamachi districts of the city. The neighborhood simply did not exist before 1923, and much of the content of local tradition is developed anew every few years. Miyamoto-chô's traditions (and the image of the neighborhood as "traditional" that many residents subscribe to) are thus present-day social constructions that owe little to historical antecedent but owe much to the interplay of contemporary political, economic, social, and cultural forces in urban Japanese life.

This creation or representation of Miyamoto-chô as a seemingly traditional community is an active product of an ideological disposition I call traditionalism, and I use the term traditionalistic to underscore distinctions between historical inertia and contemporary constructions of the venerable meanings of community life.[7] As Lebra (1992:14) puts it, "culture does not survive so much in inertia as in renewal." In Miyamoto-chô, renewal takes the form of forging a past to legitimate the present.

In many other urban societies, where racial, ethnic, religious, and class divisions are encoded in patterns of residential segregation, neighborhoods stand out starkly as significant elements of the urban landscape. In Tokyo, the broad shitamachi/yamanote dichotomy notwithstanding, residential segregation by class, religious, or other social categories is not sharply evident, and until quite recently the number of racially or ethnically distinct residents was quite small.[8] And despite the popular image of Tokyo as a collection of urban villages, urban neighborhoods themselves are often rather transparent to the view of a casual observer. Because local social relations revolve around the undramatic, mundane activities of daily life, most Japanese do not pay much attention to the real significance of neighborhood groups and social ties in contemporary Tokyo.

In part this reflects gendered and class biases. The primary participants in local life—even if not the leaders—are generally women and children, and the men who lead local associations are usually local shopkeepers and other small-scale businessmen. Neighborhood social life, therefore, revolves around people who are not defined as prestigious, influential, or particularly consequential. Neighborhoods are not arenas for elite interactions, and Japanese and foreign observers looking for the "real" action in contemporary society generally look elsewhere. In addition, the "urban village" metaphor usually implies that urban community institutions are hopelessly outdated remnants of village or preindustrial urban life, out of place and doomed to disappear in the modern industrial megalopolis. And, finally, because neighborhood groups often maintain close links to municipal agencies and local leaders are often politically conservative, neighborhood institutions are often assumed to be little more than subservient extensions of municipal governments. Such viewpoints therefore dismiss the importance of neighborhoods as a central feature of Japanese urbanism. And they ignore both the pragmatic reality and symbolic significance that local life holds for residents of a neighborhood like Miyamoto-chô.

Social Life in Miyamoto-chô

Miyamoto-chô is about a ten-minute walk from a commuter rail station that is itself about twenty minutes by train from Tokyo Station. The area is now considered an older section of the city. But Miyamoto-chô is not particularly old nor is it within the classic shitamachi districts; it was part of an outlying agricultural hamlet until 1923 when the Kantô earthquake destroyed old central Tokyo and this area was engulfed by people fleeing the destruction. By the early 1930s the region was completely urbanized, and distinct, locally organized neighborhoods began to emerge. Miyamoto-chô and six other neighborhoods dating from the late 1920s and early 1930s now occupy the area of the pre-1923 hamlet.

Miyamoto-chô is a rough rectangle measuring about two hundred by four hundred meters, bounded on the east by railway tracks and on the west by a narrow, heavily traveled road built over an old stream now channeled underground; the northern and southern boundaries are residential and shopping streets that create only barely perceptible divisions between Miyamoto-chô and the neighborhoods on either side. Square in the middle of Miyamoto-chô stands a small Shintô shrine, which is home to the tutelary deity for a parish that corresponds to the territory of the pre-1923 hamlet, now divided among Miyamoto-chô and six other neighborhoods. It is from this shrine that Miyamoto-chô derives its name.

The neighborhood covers less than a tenth of a square kilometer, with about nineteen-hundred residents in 750 households.[9] The neighborhood's population density is about twice the density for Tokyo as a whole. The neighborhood's density is all the more remarkable because Miyamoto-chô is not a high-rise district. With the exception of a handful of small luxury apartment buildings (called *manshon* or "mansions") that rise to four floors, the neighborhood is almost entirely two-story architecture: homes, inexpensive apartment buildings (called *apaato*, rather than manshon), shops, and workshops. Miyamoto-chô's tightly packed homes are interspersed with about seventy small shops and forty workshops or small-scale factories. The neighborhood is dominated socially, politically, and commercially by the self-employed merchants, craftspeople, and manufacturers for whom Miyamoto-chô is both home and workplace.

For these and for many other residents, Miyamoto-chô is an important sphere of economic activity. The neighborhood is bisected by a bustling street lined with small businesses that cater to the daily needs of residents: stores selling vegetables, fish, rice, *sake*, books, electrical appliances, and clothing; and service businesses such as laundries, news agents, plumbers, and restaurants. The shopping street's fifty stores and businesses are almost all owned and operated by local residents, generally employing only the labor of family members. Most shopkeepers, craftspeople, factory owners, and even professionals—doctors, dentists, or accountants—conduct business in shops, workshops, or offices attached to their homes, and their family members are involved in almost all aspects of the household enterprise. Their clientele is primarily local. Although the large department stores and supermarkets near the railway station a ten-minute walk away attract many shoppers from Miyamoto-chô (especially for major purchases), many local households rely on the shops in the neighborhood for miscellaneous daily shopping. The local shops, of course, are convenient, and even if they are a bit more expensive than the bigger stores, local shopkeepers can be counted on to provide extra, personalized service for their neighbors.

In addition to these and other economic ties among neighbors (such as complex landlord-tenant relations), individuals in Miyamoto-chô are linked to one another in elaborate constellations of personalized social networks. These reflect such things as family connections and school ties, at least among people who have lived most or all of their lives in the neighborhood. Other strands of affiliation emanate from people's shared political sympathies, hobbies, or tastes in recreation. And still other bonds are created out of the exigencies of living in close proximity with one another and finding common cause in the business (and the pleasures) of daily life: taking out the trash, helping a neighbor fix a fence, gossiping outside the butcher shop, having a drink together in a local bar. Within Miyamoto-chô, residents' networks intertwine and interlock thoroughly, creating an extremely high density of local interpersonal ties. Most old-time residents of Miyamoto-chô can trace ties to many other residents through several alternate paths using one or another of these sorts of connections. Put another way, people don't know someone else in Miyamoto-chô "because" of a specific connection; knowing and being known is simply a fact of the social landscape.

Of course, this knowledge of one another is kept alive through repeated interaction, and the local formal institutions of neighborhood life are major arenas in which such neighborly ties are renewed and reinforced.

Formal Neighborhood Organizations

Although their scope and complexity may be visible only locally, Miyamoto-chô's many formal organizations loom large on the social landscape to those residents for whom the services, contacts, and activities neighborhoods foster are important. At least a dozen groups take Miyamoto-chô as their basic organizational framework, including the neighborhood association (*chôkai*) and several affiliated groups such as its women's auxiliary (*fujinbu*), youth division (*seinenbu*), senior citizen's club (*rôjinkai*), and festival committee (*saireiiin*). The shopkeepers along the main shopping street have their own merchants' guild (*shôtenkai*). Other formally constituted organizations include the local schools' PTAs and alumni clubs (*dôsôkai*), a volunteer fire brigade (*shôbôdan*), a couple of ritual organizations (*kô*) centered on the Shintô shrine, and a supporters' club (*kôenkai*) for the local politician. And finally there are informal clubs and groups centered around sports, hobbies, crafts, and activities such as baseball, travel, poetry composition, traditional dance, tea ceremony, or flower arrangement.

The chôkai is unquestionably the neighborhood's most important and visible organization. Although the chôkai and its affiliates are formally autonomous, in practice their activities, leaderships, and memberships so interlock that it is difficult to disentangle one from another. The chôkai is nominally a voluntary association, but at best membership is expected if not required of all households. Probably only slightly more than a quarter of Miyamoto-chô's households enthusiastically support and participate in the events and activities sponsored by the chôkai. But the chôkai collects monthly dues of two hundred yen from almost all households[10] and virtually every household takes its annual turn as chôkai liaison representative for its immediate cluster (*kumi*) of eight or ten households. By definition all households are members of the chôkai; all adult women automatically belong to the chôkai's women's auxiliary; all children can take part in activities organized by the chôkai's youth division; and all residents over the age of sixty are presumed to belong to the senior citizen's club. Whether or not residents are enthusiastic or even voluntary participants in the chôkai and its affiliates, the chôkai's activities directly or indirectly affect the lives of every resident.

In a significant sense the chôkai acts as a semiofficial local government, providing services to residents both at neighborhood initiative and at the behest of the municipal authorities. It serves as a conduit for demands, requests, and information that flow between the municipal government and the neighborhood. The chôkai distributes pamphlets on municipal programs and regulations to residents and assists the municipal office in record keeping, census taking, and collecting information on everything from traffic patterns to the number of elderly who live alone.

The chôkai acts as a political pressure group representing what its leaders determine to be neighborhood interest. One notable success (achieved by a coalition of adjacent neighborhoods in the 1970s) was persuading the municipal government to pave over a stream that bordered Miyamoto-chô in order to build a traffic bypass. The chôkai worked hard in the 1980s to get the local government to build a new train station on a railway line near Miyamoto-chô; it was built, and now a decade later, the chôkai lobbies the municipal government for relief for local merchants who lament that the station draws more customers out of the neighborhood than it draws in.

On more modest and everyday levels, the chôkai uses its influence with the municipal office to eliminate petty nuisances. In response to the chôkai's complaints about the noise and congestion caused by mothers delivering their children to the local nursery school by bicycle, the local board of education imposed regulations that mothers must walk their children to school. In another case, a local entrepreneur who installed vending machines that sold pornographic magazines was persuaded to change his business when the chôkai orchestrated a campaign that involved visits from the principal of the local junior high school, the municipal office, and delegations of offended neighbors.

Mutual assistance, in many forms, is a major focus of chôkai activity. When a local resident dies, the chôkai notifies neighbors, organizes a group to help at the funeral, makes the chôkai meeting hall available for the wake, and sends a delegation to the funeral itself. The chôkai helps out in other kinds of emergencies as well; a few years ago when a burlap bag factory burned to the ground, a family whose adjoining house was destroyed was put up in the chôkai hall for several months while their home was being rebuilt. At the urging of the municipal office, the chôkai organizes a disaster relief team which holds regular fire drills and stages simulated earthquake evacuations each year on the anniversary of the 1923 Kantô earthquake. The chôkai cooperates with the police in annual traffic safety campaigns and provides free safety inspections of children's bicycles. Together, the volunteer fire brigade and the chôkai hold fire safety meetings and sponsor fire prevention patrols on cold winter nights when the danger of fire is at its height. When a fire does break out, the local volunteers turn out to help the professional fire department; their major contribution is their intimate knowledge of local terrain and the location of water supplies in the twisting mazes of back alleys that thread through Miyamoto-chô. The chôkai maintains street lights on back alleys, and several times each summer a chôkai work crew sprays the entire neighborhood with pesticides to eliminate mosquito breeding grounds. And the chôkai and its women's auxiliary organize a monthly recycling drive for cardboard, newspapers, bottles, and cans; the money they raise by selling these to a scrap dealer is an important source of the groups' income. The chôkai takes great pride in these mundane public service, safety, and sanitation campaigns. Its leaders argue that they improve the living environment for all residents of Miyamoto-chô and that by doing so with volunteers they lower taxes as well.

Local organizations also sponsor many recreational activities. Throughout the year, the chôkai and the PTAs organize children's outings to parks, playgrounds, beaches, and swimming pools. At least once a year every group in the neighborhood organizes a trip for adults to one or another of the famous hot springs resorts near Tokyo. Closer to home, annual events celebrated in the neighborhood include New Year's parties (actually pairs of parties, one for "forgetting the old year" in December, and one for "welcoming the new year" in January), a springtime cherry-blossom viewing party, a midsummer *Bon Odori* folk dance festival, and the autumn festival for the local Shintô shrine. And chances to relax in the company of one's neighbors pop up even in the midst of nominally nonrecreational events, such as the fire patrols, the pesticide spraying, or the earthquake drills. The hard labor is leavened by pleasant camaraderie that breaks daily life's normal routine and is usually followed by a banquet or party for the activities' planners and workers.

Through the wide variety of quasi-governmental, mutual aid, and recreational activities they sponsor, the chôkai and other formal groups contribute heavily to maintaining the fabric of local social life. The ties established among residents by their participation in local groups mutually reinforce other ties created out of personal affiliations. Many of these informal ties would exist even in the absence of groups like the chôkai, but formally constituted groups provide a focus within which informal ties multiply, and local institutions reinforce the neighborhood's density of networks by providing convenient, generally recognized social boundaries. Conversely, informal ties create a backdrop of social connectedness without which many aspects of the formal organizations' activities could not function. Without the informal ties that run throughout

Miyamoto-chô, consensual decision making would be impossible, mutual aid and social control would fail, and the chôkai and other groups would lack the means to mobilize residents to contribute time, labor, and money to neighborhood activities.

Miyamoto-chô and the Municipal Government

Neighborhoods like Miyamoto-chô also are defined through their relations with external agencies, chiefly those of the municipal government. In Tokyo, municipal administration is conducted largely by the twenty-three wards, which routinely rely on community organizations in the day-to-day delivery of services. Chôkai play a pivotal role linking internal dimensions of communities to the municipal government. Chôkai are expected to keep the citizenry informed of government programs and policies and to act as a sounding board for government proposals. At the same time, ward governments depend on chôkai to supply the labor, the organizational infrastructure, and even some of the money required for the delivery of municipal services at the local level. Relationships between neighborhood associations and municipal governments are close but also potentially exploitative. Neighborhoods can (and sometimes do) resent and resist governmental demands and the presumption that community groups are there to do the government's bidding.

Even basic definitions of boundaries can reveal sharp divisions between neighborhoods and the municipal government. The chôkai, together with other local associations, defines the basic social perimeters of Miyamoto-chô. These groups all share a common definition of the neighborhood and a common set of boundaries based on what local organizations and neighborhood residents regard as Miyamoto-chô's historically legitimate borders. As the following examples suggest, through the chôkai's insistence on maintaining these boundaries, the local definition of the community holds its own in the face of municipal government efforts to impose other definitions of community.

Miyamoto-chô's closest contacts with the municipal administration are channeled through a branch office of the ward government (one of eleven branch offices set up to cover different regions in the ward). This office handles a broad array of official transactions for individual residents, such as licensing pets, accepting passport applications, certifying residence for voting and school registration, or processing government pension forms. It also acts as a liaison between ten contiguous neighborhoods, including

Miyamoto-chô, and the ward government. The ward regards chôkai as little more than semi-official agencies of the government itself, and the branch office considers these ten chôkai to be under its jurisdiction. Chôkai leaders dispute this interpretation of their organization's role and complain (at least among themselves and to an inquiring anthropologist) about the responsibilities they are forced by the government to shoulder in pursuit of the government's rather than the neighborhoods' goals. Even at the semantic level there is disagreement over the nature of the relationship; the branch office refers to the ten chôkai together as a *burokku* (bloc) under its leadership, while the chôkai see themselves as members of a *rengô*, or federation, for which the branch office is merely a source of advice and administrative support.

Beyond coordinating administrative functions, in the past decade and a half the branch office has become the focal point for the ward's increasingly active policy of *machi-zukuri*, or "community-creation." Machi-zukuri policies reflect a point of view commonly held by government officials that sees existing patterns and institutions of neighborhood life (such as those exemplified by chôkai) as outmoded and inappropriate in contemporary society; the municipal government therefore feels it must step in and create institutions that will foster a sense of community and citizenship appropriate to a modern, democratic society. In an ironic paradox, the municipal government's attempts to dismantle existing "urban villages" and reconstitute local life in new institutional contexts take existing neighborhoods and their activities not only as the instruments but also as the models for creating "new" senses of community awareness.

For example, the events planned and sponsored by the branch office often duplicate activities of the individual neighborhoods themselves. Frequently the municipal government's versions involve much of the same traditionalistic trappings and symbolism that characterize chôkai activities. Local leaders grumble about being upstaged by the larger, more lavish events the ward government can put on. One example is the extremely elaborate *Kumin Matsuri* ("Ward Residents' Festival"), modeled on the Bon Odori folk dance festivals held in communities throughout Japan in midsummer. The municipal government first sponsored the Kumin Matsuri in 1979, and it included a specially commissioned ward residents' folk song and a folk dance, both of which conform to the conventions of contemporary, commercialized "traditional" folk song and dance genres. The ostentatiousness of this first annual festival aroused so much ill will among chôkai leaders that in subsequent years each of the eleven branch offices held separate scaled-down versions. But the ward festival(s) continued to be far more elaborate than the corresponding efforts of the chôkai, and local leaders continued to complain about the "cooperation" they felt forced to give the branch office in its planning of this event. Ultimately the amount of effort required to stage both a local Bon Odori and the Kumin Matsuri was too great for local leaders, and by the late 1980s Miyamoto-chô and the surrounding chôkai had discontinued their own neighborhood Bon Odori.

Even if this conflict with the municipal government seems a subtle one, it reflects a wider undercurrent of tension in the ongoing relationship between chôkai and the ward government. The legal disestablishment of chôkai during the years immediately after World War II[11] introduced ambiguities into the relationship that can lead to misunderstandings and disagreements on both sides. Local leaders know that the municipal government has no direct legal power over chôkai and complain of the government's overbearing attitudes. Leaders insist that local organizations must be regarded as voluntary bodies organized by and for local residents. Furthermore, the political climate since World War II has weakened citizens' subservient attitude toward government officials. Citizens now feel empowered to object to authoritarian directives from the municipal government and complain that officials often seem to forget they are public servants. Against this backdrop, the ward's machi-zukuri policies, whose apparent intention has been to supplant chôkai both as semiofficial administrative units and as focal points of local residents' activities and identification, spawn additional conflict and create the potential for dramatic rifts.

An example of such conflict is a dispute over the neighborhood's boundaries and, hence, between external and internal definitions of what the neighborhood is. In the 1960s the ward attempted to amalgamate Miyamoto-chô with an adjacent neighborhood. To an outsider almost nothing differentiates these neighborhoods, yet their residents successfully opposed the merger. True, the municipal government went ahead and redrew the boundaries, and now the two neighborhoods appear on maps as one unit. But today that larger unit is used for almost nothing but numbering houses. The chôkai and other local groups do not recognize the larger unit, nor does the ward office; since the ward office depends on the chôkai to carry out many of its tasks, it is forced to work within frameworks chôkai willingly acknowledge.

The separate political and economic interests of the two neighborhoods would not have been served by a merger. Each neighborhood routinely is able to elect a ward assembly member, so each had political *jiban* ("turf") to protect. Merchants' groups in each neighborhood strive to maintain and increase their share of local trade in the face of competition from other neighborhoods. But when residents explain their opposition to the merger, they present their resistance as an effort to preserve the "distinct" traditions and practices in the neighborhoods involved. However minimal such differences may seem to an outside observer, each neighborhood prides itself on its inventory of almost imperceptible differences: its own ways of collecting donations for the annual festival, the peculiarities of the relationship between its own chôkai and merchants' association, or its own methods of selecting neighborhood officers. These minute distinctions can become the symbolic battlegrounds *between* neighborhoods, or *among* groups within a particular neighborhood, each seeking to control the authenticity of tradition. In this instance, neither neighborhood was willing to alter practices they felt best suited their own needs and their own sense of autonomous tradition and identity.

These sentiments, in Miyamoto-chô at least, in part revolved around its neighborhood hall. The issue was not simply a question of sharing ownership of a ramshackle building but involved symbolism central to the neighborhood's self-definition. At the time, Miyamoto-chô was the only neighborhood in the area to have its own hall. During the last year of World War II, as American air raids struck Tokyo more and more frequently, the residents of Miyamoto-chô were ordered to create a firebreak along the adjacent right-of-way of a vital freight line. To create the break, the men and boys of the chôkai tore down the homes on either side of the tracks. From the lumber and roof tiles they salvaged enough to build the neighborhood hall. By the late 1970s this hall was an aging relic, and compared with newer halls built or acquired by other neighborhoods in the area, it was small and dilapidated, but it remained the center of local activity and an important symbol of the neighborhood as a community. The prospect of sharing this and other tangible or intangible cultural properties with "outsiders" was an important rallying point for opposing the ward government's plans, and ultimately this opposition proved successful.

Miyamoto-chô's Festival and Local Identity

Miyamoto-chô's annual autumn festival (*aki matsuri*) for the tutelary deity of the local Shintô shrine is a much more vivid

Ted Bestor and neighborhood leaders at the autumn ▶ festival. The lantern identifies its carrier as a festival leader.

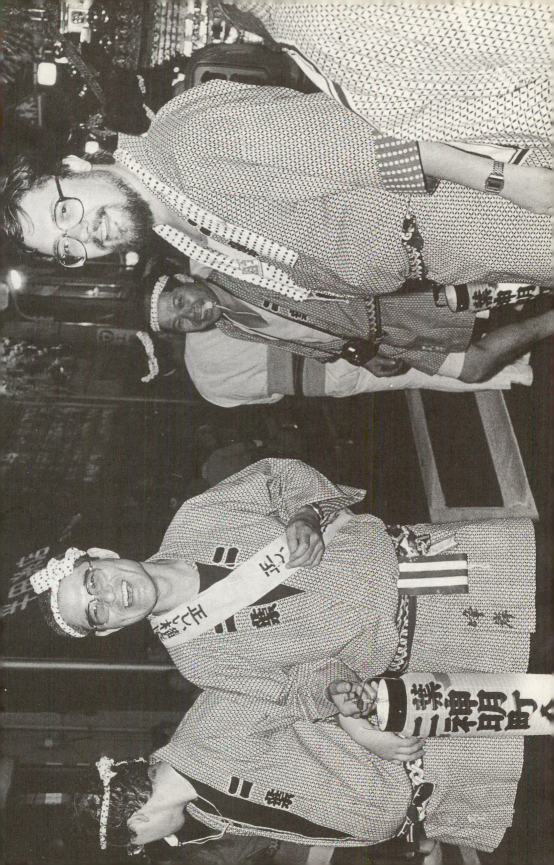

expression of community sentiment, identity, and symbolic boundaries. The two-day matsuri is a colorful event and almost every local household participates in some fashion, even if only as enthusiastic audience. The festival is, of course, a Shintô rite for which the local priest can provide a detailed theological rationale, but for most residents of Miyamoto-chô the matsuri is essentially a secular ritual, largely lacking explicit religious significance but replete with social meaning.

Through the matsuri, several important though sometimes contradictory social themes are expressed. The matsuri is organized by a festival committee (saireiiin) made up of leaders from the chôkai and other local associations as well as residents who otherwise take no active part in neighborhood affairs. Miyamoto-chô's local criteria for ranking and social stratification are clearly evident as the committee assigns positions with varying degrees of responsibility to over one hundred residents. When local businesses and households make contributions to the festival (ranging from as little as three thousand yen to as much as fifty thousand),[12] each donation is publicly recorded on an enormous panel outside the chôkai hall. Neighbors quietly comment on those who are aggressively seeking leadership by making larger donations than their social standing would warrant and on those who are shirking their responsibilities by making only token contributions. The management of the festival, and even the spatial and temporal distribution of activities during the matsuri, reflect rigid sexual and age-graded divisions of labor, and underscore distinctions between newcomers and old-timers, women and men, young and old, followers and leaders. Yet despite the social rankings that play so visible a role in the management of the festival, an overt spirit of egalitarianism and community solidarity is presented as the matsuri's dominant motif.

The matsuri also serves as a compelling marker of the community's boundaries and identity. A central feature of the festival is the *mikoshi*, a portable shrine or palanquin in which the tutelary deity temporarily resides during the two-day festival. The mikoshi, carried on a framework of poles by a group of thirty or more young men (and recently women), is taken on what amounts to an inspection tour of Miyamoto-chô. The procession carefully traces the neighborhood's boundaries. When the route of a mikoshi unavoidably must pass through the territory of an adjacent neighborhood—when roads or alleys linking parts of one neighborhood run through another, or when mikoshi are brought from other parish neighborhoods to the shrine in Miyamoto-chô for the priest's blessings—the festival committees from the neighborhoods involved

Children carrying the *mikoshi* in the neighborhood's autumn festival.
[Photo by Ted Bestor]

negotiate the route beforehand. When a mikoshi or a women's
dance troupe takes a sudden detour through another neighborhood,
leaders from the transgressed neighborhood grumble and expect
an apology from the offending neighborhood's festival committee.

Although the matsuri nominally encourages cooperation and
identification with the six other neighborhoods that make up the
shrine's parish, the mikoshi and their processions provide a venue
for interneighborhood competition. In the late 1970s, the neighborhood next-door to Miyamoto-chô triumphantly paraded its impressive large new mikoshi, hand-built by local young men over a period
of several years. During 1979–81 Miyamoto-chô successfully
countered this innovation by prominently featuring in its
processions the new spectacle of a foreign anthropologist and his
exotic red-haired, folk-dancing wife.

But, in the longer term other strategies were required to uphold
the neighborhood's standing. In the spring of 1982 younger
neighborhood leaders enthusiastically launched a drive to raise
funds for a new mikoshi. Within three months, Miyamoto-chô raised
over ten-million yen (roughly fifty thousand dollars at then-current
exchange rates) from over four hundred local households, and by

that fall Miyamoto-chô had taken delivery of the largest, most elaborate mikoshi in the area. Leaders of the fundraising campaign claim a major objective was to make Miyamoto-chô's festival more spectacular and exciting for young people, and thereby entice more people to become involved in the festival and in neighborhood affairs more generally. But they also take undisguised pleasure—perhaps even gloat—over the fact that Miyamoto-chô's new mikoshi is more impressive than the adjacent neighborhood's hand-built one and speak scornfully about another adjacent neighborhood that failed to rise to the bait.

In the festival, and dozens of other, more mundane activities throughout the year, the chôkai and other local groups staunchly defend the neighborhood's present-day boundaries and their definitions of the local community. By maintaining Miyamoto-chô's sense of identity and upholding the distinctiveness of each of the local neighborhoods, the festival and similar activities contribute to a sense of resistance to government efforts to reconstitute local social units as part of its machi-zukuri policies. Opposition to the government is not the only, nor even the most important outcome of such activities, for through their participation in events such as the festival, residents maintain the neighborhood as an arena for valued social interactions that bestow prestige, status, and recognition on their leaders and participants in ways not duplicated elsewhere in their lives.

In the general process of socially constructing its identity, institutions and residents of Miyamoto-chô rely on what I referred to earlier as "traditionalism." They define the neighborhood by referring to particular aspects of its history and its customary practices, selecting out certain events or activities with which to press their case. Although many of the events or institutions to which they refer are recent in occurrence or origin, this does not diminish their utility or significance as emblems of neighborhood distinctiveness. Japanese social institutions have a penchant for "instant tradition"—the ability to cloak new circumstances and institutions with a mantle of traditionalism, imparting depth and resiliency to what might otherwise have shaky foundations.

Epilogue

In 1988, nine years after first arriving in Miyamoto-chô, my wife and I returned to Tokyo with our twenty-one-month-old son to live in Miyamoto-chô again for a year. We arrived only days before the autumn festival and our friends took great pleasure in dressing our bewildered son in toddlers' festival garb, carrying him on their shoulders to watch the mikoshi, and taking him to the shrine to feed him snacks from the carnival stalls.

The new mikoshi had been through a few festivals already, and although it remained an object of great pride, for many residents the mikoshi itself had become a little bit matter of fact. The festival had changed in many ways, mostly subtle and cumulative, as new aspects of "tradition" had been added almost imperceptibly. In 1988 almost a third of the bearers of the mikoshi were young women. Shintô ideology historically has prohibited women from such intimate contact with the deity, and when I first arrived in Miyamoto-chô it was almost unheard of to allow women to carry mikoshi. Nine years later the most striking thing about this innovation was that no one commented on the change. The mikoshi parades had been daylight affairs in the late 1970s. By the late 1980s the parades went on until late in the night, and a local electrician had rigged the mikoshi with a set of internal spotlights powered by a car battery so that it could glitter ethereally in the autumn dusk. When I first asked about donations in the late 1970s, festival leaders were fiercely proud that in Miyamoto-chô contributions were voluntarily brought to the chôkai hall, not coerced from residents. Now, to laughter and cheers, mikoshi bearers stage mock attacks on people's homes that stop only when someone leans out a window and good-naturedly tucks a cash donation into the elaborate bamboo superstructure of the impatiently rocking mikoshi.

Even as they commented contentedly about the successful invigoration of the festival, the "young" leadership faction that had headed the drive for the expensive new mikoshi in the first place, and that now has replaced their fathers as the de facto leadership generation, was nervously aware that they are becoming a bit too old to actually hoist the heavy palanquin themselves. They joked with one another about their greying temples and aching joints and stood on the sidelines watching their sons and daughters heave the mikoshi through the streets.

As I learned that year, and in later visits in 1992 and 1994, standing on the sidelines watching their children causes the present leaders of Miyamoto-chô grave concern over the future of the neighborhood. Yes, the festival tradition is securely established, and the leaders have strengthened other aspects of the neighborhood association as well. The old chôkai hall, for example, has been replaced by a fancy new two-story building with modern kitchens, elegant meeting rooms, and a small stage; memory of the old hall and its central role in community identity for an earlier generation has faded quickly, and when it is remembered at all it is as decrepit rather than venerable. But today's leaders worry that their own children seem uninterested in taking over the reigns of community leadership. And, in the view of my middle-aged friends, other fundamental changes also threaten to hollow out Miyamoto-chô.

Many of these are local reflections of larger-scale transformations of Tokyo. Since the middle 1980s, tens of thousands of foreign workers have migrated to Tokyo to fill menial jobs in construction, manufacturing, and entertainment. Only a small handful of foreigners live in or near Miyamoto-chô, but there were none a decade earlier and their presence now shakes local confidence in the supposed homogeneity of Japanese community life. Throughout the 1980s, frenzied real estate speculators relentlessly bought up plots of land throughout the city (including Miyamoto-chô), forced out some residents, and built large new apartment buildings and parking garages. Both the foreign workers and the land speculation were products of what Tokyoites now call the "Bubble Economy." And in the late 1980s the bubble burst, plunging Japan into its first prolonged recession in recent memory, driving thousands of small, marginal companies out of business, and threatening the lifetime security of employees of some of Japan's largest companies as well. The implosion of the bubble was accompanied by the death of the Shôwa Emperor in 1989, which in Japanese thinking conclusively marked the end of the postwar period. And in the early 1990s, the conservative Liberal Democratic Party lost power for the first time since 1955, contributing to a general sense that for better or for worse Japanese society perches on the brink of massive and unpredictable change.

Locally, in Miyamoto-chô, the population has been gradually decreasing and newcomers generally seem to regard the neighborhood more as a good place to sleep than a good place to live. Residing in the new luxury apartments the old-timers have built when they remodel old homes (as they too speculated in the real estate market), the newcomers are likely to think their ties to their neighbors begin and end with their rent payments and make few efforts to put down roots. Since long before the bubble burst, the number of new shops opening has never quite made up for those that have closed, but after the bubble, the silence of shuttered shops shouts at passers-by on their way to the large new shopping complex recently completed near the local railway station. And even families that run local businesses in no danger from the economic downturn find it increasingly difficult to persuade a son or daughter to consider taking over the business in the next generation.

The leaders of Miyamoto-chô today take stock of these trends and wonder where they will all lead. Their concerns, of course, are for their own families and their own businesses, as well as for a way of life in which neighborhoods figure prominently. From their close-up perspective, the interconnections between community identity and tradition, local institutions and social ties, and family businesses and local leadership seem obvious and inevitable. And so the prospect of radical change in any element of this equation raises the immediate fear that community life as they know it cannot survive much longer.

The odd perspective of an anthropologist as someone who is both (and neither) insider and outsider, perhaps allows a longer, more dispassionate view. Certainly, my friends are right that Miyamoto-chô will never be the same kind of neighborhood it was before. Years of prosperity and rising real estate prices have altered the physical layout of the neighborhood, changed its demography, altered the nature of local business, and transformed the attitudes of the younger generation toward the local community as their sphere of activity. The sudden shock of economic downturn—however long or short it ends up being—has suddenly eroded people's ability to invest the time, energy, and money in community affairs that kept the neighborhood atop a rising wave during the boom years.

But the neighborhood remains home and workplace to hundreds of families, most of them likely to remain in place, especially if they own land here near the center of Tokyo. As residents of a densely packed neighborhood, their lives almost inevitably intertwine in dozens of mundane ways: from coordinating garbage collection schedules to worrying about the elementary school's PTA; from sharing common concerns over traffic problems to shopping together for daily necessities down the block; from helping each other when typhoons strike Tokyo to campaigning together on behalf of the local politician. None of these will disappear simply because the national economy is shaken, the political system transformed, particular local businesses disappear, or a generation of leaders has not reproduced itself. Residents of Miyamoto-chô will have common cause for a long time to come, and the neighborhood will survive as a community in some form, perhaps a more loosely integrated one.

But what of the festival and of the other activities through which the neighborhood defines itself and expresses its identity as a unit? Can such traditional aspects of local life survive in a less cohesive, less committed community? Yes, I think, because tradition and the activities that are emblematic of it are themselves products of continual transformation and innovation. Undoubtedly the expression of traditional identity in Miyamoto-chô will be transformed, but throughout the years I have studied Miyamoto-chô and in the history of its development since the early part of the twentieth century, such transformations have been the rule not the exception. Nothing, it turns out, is more traditional than innovation.

In Miyamoto-chô—and throughout Japanese society—tradition is not the antithesis of change, but a vocabulary through which identity and distinction can be maintained, bolstered, at times invented. As life in Miyamoto-chô changes, the expression of identity will undoubtedly change as the nature of the distinctions that people want to accentuate between themselves and others, between their neighborhood and the larger society, change. The festival may grow more elaborate, or less; other community rituals may fade from view; or still others may develop to take their places. But the repertoire of Japanese cultural symbolism is vast, and as long as residents of Miyamoto-chô find common cause for inter-action and cooperation, and feel a need to symbolize themselves as a distinct community, the malleability of tradition will present ample material with which to assert the continued vitality of community life.

Notes

1 It is tricky to define Tokyo because there is no single municipality that encompasses the central core of the megalopolis. For planning purposes, the Japanese government classifies four prefectures as the Tokyo metropolitan region, and in 1992 this region was home to about 32.2 million people, roughly 26 percent of the Japanese population. One of these four prefectures is the Tokyo Metropolitan Prefecture, which itself has a population of 11.9 million (Kokudochô 1993). In addition to a number of suburban towns and cities, the Tokyo Metropolitan Prefecture contains twenty-three wards that make up the central city of Tokyo. It is this core region of twenty-three wards that I refer to as "Tokyo," or for clarity's sake "central Tokyo." Together the twenty-three wards cover 618 square kilometers and in 1990 had a population of 8.16 million (Tokyo Statistical Association 1992).

2 Edo's name was changed to Tokyo ("Eastern Capital") when the Imperial Court was moved there from the ancient capital of Kyoto after the Meiji Restoration in 1868.

3 In 1978 the Tokyo Metropolitan Fire Department conducted a detailed survey of local organizations, and identified 4,067 distinct, non-overlapping, institutionally organized neighborhoods in the twenty-three wards of the central city. The mean average size of a neighborhood was only 0.14 square kilometers, and the mean average number of households per neighborhood was 801.

4 Miyamoto-chô is a pseudonym. I conducted research here from June 1979 to May 1981, followed with short research visits during the summers of 1984 and 1986, and another year of residence in 1988–89. During the winter of 1991–92, I returned

for several weeks while making an ethnographic video on the neighborhood. The community is described in depth in an ethnography titled *Neighborhood Tokyo* (Bestor 1989), in several essays (Bestor 1985, 1990, 1992a, 1992b, and 1994), and in an ethnographic video (Media Production Group 1992).

[5] Accounts of the social character of shitamachi include Dore (1958), R. J. Smith (1960), Seidensticker (1983), H. D. Smith (1986), Kondo (1990), and Bestor (1992a).

[6] Throughout the Tokugawa period (1603–1868), society was rigidly divided into four major social classes, ranked according to their social utility as defined in neo-Confucian ideology: samurai (warriors), peasants, craftspeople, and merchants. Membership in each class was hereditary, and the permissible and proscribed activities of members of each class were minutely regulated by the government. In Edo, the major social contrast was between warriors and townspeople (including both craftspeople and merchants). This class system was legally abolished in the 1870s.

[7] More detailed discussions of "traditionalism" appear in Bestor (1989, 1992a, 1992b). Several other authors also have explored the dynamics of traditionalism in Japanese society (e.g., R. J. Smith (1983); Kelly (1986); Ivy (1988); Kondo (1990); and Robertson (1991)). Hobsbawm and Ranger (1983) present similar European cases.

[8] During the 1980s, the number of foreigners in Tokyo increased several-fold, leading many Japanese accustomed to regarding their society as homogeneous to think that Tokyo has become flooded with foreigners. Actually, the number of foreigners legally resident in Tokyo is still quite small (only about 224,000 in 1992, or about 2.8 percent of Tokyo's population). Slightly over one third of these foreigners are long-term Korean residents. The new foreign population, especially of Chinese, Southeast Asian, South Asian, and Middle Eastern workers, is estimated to total somewhere between one hundred thousand and two hundred thousand people, including both legal residents and illegal immigrants. These foreigners have attracted immense media attention and are often held responsible for increasing Tokyo's crime rate (including prostitution, theft, and burglary), for disregarding public heath and sanitation standards, and for generally failing to observe the social norms that Japanese like to imagine they themselves adhere to. As their numbers have grown, some neighborhoods in Tokyo are beginning to be transformed into ethnic enclaves—of Chinese, or of Iranians, or of Bangladeshis—a development that many Tokyoites view with both alarm and incomprehension.

[9] This figure does not include the residents of two company dormitories in Miyamoto-chō that house about 180 single men who work in two large companies whose offices are several blocks away. Neighborhood organizations do not consider these men full-fledged residents, and they rarely are involved in local events.

[10] About one U.S. dollar during 1979–81; about two U.S. dollars in 1994. Apartment dwellers pay half dues.

[11] Policy makers during the American Occupation of Japan (1945–52) saw neighborhood associations as potentially undemocratic institutions, tainted by their activities as wartime agents of state control.

[12] At 1994 exchange rates, these contributions range from a low of roughly thirty dollars to a high of five hundred dollars.

Ordinary People/Everyday Life
Folk Culture in New York City

BARBARA KIRSHENBLATT-GIMBLETT

Studies of urban life often focus on those who hold the most power, whether economically, politically, or culturally; and to the extent that these studies examine culture, they are generally concerned with elite culture. Lower-income groups are typically studied in terms of so-called social problems. The analysis of folk culture offers an alternative perspective on the city by asking the question: How do ordinary people, faced with the increasing centralization of resources and power in large cities, find ways to exercise control and autonomy in their everyday lives? Though this study focuses on New York City, the issues are generally relevant to modern social life.

Vernacular culture is rooted in the immediate conditions of social life, homemade, peculiar to a locale, and often outside of, if not in opposition to, official or established culture. The street, bar, club, barbershop, vacant lot, rooftop, and kitchen are its crucible, rather than the school, museum, and symphony hall. Culture in this local sense is a reworking of the materials at hand, from oral traditions and customary practices to the products of the culture industry and elite institutions. Generally absent from the discourse of New York City Culture, vernacular culture is what ordinary people create in their everyday lives. Tacit, often small in scale and informal, vernacular cultural production can reveal how people escape bureaucratic control; create zones of autonomy and choice; resist,

Source: Article written expressly for *Urban Life*.

oppose, or subvert dominant cultural values and practices; and replace and renew what is appropriated from them by the culture industry.

Culture, as an organizing concept in the discipline of anthropology, has been variously defined in the literature (Kroeber and Kluckhohn 1952). Whereas anthropologists have tended to use the term to refer to the total way of life of a particular society, usually non-Western ones that are small in scale, scholars working in complex societies must conceptualize culture in relation to extreme social heterogeneity. Raymond Williams (1982) traces the history of the term, explaining how culture comes to be equated with civilization and the social elite.

Others have used the notion of subculture to capture the diversity of complex societies. In this study, the term *vernacular culture* focuses attention on the commonplace aspects of everyday life, in contrast with the elite culture of museums and universities and the *culture industry* that mass-produces our movies, records, and fashion.

Key thinkers, such as Theodor Adorno, Max Horkheimer, Jean Baudrillard, Pierre Bourdieu, Henry Lefebvre, Michel de Certeau, Raymond Williams, Stuart Hall, and Eric Hobsbawm have disagreed on the nature of vernacular culture and its creative and emancipatory potential. Vernacular culture is variously designated by them and others as folk, popular, residual, emergent, alternative, oppositional, subcultural, genuine, customary, or quotidian and is contrasted with official legitimate, dominant, hegemonic, high, or mass culture. The contrasts suggest relationships between vernacular culture and other kinds of cultural formations, relationships that are played out with special clarity in cities.

How then shall we constitute vernacular culture as a subject for study? Typically, the search has led to enclaves and subcultures, to vivid and legible assertions of social autonomy, whether these take the form of identifiable religious sects, such as Hasidim; deviant youth subcultures, such as Punks; artistic subcultures, such as Hip Hop; occupational groups, such as bicycle messengers; or distinctive neighborhoods, such as Chinatown or Harlem. Settings and events (clubs, parks, streets, rallies, festivals, and parades) have commanded attention as places where, for a time, vernacular culture alternatives can be enacted. Researchers have also searched the interstices in the daily round where alternative and oppositional practices can emerge—in the workplace or at times and places where formal controls are weak. Some have identified vernacular culture with the working class, others with marginal subcultures that can arise in any class, and still others with the everyday in *everyone's* life—the quotidian.

There are several recurrent questions which should be addressed in a serious investigation of vernacular culture. With the increasing centralization of both elite and mass cultural production and the massive resources they command, how can local and autonomous vernacular cultures form and survive? Where and among whom are they to be found? What is their makeup and meaning? What are their relationships to other types of cultural formation? How are vernacular values and practices deployed? What are their material consequences? Can we speak of a politics of vernacular culture?

These concerns are important in the conceptualization of urban life less in terms of the haves and have-nots and more as a struggle among diverse sectors and social worlds, where cultural capital, particularly in the form of vernacular culture, may be in greater abundance than economic resources. According to Raymond Williams and others, vernacular culture espouses what the dominant culture neglects, undervalues, opposes, represses, or even fails to recognize. In contrast, definition by negation—defining the nature of the have-nots in a society—renders certain social sectors invisible as phenomena in their own right by referring to them only in terms of others who have what they lack. Consistent with the discourse of dominant culture is the implication that success is to be measured in terms of upward mobility and economic gain, particularly as achieved through formal educational institutions and the political system. By examining vernacular culture, its processes of formation and deployment, we may be encouraged to question some of these assumptions, to see vernacular culture as commentary, critique, alternative, or resistance and to find other standards for measuring its success or failure.

Persistent themes in urban anthropology include territory, politics, social segmentation, and work. Should considerations of place be confined to neighborhood, conceptualized primarily in terms of residence? Should the concern with politics be extended to cultural politics? Should ethnic/racial segmentation be viewed not only in occupational terms, but also as highly contingent social constructions? Should the focus on labor be supplemented by attention to domestic life, leisure, religious activity, and other aspects of daily reality?

Place

"Identity of place is achieved by dramatizing the aspirations, needs, and functional rhythms of personal and group life," according to Yi-fu Tuan (1977:178). Tuan and others have stressed the effort required to transform space into place, to invest a location with meaning. Residence per se is not enough to create a sense of neighborhood: without deep emotional attachments to a location, it is difficult, if not impossible, to mobilize concerted action to protect the interests of those who live there. This is not to underestimate the economic pressures and political forces that shape neighborhoods, but to direct attention to vernacular culture as the medium through which residents make the places in which they live palpable, articulate social relations, give form to values, and discover possibilities for action.

Rather than starting with neighborhood as a self-evident unit, we might make the notion problematic. Consider a map of New York City that consists of a series of overlays, each one delineating a particular geography of the city. The boundaries and the territories they define are relevant for certain groups, activities, and occasions. They rarely converge, often conflict, and shift over time. The various areas include the *bureaucratic territories* (zip codes, area codes, police precincts, electoral districts, school districts, zoning); *areas defined by the delivery of services* (cable television, messenger services, parcel deliveries, taxis, drug traffic); *manufacturing and business areas* (fur, garment, diamond, advertising, electronics, printing, restaurant supply, luxury retail, the territorial organization of vendors and street performers); *local spheres of influence* (parishes; neighborhood associations defined by block, street, square, park, or region; gangs; organized crime); *a recreational geography of culture and entertainment* (Museum Mile, theatre district, landmarks, plaques and historic restorations, concentrations of pornography and prostitution, public spaces, vacant lots, and exotic neighborhoods); and *ceremonial centers* (Fifth Avenue, Union Square, Eastern Parkway, Washington Square). Many of these territories cannot be located by means of a map or official marker, but rather are discovered informally through social knowledge, often tacit, and through social action, whether instrumental or expressive, symbolic, and ceremonial. Clues may be found in toponomy and orientation, including the official names for areas, name changes initiated by the City Council, new names created by real estate interests, and local traditions. For whom is the area near the Port Authority bus terminal Hell's Kitchen rather than Clinton? For whom is the area below Fourteenth Street and east of the Bowery the East Village rather than the Lower East Side? Who refers to Sixth Avenue and who to the Avenue of the Americas? What conception of a territory is at work in the way that directions are given? Is an address on the Bowery to be identified in terms of Lower East Side or Little Italy/Soho cross streets? Individuals who are thoroughly familiar with Prince and Spring Streets may be at a loss if oriented in terms of Rivington and Stanton Streets; yet, all four converge within yards of each other on the Bowery.

Cognitive maps, the ways in which territories are conceptualized by their inhabitants, can offer insights into the complex ways in which space is organized in New York City. Consider the many maps of the Lower East Side that could be drawn by Chinese, Hispanic, Ukrainian, Italian, and Jewish inhabitants; children and adolescents as opposed to elderly residents; city planners; real estate developers; the art world; public historians; the tourist industry; and New Yorkers whose families once lived in the area. Is the focal point Clinton Street, with its Dominican bridal shops; Essex Street, where Jewish religious articles may be found; East Broadway, now largely a street of Chinese food shops; the art mecca of Alphabetland; the Ukrainian organizations of Second Avenue; the Italian pastry and cheese shops on First Avenue; the vacant lots and abandoned buildings awaiting development; the men's shelters and refuges for the homeless; or the points of historic interest?

Cognitive maps are also enacted in ceremonial ways. The chosen order of march, or route, and the sequence of stops, parades and processions, many of which have a long and well-documented history in the city, dramatize social relations and engage in a spatial articulation of values. As Susan Davis (1986) suggests, "Such public enactments are not only patterned by social forces—they have been part of the very building and challenging of social relations. . . . As dramatic representations, parades and public ceremonies are political acts: They have pragmatic objectives, and concrete, often material results."

The Stations of the Cross processions on the Lower East Side and in other parts of the city map sacred history onto the present social reality by establishing a convergence between each stage in Christ's passion and the places in the neighborhood of significance to the parishioners—a housing project, hospital, center of drug traffic, site of an accident or violent death. Placards held aloft at each station may carry statements of protest against abortion, United States involvements in Central America, inadequate facilities for the elderly, the lack of low-income housing, inadequate protection against crime, or drug addiction. Groups who participate in such events are also effective in mobilizing community support for

Via Crucia por las Calles (Stations of the Cross Procession) on Good Friday, 1983, St. James Church, Lower East Side. The congregation has been largely Latino since World War II. [Photo by Barbara Kirshenblatt-Gimblett]

improving conditions in their neighborhoods. Processions organized by the Church may make the parish, as a territory, visible for a moment by routing the march along the parish boundaries. Processions organized by saint societies express what Robert Orsi (1985:221) has called "the spirit of defiance in popular spirituality." Home shrines and sidewalk altars, saints' feasts and processions mobilize local communities in alternative, if not oppositional, ways and offer still other notions of territory and neighborhood.

A similar line of argument, with rather different outcomes, could be pursued in regard to other events of this kind. The lion dance processions organized for the Chinese New Year by competing martial arts clubs are viewed by the police, who issue the street activity permit, as one parade. Concerned with the practicalities of rerouting traffic in the small and crowded neighborhood, the police prescribe one route for the dancers to follow. For the dancers, however, Chinatown is a complex area, divided into highly charged provinces of power. What the police, press, and visitor consider one parade is, for Chinatown, a series of up to a dozen independent and competitive processions. Each lion dancing team has the right to pass along certain streets, but not others; obligations to go to some spots first, as a sign of deference and respect; and the good sense to avoid crossing paths with a warring team. Elaborate performances lasting almost an hour may occur at prearranged locations and can generate substantial income for the groups, who aim to pick up several thousand dollars in the course of the day. The route, the points at which the dancers stop, the time spent at each place, and the elaborateness of the performances constitute a map of social relations and power structures shaping life in the area and beyond.

The annual West Indian carnival procession each Labor Day is not only a celebration, but also an important political event. The sheer number of people who gather, estimated at about one million individuals, is itself evidence of organizational success in turning the numbers out and in coordinating their activity on such a large scale once they are present. Indeed, the West Indian Carnival Association is the largest organization in New York's Caribbean community.

In contrast with the public events staged in the places where people live are those that occur in what have evolved as the city's ceremonial centers. Fifth Avenue has, over the last hundred years, become such a ceremonial center, to the dismay of the Fifth Avenue

Charlie Barnett tells jokes to an impromptu gathering on a grassy patch, ▶
Washington Square, 1982. [Photo by Barbara Kirshenblatt-Gimblett]

Association, which sees these events as a nuisance. Dispersed populations, such as the Irish, come together from throughout the metropolitan region and claim one of the most prestigious avenues in the city for four hours in the form of the St. Patrick's Day parade, "the oldest and largest annual civic parade in the United States," according to Jane Kelton (1986).

In contrast with such highly organized, militaristic parades, are events such as the Easter Parade, a tradition for about a century on Fifth Avenue. With no formal auspices or funding; no program; no official route, map, or guide; no mailers or paid advertisements; no organizer; and no permits, tens of thousands of strangers from throughout the city and beyond gather along Fifth Avenue in their holiday best to see others and to be seen by others. This event, like the activities in Washington Square and other open spaces in the city, is important for the way that it reveals how large numbers of strangers orchestrate an exceedingly complex program of activity on the basis of tacit understanding and customary practice. These events and settings are extraordinary examples of cooperation on a large scale with a minimum of formal control. When exerted, that control is generally repressive, as in the police harassing performers for park permits or noise permits and regulating the solicitation of money (something only religious groups can do).

Events like the Easter Parade, which bring together such a heterogeneous crowd, are also important for the way in which they both crosscut boundaries of class, ethnicity, and neighborhood and lay claim to a prestigious public space. These events raise important questions about the nature of public space and the history of legislation in New York to control what can and cannot be done in the city's streets and open areas. Selectively enforced, the law over the last century has gained increasing control over what can occur in public spaces, whether at all or only by permit or license. The hanging of laundry, posting of bills, vending, playing of music, and assembly or movement through space are among the activities that can be defined as *quality of life crimes*. Attitudes toward these activities reveal competing notions of the street and differential access to public space; attitudes and notions that are frequently expressed through the rhetoric of crime, public order, and respectability.

Perhaps the most vivid, recent example of alternative conceptions of the city being enacted through a delineation of territory other than neighborhood is that of subway graffiti. The basis for association is the subway line. Writers who live near stops on the same line associate with each other, even though their neighborhoods may be widely separated. The drama of control is played out across the entire city on the moving canvas of the trains, as writers vie with each other and with city authorities to achieve the status of *all city*; that is, to have one's tag, or name, well represented on all the major lines. This youth subculture, known as Hip Hop, is worth examining for the conception of the city that it expresses and, from an historical perspective, for the ways in which its expressive modes (graffiti, rapping, breaking, language, and dress) have been contested by city authorities, while being coopted by the art world and culture industry.

Cultural Politics

Emblazoned on a subway car, the epithet "Style Wars" captures not only the spirit of urban graffiti, but also the larger point that style is meaning, that expressive behavior articulates values. Scrawled on a devastated building in Lower Manhattan, the epigraph "Semiotic Guerilla Warfare" acknowledges the conflict of value systems played out in the marks individuals make. The public nature of walls and trains and the outrage of many citizens and city officials are essential as an oppositional context for these marks. As Dick Hebdige (1979) suggests, the *crime* is only a broken code. Both "Style Wars" and "Semiotic Guerilla Warfare" are instances of expressive behavior that derive their meanings from the problematic relations between individual and institution, private and public, property and the law, autonomy and control. These relations inform a vast array of expressive forms in the city, and style provides an important arena for dramatizing these conflicts.

Oppositional styles are frequently appropriated, diffused, and defused, by those they oppose. The movement back and forth is one worth tracing, particularly in the record bin archeology and playing against the groove that are so characteristic of Hip Hop's rap music. At parties held in parks, community centers, schools, and clubs, recorded music is the raw material for performances by the DJ, a musician whose instrument is the *wheel of steel* or the turntable. As the record spins, the DJ makes the needle repeat sections, plays two records simultaneously, forces the record to play backwards, adjusts the volume of the two tracks and combines recorded sounds, often taken from obscure records found in the record bins of subway shops, with the electronic beat box or with the live verbal patter of rappers. Like so many other creations in the vernacular, Hip Hop has gained legitimacy and has been reappropriated by the mass media but with unpredictable results.

On the one hand, the legitimate theatre has featured the idiom

Semiotic

Guerrilla

Warfare

231

on its stage, a spate of main release films and videos have gained international visibility for the form, and how-to-do-it books and classes have sprung up to meet the demand for participation by suburban adults and others far-removed from the youth subculture that gave rise to Hip Hop. On the other hand, Maori and Samoan youths as far away as New Zealand, Indian and Caribbean adolescents in England, the children of Turkish migrant workers in Berlin, and *bamboo shoot* gangs in Tokyo have identified closely with Hip Hop as seen in films and video, have created their own versions of it, and have made it voice their concerns. Such cases call into question what so many critics of the culture industry have characterized as the passive and uncritical consumption of mass culture and the power of the culture industry to displace or to absorb and to domesticate vernacular creations.

Such cases are also an invitation to explore cultural politics. What role do schools, athletic leagues, and other institutions, organized and sanctioned by adults, play in homogenizing difference by imposing cultural standards? How do cultural differentiations persist in the face of efforts to eliminate them, whether in the name of respectability, democracy, or upward mobility? What are the implications of a middle-class fascination with working-class culture, particularly on the part of disaffected youth? How does style, through the media of music, dance, language, dress, and forms of association, articulate the terms in which the conflicts will be played out? With what consequences?

Social Boundaries

Rather than start with the epithets *ethnic* and *racial* as givens, it would be worthwhile to make the terms problematic, to consider other attributes that contribute to the formation of social categories (age, gender, disability, religion, class), to cast the entire question in terms of the social construction of difference and to view ethnicity in more fluid and socially contingent terms. At one extreme, cases can be cited where objective differences are not a prerequisite for social distinctions, as assimilated Jews who have faced anti-Semitism can attest. At the other extreme, observable distinctions may be inconsequential in the organization of group life. The issue is thus not the degree of cultural difference involved, objectively

◀ "Semiotic Guerilla Warfare," acknowledges the conflict of value systems played out in urban grafitti. Grafitti by artist Kenny Scharf and others on a wall on Prince Street near the Bowery, Lower Manhattan, 1983. [Photo by Barbara Kirshenblatt-Gimblett]

speaking, but the social significance attributed to any similarity or difference, however small.

Furthermore, identity is not singular and immutable. There are many bases for identifying oneself and being identified by others, and there is a degree of choice. It may not be possible to eliminate an objective difference, but it is possible to render it socially inconsequential. It is therefore important to ask how choices are made and to examine which attributes of the many that could be cited—gender, age, skin color, national origin, residence, occupation, economic status, religion, education, language, political leanings, skills, etc.—are salient in which situations. It is also important to recognize the possibility of multiple identities and multiple cultural repertoires, as well as the ability to select from and to alternate among them. This heterogeneity "brings to consciousness . . . premises or assumptions hitherto in the main covert or implicit" and is a source of cultural creativity (Keesing 1960). Evident in New York's vernacular music, dance, language, fashion, and food, this cultural creativity is worthy of study in its own right.

A promising avenue for research is how culturally specific ways of organizing time shape social identity. Discrepancies between calendars (for example, the variance between the dates of the Greek Orthodox and Roman Catholic Easters) reflect conscientious efforts to differentiate two traditions. As made so clear in the work of Eviatar Zerubavel (1981), each calendar creates its own distinctive rhythms, sequence of moods, and dramatic structure not only for those who live by it, but also for others who work and live in the area. Thus, lived calendars are both segregative and integrative, and examples abound of lives lived under more than one calendar.

Calendars are experienced territorially. Either the streets are festivalized by spectacular ceremony or deserted on holidays by those who normally work in the neighborhood:

> New York is not itself on Jewish holy days. Delicatessens are not open. The garment district is silent. All over the city, shops, offices, schools, cleaners, even entire buildings, close down for the day—like so many darkened rooms in a normally well-lighted house.

> Yesterday was Yom Kippur [Day of Atonement], the highest holy day of all, and no where was it more evident than in the diamond district along West 47th Street between Fifth and Sixth Avenues. . . . (*New York Times*, 9/28/1982)

It would be worth examining how institutions, particularly schools, government offices, and the private sector, intercalate civic, Christian, Jewish, and other calendars, and to what effect.

When activated in the forms of liturgical recitations and ritual enactments of sacred history, calendars transact the relationship between a very long stretch of history and the short annual cycle of observance. As Lloyd Warner has shown in his analysis of Yankee City, calendars manifest a particular view of history in the choice they express of what to celebrate and with what emphasis. The multiplicity of calendars and schedules in New York City is evidence of an extraordinary pluralism and offers an important contrast with the clock, traffic signal, and other efforts to synchronize and discipline large numbers of people on a strictly pragmatic basis.

Everyday Life

Though a critical factor in any consideration of New York City, work is but one aspect of the lives of New Yorkers. For many, the conditions of work are largely beyond their control. All the more reason to pay close attention to those areas where people have greater autonomy. Herein lies the importance of vernacular culture.

One of the richest areas in which to observe choice and autonomy at a local level is in that of play, the autotelic activity *par excellence*. Streets, buildings, and lots intended for purposes remote from pigeon flying and stickball are mobilized in ways that reverse the normal relations between means and ends. In play, as in art, the expressive takes precedence over the instrumental, and the constraints of necessity are suspended for a time in the interests of pure enjoyment: a sewer cap serves as homeplate, fire escape ladders become basketball hoops, fire hydrants delineate boundaries, the stoop becomes a ball court, and cars become bases. Small variations in play terminology or practice define regions of the city, while short links in long chains of transmission ensure the integrity and durability of a culture created by and for children who pass on their knowledge of the street to each other and without the intervention of adults. An activity that occurs everywhere, play takes distinctive forms in urban settings, utilizing and transforming features of the environment.

Vertical displacements, such as rooftop gardens and the *tar beach* of urban sunbathers, and aerial extensions such as the flying of pigeons and kites from rooftops, capitalize on the city's extreme verticality. The monumental view from the roof and the unlimited sky often contrast sharply with the street, which in the inner city may be the scene of litter, drugs, and devastation. The pigeon game, popular in areas where concentrations of tenements still stand, tests the loyalty of the birds, whose instincts to flock and to home are in conflict when two different flocks mix in the sky. Loyalty and honor, prized values, are dramatized daily in the pigeon game, often in areas where incomes are low, unemployment high, and opportunities for suffering personal indignities frequent.

Paradoxically, the very conditions that lead to the impoverishment of urban areas, to the abandoning of buildings and their eventual levelling, also create zones of entrepreneurial opportunity. The lots open up to the unsupervised construction of elaborate gardens and handmade buildings, often without formal sanction. In East Harlem, the South Bronx, the Lower East Side, and parts of Brooklyn, little country cabins mushroom incongruously on vacant lots between tenements and brownstones, some abandoned, others still intact.

These intentionally old-fashioned *casitas*, once common in the Puerto Rican countryside, abound where local men can no longer afford to rent storefronts or basement rooms for their social clubs. One is named *Nostalgia for My Homeland*, others are named for hometowns. The detritus of urban decay is redirected here to materialize pastoral images of another time and place. Though these environments may not significantly change the material conditions of their lives, the enacting of alternatives is both significant in itself and revealing of the larger settings in which these men find themselves.

It is essential that, in our efforts to keep the larger picture in view, we do not lose sight of life as lived in a city such as New York, with all the specificity that gives it its special character. In exploring the interaction of culture, politics, and economics, we must take care not to lose sight of processes at work outside of the formal structures and institutions. In our enthusiasm for New York's metropolitan dominance, we must not undervalue the vernacular culture of the city and all that it can reveal to us about the inner life of those who live in New York.

This essay was written with the generous support of a Guggenheim Foundation Fellowship, 1986–87. It draws on my earlier study "The Future of Folklore Studies in America: The Urban Frontier," *Folklore Forum* 16, No. 2 (1983): 175–234, and was presented as a position paper to the Committee on New York: The Dual City, sponsored by the Social Science Research Council in October, 1986.

References

Abelson, P. 1969. *Science*, 165(1).

Abey-Wickrama, I., M. F. a'Brook, F. E. G. Gattoni, and C. F. Herridge. 1969. Mental Hospital Admissions and Aircraft Noise. *Lancet*, ii:1275–1277.

Ablon, J. 1964. Relocated American Indians in the San Francisco Bay Area: Social Interaction and Indian Identity. *Human Organization*, 23:296–304.

_____. 1965. American Indian Relocation: Problems of Dependency and Management in the City. *Phylon*, 26:362–371.

_____. 1970. The Samoan Funeral in Urban America. *Ethnology*, 9:209–227.

_____. 1971. Retention of Cultural Values and Differential Urban Adaptation in a West Coast City. *Social Forces*, 49(1).

Abrams, Charles. 1964. *Housing in the Modern World*. London: Faber & Faber.

Abu-Lughod, Janet. 1962. Migrant Adjustment to City Life: The Egyptian Case. *American Journal of Sociology*, 47:22–32.

_____. 1971. *Cairo: 1001 Years of the City Victorious*. Princeton: Princeton University Press.

_____. 1980. *Rabat: Urban Aparthied in Morocco*. Princeton: Princeton University Press.

_____. 1983. Contemporary Relevance of Islamic Urban Principles. In *Islamic Architecture and Urbanism*, ed. Aydin Germen. Dammam: King Faisal University. Also summarized in *Ekistics*, January 1980.

_____. 1984. Culture, Modes of Production, and the Changing Nature of Cities in the Arab World. In *The City in Cultural Context*, eds. John Agnew, John Mercer, and David Sopher. Boston: Allen & Unwin.

_____. Preserving the Living Heritage of Islamic Cities. In *Toward an Architecture in the Spirit of Islam*, ed. R. Holod. Philadelphia: Aga Khan Foundation.

_____. 1987. The Islamic City: Historic Myth, Islamic Essence, and Contemporary Relevance. *International Journal of Middle Eastern Studies*, 19:155–161.

Abu-Lughod, Lila. 1984. Honor, Modesty and Poetry in a Bedouin Society. Ph.D. Diss. Department of Anthropology, Harvard University.

_____. 1986. *Veiled Sentiments: Honor and Poetry in a Bedouin Society*. Berkeley: University of California Press.

Abuza, N. The Paris-London-New York Questionnaires. Harvard University. Unpublished.

Adams, Bert N. 1968. *Kinship in an Urban Setting*. Chicago: Markham.

———. 1970. Isolation, Function and Beyond. *Journal of Marriage and the Family*, 32:575–597.

Agha Kahn Award for Architecture. Seminar Series. Seminar 1 (1978); Seminar 2 (1978); Seminar 3 (1979); Seminar 4 (1979); Seminar 5 (1980).

Aldous, Joan. 1962. Urbanization, the Extended Family and Kinship Ties in West Africa. *Social Forces*, 41:6–12.

Alexander, Christopher. 1966. A City Is Not a Tree. *Design*, 206:46–55.

al-Khalaf, Samir [Kanan Makiyya]. 1991. *The Monument*. Berkeley: University of California Press.

Altman, D., et al. Graduate Center, The City University of New York. Unpublished research.

Altorki, Soraya. Women in Domestic Groups: Ideology and Behavior in Jiddah Elites. Unpublished manuscript based upon doctoral diss.

———. 1986. *Women in Saudi Arabia: Ideology and Behavior Among the Elites*. New York: Columbia University Press.

Alvarez, Sonia. 1989. Women's Movements and Gender Politics in the Brazilian Transition. In *The Women's Movement in Latin America*, ed. Jane S. Jaquette, pp. 18–71. Boston: Unwin Hyman.

Alvirez, David, and Frank D. Bean. 1976. The Mexican American Family. In *Ethnic Families in America: Patterns and Variations*, eds. Charles H. Mindel and Robert W. Habenstein, pp. 271–292.

Anderson, Benedict. 1983. *Imagined Communities*. New York: Verso.

Anderson, Elijah. 1990. *Streetwise: Race, Class and Change in an Urban Community*. Chicago: University of Chicago Press.

Anderson, Nels. 1962. The Urban Way of Life. *International Journal of Comparative Sociology*, 3:175–188.

Ando, Y., and H. Hattori. 1973. Statistical Studies on the Effects of Intense Noise during Human Fetal Life. *Sound & Vibration*, 27:101–110.

———. 1977. Effects of Noise on Human Placental Lactogen (HPL) Levels in Maternal Plasma. *British Journal of Obstetrics & Gynecology*, 84:115–118.

Andreas, Carol. 1985. *When Women Rebel: The Rise of Popular Feminism in Peru*. Westport, CT: Lawrence Hill and Co.

Annest, J. L., K. R. Mahaffey, D. H. Cox, and J. Roberts. 1982. Blood Lead Levels for Persons 6 Months–74 Years of Age: United States, 1976–1980. *NCHS Advancedata*, 79:1–23.

Arensberg, Conrad M. 1961. The Community as Object and as Sample. *American Anthropologist*, 63:241–264.

———. 1968. The Urban in Crosscultural Perspective. In *Urban Anthropology: Research Perspectives and Strategies*, ed. Elizabeth Eddy. Athens: University of Georgia Press.

Arensberg, Conrad, and Solon T. Kimball. 1965. *Culture and Community*. New York: Harcourt, Brace and World.

Arizpe, Lourdes. 1975. Indigenas en la Ciudad de Mexico: El Caso de las "Marias." Mexico: Sep/Setentas.

———. 1977. Women in the Informal Labor Sector: The Case of Mexico City. In *Women and National Development*, ed. The Wellesley Editorial Committee, pp. 25–37. Chicago: University of Chicago Press.

Armelagos, George J., and John R. Dewey. 1970. Evolutionary Response to Human Infectious Disease. *Bioscience*, 20:271–275.

Aronoff, M. 1973. Development Towns in Israel. In *Israel: Social Structure and Change*, eds. M. Curtis and M. Chertoff, pp. 27–46. New Brunswick, NJ: Transaction Books.

_____. 1974. *Frontiertown: The Politics of Community Building in Israel*. Manchester: Manchester University Press.

Aronson, S. 1971. The Sociology of the Telephone. *International Journal of Comparative Sociology*, 12:153–167.

Avineri, S. 1973. Israel: Two Nations. In *Israel: Social Structure and Change*, eds. M. Curtis and M. Chertoff, pp. 281–305. New Brunswick, NJ: Transaction Books.

Avriel, A. 1979. *Everyday Life in a Hatiqua Neighborhood*. Tel Aviv: Tcherikover (in Hebrew).

Axinn, June, and Mark Stern. 1988. *Dependency and Poverty: Old Problems in a New World*. Lexington, MA: Lexington.

Ayres, Stephen M., Robert Evans, David Licht, Jane Griesbach, Felicity Reimold, Edward F. Ferrand, and Antoinette Criscitiello. 1973. Health Effects of Exposure to High Concentrations of Automotive Emissions. *Archives of Environmental Health*, 27:168–178.

Bachofen, J. J. 1861. *Das Mutterrecht*. Basel: Benno Schwabe.

Bacon, Alice M. 1902. *Japanese Girls and Women*. Boston: Houghton Mifflin.

Bailey, F. G. 1963. Closed Social Stratification in India. *Archives Europeennes de Sociologie*, IV:107–124.

Balmori, Diana, and Robert Oppenheimer. 1979. Family Clusters: Generational Nucleation in Nineteenth Century Argentina and Chile. *Comparative Studies in Society and History*, 21:231–261.

Banfield, Edward C. 1958. *The Moral Basis of a Backward Society*. New York: Free Press.

Bannister, P., and J. M. M. Mair. 1968. *Evolution of Personal Constructs*. London: Academic Press.

Barltrop, Donald. 1982. Nutritional and Maturational Factors Modifying the Absorption of Inorganic Lead from the Gastrointestinal Tract. In *Banbury Report No. 11, Environmental Factors in Human Growth and Development*, eds. V. R. Hunt, M. K. Smith, and D. Worth, pp. 35–41. Cold Spring Harbor Laboratory.

Barnes, Charles. 1915. *The Longshoremen*. New York: Russell Sage Foundation.

Barnes, J. A. 1954. Class and Committees in a Norwegian Island Parish. *Human Relations* 7:39–58.

Barth, Frederik. 1969. *Ethnic Groups and Boundaries*. New York: Allen & Unwin.

Bartlett, Donald L., and James B. Steele. 1992. *America: What Went Wrong?* Kansas City, MO: Andrews and McMeel.

Barzini, Luigi. 1965. *The Italians*. New York: Atheneum.

Bascom, William. 1955. Urbanization Among the Yoruba. *American Journal of Sociology*, 60:446–454.

Basham, Richard. 1978. *Urban Anthropology: The Cross-Cultural Study of Complex Societies*. Palo Alto, CA: Mayfield.

Bastide, R. 1964. Ethnologie des Capitales Latino-Americaines. Trans. D. G. Epstein. *Caravelle*, 3:73–89.

Basu, Dilip K., ed. 1985. *The Rise and Growth of the Colonial Port Cities in Asia*. Berkeley: Center for South and Southeast Asia Studies, University of California.

Beals, Ralph L. 1951. Urbanism, Urbanization and Acculturation. *American Anthropologist*, 53:1–10.

Bell, Charles. 1928. *The People of Tibet*. Oxford: Clarendon Press.

Bell, Colin. 1968. Mobility and the Extended Middle Class Family. In *Readings in Kinship in Urban Society*, ed. C. C. Harris, pp. 209–224. Oxford and New York: Pergamon.

Bender, D. R. 1967. A Refinement of the Concept of Household: Families, Co-residence, and Domestic Functions. *American Anthropologist*, 69:493–504.

Bendix, Reinhard. 1967. Tradition and Modernity Reconsidered. *Comparative Studies in Society and History*, 9.

Benson, Edwin. 1920. *Life in a Medieval City*. New York: Macmillan.

Berger, Bennett. 1966. Suburbs, Subcultures and the Urban Future. In *Planning for a Nation of Cities*, ed. Sam Bass Warner. Cambridge, MA: MIT Press.

Berger, S., and M. Piore. 1980. *Dualism and Discontinuity in Industrial Societies*. Cambridge: Cambridge University Press.

Berlin, Brent, Paul Kay, D. E. Breedlove, and P. H. Raven. 1968. Covert Categories and Folk Taxonomies. *American Anthropologist*, 70:290–299.

Berlin, Gordon. 1991. *The Poverty Among Families: A Service Decategorization Response*. New York: Manpower Demonstration Research Corporation. Photocopied Report.

Berreman, Gerald D. 1966. Anemic and Emetic Analyses in Social Anthropology. *American Anthropologist*, 68:346–354.

Berreman, Gerald D., G. Gjessing, and K. Gough. 1968. Social Responsibilities Symposium. *Current Anthropology*, 9:391–435.

Bestor, Theodore C. 1985. Tradition and Japanese Social Organization: Institutional Development in a Tokyo Neighborhood. *Ethnology*, 24(2): 121–135.

_____. 1986. Shitamachi and the Culture of Urbanism: Subculture, Class, and Community in Tokyo. Paper presented at the annual meeting of the American Anthropological Association.

_____. 1989. *Neighborhood Tokyo*. Stanford: Stanford University Press.

Bestor, Theodore C. 1990. Tokyo Mom-and-Pop. *The Wilson Quarterly*, Autumn.

Bieliauskas, Linas A. 1982. *Stress and Its Relationship to Health and Illness*. Boulder, CO: Westview Press.

Bielicki, Tadeusz. 1986. Physical Growth as a Measure of the Economic Well-being of Populations: The Twentieth Century. In *Human Growth*, Vol. III, eds. F. Falkner and J. M. Tanner, pp. 283–305. New York: Plenum Press.

Black, Cyril E. 1966. *The Dynamics of Modernization*. New York: Harper & Row.

Black, Francis L. 1975. Infectious Diseases in Primitive Societies. *Science*, 187:515–518.

Black, Mary, and Duane Metzger. 1965. Ethnographic Description and the Study of Law. In Anthropological Study of Law, ed. Laura Nader. *American Anthropologist*, 67:141–165.

Blake, G. H., and R. I. Lawless, eds. 1980. *The Changing Middle Eastern City*. London: Croom and Helm.

Bodde, D., ed. 1936. *Annual Customs and Festivals in Peking*. Peiping: Henri Vetch.

Boissevain, Jeremy. 1974. *Friends of Friends: Networks, Manipulators, and Coalitions*. New York: St. Martin's Press.

Bonacich, Edna. 1972. A Theory of Ethnic Antagonism: The Split-Labor Market. *American Sociological Review*, 37:547–559.

Bonilla, Frank. 1962. The Favelas of Rio: The Rundown Rural Barrio in the City. *Dissent*, 9:383–386.

Borneman, John. 1992. *Belonging in the Two Berlins: Kin, State, Nation*. Cambridge: Cambridge University Press.

Boserup, Ester. 1970. *Woman's Role in Economic Development*. New York: St. Martin's Press.

Bossen, Laurel. "Women and Dependent Development." Ph.D. Thesis. Department of Anthropology, SUNY, Albany.

Bott, Elizabeth. 1957. *Family and Social Network: Roles, Norms, and External Relationships in Ordinary Urban Families*. London: Tavistock.

Bouah, G. Niangoran. 1960. Le Village Aboure. *Cahiers d'Etudes Africaines I*, 2:113–127.

Bourgois, Philippe. 1989. In Search of Horatio Alger: Culture and Ideology in the Crack Economy. *Contemporary Drug Problems*, 16:619–649.

_____. 1995a. *In Search of Respect: Selling Crack in El Barrio*. New York: Cambridge University Press.

_____. 1995b. From Jibaro to Crack Dealer: Confronting Capitalism in Spanish Harlem. In *Articulating Hidden Histories: Anthropology, History, and the Influence of Eric R. Wolf*, eds. Jane Schneider and Rayna Rapp. Berkeley: University of California Press.

_____. 1995c. The Political Economy of Resistance and Self-Destruction in the Crack Economy: An Ethnographic Perspective. *Annals of the New York Academy of Sciences*, 749:23–44.

Bourricard, F. 1964. Lima en La Vida Politica Peruana. *American Latina*, pp. 89–96.

Braner, J. S., J. J. Goodnow, and G. A. Austin. 1956. *A Study of Thinking*. New York: John Wiley and Sons.

Brettell, Caroline B. 1982. *We Have Already Cried Many Tears: The Stories of Three Portuguese Migrant Women*. Rochester, VT: Schenkman Books.

Brettell, Caroline B., and Colette Callier-Boisvert. 1977. Portuguese Immigrants in France: Familial and Social Networks and the Structuring of Community. *Studi Emigrazione/Etudes Migrations*, 14(46): 149–203.

Brettell, Caroline B., and Patricia A. deBergeois. 1992. Anthropology and the Study of Immigrant Women. In *Seeking Common Ground: Multidisciplinary Studies of Immigrant Women in the United States*, ed. Donna Gabaccia, pp. 41–63. Westport, CT: Greenwood Press.

Bridges, Harry (President ILWU). 1957. U.S. West Coast Longshoremens' Union, interview, July.

Brody, D. J., J. L. Pirkle, R. A. Kramer, et al. 1994. Blood Lead Levels in the U.S. Population. *Journal of the American Medical Association*, 272:277–283.

Brown, C. 1983. *Black and White Britain: The Third PSI Survey*. London: Heinemann.

Brunn, Stanley, and Jack Williams. 1983. *Cities of the World: World Regional Urban Development*. New York: Harper & Row.

Brydon, L. 1987. Who Moves? Women: Migration in West Africa in the 1980's. In *Migrants, Workers and the Social Order*, ed. J. Eames, A.S.A. monograph no. 26. London: Tavistock.

Buechler, Judith M., ed. 1976. Women in the Migratory Process. *Anthropological Quarterly*, 49(1) (special issue).

Buechley, R. W., W. B. Riggan, V. Hasselblad, and J. B. VanBruggen. 1973. SO_2 Levels and Perturbations in Mortality. *Archives of Environmental Health*, 27:134–137.

Bujra, Janet. 1975. Women Entrepreneurs in Early Nairobi. *Canadian Journal of African Studies*, 9(2): 213–226.

Bundesanstalt für Arbeit. 1973. *Reprusentativuntersuchung*. Nurnberg: Bundesanstalt für Arbeit.

Burgess, J. S. 1928. *The Guilds of Peking*. New York: Columbia University Press.

_____. 1943. Community Organization in China. *Far Eastern Survey*, 14:337–371.

Burgess, R. W., and D. J. Bogue. 1964. *Contributions to Urban Sociology*. Chicago: University of Chicago Press.

Burton, Richard. 1966. *First Footsteps in East Africa*. London: Routledge & Kegan Paul.

Butterworth, Douglas, and John K. Chance. 1981. *Latin American Urbanization*. Cambridge: Cambridge University Press.

Cahn, E. S., ed. 1969. *Our Brother's Keeper: The Indian in White America*. New York: World.

Caldarola, Carlo. 1968. The Doya-Gai: A Japanese Version of Skid Row. *Pacific Affairs*, 41:511–525.

Caplovitz, David. 1963. *The Poor Pay More*. New York: The Free Press.

Caplow, Theodore, Howard M. Bahr, Bruce A. Chadwick, Reuben Hill, and Margaret Holmes Williamson. 1982. *Middletown Families: Fifty Years of Change and Continuity*. Minneapolis: University of Minnesota Press.

Carruthers, Malcom. 1976. Biochemical Responses to the Environment. In *Man in Urban Environments*, eds. G. A. Harrison and J. B. Gibson, pp. 247–273. New York: Oxford University Press.

Castells, Manuel. 1983. *The City and the Grassroots: A Cross-Cultural Theory of Urban Social Movements*. Berkeley: University of California Press.

Castles, S., and G. Kosack. 1973. *Immigrant Workers and Class Structure in Western Europe*. London: Oxford University Press.

Centers for Disease Control. 1991. Preventing Lead Poisoning in Young Children. U.S. Department of Health and Human Services, Public Health Service.

Centre International de l'Enfance. 1959. Etude des conditions de vie de l'enfant Africain en milieu urbain et de leur influence sur la delinquance juvenile. *Travaux et Documents XII*. Paris.

Cerase, F. 1970. Nostalgia or Disenchantment: Considerations on Return Migration. In *The Italian Experience in the United States*, eds. Silvano U. Tomasi and Madeleine H. Engles. New York: Center for Migration Studies.

Chandler, T., and G. Fox. 1974. *3000 Years of Urban Growth*. New York: Academic Press.

Chant, S., ed. 1992. *Gender and Migration in Developing Countries*. London: Belhaven Press.

Chase-Dunn, Christopher, and Thomas D. Hall, eds. 1991. *Core/Periphery Relations in Precapitalist Worlds*. Boulder, CO: Westview Press.

Chevalier, Dominique, ed. 1979. *L'Espace social de la ville arabe*. Paris: Maisonneuve et Larose.

Chinchilla, Norma S. 1977. Industrialization, Monopoly Capitalism, and Women's Work in Guatemala. In *Women and National Development*, ed. The Wellesley Editorial Committee, pp. 38–56. Chicago: University of Chicago Press.

Chouraqui, A. 1953. *Les Juifs d'Afrique du Nord*. Paris: Presses Universitaires de France.

Clark, Carolyn. 1980. Land and Food: Women and Power in the 19th Century. *Africa*, 50(4): 357–369.

Clarke, M. 1974. On the Concept of "Sub-culture." *British Journal of Sociology*, 25:428–441.

Clerget, Marcel. 1934. *Le Caire: Etude de geographie urbaine et d'histoire economique*, 2 vols. Paris: E. & R. Schindler.

Clignet, R., and J. Sween. 1974. Urbanization, Plural Marriage and Family Size in Two African Cities. *American Ethnologist*, pp. 221–242.

Cockburn, Aidan. 1971. Infectious Diseases in Ancient Populations. *Current Anthropology*, 12:45–62.

Cohen, A. 1965. The Social Organization of Credit in a West African Cattle Market. *Africa*, 35:8–20.

_____. 1966. Politics of the Kola Trade. *Africa*, 36:18–36.

_____. 1967. The Hausa. In *The City of Ibadan*, eds. P. C. Lloyd et al., pp. 117–127. Cambridge: Cambridge University Press.

_____. 1968. The Politics of Mysticism in Some Local Communities in Newly Independent African States. In *Local-level Politics*, ed. M. Swartz. Chicago: Aldine.

Cohen, A. 1969a. *Custom and Politics in Urban Africa*. London: Routledge & Kegan Paul; Berkeley: University of California Press.

_____. 1969b. Political Anthropology: The Analysis of the Symbolism of Power Relations. *Man*, 4:217–235.

_____. 1971. The Politics of Ritual Secrecy. *Man*, 6:427–448.

_____. 1974a. Introduction: The Lesson of Ethnicity. In *Urban Ethnicity*, ed. Abner Cohen, pp. ix–xxiv. A.S.A. monograph no. 12. London: Tavistock.

_____. 1974b. *Two-Dimensional Man*. Berkeley and Los Angeles: University of California Press.

Cohen, E. 1977. The City in Zionist Ideology. *Jerusalem Quarterly*, 4:126–144.

_____. 1984. The Dropout Expatriates: A Study of Marginal Farangs in Bangkok. *Urban Anthropology*, 13(1): 91–115.

_____. 1985a. A Soi in Bangkok: The Dynamics of Lateral Urban Expansion. *Journal of the Siam Society*.

_____. 1985b. Tourism as Play. *Religion*, 15:291–304.

Cohen, M. 1976. *House Divided House United*. New York: Columbia University Press.

Coltman, R., Jr. 1891. *The Chinese*. Philadelphia: F. A. Davis.

Conklin, Harold C. 1962. Lexicographical Treatment of Folk Taxonomies. *International Journal of American Linguistics*, 28:119–141.

_____. 1964. Ethnogenealogical Method. In *Explorations in Cultural Anthropology*, ed. Ward Goodenough. New York: McGraw-Hill.

Cook, Scott. 1968. The Obsolete Anti-Market Mentality. In *Readings in Anthropology*. Vol. II, 2d ed., ed. Morton Fried. New York: Crowell.

Coombs, Gary. 1973. Networks and Exchange: The Role of Social Relationships in a Small Voluntary Association. *Journal of Anthropological Research*, 20(2): 96–112.

Coon, Carleton. 1951. *Caravan: The Story of the Middle East*. New York: Henry Holt.

Costa, Lucia. 1957. Relatorio do Plano Pilato. *Revista Brasileira de Municipais*. Vol. 10.

Cousins, Albert, and Hans Nagpaul. 1979. *Urban Life: The Sociology of Cities and Urban Society*. New York: John Wiley and Sons.

Crawford, M. H., and George Gmelch. 1974. The Human Biology of the Irish Tinkers: Demography, Ethnohistory and Genetics. *Social Biology*, 21:321–331.

Curtin, Philip D. 1984. *Cross-Cultural Trade in World History*. New York and Cambridge: Cambridge University Press.

Davis, J. M., and D. J. Svendsgaard. 1987. Lead and Child Development. *Nature*, 329:297–300.

Davis, Kingsley. 1969. The Urbanization of the World Population. *World Urbanization, 1950–1970*. Vol. 1, *Basic Data for Cities, Countries and Regions*. Berkeley: Institute of International Studies, University of California.

Davis, Susan. 1986. *Parades and Power: Street Theater in Nineteenth Century Philadelphia*. Philadelphia: University of Pennsylvania Press.

Davison, J. 1989. *Voices from Mutira: Lives of Rural Gikuyu Women*. Boulder: Lynne Riemar Publications.

Deakin, N. 1969. *Colour Citizenship and British Society*. London: Oxford University Press.

deJesus, Carolina Maria. 1962. *Child of the Dark: The Diary of Carolina Maria deJesus*. New York: The New American Library.

Departamento Nacional de Planeacion (DNP). 1969. *La Poblacion en Colombia: Realidad, Perspectivas, y Politica*. Bogota: Imprenta Nacional.

Department of Social Sciences, University of Liverpool. 1956. *The Dockworker*. Liverpool: Liverpool University Press.

Deutsch, K. 1961. On Social Communication and the Metropolis. *Daedalus*, 90.

deVos, George, and H. Wagatsuma. 1966. The Ecology of Special Buraku. In *Japan's Invisible Race*, eds. George deVos and H. Wagatsuma. Berkeley: University of California Press.

Dickinson, Robert E. 1951. *The West European City*. London: Routledge & Kegan Paul.

Diner, Hasia. 1983. *Erin's Daughters in America: Irish Women in the Nineteenth Century*. Baltimore: The Johns Hopkins University Press.

Dohrenwend, B. P., and B. S. Dohrenwend. 1974. Psychiatric Disorders in Urban Settings. In *American Handbook of Psychiatry*, Vol. II, 2d ed., ed. G. Caplan, pp. 424–447. New York: Basic Books.

Doll, R. 1978. Atmospheric Pollution and Lung Cancer. *Environmental Health Perspectives*, 22:23–31.

Domhoff G. William. 1974. *The Bohemian Grove and Other Retreats: A Study in Ruling Class Cohesiveness*. New York: Harper & Row.

Doolittle, Justus. 1868. *Social Life of the Chinese*. London: Sampson Low.

Dore, R. P. 1958. *City Life in Japan*. Berkeley: University of California Press.

Drake, St. Clair, and Horace R. Clayton. 1945. *Black Metropolis, a Study of Negro Life in a Northern City*. New York: Harcourt, Brace.

Dray-Novey, Alison. 1993. Spatial Order and Police in Imperial Beijing. *Journal of Asian Studies*, 52:885–992.

Dubois, W. E. B. 1908. *The Negro Family*. Atlanta: Atlanta University Press.

Durkheim, E. 1964. *De la division du travail social*. Paris, 1893, 1932. (The Division of Labor in Society.) Ed. G. Simpson. New York: Free Press.

Eames, Edwin, and Judith Granich Goode. 1973. *Urban Poverty in Cross-Cultural Context*. New York: Free Press.

Eames, Edwin, and Judith Goode. 1977. *Anthropology of the City: An Introduction to Urban Anthropology*. Englewood Cliffs, NJ: Prentice-Hall.

Eco, Umberto. 1972. Towards a Semiotic Enquiry into the Television Message. *W.P.C.S.* 3, University of Birmingham.

Edgerton, Robert B. 1992. *Sick Societies*. New York: Free Press.

Ekwensi, Cyril. 1961. *Jagua Nana*. London: Hutchinson.

Engelsmann, F., H. B. M. Murphy, R. Prince, M. Leduc, and H. Demars. 1972. Variations in Responses to Symptom Check List by Age, Sex, Income, Residence, and Ethnicity. *Social Psychiatry*, 7:150–156.

Epstein, A. L. *Politics in an Urban African Community*. Manchester: Manchester University Press.

———. 1961. The Network and Urban-Social Organization. In *Social Networks in Urban Situations: Analyses of Personal Relationships in Central African Towns*, ed. J. Clyde Mitchell. Manchester: Manchester University Press, 1969.

Epstein, David G. 1972. The Genesis and Function of Squatter Settlements in Brasilia. In *The Anthropology of Urban Environments*, eds., Thomas Weaver and Douglas White, pp. 51–58. Society for Applied Anthropology monograph no. 11. Washington, DC: Society for Applied Anthropology.

———. 1973. *Brasilia: Plan and Reality*. Berkeley: University of California Press.

Erlick, June Carolyn. 1984. Women of Nicaragua. *Ms.*, Nov: 66–72; 147–150.

Evans-Pritchard, E. E. 1937. *Witchcraft, Oracles, and Magic Among the Azande*. Oxford: Clarendon Press.

———. 1940. *The Nuer*. New York: Oxford University Press.

———. 1951. *Social Anthropology*. London: Cohen & West.

Eveleth, P. B. 1986. Population Differences in Growth: Environmental and Genetic Factors. In *Human Growth—A Comprehensive Treatise*, 2d ed., eds. F. Falkner and J. M. Tanner. New York: Plenum Press.

Eveleth, P. B., and J. M. Tanner. 1990. *Worldwide Variation in Human Growth*, 2d ed. New York: Cambridge University Press.

Ewen, Elizabeth. 1985. *Immigrant Women in the Land of Dollars, 1820–1929*. New York: Monthly Review Press.

Fallers, L. A. 1957. Some Determinants of Marriage Stability in Busoga: A Reformation of Gluckman's Hypothesis. *Africa*, XXVII:106–123.

Farren, M., and E. Barker. 1972. *Watch Out Kids*. London: Macmillan.

Fawaz, Leila Tarazi. 1983. *Merchants and Migrants in Nineteenth Century Beirut*. Cambridge: Harvard University Press.

Fei, Xiaotong. 1939. *Peasant Life in China*. London: Routledge.

Fein, G. G., P. M. Schwartz, S. W. Jacobson, and J. L. Jacobson. 1983. Prenatal Exposure to Polychlorinated Biphenyls: Effects on Birth Size and Gestational Age. *Journal of Pediatrics*, 105:315–320.

Feldman, R. E. 1968. *Journal of Personality and Social Psychology*, II.

Fenner, Frank. 1970. The Effect of Changing Social Organization on the Infectious Diseases of Man. In *The Impact of Civilization on the Biology of Man*, ed. S. V. Boyden, pp. 48–68. Toronto: University of Toronto Press.

Fenner, Walter P. Nominalism and Essentialism in Urban Anthropology. *City & Society Annual Review*, I(VII): 53–66.

Ferguson, F. 1981. Interpreting the Self Through Letters. *Centrum* 1(2): 107–112.

Fernea, Elizabeth W. 1975. *A Street in Marrakech*. Prospect Heights, IL: Waveland Press.

Ferris, P. 1960. *The City*. Harmondsworth: Penguin.

Fields, F., and P. Haikin. 1971. *Black Britons*. Oxford: Clarendon Press.

Firth, R., J. Hubert, and A. Forge. 1970. *Families and Their Relatives*. London: Routledge & Kegan Paul.

Fischer, C. S. 1972. Urbanism As a Way of Life: A Review and an Agenda. *Sociological Methods and Research*, 1:187–242.

———. 1975a. The Study of Urban Community and Personality. *Annual Review of Sociology*, 1:67–89.

———. 1975b. Toward a Subcultural Theory of Urbanism. *American Journal of Sociology*, 80:1319–1341.

———. 1976. *The Urban Experience*. New York: Harcourt, Brace and Jovanovich.

Fisher, J. C. 1966. *Yugoslavia—A Multinational State*. San Francisco: Chandler.

Flannery, Kent V. 1972. The Cultural Evolution of Civilizations. *Annual Review of Ecology and Systematics*, 3:399–426.

Fleming, Patricia. 1973. The Politics of Marriage Among Non-Catholic European Royalty. *Current Anthropology*, 14:207–230.

Foner, N. 1978. *Jamaica Farewell: Jamaican Migrants in London*. Berkeley: University of California Press.

Foster, George M. 1948. *Empire's Children: The People of Tzintzuntzan*. Mexico, D. F.: Smithsonian Institution, Institute of Social Anthropology, Publication no. 6.

———. 1955. What is Folk Culture? *American Anthropologist*, 55:159–173.

———. 1988. *Tzintzuntzan: Mexican Peasants in a Changing World*. Prospect Heights, IL: Waveland Press.

Fox, Richard. 1967. Resiliency and Change in the Indian Caste System: The Umar of Uttar Pradesh. *Journal of Asian Studies*, 26:575–588.

———. 1972. Rationale and Reason in Urban Anthropology. *Urban Anthropology*, 205–233.

———. 1977. *Urban Anthropology: Cities in Their Cultural Settings*. Englewood Cliffs, NJ: Prentice-Hall.

Frake, Charles O. 1961. The Diagnosis of Disease Among the Subanam of Mindinao. *American Anthropologist*, 63:113–132.

———. 1962a. The Ethnographic Study of Cognitive Systems. In *Anthropology and Human Behavior*, eds. T. Gladwin and W. C. Sturtevant. Washington, DC: Anthropology Society of Washington.

———. 1962b. Cultural Ecology and Ethnography. *American Anthropologist*, 64:53–59.

Frank, André Gunder. 1967a. *Capitalism and Underdevelopment in Latin America*. New York: Monthly Review Press.

———. 1967b. Sociology of Development and Underdevelopment of Sociology. *Catalyst*, 20–73.

———. 1969. *Latin America: Underdevelopment or Revolution*. New York: Monthly Review Press.

Frankenberg, Ronald. 1966. *Communities in Britain*. London: Penguin.

Frazier, E. F. 1937. The Impact of Urban Civilization Upon the Negro Family. *American Sociological Review*, II:609–618.

Freeman, M. 1965. *Chinese Family and Marriage in Singapore*. London: University of London Press.

Freilich, Morris, ed. 1970. *Marginal Natives: Anthropologists at Work*. New York: Harper & Row.

Frerichs, R. R., B. L. Beeman, and A. H. Coulson. 1980. Los Angeles Airport Noise and Mortality—Fault Analysis and Public Policy. *American Journal of Public Health*, 70:357–362.

Fried, M. H. 1953. *The Fabric of Chinese Society*. New York: Praeger.

Friedl, Ernestine. 1959. The Role of Kinship in the Transmission of National Culture to Rural Villages in Mainland Greece. *American Anthropologist* 61:30–38.

Gabaccia, Donna. 1992. *Seeking Common Ground: Multidisciplinary Studies of Immigrant Women in the United States*. Westport, CT: Greenwood Press.

Gadgil, D. R. 1952. *Poona: A Socio-Economic Survey*. Poona: Gokhale Institute of Political and Economic Studies.

Gaertner, S., and L. Bickman. Unpublished research. Graduate Center, The City University of New York.

Gans, Herbert. 1962. *The Urban Villagers: Group and Class in the Life of Italian Americans*. New York: Free Press.

———. 1962a. Urbanism and Suburbanism as Ways of Life: A Reevaluation of Definitions. In *Human Behavior and Social Processes*, ed. A. M. Rose, pp. 625–648. Boston: Houghton Mifflin.

———. 1962b. The Subculture of the Working Class, Lower Class and Middle Class. *The Urban Villagers*. New York: Free Press.

———. 1992. The War Against the Poor Instead of Programs to End Poverty. *Dissent*, Fall:461–465.

Garigue, Philip. 1956. French Canadian Kinship and Urban Life. *American Anthropologist*, 58:1090–1101.

Garrison, Vivian. Social Networks, Social Change and Psychiatric Complaints among Migrants in a New York City Slum. Ph.D. Diss. Columbia University.

Gattoni, F., and A. Tarnopolsky. 1973. Aircraft Noise and Psychiatric Morbidity. *Psychological Medicine*, 3:516–520.

Geertz, Clifford. 1973. *The Interpretation of Cultures*. New York: Basic Books.

Gellner, Ernst. 1964. *Thought and Change*. London: Weinenfeld and Nicholson.

Germen, Aydin, ed. 1983. *Islamic Architecture and Urbanism*. Dammam, Saudi Arabia: King Faisal University.

Gibb, H. A. R., and H. Bowen. 1950. *Islamic Society & the West*. Vol. 1, Pt. I. London: Oxford University Press.

Giddens, Anthony. 1985. *The National-State and Violence.* Berkeley: University of California Press.

Gilad, Lisa. 1984. Community Participation in Upgrading Irregular Settlements: The Community Response. *World Development,* 12:913–922.

_____. 1989. *Ginger and Salt: Yemeni Jewish Women in an Israeli Town.* Boulder: Westview Press.

Gilder, George. 1981. *Wealth and Poverty.* New York: Bantam Books.

Giles, Wenona. 1991. Class, Gender and Race Struggles in a Portuguese Neighborhood in London. *International Journal of Urban and Regional Research,* 15(3): 432–441.

_____. 1992. Gender, Inequality and Resistance: The Case of Portuguese Women in London. *Anthropological Quarterly,* 65(2): 67–79.

Gilmore, George W. 1892. *Korea from Its Capital.* Philadelphia: Presbyterian Board of Publication.

Gist, Noel P. 1954. Caste Differentials in South India. *American Sociological Review,* 19:126–137.

Gist, Noel, and Silvia Fava. 1974. *Urban Society.* New York: Thomas Y. Crowell Company.

Gluckman, M. 1961. Anthropological Problems Arising from the African Industrial Revolution. In *Social Change in Modern Africa,* ed. A. Southall. London: Oxford University Press.

Gmelch, George. 1980. "Return Migration." *Annual Review of Anthropology.*

_____. 1985. *The Irish Tinkers: The Urbanization of an Itinerant People,* 2d ed. Prospect Heights, IL: Waveland Press.

_____. 1992. *Double Passage: The Lives of Caribbean Migrants Abroad and Back Home.* Ann Arbor: University of Michigan Press.

Gmelch, George, and Sharon Bohn Gmelch. 1974a. The Itinerant Settlement Movement: Its Policies and Effects on Irish Travellers. *Studies: An Irish Quarterly Review,* 68:1–16.

_____. 1974b. The Emergence of an Ethnic Group: The Irish Travellers. *Anthropological Quarterly,* 49:225–238.

_____. 1978. Begging in Dublin: The Strategies of a Marginal Urban Occupation. *Urban Life,* 6(4): 439–454.

_____. 1985a. The Cross-Channel Migration of Irish Travellers. *The Economic and Social Review,* 16(4): 187–196.

_____. 1985b. Gypsies in British Cities: Problems and Government Response. *Urban Anthropology,* 11(3–4): 347–376.

_____. 1987. Commercial Nomadism: Occupation and Mobility Among Travellers in England and Wales. In *The Other Nomads: Peripatetic Minorities in Cross-Cultural Perspective,* ed. Aparna Rao, pp. 133–158. Cologne: Bahlou Verlag.

_____. 1988. Nomads in the Cities. *Natural History,* 97(2): 50–61.

Gmelch, George, and Walter P. Zenner. 1978. Urban Anthropology: A Survey of the Field from a Classroom Perspective. *Urban Anthropology,* 7:207–215.

Gmelch, Sharon B. 1976. *Tinkers and Travellers: Ireland's Nomads.* Montreal: McGill-Queens University Press; Dublin: O'Brien Press.

_____. 1977. Economic and Power Relations Among Urban Tinkers: The Role of Women. *Urban Anthropology,* 6(3): 237–247.

_____. 1986. Groups That Don't Want In: Gypsies and Other Artisan, Trader and Entertainer Minorities. *Annual Review of Anthropology,* 15:307–330.

_____. 1989. From Poverty Subculture to Political Lobby: The Traveller Rights Movement in Ireland. In *Ireland From Below: Social Change in Local Communities,* eds. Chris Curtain and Thomas M. Wilson, pp. 301–319. Galway: Galway University Press.

Gmelch, Sharon B. 1991. *Nan: The Life of an Irish Travelling Woman*. Prospect Heights, IL: Waveland Press.

Goering, John M. 1978. Marx and the City: Are There Any New Directions for Urban Theory? *Comparative Urban Research*, 6:76–85.

Goffman, Erving. 1959. *The Presentation of Self in Everyday Life*. New York: Doubleday Anchor.

_____. 1972. *Encounters*. Harmondsworth: Penguin.

Goitein, S. D. 1978. *A Mediterranean Society*, Vol. III, *The Family*. Berkeley and Los Angeles: University of California Press.

Goldsmith, John R. 1980. The "Urban Factor" in Cancer: Smoking, Industrial Exposures, and Air Pollution as Possible Causes. In *Cancer and the Environment*, eds. H. B. Demopoulos and M. A. Mehlman, pp. 205–217. Chicago: Pathotox Publishers.

González, Nancie L. 1965. The Consanguineal Household and Matrifocality. *American Anthropologist*, 67:1541–1549.

_____. 1969. *The Spanish-Americans of New Mexico: A Heritage of Pride*. Albuquerque: University of New Mexico Press.

Goode, J. 1972. Poverty and Urban Analysis. *Western Canadian Journal of Anthropology*, 3:1–19.

Goode, W. 1963. *World Revolution and Family Patterns*. Glencoe, IL: Free Press of Glencoe.

Goode, William J. 1966. Industrialization and Family Change. In *Industrialization and Society*, eds. B. F. Hoselitz and W. E. Moore, pp. 237–255. Paris: UNESCO-Mouton.

Goodenough, Ward H. 1956. Componential Analysis and the Study of Meaning. *Language*, 32:195–216.

_____. 1957. *Cultural Anthropology and Linguistics*. Washington: Georgetown University Monograph Series on Language and Linguistics, 9:173.

_____. 1965. Yankee Kinship Terminology: A Problem in Componential Analysis. *American Anthropologist*, 67:259–287.

Goody, Jack. 1990. *The Oriental, the Ancient and the Primitive: Systems of Marriage and the Family in Pre-Industrial Societies in Eurasia*. Cambridge: Cambridge University Press.

Goody, Jack, ed. 1958. The Developmental Cycle in Domestic Groups. *Cambridge Papers in Social Anthropology*, No. 1. London: Cambridge University Press.

Gough, Kathleen. 1959. The Nayars and the Definition of Marriage. *Journal of the Royal Anthropological Institute of Great Britain and Ireland*, 89:23–34.

_____. 1968. Anthropology and Imperialism. *Monthly Review*, 19:12–27.

Gove, Walter R., Michael Hughes, and Omar R. Galle. 1979. Overcrowding in the Home. *American Sociological Review*, 44:59–80.

Granovetter, Mark. 1973. The Strength of Weak Ties. *American Journal of Sociology*, 78:1360–1380.

Grasmuck, S., and Patricia Pessar. 1991. *Between Two Islands: Dominican International Migration*. Berkeley: University of California Press.

Graves, Nancy, and Theodore Graves. 1974. Adaptive Strategies in Urban Migration. In *Annual Review of Anthropology*, ed. Bernard J. Siegel, pp. 117–151. Palo Alto, CA: Annual Reviews.

Grebler, Leo, Joan W. Moore, and Ralph C. Guzman. 1970. *The Mexican-American People: The Nation's Second Largest Minority*. New York: The Free Press.

Greenfield, Sidney M. 1961. Industrialization and the Family in Sociological Theory. *American Journal of Sociology*, 67:312–322.

Greer, Scott. 1956. Urbanism Reconsidered: A Comparative Study of Local Areas in a Metropolis. *American Sociological Review*, 21:19–25.

Grey, A. 1983. *Saigon*. London: Pan Books.

Guatemala. 1974. *Anuario Estadistico*. Direccion General de Estadistica, Ministerio de Economia.

Gugler, Josef, and William G. Flanagan. 1978. *Urbanization and Social Change in West Africa*. Cambridge: Cambridge University Press

Gulick, John. 1967. *Tripoli: A Modern Arab City*. Cambridge: Harvard University Press.

_____. 1968. The Outlook, Research Strategies and Relevance of Urban Anthropology. In *Urban Anthropology*, ed. E. Eddy. Athens: University of Georgia Press.

_____. 1989. *The Humanity of Cities: An Introduction to Urban Societies*. Westport, CT: Bergin and Garvey.

Gutkind, P. 1962. African Urban Family Life. *Cahiers d'Etudes Africaines*, II(10): 149–207.

_____. 1967. The Energy of Despair: Social Organizations of the Unemployed in Two African Cities: Lagos & Nairobi. *Civilizations*, 17:186–211.

Habermas, Jürgen. 1975. *The Legitimation Crisis*. Boston: Beacon Press.

Hage, Per. A Structural Analysis of Manchurian Beer Terms and Beer Drinking. Unpublished manuscript.

Hakim, Besim S. 1986. *Arabic-Islamic Cities*. London: Routledge & Kegan Paul.

Hall, E. T. 1966. *The Hidden Dimension*. New York: Doubleday.

Hall, P. 1966. *The World Cities*. New York: McGraw-Hill.

Hallowell, A. Irving. 1938. Fear and Anxiety as Cultural and Individual Variables in a Primitive Society. *Journal of Social Psychology*, 9:25–47.

Halperin, E. 1963. The Decline of Communism in Latin America. *Atlantic Monthly*, May:65–70.

Halperin, Rhoda. 1990. *The Livelihood of Kin: Making Ends Meet "The Kentucky Way."* Austin: University of Texas Press.

Halpern, Joel M. 1965. The Rural Revolution. *Transactions of the New York Academy of Sciences*, Series II, Vol. 28:73–80.

Halpern, Joel M., and Barbara Kerewsky-Halpern. 1986. *A Serbian Village in Historical Perspective*. Prospect Heights, IL: Waveland Press.

Hammel, E. A. 1969. *The Pink Yo-Yo: Occupational Mobility in Belgrade, ca. 1915–1965*. Berkeley: Institute of International Studies. University of California.

Hammel, E. A., and Charles Yarbrough. 1973. Social Mobility and the Durability of Family Ties. *Journal of Anthropological Research*, 29:145–163.

Hammill, P. V. V., F. E. Johnston, and S. Lemeshow. Height and Weight of Children: Socioeconomic Status. Department of Health, Education and Welfare Publication No. (HSM) 73–1601; Vital Health Statistics Series, 11, No. 119. Washington, DC: U.S. Government Printing Office.

Hammond, Norman. 1988. *Ancient Maya Civilization*. New Brunswick: Rutgers University Press.

Handelman, D., and L. Shamgar-Handelman. 1978. Social Planning Prerequisites for New and Expanded Communities: The Case of Israel. *Contact*, 10:86–122.

Hannerz, Ulf. 1969. *Soulside: Inquiries into Ghetto Culture and Community*. New York: Columbia University Press.

_____. 1980. *Exploring the City*. New York: Columbia University Press.

_____. 1992. *Cultural Complexity*. New York: Columbia University Press.

Hansen, A. T. 1954. Review of H. Miner's Primitive City of Timbuctoo. *American Journal of Sociology*, 59:501–502.

Hardoy, Jorge. 1975. *Urbanization in Latin America: Approaches and Issues*. New York: Doubleday and Company.

Harrington, Michael. 1962. *The Other America: Poverty in the United States*. Baltimore: Penguin.

Harris, C. C. 1969. *The Family: An Introduction*. London: Allen & Unwin.
_____. 1970. *Readings in Kinship in Urban Society*. Oxford, New York and Toronto: Pergamon Press.
Harris, Marvin. 1956. *Town and Country in Brazil*. New York: Columbia University Press.
_____. 1968. *The Rise of Anthropological Theory: A History of Theories of Culture*. New York: Thomas Y. Crowell.
_____. 1971. *Man, Nature and Culture*. New York: Thomas Y. Crowell.
Harris, Olivia. Latin American Women—an Overview. *Latin American Women Minority Rights Group*, 57:4–6.
Hay, Richard, Jr. 1977. Patterns of Urbanization and Socio-Economic Development in the Third World: An Overview. In *Third World Urbanization*, eds. Janet Abu-Lughod and Richard Hay, Jr., pp. 71–101. Chicago: Maaroufa Press.
Hebdige, Dick. 1979. *Subculture: The Meaning of Style*. London: Methuen.
Herrick, B. A. 1966. *Urban Migration and Economic Development in Chile*. Cambridge: Harvard University Press.
Hexter, A., and J. Goldsmith. 1971. Carbon Monoxide: Association of Community Air Pollution with Mortality. *Science*, 172:265–267.
Hill, T. W. 1974. From Hell Raiser to Family Man. In *Conformity and Conflict*, eds. J. Spradley and D. W. McCurdy. Boston: Little, Brown.
Ho, D. 1987. Fatherhood in Chinese Society. In *The Father's Role: Cross-Cultural Perspective*, ed. M. Lamb. Hillsdale: Lawrence Erlbaum.
Ho, Ping-ti. 1954. The Salt Merchants of Yang-Chou: A Study of Commercial Capitalism in 18th Century China. *Harvard Journal of Asiatic Studies*, 17:130–168.
Hobsbawm, E. J. 1959. *Primitive Rebels*. New York: Frederick A. Praeger.
Hobsbawm, Eric, and Terence Ranger, eds. 1983. *The Invention of Tradition*. Cambridge: Cambridge University Press.
Hollander, Nancy. 1977. Women Workers and the Class Struggle: The Case of Argentina. *Latin American Perspectives*, 4:180–193.
Holston, James. 1989. *The Modernist City: An Anthropological Critique of Brasília*. Chicago: University of Chicago Press.
Holton, R. J. 1986. *Cities, Capitalism and Civilization*. London: Allen & Unwin.
Honig, E., and G. Hershatter. 1988. *Personal Voices: Chinese Women in the 1980s*. Stanford: Stanford University Press.
Hoselitz, B. F. 1953. Social Structure and Economic Growth. *Economica Internazionale*, 6:52–57.
Hourani, Albert, and S. M. Stern, eds. 1970. *The Islamic City*. Oxford: Bruno Cassirer.
Houstoun, M. F., R. G. Kramer, and J. M. Barrett. 1984. Female Predominance of Immigration to the United States Since 1930: A First Look. *International Migration Review*, 18:908–963.
Howe, Irving. 1976. *The World of Our Fathers*. New York: Harcourt, Brace, Jovanovich.
Hoyt, H., G. W. Hoffman, and F. W. Neal. 1962. *Yugoslavia and the New Communism*. New York: Twentieth Century Fund.
Hsu, F. L. K. 1948. *Under the Ancestors' Shadow*. New York: Columbia University Press.
Hunter, Albert. 1974. *Symbolic Communities: The Persistence and Change of Chicago's Local Communities*. Chicago: University of Chicago Press.
Hurgonje, C. Snouck. 1931. *Mekka in the Latter Part of the 19th Century*. London: Luzac.
Inland Transport Committee (ILO). 1956. *Methods of Improving Organization of Work and Output in Ports*. Geneva.

Inouye, Jukichi. 1911. *Home Life in Tokyo.* Tokyo: Tokyo Printing, Co.

Ivy, Marilyn J. 1988. Tradition and Difference in the Japanese Mass Media. *Public Culture Bulletin*, 1(1).

Jackson, J. A. 1969. *Migration.* London: Cambridge University Press.

Jacobs, Jerry. 1984. *The Mall.* Prospect Heights, IL: Waveland Press.

Jacobson, David. 1971. Mobility, Continuity, and Urban Social Organization. *Man*, 6:630–645.

Jacobson, D. Fair Weather Friend: Label and Context in Middle Class Friendships. *Journal of Anthropological Research*, 31:225–334.

Jacobson, H. E. 1970. Urbanization and Family Ties: A Problem in the Analysis of Change. *Journal of Asian and African Studies*, 5:302–307.

Jacobson, J. L., S. W. Jacobson, P. M. and H. E. B. Humphrey. 1990. Effects of Exposure to PCBs and Related Compounds on Growth and Activity in Children. *Neurtoxicology and Teratology*, 12:319–326.

James, Jennifer. 1976. Motivations for Entrance into Prostitution. In *The Female Offender*, ed. L. Crites. Lexington, MA: Lexington Books.

James, Jennifer, and Nanette J. Davis. 1982. Contingencies in Female Sexual Role Deviance: The Case of Prostitution. *Human Organization*, 41:345–350.

Jankowiak, W. 1977. Migration and Labor Force Participation of Latin American Women: The Domestic Servants in the Cities. In *Women and National Development*, ed. The Wellesley Editorial Committee, pp. 129–141. Chicago: University of Chicago Press.

_____. 1990. *Women and Social Change in Latin America.* London: ZED Books.

_____. 1993. *Sex, Death and Hierarchy in a Chinese City.* New York: Columbia University Press.

Jelin, Elizabeth. 1976. The Bahiana in the Labor Force in Salvador, Brazil. In *Sex and Class in Latin America*, eds. June Nash and H. Safa, pp. 129–146. New York: Praeger.

Jelin, Elizabeth. ed. 1990. Women and Social Change in Latin America. London: ZED Books.

Jencks, Christopher. 1988. Deadly Neighborhoods. *The New Republic*, 198:23–32.

Jencks, Christopher, and Paul E. Peterson, eds. 1991. *The Urban Underclass.* Washington, DC: The Brookings Institution.

Jenner, D. A., G. A. Harrison, I. A. M. Prior, D. L. Leonetti, W. J. Fujimoto, and M. Kabuto. 1987. Inter-population Comparisons of Catecholamine Excretion. *Annals of Human Biology*, 14:1–9.

Johnson, Colleen Leary. 1974. Gift Giving and Reciprocity Among Japanese Americans in Honolulu. *American Ethnologist* 1:295–308.

Jones, F. N., and J. Tauscher. 1978. Residence Under an Airport Landing Pattern as a Factor in Teratism. *Archives of Environmental Health*, 33:10–12.

Jordan, Terry, and Lester Rowntree. 1990. *The Human Mosaic: A Thematic Introduction to Cultural Geography.* New York: Harper & Row.

Jorgensen, Joseph G. 1971. Indians and the Metropolis. In *The American Indian in Urban Society*, eds. Jack O. Waddell and O. Michael Watson, pp. 67–113. Boston: Little, Brown.

Kaplan, Temma. 1982. Female Consciousness and Collective Action: The Case of Barcelona, 1910–1918. *Signs*, 7:545–566.

Kasaba, Resat. ed. 1991. *Cities in the World-System.* Westport, CT: Greenwood Press.

Kasarda, J. D., and M. Janowitz. 1974. Community Attachment in Mass Society. *American Sociological Review*, 39:328–339.

Kasdan, Leonard. 1970. Introduction. In *Migration and Anthropology*, ed. Robert F. Spencer, pp. 1–8.

Katz, Michael, 1989. *The Undeserving Poor: From the War on Poverty to the War on Welfare*. New York: Pantheon Books.

———. 1993. *The "Underclass" Debate: Views From History*. Princeton: Princeton University Press.

Kay, Paul. 1966. Comment. *Current Anthropology*, 7:20–23.

Kaye, Barrington. 1966. *Upper Nankin Street Singapore*. Singapore: University of Malaya Press.

Keefe, Susan Emley. Urbanization, Acculturation and Extended Family Ties: Mexican-Americans in Cities. *American Ethnologist*, 6:349–365.

———. 1984. Real and Ideal Extended Familism Among Mexican Americans and Anglo Americans: On the Meaning of "Close" Family Ties. *Human Organization*, 43:65–70.

Keefe, Susan E., and Amado M. Padilla. 1987. *Chicano Ethnicity*. Albuquerque: University of New Mexico Press.

Keesing, F. M., and M. D. Keesing. 1956. *Elite Communication in Samoa: A Study of Leadership*. Stanford, CA: Stanford University Press.

Keesing, Roger. 1960. Recreative Behavior and Culture Change. In *Men and Cultures*, ed. Anthony F. C. Wallace, pp. 130–131. Philadelphia: University of Pennsylvania Press.

Kelley, Augustus M. 1949. *A Theory of Labor Movement*. New York.

Kelly, George. 1955. *The Psychology of Personal Constructs*. New York: W. W. Norton.

Kelly, Willliam. 1986. Rationalization and Nostalgia: Cultural Dynamics of New Middle-Class Japan. *American Ethnologist*, 13(4): 603–618.

Kelton, Jane. 1986. The New York City St. Patrick's Day Parade: Invention of Contention and Consensus. *The Drama Review*, 107(Fall): 93.

Kemper, Robert V. 1974. Tzintzuntzeños in Mexico City: The Anthropologist Among Peasant Migrants. In *Anthropologists in Cities*, eds. George Foster and Robert V. Kemper. Boston: Little, Brown.

———. 1977. *Migration and Adaptation: Tzintzuntzan Peasants in Mexico City*. Beverly Hills, CA: Sage.

———. 1979. Frontiers in Migration: From Culturalism to Historical Structuralism in the Study of Mexico-U.S. Migration. In *Migration Across Frontiers: Mexico and the United States*, eds. Fernando Camara and Robert V. Kemper. SUNY-Albany: Institute for Mesoamerican Studies.

———. 1981. Obstacles and Opportunities: Household Economics of Tzintzuntzan Migrants in Mexico City. *Urban Anthropology*, 10:211–230.

———. 1991a. Urban Anthropology in the 1990s: The State of its Practice. *Urban Anthropology*, 20:211–223.

———. 1991b. Trends in Urban Anthropological Research: An Analysis of the Journal *Urban Anthropology*, 1972–1991. *Urban Anthropology*, 20:373–384.

———. 1993a. Urban Anthropology: An Analysis of Trends in U.S. and Canadian Dissertations. *Urban Anthropology*, 22:1–8.

———. 1993b. Urban Anthropology: A Guide to U.S. and Canadian Dissertations. *Urban Anthropology*, 22:9–229.

———. 1994. Migración sin fronteras; el caso del pueblo de Tzintzuntzan, Michoacán, 1945–1990. In *Mesa de Antropología de la Sociedad Mexicana de Antropología*, 22:67–82. Tuxtla Guteérrez, Mexico: Gobiero del Estado de Chiapas.

Kemper, Robert V., and Benjamin Kracht. 1991. Directory of Urban Anthropologists. *Urban Anthropology*, 20:225–360.

Kemper, Robert V., Benjamin Kracht, and Stuart Campos. 1991. The Journal *Urban Anthropology*: An Index of its First Twenty Years. *Urban Anthropology*, 20:385–553.

Kemper, Robert V., and Jack Rollwagen. 1995. Urban Anthropology. In *Encyclopedia of Cultural Anthropology*, eds. Melvin Ember and David Levinson. Lakeville, CT: American Reference Publishing.

Kennedy, Jean. 1945. *Here is India*. New York: Scribners.

Khalaf, Samir, and Per Konstad. 1973. *Hamra of Beirut*. Leiden: Brill.

Khuri, Faud. 1975. *From Village to Suburb: Order and Change in Greater Beirut*. Chicago: University of Chicago Press.

King, Anthony D. 1990. *Urbanism, Colonialism, and the World-Economy*. New York: Routledge.

King, Charles E. 1945. The Negro Maternal Family: A Product of an Economic and Cultural System. *Social Forces*, 24:100–104.

Kinsey, A. C., W. B. Pomeroy, and C. E. Martin. 1953. *Sexual Behavior in the Human Female*. Philadelphia: W. B. Saunders.

Kinzer, Stephen. 1993. Yugoslavia is Suffering Loss of the Most Highly Skilled. *New York Times*, 4 May, A7.

Kleinman, J. C., V. G. DeGruttola, B. B. Cohen, and J. H. Madans. 1981. Regional and Urban Differences in Coronary Heart Disease Mortality and Risk Ractor Prevalence. *Journal of Chronic Disease*, 34:11–19.

Klimt, Andrea C. 1989. Disorderly Meetings: Arguments About Gender in a Migratory Context. Unpublished paper presented at the fourth meeting of the International Conference Group on Portugal, September 21–24, Durham, NH.

_____. 1992. Temporary and Permanent Lives: The Construction of Identity Among Portuguese Migrants in Germany. Unpublished Diss., Department of Anthropology, Stanford University.

Knipschild, P. 1977a. Medical Effects of Aircraft Noise: General Practice Survey. *International Archives of Occupational and Environmental Health*, 40:191–196.

_____. 1977b. Medical Effects of Aircraft Noise: Community Cardiovascular Survey. *International Archives of Occupational and Environmental Health*, 40:185–190.

Knipschild, P., H. Meijer, and H. Salle. 1981. Aircraft Noise and Birthweight. *International Archives of Occupational and Environmental Health*, 48:131–136.

Knipschild, P., and N. Oudshoorn. 1977. Medical Effects of Aircraft Noise: Drug Survey. *International Archives of Occupational and Environmental Health*, 40:197–200.

Koehn, Peter, and Sidney R. Waldron. 1978. Afocha: A Link Between Community and Administration in Harar, Ethiopia. *Foreign and Comparative Studies/Africa*, XXXI. Syracuse: Syracuse University.

Kokudocho. 1993. *Shutokan Hakusho* (White Paper on the Capital Region). Tokyo: Kokudocho.

Kondo, Dorinne K. 1990. *Crafting Selves*. Chicago: University of Chicago Press.

Kornblum, W. 1974. *Blue Collar Community*. Chicago: University of Chicago Press.

Krapf-Askari, Eva. 1969. *Yoruba Towns and Cities: An Enquiry into the Nature of Urban Social Phenomena*. London: Oxford University Press.

Kressel, G. M. 1975. *Individuality against Tribality: The Dynamics of a Bedouin Community in a Process of Urbanization*. Tel Aviv: Hakibbutz Hameuchad (in Hebrew).

Kroeber, A. L., and Clyde Kluckholn. 1952. Culture: A Critical Review of Concepts and Definitions. Papers of the Peabody Museum of Anthropology, Vol. 47 No. 1.

Kryter, K. 1970. *The Effects of Noise on Man*. New York: Academic Press.

Kryter, K. D. 1987. Environmental Aircraft Noise and Social Factors in Stress-Related Health Disorders. In *Inter-noise*, 87:849–952, ed. P. Li. Beijing: Acoustical Society of China.

Lagares, Calvo, M. J. 1982. *Deficit Publico y Crisis Economica*. Madrid: Instituto de Estudios Economicos.

Lambert, Jacques. 1959. *Os does Brasis*. Rio de Janeiro: Centro Brasileiro de Pesquisas Educacionais.

———. 1967. Conclusoes, Seminario sobre a Politica de Integracao de uma Populacao Marginalizada, Brasilia.

Lamphere, Louise. 1985. Bringing the Family to Work: Women's Culture on the Shop Floor. *Feminist Studies*, 11:519–555.

———. 1986a. From Working Daughters to Working Mothers: Production and Reproduction in an Industrial Community. *American Ethnologist*, 13:118–130.

———. 1986b. Working Mothers and Family Strategies: Portuguese and Colombian Women in a New England Community. In *International Migration: The Female Experience*, eds. Rita J. Simon and Caroline B. Brettell, pp. 266–283. Totowa, NJ: Rowman & Allenheld.

———. 1987. *From Working Daughters to Working Mothers: Immigrant Women in a New England Community*. Ithaca, NY: Cornell University Press.

Lamphere, Louise, Filomena M. Silva, and John P. Sousa. 1980. Kin Networks and Strategies of Working-Class Portuguese Families in a New England Town. In *The Versatility of Kinship*, eds. Linda Cordell and Stephen Beckerman, pp. 219–249. New York: Academic Press.

Lane, Edward W. 1923. *The Manners and Customs of the Modern Egyptians*, 3rd ed. New York: E. P. Dutton.

Lane-Poole, Stanley. 1902. *The Story of Cairo*. London: J. M. Dent.

Larrowe, Charles. 1955. *Shape Up and Hiring Hall*. Berkeley: University of California Press.

Laslett, Peter, et al. 1972. *Household and Family in Past Time*. Cambridge: Cambridge University Press.

Lauman, Edward O. 1973. *Bonds of Pluralism: The Form and Substance of Urban Social Networks*. New York: John Wiley.

Lauria, Anthony, Jr. 1964. "Respeto," "Relajo," and Interpersonal Relations in Puerto Rico. *Anthropological Quarterly*, 37(2): 53–67.

Leach, E. R. 1960. Introduction: What Should We Mean by Caste? In *Aspects of Caste in South India, Ceylon and North-West Pakistan*, ed. E. R. Leach, pp. 1–10. Cambridge Papers in Social Anthropology, No. 2. Cambridge: Cambridge University Press.

Lebra, Takie Sugiyama, ed. 1992. *Japanese Social Organization*. Honolulu: University of Hawaii Press.

Leeds, Anthony. 1968. Brazilian Careers and Social Structure: An Evolutionary Model and Case History. *American Anthropologist*, 70:1321–1347.

———. 1971. The Concept of the "Culture of Poverty": Conceptual, Logical and Empirical Problems with Perspectives from Brazil and Peru. In *The Culture of Poverty: A Critique*, ed. E. Leacock. New York: Simon and Schuster.

———. 1972. Urban Anthropology and Urban Studies. *Urban Anthropology Newsletter*, 1:4–5.

Leeds, Anthony, and Elizabeth Leeds. 1967. Brazil and the Myth of Urban Rurality: Urban Experience, Work, and Values in "Squatments" of Rio de Janeiro and Lima. Paper presented at the Conference on Work and Urbanization in Modernizing Societies, St. Thomas, Virgin Islands.

Leichter, H. J., and W. E. Mitchell. 1967. *Kinship and Casework*. New York: Russell Sage Foundation.

Leis, Philip, and George Hicks. 1977. *Ethnic Encounters*. North Sciutate, MA: Duxbury.

Leslie, Genevieve. 1974. Domestic Service in Canada, 1880–1920. In *Women at Work*, eds. Janice Acton, et al., pp. 71–126. Toronto: Women's Educational Press.

LeTourneau, Roger. 1949. *Fes: Avant le protectorat*. Casablanca: Societe Marocaine de Librairie et d'Edition.

Levine, Donald H., Ellwood B. Carter, and Eleanor Miller Gorman. 1976. Simmel's Influence on American Sociology: II. *American Journal of Sociology*, 81:1112–1132.

Lévi-Strauss, Claude. 1953. Social Structure. In *Anthropology Today*, ed. A. L. Kroeber, pp. 524–553. Chicago: University of Chicago Press.

_____. 1963. *Structural Anthropology*. New York: Basic Books.

Levy, Marion J. 1952. Some Sources of the Vulnerability of the Structure of Relatively Non-Industrialized Societies to Those of Highly Industrialized Societies. In *Progress of Under-Developed Areas*, ed. B. F. Hoselitz. Chicago: University of Chicago Press.

Levy, M. J., Jr., and Lloyd A. Fallers. 1959. The Family: Some Comparative Considerations. *American Anthropologist*, 61:647–651.

Lewin, Linda. 1979. Some Historical Implications of Kinship Organization for Family-Based Politics in the Brazilian Northeast. *Comparative Studies in Society and History*, 21:262–292.

Lewis, Diane. 1973. Anthropology and Colonialism. *Current Anthropology*, 14:581–602.

Lewis, Hylan. 1971. Culture of Poverty? What Does It Matter? In *The Culture of Poverty: A Critique*, ed. E. Leacock. New York: Simon and Schuster.

Lewis, O. 1952. Urbanization Without Breakdown. *Scientific Monthly*, 75:31–41.

_____. 1959. *Five Families: Mexican Studies in the Culture of Poverty*. New York: Basic Books.

_____. 1961. *The Children of Sanchez*. New York: Random House.

_____. 1965. *La Vida: A Puerto Rican Family in the Culture of Poverty*. New York: Random House.

_____. 1966. The Culture of Poverty. *Scientific American*, 215:19–25.

_____. 1969. The Possessions of the Poor. *Scientific American*, 221:114–124.

Liae, Tai Chu. 1948. The Apprentice in Chengtu During and After the War. *Yenching Journal of Social Studies*, 4:90–106.

Liebenow, J. G. 1969. *Liberia: The Evolution of Privilege*. Ithaca, NY, and London: Cornell University Press.

Liebow, E. 1967. *Tally's Corner*. Boston: Little, Brown.

Light, Ivan. 1972. *Ethnic Enterprise in America*. Berkeley: University of California Press.

_____. 1983. *Cities in World Perspective*. New York: Macmillan.

Lin-Fu, J. S. 1979. Undue Lead Absorption and Lead Poisoning in Children—An Overview. Department of Health Education and Welfare Publication No. (HSA) 79–5141, U.S. Government Printing Office.

Linton, Ralph. 1949. The Natural History of the Family. In *The Family: Its Function and Destiny*, ed. R. N. Anshen, pp. 18–38. New York: Harper and Brothers.

List, Fredrich. 1974. *National System of Political Economy*. New York: Garland (orig. in German 1841).

Little, Kenneth. 1957. The Role of Voluntary Associations in West African Urbanization. *American Anthropologist*, 59:579–596.

_____. 1960. West African Urbanization and Social Process. *Cahiers d'Etudes Africaines I*, 3:90–102.

_____. 1973. *African Women in Towns*. Cambridge: Cambridge University Press.

Litwak, Eugene. 1960a. Occupational Mobility and Extended Family Cohesion. *American Sociological Review*, 25:9–21.

Litwak, Eugene. 1960b. Geographic Mobility and Family Cohesion. *American Sociological Review*, 25:385–394.

Lofland, Lyn H. 1985. *A World of Strangers: Order and Action in Urban Public Places*. Prospect Heights, IL: Waveland Press.

Logan, Kathleen. 1984. *Haciendo Pueblo—The Development of a Guadalajaran Suburb*. Tuscaloosa: University of Alabama Press.

_____. Self-Empowerment and Urban Mobilizations in Latin America. Unpublished manuscript.

_____. 1988. Women's Political Activity and Empowerment in Latin American Urban Movements. In *Urban Life*, 2d ed., eds. G. Gmelch and W. P. Zenner, pp. 343–357. Prospect Heights, IL: Waveland Press.

_____. 1990. Women's Participation in Urban Protest. *Popular Movements and Political Change in Mexico*, eds. Joe Foweracker and Ann L. Craig, pp. 150–159. Boulder and London: Lynne Reimer.

Lomnitz, Larissa. 1974. The Social and Economic Organization of a Mexican Shantytown. In *Latin American Urban Research*, eds. W. and F. Trueblood, Vol. 4.

_____. 1977. *Networks and Marginality: Life in a Mexican Shantytown*. New York: Academic Press.

Lowenthal, D. 1972. *West Indian Societies*. New York: Oxford University Press.

Lupton, T., and S. Wilson. 1959. The Social Background and Connections of Top Decision-Makers. *Manchester University School*, 27:30–51.

Lynch, K. 1960. *The Image of the City*. Cambridge: MIT Press and Harvard University Press.

Lynch, Owen M. 1967. Rural Cities in India: Continuities and Discontinuities. In *India and Ceylon: Unity and Diversity*, ed. Philip Mason. London: Oxford University Press.

_____. 1969. *The Politics of Untouchability: Social Mobility and Social Change in a City of India*. New York: Columbia University Press.

_____. 1979. Potters, Plotters and Prodders: Marx and Meaning or Meaning vs. Marx. *Urban Anthropology*, 8:1–28.

_____. 1994. Urban Anthropology: Postmodern Cities and Perspectives. *City and Society Annual Review*, I(VII): 35–52.

Madsen, William. 1964. *The Mexican-Americans of South Texas*. New York: Holt, Rinehart and Winston.

Maine, Henry. 1861. *Ancient Law*. London: John Murray.

Mangin, William P. 1963. Urbanization Case History in Peru. *Architectural Design*, 365–370.

_____. 1964. Sociological, Cultural and Political Characteristics of Some Rural Indians and Urban Migrants in Peru. Paper presented at Wenner-Gren Symposium on Cross-Cultural Similarities in the Urbanization Process. Mimeo.

_____. 1965. The Role of Social Organization in Improving the Environment. In *Environmental Determinants of Community Well-Being*. Pan American Health Organization.

_____. 1967. Latin American Squatter Settlements: A Problem and a Solution. *Latin American Research Review*, 2:65–98.

_____. 1970. Poverty and Politics in the Latin American City. In *Power, Poverty and Urban Policy*, eds. L. Bloomington and H. Schmidt. *Urban Affairs Annual Review*, Vol. 2.

Maquet, J. 1961. *The Premise of Inequality in Ruanda*. London: Oxford University Press.

Marcuse, H. 1964. *One-Dimensional Man*. London: Sphere Books.

Marks, Carol. 1991. The Urban Underclass. In *Annual Review of Sociology*, 17:445–466.

Marmot, M. G. 1980. Affluence, Urbanization and Coronary Heart Disease. In *Disease and Urbanization*, eds. E. J. Clegg and J. P. Garlick, pp. 127–143. London: Taylor & Francis.

Marris, Peter. 1961. *Family and Social Change in an African City*. London: Routledge & Kegan Paul.

Marshall, D. 1982. Migration as an Agent of Change in Caribbean Island Ecosystems. *International Social Science Journal* 34(3): 451–467.

Marx, E. 1976. *The Social Context of Violent Behavior: A Social Anthropological Study in an Israeli Immigrant Town*. London: Routledge & Kegan Paul.

McCarthy, Patricia. 1971. Poverty and Itinerancy. Master of Arts Thesis, University College, Dublin.

McDonogh, Gary W. 1993. Empty Space. In *The Cultural Meaning of Urban Space*, eds. R. Rotenberg and G. McDonogh. Amherst, MA: Bergin and Garvey.

Mead, Lawrence M. 1992. *The New Politics of Poverty: The Non-Working Poor in America*. New York: Basic Books.

Mead, Margaret. 1928. *Coming of Age in Samoa: A Psychological Study in Primitive Youth for Western Civilization*. New York: William Morrow.

_____. 1930. *Social Organization of Manu'a, Bulletin 76*. Honolulu: Bernice P. Bishop Museum.

Media Production Group. 1992. Neighborhood Tokyo (video). Richmond, IN: Media Production Group, Institute for Education on Japan, Earlham College.

Meecham, W. C., and H. G. Smith. 1977. Effects of Jet Aircraft Noise on Mental Hospital Admissions. *British Journal of Audiology*, II:81–85.

Meier, R. L. 1962. *A Communications Theory of Urban Growth*. Cambridge, MA: MIT Press.

Meintel, Deidre. 1987. The New Double Workday of Immigrant Workers in Quebec. *Women's Studies*, 13:273–293.

Meintel, Deidre, Michiline Labelle, Genevieve Turcotte, and Marianne Kempineers. 1984. Migration, Wage Labor and Domestic Relationships: Immigrant Women in Montreal. *Anthropologica*, 26(2): 135–169.

Menahem, G. 1972. Neighborly Relations in an Urban Slum. M.A. thesis, Tel Aviv University (in Hebrew with English summary).

Mercer, Charles. 1975. *Living in Cities: Psychology and the Urban Environment*. Harmondsworth: Penguin.

Merry, Sally Engle. 1981. *Urban Danger: Life in a Neighborhood of Strangers*. Philadelphia: Temple University Press.

_____. 1984. Rethinking Gossip and Scandal. In *Toward a General Theory of Social Control*, ed. Donald Black, Vol. 11. New York: Academic Press.

Merton, Robert K. 1968. Social Structure and Anomie. In *Social Theory and Social Structure*, pp. 185–214. New York: Free Press.

Metzger, Duane, and Gerald E. Williams. 1963. A Formal Ethnographic Analysis of Tenejapa Indio Weddings. *American Anthropologist* 65:1076–1101.

Midgett, D. 1977. West Indian Migration and Adaptation in St. Lucia and London. Ph.D. Diss. University of Illinois.

Milgram, S. 1970. The Experience of Living in the Cities. *Science*, 167:1461–1468.

Milgram, S., and P. Hollander. 1964. The Murder They Heard. *Nation*, 198:602–604.

Miller, S. M., F. Reisman, and A. Seagull. 1965. Poverty and Self-Indulgence: A Critique of the Non-Deferred Gratification Pattern. In *Poverty in America*, eds. L. Ferman, et al. Ann Arbor: University of Michigan Press.

Miller, W. B. 1955. Two Concepts of Authority. *American Anthropologist*, 57:271–289.

_____. 1971. Subculture, Social Reform and the Culture of Poverty. *Human Organization*, 30:111–125.

Millon, René, Bruce Drewitt, and George Cowgill. 1973. *Urbanization at Teotihuacan, Mexico, the Teotihuacan Map, Part One.* Austin: University of Texas Press.

Milton, Gordan. 1964. The Subsociety and the Subculture. In *Assimilation in American Life.* New York: Oxford University Press.

Mims, Cedric. 1970. Stress in Relation to the Processes of Civilization. In *The Impact of Civilization on the Biology of Man,* ed. S. V. Boyden, pp. 167–181. Toronto: University of Toronto Press.

Miner, Horace. 1953. *The Primitive City of Timbuctoo.* Princeton, NJ: Princeton University Press.

Ministere des Affaires Economiques et du Plan. 1958. Recensement d'Abidjan Resultats definitifs. Abidjan.

Mitchell, J. C. 1956. *The Kalela Dance.* Manchester: Manchester University Press.

_____. 1966. Theoretical Orientations in African Urban Studies. In *The Social Anthropology of Complex Societies,* ed. Michael Banton. Association of Social Anthropologists monograph no. 4. London: Tavistock.

_____. ed. 1969. *Social Networks in Urban Situations: Analysis of Personal Relationships in Central African Towns.* Manchester: Manchester University Press.

Mitchell, William. 1978. *Mishpokhe: A Study of New York City Jewish Family Clubs.* The Hague and Paris: Mouton.

Molyneux, Maxine. 1985. Mobilization without Emancipation? Women's Interests, State and Revolution in Nicaragua. *New Movements and the State in Latin America,* ed. David Slater. Amsterdam: CEDLA.

Moreno, Jose. 1970. *Barrios in Arms.* Pittsburgh: University of Pittsburgh Press.

Moynihan, Daniel Patrick. 1965. *The Negro Family: The Case for National Action.* Washington, DC: Government Printing Office. Prepared for the Office of Policy Planning and Research of the Department of Labor.

_____. 1992. How the Great Society Destroyed the American Family. *The Public Interest,* 108:53–64.

Mullings, Leith. 1987. *Cities in the United States.* New York: Columbia University Press.

Mumford, Lewis. 1961. *The City in History.* New York: Harcourt, Brace and World.

Munson, Henry, Jr. 1984. *The House of Si Abd Allah: The Oral History of a Moroccan Family.* New Haven: Yale University Press.

Murdock, George P. 1960. Reprint. *Social Structure.* New York: Macmillan. Original edition, Glencoe, IL: The Free Press.

Murdock, George P., Clellan S. Ford, Alfred E. Hudson, et al. 1961. *Outline of Cultural Materials.* New Haven, CT: Human Relations Area Files.

Murray, Charles. 1984. *Losing Ground: American Social Policy 1950–1980.* New York: Basic Books.

Murray, Oswyn, and Simon Price, eds. 1990. *The Greek City.* New York: Oxford University Press.

Mushak, P., J. M. Davies, A. F. Crocetti, and L. D. Grant. 1989. Prenatal and Postnatal Effects of Low Level Lead Exposure: Integrated Summary of a Report to the U.S. Congress on Child Lead Poisoning. *Environmental Research,* 50:11–36.

Nadim, Nawal el Messiri. 1975. The Relationship Between Sexes in a Harah of Cairo. Ph.D. Diss., Department of Anthropology, Indiana University.

Needleman, Herbert L. 1983. Lead at Low Dose and the Behavior of Children. *Acta Psychiatrica Scandinavica,* 67(303): 26–37.

Nelson, Nici. 1978. Women Must Help Each Other. In *Women United; Women Divided,* ed. Pat Caplan. London: Tavistock.

Nelson, Nici. 1987. Rural Urban Child Fosteruns in Kenya: Migration, Kinship, Ideology and Class. In *Migrant Workers: The Social Order*, ed. J. Eames. A.S.A. monograph no. 26. London: Tavistock.

_____. 1990. The Women Who Left and Those Who Stayed Behind: Rural Urban Migration in Central and Western Kenya. In *Gender and Migration in Developing Countries*. London: Bedhaven Press.

_____. 1992. Marital Options and Gender Power in Mathare Valley, Nairobi. In *Culture and Contradictions, Dialectics, Power and Symbol*, ed. M. de Soto. Mellan Research University Press.

_____. Forthcoming. Kiambu Group: A Successful Rotating Credit Group 1970–1990. In *Money-Go-Rounds: Women's Use of Rotations, Savings and Credit Associations*, ed. S. Ardeneur. London: Berg Press.

Newman, Katherine. 1992. Culture and Structure. In *The Truly Disadvantaged City and Society*, 6:25.

Newman, Oscar. 1972. *Defensible Space: Crime Prevention Through Urban Design*. New York: Macmillan.

Newsweek. 1993. America's Poor Showing. October 18:44.

Niane, D. T. 1965. *Sudiata: An Epic of Old Mail*. Harlow, Essex: Longman.

Niargoran, G. 1960. Le village aboure. *Cahiers d'Etudes Africaines I*, 1:113–127.

Nicholaus, Martin. 1968. Radicals in the Professions. *Newsletter of the American Anthropological Association*, November, 9–10.

Ogg, Elizabeth. 1939. *Longshoremen and Their Homes*. New York: Greenwich House.

Ogien, R. Forthcoming. A Slum Area in Tel Aviv. In *A Composite Portrait of Israel*, ed. E. Marx. London: Academic Press.

Olufsen, O. 1911. *The Emir of Bokhara and His Country*. Copenhagen: Gyldendalske.

Omar, T. P. 1960. Changing Attitudes of Students in West African Society Towards Marriage and Family Relationships. *British Journal of Sociology*, 11(3): 197–210.

Omran, A. R. 1975. Epidemiological Transition in the United States: The Health Factor in Population Change. *Population Bulletin*, 32:1–42.

Ong, A. 1985. Industrialization and Prostitution in Southeast Asia. *Southeast Asia Chronicle* 96:2–6.

Orent, Amnon. 1977. *Israel: Three Studies in Urban Anthropology*. Haifa: University of Haifa.

Orsi, Robert. 1985. *The Madonna of 115th Street: Faith and Community in Italian Harlem, 1880–1950*. New Haven: Yale University Press.

Osgood, Cornelius. 1951. *The Koreans and Their Culture*. New York: Ronald Press.

Paigen, B., L. R. Goldman, M. M. Magnant, J. H. Highland, and A. T. Steegman, Jr. 1987. Growth of Children Living Near the Hazardous Waste Site, Love Canal. *Human Biology*, 59:489–508.

Palisi, Bartolomeo. 1966. Ethnic Generation and Family Structure. *Journal of Marriage and the Family*, 28:49–50.

Papanek, Hanna. 1979. Family Status Production: The "Work" and "Non-Work" of Women. *Signs*, 4:775–782.

Park, Robert E. 1952. *Human Communities*. Glencoe, IL: The Free Press.

_____. 1969. The City: Suggestions for Investigation of Human Behavior in an Urban Environment. In *Classic Essays on the Culture of Cities*, ed. R. E. Sennet, pp. 91–130. New York: Appleton-Century-Crofts (orig. pub. 1916).

Park, Robert E., and W. Burgess, et al. 1925. *The City*. Chicago.

Parker, S., and R. Kleiner. 1970. The Culture of Poverty: An Adjustment Dimension. *American Anthropologist*, 72:516–528.

Parkin, D. 1969. *Neighbours and Nationals*. London: Routledge & Kegan Paul.

Parry, G. 1969. *Political Elites*. London: Allen & Unwin.

Parsons, Talcott. 1943. The Kinship System of the Contemporary United States. *American Anthropologist* 45:22–38.

_____. 1951. *The Social System*. Glencoe, IL: The Free Press.

_____. 1975. Some Theoretical Considerations on the Nature and Trends of Change of Ethnicity. In *Ethnicity Theory and Experience*, eds. N. Glazer and D. P. Moynihan, pp. 53–83. Cambridge: Harvard University Press.

Pasternak, B., and J. Salaff. 1993. *Chinese Cowboys in Inner Mongolia*. Boulder: Westview Press.

Pastore, J. 1968. Satisfaction Among Migrants to Brasilia, Brazil: A Sociological Interpretation. Ph.D. Diss., University of Wisconsin.

Patch, Richard. 1967. La Parada: Lima's Market. American Universities Field Staff Report, West Coast of South America, Vol. 14.

Patterson, I. 1982. *Slavery and Social Death*. Cambridge: Harvard University Press.

Patterson, S. 1963. *Dark Strangers: A Study of West Indians in London*. London: Tavistock.

Paulitschke, Phillipe. 1888. *Harar: Forschungreise nach den Somal-und Gallalandern Ostafrikas*. Leipzig: F. Brockhaus.

Paulme, D. 1961. "Litterature Orale et Comportments Sociaux. *L'homme*, I, 1:37–69.

_____. 1962. *Une Societe de Cote d'Ivoire Hier et Aujourd'hui: les Betes*. The Hague: Mouton.

Pauw, B. A. 1963. *The Second Generation*. Capetown: Oxford University Press.

Peach, C. 1968. *West Indian Migration to Britain: A Social Geography*. London: Oxford University Press.

Pearse, Andrew. 1961. Some Characteristics of Urbanization in the City of Rio de Janeiro. In *Urbanization in Latin America*, ed. P. Hauser. New York: UNESCO.

Pearson, S. V. 1935. *The Growth and Distribution of Population*. New York.

Peattie, Lisa R. 1967. *The View from the Barrio*. Ann Arbor: University of Michigan Press.

_____. 1967. The Social Anthropologist in Planning. *Journal of the American Institute of Planners*, 33:266–268.

_____. 1968. Reflections on Advocacy Planning. *Journal of the American Institute of Planners*, 34:80–88.

_____. Social Issues in Housing. Joint Center for Urban Studies. Unpublished manuscript.

Pelzel, John C. 1950. Social Stratification in Japanese Urban Economic Life. Ph.D. Diss. Department of Social Relations, Harvard University.

Perin, Constance. 1977. *Everything in Its Place*. Princeton: Princeton University Press.

Peritore, Patrick. 1986. Paulo Freire's Socialism and the Worker's Party of Brazil, pp. 1–86. USFI Reports, No. 8, South America.

Perry, I. M. 1975. The New and Old Diseases. *American Journal of Clinical Pathology*, 63:453–474.

Petras, J. 1969. The New Revolutionary Politics in Latin America. *Monthly Review*, 20:39.

Phillips, Kevin. 1990. *The Politics of the Rich and the Poor: Wealth and the Electorate in the Reagan Aftermath*.

Phillips, R. E. 1956. The Bantu in the City: A Study of Cultural Adjustment on the Witwatersrand. In *Social Implications of Industrialization and Urbanization in Africa South of the Sahara*. Geneva: UNESCO.

Pilcher, William. 1972. *The Portland Longshoremen*. New York: Holt, Rinehart and Winston.

Piore, M. and C. Sabel. 1984. *The Second Industrial Divide: Possibilities for Prosperity*. New York: Basic Books.

Pirenne, Henri. 1925. *Medieval Cities*. Princeton: Princeton University Press.

Pirkle, J. L., D. J. Brody, E. W. Gunter, R. A. Kramer, D. C. Paschal, K. M. Flegal, and T. D. Matte. 1994. The Decline in Blood Lead Levels in the United States. *Journal of the American Medical Association*, 272:284–291.

Piven, Francis Fox, and Richard Cloward. 1971. *Regulating the Poor: The Functions of Public Welfare*. New York: Pantheon Books.

Pocock, D. F. 1960. Sociologies: Urban and Rural. *Contributions to Indian Sociology*, 4.

Polanyi, K. 1944. *The Great Transformation*. Boston: Beacon.

_____. 1966. *Dahomey and the Slave Trade*. American Ethnological Society monograph no. 42. Seattle and London: Washington University Press.

Polgar, Steven. 1964. Evolution and the Ills of Mankind. In *Horizons of Anthropology*, ed. S. Tax, pp. 200–211. Chicago: Aldine.

Portes, Alejandro. 1976. Latin American Class Structures: Their Composition and Change during the Last Decade. *LARR*, 20(3): 7–39.

Portes, Alejandro, and John Walton. 1976. *Urban Latin America: The Political Condition from Above and Below*. Austin: University of Texas Press.

Potash, Betty. 1986. *Widows in African Societies: Choices and Constraints*. Stanford: Stanford University Press.

Powdermaker, Hortense. 1933. *Life in Lesu: The Study of a Melanesian Society in New Ireland*. New York: W. W. Norton.

Price, John. 1972. Reno, Nevada: The City as a Unit of Study. *Urban Anthropology*, 1:14–28.

Pye, L. 1985. *Asian Power and Politics*. Cambridge: Harvard University Press.

Pye, Lucien W. 1963. The Political Implications of Urbanization and the Development Process. In Social Problems of Development and Urbanization. *Science, Technology and Development*, Vol. 7. Washington, DC: Government Printing Office.

Rabinow, Paul. 1989. French Modern: Norms and Forms of the Social Environment. Cambridge: MIT Press.

Radcliffe-Brown, A. R., and D. Ford, eds. 1950. *African Systems of Kinship and Marriage*. London: Oxford University Press.

Rainwater, Lee, and William L. Yancey, eds. 1967. *The Moynihan Report and the Politics of Controversy*. Cambridge: MIT Press.

Ramirez, Francisca. 1980. It All Depends on the Teacher. In *Latin American Women: The Meek Speak Out*, ed. June H. Turner, pp. 101–110. Silver Spring, MD: International Educational Development.

Ranum, R., and O. Forster. 1976. *Family and Society*. Baltimore: Johns Hopkins University Press.

Rao, M. S. A., Chandrashekar Bhat, and Laxmi Narayan Kadekar, eds. 1991. *A Reader in Sociology*. Hyderabad: Orient Longman.

Raum, O. F. 1969. Self Help Associations. 28:119–141.

Redfield, Robert. 1930. *Tepoztlan: A Mexican Village*. Chicago: University of Chicago Press.

_____. 1941. *The Folk Culture of Yucatan*. Chicago: University of Chicago Press.

_____. 1947. The Folk Society. *American Journal of Sociology*, 52:293–308.

Redfield, Robert, and M. Singer. 1954. The Cultural Role of Cities. *Economic Development and Cultural Change*, 3:53–77.

Reiss, A. J., Jr. 1955. An Analysis of Urban Phenomenon. In *The Metropolis in Modern Life*, ed. R. M. Fisher, pp. 41–51. New York: Doubleday.

Reiss, I. L. 1965. The Universality of the Family: A Conceptual Analysis. *Journal of Marriage and the Family*, 27:443–453.

Research Committee on Urbanism of the National Resources Committee. 1937. *Our Cities: Their Role in the National Economy*. Washington, DC: Government Printing Office.

Reynolds, V., D. A. Jenner, C. D. Palmer, and G. A. Harrison. 1981. Catecholamine Excretion Rates in Relation to Lifestyles in the Male Population of Otmoor, Oxfordshire. *Annals of Human Biology*, 8:197–209.

Rhoades, Robert E. 1978a. Intra-European Return Migration and Rural Development: Lessons from the Spanish Case. *Human Organization*, 37:136–147.

———. 1978b. Foreign Labor and German Industrial Capitalism 1871–1978: The Evolution of a Migratory System. *American Ethnologist*, 5:553–573.

———. 1979a. From Caves to Main Street: Return Migration and the Transformation of a Spanish Village. *Papers in Anthropology*, 20:57–74.

———. ed. 1979b. The Anthropology of Return Migration. Special Issue of *Papers in Anthropology*, Vol. 20. Norman: University of Oklahoma, Department of Anthropology.

Richards, Audrey. 1939. *Land, Labour, and Diet in Northern Rhodesia*. Oxford: Oxford University Press.

Richardson, B. 1983. *Caribbean Migrants: Environment and Human Survival on St. Kitts and Nevis*. Knoxville: University of Tennessee Press.

Rigdon, Susan M. 1988. *The Culture Facade: Art, Science and Politics in the Work of Oscar Lewis*. Urbana: University of Illinois Press.

Roberts, Bryan. 1970. The Social Organization of Low Income Families. In *Crucifixion of Power*, ed. R. N. Adams, pp. 479–515. Austin: University of Texas Press.

———. 1973. *Organizing Strangers*. Austin: University of Texas Press.

Robertson, Jennifer. 1991. *Native and Newcomer*. Berkeley: University of California Press.

Rodwin, L. *Evolution of a Federalist: William Loughton Smith of Charleston (1758–1812)*. Columbia: University of South Carolina Press.

Rollwagen, Jack R. 1980. Cities and the World System: Toward an Evolutionary Perspective in the Study of Urban Anthropology. In *Urban Anthropology: Cities in a Hierarchical Context*, ed. Thomas Collins. Southern Anthropological Society Proceedings No. 14: Athens: University of Georgia Press.

Romney, A. K., and R. G. D'Andrade. 1964. Cognitive Aspects of English Kin Terms. *American Anthropologist*, 66:146–170.

Romo, Frank, and Michael Schwartz. 1993. The Coming of Post-Industrial Society Revisisted: Manufacturing and the Prospects for a Service-Based Economy. In *Explorations in Economic Sociology*, ed. Richard Swedburg. New York: Russell Sage Foundation.

Rose, E. J. 1969. *Colour and Citizenship*. London: Oxford University Press.

Rosenbaum, David E. 1989. Bosh and Congress Reach Accord Raising Minimum Wage to $4.25. *New York Times*, p. A1, November 1.

Ross, Marc. 1974. *The Political Integration of Urban Squatters*. Evanston, IL: Northwestern University Press.

Rostow, Walter W. 1960. *The Stages of Economic Growth: A Non-Communist Manifesto*. Cambridge: Cambridge University Press.

Rotenberg, Robert. 1992a. The Power to Time and the Time to Power. In *The Politics of Time*, ed. Henry Rutz, pp. 18–36. American Ethnological Society monograph no. 4. Washington: American Anthropological Association.

———. 1992b. *Time and Order in Metropolitan Vienna: A Seizure of Schedules*. Washington, DC: Smithsonian Institute Press.

Rotenberg, Robert. 1995. *Landscape and Power in Vienna*. Baltimore: Johns Hopkins Press.

Rotenberg, Robert, and Gary W. McDonogh. 1993. *The Cultural Meaning of Urbn Space.*. Westport, CT: Greenwood (Bergin and Garvey).

Rusinow, Dennison. 1986. Mega-Cities Today and Tomorrow: Is the Cup Half-full or Half-empty? *USFI Reports*, no. 12:1–86.

Ryan, Mary. 1975. *Womanhood in America: From Colonial Times to the Present*. New York: New Viewpoints.

Safa, Helen Icken. 1964. From Shanty Town to Public Housing: A Comparison of Family Structure in Two Urban Neighborhoods in Puerto Rico. *Caribbean Studies*, 4.

_____. 1968. The Social Isolation of the Urban Poor: Life in a Puerto Rican Shanty Town. In *Among the People: Encounters with the Poor*. New York: Basic Books.

_____. 1974. *The Urban Poor of Puerto Rico: A Study in Development Inequality*. New York: Holt, Rinehart and Winston.

Said, Edward W. 1979. *Orientalism*. New York: Vintage.

Salmen, L. 1969. A Perspective on Resettlement of Squatters in Brazil. *American Latina*, 12:73–95.

Sampson, A. 1962. *Anatomy of Britain*. New York and Evanston: Harper & Row; London: Hodder and Stoughton.

Sanders, William T., Jeffrey R. Parsons, and Robert S. Santley. 1979. *The Basin of Mexico: Ecological Processes in the Evolution of a Civilization*. New York: Academic Press.

Sarabia, B. 1985. Historias de Vida. *Revista espanola de Investigaciones sociologicas*, 29:165–186.

Sassen, Saskia. 1992. *The Global City: New York, London, and Tokyo*. Princeton, NJ: Princeton University Press.

Sauerbrier, C. L. 1955. *Education in Cargo Operations. Progress in Cargo Handling*. London: Hiffe and Sons.

Sauvaget, Jean. 1941. *Alep*. Paris: Librairie Orientale Paul Geuthner.

Savezni Zavod za Statistiku. 1982. *Statisticki Bilten 1295* (Statistical Bulletin 1295). Belgrade: Savezni Zavod za Statistiku.

Schell, L. 1981. Environmental Noise and Human Prenatal Growth. *American Journal of Physical Anthropology*, 56:63–70.

_____. 1984. The Effect of Chronic Noise Exposure on Human Prenatal Growth. In *Human Growth and Development*, eds. J. Borms, R. Hauspie, A. Sand, C. Susanne and M. Hebbelinck, pp. 125–129. New York: Plenum Press.

_____. 1986. Community Health Assessment through Physical Anthropology: Auxological Epidemiology. *Human Organization*, 45:321–327.

Schell, L. M. 1992. Risk Focusing: An Example of Biocultural Interaction. *MASCA Research Papers in Science and Archaeology*, Vol. 9: *Health and Lifestyle Change*, ed. R. Huss-Ashmore, J. Schall, and M. Hediger.

Schell, L. M., and Y. Ando. 1991. Postnatal Growth of Children in Relation to Noise from Osaka International Airport. *Journal of Sound and Vibration*, 151:371–382.

Schmink, Marianne. 1981. Women in Brazilian "Abertura" Politics. *Signs* 7(1): 115–134.

Schneider, Betty, and Abraham Siegel. 1956. *Industrial Relations in the Pacific Coast Longshore Industry*. Berkeley: University of California Press.

Schneider, David M., and E. K. Cough, eds. 1961. *Matrilineal Kinship*. Berkeley: University of California Press.

Schwarzweller, H. K., J. Brown, and S. Mangalam. 1971. *Mountain Families in Transition*. University Park: Pennsylvania State University Press.

Seidensticker, Edward. 1983. *Low City, High City: Tokyo from Edo to the Earthquake*. New York: Knopf.

Seligman, Martin E. P. 1975. *Helplessness: On Depression, Development and Death*. San Francisco: W. H. Freeman and Co.

Selye, Hans. 1956. *The Stress of Life*. New York: McGraw-Hill.

Serjeant, R. B., ed. 1972. *The Social Construction of Communities*. Chicago: University of Chicago Press.

Service, Elman R. 1967. *Primitive Social Organization*. New York: Random House.

Shai, D. 1970. *Neighborhood Relations in an Immigrant Quarter*. Jerusalem: Szold Institute.

Shanklin, E. 1980. The Irish Go-between. *Anthropological Quarterly*, 53(3): 162–172.

Sharff, Jagna. 1987. The Underground Economy of a Poor Neighborhood. In *Cities of the United States: Studies in Urban Anthropology*, ed. Leith Mullings, pp. 19–50. New York: Columbia University Press.

Shen, Tsung-Lien, and Shen Chi-Liu. 1953. *Tibet and the Tibetans*. Stanford, CA: Stanford University Press.

Shokeid, M., and S. Deshen. *Distant Relations: Ethnicity and Politics among Arabs and North African Jews in Israel*. Typewritten manuscript.

Short, J. F., Jr. 1971. Introduction. In *The Social Fabric of the Metropolis*, ed. J. F. Short, Jr. Chicago: University of Chicago Press.

Shryrock, John K. 1931. *The Temples of Anking and their Cults*. Paris (privately printed).

Shukla, R., K. N. Dietrich, R. L. Bornschein, and P. B. Berger. 1991. Lead Exposure and Growth in the Early Preschool Child: A Follow-up Report from the Cincinnati Lead Study. *Pediatrics*, 88:886–892.

Shuttles, Gerald. 1972. *The Social Construction of Community*. Chicago: University of Chicago Press.

Shy, C. M., V. Hasselbald, R. M. Burton, C. J. Nelson, and A. A. Cohen. 1973. Air Pollution Effects on Ventilatory Function of U.S. Schoolchildren. *Archives of Environmental Health*, 27:124–128.

Siegel, Taggart, and Dwight Conquergood. 1990. *The Heart Broken in Half*. New York: Filmakers Library.

Simić, Andrei. 1973a. Kinship Reciprocity and Rural-Urban Integration in Serbia. *Urban Anthropology*, 1:205–213.

_____. 1973b. *The Peasant Urbanites: A Study of Rural-Urban Mobility in Serbia*. New York: Seminar Press.

_____. 1983. Urbanization and Modernization in Yugoslavia: Adaptive and Maladaptive Aspects of Traditional Culture. In *Urban Life in Mediterranean Europe: Anthropological Perspective*, eds. Michael Kenny and David I. Kertzer, pp. 203–224. Urbana: University of Illinois Press.

Simmel, Georg. 1908. *Soziologie*. Duncker & Humblot.

_____. 1950. The Stranger. In *The Sociology of Georg Simmel*, ed. K. Wolff, pp. 402–408. London: Free Press.

_____. 1969. Reprint. Die Grossstadte und das Geistesleben. In *Class Essays on the Culture of Cities*, ed. R. Sennet, pp. 47–60. New York: Appleton-Century-Crofts. Originally published in *Die Grossstadt*, ed. T. Petermann, Dresden: Jansch, 1905.

Simms, Ruth. 1965. *Urbanization in West Africa: A Review of the Current Literature*. Evanston: Northwestern University Press.

Simon, Rita James, and Caroline B. Brettell, eds. 1986. *International Migration: The Female Experience*. Totowa, NJ: Rowman & Allenheld.

Sjoberg, Andrée F. 1990. The Dravidian Contribution to the Development of Indian Civilization: A Call for a Reassessment. *Comparative Civilizations Review*, no. 23:40–74.

Sjoberg, Andrée F. 1994. Dravidian Features in the Religious Content of the Indian Epics. *Literature East and West*, no. 28:58–78.

Sjoberg, Gideon. 1952. "Folk" and "Feudal" Societies. *American Journal of Sociology*, 57:231–299.

_____. 1955. The Preindustrial City. *American Journal of Sociology*, 60:438–445.

_____. 1960. *The Preindustrial City*. Glencoe, IL: The Free Press.

Slotkin, James S. 1960. *From Field to Factory*. Glencoe, IL: The Free Press.

Smelser, Neil J. 1966. The Modernization of Social Relations. In *Modernization: The Dynamics of Growth*, ed. M. Weiner, pp. 110–121. New York: Basic Books.

Smith, Henry D., II. 1986. The Edo-Tokyo Transition: In Search of Common Ground. In *Japan in Transition: From Tokugawa to Meiji*, eds. M. Jansen and G. Rozman. Princeton: Princeton University Press.

Smith, M. G. 1957. Introduction. *My Mother Who Fathered Me* by Edith Clarke. London: Allen & Unwin.

_____. 1962. *West Indian Family Structure*. Seattle: University of Washington Press.

_____. 1973. Domestic Service as a Channel of Upward Mobility for the Lower Class Woman: The Lima Case. In *Female and Male in Latin America*, ed. Ann Pescatello, pp. 191–208. Pittsburgh: University of Pittsburgh Press.

Smith, Robert J. 1960. Pre-Industrial Urbanism in Japan: A Consideration of Multiple Traditions in a Feudal Society. *Economic Development and Cultural Change*, 9(1, part II): 241–257.

Sociajlistcka Federativna Republika Jugoslavia (SFRJ). 1974. *Popis Stanovnistvai Stanova 1974: Knjiga VI (Population and Housing Census 1974: Vol. VI)*. Belgrade: Savezni Zavod za Statistiku.

Solomon, R. 1971. *Mao's Revolution and the Chinese Political Culture*. Berkeley: University of California.

Sombart, Werner. 1931. Stadtische Siedlung, Stadt. In *Handworterbuch der Sociologie*, ed. Alfred Vierkandt. Stuttgart.

Sorkin, A. L. 1969. Some Aspects of American Indian Migration. *Social Forces*, 48:243–250.

Southall, Aidan. 1970. Urban Migration and the Residence of Children in Kampala. In *Peasants in Cities*, ed. William Mingin, pp. 150–159.

_____. 1973. The Density of Role Relationships as a Universal Index of Urbanization. In *Urban Anthropology*, ed. A. Southall. New York: Oxford University Press.

Sovani, N. V. 1951. *Social Survey of Kothapur*. Poone: Gokhale Institute of Political and Economic Studies.

Spasojević, Svetislav. 1984. Kuda se Slimo? (To Where Are We Moving?) *Nin*, 28 October: 26–28.

Spate, O. H. K. 1954. *India and Pakistan*. London: Methuen and Company.

Spiro, Melford E. 1954. Is the Family Universal? *American Anthropologist*, 56:839–846.

Spradley, James G. 1970. *You Owe Yourself a Drunk: An Ethnography of Urban Nomads*. Boston: Little, Brown.

Stack, Carol. 1970. The Kindred of Viola Jackson. In *Afro-American Anthropology: Contemporary Perspectives*, eds. N. Whitten and J. Szwed. New York: Free Press.

_____. 1974. *All Our Kin*. New York: Harper & Row.

Stern, Boris. 1932. Cargo Handling and Longshore Conditions. Bureau of Labor Statistics Bulletin No. 550. Washington, DC: Government Printing Office.

Stone, L. 1977. *The Family, Sex, and Marriage in England 1500–1800*. New York: Harper & Row.

Sumner, William Graham. 1906. *Folkways*. Boston.

Sussman, Marvin B. 1959. The Isolated Nuclear Family, Fact or Fiction? *Social Problems*, 6:333–340.

———. 1965. Relationships of Adult Children with their Parents in the United States. In *Social Structure and the Family: Generational Relations*, eds. Ethel Shanas and G. F. Streib, pp. 62–92. Englewood Cliffs, NJ: Prentice-Hall.

Sussman, Marvin B., and Lee Burchinal. 1962. Parental Aid to Married Children: Implications for Family Functioning. *Marriage and Family Living*, 24:320–332.

Suttles, Gerald. 1972. *The Social Construction of Community*. Chicago: University of Chicago Press.

Sutton, Joseph A. D. 1979. *Magic Carpet: Aleppo-in-Flatbush*. Brooklyn: Thayer-Jacoby.

———. 1987. *Aleppo Chronicles*. Brooklyn: Thayer-Jacoby.

Swanstrom, Edward. 1938. *The Waterfront Labor Problem*. New York: Fordham University Press.

Taira, Koji. 1968. Ragpickers and Community Development: Ant's Villa in Tokyo. *Industrial and Labour Relations Review*, 22:11.

Tarnopolsky, A., and C. Clark. 1984. Environmental Noise and Mental Health. In *Mental Health and the Environment*, ed. Hugh L. Freeman, pp. 250–270. New York: Churchill Livingstone.

Taylor, Lee. 1968. *Occupational Sociology*. New York: Oxford University Press.

Tedlock, Barbara. 1982. *Time and the Highland Maya*. Albuquerque: University of Mexico Press.

Thiebault, H., L. LaPalme, R. Tanguay, and A. Demirjian. 1985. Anthropometric Differences between Rural and Urban French-Canadian Schoolchildren. *Human Biology*, 57:113–129.

Thomas, W. I., and F. Znaniecki. 1927. *The Polish Peasant in Europe and America*. New York: A. A. Knopf.

Thompson, James W., and Edgar N. Johnson. 1937. *An Introduction to Medieval Europe*. New York: Norton.

Thomson, Marilyn. 1986. *Women of El Salvador: The Price of Freedom*. Philadelphia: ISHI Press.

Thrupp, Sylvia L. 1942. Medieval Guilds Reconsidered. *Journal of Economic History*, 2:164–173.

Thurston, Edgar. 1909. *Castes and Tribes of Southern India*. Vol. VI. Madras: Government Press.

Tisdale, H. 1942. The Process of Urbanization. *Social Forces*, 20:311–316.

Tokyo Shobocho. 1978. *Chokai Jichikai oyobi Bosai Shimin Soshiki nado Ichiranhyo*. Tokyo: Tokyo Shococho.

Tokyo Statistical Association. 1992. *Tokyo Statistical Yearbook*. Tokyo: Tokyo-to Tokei Kyokai.

Tokyo-to Tokei Kyokai. 1984. *Dai-34-kai Tokyo-to Tokei Nenkan*. Tokyo: Tokyo-to Kyokai.

Totti, Xavier F. 1986. A Face-Threatening Act: Ideology, Language, and Power in the Caribbean. Paper presented at the 85th annual meeting of the American Anthropological Association, December 3–7.

Tracy, James D., ed. 1990. *The Rise of Merchant Empires*. Cambridge: Cambridge University Press.

Tuan, Yi-fu. 1977. *Space and Place: The Perspective of Experience*. Minneapolis: University of Minnesota Press.

Turner, J. 1963. Dwelling Resources in South America. *Architectural Design*, August: 389–393.

Turner, June H., ed. 1980. *Latin American Women: The Meek Speak Out*. Silver Spring, MD: Inter-Educational Development.

U.S. Senate Committee on Labor and Public Welfare, Subcommittee on Indian Education. 1969. *The Education of American Indians: Field Investigations and Research Reports*. Vol. 2. Washington, DC: Government Printing Office.

Uzzell, Douglas. 1975. The Interaction of Population and Locality in the Development of Squatter Settlements in Lima. In *Latin American Urban Research*, eds. W. Cornelius and F. Trueblood, Vol. 4, pp. 113–134. Beverly Hills: Sage Publications.

Valentine, Bettylou. 1978. *Hustling and Other Hard Work*. New York: Free Press.

Valentine, C. 1968. *Culture and Poverty: A Critique and Counterproposals*. Chicago: University of Chicago Press.

Van Der Velden, L. 1982. *Tussen Prostituee en Maitresse: De Hospitality Girls van Ermita Manila*. Amsterdam: Anthropologisch Soziologisch Centrum, Amsterdam University.

Vatuk, Sylvia. 1972. *Kinship and Urbanization*. Berkeley and Los Angeles: University of California Press.

Verster, J. 1967. Social Survey of Western Township. *African Studies*, 26:175–246.

Vieille, A. (Michel). 1970. Relations with Neighbours and Relatives in Working Class Families of the Department de la Seine. In *Readings in Kinship in Urban Sociology*, ed. C. C. Harris, pp. 99–117. Oxford and New York: Pergamon.

Vogel, Ezra. 1967. *Japan's New Middle Class*. Berkeley and Los Angeles: University of California Press.

Wagenfeld, M. O. 1982. Psychopathology in Rural Areas: Issues and Evidence. In *Handbook of Rural Community Mental Health*, eds. P. Keller and J. D. Murray, pp. 30–44. New York: Human Sciences Press.

Wagley, Charles. 1964. Luzo-Brazilian Kinship Patterns: The Persistence of a Cultural Tradition. In *Politics of Change in Latin America*, eds. J. Maier and R. Weatherhead. New York: Frederick A. Praeger.

Wagley, Charles, and Marvin Harris. 1955. A Typology of Latin American Sub-cultures. *American Anthropologist*, 57:428–451.

Waldbott, G. L. 1978. *Health Effects of Environmental Pollutants*, 2d ed. St. Louis: Mosby.

Waldron, Sidney R. 1974. Social Organization and Social Control in the Muslim Walled City of Harar, Ethiopia. Unpublished Ph.D. Thesis. Department of Anthropology, Columbia University.

Wallace, Anthony F. C., and J. Atkins. 1960. The Meaning of Kinship Terms. *American Anthropologist*, 62:58–80.

_____. 1961. *Culture and Personality*. New York: Random House.

_____. 1962. Culture and Cognition. *Science*, 135:351.

Wallerstein, Immanuel. 1974. *The Modern World-System*. Vol. I. New York: Academic Press.

_____. 1976. *The Modern World-System: Capitalist Agriculture and the Origins of the European World-Economy in the Sixteenth Century*. New York: Academic Press.

Walton, John. 1979. Urban Political Economy: A New Paradigm. *Comparative Urban Research*, 7:5–17.

Ward, Kathryn B. 1993. Reconceptualizing World System Theory to Include Women. In *Theory of Gender/Feminism of Theory*, ed. Paula England. New York: Aldine de Gruyter.

Waters, J. Graduate Center, The City University of New York. Unpublished research.

Watson, James L. 1974. Restaurants and Remittances: Chinese Emigrant Workers in London. In *Anthropologists in Cities*, eds. George Foster and Robert Kemper. Boston: Little, Brown.

Watson, James L. 1975. *Emigration and the Chinese Lineage*. Los Angeles and Berkeley: University of California Press.

Weathorford, D. 1986. *Foreign and Female: Immigrant Women in America, 1840–1930*. New York: Schocken Books.

Weaver, Muriel Porter. 1993. *The Aztecs, Maya, and Their Predecessors*, 3d ed. San Diego: Academic Press.

Webb, S. D. 1978. Mental Health in Rural and Urban Environments. *Ekistics*, 266:37–42.

———. 1984. Rural-Urban Differences in Mental Health. In *Mental Health and Environment*, ed. Hugh L. Freeman, pp. 226–249. New York: Churchill Livingstone.

Weber, Max. 1892. *Die Verbaltnise der Landarbeiter in Ostelbischen Deutschland*. Berlin: Drucker and Humbolt.

Weinberg, Ian. 1969. The Problem of Convergence of Industrial Societies: A Critical Look at the State of Theory. *Comparative Studies of Society and History*, 11:1–15.

Weintrub, D., M. Lissak, and Y. Atzmon. 1970. *Mosbava, Kibbutz and Mosbav: Patterns of Jewish Rural Settlement and Development in Palestine*. Ithaca: Cornell University Press.

Welch, B. L., and A. S. Welch. 1970. *Physiological Effects of Noise*. New York: Plenum Press.

Wellman, Barry. 1979. The Community Question: The Intimate Networks of East Yorkers. *American Journal of Sociology*, 84:1201–1231.

Weulersse, J. 1954. Antioche: Essai Geographie Urbane. *Bulletin d'etudes orientales*, 4:27–79.

Wheatley, Paul. 1970. The Significance of Traditional Yoruba Urbanism. *Comparative Studies in Society and History*, 12:393–423.

———. 1971. *The Pivot of Four Quarters*. Chicago: Aldine.

White, Luise. 1990. *Comforts of Home: Prostitution in Colonial Nairobi*. Chicago: University of Chicago Press.

Whiteford, Andrew H. 1960. *Two Cities in Latin America: A Comparative Description of Social Classes*. Beloit, WI: Beloit College, Logan Museum. Reissued 1991, Waveland Press.

Whiteford, Michael B. 1976a. *The Forgotten Ones: Colombian Countrymen in an Urban Setting*. Gainesville: University Presses of Florida.

———. 1976b. Avoiding Obscuring Generalizations: Differences in Migrants and Their Adaptations to an Urban Environment. In *New Approaches to the Study of Migration*, eds. D. Guillet and D. Uzzell. Houston: Rice University Press.

Whitten, Norman E., and James F. Szwed. 1968. Negroes in the New World: Anthropologists Look at Afro-Americans. *Transaction*, 5:49–56.

Whyte, M. 1988. Changes in Mate Choice in Chengdu. In *Center for Research in Social Organization*. Working Paper series. Ann Arbor: University of Michigan.

Whyte, M., and W. Parish. 1984. *Urban Life in Contemporary China*. Chicago: University of Chicago Press.

Whyte, Martin K. 1978. *The Status of Women in Preindustrial Societies*. Princeton: Princeton University Press.

Whyte, William F. 1955. *Street Corner Society*. Chicago: University of Chicago Press.

Wilcox, Walter F. 1926. A Definition of "City" in Terms of Density. In *The Urban Community*, ed. E. W. Burgess.

Williams, Edward T. 1952. *China Yesterday and Today*, 5th ed. New York: T. Y. Crowell.

Williams, Louise, M. Anne Spence, and Susan C. Tideman. 1988. Implications of the Observed Effect of Air Pollution on Birth Weight. *Social Biology*, 24:1–9.

Williams, Raymond. 1082. Base and Superstructure in Marxist Theory. In *Problems in Materialism and Culture*, ed. Raymond Williams. London: Verso.

Willis, Paul. 1977. *Learning to Labour*. New York: Columbia University Press.

Wilson, R. 1974. The Moral State: A Study of the Political Socialization of Chinese and American Children. In *Normal and Abnormal Behavior in Chinese Culture*, eds. A. Kleinman and T. Y. Lin. Holland: Reidel.

Wilson, William J. 1987. *The Truly Disadvantaged: The Inner City, the Underclass and Public Policy*. Chicago: University of Chicago Press.

Winch, Robert F., Scott Greer, and Rae Lesser Blumberg. 1967. Ethnicity and Extended Familism in an Upper-Middle-Class Suburb. *American Sociological Review*, 32:265–272.

Wirth, L. 1938. Urbanism As a Way of Life. *American Journal of Sociology*, 44:3–24.

_____. 1956. *The Ghetto*. Chicago: University of Chicago Press (orig. pub. in 1928).

Wolf, Eric. 1956. San Jose: Subcultures of a "Traditional" Coffee Municipality. In *The People of Puerto Rico*, ed. Julian Steward, pp. 171–264. Chicago: University of Illinois Press.

_____. 1982. *Europe and the People Without History*. Berkeley: University of California Press.

Wolf, M. 1972. Uterine Families and the Women's Community. In *Women and the Family in Rural Taiwan*, ed. M. Wolf. Stanford: Stanford University Press.

_____. 1985. *Revolution Postponed*. Stanford: Stanford University Press.

Wolfe, Alvin W. 1980. Multinational Enterprise and Urbanism. In *Urban Anthropology: Cities in a Hierarchical Context*, ed. Thomas Collins. Southern Anthropological Society Proceedings no. 14. Athens: University of Georgia Press.

_____, et al. 1974. Social Network Effects on Employment. Prepared for Department of Labor, U.S. Department of Commerce, National Technical Information Service, Springfield, VA (No. PB-231-900).

Young, Michael, and P. Willmott. 1957. *Family and Kinship in East London*. London: Routledge & Kegan Paul.

_____. 1973. *The Symmetrical Family*. New York: Pantheon Books.

Zborowski, M., and E. Herzog. 1952. *Life Is with People*. New York: International Universities Press.

Zenner, Walter P. 1966. Syrian Jewish Identification in Israel. Ph.D. Diss. Department of Anthropology, Columbia University. Ann Arbor: University Microfilms.

_____. 1970. International Networks of a Migrant Ethnic Group. In *Anthropology & Migration*, ed. Robert F. Spencer, pp. 36–48. Seattle: University of Washington Press.

_____. 1978. Jewish State Employees in the Albany Area. Albany: State University of New York at Albany, Anthropology Department. Working Paper No. 1.

_____. 1982. Arabic Speaking Immigrants in North America as Middleman Minorities. *Ethnic and Racial Studies*, 5:457–477.

Zentrum Fur Entwicklungsbezogene Bildung (Zeb). 1981. *Tourismus, Prostitution, Entwicklung*. Stuttgart: Zentrum fur Entwicklungsbezogene Bildung.

Zerubavel, Eviatar. 1981. *Hidden Rhythms and Calendars in Social Life*. Chicago: University of Chicago Press.

Zerubavel, Yael, and Dianne Esses. 1987. Reconstructions of the Past: Syrian Jewish Woman and Maintenance of Tradition. *Journal of American Folklore*, 100(398): 528–539.

Zinsser, H. 1935. *Rats, Lice, and History*. Boston: Little, Brown.

Zolberg, A. R. 1964. *The One Party Government in the Ivory Coast*. Princeton: Princeton University Press.

About the Authors

JANET L. ABU-LUGHOD is Professor of Sociology and Historical Studies at the Graduate Faculty of the New School. She formerly headed programs in urban studies and in comparative urban studies at Northwestern University where she taught for twenty years. She is the author or editor, inter alia, of: *Housing Choices and Constraints*; *Cairo: 1001 Years of the City Victorious*; *Rabat: Urban Apartheid in Morocco*; *Third World Urbanization*; *Before European Hegemony: The World System A.D. 1250–1350*; *Changing Cities*; and most recently, *From Urban Village to East Village: The Battle for New York's Lower East Side*. She is currently writing a book comparing New York, Chicago, and Los Angeles as well as world cities.

THEODORE C. BESTOR is an Associate Professor of Anthropology at Cornell University. His first book, *Neighborhood Tokyo* (Stanford University Press 1989), won the Hiromi Arisawa Award for Japanese Studies from the American Association of University Presses and the Robert E. Park Award for Urban and Community Studies from the American Sociological Association. In 1992, he narrated a half-hour ethnographic video about contemporary life in Tokyo (also entitled *Neighborhood Tokyo*), which is distributed by the Institute for Education on Japan at Earlham College. He is now completing an ethnography of Tokyo's massive Tsukiji wholesale seafood market, focused on the institutions and culture of Japanese economic behavior. Bestor is the president of the Society for Urban Anthropology.

LAUREL BOSSEN is an Associate Professor at McGill University. Raised in Chicago, she received her B.A. from Barnard College and her Ph.D. from the State University of New York at Albany, and taught for several years at the University of Pittsburgh. She has conducted extensive research in Guatemala in both Maya and Ladino communities, and is the author of *The Redivision of Labor: Women and Economic Choice in Four Guatemalan Communities* (1984). Her research interests include economic anthropology, development and gender in complex societies, Mesoamerica and China.

PHILIPPE BOURGOIS is a Research Fellow at the San Francisco Urban Institute, and an Associate Professor of Anthropology at San Francisco State University. Cambridge University Press published his book *In Search of Respect: Selling Crack in El Barrio* in 1995. He has also worked on ethnic relations in Central America, publishing *Ethnicity at Work: Divided Labor on a Central American Banana Plantation* with Johns Hopkins University Press in 1989.

CAROLINE BRETTELL is Professor of Anthropology and Director of Women's Studies at Southern Methodist University. She is the author of *Men Who Migrate, Women Who Wait: Population and History in a Portuguese Parish* and *We Have Already Cried Many Tears: The Stories of Three Portuguese Migrant Women*. She is the editor of *When They Read What We Write: The Politics of Ethnography* and coeditor of *International Migration: The Female Perspective* and *Gender in Cross-Cultural Perspective*.

EDWIN EAMES recently retired his position as Professor of Anthropology at Baruch College of the City University of New York. He is a native of New York City, where he was born in 1930. After receiving a B.A. from City College in New York, he received his graduate training and Ph.D. at Cornell University. His major fieldwork has been on rural-urban migration in India and the migration of south Asians to British and American cities. As a result of his disability (he is blind and travels with a guide dog) he has shifted his research interests to the anthropology of disability and disability advocacy.

DAVID EPSTEIN was born in New York in 1943. He received both his B.A. and his Ph.D. from Columbia University. He has been a visiting professor at Queens College and is author of *Brasília: Plan and Reality*.

GEORGE M. FOSTER became Professor Emeritus at the University of California (Berkeley) in 1979, after teaching for twenty-six years on that campus. Born in 1913, he graduated from Northwestern University in 1935 and took his Ph.D. in anthropology at Berkeley in 1941. His research interests include peasant society, Latin America, sociocultural change and development, applied anthropology, and medical anthropology. Currently he is continuing a long-term longitudinal study of Tzintzuntzan, Michoacán, Mexico.

GEORGE GMELCH is Professor and Chair of Anthropology at Union College in upstate New York. He was raised in the San Francisco bay area and did his undergraduate studies in anthropology at Stanford University and his graduate studies at the University of California in Santa Barbara. Before going to graduate school he played several seasons of professional baseball in the Detroit Tigers organization. He has conducted field research on Irish Travellers, English Gypsies, Alaskan fishermen, and return migrants in

Ireland, Newfoundland, and Barbados. Among his books are *The Irish Tinkers: The Urbanization of an Itinerant People* and *Double Passage: The Lives of Caribbean Migrants Abroad and Back Home*.

SHARON GMELCH is Professor of Anthropology and Director of Women's Studies at Union College. She received her anthropological training at the University of California, Santa Barbara. She has done extensive field research with Travelling People in Ireland as well as research in Alaska, Barbados, and Quebec. Her chief research interests are interethnic relations, ethnic group formation, culture change, and sex roles. She is the author of *Nan: The Life of an Irish Travelling Woman* and three other books.

JUDITH GOODE is Professor of Anthropology at Temple University. She received her doctorate at Cornell University. She is a former president of the Society for Urban Anthropology. She has done urban ethnographic research in Medellín and Bogotá, Colombia and has been working recently in Philadelphia. Her projects focus on work and class as well as immigration, ethnic group formation, and intergroup relations. Her most recent book is *Reshaping Ethnic and Racial Relations in Philadelphia: Immigrants in a Divided City* (1994, with Jo Anne Schneider).

WILLIAM JANKOWIAK is an Associate Professor of Anthropology at the University of Nevada, Las Vegas. Besides studying aspects of Chinese society, he has explored and written on American gender relations, New Orleans second-line street festival, and family life in a contemporary Mormon polygamous community. Presently, he is at work on a book that examines the cross-cultural significance of lust and love and the challenges it presents to human understanding and scientific analysis.

SUSAN EMLEY KEEFE is Professor and Chairperson of the Department of Anthropology at Appalachian State University in the Blue Ridge Mountains of North Carolina. Her research on Mexican-American families was completed following her graduate work at the University of California, Santa Barbara. Her research interests also include ethnicity, mental health, education, and inequality. She has recently examined the concepts of ethnicity and ethnic identity as applied to Appalachians and the implications for their educational opportunities. She is the author of *Chicago Ethnicity* (with Amado M. Padilla) and editor of *Appalachian Mental Health*.

ROBERT V. KEMPER is Professor of Anthropology at Southern Methodist University. Born in San Diego, California, in 1945, he received his B.A. degree from the University of California (Riverside) in 1966 and his Ph.D. degree from the University of California (Berkeley) in 1971. His research interests include migration and urbanization, tourism, and Latin America. He is Associate Editor of the journal *Urban Anthropology*.

BARBARA KIRSHENBLATT-GIMBLETT is Professor of Performance Studies and of Hebrew and Judaic Studies, at New York University. She is a research associate at the YIVO Institute for Jewish Research. Born and raised in Toronto, she studied at the University of Toronto before completing her B.A. and M.A. at the University of California, Berkeley, and her Ph.D. at Indiana University in 1972. Her research on urban vernacular culture has been supported by a Guggenheim Foundation Fellowship (1986–87), and though focused on New York City, includes comparative material based on her fieldwork in Japan, India, Kenya, Egypt, Israel, and New Zealand. Her research interests include Ashkenazic Jewry, tourism, and food as a symbolic system. She is the author, with Lucjan Dobroszycki, of *Image Before My Eyes: A Photographic History of Jewish Life in Poland, 1864–1939*.

OSCAR LEWIS (1914–1971) was born in New York City. He received his B.S. from the City College of New York and his Ph.D. from Columbia University. He did research in Canada among the Blackfoot Indians and in India. He is best known for his in-depth study of the Mexican village of Tepoztlán and for his use of life histories in studying the poor in Mexico, the United States, and Cuba. He was Professor of Anthropology at the University of Illinois from 1948 until his death.

KATHLEEN LOGAN is an Associate Professor in the Department of Sociology/Anthropology and faculty member of the Latin American and Caribbean Center at Florida International University. She earned her doctorate at Bryn Mawr College. She is the author of *Haciendo Pueblo: The Development of a Guadalajaran Suburb* and a co-editor of *Americas, an Anthology* with Mark Rosenberg and Douglas Kincaid. Working in Mexico, she has written about feminism, urbanization, community mobilizations, women's political participation, and medical practices among lower income groups. Her current research project is women's participation in the democratic transformation of Mexico, funded by a grant from the North-South Center, University of Miami. She is a former president of the Society for Urban Anthropology.

OWEN M. LYNCH is Charles F. Noyes Professor of Urban Anthropology at New York University in New York City. His most important research has been done in India, where he studied untouchables and neo-Buddhists in Agra city and shantytown dwellers in Bombay. He has also directed a study of block associations in New York City. He is the author of *The Politics of Untouchability: Social Mobility and Social Change in a City of India* as well as editor of *Divine Passions: The Social Construction of Emotion in India*, and *Culture and Community in Europe*. He has published numerous articles on his research interests: urban society and theory, untouchables in India, pilgrimage, and the cultural construction of emotion.

SALLY ENGLE MERRY is Professor of Anthropology at Wellesley College. She received her Ph.D. in Anthropology from Brandeis University in 1978. She is the author of *Urban Danger: Life in a Neighborhood of Strangers*, *Getting Justice and Getting Even: Legal Consciousness among Working-Class Americans*, and co-editor of *The Possibility of Popular Justice: A Case Study of American Community Justice* with Neal Milner. She has published numerous articles and review essays on legal ideology, mediation, urban ethnic relations, and legal pluralism. She is president of the Law and Society Association. She is currently working on a project on the meanings of law and violence in the American colonization of Hawaii in the nineteenth and twentieth centuries and on the contemporary problems concerning the legal management of domestic violence.

STANLEY MILGRAM (1933–1984) was Professor of Psychology at the Graduate Center of the City University of New York. After receiving his Ph.D. from Harvard in 1960, he trained students in urban research and experimental social psychology. Along with Henry From, he produced the award-winning film, *The City and the Self* (distributed by Time-Life Films). He published numerous papers on urban life from a social psychological viewpoint. His book, *The Individual and the Social World* (Addison-Wesley) was published in 1979.

NICI NELSON is in the Anthropology Department at Goldsmith's College, University of London. She has worked in Eastern Africa for the last 25 years. Her publications have covered the areas of African urbanization and issues relating to gender-power and gender and development.

ROBERT E. RHOADES was born in rural Oklahoma and early in life experienced migration through the westward "Okie" movements. Like many migrant families of the period, however, he returned to the family farm. Rhoades' academic interests naturally focus on migration and agricultural anthropology. He has studied agriculture (Oklahoma State University), sociology (University of Hawaii) and anthropology (University of Oklahoma), in which he received his Ph.D. in 1976. Rhoades has also worked in Nepal (1962–1964), the Philippines (1976–1978) and is now Chairman of the Anthropology Department at the University of Georgia.

ROBERT ROTENBERG is Professor of Anthropology and Director of the International Studies Program at DePaul University in Chicago. He has written two books, *Time and Order in Metropolitan Vienna* and *Landscape and Power in Metropolitan Vienna*, and co-edited *The Cultural Meaning of Urban Space*. His current research concerns the interactions between media, local knowledge, and social movements in shaping religious experience.

LAWRENCE M. SCHELL is Professor of Anthropology at the State University of New York at Albany. He is also a professor in the Department of Epidemiology in the School of Public Health at Albany, and is affiliated with the Department of Pediatrics at Albany Medical College. His research interests are the impact of urbanism on health, and the interaction of culture and biology generally. He is conducting two research projects, one on the effect of maternal lead burden on neonatal and infant development, and another on the effect of several pollutants (PCBs, lead, mercury, and fluoride) on the growth and development of Mohawk adolescents. He received his B.A. from Oberlin College and his Ph.D. from the University of Pennsylvania.

602 About the Authors

ANDREI SIMIĆ is Professor of Anthropology at the University of California. He received his B.A. degree in Slavic languages and Ph.D. in anthropology from the University of California at Berkeley. He has carried out extensive fieldwork in Yugoslavia and among Euro-American ethnic groups in the United States. His areas of interest include: urbanization and modernization, ethnicity, social gerontology, and ethnographic film. Dr. Simić's geographic regions of specialization are Eastern Europe and the Mediterranean, Latin America, and the United States. He has currently completed a 60-minute documentary film on Serbians in America.

ANDRÉE F. SJOBERG is Associate Professor in the Department of Oriental and African Languages at the University of Texas at Austin. In addition to her cross-cultural interests, she has specialized in the Uzbeks of Central Asia and the Dravidians of South India. In recent years she has been writing a set of articles that document the role of the Dravidians in shaping Indian culture, Hinduism in particular.

GIDEON SJOBERG is Professor of Sociology at the University of Texas at Austin. He is author of *The Preindustrial City* (1960) and co-author of *A Methodology for Social Research* (1968). In recent years he has co-edited *A Case for the Case Study* (1991) and *A Critique of Contemporary American Sociology* (1993). He continues to write on bureaucracy, methodology, and human rights.

CAROL B. STACK is a Professor in the School of Education at the University of California (Berkeley). She received her Ph.D. in anthropology from the University of Illinois at Urbana, and is author of *All Our Kin: Strategies for Survival in a Black Community* (1974). Her research interests include social anthropology of complex societies, black families, foster care, welfare, and education.

SIDNEY R. WALDRON is Professor of Anthropology at the State University of New York at Cortland. He worked among the Harari in 1962–63, 1975, and 1977, and he is presently completing a monograph on the Harari. In 1981–82 he worked with refugees in Somalia, and in 1985–86 he was a visiting fellow at Oxford University's Refugee Studies Programme. During that period he helped establish a Refugee Studies Center at the University of Juba in the Sudan. He is a member of the advisory board of the American Anthropological Association's Task Force on African Hunger.

MICHAEL B. WHITEFORD is Professor of Anthropology and Professor-in-Charge of the Anthropology Program at Iowa State University. Born in 1945, he received his B.A. degree from Beloit College in 1967 and his Ph.D. degree from the University of California (Berkeley) in 1972. In addition to migration and urbanization, his research interests include medical anthropology, particularly focusing on the social epidemiology of nutritional status. He has done fieldwork in Colombia, Costa Rica, Honduras, and Mexico.

LOUIS WIRTH (1897–1952) was born in Germany. He attended public school in Omaha, Nebraska. He received his B.A., M.A., and Ph.D. from the University of Chicago. Until his death he was Professor of Sociology at the University of Chicago. He was interested in social theory, the social ecology of the human community, and the application of sociology to public policy. In addition to his work on urbanism, he focused attention on the role of thought and ideology in social life and on minority problems. His book *The Ghetto* (1928), which is a study of the Jewish immigrant community in Chicago, is a classic.

WALTER P. ZENNER is Professor of Anthropology at the State University of New York at Albany. He has specialized in the study of ethnic identity. He has done research on Arabs and Jews in Israel, Great Britain, and the United States. He has authored numerous articles and written and edited several books, including *Persistence and Flexibility: Anthropological Perspectives of the American Jewish Experience* and *Minorities in the Middle: A Cross-cultural Analysis*. He is currently continuing his research on Syrian Sephardim in various parts of the world, including Jerusalem, Manchester (England), and Chicago. He was president of the Society for Urban Anthropology from 1992 through 1994.